THEY STAND TOGETHER

THEY STAND TOGETHER

The Letters of
C. S. Lewis to Arthur Greeves
(1914-1963)

Edited by Walter Hooper

MACMILLAN PUBLISHING CO., INC.
New York

Macmillan Publishing Co., Inc.
866 Third Avenue, New York, N.Y. 10022

Library of Congress Catalog Card Number: 79-88793
ISBN 0-02-553660-5

First American Edition 1979

Printed in the United States of America

To the memory of
Arthur Greeves

That we may mark with wonder and chaste dread
At hour of noon, when, with our limbs outspread
Lazily in the whispering grass, we lie
To gaze out fully upon the windy sky –
Far, far away, and kindly, friend with friend,
To talk the old, old talk that has no end,
Roaming – without a name – without a chart –
The unknown garden of another's heart.

(Poem written by C. S. Lewis for Arthur Greeves, 1917)

CONTENTS

INTRODUCTION

It was in April 1914 that C. S. Lewis, at home in Strandtown, on the eastern outskirts of Belfast, wondered whether he should walk across the road and meet Arthur Greeves. Their families were friends, Arthur was ill, and a message had been sent to say that he would welcome a visit. Lewis rarely accepted such a summons, but with the end of his schooldays in sight his day-to-day melancholy was for once lifted, and he accepted. One ponders – this meeting could easily have never taken place and these letters never written; and yet they were.

Everything had shown Lewis to be bright, but he nevertheless hated all the schools he was forced to attend. First, there was Wynyard School in Watford, Hertfordshire, which establishment consisted of a pair of semi-detached houses with outdoor lavatories. It was fast sliding into irreversible squalor and ruin when Lewis went there in 1908. Judging from all the accounts of it I have read, it was 'at once brutalizing and intellectually stupefying' to Lewis and the other half-dozen unfortunates who suffered from a crazed headmaster who wielded the cane at the slightest provocation and rewarded good behaviour by allowing one to carry a parcel of foul linen to the laundress before morning classes began. Lewis and his contemporaries won their freedom in 1910 when the headmaster, Robert Capron (1851–1911), had a High Court action brought against him. At the same time that Wynyard fell apart, the headmaster was certified insane and died shortly afterwards in an asylum of brain fever. Those who have read Lewis's autobiography, *Surprised by Joy*,[1] will understand why he chose 'Belsen' as a pseudonym for the school. Years later, when I was living in Lewis's Oxford home as his private secretary, he told me that the blanket on my bed was the same he had shivered under in that curtainless dormitory of Wynyard. And for this, I have preserved it as the last surviving memento of Wynyard to which no unhappy memories are attached.

[1] *Surprised by Joy: The Shape of My Early Life* (1955).

All the other schools he attended were by past and present standards better than most. But Lewis had a congenital distaste for collectivism of almost every kind, and though he liked walking and swimming, he hated being made to play games.

After Wynyard came one term at Campbell College, Belfast, in 1910 which he might have liked more than he did had it not seemed to him, as a day boy, 'very like living permanently in a large railway station'.[2] Next came Cherbourg School, a tall, white building perched high up on the beautiful Malvern Hills overlooking Malvern College. During his two years there (1911–13) his education began in earnest under the kind and sensible guidance of the headmaster, Arthur C. Allen. When the boy's father heard of his quite extraordinary success in Latin and Greek he wrote to him on 27 October 1912 saying, 'Strange to say I dreamt one night last week of a brilliant star falling through the sky. I suppose I must have been thinking of you when I fell asleep. I certainly woke up with a start thinking of you. Not that you are a "brilliant star falling thro' the sky". But perhaps that is the dream message of coming success.' Meanwhile, terrible harm was coming to the lad from an unexpected quarter – the school matron, Miss G. E. Cowie. Well-intentioned though she was, her floundering in the mazes of Theosophy, Rosicrucianism and Spiritualism neutralized and finally smothered the truth of Christian revelation and left the boy an unbeliever. But Lewis persevered as a scholar and at the end of Summer Term 1913 he won a classical scholarship to Malvern College. Allowed to name his own prize, he was given a copy of Donald A. Mackenzie's *Teutonic Myth and Legend* containing the inscription 'C. S. Lewis. Scholarship Prize. June 1913, Cherbourg, Malvern. Arthur C. Allen' – which schoolboy treasure he passed on to me.

Malvern College, which Lewis entered in September 1913, is set in one of the loveliest spots in England, and if (impossibly) he had been the only pupil there Lewis would have found the library and many of the masters all he could have wanted. But he detested the games, the 'preparation for public life', the absorbing preoccupation of most of the boys to achieve a place in the school's 'inner ring', and the fagging – the system by which, without breaking any rules, the older boys can tyrannize the younger ones. Exhausted, Lewis pleaded with his father to have him removed. Until that could take place, however, if it ever would, Lewis held on to the only life-raft he knew.

His greatest pleasure lay in literature. School organization

2 *ibid.*, ch. iii, p. 55.

brought only deeply felt melancholy, and for solace he retreated mentally into 'a many-islanded sea of poetry and myth'.[3] He was deeply, but at this time secretly, in love with Norse mythology which to a boy his age was already an old passion as it began as far back as 1912 when he was ravished by the vast, cool, 'northerness' of it. It had worked on him through the *Nibelung Saga* as adapted by Wagner, the Icelandic *Eddas* and modern historical works such as H. M. A. Guerber's *Myths of the Norsemen*. When he reached home for his Easter holidays in March 1914 he had written 819 lines of a pessimistic epic called *Loki Bound* which was Norse in subject and Greek in form.

Though his father, Albert Lewis, had received no unflattering reports of these schools (excepting Wynyard) from his elder, more gregarious son Warren who had preceded his brother to all of them but Campbell, he was now convinced that the younger boy's pessimism was not feigned. The schools were causing him considerable damage, and something had to be done. During the Easter vacation of 1914 he wrote to William T. Kirkpatrick who had been his headmaster when Albert was a pupil at Lurgan College in Co. Armagh, and asked him to take him. Kirkpatrick, then 66 and living in the wilds of Surrey, was taking one or two boarding pupils, and as he had already prepared Warren for Sandhurst, he consented to 'cram' Clive Lewis for Oxford. The one condition he insisted on was that Clive return to Malvern for one final term, and come to him in the Autumn of 1914. 'If you want to know how I felt,' Lewis was to say about this decision, 'imagine your own feelings on waking one morning to find that income tax or unrequited love had somehow vanished from the world.'[4] With the worst nearly behind him and transported by the thoughts of things to come, he decided to visit Arthur Greeves. Of this first momentous meeting he was to write in *Surprised by Joy* (ch. viii, pp. 125–6):

> Many chapters ago I mentioned a boy who lived near us and who had tried, quite unsuccessfully, to make friends with my brother and myself. His name was Arthur and he was my brother's exact contemporary; he and I had been at Campbell together though we never met. I think it was shortly before the beginning of my last term at Malvern that I received a message saying that Arthur was in bed, convalescent, and would welcome a visit. I can't remember what led me to accept this invitation, but for some reason I did.
>
> I found Arthur sitting up in bed. On the table beside him lay a copy

[3] *ibid.*, ch. xi, p. 161.
[4] *ibid.*, ch. viii, p. 125.

of *Myths of the Norsemen*.

'Do *you* like that?' said I.

'Do *you* like that?' said he.

Next moment the book was in our hands, our heads were bent close together, we were pointing, quoting, talking – soon almost shouting – discovering in a torrent of questions that we liked not only the same things, but the same parts of it and in the same way; that both knew the stab of Joy and that, for both, the arrow was shot from the North. Many thousands of people have had the experience of finding the first friend, and it is none the less a wonder; as great a wonder (*pace* the novelists) as first love, or even a greater. I had been so far from thinking such a friend possible that I had never even longed for one; no more than I longed to be King of England . . . Nothing, I suspect, is more astonishing in any man's life than the discovery that there do exist people very, very like himself.

Most of us first heard of Arthur Greeves from *Surprised by Joy* However, as Lewis's main reason for writing that book was to tel how he passed from atheism to Christianity, what is said about Greeves and other of Lewis's friends was to a large extent dictated by the limitations Lewis set himself in describing the effect those friends had on his conversion. Who then, many still ask, *was* Arthur Greeves?

The question may never be answered satisfactorily until, and if, a biography of Greeves is attempted. For the time being, I believe that this book comes as close as anything to being a 'biography' of Lewis's 'first friend' even though it comes to us through the 'borrowed' voice of the letter writer. It comprises the largest collection of letters Lewis ever wrote to anyone, though, for reasons which I have never been able to discover, only four of Greeves's letters to Lewis have survived. Still, I do not think this book lop-sided on that account. Lewis was one of the most lucid writers of this century, and he had the knack of answering in such a way that in most instances one can know what the questions and observations of his correspondents were. Such being the case, I make two claims for this book. It is the greatest source of written information there is about Arthur Greeves, and, considering the intimacy and informality of their long friendship, I believe these letters may be as close as we shall ever get to Lewis himself.

The friends wrote to one another less frequently as they grew older, but there is a continuous narrative thread running through the book, and I believe that even those only mildly familiar with Lewis's life will have no difficulty in following it. I have become so familiar with the *story* the letters tell that I have come to look upon it as a parallel autobiography to *Surprised by Joy*, but with an important difference. Whereas *Surprised by Joy* was written to tell the story of Lewis's conversion and breaks off at 1931, these letters, though not written for publication, and with only one reader in mind, carry us up to within two months of the author's death on 22 November 1963.

It is not, I feel, necessary to give here many of the generally known facts of C. S. Lewis's life as there exists, besides his autobiography, these letters, and *C. S. Lewis: A Biography* (1974) by Roger Lancelyn Green and myself, many other sources of information which have resulted from his wide and growing fame. But Lewis and Greeves were so close, that as the editor of these letters, I have felt that there were two offices I had a duty to perform in order to make this a clear and coherent narrative. First, I have, perhaps to the frustration of those who like what they call a 'nice, clean page', supplied such footnotes as I have thought necessary and the occasional longer note to fill some gap not covered in the letters. And, second, I have felt that in this Introduction I should provide a background for those people who appear most prominently in this book. Tedious as genealogies are to read (and to write), I do not believe those of Lewis and Greeves can be omitted without causing the reader some inconvenience later on. These letters when savoured with the fullness of the footnotes tell the quiet story of Lewis's life with far more subtlety and unbought eloquence than any attempt of the biographer.

Lewis's grandfather, Richard Lewis (1832–1908), emigrated to Ireland from Wales about the middle of the last century. In 1868 he moved his family to Belfast where he and John H. MacIlwaine entered into a partnership under the firm-name of 'MacIlwaine and Lewis: Boiler Makers, Engineers, and Iron Ship Builders'. Of his six children, Martha, Sarah Jane, Joseph, William, Richard and Albert James (1863–1929), it is Albert who comes most into this story.

In 1885 Albert qualified as a solicitor and in 1894 he married Flora Augusta Hamilton (1862–1908) whose family was of the professional class and had emigrated from Scotland to Ireland as far back as 1616. Her father was the Reverend Thomas Robert Hamilton (1826–1905), the Rector of St Mark's Church, Dundela, and one of a long line of distinguished ecclesiastics in the Church of Ireland. On her mother's side Flora was related to a family which, if not more distinguished, was more aristocratic than her father's – the family of Sir William Quartus and Lady Mary Ewart (Flora's cousin) who lived in Glenmachan House with their children, Robert Heard,

Gordon, Charlotte Hope, Isabella Kelso and Mary Gundreda.[5]

Albert and Flora were to have two children, Warren Hamilton (1895–1973) and Clive Staples (1898–1963) who gave himself the name 'Jack' and who is of course the author of these letters. The family lived in one of a pair of semi-detached houses called Dundela Villas (now extinct) until 1905 when Albert built a new house for his family near Glenmachan and St Mark's Church – all in an area of Belfast called Strandtown. The house was named Little Lea, and though the Lewises, Hamiltons and Ewarts were connected by family ties, they now lived in close proximity to one another as well as to the Greeves family whose home was called Bernagh. Albert never recovered from the death of his beloved Flora in 1908, but the event nevertheless served to strengthen family ties and make him in some ways dependent on his neighbours at Bernagh, which stood midway between Little Lea and Glenmachan House.

Burke's Irish Family Records (1976) contains a complete genealogy of Arthur Greeves's family. As family trees tend to be somewhat complicated, I have decided to do some disentangling and thus show more clearly what Arthur Greeves's descent looks like. Even at the expense of a few minutes' tedium, I think the reader will benefit from the family's history of non-conformity as this was to play an important part in Arthur's spiritual odyssey and, to a considerable extent, his theological arguments with C. S. Lewis.

The first of Arthur Greeves's ancestors to emigrate from Rock, in Northumberland, to Ireland was (*1*) Henry Greer or Greve who married Marye Torner in 1649. They arrived in Ireland in 1653 and obtained a lease of land near Red Ford, not far from Dungannon, in Co. Tyrone, which land remained in the family for 170 years thereafter. Henry and his wife were early members of the Meeting of the Society of Friends whose central doctrine of the 'Inner Light', or direct working of God in the soul, is considered superior to the Scriptures and the Church. As a result of their non-conformity, they suffered like other Quakers from their refusal to pay tithes. Henry and Marye had three sons and a daughter.

(*2*) Their second son, Robert Greer or Grives of Red Ford, who was born about 1660, was a linen bleacher, merchant farmer and, like his father, a prominent member of the Friends. His wife Mary Whitsitt of Grange, Dungannon, was at least as zealous as her

---

[5] For more details about the Lewis and Hamilton families see the 'Prologue' in Roger Lancelyn Green and Walter Hooper's *C. S. Lewis: A Biography*. For information about the Ewarts of Glenmachan see *Burke's Peerage, Baronetage and Knightage* (1970).

husband and was for 43 years a 'minister' of the Society of Friends. Robert and Mary (who died in 1730 and 1742 respectively) had nine children. (3) Their second son, John Greer or Greeves of Grange (having inherited lands which had belonged to his maternal grandfather) married in 1715 his cousin, who was also named Mary Whitsitt. John (d. 1742) and Mary had two sons and a daughter. (4) Their second son, William Greer or Greeves (1719?–76) of Grange, Co. Tyrone, was a merchant, tanner and farmer and continued in the family's religious tradition by becoming a Trustee of the Friends' Meeting House at Grange. When in 1744 he married Mary Morton (1725–1814), who was his cousin on both sides of the family, he assumed the name *Greeves*, which spelling the family was to use thereafter. William and Mary had eight sons.

(5) The eighth son, John Greeves (1761–1843) built himself a house called 'Bernagh' in Co. Tyrone. He was a linen bleacher and merchant and married one Margaret Sinton (1767–1824) of Mayallon, Co. Down. Of the four sons born to them, the eldest was (6) Thomas Greeves (1792–1852) of 'Bernagh', Co. Tyrone, who married Rachel Malcomson (1795–1871) of Lurgan, Co. Armagh, and was to become even more prosperous than his father as a linen merchant.

Of their two sons and three daughters, it was their first son (7) John Greeves (1831–1917) of 'Lismachan', Strandtown, Co. Down, who was to become the only paternal grandfather that Arthur Greeves knew personally. He married Elizabeth Pim Jackson (1837–95) of 'Altona', Strandtown, and he and his brother Thomas Malcomson Greeves (1835–1924) together founded the firm of J. & T. M. Greeves Ltd., Flax Spinners, Belfast, which business was to remain in some branch of the family up to 1961 when it was amalgamated with Herdmans Ltd. of Strabane. John and Elizabeth had seven sons, and though the parents were brought up Friends, they were early converts to the Plymouth Brethren, which religious sect was established in 1830 and was then, as now, noted for its rigorous and uncompromising nature.

Their eldest son was (8) Joseph Malcomson Greeves (1858–1925) of 'Bernagh', Strandtown, and he became the next director of J. & T. M. Greeves Ltd. He married an American of the Baptist persuasion, Mary Margretta Gribbon (1861–1949) of Brooklyn, New York and – finally – it is they who were the parents of Lewis's close friend Joseph Arthur Greeves (1895–1966) and four other children, Thomas Jackson (1886–1974), Mary Elizabeth or 'Lily' (1888–1976), William Edward (1890–1960) and John (1892–1969), all of whom are mentioned in the course of these letters.

'Jack' Lewis was to achieve greater fame than his brother, but Warren had the greater 'sense of family' and it is to him that we must be indebted for the verbal 'portraits' he encouraged his brother to draw of the Greeves family. Warren's temporary retirement from the Army coincided almost exactly with their father's death in 1929. Following the break-up of Little Lea, a vast accumulation of family letters, diaries and memorabilia came to light and these papers were transferred to Oxford. With painstaking care and a patience to be marvelled at, Warren arranged the documents in chronological order and spent, as he told me, more than five years typing them into eleven volumes containing over 300 pages each. This unpublished work, the original of which is in Wheaton College, Wheaton, Illinois, and a copy of which is in the Bodleian Library, Oxford, is entitled the *Lewis Papers: Memoirs of the Lewis Family 1850-1930*.[6] In 1933 at which time Warren was at work on Vol. III, which covers the years 1901–12, he persuaded his brother to write the following sketches of Arthur's parents. I cannot say whether or not they are 'true' in every detail, but they are valuable in having been written by C. S. Lewis after many years of friendship with Arthur and seeing him in the context of his family:

Joseph was a Plymouth Brother, and one of a large and wealthy family in Belfast, who claimed to have been members of this sect for many generations. He was a tall, straight sort of a man, severe in his dress and in his expression. I have been told he was handsome in his youth, and his beard, when I knew him, did not conceal a certain cold and heavy regularity of features which might have been admired if you could forgive them for their lack of all that makes a face alive. 'There was no speculation in his eyes' – the face, like the man, was timid, prim, sour, at once oppressed and oppressive. He was a harsh husband and a despotic father. His wife was 'in tears half the time' while he lived, as one of his sons told me. He died of anaemia. In his declining years his habits became very gross, and I have heard that he commonly broke wind without restraint in the presence of his wife and children. My own father described his funeral as 'the most cheerful funeral he ever attended'.

Outside his own house, he was civil and even friendly, as far as his powers would let him be. He had however no conversation. Even on religious subjects he was a deadweight, and my father thought his knowledge of Scripture by no means extensive. I have heard that at

[6] After this colossal effort at transcribing, Warren Lewis, always in the habit of 'travelling light', destroyed nearly all the original documents which went into the *Lewis Papers*.

family prayers in his own house, where he daily read and then expounded a passage from the Bible, he went over and over the same passages and gave always the same explanations. His chief intellectual interests were those of an antiquary, and he had on his shelves a few volumes of local history and archaeology. It is also worth recording that his was the only private house in which I have ever seen a copy of Alison's *French Revolution*,[7] a work endlessly familiar in the second-hand bookshops of my day. He was also a sportsman, and sometimes went shooting on the islands of Strangford Lough.

His wife had unmistakably been a beauty in her youth, and was a comely matron when I first remember her. Her character is not easy to describe. I think it changed a good deal during the period of my acquaintance with her. Her sincere and almost motherly affection for myself was however the same at the end as at the beginning. This perhaps gave the key to one side of her nature. She was (at first sight – or shall I say, at certain periods) the very type of the simple, warm hearted, confiding wife and mother. 'All was conscience and tendre herte.' Such was her naivete that she would pour out to any acquaintance met on the road, the whole plot of the last novel she had read: and her comments on her neighbours were of such a kind that one was left wondering whether quite that amount of simplicity was possible. Could it be that the sheep's clothing concealed a cat? Yet no sooner had you veered towards this hypothesis, than the next remark would fling you back on the original view – 'naivete, not to say mental deficiency'. Succeeding years tended to bring the truth to light, that Mrs Greeves had, with all her benevolence, a genuine streak of ill nature in her. Her unfair and partial treatment of her son John, when I last stayed in Bernagh, is the heaviest count against her. And yet, like Chaucer, 'me ne list this silly woman chide', for silly she was and sillier she steadily became.

Her chief reading after her husband's death, was such books as prophesy the end of the world. One of them, I remember, opened with the remarkable BONA FIDE that indeed there had been many previous prophecies, but the difference about the present one was that it was really true. Her conversation came to consist more and more of a perpetual attempt, and a perpetual failure, to tell stories and riddles. A more complete triumph of hope over experience it would be impossible to imagine. NEVER ONCE have I heard her reach the end of her anecdote without either missing the point or frankly breaking down – but with scarcely a pause she would embark upon another. If stories ceased for a moment, she would talk about the Kaiser – for whom, years after the war, she retained the pious hatred of 1915. I once remarked to her that we must remember the bad upbringing he had had. She replied, 'I don't want to hear anything of that sort.' The nearest meeting

[7] Sir Archibald Alison, *History of Europe during the French Revolution* (1833–42).

between her religious and patriotic views was a half tearful complaint, 'And yet it says you ought to forgive your enemies!' . . . I do not know how it is – Mrs Greeves was a better woman than any true account of her would lead you to believe. Much she did that was bad, and all that she said was foolish: but somehow it was all forgiveable. One does not love the domestic cat less because it is greedy and thievish. Somehow these facts do not reach the heart of the mystery.

The children all (I believe) abandoned the religion of their parents. They had all been subjected to a baptism by total immersion EN MASSE when the youngest was about 12. It had been carried out in the bathroom where the young men, the young woman, and the boys, in their bathing suits, had been plunged one by one in a bath of tepid water. But I do not think that their religion had at any time been practised with much devotion by the younger generation. Certainly all, except Willie, bore the ugly marks of ex-Puritanism – of those who are brought up in a crude antithesis of Grace and Nature, and who there-fore, when they abandon the Grace, straightway become startlingly natural. All revealed each passing sensation of greed, jealousy, anger, pleasure, or disappointment in an almost savage nakedness. Their up-bringing gave them no HUMANE tradition to turn to when once their theology was gone.[8]

Lewis went on to describe all the younger members of the family with the exception of Arthur about whom he said (Vol. III, p. 305): 'Of Arthur, the youngest child, I shall give no account. He is, after my brother, my oldest and most intimate friend. I know more of him than any historian has a right to know of his subject, and I therefore leave him to those [who] can discover his faults more properly and his virtues less partially than I.' In the end, he was forced to draw Arthur's portrait as a corrective to the one supplied by Warren. Why this reticence?

As mentioned earlier, Lewis had been 'astonished' at discovering in Arthur Greeves that 'there do exist people very, very like himself'. If one were to judge friendship merely by what people *do* this might seem an odd thing for Lewis to have said. Given the common *milieu* in which they grew up – the same neighbourhood and many of the same friends and acquaintances – perhaps it is 'odd'. But I think most of this 'oddness' seems so to us, not merely because their lives were to take such different directions, but because Lewis achieved great fame through his books and Greeves lived and died (like most of us) without being heard of outside his immediate circle. It was Lewis's belief that anyone who is surprised at the kind of friends his friends have will, upon reflection, be no less surprised at the kind of

[8] *Lewis Papers*, Vol. III, pp. 302–4.

friends *he* has. However, leaving aside Lewis's 'reticence' for a moment, it will help to know something of what both men had been doing up to the point when Warren began asking for a 'portrait' of Arthur Greeves for his *Lewis Papers.*

Greeves was discovered to have a bad heart when he was a small boy, and as a result of his mother's excessive coddling and his own natural indolence, he was a confirmed valetudinarian by the time he and Lewis met. What formal education he had was received at Campbell College between 1906 and 1912. He worked for a short while, with frequent 'sick leaves', for his brother Tom in his firm 'Greeves & Morton: Linen Merchants'. After this, being independently wealthy, he never took another job. Partly through Lewis's coaxing, he enrolled at the Slade School of Fine Art, in London, and left there after two years (1921–3) with a Certificate. Some time later he studied art in Paris for a short while. Those paintings of his which I have seen seem to me quite good – some of his landscapes are beautiful – and it is worth noting that two of his pictures were exhibited in the Royal Hibernian Academy, Dublin, in 1936.

Lewis, by any comparison, was an intellectual giant. Before he went up to Oxford, his tutor, Mr Kirkpatrick, who distrusted sentiment and was ruthlessly honest, told his father that Clive – not yet eighteen – was the most brilliant translator of Greek plays he had ever met. He took a triple 'First' at Oxford, and in 1925 was elected a Fellow and English Tutor of Magdalen College. By 1933 he had published two volumes of verse and an allegorical apology for Christianity, Reason and Romanticism, *The Pilgrim's Regress.* He was already at work on his famous *Allegory of Love* and even those who knew him best could not foresee the consequence of his intellect.

Those who knew Lewis best in the mid-1930s were Owen Barfield, Cecil Harwood, J. R. R. Tolkien and of course his brother. But none of these – not even Warren – knew as much about some things which had happened to Lewis between 1914 and 1929 as did Arthur Greeves, and I think this accounts for Lewis's reticence regarding what was and what was not going into the *Lewis Papers.*

As will be seen from Lewis's letters to Greeves of 22 September and 1 October 1931, Lewis himself wanted for the purpose of the family history to have the loan of the letters he had written during his years at Great Bookham. He wished, as he said in his letter of 22 September, to 'renew those glorious years whenever I read them'. Greeves duly sent all those letters to him, and Lewis wrote back at once (1 October) to assure Greeves that he would not allow his brother to read those dealing with 'It' – by which he meant those dealing with the sexual fantasies of his youth. 'I am surprised,' he went on to say, 'to find what a large percentage of the whole they are. I am now inclined to agree with you in *not* regretting that we confided in each other even on this subject, because it has done no harm in the long run – and how could young adolescents really be friends without it? At the same time, the letters give away some of your secrets as well as mine: and I do not wish to recall things of that sort to W[arren]'s mind, so that in every way they had better be kept out of the final collection.' He might have added, except that Arthur already knew, that they belonged to his unregenerate youth, years before he became a Christian. The sweet and poignant memories of Bookham he would always want to retain, but 'It' was not so much like an albatross tied round his neck as something which had served its purpose and had now lost both its interest and significance.

Those who have seen the originals of the Bookham letters will have noticed that the passages relating to the sexual fantasies have been scratched through. I do not think Lewis did any of the scratching as there was, from his point of view, no one to hide the matter from. He selected from the – I think – 60 or so letters returned to him those I have numbered 21, 23–25, 27–37 and returned all the others to Arthur. I am a little puzzled as to why, in releasing these to his brother, he did not include any of the many letters he had received from Greeves. It is possible that they had already been lost, but whether they had or not I suspect that he did not wish to expose either Arthur's secrets or the fact that he was not in fact a very interesting or articulate writer to Warren or anyone else who some day might read the *Lewis Papers*. It is perhaps worth mentioning that shortly after the death of Arthur Greeves, when the bulk of this correspondence was put into Warren's hands, he did not bother to read it; so that the only ones he ever *did* read were those he copied into the *Lewis Papers*.

Those who knew 'Warnie' Lewis will recall with pleasure his easy and good-natured conversation. During the nine years in which I knew him I found him almost totally uninquisitive about people's private affairs and I cannot recall him ever saying anything to embarrass or annoy anyone, but for one notable exception. He confessed to having disliked Mrs Moore intensely. Whenever her name came up he admitted that, after living in the same house with her for over twenty years, he still could not fathom what it was about her that had so attracted his brother. In assisting Roger Lancelyn Green and me with our biography of his brother he was glad for us to quote the following passage from his private writings: 'What had actually happened was that Jack had set up a joint establishment which bound him to her service for the next thirty years and ended only with her death in January 1951. How the arrangement came into being no one will ever know, for it was perhaps the only subject which Jack never mentioned to me; more than never mentioned, for on the only occasion when I hinted at my curiosity he silenced me with an abruptness which was sufficient warning never to re-open the topic.'[9]

There has already been so much speculation about Lewis's relationship with Mrs Moore that I would gladly say nothing more about it. I have known, however, for years that if these letters were published the 'light' they shed on the relationship would require that that very complex story be opened up at least once more so that the many things said about Mrs Moore in these letters could be put into what I hope is a fair and suitable framework.

When, as I have said, the bulk of these letters came into his hands, Warren showed not the slightest interest in reading them. Indeed, when I suggested that they would almost certainly clear up some of the 'problems' he saw in the Lewis-Moore friendship he made it clear that he did not wish to read the letters, much less hear them discussed. But, oddly, he had no objection whatever to my editing them for publication. While he confessed to liking Arthur Greeves, I am nearly sure that I detected some cool, but never fully expressed, disdain for what I think he believed was Arthur Greeves's part in the 'secret' behind this curious relationship. He was wrong in supposing that Greeves took 'part' in the matter, except that he was invariably kind to Mrs Moore. But he was right in supposing that Greeves *knew* more than either Warren or his father about Lewis's youthful infatuation for the lady. It is not my business, nor I dare say anyone else's, to get to the 'bottom' of what must always remain something of a mystery – but it is perhaps as well to set the stage, so to speak, for the letters themselves.

Near the end of his first term at University College, Oxford, Lewis joined the Officers' Training Corps and was billeted in Keble College where his room-mate turned out to be E. F. C. 'Paddy' Moore. Paddy's home was in Bristol, and his mother and sister came down and took temporary lodgings in Oxford to be near him. Paddy introduced Lewis to them in June 1917 and thereafter they were to see one another frequently. Lewis – as he makes clear in *Surprised by Joy* – had never been entirely comfortable with his father, and Albert Lewis was deeply hurt when his son, having been given a month's leave (18 September–18 October 1917) before he went

[9] *C. S. Lewis: A Biography* (1974), ch. ii, p. 66.

overseas, spent the first three weeks of it with the Moores in Bristol. This was the last time Lewis and Paddy were to be together before they were shipped to France with their separate battalions. Paddy's sister Maureen (now Lady Dunbar of Hempriggs) was twelve at the time, but she told me years later that she could recall very distinctly hearing Lewis and her brother promise most solemnly that if one or the other of them survived the war the survivor would look after Paddy's mother and Lewis's father. Paddy, whom none of them was ever to see again, was killed in March 1918; and Lewis, having been wounded, was returned to England in May of that same year. The old affection was still there and Lewis fulfilled his promise by taking Mrs Moore and Maureen with him to Oxford as his 'adopted mother and sister'.

Anticipating his father's objections, Lewis kept most of this from him and – as the letters to Greeves will show – this inevitably led to duplicity on Lewis's part and painful feelings on both sides. If it had been merely a matter of Lewis fulfilling a promise Albert Lewis, Warren and even Arthur might not have been so puzzled. But it was clear to all – and specially to Arthur whom Lewis confided in – that Lewis preferred Mrs Moore's company to that of anyone. Warren was overseas when this joint ménage was being set up and he was quite as troubled as his father by the strange 'trap' which, to them, Lewis seemed to have been drawn into by Mrs Moore. When the pieces began to come together Warren was deeply stung that his father – so far away – was receiving so little and infrequent attention from his other son. It also signalled the end of the Lewises as a small but closely-knit family.

When Warren returned to England in 1922 from the Far East he went to Oxford to see his brother. On discovering that he was living in a rented house with 'the family' Warren took rooms in a hotel. Interestingly, Arthur had been there shortly before him and he and Mrs Moore seemed to have liked one another from their first meeting in 1919. But Warren could not forget the pain caused his father and the rupture Mrs Moore, perhaps unintentionally, had caused in the family. On 4 August 1922 Lewis was to say in his diary that during the meal he had with Warren 'I thought I had arranged for him to come and meet the family at tea: but quite suddenly while sitting in the garden of the Union he changed his mind and refused pertinaciously either to come to tea or to consider staying with us'. But when he saw him again that evening Lewis was able to record that his brother 'was now totally changed. He introduced the idea of coming to stay off his own bat and promised to come out tomorrow.' The next day he was able to write, 'I met W. again at the Roebuck and [he] came up here. Everyone present for tea and got on well.'[10]

Later, when Albert died – after being perfectly reconciled with his younger son – and Warren retired from the Army, Mrs Moore was as enthusiastic as Lewis in wanting him to make his home with them. They seem to have jogged along quite well, partly I think because Warren spent most of the day in one of his brother's Magdalen rooms. But after Mrs Moore died in 1951 and his brother in 1963, Warren confessed to having always disliked her. I was living with him at the time, and considering his loneliness and the misery caused by his alcoholism, I believe that his worst memories of Mrs Moore somehow caused him to make her the scapegoat for nearly all his troubles. At the same time he liked Lady Dunbar with a sincere and unwavering brotherly affection. It was, therefore, all the more surprising when he began writing the Memoir for his edition of his brother's *Letters* (1966) that he should be so scathing in his criticism of Mrs Moore that Mr Barfield and I urged him to moderate his criticism – which he did.

In so far as there is any 'mystery' to Lewis's devotion to Mrs Moore it is probably that, like everyone else, she struck each person differently, and that, like everyone else, she changed over the 34 years that Lewis and many of his friends knew her. Indeed, the only other person I have known who can be said to have disliked Mrs Moore was Professor Tolkien. He did not know her well, and I think it was because he was so protective of his friend and so alarmed that Lewis should have to sacrifice so much of his time and energy into caring for her that he once said to me 'Even if Jack had not been the very good man that he was he would deserve an instant apotheosis for having put up with that woman all those years!'

For every one who did not like Mrs Moore, I have come across a dozen who seemed genuinely devoted to her. This includes many of her neighbours who were still living near the Kilns when I was there, as well as old friends such as Mr and Mrs Owen Barfield. The Barfields knew Mrs Moore well over a long period, and they still recall her as a tireless and generous hostess who contributed enormously to the domestic happiness which Lewis enjoyed.

It was not my intention to wander from the friendship which these letters celebrate, but I think Lewis's initial reticence in writing about Arthur Greeves was due mainly to their confidences about sexual fantasies and especially the nature of this strange relationship with a friend's mother.

[10] *Lewis Papers*, vol. VII, p. 191.

There is not space enough to include here the portrait of Arthur which Warren felt obliged to write for the family history. Those who are interested will find it in vol. IV, pp. 181–2 of the *Lewis Papers*. It contributes little to our knowledge of Greeves and in the main deals with the weaknesses of his brother's friend of whom Warren confessed that he 'knew very little about'. Perhaps the chief value of it was to force Lewis to pick up his pen – which had been Warren's intention all along – and supply one which is, at the same time that it is more complimentary, also more rounded and is perhaps as definitive a portrait as we are likely to come by. It is impossible to date exactly, but I think Lewis wrote it some time around 1935:

My refusal to draw the character of Arthur Greeves has resulted in a portrait of him by another hand, which justice and charity oblige me to supplement. I do not contradict it, nor do I accuse it of malice. It is the work of one who knew the subject less intimately than myself and who saw only the surface of a character whose faults lay very obvious to the eye.

Arthur was the youngest son of a doting mother and a harsh father, two evils whereof each increased the other. The mother soothed him the more, to compensate for the father's harshness, and the father became harsher to counteract the ill effects of the mother's indulgence. Both thus conspired to aggravate a tendency (not rare in human nature) towards self pity, and some supernumerary bullying from an older brother was hardly likely to cure it. It can easily be imagined how such a child grew up: but who could have foretold that he would be neither a liar nor a tale bearer, neither a coward nor a misanthrope? He was the frankest of men. Many of the most ludicrous episodes which could be told against him, turn on his failure to acquire that 'visor to the human face' which such a training usually teaches a man to wear. He was the most faithful of friends, and carried the innumerable secrets of my own furtive and ignoble adolescence locked in a silence which is not commonly thought effeminate. Under illness or inconvenience he was impatient – a loud and violent, but not a lengthy grumbler: but danger left him unmoved. He was careless of heights and as a motorist was a rash though surprisingly competent driver. He was much isolated from his fellow men, not only by real and supposed ill health, but by literary and artistic tastes which none of his family and few of his neighbours shared.

Until I met him, and during my frequent absences, his position was much the same as that of an imaginative boy in one of our public schools. Yet he never showed any inclination to revenge himself after the fashion so familiar among our modern *intelligentsia*. He continued to feel – indeed he taught me to endeavour to feel with him – at once a human affection and a rich aesthetic relish for his antediluvian aunts, his mill-owning uncles, his mother's servants, the postman on our roads, and the cottagers whom we met in our walks. What he called the 'Homely' was the natural food both of his heart and his imagination. A bright hearth seen through an open door as we passed, a train of ducks following a brawny farmer's wife, a drill of cabbages in a suburban garden – these were things that never failed to move him, even to an ecstasy, and he never found them incompatible with his admiration for Proust, or Wyndham Lewis, or Picasso.

He was completely unworldly. He never in his life read an 'advanced' book or imitated a 'modern' painter because he felt that he could thus become a superior being. The motive was always either his genuine pleasure in them, or else the advice of ill-chosen friends. For Arthur was both humble and unstable. He could be persuaded to read, or at least begin, any book: to adopt (for a time) any canon of taste. The last speaker was always right to him. But all these fluctuations went on over a fundamental constancy: to the charm of the 'homely' he was never untrue, and if he was easily drawn into the follies of any and every coterie, he could not, by any process, be infected with its pride.

During the earlier years of our acquaintance he was (as always) a Christian, and I was an atheist. But though (God forgive me) I bombarded him with all the thin artillery of a seventeen year old rationalist, I never made any impression on his faith – a faith both vague and confused, and in some ways too indulgent to our common weaknesses, but inexpugnable. He remains victor in that debate. It is I who have come round. The thing is symbolical of much in our joint history. He was not a clever boy, he was even a dull boy; I was a scholar. He had no 'ideas'. I bubbled over with them. It might seem that I had much to give him, and that he had nothing to give me. But this is not the truth. I could give concepts, logic, facts, arguments, but he had feelings to offer, feelings which most mysteriously – for he was always very inarticulate – he taught me to share. Hence, in our commerce, I dealt in superficies, but he in solids. I learned charity from him and failed, for all my efforts, to teach him arrogance in return.

And since I have mentioned charity, I must speak of his 'charity' in the narrower sense. This was all his own, all virtue, and no nature. Heredity and early training had laid upon him as a natural curse the love of money, but he conquered it. He came to support, almost entirely, an unemployed man, and to offer me assistance in my lean times. He came (perhaps a harder thing for a constitutionally lazy man) to discharge regular duties in a charitable organisation. In this respect he defeated his nature. Against gluttony – another hereditary vice – he was less successful: he remained always a valetudinarian, though he was as much the dupe of doctors as of his self pity.

But if I had to write his epitaph, I should say of him what I could say of no one else known to me – 'He *despised* nothing.' Contempt – if not the worst, surely the most ludicrously inappropriate of the sins that men commit – was, I believe, unknown to him. He fulfilled the Gospel precept: he 'judged not'.[11]

One has only to read Lewis's letter of 12 October 1916 and some of those which follow to understand what he meant by 'the thin artillery of a seventeen year old rationalist'. Following the war and his return to Oxford in 1919, his 'artillery', while more formidable, met equally powerful opposition from Owen Barfield and others. While all this was going on, Lewis's attacks upon the Faith caused Greeves acute agony and it redounds to his credit that he endured it so patiently. When Lewis was finally brought to his knees and forced to admit that God is God – which long and involved surrender is recounted in *Surprised by Joy* – it was to Arthur that Lewis first broke the news. 'I have,' he wrote on 1 October 1931, 'just passed from believing in God to definitely believing in Christ – in Christianity,' which news, one of Arthur's cousins has said, caused him to weep with pleasure.

If it is true, as Lewis believed, that there are no 'accidents' with God, this would seem to apply in a marked degree to Lewis himself. The hard knocks he had given and received as an atheist were later to serve as some of the finest weaponry he was to use in his long and spectacular career as a Christian apologist. Remarking on the way God closed in on him, he said, 'Really, a young atheist cannot guard his faith too carefully.'[12]

Meanwhile, before Lewis's career was extended to defending the Faith – something still unforeseen when he published *The Pilgrim's Regress* – he enjoyed some of the most pleasant years of his life as his letters to Greeves show. Lewis was essentially a private man, delighting in the company, especially as Mrs Moore began to suffer the disabilities of age, of small and intimate groups of friends which included his brother, Owen Barfield, Professor Tolkien, Hugo Dyson and others. Though we have all been discomforted lately by those who are unable to understand the difference between 'preference' and 'prejudice', and out of mistaken notions about human nature and the natural canalization of social intercourse confound the two as 'prejudice', it nevertheless remains true that Lewis was a man of simple *preferences*. 'My happiest hours,' he wrote, 'are spent with three or four old friends in old clothes tramping together and putting up in small pubs – or else sitting up till the small hours in someone's college rooms, talking nonsense, poetry, theology, metaphysics over

[11] *Lewis Papers*, vol. X, pp. 218–20.
[12] *Surprised by Joy*, ch. xiv, p. 213.

beer, tea, and pipes. There's no sound I like better than adult male laughter.'[13] Lewis was here referring both to his walking-tour companions as well as to a small group (some of which were the same) now immortalized in Oxford history as 'The Inklings'.

Humphrey Carpenter, the biographer of Tolkien, has given us such a full and readable account of this group in his book *The Inklings: C. S. Lewis, J. R. R. Tolkien, Charles Williams, and their Friends* (1978), that it would be superfluous to say much about them here. The Inklings seem to have evolved from the Monday morning meetings between Lewis and Tolkien in 1931 until, a few years later, an unelected group of friends was gathering round Lewis in his Magdalen College rooms every Thursday evening in term. They were well established by the time Charles Williams joined them in 1939. Then the more or less 'regular' members included not only Williams, and the Lewis brothers, but Professor Tolkien, Christopher Tolkien, Owen Barfield, Hugo Dyson, Nevill Coghill, Adam Fox, Dr R. E. Havard, Lord David Cecil, Father Gervase Mathew, Colin Hardie and John Wain. Most of these Inklings met, as well, every Tuesday morning in their favourite pub, 'The Eagle and Child' – better known as the 'Bird and Baby' – in St Giles's. There was no regular 'programme' at either of these gatherings, but more often than not the Thursday evenings' entertainment consisted of one or other of the Inklings reading aloud some portion of a book he was writing. The fare often included portions of Tolkien's *Lord of the Rings*, and one of the first books Lewis read aloud was his *Problem of Pain* (1940).

The Problem of Pain is not, in my opinion, the best of Lewis's theological books but it caught the attention of the BBC and led to Lewis's extraordinarily successful series of broadcast talks, now collected under the title *Mere Christianity* (1952). It is perhaps to be regretted that Lewis did not tell Greeves more about the actual writing of his books, but this is typical of the man. Arthur, for all his attempts, did not succeed in publishing anything, and even if Lewis had *wanted* to discuss his own successes I think he would have resisted the temptation lest they detract from the pleasure Greeves had from his own modest achievements.

The odd thing is that if, in the unlikely event this volume of letters were the only book of Lewis's someone were to read, he could put it down knowing little of the reason for Lewis's fame. That is, much as I hope he would enjoy the letters by themselves, he might

[13] From a letter to the publisher quoted on the dust cover of the American edition of Lewis's *Perelandra* (New York, 1944).

not realize that Lewis was a polymath such as we may never see again. Besides being perhaps the greatest literary critic of our times, Lewis wrote a famous trilogy of science fiction novels, what is certainly the most popular set of 'children's stories' in the English-speaking world – *The Chronicles of Narnia* – and a score of theological books of such wisdom and imaginative beauty that it is apparent that he understood what Christianity is *about* better than any of the professional 'critics' of the Faith.

This is not intended as an unfair comparison between Lewis and Greeves, but a means of introducing what must be one of the strangest paradoxes of their friendship. As Lewis pointed out in his sketches of the Greeves family, Arthur had been infected from his earliest days by what Lewis called a 'crude antithesis of Grace and Nature'. He was as well, so Lewis informs us, 'both humble and unstable', easily persuaded 'to adopt (for a time) any canon of taste' but that 'all these fluctuations went on over a fundamental constancy'. This doubtless helps explain what Lewis had said earlier, in his letter of 6 December 1931, where he wrote 'I begin to see how much Puritanism counts in your make up – that both the revulsion from it and the attraction back to it are strong elements . . . Your relations have been found very ill grounded in the Bible itself and as ignorant as savages of the historical and theological reading needed to make the Bible more than a superstition.'

It is indeed very sad that, coincidental with Lewis's acceptance of thoroughgoing, supernatural Christianity – due in part to Arthur's perseverance years before – Arthur now began to vacillate between various expressions of non-conformity, some of whose beliefs can hardly be called Christianity at all. While the original damage seems to have been caused by his Plymouth Brethren parents, other forces were at work as well. It will perhaps seem odd that a man with such deep feelings for God and tradition simply could not settle down in the Anglican Church. He attended St Mark's for a while, but he disliked even the moderate amount of ritual he found there and he was generally uncomfortable in the company of priests. At this time Arthur's main travelling companion was his cousin, Sir Lucius O'Brien (1895–1974), who had been brought up a Quaker but who, about the time of Lewis's conversion, had lost interest in Christianity. I would not wish to malign that good man and devoted public servant, but judging from the mention of Sir Lucius in the letter of 6 December 1931, and what I have heard about the effects of his agnosticism on Arthur, it would appear that he did indeed play some part in causing Arthur to waver more than he might have done had it not been for Sir Lucius's influence.

Lewis's letters of the 1930s and early 1940s seem to have had a steadying influence on Arthur. But his vacillations soon began again and in 1944 he seems to have taken up with the Unitarians. Continually searching for the 'way' that suited his temperament, he later became interested in the Baha'i Faith of which his cousin, Mrs Lisbeth Greeves, was a member. The founder of this contemporary Eastern faith was Mirzā Hoseyn Alī Nūri (1817–92) who after breaking away from orthodox Mohammedism, took the name Baha'u'llah, meaning 'The Glory of God', and announced himself to be the one foretold in the holy books of all religions as the one who would inaugurate an era of peace and well-being for all mankind. One of the central tenets of this faith is the belief in successive 'progressive revelations' of God, none of which is final. Thus Mohammed was a great prophet but neither his revelations nor those of Baha'u'llah is believed to preclude God from revealing himself in future ages. It is easy enough for those interested to discover the teachings of the Baha'u'llah for themselves. Whether Arthur discussed the Baha'i Faith with Lewis is not known. There is no mention of it in Lewis's letters, but it could have been that they talked about it during some of their holidays together. In any event, Arthur did not in the end, despite its attractions for him, become a member.

Meanwhile, during Arthur's spiritual meanderings Lewis was having domestic problems which, while they drew him closer to Arthur, may have precluded their talking much about these matters. As far back as the late 1930s Professor Tolkien and others of the Inklings had observed that on the Inkling evenings at which Warren was present Lewis restricted the refreshments to tea. As many of the Inklings were to tell me later, Lewis did not explain this to his Oxford friends but they supposed (rightly) that Warren was an alcoholic. The problem, which had been building up steadily ever since he retired from the Army seems suddenly to have become very serious in the late 1940s. Arthur doubtless had known about it from the beginning, but the first mention of it in the letters occurs in that of 2 July 1949 where Lewis warns Arthur that in talking to Irish friends and relations Warren's trouble had to be disguised as 'nervous insomnia'. Thereafter, as Lewis found his coveted holidays with Arthur jeopardized by his brother's alcoholism, he had of necessity, and partly out of a need for Arthur's sympathy, to refer to it more explicitly. I should however inform the reader that some of the letters in which Lewis described Warren's alcoholic bouts in detail were destroyed shortly after Arthur's death and before any of these letters were made public.

His brother's problem makes one wonder how Lewis managed to keep his sanity much less do all he did during the last uncomplaining fifteen years of his life. Besides the care of Mrs Moore, and later his cancer-ridden wife, dashing all over the country giving talks to the RAF and almost every religious or literary society that asked him, he had as well to keep up his teaching at Oxford and, later, his lecturing at Cambridge. All this time books poured from his pen and he took the time to push a rheumatic hand across tens of thousands of sheets of paper in an attempt to answer nearly every enquiry he received.

Where did he find the energy? The continuous letter-writing he admits was a chore – but who would guess that from the letters themselves? – letters which reveal a far greater and more serious effort on his part than in almost any of those he received. As to where he found the time – well, it was just that for him writing books was his recreation, his solace, quite as natural as breathing.

In any case, just as Warren had looked after his younger brother when they were little lads together in Strandtown, now it was Jack's turn – in an old-fashioned way that did him credit – to do the protecting. When I first set about editing these letters those dealing with Warren's alcoholism had not come to light and I thought it right to keep it to myself. But now the one-time 'secret' is out. Besides, the missing letters were found where Arthur had left them, away from the rest, and it became clear that a first-hand account was at last called for.

I met C. S. Lewis early in 1963 and Warren had already gone off on what was to me (then) one of his inexplicable binges. Meanwhile, Lewis and I became more intimate, and finally he asked me to become his companion-secretary and I moved into his house. It was then that the facts about Warren came to light. They did indeed explain why Jack was in such open need of help. No one knew any more than that Warren was somewhere in Ireland on one of his more or less regular sprees. Jack himself was suffering from a combination of illnesses and the doctors told us that while there was a strong possibility that he might live for years, he could die at any moment. I wanted desperately for him to live, and even imagined that if he 'tried a little harder' he might have those extra years. Lewis, though, accepted things as they were, and spent more time comforting me than I him. 'I see myself,' he said, 'as a sentinel on duty. I'm willing to stay until I'm called – but, mind, I would sooner be called. Till such time as that happens, I'll willingly do whatever the doctors tell me.' Meanwhile, as it appeared that Jack *would* live for several more years, we got on with our work, the Monday morning Inklings meetings, the pints of beer, the steady conversations over cups of tea and all the rest. One day with another, it was the happiest time of my life for I, like Lewis, now knew what it was to be 'King of England'.

But Jack, with his great royal heart, worried for the welfare of his brother. He was anxious as to what would happen to him after his own death. In an effort to be as generous and, yet, as practical as possible he made Warnie the sole beneficiary of his literary Estate, having also appointed two of his friends as Executors and Trustees to prevent his brother converting that Estate, for as long as he should live, into ready cash. Even then the thought of Warnie's future so troubled him that he told me he wished, for Warnie's sake, that his brother might die first to prevent him ending up in a ditch uncared for and unloved. He always lamented, '*Who* is there to look after him when I'm gone?' The thought that I might be the one to do that never entered my head.

Going on the assumption that Lewis would live for some time yet, I went to the United States in September to clear up certain affairs before I returned after Christmas to resume (as I expected) my duties as Jack's secretary. Warnie returned home in October, and before Jack told him of the arrangements he and I had reached, he wrote to me on 11 October 1963 warning me of complications which might result from our reunion: 'There's always the chance W. might resent your presence (if he did, *you* wd. never know. He is the politest of men). Also, that he might *welcome* it as finally excusing him from all responsibilities to me, and so go more often on the binge. All this my *prudence* says. Don't ever doubt that the day of your return, whenever and on whatever conditions, will be one of re-joicing to me. Your absence makes a cavity like a drawn tooth!'

I was never to see Jack again, but be that as it is. When I returned after Christmas Warnie welcomed me as though I were already as much his friend as I had been Jack's, and it soon became clear that it had been given to me to care for Warren Lewis. Jack could never have known it in the anxious days of the previous summer, but as it turned out he needn't have worried.

During his early years Jack Lewis had sought privacy until his conscience drove him into becoming a public figure. For Warnie it had worked the other way round. After many happy and sociable years at Malvern, Sandhurst and in the Army, he was perfectly content to settle down to the twice-weekly meetings with the Ink-lings, the occasional walking-tour and a holiday in Ireland. The rest of the time went into his own absorbing hobby which was the study of the *Grand Siècle* and which resulted in his book *The Splendid Century: Some Aspects of French Life in the Reign of Louis XIV* (1953) and five other works on that same period. Jack loved the 'homely', but Warnie the 'cosy'. His daily routine was a short walk round the neighbourhood of the Kilns and sitting in his study reading and re-reading his 'French books' and the Kiplings and Trollopes he had inherited from his father. Like Jack, Warnie smoked pipes between numerous cigarettes, so that there was always a bluish haze in the room and everything, including the man, exuded the rich, male smell of old books and pipe tobacco. 'I like a man who *smokes* with me' he once said reprovingly when I talked of breaking the habit, and he often defended smoking on the interesting grounds that expensive cigarettes are '*better* for you than the cheaper brands'. Again, like his brother, he drank vast quantities of tea and he even carried a flask up to bed with him every night so that he could enjoy an 'early-early-morning cup' without having to get up. Jack's conversation was brilliant almost to the point of intoxicating. Warnie was much more relaxing and, despite all the ups and downs caused by his drinking, he was at all times the most courteous man I have ever known.

Though endlessly generous (Jack had for years been giving two-thirds of his royalties to charity) both Lewis brothers lived in fear of penury which Jack told me had been instilled into them by their father who frequently warned them that they were likely to end up in a 'work house'. Jack could be made to see how unfounded his fears were, but Warnie often described himself as a 'bankrupt' even when his bank-balance flatly contradicted it. By the time I returned to Oxford, Warnie had decided to move out of the Kilns (which, though it belonged to Lady Dunbar, was legally his home as long as he lived) and settle into a small semi-detached house nearby in 51 Ringwood Road. Having already bought the new house as an economy measure, he was reluctant to move into it, not wishing to upset his old routine. Meanwhile, I began reading theology at St Stephen's House in Oxford with a view towards serving my title at Headington Quarry and settling down with Warnie in Ringwood Road.

Early in 1964 Warnie began editing a volume of his brother's *Letters* – eventually published in 1966 – as a tribute to his brother, and to keep himself out of the forever threatening 'work house'. During my daily visits to the Kilns we usually had a pint or so of beer together in one of the local pubs, and from what I could see there was no threat of a 'binge'. He was a man who simply liked drink and felt better from it. Then, suddenly, he wearied of the editing, and with some of our belongings in the Kilns and some in the new house, he took off for Ireland. Some arrangements had to be made regarding the future of the Kilns, and as nothing had been heard from Warnie for six weeks, Lady Dunbar asked me to go to Ireland and try to fetch him home.

When he was drinking heavily Warnie preferred Ireland to being at home as there the pubs – unlike the ones in England – are open nearly all the time. In any case, as I had learned from Jack, Warnie had used up his 'credit' with the nursing homes and hospitals in Oxford which would no longer accept him as a patient.

When I arrived in Drogheda, in Co. Louth, on 21 July 1964 I discovered that Warnie had been, ever since about 1947, stopping in 'The White Horse Inn' until he required hospitalization. When that time came the Medical Missionaries of Mary, founded in 1937 by Mother Mary Martin – the best and most gracious lady I have ever known – gave him a bed in Our Lady of Lourdes Hospital in Drogheda. They did all in their power to help Warnie Lewis and never gave up hope that he would one day recover. He was in fact kept alive by Mother Mary and the nuns, but, Our Lady of Lourdes being a general hospital, they could not keep him there against his will. The result of this was that while Warnie 'pub-crawled' all day, he returned to the hospital to roost at night. Expecting that he would regard me as his 'gaoler' come to take him home, I was surprised to be welcomed with open arms. He – no longer fearing the 'work house' – had hired a taxi, and for the next seven days we motored from one village pub to another. The routine was nearly always the same. He left the hospital at 10.30 a.m., consumed a 'breakfast' of three triple-gin-and-tonics, and with our driver in attendance, we went – always on the move – from one pub to another where Warnie drank three triple-whiskies at each. I lived off sandwiches except when the nuns fed me, and he off spirits, but never then or any time else over the next nine years did I find that drink made him nasty or brutish. The schoolboy assumption that if one drink makes you feel pleasant twenty drinks will make you feel twenty times as pleasant seemed to work for him. He was never ill-tempered, and though he could not recall our conversations afterwards, they were always interesting and perfectly civilized. I don't know how it is, but he was more like his brother in wit and conversation when he was drunk than when sober.

By the time of my ordination in September 1964 the Kilns was let and I moved with my friend into our new house. Over the next few months we were to make three more trips to Drogheda, always

avoiding Belfast lest we run into any of Warnie's cousins or acquaintances – and thus it was that I never met Arthur Greeves. The fact
was that while I was forced to be a 'gaoler' of sorts I hadn't the
authority to do it well and Warnie often reminded me, when I tried
to curb his drinking, 'Walter, remember that you are not Jack, and
therefore you can't *force* me to do anything!' The saddest part of all
was that the poor man, his ageing body stiff with rheumatism and
needing to be helped out of the car, would nevertheless drag me to
the top of a hill to admire a statue of St Patrick, with the result that,
neither of us knowing the terrain, we would suddenly tumble into a
hollow, pull ourselves out, and so go on till we reached the statue,
and then begin our even more perilous descent. At other times we
couldn't help laughing at ourselves. During one of these trips we
were taken by an old family friend, Major Frank Henry, to a lovely
inn for a celebration meal before we returned to England. The place
was filled with high-ranking clerics and American tycoons. After a
few glasses Warnie slipped off to the lavatory. A moment later I
heard him bellowing 'Walter! Walter, come here!' I rushed in to
discover that a well-meaning nun who dressed him that morning
had put his trousers on back to front – and a possible disaster was
narrowly avoided.

In December 1964 Mother Mary Martin had to inform me that
the patient she had done everything in her power to help had become
too great a burden on the other patients. We had then, out of charity
to them, to end our visits to Drogheda.

This threw us on the only resource that Oxford offered, the
Warneford Hospital which is a mental institution but which affords
treatment to alcoholics when there is nowhere else for them to go.
Warnie resisted this as long as he could, with unfortunate results for
both of us. His 'resistance' meant that he would sit in his study chair
for as long as a fortnight without getting up, eating nothing, and
drinking as much as six bottles of whisky a day. As he could not distinguish night from day I had to be constantly on call, and as a
result I passed more than a year without a single night of unbroken
sleep. Not even then could I bear him any ill will. His courtesy never
wavered, and I still recall his conversation as some of the best I had
ever heard: he described French battles and Court intrigues with
more vividness than one finds even in his books; at other times he
sang snatches of songs he remembered from the old music hall days.

One advantage of the Warneford was that he hated it so much that
it made him want to get better. Once as we were walking round the

grounds, I found him so unsettled that I asked if he would like to enrol in a handicraft course – it seemed the only thing left. 'Pasting pansies on an empty gin bottle is not *my* idea of fun!' he snapped and immediately set about begging my pardon. Still, much as I loved him, I had suffered enough to recognize the strong element of selfishness in his character. After being in and out of the Warneford more times than I care to remember, I threatened on one of his visits home to nail a giant-sized photograph of the Warneford over his mantel-piece to remind him of our joint agony – and he immediately began to improve.

The bouts continued but there were longer periods of sobriety in between. When I was made Chaplain of Wadham College, and so had to move into Oxford, we still saw one another frequently. This coincided with Warnie's recovery of the Kilns, and he was extremely fortunate in having with him in the house Mrs Molly Miller (the Lewises' housekeeper since 1952) and her equally valuable husband Len Miller. They cared for him with great tenderness, and back in his old surroundings – especially the smoke-filled study – we en-joyed some of the most pleasant, even restful, days I can remember. All the former weariness and anxiety now seemed worth it. Warnie loved the annual 'Friends of Jack Lewis Party' which I organized to keep the Inklings and their friends in touch, and our little 'family' of four, with the occasional addition of Lady Dunbar, had many happy times together.

We all knew that anticipation – even anticipation of things he liked – sometimes sent him to the bottle, and thus the necessity of avoiding anything that was likely to set him off. Professor Tolkien most kindly invited us to his 80th birthday party celebrated in Merton College on 2 January 1972. The Professor and I both knew that Warnie would be hurt if he weren't invited, and so it was de-cided to risk it. Warnie and I planned to meet at the party. He didn't appear and I was to learn later that shortly before he was to set out he drank a bottle of brandy. This led to a full-scale binge which damaged his heart to such an extent that a pace-maker had to be implanted in his chest.

This caused him to worry more about himself than was really justified. However, shortly afterwards Mrs Miller suffered a stroke and – characteristically – he treated her with the tenderness she had always shown him. I was very fond of Mrs Miller too, and their troubles served only to strengthen our ties. It looked for a while that Warnie might continue in his sobriety. However, by the summer he so longed for a jaunt in his native Ireland that there was nothing to do but let him go. Once there he began drinking, collapsed, and his dear nuns at Drogheda could not turn him away. They cared for him with the affection and high spiritual comforts they had always shown him. There he had to remain throughout the winter suffering from his heart and other ailments. By the spring he felt well enough to come home, and indeed insisted on it. He arrived back in Oxford the first week of April 1973, began drinking and died in his bed on the 9th, a few months short of his 78th birthday. None of those of us who loved him succeeded as well as we should have liked. Still, I often wish I could have told all this to Jack Lewis before his death. It would have made his last few weeks in the Kilns with his brother so much easier.

But there is no getting round it, C. S. Lewis's last days were spent thinking a great deal about his brother and of the good times they had had when they were boys. Warnie himself had felt this too, and it is right that this account leaves off with them together. Of the last few weeks in the Kilns together Warnie was to write:

. . . once again – as in the earliest days – we could turn for comfort only to each other. The wheel had come full circle: once again we were together in the little end room at home, shutting out from our talk the ever-present knowledge that the holidays were ending, that a new term fraught with unknown possibilities awaited us both.

Jack faced the prospect bravely and calmly. 'I have done all I wanted to do, and I'm ready to go', he said to me one evening. Only once did he show any regret or reluctance: this was when I told him that the morning's mail included an invitation to deliver the Romanes lecture. An expression of sadness passed over his face, and there was a moment's silence: then, 'Send them a very polite refusal'.

Our talk tended to be cheerfully reminiscent during these last days: long-forgotten incidents in our shared past would be remembered, and the old Jack would return for a moment, whimsical and witty. We were recapturing the old schoolboy technique of extracting the last drop of juice from our holidays.

Friday, the 22nd of November 1963, began much as other days: there was breakfast, then letters and the crossword puzzle. After lunch he fell asleep in his chair: I suggested that he would be more comfortable in bed, and he went there. At four I took in his tea and found him drowsy but comfortable. Our few words then were the last: at five-thirty I heard a crash and ran in, to find him lying unconscious at the foot of his bed. He ceased to breathe some three or four minutes later.

The following Friday would have been his sixty-fifth birthday. Even in that terrible moment, the thought flashed across my mind that whatever fate had in store for me, nothing worse than this could ever happen to me in the future.[14]

Arthur was unable to get over for Jack's funeral, but these letters are evidence enough of the heartbreak he suffered, a heartbreak that Warnie knew he shared to a special extent with his brother's 'first friend'. Upon receiving his letters of sympathy, Warnie wrote to Arthur on 5 December 1963 saying, 'Of all the letters I have dealt with . . . yours is outstanding. For the simple reason that you and I knew Jack as no other people did. No doubt we both saw a different Jack, but still we share memories of him which go back further than those of anyone . . . of all the people I know, we two are the only ones who can really sympathize with each other.'

Without any change in his appearance that was particularly noticeable, Arthur's heart trouble began to worsen. He was able to make one more trip to London in the spring of 1966 before he settled down in his native Co. Down. He lived alone, except for a housekeeper, at Crawfordsburn where he moved in 1949, after the death of his mother, to be near those he loved most. They were his first cousin Lt-Colonel John Ronald Howard Greeves and his wife Lisbeth who had long been one of his closest confidants. From them he received kind and protective attention.

From all that Lt-Colonel and Mrs Greeves have told me, it would seem that Arthur was the archetype of the person Dr Johnson could have had in mind when he remarked that 'There is nothing too little for so little a creature as man'.[15] He never lost his relish for the 'homely', for what, then as now, would strike us as modest pleasures – walks, short rambles by car to quiet resorts near his home, and little supper parties with those he loved. The one-time urgency of his spiritual quest seems to have found fulfilment when he began attending, near the end of his life, Quaker services of about five elderly friends in a small meeting-room in Bangor. There, on Sundays, he enjoyed the silence, the quiet and the peace which (like his ancestors before him) he seems to have been looking for throughout his life.

Two weeks before he died he asked Lisbeth Greeves to lunch with him – 'after which,' as she recalls, 'although seemingly very well he must have "sensed" that he was near his passing, as he asked me to pray with him that he would, when his time came, die during his sleep.' She further recalls that on 27 August 1966 he was invited to the home of another old friend, Mrs Ethel Sumner, for what was to

[14] 'Memoir' in *Letters of C. S. Lewis*, ed. W. H. Lewis (1966), pp. 24–5.
[15] James Boswell, *The Life of Samuel Johnson*, 9 July 1763 (1791).

be a very pleasant birthday dinner. Two days later 'he died in his sleep – just like a happy child sleeping peacefully – with a linen handkerchief over his eyes, to shade them from the early morning sun'.[16]

'It is not,' Lewis had written, 'settled happiness but momentary joy that glorifies the past.'[17] These letters have both.

[16] Lisbeth Greeves to Walter Hooper of 6 January 1978. This and many other letters Mrs Greeves wrote to me about Arthur Greeves are in the Bodleian.

[17] *Surprised by Joy*, ch. i, p. 15.

EDITOR'S NOTE

The only letter I actually saw C. S. Lewis write to Arthur Greeves is that of 11 July 1963, though Lewis told me that the two friends had been corresponding for most of their lives. After his death, when I was living with his brother Major Warren Hamilton Lewis during 1964–5, Warren invited me to read his eleven unpublished volumes called the *Lewis Papers: Memoirs of the Lewis Family 1850–1930*. There I found transcribed 25 letters from 'Jack' (C. S.) Lewis to Arthur Greeves written between 1915 and 1916. Greeves was still alive and I assumed that if he had preserved his other letters from Lewis they were still with him in Northern Ireland. As I have pointed out in the Introduction, Warren Lewis was at this time undergoing a serious bout of alcoholism, which often led to very erratic behaviour on his part. I hoped that when he was better he would tell me more about his family and friends in Ireland – especially Arthur Greeves whom Jack Lewis had spoken of with so much affection during his last days.

Arthur died on 29 August 1966 and I regretted bitterly that I had never met him. Then, on a dank day in November 1966 – I remember there was a good fire in the grate – I was on one of my daily visits to see Warren. A letter and a registered parcel arrived from Belfast and, as I was coping with most of his post at the time, I was asked to open them. The letter accompanying the parcel was from Lisbeth Greeves, Arthur's cousin by marriage. Mrs Greeves had, she explained, been appointed by Arthur's executors to deal with all his personal effects, and in carrying out her duties she had come across this parcel addressed to Major Lewis.

Few literary finds could have excited me more. Inside the parcel were the two letters from Warren, the single letter from Joy Davidman and the 225 letters from Jack Lewis to Arthur Greeves that we were all, for some years, to suppose comprised the complete manuscript collection of the Lewis side of this long correspondence. With the manuscripts was a letter to Warren from Arthur's sister Lily Greeves Ewart. Because of Warren's general inattentiveness at this time I read Lily's letter to him several times, and, in view of what followed, I am glad I made a point of remembering as much of it as I could. Mrs Ewart said that her brother had attempted to arrange the letters into their proper chronological sequence and she stressed the point (which I copied into my diary) that 'it was my brother's wish that these letters be given to the University of Oxford Library'. As she didn't know the Library's address, she asked if Warren would put them there. Lily thought it a small favour to ask and, as she said, she believed he would wish to perform this small but important task on behalf of his brother's oldest friend.

Major Lewis was interested in the newly-formed C. S. Lewis Collection (now part of the Wade collection) at Wheaton College in Illinois. To my astonishment, he destroyed Lisbeth Greeves's and Lily Ewart's letters that very morning, never acknowledging either. He dismissed the fact that the letters from his brother were not his, and directed that they be sent to Wheaton. The Trustees of Lewis's Estate felt it only fair to inform the Bodleian and Wheaton of Arthur's intention, and that Warren had nevertheless appropriated the letters. In the absence of any legal obligation, however, no one was able to prevent Warren from disposing as he thought fit of the parcel Lisbeth Greeves had sent him, and the letters were sent to Wheaton where they have remained.

The Bodleian is an assiduous collector of Lewisiana. In 1968 an amicable arrangement was agreed upon between the Bodleian and Wheaton, and the two libraries began sending one another copies of the Lewis manuscripts in their possession. After the Bodleian had obtained copies of the letters written to Arthur, I was appointed by Warren Lewis and my fellow Trustees of the Lewis Estate, Owen Barfield and A. C. Harwood, to edit them for publication. This mammoth project had to be fitted into a very busy schedule so, doing the best I could, it has taken me ten years to complete.

Warren Lewis died on 9 April 1973. The following January I wrote to Mr Robin Morgan, the Headmaster of Campbell College, Belfast, requesting information about Jane McNeill, pointing out that it was relevant to an edition of Lewis's letters to Greeves – both of whom were former Old Boys of Campbell College. Mr Morgan – to whom I am deeply indebted for what was to follow – turned out to be a friend of Arthur's first cousin, Lt-Colonel John Ronald Howard Greeves, and his wife Lisbeth. Lt-Colonel and Mrs Greeves were unhappy to learn that Arthur's original gift to the Bodleian had gone elsewhere but, unknown to me at the time, they were intrigued by the possibility of the Bodleian still having some of Lewis's letters to Arthur. The Headmaster of Campbell College wrote to me on 23 January 1974 saying 'Colonel Greeves's wife, Elizabeth, has a number of poems written by Lewis to Arthur, and also a quantity of letters written by Lewis to Arthur and given by him to her. Some of the letters are, I understand, of a deeply personal nature and show Lewis's profound, even agonizing, concern over his brother's decline into alcoholism. Mrs Greeves feels that to reveal their contents would be a breach of the trust reposed in her by Arthur, but she is considering, quite enthusiastically it seems, sending the bulk of the letters to you since you are Lewis's Trustee and a clergyman.'

This left me thinking 'Would I ever see these letters?' and 'What would they say?' It was in all events a pleasing state of anxious expectancy. On 12 February 1974 I received a parcel and a letter dated the 11th in which Mr Morgan said 'I have very great pleasure in enclosing a collection of letters from C. S. Lewis to Arthur Greeves'. With it was a letter from Lisbeth Greeves of 2 February in which she wrote 'My husband & I are very pleased to hand over all the letters we have, that C. S. Lewis wrote to my cousin and friend Arthur Greeves'. This new treasure consisted of 50 letters written between 1949 and 1961 when, as has been said, Lewis was particularly troubled by his brother's 'decline into alcoholism'.

I was later to learn that, shortly after Arthur's death, Mrs Greeves had thought it best to destroy a few of those letters A little later still it was remembered that two of Lewis's letters had been given to Lt-Colonel and Mrs Greeves's daughter, Mary Nash, who has kindly allowed the Bodleian and Wheaton to have copies. As Major Lewis was already dead we agreed that there was now no 'face to be saved'. Still, we didn't want to act precipitately, and it was Mrs Greeves's decision that the 50 letters should remain under seal in the Bodleian until the whole of the correspondence was published. There are now in the Bodleian the originals or copies of all the letters from Lewis to Greeves that are known to exist. The 296 letters fall into the following groups:

1. Letters numbered 1–23, 26, 43–212, 214–19, 238–9, 262, 265–6, 270–1, 274–80, 284–5, 287–96 exist in manuscript and they are in Wheaton, with copies in the Bodleian.
2. Letters numbered 24–5, 27–42 exist only in the unpublished *Lewis Papers*, the original of which is in Wheaton and a copy of which is in the Bodleian.

3. Letters numbered 213, 286 exist in manuscript and are the property of Mary Nash of London. Copies are in the Bodleian and Wheaton.

4. Letters numbered 220–37, 240–61, 263–4, 267–9, 272–3, 281–3 exist in manuscript. They are owned by the Bodleian, and there are copies in Wheaton.

It is as well to record here a curiosity regarding those letters in the *Lewis Papers*. In 1931, when Warren began typing these family papers, Jack Lewis asked Arthur for the loan of the letters he had written from Great Bookham. Lewis screened the letters carefully (see Letter 171) and Warren was allowed to copy into the *Papers* those numbered 21, 23–5, 27–47. All except those numbered 24–5, 27–42 were returned to Arthur, and I suspect that the originals of these became intermingled with all the other documents which Warren destroyed after copying them into the *Lewis Papers*.

This, in turn, raises the even more perplexing question of what happened to the letters from Arthur to Jack Lewis. It is possible that Lewis had not preserved them. However, when, in 1964, Warren was moving out of the Kilns into a much smaller house he kept a bonfire of papers burning for three days. Regretfully, I had not been out to see him since the desecration began, but when I turned up at the Kilns the day following I was given a vast quantity of Lewis's notebooks and other papers which, had I not been there, Warren assured me, would have gone on to the fire. I found the four letters from Arthur which are printed in this collection in one of the notebooks. While I cannot be certain that Lewis saved the others, I can only suppose that if they had not disappeared earlier they almost certainly went into the bonfire.

Those who have seen the letters Lily Ewart sent to Warren in 1966 will have noticed that nearly all those written during 1914–29 were not dated. Lewis was later to regret this, but he could hardly have regretted it more than his correspondent. Arthur was an old man when he began trying to put the letters into their proper order for the Bodleian, and the only alternative to dating them was to order them by number. He did the best he could, but when I began my work I discovered that his numbering was so far out as to be more confusing than helpful. Thus, my first labour was to try and date the letters, which task struck me as the most complex jigsaw puzzle I could imagine. However, I began with advantages which Arthur did not have – the *Lewis Papers*, Lewis's letters to others, and the invaluable resources of the Bodleian. Even then, it sometimes took me weeks to date a single letter, and each piece of this jigsaw required a different method of detection.

I recognized soon after I began this part of my work that Lewis and Greeves were, during the Bookham period, writing to one another weekly. At first I thought that the frequent occurrence of 'Wednesday' at the letter-head was the day on which Lewis normally wrote. Later when I discovered that he usually penned his letters on Tuesdays, I realized that such scanty information as, say, 'Wednesday' or 'Saturday' on a letter was only meant to explain why it was late getting to Arthur. Of great advantage to me was the information from Albert Lewis's letters and diaries (all transcribed in the *Lewis Papers*). Having discovered from Mr Lewis's diaries when his son was in Belfast, I was better able to know when he was at Great Bookham or Oxford, and thus likely to write to his friend.

In some instances, even when I knew the month and perhaps the day, it was very difficult to know which *year* certain letters were written. Lewis's father saved all the letters he had from his sons, and Warren kept those from his father. Comparisons between them turned out to be useful. Lewis did not date the letters to his father, but Mr Lewis, a stickler for detail, preserved the post-marks found on the envelopes. Thus, if Jack Lewis told both Arthur and his father that he was reading a particular book for the first time, the post-mark on the letter to his father would sometimes furnish both the year and the precise week in which the letter to Arthur was written.

Frequently I was helped by a combination of things. After puzzling for a long while over Letter 11 in which Lewis complained of 'this submarine nonsense' which might prevent him getting home for a holiday, I discovered from Albert Lewis's letter to Warren of 3 February 1915 that a collier named the *Kilcoan*, designed by his brother Joseph Lewis, had been sunk by a German submarine in the Irish Sea. From other clues which indicated that Jack Lewis was thinking of this event in particular, I was able to go on to discover from *The Times* that the *Kilcoan* was torpedoed on 30 January 1915, and this helped me date the letter exactly.

Often when there were no clues to be had from these kinds of sources, I was helped by something likely to strike those who rely on typewriters as trivial. Besides being very familiar with Lewis's handwriting, I happen, by preference, to write with the nearly obsolete nib pen which is dipped in an inkwell. Lewis nearly always wrote with one. Those of us who prefer this method of writing have at least one advantage over those who use fountain pens and the ballpoint sort. Nibs have to be changed every few weeks, and each nib being slightly different, and there being many kinds of them, it is fairly easy to tell which letters were written with the same one.

And so it went on. The dating of the letters took me over a year, though, in retrospect, I know I enjoyed this part of the job more than anything. I regret that I cannot supply an exact date for every letter, but I believe the letters as I have them are in their correct chronological sequence.

From the beginning it had been my intention to make this book as much like a facsimile of the letters as was possible. In his early years Lewis was not a good speller, but as he was writing to a friend he was too interested in what he had to say to bother with a dictionary. I have preserved his actual spelling and abbreviations because they add to the charm of the letters and because they were his. There is, however, one alteration which I felt bound to make. Generous as Lewis always was, he was extremely paper-paring. Most of the letters were written without any paragraphing at all, and when transcribed on to the typewriter, *looked* unreadable. In the end I decided to divide the individual letters into paragraphs, so that the well-ordered ideas, with a natural sequence, fell instantly into place. They now appear more as Lewis would have designed them if he had been the confident owner of a paper mill.

It is one of life's most pleasant comedies that old age is often embarrassed by the excesses of youth. Arthur as an old man, idling before death and posterity, sought charmingly to make the letters more 'respectable'. As a consequence, many of the sentences having anything at all to do with 'That' were thoroughly scribbled over. And wasn't this typical? For what Lewis had in high-flown intellect his friend returned with earthly grace. But for Arthur embarrassment was soon to lose its meaning and for the editor – he is left to tell the story as it was.

Using the techniques of infra-red and ultra-violet fluorescence photography the deleted passages, for what they are, have been almost completely restored, and stand within brackets shaped thus – ⟨ ⟩.

In my quest through that mist of the past, I have been directed by many who, seeing me lost, knew the way better than I. They know who they are. Ronald and Lisbeth Greeves have been more magnanimous than any editor would have the right to expect. Except that I know they want it to be as it is, this book would have been dedicated to them. Lewis's finest legacy to me – my friend Owen Barfield has stood by me all the way. I am indebted to the Trustees of the Estates of W. H. Lewis, Joy Davidman and Arthur Greeves for permission to include their letters here. Familiar as I am with the Bodleian I should many times still have been completely lost had it not been for my two ladies who know everything, Miss Georgina Warrilow, Superintendent of the Upper and Lower Reading Rooms, and Miss Mary Sheldon-Williams, Assistant Librarian in charge of the Classics and Theology Reading Rooms. I suspect they are related to one 'S.H.' who once lived at 221B Baker Street, London. I am fortunate beyond all covenant in living in the same house and being helped so much by Anthony Marchington who is, as Lewis said of one of his contemporaries, 'the sole Horatio known to me in this age of Hamlets'. Lastly, I am grateful to Professor Clyde S. Kilby, Curator of the Marion E. Wade Collection at Wheaton, for allowing the 'deleted passages' to be photographed, and to Mr Bob O'Donnell and Mr David Elders of Lord and King Associates of West Chicago for photographing them. I acknowledge you all.

Oxford   WALTER HOOPER
26 April 1978

I

[Malvern College,
Malvern.
June? 1914]

Dear Arthur,

I really must apologize for having kept such a long and unjustifiable silence. But the readiest means of mending that fault are those of writing fully and at once – which I now propose to do. To begin at the beginning, you had hardly been outside Little Lea[1] for twenty minutes when a chance of not going back[2] seemed to be held out to me, only, as you may guess, to be snatched away again. When we came to pack up my last few belongings, what should happen but that no key was to be found for my trunk! High and low we searched, but not a sign of it. My father was in despair: how was I to go back? How long would it take to have a new lock fitted? For a few moments I had a wild hope of staying at home. What was my disgust, when, almost at the last moment, Annie[3] turned up with the required artical, and off I had to go!

Since then, I have lived or existed as one does at School. How dreary it all is! I could make some shift to put up with the work, the discomfort, and the school feeding: such inconveniences are only to be expected. But what irritates me more than anything else is the absolute lack of appreciation of anything like music or books which prevails among the people whom I am forced to call my companions. Can you imagine what it is like to live for twelve weeks among boys whose thoughts never rise above the dull daily round of cricket and work and eating? But I must not complain like this, I suppose. Malvern has its good points. It teaches one to appreciate home, and to despise that sort of lifelessness. If I had never seen the horrible spectacle which these coarse, brainless English schoolboys present, there might be a danger of my sometimes becoming like that myself. But, as it is, I have had warning enough for a lifetime. Another good point about Malvern is the Library, which is one of the best-stocked I have ever been in – not that anyone but myself and two or three others care twopence about it, of course! I have here discovered an author exactly after my own heart, whom I am sure you would delight

---

[1] The Lewises' home in Belfast.
[2] For his last term at Malvern College.
[3] Annie Strahan was the cook-housekeeper at Little Lea from 1911 to 1917.

in, W. B. Yeats. He writes plays and poems of rare spirit and beauty about our old Irish mythology. I must really get my father to buy his books when I come home. His works have all got that strange, eerie feeling about them, of which we are both proffessed admirers. I must get hold of them, certainly.

You can hardly tell how glad I was to hear that you were learning theory. It is a positive shame that you should go about with all those lofty strains running in your head, and yet never set pen to paper to perpetuate them. Of course, take the 'Loki Bound' MS.[4] over to Bernagh,[5] anytime you feel inclined to compose a little operatic music. Thank you very much indeed for undertaking the job of the gramaphone. I suppose by this time it is restored to its former condition. It makes me furious to think of your being able to walk about your house and ours and all the beautiful places we know in the country, while I am cooped up in this hot, ugly country of England. Where is your favourite walk? I hope that by this time you are quite recovered and are able to go about freely without fear of injury. County Down must be looking glorious just now: I can just picture the view of the Lough and Cave Hill from beside the Shepard's Hut. Sometime next holydays, you and I must make a journey up their before breakfast. Have you ever done that? The sunrise over the Holywood Hills, and the fresh stillness of the early morning are well worth the trouble of early rising, I can assure you.

Since I have touched on the subject of health, I must ask a few questions of a disagreeable nature, on a matter which I have very near my heart. I have now had no direct letter from my father for over three weeks, and I hear that he is very ill. I would be very thankful indeed if you would go over and see him sometimes, and try and cheer him up: then you could tell me exactly how he is, and whether what I have heard has been exagerated or not – although I really don't deserve a reply to this after the shameful way I have treated you with regard to letters. But I feel sure you won't mind writing just a few lines, to tell me about yourself and family, and the state of various other things, besides my father's health. As I am sure you are tired by this time of a long and melancholy letter, I will stop.

Yours affectionately
Jack Lewis

---

[4] A tragedy, Norse in subject and Greek in form, which Lewis was writing.
[5] The Greeveses' home in Belfast.

2

'Gastons'
Grt. Bookham.
Surrey.
Saturday
Sept / 14
[26 September 1914]

My dear Arthur,

if it were not that you could answer me with my own argument, I should upbraid you with not having written to me. See to it that you do as soon as you have read this.

And now – what do I think of it? After a week's trial I have come to the conclusion that I am going to have the time of my life: nevertheless, much as I am enjoying the new arrangement, I feel sure that you would appreciate it even more than I. As for the country, I can hardly describe it. The wide expanse of rolling hill and dale, all thickly wooded with hazel and pine (so different from our bare and balder hills in Down) that is called Surrey, is to me, a great delight. Seen at present, in all the glory of a fine Autumn, it may be better imagined than described. How I wish that I could paint! Then I could carry home a few experiences on paper for my own remembrance and your information. But the village wd. please you even better. I have never seen anything like it outside a book. There is a quaint old inn that might have stepped out of the 'Vicar of Wakefield',[1] and a church that dates from before the conquest. But it is no good enumerating things: I cannot convey the impression of perfect restfulness that this place imparts. We have all often read of places that 'Time has forgotten' – well, Great Bookham is one of these!

I have only just discovered that you put my name in that book. If I had seen it earlier I shd. have sent it back. You have no right to be so foolishly generous! However – many, many thanks. When one has set aside the rubbish that H. G. Wells always puts in, there remains a great deal of original, thoughtful and suggestive work in it. The 'Door in the Wall', for instance, moved me in a way I can hardly describe! How true it all is: the *SEEING ONE* walks out into joy and happiness unthinkable, where the dull, senseless eyes of the world see only destruction & death. 'The Plattner Story' & 'Under the Knife' are the next best: they have given me a great deal of pleasure. I am now engaged in reading 'Sense & Sensibility'. It is,

[1] Oliver Goldsmith (1766).

undoubtedly, one of her best. Do you remember the Palmer family?[2]

In Greek, I have started to read Homer's Iliad, of which, of course, you must often have heard. Although you don't know Greek & don't care for poetry, I cannot resist the temptation of telling you how stirring it is. Those fine, simple, euphonious lines, as they roll on with a roar like that of the ocean, strike a chord in one's mind that no modern literature approaches. Better or worse it may be: but different it is for certain.

I hope everything went off successfully on the eventful Teusday, and also that you are now recovered from your cold. You know my address: you have no excuse for silence, Sir!! No Philip's concerts this year at Belfast, I am told.

Yrs. (Expecting a letter)
C. S. Lewis

3

Gt. Bookham
[6 October 1914]

Dear Arthur,

I will begin by answering your questions & then we can get on to more interesting topics. The plot of my would-be tragedy is as follows: (The action is divided into the technical parts of a Grk. tragedy: so:)

I. Prologos.

Loki, alone before Asgard, explains the reason of his quarrel of the gods: 'he had seen what an injustice the creation of man would be and tried to prevent it! Odin, by his magic had got the better of him, and now holds him as a slave. *Odin* himself now enters, with bad news. *Loki* (as is shewn in the dialogue) had persuaded the gods to make the following bargain with the Giant, Fasold: that if F., in one single winter, built a wall round Asgard, the goddess Freya should be given him as his concubine. The work is all but finished: the gods, repenting of the plan, are claiming Loki's blood.

II. Parodos.

Thor, *Freya* & the *Chorus* enter. After a short ode by the latter, Thor complains that *Loki*, who is always the gods' enemy has persuaded them to this plan, well knowing that it would come to no

[2] In Jane Austen's *Sense and Sensibility* (1811).

good. *Loki* defends his actions in a very scornful speech, and the two are only kept from blows at the request of *Odin* & *Freya*. *Odin*, though feeling qualms on account of their ancient friendship, agrees to *Loki's* being punished if the latter cannot devise some way out of the difficulty by the next day, (when 'the appointed Winter' is up). The others then withdraw leaving Loki alone with the *Chorus*. He has been cringing to Odin up till now, but on his exit bursts out into angry curses.

III. Episode I.

The *Chorus* pray to the 'spirits of invocation' to help *Loki* to find a plan. His only desire is to be able to save his own head and plunge the gods into even deeper morasses. A long dialogue ensues between him & the *Chorus*, the result of which is this plan: that *Loki* will send a spirit of madness into *Fasold's* horse which always accomplishes the greater part of the work. (Vide 'Myths of the Norsemen').[1] The *Chorus* agree & Loki sets off to Jarnvid (Iron-wood) to instruct the spirit.

IV. Episode II.

It is now quite dark. The *Chorus* are singing a song of hope & fate, when *Fasold* enters with his horse, dragging the last great stone. He stops & converses with the *Chorus*. In the dialogue which follows, the genial, honest, blundering mind of *Fasold* is laid open: and his frank confession of his fears & hopes for *Freya*, and his labours, forms a contrast to the subtle intrigues of the gods. At last he decides to move on. He urges the horse: but at that moment the frenzy siezes it: it breaks from its traces & gallops off, kicking its master and leaving him senseless in the snow. Presently he recovers, and after a very sad & indignant accusation of the gods, goes off to mourn 'his vanished hope'. He cannot now hope to gain the 'dear prize' for which 'he laboured all those months'! The morning is all ready at hand

V. Episode III.

Loki, *Thor* & *Freya* return. All are in high spirits, and exult over the success of the plan. To them enters *Odin*. By the appearance of the god, we guess that something is wrong. On being questioned his explanation (greatly condensed) is this. 'The gods' empire rests on

[1] H. M. A. Guerber, *Myths of the Norsemen from the Eddas and Sagas* (1908).

treaties. Therefore on honour. When that honour is broken their doom is at hand. Loki has conquered the Giant, how? By Fraud. We have broken faith and must prepare for the twilight of the gods.' As soon as the general shock has passed off, *Thor* turns upon *Loki* and says that he is the cause of all this. *Loki*, seeing that he has accomplished his design, throws off the mask of humility that he has been wearing, and, confessing that it was all his plan, bursts forth into fearful [cursings?] upon *Thor* and *Odin*. Since *Loki* cannot be killed by any known weapon, *Thor* purposes to pinion him on an adjacent boulder (etc. Vide 'Myths of the N's') as a punishment. *Odin*, though without enthusiasm consents, and he is bound. (Thor, Freya, Odin go off).

VI. Exodos.

Loki, bound to the rock, is indulging in a satyric dialogue with the *Chorus*, when Odin returns. As soon as *Loki* sees him he bursts into violent abuse. *Odin* has come to offer him pardon & release: 'He (*Odin*) is a lonely god: men, gods, & giants are all only his own creatures, not his equals & he has no friend – merely a crowd of slaves. *Loki*, who had been brought forth *with* & (not *by*) him by Fate, had supplied one. Will he be reconciled?' *Loki*, however, casts his offer back in his teeth, with many taunts. Seeing that they can effect nothing *Odin* & *Chorus* withdraw & the tragedy ends.

Such then, in brief, is the skeleton of my poor effort: poor indeed in its intrinsic worth, and yet not so poor if you could set it to soul-stirring music. As an opera the parts would be like this.

LOKI	Tenor (?)
ODIN	Baritone
THOR	Basso (of course)
FREYA	Soprano
FASOLD	Basso
LEADER of the CHORUS	Contralto (she has quite a lot to do, here & there)

Of course you would readily see what musical points could be made. Nevertheless I cannot refrain from giving you a few of my ideas. To begin with, Loki's opening speech would be sombre and eerie, – expressive of the fire-god's intrigueing soul, and endless hatred. Then (*Parados*) the first song of the chorus would be bright and tuneful, as a relief to the dramatic duet that precedes it. The next great opportunity for 'atmospheric' music comes (Episode I) where the theme of the 'spirit of madness' is introduced. *You* can well imagine what it ought to be like. Then (Episode II) we would have a bluff, swinging ballad for the huge, hearty giant; and of course the 'madness motive' again, where the horse breaks lose. Then some 'Dawn' music as a prelude to (Episode III) and Odin's speech about their position! What an opening for majestic & mournful themes. But the real gem would be some inexpressibly sad, yearning little theme, where (Exodos) Odin expresses his eternal loneliness. But enough!, enough! I have let my pen run away with me on so congenial a subject & must try & get back to daily life.

As for my average 'Bookham' day, there is not much to tell. Breakfast at 8.0, where I am glad to see good Irish soda-bread on the table begins the day. I then proceed to take the air (we are having some delightful, crisp autumn mornings) till 9.15, when I come in & have the honour of reading that glorious Iliad, which I will not insult with my poor praise. 11–11.15 is a little break, & then we go on with Latin till luncheon, at 1.0. From 1.–5.0, the time is at my own disposal, to read, write or moon about in the golden tinted woods and vallies of this county. 5–7.0, we work again. 7.30, dinner. After that I have the pleasant task of reading a course of English Literature mapped out by Himself.[2] Of course, that doesn't include novels, which I read at other times. I am at present occupied with (as Eng. Lit.) Buckle's 'Civilization of England',[3] and (of my own accord) Ibsen's plays.

Hoping to hear from you soon, with all your views & suggestions for Loki, I am.

Yrs. sincerely
C. S. Lewis

P.S. If you begin composing in earnest, you'll find the libretto in my study upstairs. J.

---

[2] His tutor William T. Kirkpatrick (1848–1921).
[3] H. T. Buckle, *History of Civilization in England* (1857; 1861).

4

My dear Arthur,

Although delighted, as always, to find your letters on my plate, I was very sorry to hear that you were once again laid up: I hope, however, that it is nothing more than a cold, and will soon pass away.

I was very glad to hear your favourable criticism of 'Loki' (and I hope it is genuine) and to see that you are taking an interest in it. Of course your supposed difficulty about scoring is a 'phantasm'. For, in the first place, if we do compose this opera, it will in all probability never have the chance of being played by an orchestra: and, in the second place, if by any chance it were ever to be produced, the job of scoring it would be given – as is customary – to a hireling. Now, as to your budget of tasteful and fascinating suggestions. Your idea of introducing a dance after the exit of Odin etc, is a very good one, altho' it will occasion some trifling alterations in the text: and, speaking of dances in general, I think that you are quite right in saying that they add a certain finish to both dramatic & operatic works. Indeed, when I was writing them, there were certain lines in the play which I felt would be greatly 'helped out' by appropriate movements. Thus the lines

'The moon already with her silvery glance, –
The hornèd moon that bids the high gods dance'

would suggest some good moonlight music both in motion and orchestra.

Turning to your remarks about illustrations, I must confess that I have often entertained that idea myself; but, thinking that, since you never spoke of it, there was some radical objection on your part, I never liked to suggest it. Now that I am undeceived in *that* direction, however, need I say that I am delighted with the idea? Your skill with the brush, tho' by no means superior to your musical abilities, has yet a greater mastery of the technical difficulties. I have only to cast my eyes over the libretto to conjure up a dozen good ideas for illustrations. (1) First of all, the vast, dreary waste of tumbled volcanic rock with Asgard gleaming high above in the background, thrown out into sharp relief by the lurid sunset: then in the foreground there is the lithe, crouching figure of Loki, glaring with satanic malignity at the city he purposes to destroy. That is my conception of the Prologos. (2) Then Odin, thundering through the twilit sky on his eight footed steed! (what a picture.) (3) Again, Freya, beautiful, pathetic and terrified making her anguished entreaty for protection. (4) A sombre study of the moonlight choral dance that you so wisely suggested. (5) The love-sick Fasold raging in impotent fury when he discovers that he has been cheated. And (6) last of all, Loki, bound to his rock, glaring up to the frosty stars in calm, imperturbable and deadly hatred! And so on & so on. But you, with your artist's brain will doubtless think of lots of other openings. I do sincerely hope that this idea will materialise, and that I shall find on my return a whole drawer full of your best.

I am afraid this is rather a 'Loki' letter, and I know that I must not expect others to doat on the subject as foolishly as do I. I am going to ask for 'Myths and legends of the Celtic Race'[1] as part of my Xmas box from my father: so that, as soon as I put the finishing touches to 'Loki Bound', I can turn my attention to the composition of an Irish drama – or perhaps, this time, a narrative poem.[2] The character of Maeve, the mythical warrior Queen of Ireland, will probably furnish me with a dignified & suggestive theme. But, we shall see all in good time.

Mrs Kirkpatrick, the lady of this house, had not played to me at the time of writing my last epistle. But since then she has given me a most delightful hour or so: introducing some of Chopin's preludes, 'Chanson Triste', Beethoven's moonlight Sonata, Chopin's March Funèbre, The Peer Gynt Suite & several other of our old favourites. Of course I do not know enough about music to be an authoritative critic, but she seemed to me to play with accuracy, taste & true feeling. So that there is added another source of attraction to Great Bookham. For the value of Mrs K's music is to me two fold: first it gives me the pleasure that beautiful harmonies well executed must always give: and secondly, the familiar airs carry me back in mind to countless happy afternoons spent together at Bernagh or Little Lea!

Strange indeed is my position, suddenly whirled from a state of abject terrorism, misery and hopelessness at Malvern, to a comfort

---

[1] Presumably *Celtic Myth and Legend* by Charles Squire.

[2] Whether Arthur Greeves ever attempted any part of his share in the musical drama is not known, but Lewis's lyric text of *Loki Bound* filled thirty-two pages of a notebook. The only part of this which has survived consists of 119 lines reproduced in the unpublished *Lewis Papers*, vol. IV, pp. 218–20.

and prosperity far above the average. If you envy my present situation, you must always remember that after so many years of unhappiness there should be something by way of compensation. All I hope is that there will not come a corresponding depression after this: I never quite trust the 'Norns'.[3]

I have come to the end now of *my* time & paper and, I daresay, of *your* patience. While I remember; it would be as well for you to keep that sketch of the plot of Loki, so that we can refer to it in our correspondence, when necessary.

Yrs. very sincerely
Jack Lewis

P.S. Have the Honeymooners come home from Scotland yet? (J.)[4]

5

[Gastons
20 October 1914]

My dear Arthur,

Many thanks for the letter, which I hope is becoming a regular 'institution', and apologies for my comparative slackness in replying. When I read your description of the boring evening I thought for a while of writing you a letter full of 'war' – to hear your views afterwards. But, to be serious, what would you? Is the trivial round of family conversation ever worth listening to, whether we are at war or no? I can promise you that it is not at Little Lea: and if Bernagh is different it must be an exceptional household. The vast majority of people, too, whom one meets outside the household, have nothing to say that we can be interested in. Their circle of interests is sternly practical, and it is only the few who can talk about the really important things – literature, science, music & art. In fact, this deadly *practicalness* is so impressed on my mind, that, when I have finished Loki, I am resolved to write a play against it.

The following idea has occurred to me: in Irish mythology the ruling deities are the light & beautiful Shee: but, we are told, before these came, the world was ruled by the Formons, hideous and monstrous oppressors. What are the exact details of the struggle between the two parties I do not know. But it ought to make a good

---

[3] The female Fates of Norse mythology.

[4] The 'Honeymooners' were probably Arthur's brother, Thomas Greeves, and Winefred Lynas who were married on 22 September 1914.

allegorical story, in which the Formons could be taken as typical of the stern, ugly, money grubbing spirit, finally conquered by that of art & beauty, as exemplified by the lovely folk of the Shee. However, of course, this is only a castle in the air.

I sympathize with your difficulty in drawing a horse, as I have often made the attempt in the days when I fancied myself in that line. But of course that counts for nothing: as the easiest of your sketches would be impossible for me. But there are heaps of pictures in which you need not introduce the animal. I hope the music has started in real earnest by now. The longer I stay at this place, the better I like it. Mrs. K., like all good players – including yourself – is lazy and needs a lot of inducement before she performs.

yours sincerely
C. S. Lewis

6

Gt. Bookham
Wednesday
[28 October 1914]

Dear Arthur,

You ask me what a shee is: I reply that there is no such thing as '*A*' Shee. The word (which, tho' pronounced as I have spelled it, is properly in Irish spelled 'Shidhe') is a collective noun, signifying 'the fairies', or the gods, – since, in Irish these powers are identical. The common phraze 'Banshee', is derived from 'Beän Shidhe' which means 'a woman of the Shee': and the gods, as a whole, are often called 'Aes Shidhe', or 'people of the S.' The resemblance between this word '*Aes*' and the Norse '*Aesir*' has often been noted as indicating a common origin for Celtic & Teutonic races. So much for the etymology. But the word has a secondary meaning, developed from the first. It is used to indicate the 'faery forts' or dwelling places of the Shee: these are usually subterranean workings, often paved and roofed with stone & showing an advanced stage of civilization. These can be seen in a good many parts of Ireland. Who *really* built them is uncertain: but scholars, judging by the rude patterns on the door posts, put them down to the Danes. Another set say that they were made by the original inhabitants of Ireland, previous *even* to the Celts, – who of course, like all other Aryan people primarily came from Asia.

I am sorry that my epistle is rather late in arrival this week: but what with people bothering from Malvern, and letters to be written home, I have not had many free evenings. I feel confidant of your always understanding that, when my letters fail to arrive, there is a good, or at least a reasonable explanation. Now that I have threshed out the question of Shee, and apologized, I don't know that there is much to write beyond hoping that 'Loki' is proceding expeditiously in music & illustration.

Last week I was up with these people to the Coliseum: and, though of course (which by the way I see no prospect of) I had sooner have gone to some musical thing, yet I enjoyed myself. The Russian Ballet – and especially the music to it – was magnificent, and G. P. Huntley in a new sketch provoked some laughter. The rest of the show trivial & boring as music halls usually are.[1] At 'Gastons' however, I have no lack of entertainment, having been recently introduced to Chopin's Mazurkas, & Beethoven's 'Sonate Pathétique'.

No: there is no talk yet of going home. And, to tell you the truth, I am not sorry: firstly, I am very happy at Bookham, and secondly, a week at home, if it is to be spent in pulling long faces in Church & getting confirmed, is no great pleasure – a statement, I need hardly say, for yourself alone.

Yrs.

Jack Lewis

7

[Gastons
4 November 1914]

Dear Arthur,

I suppose that I should, as is usual in my case begin my epistle with an apology for its tardiness: but that form of adress is becoming so habitual as to be monotonous, so that it may be taken for granted.

I was, if I may say so, not a little amused to hear you say in an off-hand manner 'The Celts used to retire to them in time of war', when antiquarians have been disputing for ages: but of course you have grounds for your statement I admit. Your souteraines are, I imagine, but another variety of the same phenomena as my Shidhes: when I said 'doorposts' I did not imply the existence of doors, meaning only the stone pillars, commonly (I believe) found at the entrances to these excavations.

---

[1] The programme at the London Coliseum between 19–24 October included the Imperial Russian Ballet's performance of *Fleurs d'Orange* and G. P. Huntley acting in Eric Blore's *A Burlington Arcadian*.

Great Bookham and the present arrangement continue to give every satisfaction which is possible. But there is one comfort which must inevitably be wanting anywhere except at home – namely, the ability to write whenever one wishes. For, though of course there is no formal obstacle, you will readily see that it is impossible to take out one's manuscript and start to work in another's house. And, when ideas come flowing upon me, so great is the desire of framing them into words, words into sentences, and sentences into metre, that the inability to do so, is no light affliction. You, when you are cut off for a few weeks from a piano, must experience much the same sensations. But it would be ridiculous for me to pretend that, in spite of this unavoidable trouble, I was not comfortable. Work and liesure, each perfect and complete of its kind, form an agreeable supplent to the other, strikingly different to the dreary labour and compulsory pasttimes of Malvern life. The glorious pageant of the waning year, lavishing her autumn glories on a lovely countryside, fills me, whenever I take a solitary walk among the neighbouring hills, with a great sense of comfort & peace.

So great is the selfishness of human nature, that I can look out from my snug nest with the same equanimity on the horrid desolation of the war, and the well known sorrows of my old school. I feel that this ought not to be so: but I can no more alter my disposition than I can change the height of my stature or the colour of my hair. It would be mere affectation to pretend that sympathy with those whose lot is not so happy as mine, seriously disturbs the tenour of my complacence. Whether this is the egotism of youth, some blemish in my personal character, or the common inheritance of humanity, I do not know. What is your opinion?

I am reading at present, for the second time, the Celtic plays of Yeats. I must try & get them next time I am at home. Write soon, and tell me all that you are doing, reading & thinking.

Yours,
C. S. Lewis

8

Dear Arthur,

It is the immemorial privilege of letter-writers to commit to paper things they would not say: to write in a more grandiose manner than that in which they speak: and to enlarge upon feelings which would be passed by unnoticed in conversation. For this reason I do not attach much importance to your yearnings for an early grave: not, indeed, because I think, as you suggest, that the wish for death is wrong or even foolish, but because I know that a cold in the head is quite an insufficient cause to provoke such feelings. I am glad Monday found you in a more reasonable frame of mind.

By the way, I hear nothing about music or illustrations now! Eh? I hope that this can be accounted for by the fact that both are finished. I suppose the former has been performed in the Ulster Hall, by this time, and the latter exhibited – where? Here the sentence comes to a stop: for I have suddenly realized that there is no picture gallery in Belfast. It never occurred to me before what a disgrace that was. I notice, too, that you answer my questions about 'doing' and 'reading' but keep a modest silence about 'thinking'. It is often difficult to tell, is not it? And seldom advisable: which makes me think about the hard question of truth. Is it always advisable to tell the truth? Certainly not, say I: sometimes actually criminal. And yet, useful as it is for everyday life, that doctrine will land one in sad sophistries if carried to its conclusion. What is your view?

The other day I was in Guildford (it is a glorious old English town with those houses that [get] bigger towards the top; a Norman castle; a street built up a preposterous hill; and beautiful environments) where I picked up a volume of Wm. Morris's lyric poems in that same edition in which you have 'The Wood at the Worlds end'.[1] So delighted was I with my purchase, that I have written up to the publisher for the same author's 'Sigurd the Volsung': which, as I need hardly tell you, is a narrative poem, dealing with Siegfried (=Sigurd) & Brünhilde, as described in the legends of Iceland, earlier than those of Germany. What is your opinion of Ainsworth? I see you are reading his 'Old St. Pauls'. I must confess I find him dreary – a faint echo of Scott, with all the latter's faults of lengthiness

---

[1] He meant William Morris's *The Well at the World's End* (1896).

and verbosity and not of his merits of lively narrative & carefully-welded plots.

When you talk about the difficulty of getting the necessary materials for one's pursuits, I am thankful that, in my case, when the opportunity is at hand, the means – paper & pen – is easily found. Whereas you, unfortunately, need a piano or a box of paints and a block of drawing paper.

I hope there will be some relics of us left when we have settled that question of souteraines.

Yrs sincerely
Jack Lewis

9

[Gastons
17 November 1914]

My dear Arthur,

Do you ever wake up in the morning and suddenly wonder why you have not bought such-and-such a book long ago, and then decided that life without it will be quite unbearable? I do frequently: the last attack was this morning à propos of Malory's 'Morte D'Arthur', and I have just this moment written to Dent's for it. I am drawing a bow at a venture and getting the Everyman two-shilling 'Library' edition. What is it like, do you know? As for the book itself, I really can't think why I have not got it before. It is really the English national epic, for Paradise Lost is a purely literary poem, while it is the essence of an epic to be genuine folk-lore. Also, Malory was the Master from whom William Morriss copied the style of his prose Tales.

Which reminds me of your criticism of the 'Well'. I quite see your point, and, of course, agree that the interests of the tale reach their climax in the great scene at the World's End: my reply is that the interest of the journey home is of quite a different nature. It is pleasant to pick up all the familiar places and characters and see the same circumstances applied to the heroe's new rôle of 'Friend of the Well'. The Battle-piece at the end is very fine, and the ending, tho', as was inevitable, conventional, leaves one in a pleasant, satisfied state of mind. The only part that I found really tedious was Roger's historical survey of the Burg & the Scaur. In fact, Roger was only a lay-figure brought in to conduct the Ladye's machinations with Ralph, and why he was not allowed to drop into oblivion when they were over, I cannot imagine.

How I run on! And yet, however many pages one may fill in a letter, it is only a tithe of what ten minutes conversation would cover: it is curious, too, how the thoughts that bubble up so freely when one meets a friend, seem to congeal on paper, when writing to him.

I wonder what you, who complain of loneliness when surrounded by a numerous family and wide circle of friends, would do if you could change places with me. Except my grinder and his wife, I think I have not spoken to a soul this week: not of course that I mind, much less complain; on the contrary, I find that the people whose society I prefer to my own are very few and far between. The only one of that class in Bookham, is still in the house, though they tell me she is up and about.[1] Of course, as they say at home, this solitude is a kind of egotism: and yet I don't know that they are right. The usual idea is that if you don't want to talk to people, you do so because you think they're intellectually your inferiors. But its not a question of inferiority: if a man talks to me for an hour about golf, war & politics, I know that his mind is built on different lines from mine: but whether better or worse is not to the point.

My only regret at present is that I cannot see Co. Down in the snow: I am sure some of our favourite haunts look very fine. We have been deeply covered with it all week, and the pine wood near hear, with the white masses on ground and trees, forms a beautiful sight. One almost expects a 'march of dwarfs' to come dashing past! How I long to break away into a world where such things were true: this real, hard, dirty, Monday morning modern world stifles one. Progress in health and spirits and music! Write soon and give all your thoughts, actions, readings and any local gossip, for the benefit of

yours sincerely
Jack Lewis

---

[1] This was probably Mrs Kirkpatrick's 'theatrical' friend, Miss MacMullen, who, Lewis wrote to his father on 13 October, 'Altho' perfectly well sees fit to travel down to Gastons with a bath chair, a maid and a bull dog'.

10

[Gastons
26 January 1915][1]

My dear Arthur,

I wonder would hunting be good sport? The matter occurred to me, not because I am really interested in it, but because I have just returned from a compulsory chase – trying to find out where the bit at the top of page 2 of your letter was meant to come in. Now, faint & perspiring, I am enjoying the fruits of my labours.

By this time you will probably have finished 'Villette'.[2] What do you think of the ending? I can just hear you saying, 'Cracked – absolutely!'. It certainly is most unsatisfactory, but yet a touch of genius. I fancy it is the only novel in existence that leaves you in a like uncertainty. Merriman is a far cry from the Brontës. Both of course are good, but while they should be sipped with luxurious slowness in the winter evening, he may be read in a cheap copy on top of a tram. And yet I don't know: of course his novels are melodrama, but then they are the best melodrama ever written, while passages like the 'Storm' or the 'Wreck' in the Grey Lady, or the Reconciliation between the hero and his father in 'Edged Tools', are as good things as English prose contains.[3]

The remark about the Maiden Islands was really quite smart for you. You might have it framed? Also such gems of orthography as 'simpathise' and 'phisically' which appeared in your last correspondance, tho' of course I, being almost as bad, have no right to complain.

The weather here is perfectly damnable, there having been scarcely a couple of hours' sunshine since I left home. Now that my friends have gone, there is nothing to do but sit & read or write when it rains, and consequently I have nearly finished The Morte D'arthur. I am more pleased at having bought it every day, as it has opened up a new world to me. I had no idea that the Arthurian legends were so fine (The name is against them, isn't it??) Malory is really not a

---

[1] Lewis returned home on 28 November and was confirmed in the Church of St Mark's, Dundela, on 6 December. Albert Lewis, like so many others, had for some months previously feared that England would be invaded by the Germans, and this explains why his son was not allowed to return to Great Bookham till 16 January 1915.

[2] Charlotte Brontë, *Villette* (1853).

[3] Henry Seton Merriman, *The Grey Lady* (1895); *With Edged Tools* (1894).

great author, but he has two excellent gifts, (1) that of lively narrative and (2) the power of getting you to know characters by gradual association. What I mean is, that, although he never sits down – as the moderns do – to describe a man's character, yet, by the end of the first volume Launcelot & Tristan, Balin & Pellinore, Morgan Le Fay & Isoud are all just as much real, live people as Paul Emanuel or Mme Beck.[4] The very names of the chapters, as they spring to meet the eye, bear with them a fresh, sweet breath from the old-time, faery world, wherein the author moves. Who can read 'How Launcelot in the Chapel Perilous gat a cloth from a Dead corpse' or 'How Pellinore found a damosel by a Fountain, and of the Jousts in the Castle of Four Stones', and not hasten to find out what it's all about?

To obey my own theory that a letter should tell of doings, readings, thinkings, I will conclude by saying that I am trying to find some suitable theme for my Celtic narrative Poem: there are heaps of stories but mostly too long. Fare-thee-well.

Yours sincerely
C. S. Lewis

N.B. This was written on the same day as I got your letter, but I forgot to post it. Mille pardons. J.

11

[Gastons
2 February 1915]

Dear Arthur,

The first essential point for a letter writer to master is that of making himself intelligible to his reader. Or, to come down from my high horse, what was the (it?) in brackets meant for? A thousand pardons for my dulness, only I utterly failed to follow your wheeze: please explain in your next epistle.

I am deep in Morte D'Arthur by this time, and it is really the greatest thing I've ever read. It is strangely different from William Morris, although by subject & language they challenge comparison. One is genuine, and the other, tho' delightful, must, of course, be only an artificial reproduction. You really ought to read your copy of it, or at any rate parts of it, as the connecting chain between book and book is not very tightly drawn. I don't think it can be the

---

[4] These last two are characters in *Villette*.

Library Edition, that those people have sent me, as it does not agree with your description at all, being bound in plum-coloured leather, with pale-blue marker attached. However, partly through my keenness to read the book & partly because it was a very handsome binding, I did not send it back.

By the way, is there anything the matter with my father, as I have not heard from him for some time now? Or perhaps it is only this submarine nonsense that makes the conveyance of letters uncertain: which reminds me, that, though I do not usually take much interest in the war, yet it would be unpleasantly brought home to me if I had to spend my holydays in England.[1]

Your remarks á propos of loneliness are quite true, and I admit that what I said before was rather not, as uncongenial companions produce in reality a worse desolation than actual solitude.

I am glad to hear you have read Esmond:[2] it is one of my favourite novels, and I hardly know which to praise most, the wonderful, musical, Queen Anne English, or the delicate beauty of the story. True, I did rather resent the history, and still maintain, that when a man sets out to write a novel he has no right to ram an European War down your throat – it is like going back to Henty! Did you ever try that arch-fiend?

I am surprised that there is no snow in Ulster as we had a week of good, thick, firm, 'picture' snow – and very much I enjoyed it. And other things too! She is better now, up & about, and we have progressed very rapidly. In fact the great event is actually fixed – fixed! – do you realize that? I don't think I've ever been so bucked about anything in my life, she's an awfully decent sort.[3] But I suppose this is boring you, so I must cut short my raptures – & my letter.

Yours
Jack

---

[1] There were, in fact, a good many German submarines operating in the Irish Sea at this time. Lewis's father was particularly upset over the raid near Fleetwood on 30 January 1915 when the Germans sank the *Kilcoan*, a collier designed by his brother Joseph.

[2] William Makepeace Thackeray, *Esmond* (1852).

[3] A family of Belgian refugees were evacuated to Great Bookham in the autumn of 1914. Lewis began visiting them with Mrs Kirkpatrick, and became infatuated with one of the young girls in the family. He, doubtless, discussed his feelings for her with Arthur Greeves during the Christmas holidays. As to how much truth there was in what he wrote and said about the Belgian girl, see Lewis's letter of 1 October 1931.

T.S.T.–C

12

[Gastons
16 February 1915]

Dear Arthur,

When I received your epistle, which certainly did not weary one
by its length, I was in one of my black moods: like Saul, my evil
spirit was upon me. Having just had a sufficient glimpse of home and
of my brother to tantalize but not to satisfy:[1] having lost, if not for
good, at least for this term, an unparalleled opportunity: and finding
a very objectionable visitor in possession of my grinder's house, you
may well imagine that I was in no mood for an extra irritation. I had
just, too, been out for a walk, mon dieu, a nightmare! Splashing
thro great puddles beneath a leaden sky that rained and rained!
However, enough of this.

You ask me what was the matter with me when I was at home.
Thank you: I believe I enjoyed excellent health. Of course it is true,
that we saw a good deal more of our relations than we wanted, and
had none too much time to ourselves: but of course, you, or any
member of your household, are always welcome.

As to the other grievance, it really is phenominal ill luck. Of
course, like all the rest of her sex she is incapable of seeing anything
fair, and when she had been persuaded after a good deal of difficulty
to do this, and then I failed to turn up, it is only to be expected that
I am 'left'. In any case, it would be impossible now; as she has gone
with her mother for a week to visit some other Belgians in Birmingham.[2] But perhaps you are tired of my 'affaires'.

To go back to the question of holydays (I started to try and write
an 'essay-letter', but can't keep it up; excuse me if I meaunder a bit),
the last straw came on Sunday afternoon when we were snatching a
few moments rest before going off to visit our various relations: who
should walk in – but – but – but – Henry Stokes!!!! Dear boy! How
thoughtful of him! How kind! What a pleasure for us all! After that,
my brother suggested that if ever he got another week's leave, we
should spend it on the Maidens.

You must imagine me writing this in my bedroom at about 11
o'clock, as that damned guest makes it impossible to be comfortable

[1] Lewis's brother, Warren, had only just returned from France, and
having a week's leave, they spent part of it together at home. Lewis returned
to Great Bookham on 9 February.
[2] Presumably the Belgian girl he had written about earlier.

downstairs. Although it was quite spring weather before I went home, a thin snow mixed with rain is falling outside. In spite of all my troubles, I am quite bucked with life to night, and if only the water were hot enough for a bath I should be in heaven. I wonder what you are doing just now?

Which reminds me, you are drifting into a habit of morbid self-pity lately: all your letters are laments. Beware of the awful fate of growing up like that. I never, for my part, saw what was meant by such terms as 'the releif of confiding ones troubles' and the 'consolations of sympathy': my view is, that to mention trouble at all, *in a complaining way*, is to introduce into the conversation an element equally painful for everyone, including the speaker. Of course, it all depends on the *way* it is done: I mean, simply to mention them, is not wrong, but, by words or expression to call for sympathy which your hearer will feel bound to pump up, is a nuisance.

What a good friend I am, to sit up writing all this stuff to a creature who, just because he 'doesn't feel like it' gives me no more than a couple of lines. Write soon, like a good friend, and tell me all about yourself, and all the local gossip. I am damnably tired, and there's something the matter with the gas, and I've come to the end of my paper. So I must dry up.

Yours
Jack

13

[Gastons
30 March 1915]

Dear Arthur,

How I pity you people who never have known the pleasures and the pains – which are an integral part of the pleasures – of a regular interchange of home-coming and school going. Even the terrors of Malvern were almost justified by the raptures with which one hailed the periodic deliverance. Here, where the minor disadvantages of my sojourns at Bookham are just enough to act as a foil to the pleasures of home, but not so great as to make the earlier part of the term unhappy, the arrangement is ideal. The satisfaction with which a day boy looks forward to a period of rest from his work, can be but the faintest shadow of a boarder's feeling towards his return from temporary exile.

These last few days! Every little nuisance, every stale or tiresome bit of work, every feeling of that estrangement which I never quite get over in another country, serves as a delightful reminder of how different it will all be soon. Already one's mind dwells upon the sights and sounds and smells of home, the distant murmuring of the 'yards', the broad sweep of the lough, the noble front of the cave hill, and the fragrant little glens and breazy meadows of our *own* hills! And the sea! I cannot bear to live too far away from it. At Belfast, whether hidden or in sight, still it dominates the general impression of nature's face, lending its own crisp flavour to the winds and its own subtle magic to horizons, even when they conceal it. A sort of feeling of space, and clean fresh vigour hangs over all in a country by the sea: how different from the stuffiness of Bookham: here the wind – that is to say, the true, brisk, boisterous irresistable wind – never comes.

And yet, I would not for a moment disparage the beauty of Surrey: these slumbering little vallies, and quaint farmsteads have a mellow charm of their own, that Ulster has not. But just now my End-of-Term feelings will not allow me to think of that.

'But why', you will ask 'am I treated to these lyrical raptures?' Indeed, Sir, I hardly know. My father wrote a few days ago, and asked if we should risk the submarines and come home, or not. I of course said that we should, – advancing many sage arguments thereto, and suggested leaving here next Friday.[1] I have not been answered yet, but hope to goodness it is coming off. Anyway, a wave of End-of-Terminess came over me to night, and, as I had to communicate with someone, so you, poor fellow, got let in for this!

I had a letter from 'Her'[2] the other day, which is all satisfactory, Must shut up now.

Yours
Jack

14

[Gastons
4 May 1915]

Dear Galahad,

I am surprised! Have you actually come down to enjoying such stuff as 'The Bread of the Treshams'? I never (for which the gods be thanked) saw or read it, but the name is enough. I admit, I should like to have seen The Shrew, and novelties in the way of staging are

---

[1] Lewis arrived home for his Easter holidays on 1 April and was there till 30 April.
[2] The Belgian girl.

always rather interesting. I much prefer on the stage – and everywhere for that matter – quiet, tasteful, plain decorations, to tawdry,
splendid things.

I feel my fame as a 'Man-about-the-Gramaphone' greatly put out
by your remarks à propos of Lohengrin Prelude Act III, as, I must
confess, I never heard of it on Columbia. I do hope it is a good
record, as I should like to have it very much: what is the Venusbury
music like? Is it that wild part that comes at the end of the Tannhaüser overture? Of course you know the Columbia edition of
Schubert's Rosamunde has long been at Little Lea, but when last I
played it to you, I seem to remember a *non* favourable verdict from
you. I am so glad that you have gotten (That's correct, you know.
'Got' isn't) the Fire Music, as I have been hesitating over it for ages,
and your success or failure will decide me. Oh! I had better stop
writing about this, as it makes me 'think long': not, if you please, in
a sentimental way, but with a sensible desire for my books and you
and our Gramaphone*S* etc.

However, I have gotten (notice – again) one great addition to my
comfort here, in the discovery of a 'Soaking-machine', which con-
veniences are very scarce in England, owing to the strict customs
which prevent the mildest trespassing. My new palace, is at the foot of
a great oak, a few yards off a lane, and hidden therefrom by a little
row of shrubs and small trees. Completely private, safe from sun,
wind or rain, and on the ridge of the only rising ground (you wouldn't
call it a hill) about here. There, with a note book and pencil, I can be
as free to write, etc, as at home. So if your next letter comes in
pencil, on a sheet torn from a pocket book, you needn't be surprised.
I must find some more of these places as summer goes on, for it is
already too hot to walk far.

I bought yesterday a little shilling book about Wm. Morris, his life
and his work, which is rather interesting. To me, at least, for I am
afraid *you* have given up that old friend of ours.

To say that you have something 'sentimental' to say, and not to
say it, is to be like Janie McN. with the latest scandal, that everyone
is told *about* and no one is told.[1] I don't quite follow your letter in
places. What is the connection between all the rubbish about 'that
nuisance Arthur' (you know how all your friends ridicule and dislike
that sort of talk) and the wish that I should become sentimental per-

[1] Jane ('Janie') Agnes McNeill (1889–1959) was the daughter of James
Adams McNeill who at one time had Lewis's mother as his pupil and was
later Lewis's favourite master at Campbell College in 1910. Lewis was fond
of all the McNeills and dedicated *That Hideous Strength* to Janie.

force? By the way, I am perhaps more sentimental than you, but I don't blow a trumpet about it. Indeed, I am rather ashamed of it. Feelings ought to be kept for literature and art, where they are delightful and not intruded into life where they are merely a nuisc- ance.

I have just finished 'Shirley'; which I think better than either 'Jane Eyre' or 'Villette'.[2] You must read it.

What a letter; every sentence seems to begin 'I'. However, a good healthy dose of egotism is what *you* need, while you might pass on a little of your superfluous modesty to Bookham. Sorry you've re- turned the old Meistersingers, but think the Beka better value.

Yours
Jack

P.S. What is the name of the 'Galloping Horse' piece by Chopin? I want to make Mrs K. play it.

J.

15

[Gastons
11 May 1915]

Dear Galahad,

Tut! Tut! Must I change your soubriquet? From being the spotless knight of the Grail, are you going to turn philosopher and meet me on my own ground to dispute my shadowy quibbles about the proper sphere of sentiment? Galahad becomes Merlin: who knows but that you may 'grow besotted of a damosel', like him, and like him, I may find you when I come home bound fast under a great stone, making a piteous wail to all who pass. And what a relief for the neighbourhood! I think I shall nominate a suitable damosel – say Miss Bradley or Sal Stokes – to besott and bind you. By the way, à propos of Miss Bradley, has she yet recovered (or better still died) from that peculiarly inter- minable complaint of hers, which prevents the gramaphone being played up at Glenmachen?

But to go back to the sentiment controversy, your objection is nonsense. You argue that sentiment is delightful in art, because it is a part of human nature. Quite right. From that, you deduce that it ought not to be confined to that sphere of human nature where it *is* delightful – viz. art. That is almost as sensible as to say that trousers

[2] Charlotte Brontë, *Shirley* (1849); *Jane Eyre* (1847); *Villette* (1853).

are delightful only because they are a part of human clothes: therefore they ought to be worn, not only on the legs, but every where else. Do you maintain that it is a highly commendable and philosophical act to wear trousers, say, on your head? My point is that art is a recepticacle of human thought: sentiment, emotion etc make up that section of human thought which are best suited to fill that definite receptical – and no other. For why, when we have found the best place to keep a thing, should we keep it in other places as well, or instead? By the analogy of the trousers I have shown how ridiculous that would be. As for your idea that to be young, one must be sentimental, let us go into it. Young children are practically devoid of sentiment: they are moved only by bodily pain: young men are a little more sentimental, middle aged ones considerably more so, and old ones the most mawkishly so of all. Sentiment, you see, is a distinct mark of age.

Ah!! Having gott*en* (N.B.) that off our chest, we can proceed to other matters. That little book about Wm. Morris has interested me so much – or re-awakened the old interest – in him, that I have just written up for 'The Roots of the Mountains' in Longman's pocket edition: it is about the Goths, and is praised in that book as one of the best of the prose Romances. What is the good of getting Anderson in Everyman? It is true, the tales have considerable merit in ipso (that's Latin and means 'in themselves', Ignorant!): but yet, if any book ever needed or was greatly improved by fancy binding, that is it.

The word Soaking-Machine can hardly be styled 'slang', being, as it is, coined by myself for private circulation: I thought you knew what it meant. The word 'soak' means to sit idly or sleepily doing nothing, and a S'ing machine is [a] place for this operation, i.e. a comfortable seat. Surely I must often have said to you in the course of our walks 'Let's find a soaking-machine' or 'Here's a good soaking-machine'?

I despair of making head or tail of any of your gramaphonic talk, where your extraordinary loose and obscure use of words like 'latter' etc makes havoc of the sense. Do you mean that you had another record of the Venusburg music, before you heard it with Lohengrin, à l'autre côté? Or do you know what you mean? Or, lastly, do you mean anything at all? I write such enormous letters (which you probably never read to the end) that, from the way Mrs K. keeps looking at me, I believe she fancies it a billet doux. Why didn't you give me the number of the Polonaise: and what cheek to say 'I think it is in A Flat', when a journey downstairs would make sure.

It has been raining for almost 36 hours here, which is not very cheerful. The idea of spelling melodrama 'mello-drama' is really quite 'chic': I should take out a patent on it, if I were you. I hope you are in good spirits these days, and that the lady of the office window is kind & in good health. Write soon: you've know idea how welcome your letters are. By the by, you might tell the girl in Osborne's to send on the monthly catalogues to my address here, which you can tell her – Columbia, H.M.V., Zono, Beka, are the chief. Valde.

Yours
Jack

16

[Gastons
25 May 1915]

Dear Galahad,

B-r-r-r! Behold me coming with locusts & wild honey about my loins (or is it sackcloth & ashes) to kneel and tremble and apologise for my letterless week. However, qui s'excuse, s'accuse, as the French say, and if you want to seek the real author of the mischief you must go up to heaven, and find the four and twenty elders sitting in a row, as St John says, falling on their faces on the sea of glass (which must hurt rather but apparently is the 'thing' up yonder), and William Morris in white raiment with a halo.

Or, in other words, 'The Roots of the Mountains' is the chief cause of my silence. It is not, however, in spite of all this, nearly so good as the first volume of 'The Well at the World's End', although the interest is better sustained throughout. To begin with, I was desparately dissapointed to find that there is nothing, supernatural, faery or unearthly in it at all: in fact, it is more like an ordinary novel. And yet there are many compensations: for, tho' more ordinary than the 'Well', it is still utterly different from any novel you ever read. Apart from the quaint and beautiful old English, which means so much to me, the supernatural element, tho' it does not enter into the plot, yet hovers on the margin all the time: we have 'the wildwood wherein dwell wights that love not men, to whom the groan of the children of men is as the scrape of a fiddle-bow: there too abide the kelpies, and the ghosts of them that rest not', and such delightful names as The Dusky Men, The Shadowy Vale, The Shivering Flood, The Weltering Water etc. Another thing I like about it is that the characters are not mediaeval knights but Norse mountain tribes with axe & long-sword instead of horses & lances and so forth. However, though it is worth having and well worth reading, I don't know if its really worth buying. The next time I get a Morris Romance it will be one of the later ones, as the 'Roots' is one of the first, when, apparently, he hadn't yet found his feet in prose work.

On Saturday last we were over at a little village near here, where Watts the painter lived:[1] there is a little gallery, a lovely building, designed by himself, containing some of his quite famous pictures like 'Orpheus & Euridyce', 'Endymion', 'Sir Galahad' etc, which I always thought were in the Louvre or the Tate or some such place. Of course I don't really quite understand good painting, but I did my best, and succeeded in really enjoying some myself, & persuading the other people that I knew a tremendous lot about them all.

What a grand dialectician, our Little Arthur is!! You reply to my elegant tirade against sentiment by stating your old thesis that it ought not to be suppressed, without a single reason. You don't admit my arguments, and yet make no endeavour to answer them. And because I choose trousers for an example you say that it is 'very funny'. Moi, I didn't know trousers were funny. If you do, I picture your progress from the tram to the office something thus: 'Hullo! Good lord, there's a fellow with trousers over there! And there's another. Ha-Ha – Oh this is too screaming. Look – one-two-three more – ' and you collapse in a fit of uncontrollable merriment. Doesn't this sort of truck fill up the paper? But in point of fact, I've lost your last letter, and so don't quite know what to talk about.

Thanks for carrying out my message to Miss Whatdoyoucallher? about the monthly catalogues, which are now arriving in due order. That's rather a pretty girl, the H.M.V. infant prodigy 18 year old soprano, but she doesn't seem to sing anything worth hearing.

'Hear your brethren are going to join a friend's ambulance corps, whatever that may be. Give them my congratulations and all the usual nonsense one ought to say on such an occasion. I hope they will get on famously and come back with Victoria crosses and eye-glasses, which seem to be the two goals of military ambition.

It is hot as our future home down below, here, but the country is looking delightful, & I have found one or two more SOAKING MACHINES (I *will* use that word if I want to) and so am quite comfortable. I hear you have taken to getting heart fits in the middle of the sermon at Saint Marks and coming out – I only wish you'd

[1] The painter and sculptor George Frederic Watts (1817–1904) who lived for some years at 'Limneslease' near Compton in Surrey.

teach me the trick.[2]

And now, the kind reader, if there still is one, is going to be left in peace. Do write soon, and forgive your suppliant

Jack

17

[Gastons
1 June 1915]

Dear Galahad,

Your interesting epistle which I have read with wonder and delight, contains the following gems of Arthurian style

A. 'I don't suppose you will object to *my* coming with *me*.'

B. 'Read this with *discust*.'

C. 'I am talking now of *sensulity*.'

Dear old Galahad! That's an unusually good budget even for you: I am afraid this 'sensulity' of yours – I never saw the word before but I suppose you know what it means – must be beginning to tell on you.

As to your first question, the only holyday I propose to take is a week or so with my relations at Larne, and my father's offer, which I take to be purely formal, I would not much care to accept. I hope you will be sensible enough to spend your holydays at home with me, seeing each other and talking & going for long walks over the hills, instead of going off to some godless place by the sea. My point is that I should be going to my Aunt's in any case, and 1 week or so from home is quite enough for me: as well, I don't think it very decent to leave my father any longer. But don't let this prevent your going somewhere. All I want to point out is, that my refusal of a joint holyday, is not from a design to avoid you, but because I don't want to be away from home too long. Of course, if you would condescend to honour Larne with your presence while I am at my Aunt's, I should be very bucked to see you: but you might be bored. However, we can talk all this over when we meet at the end of July.

Odeon records are the most fascinating and delusive bait on the Gramaphone market. Cheap, classical, performed by good artistes, they present a jolly attractive list: but they wear out in a month. Of

[2] The Lewises were parishioners of St Mark's Church, Dundela. The Rev. Arthur William Barton was Rector there from 1914 to 1925, and in 1930 he was consecrated Lord Bishop of Kilmore, Elphin and Ardagh. This much loved man had, like the Lewis brothers, been a pupil at Wynyard School in Watford.

course there are exceptions, and I can play you some selections from Lohengrin which I have on that make, and which have worn well. On the whole however, I wouldn't advise anyone to get Odeon records, as a short-lived record is one of the most dissapointing of things. I foresee, by the way, that your way of getting records is like Jane McNeil's way of getting books – that is you use a shop like a free library: whenever a record is worn out, back it goes to the shop, and you have a new one in its place. Which reminds me, my monthly catalogues for this month haven't turned up yet, so you must shout at Miss Thompson.

With reference to your remarks about sensuality – je vous demande pardon – '*sensulity*', I don't know I am sure, why you have been suffering especially in this way just now. Of course when I was particularly so last term, there was a reason, about whom you heard perhaps more than you wanted. You ought to be past the age of violent attacks of 'ΕΡΩΤΙΚΑ (Greek); as well you are Galahad the spotless whose 'strength is as the strength of ten, because your heart is pure'. Perhaps you would understand now, what you didn't understand when I started the subject last hols, ⟨what I mean by the 'sensuality of cruelty': again perhaps you would not.⟩

Last week I got a copy of that little book of yours on Icelandic Sagas, which I found very interesting, and as a result I have now bought a translation of the 'Laxdaela Saga' in the Temple Classics edition. I never saw a Temple Classic before; did you? In binding, paper, & 'forma' (by which I include the aspect of a typical page, its shape, spacing, lettering etc) they are tip top, and justify the boast of 'elegance' made in their advertisements. They are, I think, far better value than Everyman's at the same price.

As to the Saga itself I am very pleased with it indeed: if the brief, simple, nervous style of the translation is a good copy of the original it must be very fine. The story, tho', like most sagas, it loses unity, by being spread over two or three generations, is thoroughly interesting. Just as it was interesting after the 'Well at the World's End' to read the 'Morte', so after the 'Roots', a real saga is interesting. I must admit that here again the primitive type is far better than Morris's reproduction. But that of course is inevitable, just as Homer is better than Vergil.

Sorry to hear my father is so low, but I write to him regularly, and the last was really rather a long and good effort. Hope you're all well at Bernagh.

Yours
Jack

18

Dear Galahad,

I seem to have trod on somebody's corns over this question of a holyday: I expressly said that I did not wish to keep you at home on my account if you wished to go elsewhither. To be brief, my whole answer was that I refused your kind proposal because I was already booked, adding that I should not care to take another holyday in addition to that at Larne. Now what is your grievance – for grievance you must have or you would not write such good grammar. Is it because I won't throw up my previous invitation in favour of yours? That would be rude. Is it because I will not accompany you on another holyday? That is selfish of you, to expect me to give [up] my fleeting sojourn at Leeborough [Little Lea] for your amusement. Is it because I mildly suggested that you need not go for a holyday? There was never any obligation on you to accept such a scheme. And as for your hot weather – je me moque de cette là, it is bitterly cold to-night! How funny that I always prove everything I want in argument with you but never convince you!

Now, having despatched our inevitable weekly dialectical passage-at-arms (by the way, you have never replied to my theory of trousers), we may proceed to the letter. I admit that the 'I hope you are all well' is a blot on my character that can hardly be wiped out: I didn't think I had sunk*en* so low as that, and will try to reform.

I thought you would agree with me about Mansfield park: I should almost say it was her best.[1] I don't remember the names very well, but I think I rather liked Edmund. Do get a Temple Classic. You will bless me ever after, as they are really the best shillings worth on the market. I hope I may prove a false prophet about the Odeon records, and that you will have better luck in them than I. Now that it is drawing a little nearer my return, I begin to hanker again for my gramaphone: but I am not consoled even with the catalogues, so you must stir up the damosel again. I am still at the 'Laxdaela Saga' which is as good as ever, and I insist upon your reading it too.

On Saturday I met the prettiest girl I have ever seen in my life (don't be afraid, you're not going to have to listen to another love-affair). But it is not her prettiness I wanted to tell you about, but the

[1] Jane Austen, *Mansfield Park* (1814).

fact that she is just like that grave movement in the Hungarian Rhapsody (or is it the 'dance'?) that I love so much. Of course to you I needn't explain how a person can be like a piece of music, – you will know: and if you play that record over, trying to turn the music into a person, you will know just how she looked and talked. Just 18, and off to do some ridiculous war-work, nursing or something like that at Dover of all places – what a shame!

By the way, that would be a rather interesting amusement, trying to find musical interpretations for all our friends. Thus Gordon is like the Pilgrims chorus from Tannhaüser, Kelsie a bit like the Valkyries only not so loud, Gundred like the dance-movement in Danse Macabre, and Bob like a Salvation army hymn.[2] We might add yourself as a mazurka by Chopin, wild, rather plaintful, and disjointed, and Lily[3] like, well – a thing of Grieg's called 'The Watchman's Song' that you haven't heard. I think I must write a book on it.

By the way (all my sentences seem to begin like that) I am very sorry this is a bit late, but I was writing to my father and brother last night. Now, good night, Galahad, and be good and talk sense the next time you do me the honour of arguing with me.

Yours
Jack

P.S. What about the question of 'sensulity'?

19

[Gastons
29 June 1915]

Dear Galahad,

Did the Norns or Dana holy mother of them that die not, weave for us in that hour wherein our mothers bare us, that never should we write to each other without the first page being occupied by argument? Because, whether by the decree of fate or no, this has always been the case. First it was Shee v. Souteraines, then Tears v. Trousers, and now Larne v. Leeborough – which by the way means Little Lea. How you can have known me so long without picking up the words & tags which I use every day passes my understanding –

[2] Gordon, Isabella Kelso, Gundreda and Robert Ewart were the children of Sir William and Lady Ewart, Lewis's cousins, who lived at 'Glenmachan'.
[3] Arthur's sister, Lily Greeves.

unless I am to conclude that you are asleep half the time I am talking to you, which is very probably so.

Well about this infernal holyday: as your infantile brain – for which I have catered on this envelope – is incapable of swallowing my previous very elementary argument, I will explain my position once more in very simple terms, as follows: –

I have eight weeks vacations.

I have been invited to stay 10 days with Mrs Hamilton.

I have accepted her invitation.

I intend to keep that promise

I don't want to be any longer away than 10 days.

I don't want to keep you at home on that account.

I therefore decline your kind proposal.

I am very sorry

I hope you understand. How's that?

It may be true that it is easier to assign music to people we know, than to conjure up people to fit the music, but I deny that anyone's character is really unlike their appearance. The physical appearance, to my mind, is the expression and result of the other thing – soul, ego, ψῡχη, intellect – call it what you will. And this outward expression cannot really differ from the soul. If the correspondence between a soul & body is not obvious at first, then your conception either of that soul or that body must be wrong. Thus, I am 'chubby' – to use your impertinent epithet, because I have a material side to me: because I like sleeping late, good food & clothes etc as well as sonnets & thunderstorms. The idealistic side of me must find an outlet somewhere, perhaps in my eye, my voice or anything else – you can judge better than I. And the other side of me exists in my countenance because it exists also in my character.

'But', I hear you saying, 'this is all very well. Only what about the practised flirt with the innocent schoolgirl face & the murderer with a smile like an old woman?' These are only seeming exceptions. The girl has or imagines she has that sort of disposition somewhere in her, or it wouldn't be on her face: as a matter of fact, it is always 'innocent' (which means ignorant) people who do the most outrageous things. The murderer too, may be really a peaceful, kindly 'crittur', and if circumstances drive him to violence, the initial mould of the character and therefore of the face remain just the same.

I remember reading in a book called 'The open Road' an extract from Hewlet's 'Pan and the Young Shepherd', which I thought splendid.[1] Thanks to our Galahad's detestable handwriting I can't

[1] *The Open Road*, compiled by E. V. Lucas (1905).

tell whether your book is the 'Lore' or the 'Love' of P. In any case I have never heard of it before, but, from your description, am very eager to read it. I also saw a copy of this author's 'Forest Lovers' in Carson's last hols, but it did not attract me much.[2] Is this new one in a decent edition?

I am glad to hear that you are keeping up the 'illustrative' side of your art, and shall want you to do some for my lyric poems. You can begin a picture of my 'dream garden' where the 'West winds blow'. As directions I inform you it is 'girt about with mists', and is in 'the shadowy country neither life nor sleep', and is the home of 'faint dreams'. With this Bädekers guide to it, you can start a picture. You remember, I scribble at pen and ink sketches a bit, and have begun to practise female faces which have always been my difficulty. I am improving a very little I think, and the margins of my old Greek lexicon as well as my pocket book now swarm with 'studies'.

Only four weeks now till I shall be home again! Isn't that a buck, at least for me – and no one else in the world really counts of course. What nonsense you talk about that 'poor man', my father. I am afraid it is true that he must bore Lily, but there is no fear of her boring him. I sympathize however, with the havoc which he must have wrought with a serious musical evening.

How is your gramaphone progressing, by the way, and how many records have you listed up to date? I am so sorry if this Liliputian writing has blinded you for life, but we have run out of the other sort of note paper.

Well – καῖρε μοὶ, (Farewel)

Jack

P.S. Have begun the 'Proffessor' and as read far as the heroe's arrival at Brussels.[3] It is shaping very well. I believe you have read it have you not – J.

---

[2] Maurice Hewlett, *Pan and the Young Shepherd* (1898); *Lore of Proserpine* (1913); *Forest Lovers* (1898).
[3] Charlotte Brontë, *The Professor* (1857).

20

Dear Galahad,

I have debated more than once as to whether you would prefer a tired and perfunctory letter written in good time during the week, or a fresh and willing [one] a few days late on Saturday evening. Thinking that you would choose the latter, and knowing I would – here we are.

What on earth are you doing reading the Sowers?[1] A Russian mystery-story full of wise diplomatists and impossible women – it ought to be clad in a bright red cover, with a crude picture of Steinmitz saying 'The Moscow Doctor – and your prince!!!' from the head of the stairs, and set on a railway bookstall. But, perhaps I am wrong. Of course it has points, but you are worthy of better things. Never read any George Eliot myself, being no great hand at novels but admire your energy in that line.

Talking about books, I am determined to teach you to like poetry, and will begin next hols. on Coleridges 'Christabel'. Don't be put off by the name. It is exactly the sort of romantic strangeness and dreaminess you & I like, a sort of partner to the Ancient Mariner, as Danse Macabre is to the March of the Dwarfs.

Also – I hope all these schemes aren't boring you – you are going to help me to improve my drawing next hols. Figures I can do tolerably, but from you I must learn the technique of the game – shading, curves, how to do a background without swamping the figures etc. Of course this will all be in pen and ink which is the best medium for my kind of work – I can imagine your smile at my calling such scribbles 'work', but no matter. I am longing to get home again now, and expect I shall arrive next Saturday.[2]

Yes Mrs K. has played the Polonaise; we found the right one without difficulty, and tho' she made some remarks about the hardness of it I at length persuaded her. Now, you know, I never flatter: so you may take it as solemn truth when I tell you that, if I admired your playing before, I understood its true value far better when I compared [it] with Mrs K. – by no means a contemptible craftsman. To hear the lovely galloping passages rendered correctly, even well,

---

[1] Henry Seton Merriman, *The Sowers* (1896).
[2] He arrived in Belfast on 31 July and was there for the next two months.

but without your own frank enjoyment of the work, your sympathy
with the composer and your inimitable fire and abandonment (this
sounds like an essay but I mean every word of it), was a revelation.
You threw yourself into it, and forgot yourself in the composer: Mrs
K sat there, amiable, complacent and correct, as if she were pouring
out tea. Now, while they're not all as bad as she, still you alone of the
people I have heard play set to the matter properly. And for that
reason, a piece, by you, if it were full of mistakes (tho' of course it
wouldn't be) would be better than the same piece faultlessly played
by – say, Hope Harding.³ This is a rare gift of yours: you should yet
do great things with it: you are a fool if you don't cultivate it. Perhaps, because you paint and read as well as play, you realize the
imagination of a composer's mind perfectly, and can always bring
out to a sensible (in the old sense of the word) listener anything at all
that there is in the notes. Of course, all this is the praise of an amateur: but the praise of an honest amateur who has a genuine, tho'
non-techniqual taste for music, is worth something at least.

I agree with you that the music of Lohengrin, so far as I know it is
delightful: nor do I see what is wrong with the story, tho' of course
the splendid wildness of the 'Ring' must be lacking. On the whole,
however, I am not sure that any music from it I know, is not perhaps
cast in a lower mould than 'Parsifal' & the 'Ring'. Although, indeed,
the prelude – which you wouldn't listen to when I played it – is quite
as fine I think as that from 'Parsifal'.⁴

What is your opinion of W. Jaffe – little Vee-Lee?⁵ He did one
thing for which he can never be forgiven – dropping in and staying
till eleven on the first night of my brother's leave. The Hamiltons
came over on another, so we had only one evening alone together in
peace and comfort.⁶ On the whole, tho', he is a decent crittur, I
suppose. Have you ever heard their gramaphone? I wonder what its
like.

Which reminds me, did you hear the new Glenmachen⁷ record –
a solo by the Russian base – Chaliapin from 'Robert Le Diable'.
The orchestration is absolutely magnificent and the singing as good.

³ Lewis's cousin, Mrs George Harding (*née* Charlotte Hope Ewart –
1882–1934).

⁴ Lewis loved all Richard Wagner's music, especially the *Ring of the
Nibelung* cycle.

⁵ William Jaffé, a friend of Albert Lewis, was the son of Sir Otto Jaffé who
was twice Lord Mayor of Belfast.

⁶ Warren was again on leave. Lewis spent a few days with him at Little
Lea, returning to Great Bookham on 9 July.

⁷ The home of Sir William and Lady Ewart.

I only wish I could afford 'the like of them', don't you?

I shan't write again this term now – jolly glad it's so near the end.

Yours

Jack

21

[Gastons
5 October 1915]

My dear Galahad,

I can't really see why you have any more right to grouse at my not writing than I at you, but we will let it pass. And in the meantime, what do you think? It is a bit thick when one has fled from Malvern to shun one's compeers in the seclusion of Surrey wilds, to be met by a damned fellow pupil of my own age – and sex! Isn't it the limit? Moreover he is a hopeless fellow with whom I despair of striking up any friendship that can be at all amusing – you know, the usual sort with absolutely no interest in any of the things that matter. Luckily, however, he spends the greater part of his time taking special classes at Leatherhead, so that I still have my afternoon walk alone. Indeed, I suppose it is easier to put up with one philistine at Bookham than with five-hundred at Malvern, but still, the thing is a nuisance on which I had not counted.[1]

I wish indeed that I had been with you at Portrush, of which your description sounds most attractive. I once visited Dunluce Castle years ago when I was staying at 'Castle Rock', but being a kid did not of course appreciate it as much as I would now.

It is very annoying that after waiting all the holydays for those Columbia records, I should just manage to miss them: mind you tell the girl to send me on the monthly lists of Zono, Columbia & H.M.V. I noticed by the way that the Zono list contains an attractive record with the 'Seranade' and 'Church Scene' from Faust. Do you remember the latter – that magnificent duet outside the Church, with organ accompaniment where Gretchen is hunted about the stage with Mephisto behind her? You must hear it and tell me your impressions.

I thought you would enjoy 'Shirley'. Don't you see now what I meant when I said that love, apart from physical feelings, was quite different to friendship? If not you must have a brain like a cheese. There is not really much resemblance either between Louis &

[1] The fellow pupil was Terence Forde. He had been brought up in Manchester, and after moving to Ireland he attended Campbell College, from which school he was sent to Mr Kirkpatrick.

Gordon or Shirley & Lily. Can you imagine G. behaving to Lily the way Louis does at times to Shirley? I am afraid that, much as I like him, G. hasn't got it in him. Lily of course is not unlike S., but not so much of a 'grande dame', if you know what I mean.[2] When I said that K.[elsie Ewart] was like a valkyrie I meant of course in her appearance – or rather in her open-air appearance. When however you see her in artificial light, both in clothing & natural colouring she is like some thoughtful, exquisite piano piece of Chopin's – you'd know which better than I.

By the way, tell your sister that I have already written to thank her for the boot-bags, and that when the love she says she's sending arrives I will write and thank her for it too.

I have been reading the 'Faerie Queen' in Everymans both here and at home ever since I left you and am now half way thro' Book II. Of course it has dull and even childish passages, but on the whole I am charmed, and when I have made you read certain parts I think you will appreciate it too.

Talking about poetry, if you have not done so already, go over to Little Lea and borrow Swinburne's 'Poems and Ballads' 2nd Series at once. Read 'The Forsaken Garden', 'At Parting' (I think that is the name, it begins 'For a day and a night love stayed with us, played with us') 'Triads' 'The Wasted Vigil' and 'At a month's End'. The latter especially you must read from end to end as a commentary on the love parts of 'Shirley', only that in this case the man who tried to tame some such fierce & wonderful character failed instead of succeeding. Then you will relish all the lovely verses at the end, especially that beginning 'Who strives to snare in fear and danger / Some supple beast of fiery kin'. Then tell me your impressions. Hope this hasn't bored you.

I am jolly glad to hear that you are at last starting with Dr Walker and shall expect to find great 'doings' in your musical line when I come back. Write soon and don't forget the catalogues

Yours
Jack

---

[2] The comparison is between Louis and Shirley, characters in Charlotte Brontë's *Shirley*, and Gordon Ewart and Lily Greeves who were to be married on 14 December 1915.

22

[Gastons
12 October 1915]

My dear Galahad,

I am frightfully annoyed. I have just been to Guildford to hear Ysaye[1] and enjoyed it no more than I do the barking of a dog. The apalling thought comes over me that I am losing by degrees my musical faculty: already, as you know, I cannot enjoy things that used to drive me wild with delight, and I suppose in the course of time I shall become absolutely insensible – just like Henry Stokes or my brother or anyone else. There was also a woman called Stralia, a soprano, who sang one lovely thing from 'Madame Butterfly' and lots of stuff I didn't understand. I havenot the faintest idea what Ysaye played, and I never want to hear it again. I listened as hard as I could, shutting my eyes and trying in vain to concentrate my attention, but it was all just meaningless sound. Of course violin solos were never much in my line but even so, it should not be so bad as this. Now I suppose I have lost your sympathy forever and am set down – who knows but it may be rightly – as a Goth and philistine. But it really is torture to feel things going out of you like that. Perhaps after all, the taste in music developed by a gramaphone is a bad, artificial, exotic one that dissapears after a certain point . . . The Lord knows!

You ask me how I spend my time, and though I am more interested in thoughts and feelings, we'll come down to facts. I am awakened up in the morning by Kirk splashing in his bath, about 20 minutes after which I get up myself and come down. After breakfast & a short walk we start work on Thucydides – a desperately dull and tedious Greek historian (I daresay tho', you'd find him interesting) and on Homer whom I worship. After quarter of an hour's rest we go on with Tacitus till lunch at 1. I am then free till tea at 4.30: of course I am always anxious at this meal to see if Mrs K. is out, for Kirk never takes it. If she is I lounge in an arm chair with my book by the fire, reading over a leisurely and bountiful meal. If she's in, or worse still has 'some people' to tea, it means sitting on a right angled chair and sipping a meagrue allowance of tea and making intelligent remarks about the war, the parish and the shortcomings of everyones servants. At 5, we do Plato and Horace, who are both charming, till

[1] Eugène Ysaÿe (1858–1931), the Belgian violinist and conductor whose style of playing was considered unconventional and highly original.

supper at 7.30, after which comes German and French till about 9. Then I am free to go to bed whenever I like which is usually about 10.20.

As soon as my bed room door is shut I get into my dressing gown, draw up a chair to my table and produce – like Louis Moore, note book and pencil. Here I write up my diary for the day, and then turning to the other end of the book devote myself to poetry, either new stuff or polishing the old. If I am not in the mood for that I draw faces and hands and feet etc for practice. This is the best part of the day of course, and I am usually in a very happy frame of mind by the time I slip into bed.

And talking about bed, I wish you and your family would have the goodness to keep out of my dreams. You remember my telling you that I dreamed that you and Lily & I were walking along North Street when I saw a ghost but you & she didn't? That was at Port Salon. Well, last night found the same 3 walking somewhere in town, only this time the place had been captured by the Germans. Everyone had escaped and we were hurrying along in terror through the deserted streets with the German soldiers always just round the corner, going to catch us up and do something terrible. Dreams are queer things.

You ask me whether I have ever been in love: fool as I am, I am not quite such a fool as all that. But if one is only to talk from first-hand experience on any subject, conversation would be a very poor business. But though I have no personal experience of the thing they call love, I have what is better – the experience of Sapho, of Euripides of Catullus of Shakespeare of Spenser of Austen of Bronte of, of – anyone else I have read. We see through their eyes. And as the greater includes the less, the passion of a great mind includes all the qualities of the passion of a small one. Accordingly, we have every right to talk about it. And if you read any of the great love-literature of any time or country, you will find they all agree with me, and have nothing to say about your theory that 'love=friendship+sensual feelings'. Take the case I mentioned before. Were Louis & Shirley ever friends, or could they ever be? Bah! Don't talk twaddle. On the contrary, the mental love may exist without the sensual or vice versa, but I doubt if either could exist together with friendship. What nonsense we both talk, don't we? If any third person saw our letters they would have great 'diversion' wouldn't they?

In the meantime, why have no catalogues reached me yet? By the time this reaches you, you will I hope have read your course of Swinburne I mapped out, and can send me your views. So glad you too like the 'Faerie Queen', isn't it great? I have been reading a horrible book of Jack London's called 'The Jacket'. If you come across [it] anywhere, don't read it. It is about the ill-treatment in an American prison, and has me quite miserabl. Write soon.

Yours
Jack

23

[Gastons
16 November 1915]

My Furious Galahad,

Horace has pointed out that if you buy an article after knowing all its defects, you have no right to quarrel with the seller if you are dissatisfied. In the present case, since I told you how slack I was, and openly admitted that I could not promise to keep up a regular correspondance, you have no ground for grumbling if you find that I was speaking the truth. Should you, however, show any disposition to a brief exercise in that fascinating art, I have another excellent excuse: your letters are always shorter than mine: so much so that if I remain silent for a week or so, my amount of letter-writing for the term will still be a good bit bigger than yours.

As a matter of fact I have really had nothing to say, and thought it better to write nothing than to try and pump up 'conversation' – in the philistine sense of the word. I have read nothing new and done nothing new for ages. I am still at the Faerie Queene, and in fact have finished the first volume, which contains the first three books. As I now think it far too good a book to get in ordinary Everyman's I am very much wondering what edition would be the best. Of course I might get my father to give me that big edition we saw in Mullans' for a birthday or Xmas present: but then I don't really care for it much. The pictures are tolerable but the print, if I remember, rather coarse (you know what I mean) and the cover detestable. Your little edition is very nice, but rather too small, and not enough of a library-looking book. How much is it, and what publisher is it by? I believe I have heard you say that it can be got in the same edition as your 'Odyssey', but then that is rather risky, because the illustrations might be hopeless. Write, anyway, and tell me your advice.

By the way those catalogues have never come yet; you might wake the girlinosborne's up. I hope you are right about my music not being a whim: could you imagine anything more awful than to have all your tastes gradually fade away? Not a bad subject for a certain sort of novel! And talking about music, how did *you* enjoy Ysaye: you don't say in your letter. Yes: his brother did play when they were at Guildford: one of his things was a Liebestraum by Liszt, which I did appreciate to a certain extent.[1] Mrs K. has got a new book of Grieg's with a lot of things in it that I am just longing to hear you play: the best is 'Auf den Bergen', do you know it? A lovely scene on mountains by the sea (I imagine) and belled cattle in the distance, and the snow and pines and blue sky, and blue, still, sad water. There's a sort of little refrain in it that you would love. You must try and get hold of it.

Since finishing the first volume of Spenser I have been reading again 'The Well at the World's End', and it has completely ravished me. There is something awfully nice about reading a book again, with all the half-unconscious memories it brings back. 'The Well' always brings to mind our lovely hill-walk in the frost and fog – you remember – because I was reading it then. The very names of chapters and places make me happy: 'Another adventure in the Wood Perilous', 'Ralph rides the Downs to Higham-on-the-Way', 'The Dry Tree', 'Ralp reads in a book concerning the Well at the World's End'.

Why is it that one can never think of the past without wanting to go back? We were neither of us better off last year than we are now, and yet I would love it to be last Xmas, wouldn't you? Still I am longing for next holydays too: do you know they are only five weeks off.

By the way, I hope you have read 'your Swinburne' by now: anyway, when you go up to night to the room I know so well you must go and have a look at the 'Well at the W's End'. Good-night.

Yours
Jacks

24

[Gastons
1 February 1916][1]

Dear little Archie,

Oh Gods of friendship, has such devotion ever been witnessed as mine! I am just at the beginning of a heavenly new book, I am just

---

[1] This is Théo Ysaÿe (1865–1918), a pianist and composer.

[1] Lewis went home for Christmas on 21 December 1915, and returned to Great Bookham on 21 January 1916.

at the end of a long day's work, and yet I spend my spare time in writing letters. I hope you duly appreciate the sacrifice of a fresh young heart offered up on the savage altar of – well to get on.

On the Saturday in London[2] I wasted 7/6 on going to a matinee of Carmen. There was no one in the caste of whom I had heard before and no one whom I want to hear again. Carmen herself was tolerable, but the rest, especially the Toreador, were fiendish. With the opera too I was awfully disappointed, although there is certainly a lot of beautiful music in it – particularly in the preludes to the acts (oh, one thing was good – the orchestra: they played that intermezzo that I have exquisitely) and in the scene among the mountains. But one does get so sick of all the tedious melodrama, all the blustering orchestration, and sticky tunes of good old fashioned operas. Then too there are a pair of villains in it who have a ghastly resemblance in their clownings to that other pair in Fra Diavolo – do you remember those awful creatures? So on the whole I was very fed up with this world by the time I reached dear Bookham. I find – of course – my beloved fellow pupil.

Since then I have been cheered up by the arrival of my new 'Faerie Queen' in the red leather Everyman. I can't see why you so dislike this edition: and if you have noticed the effect that their backs have when two or three are together in a shelf I am sure you do really appreciate them. I have read a good chunk of this and have also re-read Jane Eyre from beginning to end – it is a magnificent novel. Some of those long, long dialogues between her and Rochester are really like duets from a splendid opera, aren't they? And do you remember the description of the night she slept on the moor and of the dawn? You really lose a lot by never reading books again.

The other book – which I am denying myself to write to YOU, yes YOU of all people – is from the library by Blackwood called 'Uncle Paul'.[3] Oh, I have never read anything like it, except perhaps the 'Lore of Proserpine'. When you have got it out of your library and read how Nixie and Uncle Paul get into a dream together and went to a primaeval forest at dawn to 'see the winds awake' and how they went to the 'Crack between yesterday and tomorrow' you will agree with me.

It was most annoying not getting my new records before I came back, wasn't it? Tell the girlinosbornes – the next time you go to see Olive – to send the bill for them to my address here at once. I do hope my Caruso 'E lucevan e stella' is going to be a success. Talking

[2] 29 January 1916.
[3] Algernon Blackwood, *The Education of Uncle Paul* (1909).

about that thing, does it convey anything to you? To me it seems to be just abstract melody. The actual scene I believe is a man on the battlement of a castle writing a letter – but you have probably read Tosca in that beastly potted opera book.

I was interested in what you said about the 'Brut'.[4] You ought to get it in Everyman.

Yours
Jack

25

[Gastons
8 February 1916]

My dear Arthur,

You lucky devil! It makes me very envious to hear of all these good things going on at home while I am languishing in the wilds of Surrey.

I am surprised to hear that you never heard of Barkworth, as I have seen his name in the musical part of the Times and other papers:[1] I believe he is one of the promising musicians of the day – that is if there are ever going to be English musicians and an English school of opera. Personally I should have been very much interested to hear his 'Romeo and Juliet'. If the only fault is that it is blustering, you might say the same of the 'Flying Dutchman' or the 'Valkyrie', mightn't you? What did poor Willie Jaffe think of it? (I suppose you mean him by W.J. –) Hardly in his line I should fancy. I am sure 'Pagliaci' and 'Cavalleria' were lovely, and I would especially like to have seen 'Rigoletto', because I know the plot.

I quite agree with you that a gramophone spoils one for hearing opera: the real difficulty is to find for what a gramophone does not spoil one. True, it improves your musical taste and gives you opportunities of hearing things that you might otherwise never know: but what is the use of that when immediately afterwards it teaches you to expect a standard of performance which you can't get, or else satiates you with all the best things so that they are stale before you have heard them once on the stage? Or in other words, like everything else it is a disappointment, like every other pleasure it just slips out of your hand when you think you've got it. The most striking example of this is the holiday which one looks forward to all the

---

[4] By Layamon (*fl.* 1200).

[1] John Edmund Barkworth (1858–1929), a composer whose chief work is an opera based on Shakespeare's *Romeo and Juliet*.

term and which is over and gone while one is still thinking how best to enjoy it.

By all this you will gather that I am in a bad temper: well, so I am – that bloody little beast my fellow pupil has sneaked upstairs for a bath and I can now hear him enjoying it and I know there will be no hot water left for me. They only raise hot water here about once a month.

However. Let us proceed: do you read Ruskin at all? I am sure you don't. Well I am reading a book of his at present called 'A joy for ever', which is charming, though I am not sure you would care for it.[2] I also still employ the week ends with the Faerie Queene. I am now in the last three books, which, though not much read as a rule, are full of good things. When I have finished it, I am going to get another of Morris' romances, or his translation of one of the sagas – perhaps that of Grettit the Strong. This can be got either for 5/– in the Library edition (my 'Sigurd the Volsung' one) or for 3/6 in the 'Silver Library' (like my 'Pearl Maiden'). Which would you advise?

By the way, why is your letter dated Wednesday? It has arrived here this evening – Tuesday – am I to understand that you posted it tomorrow, or that you have been carrying it about in your pocket for a week?

Isn't it awful about Harding? I hear from my father that Hope is going out.[3] I suppose that by this time the jeunes mariés have got into Schomberg.[4] Why are your letters always so much shorter than mine? Therefore I stop.

Yours,
Jack

---

[2] John Ruskin, *The Political Economy of Art* (1857), the title of which was later changed to *A Joy for Ever*.

[3] Major George Harding, who was married to the former Charlotte Hope Ewart, had contracted double pneumonia in Sicily, where he had been sent to make the preliminary administrative arrangements for the transfer of a British Expeditionary Force to the Italian front. His wife was allowed to join him in Sicily, and she travelled overland alone via France and Italy.

[4] The home of the newly-weds, Gordon and Lily Ewart.

26

My dear Galahad,

I suppose that by this time there is wrath and fury against me: however, there is no excuse, and you must just thole, as they say.

I don't know what it is like with you, but for this last week we have had the most lovely snow here. There is no wind, so where the snow 'falleth, there shall it lie': which means that when you walk through the woods every branch is laden like a Christmas tree, and the mass of white arranged in every fantastic shape and grouping on the trees is really wonderful. Don't you love to walk while it *is* actually snowing? I love to feel the soft, little touches on your face and see the country through a sort of haze: it is so exquisitly desolate. It reminds one of that scene in 'The Lore of Prosperpine'.

Poor thing! I do like the way, because a fellow asks you to join a corps, that you complain about 'your troubles'. May you never do worse! It reminds me of the story of Wellesly and his rich friend: W. had been going on one of his preaching tours round the country, riding alone in all weather, being put in the stocks, insulted, & stoned by the mob, in the course of all which he stayed for a night at the luxurious mansion of the friend. During the evening, a puff of smoke blew out of the grate, whereupon the host exclaimed 'You see, Sir, these are some of the crosses which I have to bear!' Indeed, however, I 'can't talk' as you would say, for of course I am an inveterate grumbler myself – as you, of all people have best reason to know.

By the way, do you know a series of rather commonplace little volumes at 1/6 each called the Walter Scott Library? I have just run across them: they are not particularly nice – though tolerable – but the point is that they sell some things I have often wanted to get: among others Morris' translation of the 'Volsunga Saga' (not the poem, you know, that I have, but a translation of the old Icelandic prose saga) which cannot be got in any other edition except the twelve guinea 'Works', of which you can't get the volumes separately. If only the edition were a little decenter I'd certainly get it.

Perhaps you laugh at my everlasting talk about buying books which I never really get: the real reason is that I have so little time here – indeed only the week-ends as I spend all the spare time on

week-days in reading French books, which I want to get more fluent
in. However, I am now nearing the end of the 'Faerie Queene', and
when that is done the Saturdays & Sundays will be free for something else. Really, whatever you say, you have much more time than
I.

I wonder why Osborne's have sent no bill to me yet? I am not sure
whether I asked you to give them my adress and tell them to send
in the account or not: anyway, be a sport, and do so – AT ONCE.

I have had a grisly dissapointment this week: Mrs K. said she was
going away for a fortnight & I was gloating in the prospect of privacy
& peace. But it has turned out a mare's nest. Ochone!

be good,
Jack

27

[Gastons
7 March 1916]
Tuesday

My dear Galahad,

I was very glad to get your interesting letter – which was fortunately longer than some of them – as I was beginning to wonder what
had become of you; I think your 'lapse' this term puts you on a level
with mine last, so that we can cry quits and admit that we are both
sinners.

I have had a great literary experience this week. I have discovered
yet another author to add to our circle – our very own set: never since
I first read 'The well at the world's end' have I enjoyed a book so
much – and indeed I think my new 'find' is quite as good as Malory
or Morris himself. The book, to get to the point, is George Macdonald's 'Faerie Romance', *Phantastes*,[1] which I picked up by
hazard in a rather tired Everyman copy – by the way isn't it funny,
they cost 1/1d. now – on our station bookstall last Saturday. Have
you read it? I suppose not, as if you had, you could not have helped
telling me about it. At any rate, whatever the book you are reading
now, you simply MUST get this at once: and it is quite worth getting
in a superior Everyman binding too.

Of course it is hopeless for me to try and describe it, but when you
have followed the hero Anodos along that little stream to the faery
wood, have heard about the terrible ash tree and how the shadow of
his gnarled, knotted hand falls upon the book the hero is reading,
when you have read about the faery palace – just like that picture in

[1] George MacDonald, *Phantastes: a faerie romance* (1858).

the Dulac book – and heard the episode of Cosmo, I know that you will quite agree with me. You must not be disappointed at the first chapter which is rather conventional faery tale style, and after it you won't be able to stop until you have finished. There are one or two poems in the tale – as in the Morris tales you know – which, with one or two exceptions are shockingly bad, so don't TRY to appreciate them: it is just a sign, isn't it, of how some geniuses can't work in metrical forms – another example being the Brontes.

I quite agree with what you say about buying books, and love all the planning and scheming beforehand, and if they come by post, finding the neat little parcel waiting for you on the hall table and rushing upstairs to open it in the privacy of your own room. Some people – my father for instance – laugh at us for being so serious over our pleasures, but I think a thing can't be properly enjoyed unless you take it in earnest, don't you? What I can't understand about you though is how you can get a nice new book and still go on stolidly with the one you are at: I always like to be able to start the new one on the day I get it, and for that reason wait to buy it until the old one is done. But then of course you have so much more money to throw about than I.

Talking about finishing books, I have at last come to the end of the Faerie Queene: and though I say 'at last', I almost wish he had lived to write six books more as he hoped to do – so much have I enjoyed it. The two cantos of 'Mutabilitie' with which it ends are perhaps the finest thing in it, and if you have not done so already, you should read them whenever you have the time to spare.

I am now – by the same post – writing for a book called 'British Ballads' (Everyman) in the chocolate binding of which I used to disapprove: so you see I am gradually becoming converted to all your views. Perhaps one of these days you may even make a Christian of me.

Yes: I have at last heard from the girlinosbornes: but like the minstrel in Scott,

'Perhaps he wished the boon denied'

as the bill is rather a staggerer and my finances are not very blooming at present – I am thinking of sending it out to my brother to pay.

I well remember the glorious walk of which you speak, how we lay drenched with sunshine on the 'moss' and were for a short time perfectly happy – which is a rare enough condition, God knows. As Keats says 'Rarely, rarely comest thou, spirit of Delight'.[2] I do hope

[2] The lines are from Shelley's poem 'Rarely'.

we shall have many more pleasant hours such as that: the days are running in so fast now, and it makes me so sad to think that I shall have only two more sets of holidays of the good old type, for in November comes my 18th birthday, military age, and the 'vasty fields' of France, which I have no ambition to face. If there is good weather and you get some days off next hols., we should go for some walks before breakfast – the feel of the air is so exquisite. I don't know when I can expect to come home.

Jack

28

[Gastons
14 March 1916]
(You ought to know the date.)

My dear Galahad,

It must have been a very old Everyman list on which you found 'Phantastes' as one of the new ones, since, to my knowledge, the copy I got had been on the bookstall for weeks. Everymans with us have gone up 1d. in the shilling: I suppose it is just the same at home? By the time you get this you will probably have finished Phantastes, so you must give me your verdict on it as a whole: when one has read a book, I think there is nothing so nice as discussing it with some one else – even though it sometimes produces rather fierce arguments.

I too am rather disappointed. The 'British Ballads' has come, and though I am awfully bucked with the edition – I can't think why I didn't appreciate it before. This must be a triumph for you – the reading matter is not nearly so good as I expected. For one thing, instead of being all made up of real old ballads as I hoped, it is half full of silly modern imitations and even funny ones. Don't you loathe 'funny' poetry? However, as it is not your style of book, I suppose I am boring you.

All the same, when you begin to write a letter you just go on babbling – at least I do – without thinking whether the person at the other end is interested or not, till you come to the last page and find that you haven't really said what you wanted to. But perhaps that sort of rambling is the right kind of letter. I don't know whether you personally write that way or not, but the result is charming, and you can't think how eager I am to see the atrocious but familiar scroll waiting for me on the hall table. And yet, every letter is a disappointment: for a minute or two I was carried back to your room at Bernagh

– don't you remember rooms by their smells? Each one has its own – and seem to be talking to you, and then suddenly I come to the end and it's all only a little bit of paper in my hand and Gastons again. But come. We are being mawkish. I think you and I ought to publish our letters (they'd be a jolly interesting book by the way) under the title of lamentations, as we are always jawing about our sorrows.

I gather it was that beastly girl in Mayne's who 'flared up' as you say. Aren't they rude in that place? I think we ought to start a movement in the neighbourhood to boycott them. Only we'd have to join in it ourselves, which would be a pity.

No: I have never yet seen Kelsie's book. I daresay she doesn't know that I take an interest in such things, and you are lucky in having a reputation as a connoisseur which makes you free of every library in Belmont – tho' there aren't very many to be sure. I am afraid our Galahad will be growing a very stodgy mind if he reads nothing but Trollope and Goldsmith and Austen. Of course they are all very good, but I don't think myself I could stand such a dose of stolidity. I suppose you will reply that I am too much the other way, and will grow a very unbalanced mind if I read nothing but lyrics and fairy tales. I believe you are right, but I find it so hard to start a fresh novel: I have a lazy desire to dally with the old favourites again. I think you'll have to take me in hand and set me a 'course' when I come home.

By the way what about the piano and the gramophone these days? We don't seem to talk of music so much now as we did: of course your knowledge on that subject is so much greater than mine that I can really only express a philistine's taste. Are you still going to Walker? For my part, I have found my musical soul again – you will be relieved to hear – this time in the preludes of Chopin. I suppose you must have played them to me, but I never noticed them before. Aren't they wonderful? Although Mrs K. doesn't play them well, they are so passionate, so hopeless, I could almost cry over them: they are unbearable. I will find out the numbers of the ones I mean and we will have a feast next holidays.

By the way, you speak in your last letter of the difference between music and books: I think (to get back to an old argument) it is just the same difference as between friendship and love. The one is a calm and easy going satisfaction, the other a sort of madness: we take possession of one, the other takes possession of us: the one is always pleasant, the other in its greatest moments of joy is painful. But perhaps I am rating books and friendship too low, because poetry and great novels do sometimes rouse you almost as much as music:

the great love scenes in Shirley for instance, or the best parts of
Swinburne etc.

I am sorry I always make the mistake about your address. Hullo.
I've done it again.

Yours,
Jack

29

[Gastons
21 March 1916]

My dear Galahad,

So here we are at the weekly letter, and very glad I am too; but
Heavens! – how the weeks run on don't they? While I was at Malvern
I used to count the days and long for the end of term, so of course
time crawled; now-a-days when I am quite comfortable the whole
thing goes on far too quickly. And it's all so many days, months etc.,
not of the term or the year, but of one's life – which is tiresome.
'Help!' I hear you muttering, 'Is he going to moralize for four
pages?' (Cheer up, I'll try to hold it in.)

I'm awfully bucked to hear that you think the same about Phantastes as I, though if you only began to enjoy it in the eleventh
chapter, you must have missed what I thought were the best parts –
that is to say the forest scene and the faery palace – or does that come
after chapter XI? You will gather that the book is upstairs and that I
am too lazy to go and get it. I hope that by this time you have bought
'Sir Gibbie' and will be able to advise me on it. Some of the titles
of his other books are, to me at least, even more alluring than the one
you quote: for instance 'At the back of the north wind'.[1]

Isn't it funny the way some combinations of words can give you –
almost apart from their meaning – a thrill like music? It is because I
know that you can feel this magic of words AS words that I do not
despair of teaching you to appreciate poetry: or rather to appreciate
all good poetry, as you now appreciate some. This is however off the
point: what I meant to say was that lots of his titles give me that feeling. I wish there were more in Everymans, don't you?

Talking about Everymans, do you know what their 1/6 binding is
like? I can't remember whether you have anything in it or not, but I
have been thinking of trying it, so tell me what you know on the

---

[1] George MacDonald, *Sir Gibbie* (1879); *At the Back of the North Wind*
(1871).

subject. What? you ask, still new books? Well really the length of the Faerie Queene was a godsend, because so long as I turned to it every week-end with the regularity of clockwork I could keep my money in my pockets: now however the temptation to get a nice new book for the longed for Sunday rest is overwhelming.

I am glad to hear that you have moved into Lily's room as I think you – or 'we' shall I say in selfishness – will be more comfortable there: at the same time I have a sort of affection for the old one where we have had such good times: we should call it 'joyous garde'. Still, I am longing to find myself in your new quarters with all the old talk, the old music, and the old fingering of rich, friendly books.

You know, Galahad, that though I try to hide it with silly jokes that annoy you, I am very conscious of how unfair our friendship is, and how you ask me over continually and give me an awfully good time, while I hardly ever bring you to us: indeed though he is a good father to me, I must confess that he – my father – is an obstacle. I do hope you understand? You know how I would love if I could have you any time I liked up in my little room with the gramophone and a fire of our own, to be merry and foolish to our hearts content: or even if I could always readily accept your invitations without feeling a rotter for leaving him alone. I don't know why I've gone off into this discussion, but perhaps it is just as well. Indeed the only thing to be done is to get my father married as quickly as may be – say to Mary Bradley. Or lets poison old Stokes and give him the widow. In which case of course our imagined snuggery in the little end room would be brightened up by a charming circle of brothers and sisters in law.

I know quite well that feeling of something strange and wonderful that ought to happen, and wish I could think like you that this hope will some day be fulfilled. And yet I don't know: suppose that when you had opened the door the Ash had REALLY confronted you and turning to fly, you had found the house melting into a haunted wood – mightn't you have wished for the old 'dull' world again? Perhaps indeed the chance of a change into some world of Terreauty (a word I've coined to mean terror and beauty) is in reality in some allegorical way daily offered to us if we had the courage to take it. I mean one has occasionally felt that this cowardice, this human loathing of spirits just because they are such may be keeping doors shut? Who knows? Of course this is all nonsense and the explanation is that through reading Maeterlink, to improve my French, too late at night, I have developed a penchant for mystical philosophy – greatly

T.S.T.–D

doubtless to the discomfort of my long suffering reader.

By the way, is the girlinosbornes beginning to ask about my bill yet – which is not paid? Write soon AND LONG mon vieux, to,

yours,

Jack

30

[Gastons
16 May 1916][1]

My dear Galahad,

I wonder what you are doing tonight? It is nearly ten o'clock and I suppose you are thinking of bed: perhaps you are at this moment staring into the good old bookcase and gloating over your treasures. How well I can see it all, exactly as we arranged it a few days ago: it is rather consoling for me to be able to follow you in imagination like this and feel as if I were back in the well-known places.

Now let us get on with what you really want to hear; no, I did not go to the 'Starlight Express' nor could I see it in the 'Times' list of entertainments. Perhaps after all it is not an opera but a cantata or something. What I did go to see was a play called 'Disraeli'[2] which I liked immensely, though I am not sure the Meccecaplex would have cared for it. It's about the real Disraeli you know, the part being taken by Dennis Eadie – whom you saw in 'Milestones'[3] didn't you; he looks exactly like the pictures of the said politican in the old Punches. However, it is a thoroughly interesting play and I shall never repent of having seen it: I think you agree with me that a good sensible play is far better than a second rate opera, don't you?

By the way, you have really no right to this letter, old man: that one of yours which you have been talking about all the holidays is not here, and Mrs K. says that nothing came for me while I was away. So now I shall be no longer content with your continual 'as I said in my letter', but will expect it all over again – especially the remarks about 'The Back of the Northwind' (by the way doesn't it sound much better if you pronounce that last word 'Northwind' as one word, with the accent slightly on the first syllable?).

Talking of books – you might ask, when do I talk of anything else – I have read and finished 'The Green Knight', which is absolutely

[1] Lewis was at home on holiday from 5 April to 11 May 1916.
[2] By Louis Napoleon Parker (1911).
[3] By Arnold Bennett and Edward Knoblauch (1912).

top-hole:[4] in fact the only fault I have to find with it is that it is too short – in itself a compliment. It never wearies you from first to last, and considering the time when it was written, some things about it, the writer's power of getting up atmosphere for instance, quite in the Bronte manner, are little short of marvellous: the descriptions of the winter landscapes around the old castle, and the contrast between them and the blazing hearth inside, are splendid. The last scene too, in the valley where the terrible knight comes to claim his wager, is very impressive.

Since finishing it I have started – don't be surprised – 'Rob Roy',[5] which I suppose you have read long ago. I really don't know how I came to open it: I was just looking for a book in the horribly scanty library of Gastons, and this caught my eye. I must admit that it was a very lucky choice, as I am now revelling in it. Isn't Die Vernon a good heroine – almost as good as Shirley? And the hero's approach through the wild country round his Uncle's hall in Northumberland is awfully good too.

In fact, taking all things round, the world is smiling for me quite pleasantly just at present. The country round here is looking absolutely lovely: not with the stern beauty we like of course: but still, the sunny fields full of buttercups and nice clean cows, the great century old shady trees, and the quaint steeples and tiled roofs of the villages peeping up in their little valleys – all these are nice too, in their humble way. I imagine (am I right?) that 'Our Village'[6] gives one that kind of feeling. Tell me all about your own 'estate' as Spenser would say, when you write.

Have you finished 'Persuasion'[7] and has the De Quincy come yet, and what do you think of both? Have there been any particular beauties of sun and sky since I left? I know all that sounds as though I were trying to talk like a book, but you will understand that I can't put it any other way and that I really do want to hear about those kind of things.

This letter brings you the first instalment of my romance: I expect you'll find it deadly dull: of course the first chapter or so must be in any case, and it'll probably never get beyond them. By the way it is headed as you see 'The Quest of Bleheris'. That's a

[4] The fourteenth-century poem *Sir Gawain and the Green Knight*. Lewis was reading the prose translation by E. J. B. Kirtlan (1912).

[5] By Sir Walter Scott (1818).

[6] Mary Russell Mitford, *Our Village: Sketches of Rural Life, Character, and Scenery*, 5 vols. (1824–32).

[7] By Jane Austen (1818).

rotten title of course, and I don't mean it to be permanent: when it's got on a bit, I must try to think of another, really poetic and suggestive: perhaps you can help me in this when you know a bit more what the story is about.

Now I really must shut up. (That's the paper equivalent of 'Arthur, I'm afraid I shall have to go in a minute'.) Oh, I was forgetting all about Frankenstein.[8] What's it like? 'Really Horrid'?, as they say in 'Northanger Abbey'.[9] Write soon before I have time to feel lonely.

Yours,
Jack

31

[Gastons
22 May 1916]
Monday.
10 o'clock.

My dear Arthur,

Many, many thanks for the nice long letter, which I hope you will keep up for the rest of the term, in length. I see that it has taken four days to reach me, as it came only this morning, so I don't know when you will be reading this.

I am rather surprised at your remark about 'Persuasion', as it seemed to me very good – though not quite in her usual manner. I mean it is more romantic and less humorous than the others, while the inevitable love interest, instead of being perfunctory as in 'Emma' and 'Mansfield Park'[1] is the real point of the story. Of course I admit that's not quite the style we have learned to expect from Jane Austen, but still don't you think it is rather interesting to see an author trying his – or her – hand at something outside their own 'line of business'? Just as it is interesting to see Verdi in 'Aida' rising above himself – though I suppose I have no right to talk musical criticism to you – or indeed to anybody.

I am glad that you are bucked with your De Quincy, and am eager to see the paper. By the way I suppose you notice that the same series can be got in leather for 5/–. I wonder what that would be like. I am thinking of getting the two volumes of Milton in it, as soon as I am flush or have a present of any sort due to me: one wants to get a person like Milton in a really worthy edition you know. Tell me what

[8] Mary Wollstonecraft Shelley, *Frankenstein* (1818; 1831).
[9] By Jane Austen (1818).
[1] Jane Austen, *Emma* (1816); *Mansfield Park* (1814).

you think about this.

On Wednesday I had a great joy: I went up to town with the old woman[2] (by the way I have just seen the point of your joke about 'byre' and liar. Ha! Ha!) to see the Academy. I have never been to one before, and therefore cannot say whether this year's was good as they go: but anyway I enjoyed it immensely and only one thing – your company – was lacking to make it perfect. How I wish we could have been there to enjoy some things together – for there were ones that would have sent you into raptures. Particularly there was a picture called 'Nature groaning' that exactly reminded me of that wet walk of ours, although the scene was different: it represented a dull, gloomy pool in a wood in autumn, with a fierce scudding rain blown slantways across it, dashing withered leaves from the branches and beating the sedge at the sides. I don't suppose that makes you realize it at all, but there was a beautiful dreariness about it that would have appealed to you. But of course it is really no good trying to describe them: I wish you would get that Academy book which one always finds in a dentist's waiting room so that we could compare notes. If you do, you must particularly notice 'The Egyptian Dancers' ['A Dancer of Ancient Egypt'], 'The Valley of the Weugh or Sleugh' or something like that ['The Valley of the Feugh'] (a glorious snow scene), 'The deep places of the earth', 'The watcher' and a lovely faery scene from Christina Rosetti's 'Goblin Market'. It costs only a shilling I think and tho' of course the black and white reproductions lose a lot, still they are quite enjoyable.[3]

Talking about pictures etc., I was very pleased with your description of the mist and the night sky: you are by no means such a contemptable artist in words as you would like people to believe – in fact to be honest, if you weren't lazy you could do big things – and you have brought a very clear picture to my mind: one does get topping effects over the Lough sometimes, doesn't one? Really, after all, for sheer beauty of nearly every kind, there is no place I know like our own good county Down.

I am still at 'Rob Roy' which I like immensely, and am writing by this post for the first volume of Chaucer's 'Canterbury Tales' in the Everyman 2/2 edition: am I wise? I have dipped into them very often latterly in the Kirk's horrible old copy, and think I shall like them,

[2] Mrs Kirkpatrick.

[3] A complete list of the art works at the Royal Academy Exhibition can be found in *The Exhibition of the Royal Academy of Arts*, no. 148 (1916). But Lewis is referring to *The Royal Academy Illustrated* (1916) which contains photographs of most of the paintings mentioned here.

while, as I told you before, the paper of that Everyman is especially
nice. I have also got a French prose romance of 'Tristan and Iseut'
which promises very well as far as I can see: in the meantime however since like all French firms' books it is paper back, I have sent it
away to be bound in a very tasty binding of my own choice. Tell me
more about 'Frankenstein' in your next letter so that I may decide
whether to buy it or no. Any new records? I imagine that the success
of your late venture may buck up your taste for your gramophone
may it not?

This brings you the next chapter of my infliction. By the way I
don't know how I actually wrote it, but I certainly meant to say 'The
quest of Bleheris' and [not] 'of THE Bleheris', since Bleheris is a
man's name. However, as I wrote to you before, that title is only
waiting until I can get another better one. Your advice as to fighting
and brasting exactly falls in with my own ideas since like Milton I
am,

> 'Not sedulous by nature to indite
> Wars' . . . .[4]

I am afraid indeed that like 'Westward Ho'[5] my tale will have to
dawdle about a bit in the 'City of Nesses' before I can get poor
Bleheris off on his adventures: still you must do your best.

Oh vanity! vanity! to think that I can waste all this time jawing
about my own work. Oh, one thing: I can't agree with you that
Kelsie is at all like Diana Vernon: for if – to talk like Rashleigh,[6] 'My
fair cousin' has a fault, it is a certain deadly propriety and matter-of-
factness that will creep in even when she's at her best, don't you
think so.

And now I've scrawled for a whole hour (it's just striking) so good
night.

Jack

32

[Gastons
30 May 1916]

My dear Galahad,

I don't know whether you quite realized how mysterious your last
letter was: on page III I read 'have just begun a tale called "Alice for
short" '. Very good, say I, remembering William de Morgan's novel

---

[4] *Paradise Lost*, IX, 27.
[5] By Charles Kingsley (1855).
[6] Diana Vernon and Rashleigh are characters in *Rob Roy*.

of that name:[1] but you are 'doubtful whether you'll finish it': remembering the size of the volume on our landing book case I am not surprised: then I read on a bit and see that you 'daren't let it out of your hands, even to me'. Ah! Ce devient interèssant (is there an accent on that word?), I think something tremendously improper. But imagine my even greater confusion on learning that de Morgan's long and heavy looking novel is a continuation of Alice in Wonderland! Of course as soon as I turned the page I saw that you meant 'began to write' and not 'began to read' as I had naturally thought, being as you know cracked absolutely.

Well as to the information itself: I cannot urge you too strongly to go on and write something, anything, but at any rate WRITE. Of course everyone knows his own strength best, but if I may give any advice, I would say as I did before, that humour is a dangerous thing to try: as well, there are so many funny books in the world that it seems a shame to make any more, while the army of weird and beautiful or homely and passionate works could well do with recruits. But perhaps your 'Alice' is not so much humorous as lyric and fantastic? Anyway, you might as well send me along what you have done and let me have a look at it: at the worst it can't be more boring than 'Bleheris' and of course it's much easier to criticise each other's things on paper than viva voce: at least I think so.

And by the way, while I'm on this subject, there's one thing I want to say: I do hope that in things like this you'll always tell me the absolute truth about my work, just as if it were by someone else whom we did not know: I will promise to do the same for you. Because otherwise there is no point in sending them, and I have sometimes thought that you are inclined not to. (Not to be candid I mean). So I shall expect your MS – 'Alice' or anything else you have done – next week.

'Rob Roy' is done now, and (to pay you out for your remarks about 'Persuasion') I must admit that I only skimmed the last three or four chapters: the worst of a book with a plot is that when the plot is over, the obvious 'fixing up' is desperately tedious. On the whole however it was jolly good, and some of the scenery passages, as you say, are gorgeous: particularly where Frank is riding 'near the line' with the Bailey and the latter points out the Highland Hills – do you remember? That bit is almost as good as the scene where Clement Chapman shows Ralph the Wall of the World. But I suppose you would think it sacriledge to compare Morris to Scott. So would I for that matter, only the other way round.

[1] William De Morgan, *Alice-for-Short* (1907).

You ask about the binding of my 'Tristram': well of course, apart from the binding itself, all French books are far poorer than ours: this one for instance cost 2/– (2fr.50) although it was only a paper back, of about the same size as my Gawain: the binding will come to another 2/– or perhaps 2/6. That sounds a lot: but after all if you saw a nice leather bound book in a shop of that size and were told it cost 4/–, I don't think it would seem very dear. Of course it is true I may very likely be disappointed in it, but then, not being a prudent youth like you, I have to take risks occasionally.

With the Chaucer I am most awfully bucked: it is in the very best Everyman style – lovely paper, strong boards, and – aren't you envious – not one but two bits of tissue paper. When I've collected enough in that way, I shall be able to put tissue in all my better class Everymans. As to the contents, although I looked forward to them immensely, they have proved even better than I hoped: I have only had time so far to read the 'Prologue' and 'The Knight's Tale' (that's Palamon and Arcite you know), but I adore them. The tale is a perfect poem of chivalry, isn't it? And the pathos of Arcite's death is really wonderful, with the last broken appeal,

'Forget nat Palamon that gentil man'

and the cry of 'Mercy Emelye'.

But God! there I go on talking like a book again, and you a poor invalid who ought to be consoled. Seriously though, I hope you'll be quite alright by the time you read this: I don't like to hear of your being in bed so often, especially as it affects your spirits so. However, cheer up, and whenever you are fed up with life, start writing: ink is the great cure for all human ills, as I have found out long ago.

I quite appreciate what you say about my father, to whom I wrote on Sunday: but after all he hasn't written to me, and as he had Warnie with him I thought he could 'thole'. Still you are quite right in what you say and I must be more regular in future.

I thought you would like De Quincy, and hope you will go on reading him: it is always nice to feel that one has got a new friend among the book world, isn't it? What an old miser you are though. I suppose I shall have to buy the Academy book myself now: and rest assured that you will never see one page of it. It is strange that 'Frankenstein' should be badly written: one would expect the wife of Shelley to be a woman of taste, wouldn't one?

As to my brother's talk about another 'E Lucevan le Stelle' I'm afraid the front must have turned the poor boy's brain:[2] considering

[2] Lieutenant Warren Lewis, who had been in France most of the time

how I pined after your copy for over a year it wasn't very likely that I should have forgotten one if I had it. What put the idea into his head I can't think.

Have been to Leatherhead baths for a swim today and am terribly stiff, as I always am after the first bathe of the year. Sorry this is not much of a letter this week, old man, but it's after 11, and everyone is going to bed. This brings you the next instalment of Bleheris – criticise freely.

Yours,
Jack

33

[Gastons
6 June 1916]

My dear Arthur,

I was rather surprised to see the note paper of your last letter, and certainly wish that I could have been with you: I have some vague memories of the cliffs round there and of Dunluce Castle, and some memories which are not vague at all of the same coast a little further on at Castlerock, where we used to go in the old days. Don't you love a windy day at a place like that? Waves make one kind of music on rocks and another on sand, and I don't know which of the two I would rather have.

As to your remarks about my 'promise' to join you on some future holiday, I must call your attention to the fact that all I promised was not to contract any engagement with my Aunt that could stand in the way of it, always warning you that I might not go anywhere. However I hope to do so, and will certainly try my best.

By the way, in future, if possible, don't write your letter on so many different 'levels', so to speak: I keep them all on a pin now, and so far, all being written the same way up, I have been able to turn to any one I wanted, like a book: the latest one is a hard nut to crack. Always grumbling you see.

You may well ask 'when' my 'Tristan' is coming: I have asked the same question myself more than once, and it's beginning to be like those famous Columbia records the holydays before last. As to the binding, if it is what the girl in the shop told me, it will be boards with leather back, and those little triangular pieces of leather on the

since 1914, was now with the 7th Division. He had been at home on leave from 19 to 25 May, and on the way back to join his Division he spent a day in London with his brother.

corners. I don't know if you understand this description, so I have
drawn it for you: though perhaps indeed you find the picture quite as
hard. In other words it is a glorified edition of the 2/– Everyman. The
reason I'm not quite certain is that the girl showed me a much larger
book done in the same style, only red. As I didn't care for the colour,
she said she thought it could be done like that in brown; so I'm still
waiting the result.

With my last parcel – the Canterbury Tales – I got Macmillan's
and Dent's catalogues, where I find much of interest: I suppose you
know it all already however. For instance I never knew before that
Macmillans would send you – through a bookseller – books on approval. Of course when things are so out of joint as you're only
allowed to keep them for a week, perhaps you could hardly manage it
over in Ireland. Being so near town myself, I think I shall try it,
wouldn't you? I also notice that Dents have a series of 'Classiques
Francaises' corresponding to the English Everymans Library. Does
that mean that they'd be bound the same way? Among them I'm very
pleased to find a rendering of the 'Chanson de Roland' into modern
French: this, as you probably know, is the old French epic, equivalent to our Beowulf, and for years I have been wondering how to get
it. Now, as things sometimes do, it just turns up. Of course talking
about Beowulf reminds me again what hundreds of things there still
are to buy: if you remember it has been 'the next book I'll get' ever
since you have known me.

I know very well what you mean by books getting tiresome half
way through, but don't think it always happens: for instance 'Phantastes', 'Jane Eyre', 'Shirley' (which in fact only begins to get
interesting about then) might be cited – good word that – as examples. Tell me more about 'John Silence'[1] when you write, and
also let me know the publisher and price, as I have forgotten again
and may want it one of these days.

I don't like the way you say 'don't tell anyone' that you thought
'Frankenstein' badly written, and at once draw in your critical horns
with the 'of course I'm no judge' theory. Rot! You are a very good
judge for me because our tastes run in the same direction. And you
ought to rely more on yourself than on anyone else in matters of books
– that is if you're out for enjoyment and not for improvement or any
nonsense of that sort. Which reminds me, I came on a phrase in
Maeterlinck the other day which just suits my views about youth and
silly scientific learning. 'L'ignorance lumineuse de la jeunesse',[2]

[1] Algernon Blackwood, *John Silence: Physician Extraordinary* (1908).
[2] The phrase is from Maurice Maeterlinck's 'L'Intelligence des Fleurs'

the luminous ignorance of youth is exactly our strong point, isn't it?

Great God, how I must be boring you! But you ought to know by now that your friend Chubs with a pen in his hand is a very dangerous object: that extemporising goes a bit far at times: though seriously, to harp back to the eternal subject of self – I think Bleheris has killed my muse – always rather a sickly child. At any rate my verse, both in quality and in quantity for the last three weeks is deplorable!! Before you get any further in the aforesaid romance, let me hasten to warn you that when I said the first chapter, that Bleheris was like you, I hadn't really thought of what I should make him. However I take that back, so that in future when my poor hero does anything mean you won't think I am covertly preaching at you.

In odd moments last week I read an excellent novel by – you'd never guess – Bernard Shaw. It is called 'Love among the Artists', and is published in Constable's shilling series. I want you to get it: there are one or two extraordinary characters in it, and I think the whole gist of the thing, all about music, art etc. would appeal to you very strongly. Tell me if you do. I wonder what the good author who takes his own works so seriously would think if he knew that he was read for pleasure to fill up the odd moments of a schoolboy. If you do get the book, don't forget to read the preface which is very amusing.

I can't understand why you are willing to let me see your tale in the holydays, but are unwilling to send it by post. I refuse point blank to read it in your presence: that means that you spend your time thinking of what the other person is thinking and have no attention left to give to the work itself. So you may as well send it along.

Since I last wrote to you I have found the thought of a book done and yet not done intolerable, and therefore gone back and finished 'Rob Roy'. I am very glad I did so, as otherwise I should have missed the very vigorous scene in the library, and the equally satisfactory death of Rashleigh.

I have written from 10 to quarter past 11 and the others are going up; so good night my Galahad,

from yours,
Jack

which Lewis found in his *Morceaux Choisis*, with an Introduction by Georg-ette Leblanc (Paris, 1911), p. 181.

34

My dear Arthur,

I must begin by apologizing for being a day late this week: I suppose by this time you have worked up quite a flourishing griev- ance. However, you will be glad to know that there is a genuine excuse this time – not just laziness. The reason is that there were visitors here last night, and tho' I don't usually turn up on these occasions, I was so warmly urged 'just to come into the drawing room for a minute or two when I had finished my work' that I really couldn't refuse. So the hour between 10 and 11 which on Tuesday nights is usually taken up with your letter was lost.

The reason why Mrs K. pressed me was that the visitors were some neighbours of ours and with them a girl who is staying with them – that's an elegantly arranged sentence for a literary man – who has a voice and is being trained for opera. Well I am certainly glad I didn't miss it, as she has a very fine contralto and sang two good songs – your record from 'Orfeo' and a very queer thing of Debussy's which I would like to hear again. Of course with that exception she sang rubbish, as the fools asked for it: horrible old ballads like 'Annie Laurie' etc. Still it was worth sitting talking about the war and wasting my time even for two good things. Why are singers always so plain I wonder?

I can't help smiling at the thought of your sitting in the garden on Sunday morning, as we have had nothing but thunderstorms for the last week and it has just now turned so cold that we've gone back to fires. There, I'm talking about the weather! By the way I don't know if you ever noticed how topping it is to see a fire again suddenly in the middle of June: it is so homely and cozy and is like having a bit of the good old Winter back again.

The remark about the cows with which you credit me really comes from your newly made friend De Quincy. I think it is just before the description of the flood – the 'Bore' as he calls it. Look it up and see if I'm right.[1] Anyway I quite agree with it: but perhaps even nicer is a humorous looking old horse, living contentedly in a field by himself, it's those little things that keep one from being lonely on a walk: there is one horse here that I have got to know quite well by giving

---

[1] The passage occurs in the 'Introductory Narration' of Thomas De Quincey's *Confessions of an English Opium Eater* (enlarged edition, 1856).

him sugar. Perhaps he may save me from a witch some day or lead me home in a fog?

You will be amused to hear that my 'Tristen' has not YET come: that is nearly three weeks now, and I am beginning to get angry. You ask at what shop it's being done: well you see it's being worked indirectly through the village stationer here who will send books to be bound for you in London, I don't know where. The reason for its taking so long, I imagine is that the wretch really waits until he has several to do and then makes one parcel of them so as to save himself the postage. In any case I shall not give him another opportunity, as there are people in the neighbouring town of Leatherhead who bind books themselves.

I am glad you like 'John Silence' and must get it too. I have now read all the tales of Chaucer which I ever expected to read, and feel that I may consider the book as finished: some of them are quite impossible. On the whole with one or two splendid exceptions such as the Knight's and the Franklin's tales, he is disappointing when you get to know him. He has most of the faults of the Middle Ages – garrulity and coarseness – without their romantic charm which we find in the 'Green Knight' or in Malory. Still, I only really expected to enjoy some of the Tales, and feel that the book was worth getting for their sake. I am not sure whether you would like him or not, but you should certainly not start poetry with him.

Which reminds me, have you ever carried out your plans of reading 'Jason'?[2] I am wondering what I ought to get next, or whether I ought to save money and read some of the Gastons books – perhaps finish the Brontes or take up another Scott. I have found that Sidney's romance the 'Arcadia'[3] is published at 4/6 by the Cambridge University Press (what are they like?) and am strongly tempted to get it. One thing that interests me is that Sidney wrote it for his sister, the Countess of Pembroke, sending it to her chapter by chapter as he wrote it as I send you 'Bleheris'. Perhaps we were those two in a former state of existence – and that is why your handwriting is so like a girl's. Though even my self conceit will hardly go as far as to compare myself with Sidney.

What a queer compound you are. You talk about your shyness and won't send me the MS of 'Alice', yet say that you are willing to read it to me – as if reading your own work aloud wasn't far more of an ordeal. By the way I hope that you are either going on with 'Alice' or starting something else: you have plenty of imagination, and what

[2] William Morris, *The Life and Death of Jason* (1867).
[3] Sir Philip Sidney, *The Countesse of Pembrokes Arcadia* (1590).

you want is practice, practice, practice. It doesn't matter what we write (at least this is my view) at our age, so long as we write continually as well as we can. I feel that every time I write a page either of prose or of verse, with real effort, even if it's thrown into the fire next minute, I am so much further on. And you too who have been so disappointed at the technical difficulties of composing, won't you find it a relief to turn to writing where you can splash about, so to speak, as you like, and gradually get better and better by experience? Or in other words, I shall expect an MS of some sort with your next week's letter: if I don't get it, I may have recourse to serious measures.

I like the way you say 'why don't' I 'take' a day in town! As if I could just stroll down one morning and say that I wasn't going to do any work today: no Galahad, that sort of thing may do in Franklin Street, but where people WORK – note that word, you may not have met it before – it can't be did.

I am being fearfully lacerated at present: thinking that Pindar is a difficult author whom we haven't time to read properly, Kirk has made me get it in the Loeb library – nice little books that have the translation as well as the text. I have now the pleasure of seeing a pretty, 5/– volume ruined by a reader who bends the boards back and won't wash his filthy hands: while, without being rude, I can't do anything to save it. Of course it is a very little thing I suppose, but I must say it makes me quite sick whenever I think of it.

In case you despair of ever getting rid of the 'City of the Nesses', I promise you that in the next chapter after this one Bleheris actually does get away. Don't forget the MS when you write, and tell me everything about yourself. Isn't this writing damnable?

Yours,
Jack

35

[Gastons
20 June 1916]

My dear Arthur,

I do wish you would be serious about 'Alice': whatever else is a matter for joking, work – in this particular sense of the word – certainly is not. I do really want to see something of yours, and you must know that it is impossible to write one's best if nobody else ever has a look at the result.

However, I told you I would proceed to serious measures, so here is my manifesto. I, Clive Staples Lewis, student, do hereby give

notice that unless some literary composition of Arthur Greeves be in
my possession on or before midnight on the last night of June in the
year nineteen hundred and sixteen, I shall discontinue from that date
forward, all communication to the said Arthur Greeves of every kind,
manner, and description whatsoever, until such composition or
compositions be forwarded. 'So there' as the children say. Now let us
go on.

'Oh rage, Oh desespoir!' Alas! I am undone. All men are liars.
Never, never get a book bound. You will gather from this that
'Tristan' has arrived and is a complete and absolute failure. When I
told them to bind it in brown leather, with corner pieces etc., I
imagined that it would look something like Kelsie's Dickens or like a
2/- Everyman. Wouldn't you have thought so? Well as a matter of
fact, though in a sense they have done what I told them, yet the total
effect, instead of being booky and library like, is somehow exactly like
a bank book or a ledger. For one thing the leather – though I must
say excellent in quality – is very dark and commercial looking, and
the cloth between the back and triangular bits is the absolute abomination of desolation. As if this wasn't enough – the edges of the
paper were before nice, and artistically rough. Well what do you
think the brutes have done? They have smoothed them down and
coloured them a horrible speckled red colour, such as you see in
account books. You can imagine my absolute fury.

True, it is some consolation to find the book itself good beyond
what I had expected: it gets the romantic note (which the French
don't usually understand) very well indeed. One or two little descriptions are full of atmosphere. In particular, what could be better
for Lyonesse – glorious name – as we imagine it, than this simple
sentence: 'Climbing to the top of the cliff he saw a land full of vallies
where forest stretched itself without end.' I don't know whether you
will agree with me, but that gives me a perfect impression of loneliness and mystery. Besides its other good points, it is very, very
simple French, so that if you think of starting to read that language
this would make a very good beginning.

I am sorry to hear about the 'Beowulf', and if it is at all like what I
imagine, surprised as well. Of course you were always less patient of
the old fashioned things than I, and perhaps it is not a good translation. However (seriously) I may buy it from you at a reasonable price,
if I like the look of it, just to match my 'Gawaine' – that is unless I
get Morris's 'Beowulf'[1] instead, which is rather too dear at 5/-.

Your remarks about music would seem to lead back to my old idea

[1] *Beowulf*, translated by William Morris and A. J. Wyatt (1892).

about a face being always a true index of character: for in that case, if you imagined from the music of the soul either of Gordon or of this mysterious 'fille aux cheveux de lin' one would be bound to imagine the face too – not of course exactly, but its general tone. What type of person is this girl of whom Debussy has been talking to you? As to your other suggestions about old composers like Schubert or Beethoven, I imagine that, while modern music expresses both feeling, thought and imagination, they expressed pure feeling. And you know all day sitting at work, eating, walking etc., you have hundreds of feelings that can't (as you say) be put into words or even into thought, but which would naturally come out in music. And that is why I think that in a sense music is the highest of the arts, because it really begins where the others leave off. Painting can only express visible beauty, poetry can only express feeling that can be analysed – conscious feeling in fact: but music – however if I let myself go on such a fruitful subject I should take up the rest of this letter, whereas I have other things to tell you.

What is nicer than to get a book – doubtful both about reading matter and edition, and then to find both are topping? By way of balancing my disappointment in 'Tristan' I have just had this pleasure in Sidney's 'Arcadia'. Oh Arthur, you simply must get it – though indeed I have so often disappointed you that I oughtn't to advise. Still, when you see the book yourself, you will be green with envy. To begin with, it is exactly the sort of edition you describe in your last letter – strong, plain, scholarly looking and delightfully – what shall I say – solid: that word doesn't really do, but I mean it is the exact opposite of the 'little book' type we're beginning to get tired of. The paper is beautiful, and the type also.

The book itself is a glorious feast: I don't know how to explain its particular charm, because it is not at all like anything I ever read before: and yet in places like all of them. Sometimes it is like Malory, often like Spenser, and yet different from either. For one thing, there is a fine description of scenery in it (only one so far, but I hope for more) which neither of them could have done. Then again the figure of the shepherd boy, 'piping as though he would never be old'[2] rather reminds me of the 'Crock of Gold'.[3] But all this comes to is that Sidney is not like anyone else, but is just himself. The story is much more connected than Malory: there is a great deal of love making, and just enough 'brasting and fighting' to give a sort of impression of all the old doings of chivalry in the background

[2] *Arcadia*, Bk. I, ch. 2.
[3] By James Stephens (1912).

without becoming tedious: there is a definite set of characters all the time instead of a huge drifting mass, and some of them really alive. Comic relief is supplied by the fussy old king of Arcadia – rather like Mr Woodhouse in Emma – and his boor, Dametas. The only real fault is that all the people talk too much and with a tendency to rhetoric, and the author insists on making bad puns from time to time, such as 'Alas, that that word last should so long last'.[4] But these are only small things: true, there is a good deal of poetry scattered through it which is all detestable, but then that has nothing to do with the story and can be skipped. I'm afraid this description won't help much, but I am just longing for Saturday when I can plunge into it again. (I mean the book, not the description.)

So much have I chattered that I have hardly any more room left. No, I have never yet read any of Christina Rosetti's poems, though, as you have heard me say, I love her brother Gabriel Rosetti. I believe she is very good, and a faery picture illustrating the 'Goblin market'[5] which I saw in the Academy attracted me very much. That is certainly a lovely edition of Lily's, though of course not worth [getting], unless somebody presented it to you. A nice sentiment truly! But you understand.

I see that I have scribbled a note about illustrations on this week's instalment (of course each is written a fortnight before you get it). Well do have a try: or rather that is a patronizing thing to say: I mean, do exert yourself. I am afraid my poor description won't inspire you much. I wonder do you really know what Cloudy Pass[6] looks like?

Well, they're going to bed now. It is eleven o'clock so I suppose you yourself are already in that happy place. Don't forget my manifesto.

Yours,
Jack

36

[Gastons
28 June 1916]

My dear Arthur,

For some reason your letter didn't reach me until this morning (Wednesday) so I am afraid that this will be a day late. I have been

---

[4] *Arcadia*, Bk. I, ch. 1.
[5] By Hilda Hechle.
[6] In his story *The Quest of Bleheris*.

longing to get to my answer all day: and now that the time is come I hardly know how to collect my thoughts – they have been buzzing so in my head ever since breakfast.

First, ten thousand thanks for the enclosure. You know that I never flatter my friends – in fact my faults are in the other direction: so you may accept as a truth how this first sample of your work has knocked me all of a heap. Really, Galahad, I had no idea you could do anything like this: it is splendid. The only fault I have to find is that there is not enough of it. The idea of all the things round the river being in love with your hero – and I suppose the river too – showing their affection – is beautifully suggestive: I am longing to see it worked out – for by the way, on no account must you think of giving up after so happy a beginning. What I like particularly is the way which – according to the advice of friend Horace – you get straight into the middle of your theme right away, without any such dull descriptions as open Bleheris. The whole description of the river, etc., is done (in my poor opinion) with great skill: it sort of carries you away from the world into a dim, summery dream in some landscape more lovely than reality. Isn't the very word 'punt' very descriptive of summer and cool green reaches?

And now I am going to be so bold as to make a few suggestions: not that I think I am better 'up' in such things than you, but because it is good for both parties to be criticised, and I wish you would do the same to me. Well then, I don't know if it be true with other people, but in my own case, I have always found that if you are in at all good form when you write, corrections made afterwards are usually for the worse. Certainly most of yours are not improvements: for instance in several cases you have changed the word 'that' to which, as

that) happened long ago.
which)

Of course it is a small point, but don't you think 'that' is more simple, natural, and dignified than 'which'? The latter is indeed rather business like. Nor do I see why 'extremely old' should be written over the plain 'very old'. The second point is this: does your own judgement approve the sentence, 'shook her silvery sheen'? The alliteration, I think, would be a bit daring even in verse, and I am sure cannot be allowed in prose.

Now, I suppose you think me meddlesome and impudent. Well, though perhaps I am given to finding spots in the sun, I still appreciate its brightness: I repeat, though my opinion of you as a friend could not be higher than it was, my opinion of you as an author has risen by leaps and bounds since this morning. You MUST go on with this exquisite tale: you have it in you, and only laziness – yes, Sir, laziness – can keep you from doing something good, really good. By the way, before we go any further, I must say in fairness, that when you find those roses playing a more prominent part in the life of my Bleheris, it is not cribbed from your willow tree: I had thought out my plot – what there is of it – before I left home.

I am very glad to hear that you have bought C. Rossetti's poems: partly because I want to be able to look at it myself in the comfort of your sofa – mind the springs – and also I am glad you are beginning to read poetry. Which reminds me, a propos of your tale, you should read the bit in Morris's 'Jason' about Hylas and the water nymphs. I think it is in Book II – at any rate you can see from the headings – and it would not take you more than half an hour. As to the illustrated edition of his early poems, I believe we once saw it together in Mullen's, but so far as I remember, weren't greatly impressed; or am I thinking of something else? You don't tell me what you are actually reading at present, for you can't be living entirely on lyrics: have you finished 'John Silence' yet, and what is your final verdict on it?

In the mean time the 'Arcadia' continues beautiful: in fact it gets better and better. There has been one part that Charlotte Bronte could not have bettered: where Philoclea the heroine, or rather one of the heroines, is beginning to fall in love unconsciously with a man disguised as a girl: and she does not know the secret: the delicacy and pathos of her wrestlings with a feeling which of course she can't understand, as told by Sidney are – well I can't explain what they are like: there is one scene where she goes out by moonlight to an old grove, an haunted place, where there is an altar to 'the wood gods of old',[1] and lies looking up at the stars and puzzling about things, that is equal to if not better than the scene where Jane Eyre wakes up on the moor – do you remember? On the other hand, of course there are parts YOU might not have patience with: in the old style, where people relate their own adventures with no direct bearing on the main story: yet even this, to me, is interesting – so quaint and so suggestive of the old romantic world.

Besides this, I have read nothing lately, except a foolish modern novel which I read at one sitting – or rather one lying on the sofa,

[1] *Arcadia*, Bk. II, ch. 4.

this afternoon in the middle of a terrible thunderstorm. I think, that if modern novels are to be read at all, they should be taken like this, at one gulp, and then thrown away – preferably into the fire (that is if they are not in one's own edition). Not that I despise them because they are modern, but really most of them are pretty sickly with their everlasting problems.

I am glad to hear that you have started illustrating my tale: your criticism about not making long conversations is a very sound one, though I fear I can't keep up to it. For instance, after this chapter the next two are, I am afraid, taken up with a conversation between Bleheris and the people he meets at an inn. Still, as it is necessary to what follows, you must try and get through it. This chapter is a failure: I particularly wanted to show what sort of a person he is and how he develops, but have only made him ridiculous.

I am interested in what you tell me of the Bronte country. Fancy a real living original of Heathcliffe? What must he have been like.

Now it is time for bed, so good night mon vieux, and don't forget another instalment in your next letter.

Yours,
Jack

37

[Gastons
4 July 1916]

My dear Arthur,

So you feel hurt that I should think you worth talking to only about books, music, etc.: in other words that I keep my friendship with you only for the highest plane of life: that I leave to others all the sordid and uninteresting worries about so-called practical life, and share with you those joys and experiences which make that life desirable: that – but now I am getting rhetorical. It must be the influence of dear Sidney and his euphuism I suppose. But seriously, what can you have been thinking about when you said 'only' books, music, etc., just as if these weren't the real things!

However, if I had thought for a moment that it would interest you, of course you are perfectly welcome to a full knowledge of my plans – such as they are. Indeed I imagined that you had a pretty clear idea about them: well, 'let us go forward', to quote from a certain romance: being Irish, I hear from my father that the fact of my being educated in England will not bring me under the new act. I am therefore going to remain as I am until December when my Oxford exam comes off.

After that, I shall of course join the army: but in what exact way, I don't at present know any more than you do. So there you have the whole yarn.[1]

I may just remark in passing that you should by this time know better than to waste pity on your friend Chubs for 'worrying' about it: did you ever see him worrying about anything? I have learnt by now that whatever plans you make in this world, everything always turns out quite differently, so what is the use of bothering? To be honest, the question has hardly crossed my mind once this term. Now I don't mind in the least telling you all this, and if you wanted to know I don't see why you never asked before. But then I am a coarse-grained creature who never could follow the feelings of refined – might I say super-refined? – natures like my Galahad's.

The annoying part is that you have taken up your letter (and here am I taking up mine!!) with this, to the exclusion of all sorts of interesting things that I wanted to hear: for instance, you must tell me more about Hardy. We have all heard of him till we are sick of it, and so I should like to hear the opinion of someone I know. What sort of a novel is it? Would I like it?

But of course the first thing I looked for in this evening's letter was to see if there was an instalment there. I have now read it over again with last week's to get the continuous narrative, and with the same pleasure. Did you quite realise what a splendid touch it was for Dennis to hope 'nobody would steal his clothes'? Somehow the practical, commonsense realism of that, increases the fairy-like effect of what follows enormously. I don't know if I can explain it, but it sort of brings the thing just enough in touch with reality to make it convincing, without spoiling its dreaminess. Also the idea of his seeing her face not directly, but in the water, is somehow very romantic. By the way, I hope you don't really think that I hinted for

[1] For some months now many letters had been passing between father and son, and father and Mr Kirkpatrick, regarding Lewis's future. All were agreed that he should try for a place at Oxford, and Lewis was due to sit for a scholarship examination there on 5 December. However, with one son already in the Army, and the war growing worse every day, Albert Lewis was very anxious to keep Clive out of the service. According to the Military Service Act in effect at this time, this would not have been difficult. Whereas it stated that every male British subject who had attained the age of eighteen and 'ordinarily resident in Great Britain' was liable for enlistment in the Army, it further stated that a subject 'who is resident there for the purposes of his education only' was exempt from serving. Contrary to his father's wishes, Lewis insisted that he would *not* apply for this exemption, and, having made up his mind, he would not be talked out of it by either father or tutor.

a moment that your willow was borrowed from my roses: how could you know what my roses were going to do about five chapters ahead? Above all, don't change anything in the plan of your tale on that account. Perhaps, as you say, we both took it unconsciously from 'Phantastes', who in his turn borrowed it from the dryads, etc. of classical mythology, who are a development of the primitive savage idea that everything has a spirit (just as your precious Jehovah is an old Hebrew thunder spirit): so we needn't be ashamed of borrowing our trees, since they are really common property.

Your reply to my criticism is typically Galahadian: but though in your case I am sure it is more sincere than it looks, still this excessive modesty is rather absurd. You may be dissatisfied with it (though I don't see why), you may be uncertain of yourself, but still in your heart of hearts you don't think of 'The Water Sprite' as 'that rubbish of mine', now do you?

Do you know what your tale has done? It has made me sorry that I began Bleheris in the old style: I see now that though it is harder to work some effects in modern English, yet on the whole my way of writing is a sort of jargon: however, we must do the best we can. I was very glad to hear that you liked the Sunken Wood, especially as the next two chapters are stodgy conversation. I am afraid Bleheris never gets into the wood: but you ought to know that the 'little, hobbling shadow' doesn't live more in that wood than anywhere else. It follows nervous children upstairs to bed, when they daren't look over their shoulders, and comes and sits on your grandfather's summer seat beside two friends when they have talked too much nonsense in the dark. I hope you have an illustration ready for this chapter?

I am still at the 'Arcadia', which you will gather from this is a long book, though not a bit too long. I won't make you sick of it before you see it by starting to sing its praises again: I only promise you that I am still as keen on it as when I began. By the way, now that we are both writing, and know how much work there is in a short instalment that can be read in a few minutes, you begin to realize the labour of writing a thing say like the 'Morte D'Arthur'.

I gather from your silence that you are doing nothing in the gramophone way? Ask the Girlinosbornes whether my new record of 'Is not His word like a fire' (ordered last holidays) has come yet or not. I hope it will be waiting for me when I get home: which event – do you realize – will happen in about a month. This term has gone terribly quickly and been very pleasant, but all the same I shall not be sorry to take up my other life again.

What new books are there of yours to see? I am longing to have a look at your De Quincey and 'Rossetti'. By the way, I suppose you never looked up the passage about the 'bore' nor the one in William Morris about Hylas and the nymphs? I have now finished my Tristan, which is really delightful: it is the saddest story on earth I think, don't you? I have written for the French Everyman translation of 'Roland' which ought to have come by now, but hasn't. I am interested to see what the binding is like, aren't you?

You will see by the scrawl that I am trying to write about a million miles an hour as everyone has gone to bed. So goodnight old man: send another instalment next week, I am so interested in your adorable fairy.

Yrs.,
Jack

P.S. By the way, one criticism just to keep you from getting your head turned. Don't talk about Dennis as 'our young friend' or 'our hero' – the last is like a newspaper: at least you may take it as a suggestion just for what it is worth. – J.

38

[Gastons
11 July 1916]

My dear Arthur,

I am very glad to hear that you are getting to like Jason: I agree with you that the whole description of Medea – glorious character – going out by night, and of her sorceries in the wood is absolutely wonderful, and there are other bits later on, such as the description of the 'Winter by the Northern River' and the garden of the Hesperides, which I think quite as good. Curiously enough I have just started the 'Argonautica'[1] the Greek poem on the same subject, and though I haven't got very far – only in fact to the launching of Argo – it is shaping very well. It will be interesting to compare this version with Morris's, although indeed the story of the Golden Fleece is so perfect in itself that it really can't be spoiled in the telling. Don't you find the very names 'Argo' and 'Argonauts' somehow stirring?

I thought a person like you would sooner or later come to like poetry: by the way, of course you are quite right when you talk about thinking more of the matter than of the form. All I meant when I

[1] By Apollonius Rhodius.

talked about the importance of form was to carry a little further what you already feel in prose – that is how some phrases such as the Wall of the World, or at the Back of the North Wind affect you, partly by sound partly by association, more than the same meaning would if otherwise expressed. The only difference is that poetry makes use of that sort of feeling much more than prose and produces those effects by metre as well as by phrase. In fact, the metre and the magic of the words should be like the orchestration of a Wagnerian opera – should sort of fill the matter by expressing things that can't be directly told – that is, it expresses feeling while the matter expresses thought. But I daresay I have given you my views on the subject before. I am very flattered that you remember that old line about the 'garden where the west wind' all these months, and will certainly copy out anything that is worth it if you can find me a shop in dear Belfast where I can buy a decent MS book: I have failed in that endeavour so far.

So we are to be treated to more and more modesty? Indeed Arthur if I could get a little of your diffidence, and you a little of my conceit we should both be very fine fellows. This week's instalment is quite worthy of the other two, and I was quite disappointed when it broke off. The reeds 'frightened out of their senses' and shouting in 'their loudest whisper' are delightful. 'Our Lady of the Leaf' might be kept in mind as a possible title if you don't care for the present one.

You are rather naive in telling me that you 'have to sit for a minute thinking' and 'find the same word coming in again' as if these weren't the common experiences of everyone who has ever written. I haven't noticed any smallness in the vocabulary you employ for your tale, and anyway that's just a matter of practice. By the way, even if you didn't mean it, I hope you see now what I am driving at about the remark of Dennis as to his clothes. As to the 'sitting for ten minutes', I don't believe that good work is ever done in a hurry: even if one does write quickly in a burst of good form, it always has to be tamed down afterwards. I usually make up my instalment in my head on a walk because I find that my imagination only works when I am exercising.

Can you guess what I have been reading this week? Of all things in the world 'Pendennis'![2] Isn't this the one you find too much for you? I am nearly through the first volume and like it well so far: of course one gets rather sick of Pen's everlasting misbehaviour and the in-evitable repentance going round and round like a mill wheel, and there doesn't seem much connection between one episode and another. All the same, it has a sort of way with it.

[2] William Makepeace Thackeray, *The History of Pendennis* (1849–50).

That feast the 'Arcadia' is nearly ended: in some ways the last book is the best (though a little spoiled I admit by brasting) and here the story is so like the part of Ivanhoe where they are all in Front-de-Boeuf's castle, that I think Scott must have borrowed it. Your remarks about C. Rosetti's poems are very tantalizing and I am longing to see them. How I do love expensive books if only I could afford them. Apropos of which, do you know anything of the artist Beardesley?[3] I fancy he was the man who started the modern school of 'queer' illustrations and the like: well I see you can get for £1.5s. a I vol. edition of Malory with his illustrations, published by Dent. What do you think it would be like? I only wish it was Macmillan and so we could have it on approval.

You are quite wrong old man in saying I can draw 'when I like'. On the contrary, if I ever can draw, it is exactly when I don't like. If I sit down solemnly with the purpose of drawing, it is a sight to make me 'ridiculous to the pedestrian population of the etc.'. The only decent things I do are scribbled in the margins of my dictionary – like Shirley – or the backs of old envelopes, when I ought to be attending to something else.

I am quite as sorry as you that I can't see my way to working Bleheris back into the Sunken Wood, for I think the idea might be worked a bit more: but don't see how it is to be done without changing the whole plan of the story.

The immediate prospects of my getting married 'agreeably or otherwise' as you kindly suggest, are not very numerous: but if you are getting uneasy about an invitation, rest assured, when the event comes off, if you behave you shall have one.

It was strange that Mrs K. should get Hardy's 'Under the Greenwood Tree' out of the library last week, though I never got a chance of looking into it: somehow I don't fancy Hardy is in my line, but then I always have a prejudice against people whom you're always hearing about.

You say nothing about music now-a-days, and I am afraid I scarcely think of it: it annoys me hugely to think of the whole world of pleasures that I used to have and can't enjoy now. Did you see a long article in the Times Literary Supplement about the 'Magic Flute' which is on at the Shaftesbury?[4] How I wish I could go up and hear it and also 'Tristan and Isolde' – though if I did it would be a disappointment in all probability.

[3] Aubrey Vincent Beardsley (1872–98).
[4] 'The Magic Flute' (unsigned), *The Times Literary Supplement* (29 June 1916), pp. 1–2.

I am furious because in answer to my order for the 'Chanson de Roland' I am told it is out of print, which is very tiresome. Here I enclose another chapter, really all conversation this time, but can promise you a move next week. Don't forget your own instalment which I look forward to very eagerly. Good night.

Yours,
Jack

39

[Gastons]
Tuesday evening, the I
don't know whath, [18] July /16.

My dear Arthur,

I can't understand why you should want to know the dates on which these gems of wit were written: if you should ever happen to look at them in the future, a date is a meaningless thing and it won't really help you to see a few numbers written on the top. For my part, when I read your old letters, I don't think about such nonsense. I classify them not by time but by the stage in our thoughts at which they were written: I say 'Ah, that was when we were talking about Loki, this was when we talked much about music and little about books, we didn't know each other so well when this was written' and so on. Which is far more sensible than saying, 'This was September 1914, that was August 1915.' As well, the fact that everyone else puts a date on their letters is to me an excellent reason for not doing so. Still, if you are really concerned about it, I suppose I must 'bow myself in the house of Rimmon'.[1] Since I have gone so far as to put a date however, you can't be so unreasonable as to suggest that it should be the right one.

I am awfully bucked about 'Twelfth Night':[2] I thought at the time you remember, that Heath Robinson's illustrations were absolutely perfect – quite as good as Rackham's, though of course in a different style. If I remember aright there is a splendid one on the line 'How full of shapes is fancy'[3] and also some fine evening cloud effects – not to mention the jester in the rain and the delightfully 'old English' garden scenes.

I am longing, as you say, to be at home and to go over all our

---

[1] 2 Kings, v.18.
[2] *Shakespeare's Comedy of Twelfth Night*, With Illustrations by W. H. Robinson [1908].
[3] *Twelfth Night*, I, i, 14.

treasures both old and new: – so of course we shall be disappointed in some way. As you say, you are extravagant, but I too at present buy one book as soon as I have finished another.

The 'Arcadia' is finished: or rather I have read all there is of it, for unfortunately it breaks off at a most exciting passage in the middle of a sentence. I will not praise it again, beyond saying that this last 3rd. book, though it has no such fine love passages as the 2nd., yet (despite the brasting), for really tip-top narrative working the interest up and up as it goes along, is quite worthy of Scott.

This week's new purchase consisted of Milton's 'Paradise Lost' – in the same edition as my Mandeville[4] – and 'John Silence' in the 7d. edition. Just as one sometimes has a spell of being disappointed in new books, so at other times you keep on getting one treat after another. For the first few pages of John Silence I was hardly in the right mood: but after that it fairly swept me off my feet, so that on Saturday night I hardly dared to go upstairs. I left off – until next week end – in the middle of the 'Nemesis of Fire' – Oh, Arthur, aren't they priceless? Particularly the 'Ancient Sorceries' one, which I think I shall remember all my life. Oh, that evil dance, and the 'muttering the old, old incantation'! The feeling of it all chimed with a lovely bit of 'Paradise Lost' which I read the same evening where it talked of the hounds that,

> '. . . Follow the night hag, when, called
> In secret riding through the air she comes
> Lured with the smell of infant blood, to dance
> With Leopard witches, while the labouring moon
> Eclipses at their charms.'[5]

Don't you like the Leopard witches? How you will love Milton some day! By the way we may remark in passing that John Silence is one of the nicest 7d's in paper and so forth that I have ever seen. I wonder how people would laugh if they could hear us smaking our lips over our 7d's and Everymans just as others gloat over rare folios and an Editio Princeps? But after all, we are surely right to get all the pleasure we can, and even in the cheapest books there is a difference between coarse and nice get up. I wonder what a book called 'Letters from Hell' published at 1/– by Macmillan would be like?[6]

[4] *The Travels of Sir John Mandeville*, modernized and edited by A. W. Pollard (1900).

[5] *Paradise Lost*, II, 662.

[6] [Valdemar Adolph Thisted], *Letters from Hell*, Given in English by Julie Sutter, with a Preface by George MacDonald (Richard Bentley & Son, 1885; reprinted by Macmillan, 1911). This curious book was first published

This week's instalment I enjoyed especially: the idea of the hair so beautiful to the eye so coarse to the touch is very suggestive, and you keep us in fine doubt as to whether your faery is going to turn out good and benevolent or terrible. You complain that your tale is commonplace, but I don't know anything that you think is like it, and I hope that you will really never think of giving it up unfinished – all the same, if you do – for which I can see no earthly reason – don't be discouraged, because we very rarely succeed in finishing a first work. If you saw the number of 'beginnings' I have made! By the by, there is one little point I must grouse at this week. You say that the faery resumed her 'normal' size. What was her normal size? We saw her first as a little figure on a leaf, and she hasn't changed since. Do you mean that she took on human size? Of course a few trifling changes when you revise will make this quite clear. The point of names is rather difficult: 'Dennis' I like, but the old Irish attractions of 'Desmond' are very strong. I really don't know what I should advise.

I am sorry you disapprove of my remarks in the romance. But you must remember that it is not Christianity itself I am sneering at, but Christianity as taught by a formal old priest like Ulfin, and accepted by a rather priggish young man like Bleheris. Still, I fear you will like the main gist of the story even less when you grasp it – if you ever do, for as is proper in romance, the inner meaning is carefully hidden.

I am really very sorry to hear about your new record, but so many of your Odeons have been successful that I cannot reasonably have the pleasure of saying 'I told you so'. Talking about music, I have at last found out the exact number of the Chopin piece I like so well – it is the 21st Prelude. Look it out, and tell me if it is not the best music in the world?

I am afraid it is mere foolishness to praise that rhyme of mine as you do. Remember, you know exactly the occasion that gave rise to it, and can read between the lines, while to others it would perhaps be scarcely intelligible: still it is nice to be able to please even one reader – as you do too, for all your talk. In a way that sort of double-meaning in the title 'Lady of the Leaf' would be rather fascinating I think.

I am glad to hear your remarks about the different pleasures of painting, writing etc. I quite agree with you, 'work' of this kind, though it worries and tortures us, tho' we get sick of it and dis-

in Denmark in 1866, and later translated into German. Julie Sutter's English translation of 1885 was made from the German version.

satisfied with it and angry, after all it is the greatest pleasure in life – there is nothing like it. Good night old man.

Jack

P.S. Is Dennis in bathing things all this time, or 'au naturel'? The point is not without interest.

P.P.S. Up in my room I have just read over the whole 'Watersprite' again. I have not done it justice in this letter, the whole story is topping and the air of mystery that hangs about Her makes one very keen to go on. I am not putting this in because I want to pleasure you, but because it just strikes me at the moment and must come out. Go on and prosper – there goes half past. So gute nacht du lieber kamarad, bon soir mon vieux.

J.

40

[Gastons]
July 25, 1916 and be d–d to you.

My dear Arthur,

That thrice accursed fellow pupil of mine is at present sitting up in the work room so I cannot go and steal a page from his exercise book to write on, as I have been doing all the term – you must be content therefore with these odd scraps: indeed I don't see why I should write at all, as by writing both the first and the last letter of this term I have treated you to two more than you deserve; however, I will make a note that it is your turn to begin after the holidays.

You are quite mistaken if you suppose that in asking about Dennis' bathing things I suggested that he OUGHT to have them on – I only wanted to get a perfectly clear picture: still I don't see any parallel between him and Bleheris in knickerbockers (a very funny word – that or Bickerknocker would be a good name for a dwarf if either of us should want one), because I take it your story is modern. But of course I quite agree that your hero is far better without them. It seems rather unnatural though to pass over any question of embarrassment in absolute silence: the fey of course, as a non-human being, may be excused, but poor Dennis might at least be allowed to blush when he comes round. Handled delicately and without any foolish humour – I am quite serious – the point might be worked a little more: what think you? Morris – who I always think manages to be as good as gold and at the same time beautifully sensuous, would have revelled in it. This week's instalment is excellent, and your references to the Sea and the sea gods give me great anticipation of what may happen next: that next number which I am longing to get – from your own hand.

You must be easily satisfied if you think that I flatter you – when I scarcely let a sentence go past without pricking holes in it: you must also have funny ideas about my rate of composition if you think I have already finished Bleheris. As a matter of fact I write one chapter every Sunday afternoon, and having started before I came back, am always two instalments ahead of the one you get: the general course of the story was mapped out from the start, but of course is changed pretty freely whenever I like. When I said that you wouldn't like the 'gist' of the thing, I meant nothing to do with what you call 'shocked' or 'immodest' (though I admit that when the heroine turns up she is in fairly sharp contrast to Alice the Saint), but that the meaning of it all is somewhat anti-Christian: however, the story and not the allegory is the important part.

I have now finished that adorable (to quote our friend Ch-anie)[1] 'John Silence': I still think 'Ancient Sorceries' the best, though indeed all, particularly the 'Fire' one, are glorious. In the last one the opening part, all about those lovely Northern Islands and the camp life – wouldn't you love to go there? – is so very beautiful that you feel almost sorry to have the supernatural dragged in. Though the idea of the were-wolf is splendid. At what point of the story did you begin to guess the truth?

My last budget of books includes a French Everyman copy of a poet called Chenier[2] (a poet you might perhaps like some day, when you come to read French verse) and a 13d. Macmillan copy of Walter Pater's 'Renaissance',[3] in the same edition as the 'Letters from Hell' I suppose. That book (Hell) by the way is not by Dostoevsky I think, because I fancy I read somewhere that it is translated not from the Russian but from the Swedish: I have noticed too (did I tell you before) that this edition has a preface by our friend Macdonald, the author of Phantastes. We must certainly get it, as the Macmillan 1/- series are, to my mind, very nicely got up. The French Everyman is quite different from the English one – I am not sure yet whether I like it more, or less – you must judge for yourself.

[1] The pronunciation of the name of their friend Jane or 'Janie' (thus 'Ch-anie' and even 'Tchanie') McNeill by 'Ch-anie's' mother – which pronunciation Lewis delighted in imitating.
[2] André Chénier (1762–94).
[3] Walter Pater, *Studies in the History of the Renaissance* (1873).

It is a terrible responsibility to have to guide my Galahad in poetry: a false step might turn you away altogether! I don't think I should advise Milton: while there are lots of things in him you would love – the descriptions of Hell and Chaos and Paradise and Adam and Eve and Satan's flight down through the stars, on the other hand his classical allusions, his rather crooked style of English, and his long speeches, might be tedious. Besides it is written in blank verse (without rhymes) and people who are beginning to read poetry don't usually care for that. But of course you are different, and for all I know you might. You must have a good look at it in my copy and see what you think.

Endymion[4] is top-hole in places, in fact nearly all the time, though somewhat 'sticky': it would be a very good thing to try, I think, if you would not scruple to skip whenever you found it dull: the third book especially, where he wanders at the bottom of the sea, would appeal to you strongly. The only other poems I can suggest are Arnold's 'Tristan and Isolde' or 'Balder Dead'[5] (though this is in blank verse) or some of the stories in Morris' 'Earthly Paradise' or perhaps some of the other Rossetti's pieces; these of course you could finish in a few hours, and some of them are not really very good. If you get an edition of Keats perhaps you would like 'St Agnes Eve'[6] – it is shorter than Endymion, written in Spenser's metre, and very romantic – though perhaps rather 'sticky' also. In sympathy with your new investment, having finished 'Pendennis' of which I am heartily sick by now, I have begun to read 'Twelfth Night' which is a charming little romance, don't you think? The opening speech about the music is the best.

Can't understand it being 'too hot to practise' as it is absolute winter here. Bah, there you see I am talking about the weather, like any fool! If I can get away – I haven't promised, mind – I should be pleased with all my heart to go to Portsalon: indeed whenever (correctly used in this sentence) I have thought of a holiday with you, that place has come into my mind: however, we can discuss all this when we meet – next week. Can you realize? I am so looking forward to seeing you again old man, and I do hope and pray that nothing will turn up to disappoint us. I expect to arrive home on Tuesday: there is some faint danger of my father's staying at home, but if not, perhaps you could get a day off? Oh, how we will look over all these new books together: I have something ravishing to show you

---

[4] John Keats, 'Endymion' (1818).
[5] Matthew Arnold, *Tristram and Iseult* (1852); *Balder Dead* (1853).
[6] John Keats, 'The Eve of St Agnes' (1820).

in the way of paper, but that can wait.

I am writing at present a rather lengthy (for me that is) poem about Hylas, which you shall see if it is a success: but perhaps it will never be finished. By the way, I have come to the Hylas part in the Greek Argonautica. He doesn't go into it nearly as fully as Morris, but in some ways it is better. In this version the various nymphs – mountains, Oreads, wood nymphs etc., are dancing by moonlight when they hear a mortal blundering through the wood. So they all scatter to their various trees, streams etc., and this particular one, as Hylas bent down to fill his pitcher, caught him round the neck and pulled him down; and so to bed, bon soir tu excessivement pudibonde.

Jack

41

[Little Lea,
Strandtown,
Belfast.]
18/9/16.[1]

My Dear Galahad,

It seems a mockery to think that we were talking so lately about how much better we were in our letters than in conversation – I don't feel like that when I actually sit down to write for the first time. Somehow my being at home instead of at Bookham makes it seem strange to be away from you: it is only so few days ago that we were ragging about together in your bedroom. And now you must brush your teeth alone!

But first of all I will answer your questions. The journey home was absolutely damnable: I had to wait an hour at Letterkenny, and an hour and a quarter at Strabane. You may judge of my boredom when I tell you that I was reduced to buying a 'Novel' magazine – because everything else on the bookstall was even more impossible. My father seemed in very poor form when I got home, and fussed a lot about my cold: so everything is beastly, and I have decided – of course – to commit suicide again.

This morning I visited Mullans on your little job, but their copy of the Kaleva[2] was much too old and shop-soiled to satisfy you,

---

[1] Some time after Lewis arrived home on 1 August, he and Arthur went on holiday to Portsalon in Co. Donegal. While Arthur stayed on at Portsalon – this letter being addressed to him there – Lewis returned to Belfast. He crossed over to England on 22 September.

[2] *Kalevala* ('Land of Heroes') is the national epic poem of Finland.

while I couldn't find one in Maynes at all: this being so, I didn't know quite whether you meant me to order one or not – at any rate I did NOT. I am sending you – as a peace offering – a little present, which may arrive by the end of this week: change it if you don't care for it – or when you have read it.

I was very much interested in your description of those lakes, tho' I must say that considering my eager desire to see them, both this year and last, it was particularly kind of you to go just after I had left – but not a word of that to the others. I can quite imagine how fine it must have been – rather like the 'Star Bath'[3] as I picture them. The mist's gradual creeping up would have been great. After all, mountain scenery is in some ways the best, isn't it – excepting our own hills with their exquisite little corners of such homely and 'intime' beauty, which are in a different class. How I do wish I could still be with you during the next fortnight! You must let me know whatever you do, and tell me all the funny or exciting 'adventures' that turn up, and I won't feel quite out of it.

To go back to books: I found my Milton Vol. II waiting at Mullans and am very pleased with it, except that the yellow wrapper is in bad condition and can't be worn when it is on its shelf. I have also bought a 7d. Macmillan book by Algernon Blackwood called 'Jimbo, a fantasy'. Although you have never mentioned it, I dare say you know that there is such a book – I never heard of it myself. I am keeping it to read in the train when I go back (Friday night), but I have to restrain myself every moment – it looks so awfully appetizing. If it turns out to be good, of course I will let you know. What are you reading? Try Phrynette[4] if you can't get anything else. I am still at The Newcomes[5] and the Faerie Queene, reserving the Milton for next term, while in the mornings in bed I am going over 'Sense and Sensibility' again – which I had nearly forgotten. Do you remember Mrs Jennings and Marianne Dashwood and the rest?

On Sunday night my father and I had supper at Glenmachan, whither came the Hamiltons from Knock. K.[elsie] has a scheme for going down with them and me to Larne for a day, which I hope will come off, as I am very dull, and lonely and fed up – indeed I shall

---

[3] In April 1915 Lewis began a manuscript volume of his poems entitled *Metrical Meditations of a Cod*. The manuscript no longer exists, but many of the poems, such as 'Star Bath' which was possibly suggested by an account of some lakes near Portsalon, found their way into his first published work, *Spirits in Bondage: A Cycle of Lyrics* (1919).

[4] Marthe Troly-Curtin, *Phrynette and London* (1911); *Phrynette Married* (1912).

[5] William Makepeace Thackeray, *The Newcomes* (1854–5).

not be sorry to leave home.

I needn't apologize for giving you no instalment this week, as you are in the same state, but I will try and do better next time. This letter is perhaps a bit short, but so is yours – we have neither of us yet got our sea legs. Let me hear from you by Tuesday at the very latest, a good long one, as I need a lot of cheering up. Good bye old man,

yours,
Jack

42

[Gastons]
27th./9/16.

My dear Galahad,

I think you must be going dotty with all your talk about when I'm going back, seeing that I said in my first letter that Friday (last) was already fixed. At any rate you must have found out by now, and will understand why I am late in answering your letter, which only reached me today. As you say, it seems years and years since I left: I have quite dropped back into the not unpleasant, though monotonous routine of Bookham, and could almost believe that I had never left it. Portsalon is like a dream. I heartily agree with you that it must have been nice to have the Lounge all to yourselves.

Now to books: I told you didn't I that I had bought Blackwood's Jimbo did I not? I finished it on Sunday and am awfully bucked with it – a very good 7d. worth. It is quite in Blackwood's best manner, and you will specially love the last thirty pages or so – they are terrific. Get it at once. I hope you are not praising 'Letters from Hell' out of politeness, for I really want to know what it is like. I saw it once in a second hand bookshop at Guildford nearly a year ago: looking over the first few pages I thought it excellent, but of course it may not be so good later on. How many books seem to promise such a lot at the start and then turn out disappointing. Whereas good, stodgy books like Scott have all their interesting parts in the middle and begin with reams of dry-as-dust. Talking about stodge, I finished 'The Newcomes' before leaving home, and certainly enjoyed the end better than any parts except the scenes at Baden. Of course it is a great novel, but I am very thankful to have got it off my chest. I should advise you to get the 2/6 volume containing Milton's minor poems, which I am now reading: I am sure they are better to begin on than P.L. I am now at 'Comus', which is an absolute dream of delight. I am sure you would love it: it is like a play written on an episode from the Faerie Queene, all magic and distressed ladies and haunted woods. It is lovely in books the way you can just turn from one sort of beauty to another and never get tired.

I was sorry to find no instalment in your last letter, tho' of course if you have completely lost interest in poor Papillon it is no good forcing yourself. I will consent to your trying a novel only on the condition that it be sent to me, chapter by chapter. I too am wondering whether I should not chuck Bleheris and start something else: partly I have so many ideas and also I think the old fashioned English is a fatal mistake. Any good things that are in it or would be later on, can be worked in elsewhere. In a way it is disheartening to remember how keenly we were both starting out on our tales this time last term and see the result. But still we have both much experience and practice gained, and we got a lot of pleasure out of them while they lasted: the danger is that we get to turn too easily from one thing to another and never get anything done.

I didn't go to see anything in London, I really don't know why – I was a bit tired, nothing seemed to attract me much, and also, having started 'Jimbo' in the train, was eager to get to it again. One part of my journey I enjoyed very much was the first few miles out of Liverpool: because it was one of the most wonderful mornings I have ever seen – one of those lovely white misty ones when you can't see 10 yards. You could just see the nearest trees and houses, a little ghostly in appearance, and beyond that everything was a clean white blank. It felt as if the train was alone in space, if you know what I mean.

I think you are very wise not to take that puppy from K[elso Ewart]. Unless you are a person with plenty of spare time and real knowledge, it is a mistake to keep dogs – and cruel to them. Have you got the Kaleva yet, tell me when you do and what you think of it. I wonder where you are at this moment? Have you reached home yet? Tell me all the news when you write, what you're reading etc. and whether you are going back to your taskmaster Tom at once.[1] I am not nearly so fed up now as I was, and hope you are the same. The country at home was beginning to look nice and autumn-y, with dead leaves in the lanes and a nice nutty smell (you know what I mean) so I suppose it is getting better still. Here it is horrible bright summer which I hate. Love to all our friends such as the hedgepig etc.

Yours,
Jack.

[1] Arthur was assisting Tom Greeves in his brother's business concern.

43

My dear Arthur,

I believe it is Lamb who says somewhere that he does not know whether it is more delightful to set out for a holiday or return from one: perhaps you hardly agree with him! Though I am sure he hated his office (read 'The Superannuated Man')[1] quite as much as you do. But of course he means, I suppose, the getting back to home, to ones books etc and not to work. However I suppose you are gradually getting 'broken in'.

The beastly summer is at last over here, and good old Autumn colours & smells and temperatures have come back. Thanks to this we had a most glorious walk on Saturday: it was a fine cool, windy day & we set out after lunch to go to a place called 'Friday Street' which is a very long walk from here through beautiful woods and vallies that I don't know well.[2] After several hours wandering over fields & woods etc. with the aid of a map we began to get lost and suddenly at about 4 o'clock – we had expected to reach the place by that time – we found ourselves in a place where we had been an hour before! *You* will understand that, while the others were only annoyed at this, I felt je ne sais quoi de dreamlike and terrifying sensation at the idea of wandering round in circles through these big, solemn woods; also there was a certain tinge of 'Alice-in-W-ism' about it. We had a lot of difficulty in at least reaching the place, but it was glorious when we got there. You are walking in the middle of a wood when all of a sudden you go downwards and come to a little open hollow just big enough for a little lake and some old, old red-tiled houses: all round it the trees tower up on rising ground and every road from it is at once swallowed up in them. You might walk within a few feet of it & suspect nothing unless you saw the smoke rising up from some cottage chimney. Can you imagine what it was like? Best of all, we came down to the little inn of the village and had tea there with – glory of glories – an old tame jackdaw hopping about our feet and asking for crumbs. He is called Jack and will answer to his name.

The inn has three tiny but spotlessly clean bedrooms, so some day,

---

[1] Collected in Charles Lamb's *Essays of Elia* (1823).
[2] Friday Street, Surrey, in the Dorking rural district.

if the gods will, you & I are going to stay there. The inn is called the 'Stephen Langton' and dates from the time of that gentleman's wars against the king or the barons or somebody (you'll know I expect),[3] tho' of course it has been rebuilt since. I don't like playing the guide-book, but it was so ravishing that I had to tell you. We were so late getting there that it was dark soon after we left, and often going astray we didn't get home till ten o'clock – dead beat but happy.

Partly because the country we saw that day was so like it I have been reading again the second volume of Malory, especially the part of the 'Sangreal' which I had forgotten. With all its faults, in small doses this book is tip-top: those mystic parts are very good to read late at night when you are drowsy and tired and get into a sort of 'exalted' mood. Do you know what I mean? You so often share feelings of mine which I can't explain that I hope you do: mention this subject when you next write. Besides this I have finished 'Comus' with great enjoyment: I have also re-read for the thousandth time 'Rapunzel' and some other favourite bits of Morris, while through the week I have read an excellent novel of Vachell's 'The Paladin'[4] which you have probably read too and also dipped often into Boswell's 'Life of Johnson'.[5] Being entirely made up of conversation I don't think it is a book to be read continuously, tho' it is very good fun in bits: you are thinking of getting it I believe. I agree with you that I must read some more books in the particular 'genre' of 'Our Village' etc, but there are so many things to read that I don't know where to begin. I forget what edition you are getting of the 'Scenes of Clerical life'.[6]

As to the fate of sad Papillon, I will look at the exact place of leaving-off when I go upstairs & write it down somewhere in pencil: unless you decide to go on with it don't waste time & energy copying the rest but send me instead the first drafts of your new work. I should be glad, though, to see you going on with it and have the complete tale, for there is good stuff in it: however, I can't preach in this respect now! Loki & Dennis & Bleheris, all our operas, plays etc go one way; perhaps they are caught like Wan Jadis in the Grey Marish on the way to the country of the past! For my part I am at present engaged in making huge plans both for prose and verse none of which I shall try. I begin to see that short, slight stories & poems

[3] Stephen Langton (d. 1228), Archbishop of Canterbury, in his later life supported the regency in its struggles against baronial insubordination.
[4] Horace Annesley Vachell, *The Paladin, As Beheld by a Woman of Temperament* (1909).
[5] James Boswell, *The Life of Samuel Johnson* (1791).
[6] By George Eliot (1858).

are all I am fit for at present & that it would be better to write & finish one of such than to begin & leave twenty ambitious epic-poems or romances. I wait eagerly either for another instalment of the Watersprite or else some new venture from you: you shall have the first thing I do, if I ever do anything.

How I wish I had been with you at Mr Thompson's.[7] Everything seems to have happened well after my departure – I suppose you say no wonder! What a female-minded person I am getting! I would cross out that remark as peevish & 'cattish', but it would make a mess and you would only wonder what was underneath. Take it as unsaid.

Have you got or begun the 'Kalevala' yet? Give me your first impressions when you do. Papillon has got to where they are both under the water and ends with the words 'it shot him much farther than he had intended so that he nearly lost sight of the fairy'. Looking at it revives my enthusiasm. Do go on with it if you can: certainly send me the rest provided this doesn't interfere with any new work. Now good night Galahad the 'haut prince' as Malory [would] say,

yours

Jack

P.S. Poor puppy!! What a life it'll have! I shall poison it in kindness when I come home!

P.P.S. Why do your letters never come till Wednesday now?

44

[Gastons]

(The 12th. Oct., I think) [1916]

My dear Arthur,

It was unfortunate that I should choose a word like 'exaltation' which is so often used in connection with religion and so give you a wrong impression of my meaning. I will try to explain again: have you ever sat over the fire late, late at night when you are very drowsy & muddle headed, and it is no use trying to go on with your book? Everything seems like a dream, you are absolutely contented, and 'out of the world'. Anything seems possible, and all sorts of queer ideas float through your mind & sort of vaguely thrill you but only mildly & calmly. It is in this sort of mood that the quaint, old

---

[7] James A. Thompson was a resident of Strandtown and of some consequence in the congregation of St Mark's, Dundela.

mystical parts of Malory are exactly suitable: you can read a chapter or two in a sort of dream & find the forests of 'Logres & of Lyonesse' very agreeable at such a time – at least I do.

As to the other question about religion, I was sad to read your letter. You ask me my religious views: you know, I think, that I beleive in no religion. There is absolutely no proof for any of them, and from a philosophical standpoint Christianity is not even the best. All religions, that is, all mythologies to give them their proper name are merely man's own invention – Christ as much as Loki. Primitive man found himself surrounded by all sorts of terrible things he didn't understand – thunder, pestilence, snakes etc: what more natural than to suppose that these were animated by evil spirits trying to torture him. These he kept off by cringing to them, singing songs and making sacrifices etc. Gradually from being mere nature-spirits these supposed being[s] were elevated into more elaborate ideas, such as the old gods: and when man became more refined he pretended that these spirits were good as well as powerful.

Thus religion, that is to say mythology grew up. Often, too, great men were regarded as gods after their death – such as Heracles or Odin: thus after the death of a Hebrew philosopher Yeshua (whose name we have corrupted into Jesus) he became regarded as a god, a cult sprang up, which was afterwards connected with the ancient Hebrew Jahweh-worship, and so Christianity came into being – one mythology among many, but the one that we happen to have been brought up in.

Now all this you must have heard before: it is the recognised scientific account of the growth of religions. Superstition of course in every age has held the common people, but in every age the educated and thinking ones have stood outside it, though usually outwardly conceding to it for convenience. I had thought that you were gradually being emancipated from the old beliefs, but if this is not so, I hope we are too sensible to quarrel about abstract ideas. I must only add that ones views on religious subjects don't make any difference in morals, of course. A good member of society must of course try to be honest, chaste, truthful, kindly etc: these are things we owe to our own manhood & dignity and not to any imagined god or gods.

Of course, mind you, I am not laying down as a certainty that there *is* nothing outside the material world: considering the discoveries that are always being made, this would be foolish. Anything MAY exist: but until we know that it does, we can't make any assumptions. The universe is an absolute mystery: man has made many guesses at it, but the answer is yet to seek. Whenever any new light can be got as to such matters, I will be glad to welcome it. In the meantime I am not going to go back to the bondage of believing in any old (& already decaying) superstition.

See! I have wasted ¾ of my letter on all these dry bones. However, old man, you started the subject and I had to have my turn. Yes, I wish you had really been with me on the walk to Friday-Street: how you and I, alone, would have gloried in those woods and vallies! But some day we will go and spend a week there at the inn, get up at 5 every morning & go to bed at 8, spending the interval sitting by the lake and talking to the Jackdaw. He can only say 'Caw' so that will be a nice change after my torrents of conversation!

I have written up for 'Letters from Hell' and it ought to be here by the end of the week. I am looking forward to it immensely and will enjoy being able to talk it over with you. You ask me what 'special' book I am reading at present: you must remember that I read seriously only on week-ends. When I last wrote my week-end books were 'Comus' and the Morte Darthur; last week-end, 'Comus' being finished, its place was taken by Shelley's 'Prometheus Unbound' which I got half through. It is an amazing work. I don't know how to describe it to you; it is more wild & out of the world than any poem I ever read, and contains some wonderful descriptions. Shelley had a great genius, but his carelessness about rhymes, metre, choice of words etc, just prevents him being as good as he might be. To me, when you're in the middle of a fine passage and come to a 'cockney' rhyme like 'ru*in*' & 'pursu*ing*', it spoils the whole thing – makes it vulgar and grotesque. However some parts are so splendid that I could forgive him anything. I am now, through the week, reading Scott's 'Antiquary'.[1] I suppose you have read it long ago: I am very pleased with it, especially the character of the Antiquary himself, the description of his room, and the old beggar. Tell me your views when you write – it is nice gradually to get more & more into each other's style of reading, is it not – you with poetry and I with classical novels?

As to Bleheris, he is dead and I shan't trouble his grave.[2] I will try and write something new soon – a short tale, I expect – but am rather taken up with verse at present, in my spare-time; which gets less and less as the exam. draws nearer. However I look eagerly for

---

[1] Sir Walter Scott, *The Antiquary* (1816).

[2] *The Quest of Bleheris* lies, however, in a very distinguished 'grave'. The manuscript is now in the Bodleian Library (MS. Eng. lett. c. 220/5, fols. 5–43).

the first chapter of your novel, or failing that, the next leaf of Dennis.

It is an amazing thing to call the 'Kalevala' tame: whatever else it is, it is not tame. If a poem all about floods & primeval spirits and magic and talking beasts & monsters is not wild enough, I really don't know what to say! However, chacun à son goût! As to the Milton I daren't advise you – both volumes are so good, if you care for him. You don't give any criticism on 'Evelina';[3] do so, when you write.

It is a lovely moonlight night (a brau' brich' minlich' nicht, do you remember). I wish you were here. Goodnight

J.

45

[Gastons]
(Forgotten the date) [18 October 1916]

My dear Arthur,

Frequently in arguing with you by letter I have had to ask you to read what I say carefully before you rush on to answer it. I distinctly said that there was once a Hebrew called Yeshua, I think on p. 2 (II!!) of my letter: when I say 'Christ' of course I mean the mythological being into whom he was afterwards converted by popular imagination, and I am thinking of the legends about his magic performances and resurrection etc. That the man Yeshua or Jesus did actually exist, is as certain as that the Buddha did actually exist: Tacitus mentions his execution in the Annals.[1] But all the other tomfoolery about virgin birth, magic healings, apparitions and so forth is on exactly the same footing as any other mythology. After all even your namesake king Arthur really lived once (if we are to believe the latest theories) but it doesn't follow that Malory's old book is history. In the same way there was such a person as Alexander the Great, but the adventures which the Middle Ages related of him are nonsense. It is generally thought, too, that there was such a man as Odin, who was deified after his death: so you see most legends have a kernel of fact in them somewhere. Indeed, these distinctions are so very obvious, that if you were not my best friend I should almost suspect you of wilfully misunderstanding me through temper.

Later on you ask me why I am sad, and suggest that it is because I have no hope of a 'happy life hereafter'. No; strange as it may appear I am quite content to live without beleiving in a bogey who is prepared to torture me forever and ever if I should fail in coming up to

[3] Frances Burney, *Evelina* (1778).
[1] Cornelius Tacitus (c. 55–120), *Annals*, Bk. XV, sect. 44.

an almost impossible ideal (which is a part of the Christian mythology, however much you try to explain it away). In fact I should
think it horrible to feel that if life got too bad, I daren't escape for
fear of a spirit more cruel and barbarous than any man. Then you
are good enough to ask me why I don't kill myself. Because – as I
have said to you before – in spite of occasional fits of depression I am
very well pleased with life and have a very happy time on the whole.
The only reason I was sad was because I was dissapointed in my hope
that you were gradually escaping from beleifs which, in my case,
always considerably lessened my happiness: if, however, it has the
opposite effect on you, tant mieux pour vous! As to the immortality
of the soul, though it is a fascinating theme for day-dreaming, I
neither beleive nor disbeleive: I simply don't know anything at all,
there is no evidence either way. Now let us take off our armour,
hang up our swords and talk about things where there is no danger of
coming to blows!

Yes, I quite agree that the metre of the Kalevala is tedious & the
word 'tame' exactly describes it. It doesn't sort of rise to the subject
at all, but is always the same whatever is happening. If you give this
up – and there is no point in going on unless it takes your fancy –
don't let it quench your rising taste for poetry. I must really fulfill
my long standing purpose and settle down to some more books of
the 'Cranford' type:[2] your description has made me quite enthusiastic, so *without fail* tell me the edition you have got it & all your
Austens etc in? I finished 'The Antiquary' this afternoon, and it
thoroughly denies our old wheeze about most books getting tiresome
halfway through. It gets better and better as it goes on, and I have
not enjoyed anything so much for a long time. I believe I shall soon
become almost as devoted to Scott as you are: I begin to feel that
sort of 'repose', which you like, in turning to him. Which of his
should I try next? I shall be glad to hear your views on 'Lavengro'[3]
when you have read it, also by whom this mysterious 1/- edition is
published.

And now I must turn to 'Letters of Hell'. I suppose I must have
looked forward to it too much: at any rate – I will tell the truth – I
have failed to read it, have not enjoyed it a bit and have put it away
in my drawer unfinished. There! Am I fallen in your eyes forever?
I don't really know why I disliked it so much, because I could see all
the time that there was good in it if only I could appreciate it –
which makes it all the more annoying. For one thing I expected

[2] Elizabeth Cleghorn Gaskell, *Cranford* (1853).
[3] George Borrow, *Lavengro* (1851).

beauties of the phantastic type, and in reality it turns out only a novel. For the parts about Hell are after all only a setting for the story of his previous life – a story which seemed to me so far as I read it supremely commonplace. The characters are all absolutely crude – wicked rich men of the melodramatic type and miraculously innocent angels of heroines. The only part I liked was the vision of paradise, which struck me as good. Still, when both you and Macdonald praise the book, I am ready to beleive that the fault must be in me and not in it.

Thanks for the instalment: as the post only came in at 9 o'clock I can't read it yet or I won't get my letter to you done till bedtime – but you shall have my verdict ('impudence' say you) next week. Do either go on with this tale or start something new: I am trying to make out the plan of a short tale but nothing 'comes'. That is an awful waste, that book W[arnie] gave my father: wouldn't you love an edition with that binding and paper, only the size of my Kipling, say of the Brontës or James Stephens or Macdonald? Talking about Kipling it is time you began him: try 'Rewards & Fairies' and if the first story in it 'Cold Iron' doesn't knock you head over heels, I don't know what will. Good night, they're all gone up, and I have tired you by now 'I *do* talk *so*.'

Jack

P.S. (In the bedroom) It is much more wintry to night, and when I came up the curtains were not drawn and the room was full of moon-light, bright bright as anything. It is too cold to sit looking at the glorious night but it *is* beautiful! I shake your hand. Goodnight. I wish you could come & 'grind' at Gastons. Ugh. Horrible cold sheets now

J.

46

[Gastons]
25th Oct 1916

My dear Galahad,

As usually happens in these sort of things the violent controversy that we have been having for the last three weeks (& which I quite agree with you in giving up) has obscured the original subject of the discussion 'exaltation'. I want to know if you understand that sort of 'fey' state of mind which I described, or tried to describe, as coming on when one is very drowsy. Say what you think of this in your next letter. The question arose out of the 'Morte' which I have now read from the beginning of the Quest of the Grael to the end, thus finishing the whole thing. I certainly enjoyed it much better than before, and wished that I had the first volume here as well. The quietness of the end, and the description of Arthur's death are particularly good – you must give it another try sometime.

It was silly of me to ask you about 'Cranford' etc, as I have a MacMillan's list here and could have looked them up myself if I had had the sense: but I suppose you regard that as a big 'if'! I can understand that it is not pleasing to have these in the same edition as the Jane Austens, tho' for me of course it would make a nice change. I don't know when I shall buy some new books, as I am at present suffering from a flash of poverty – poverty comes in flashes like dulness or pleasure. When I do it will be either 'Our Village', 'Cranford' or Chaucer's 'Troilus & Cressida',[1] if I can get a decent edition of it. By all accounts it is much more in my line than the 'Canterbury Tales', and anyway I can take no more interest in them since I have discovered that my Everyman edition is abridged & otherwise mutilated. I wish they wouldn't do that ('Lockhart',[2] you say, is another case) without telling you. I can't bear to have anything but what a man really wrote.

I have been reading the quaintest book this week, 'The Letters of Dorothy Osborne to Sir William Temple'[3] in Everyman. I suppose, as a historian you will know all about those two, but in case you don't they lived in Cromwell's time. It is very interesting to read the ordinary everyday life of a girl in those days, and, tho' of course they are often dull there is a lot in them you would like: especially a description of how she spends the day and another of a summer evening in the garden. It is funny too, to notice that, just like us, she says that she never wished very hard for anything in her life without being dissapointed. But then I suppose everyone in the world has said that sometime or other. It is perhaps not a book to read straight through but well worth having.

My other reading – in French – has been Maeterlinck's 'Oiseau Bleu':[4] of course I have read it before in English and seen it on the stage, as you know, but I am absolutely delighted to read it again.

[1] Geoffrey Chaucer, *Troilus and Criseyde* (1482?).
[2] John Gibson Lockhart, *Memoirs of the Life of Sir Walter Scott*, 7 vols. (1837–8).
[3] *Letters from Dorothy Osborne to Sir William Temple: 1652–4*, ed. E. A. Parry (1888).
[4] Maurice Maeterlinck, *L'Oiseau Bleu* (1903).

Now that I have the original I wish you would adopt my English version, which is yours forever for the taking whenever you care to walk up to my room at home and find it on the little open bookcase. You could do it to day when you are home for lunch: I don't know why you have never read this glorious book before, but please do as I suggest & (though it is always dangerous, as we know, to recommend) I think you will have some real joy out of it. The scenes in the Temple of Night and in the Kingdom of the Future are exactly in our line.

Unfortunately we have not got a complete set of Scott here – only odd Everyman copies of which 'The Fair Maid of Perth' is not one. The earlier period is of course all the better for me, in fact to be honest I am childish enough to like 'Ivanhoe' better than any of his, and next to it 'Quentin Durward'. What is 'Guy Mannering' like? The alternative title of 'The Astrologer' sounds attractive but of course it may not have much to do with it.[5]

How's the poor, miserable, ill-fated, star-crossed, hapless, lonely, neglected, misunderstood puppy getting along? What are you going to call him, or rather, to speak properly, how hight he? Don't give him any commonplace name, and above all let it suit his character & appearance. Something like Sigurd, Pelleas or Mars if he is brisk and warlike, or Mime, Bickernocker or Knutt if he is ugly and quaint. Or perhaps he is dead by now, poor little devil!

The book you refer to is 'How to Form a Literary Taste' by Arnold Benett:[6] the edition is pretty but the book is not of any value. The very title – as if you set out to 'learn' literature the way you learn golf – shews that the author is not a real book-lover but only a priggish hack. I never read any of his novels & don't want to. Have you? By the way, he is a rather violent atheist, so I suppose I shall meet him by

'The fiery, flaming flood of Phlegethon',[7]

as good old Spencer has it.

I am sure Lockhart's Life of Scott would be good, but 5 vols. at 3/6 each is too much: at any rate I had sooner get Boswell if I were going to make a start on biography. I have read to day – there's absolutely·no head or tale in this letter but you ought to be used to

[5] Sir Walter Scott, *The Fair Maid of Perth* (1828); *Ivanhoe* (1820); *Quentin Durward* (1823); *Guy Mannering* (1815).

[6] Arnold Bennett, *Literary Taste: How to Form It, with Detailed Instructions for Collecting a Complete Library of English Literature* (1909).

[7] Edmund Spenser, *The Faerie Queene*, I, v. 33, 3: 'And come to fiery flood of *Phlegeton*.'

that by now – some 10 pages of 'Tristam Shandy'[8] and am wondering whether I like it. It is certainly the maddest book ever written or 'ever wrote' as dear Dorothy Osborne would say. It gives you the impression of an escaped lunatic's conversation while chasing his hat on a windy May morning. Yet there are beautiful serious parts in it though of a sentimental kind, as I know from my father. Have you ever come across it?

Tang-Tang there goes eleven o'clock 'Tis almost faery time'. Don't you simply love going to bed. To curl up warmly in a nice warm bed, in the lovely darkness, that is so restful & then gradually drift away into sleep . . . Perhaps to enjoy this properly you must stay up till 11 working fairly hard at something – even a letter like this – so as to be really hungry for sleep. At home, like you, I often get started off on a train of thought which keeps me awake: here I am always too tired tho' goodness knows, eleven is early enough compared with some peoples times. It is strange, somehow, to read about concerts & Bill Patterson's visits etc;[9] when I am at Bookham everything at home seems a little unreal. Each of you (i.e. my friends) is quite real by him or herself but 'en bloc' you seem like something out of a book. I wish I had been with you at D. Garrick.[10] I have always heard it was good. I shall not soon forget that morning at the far end of the strand, with the pleasant 'Frightfulness' of the Waves. I can still remember exactly what it felt like in the water and also running up to the cave. Take it all in all, we've had many pleasant times in our lives, & of these many (in my case) the most part together. You'd think I was bidding you an eternal farewell the way I'm going on. There's quarter past, so I'll say 'Good morning' not 'Night' for you read this at breakfast, don't you? I'm turning out the gas. Bon soir!

Jack

By the way, what sort of voice has a 'cracked turnip'. See your last letter.

[8] Laurence Sterne, *The Life and Opinions of Tristram Shandy*, 9 vols. (1760–7).

[9] William Hugh Patterson (1835–1918), who was in the ironmongery business, was a close friend of the Lewis family. His liberal curiosity led him to take up many antiquarian hobbies and he published *A Glossary of Words in Use in the Counties of Antrim and Down* (1880), a book much appreciated by Clive. His son, William H. F. 'Bill' Patterson, was addicted to puns and was a recognized Strandtown wit. He published a volume of verse under the initials W. H. F., *Songs of a Port* (Belfast, 1920).

[10] Thomas William Robertson, *David Garrick* (1864), a comedy in three acts.

47

[Gastons
1 November 1916]

My dear Galahad,

I can't let it pass unchallegend that you should put 'Boewulf' and 'Malory' together as if they belonged to the same class. One is a mediaeval, English prose romance and the other an Anglo Saxon epic poem: one is Christian, the other heathen: one we read just as it was actually written, the other in a translation. So you can like one without the other, and any way you must like or dislike them both for different reasons. It is always very difficult of course to explain to another person the good points of a book he doesn't like. I know what you mean by that 'crampy' feeling: you mean there are no descriptions in Beowulf as in a modern book, so little is told you & you have to imagine so much for yourself.

Well, for one thing, remember that nearly all your reading is confined to about 150 years of one particular country: this is no disgrace to you, most people's circle is far smaller. But still, compared with the world this one little period of English literature is very small, and tho' you (and I of course) are so accustomed to the particular kinds of art we find inside it, yet we must remember that there are an infinite variety outside it, quite as good in different ways. And so, if you suddenly go back to an Anglo-Saxon gleeman's lay, you come up against something absolutely different – a different world. If you are to enjoy it, you must forget your previous ideas of what a book should be and try and put yourself back in the position of the people for whom it was first made. When I was reading it I tried to imagine myself as an old Saxon thane sitting in my hall of a winter's night, with the wolves & storm outside and the old fellow singing his story. In this way you get the atmosphere of terror that runs through it – the horror of the old barbarous days when the land was all forests and when you thought that a demon might come to your house any night & carry you off. The description of Grendel stalking up from his 'fen and fastness' thrilled me. Besides, I loved the simplicity of the old life it represents: it comes as a relief to get away from all complications about characters & 'problems' to a time when hunting, fighting, eating, drinking & loving were all a man had to think of it. And lastly, always remember it's a translation which spoils most things.

As to 'Malory' I liked it so awfully this time – far better than

[Enter Grendel]

reading it I tried to imagine myself as an old ··ed and the
ry hall of a winter's night, with the wolves o storm is different: ·
llow singing his story. In this way you get the lence. It na
at runs through it - the horror of the old barbarous seems to me.

See page 143

·ing' on Saturday but some
· to the 'mist scene' I am afraid
at the time it will hardly

COLD GREEN

BLOOD COLOUR

DEAD BLACK→

·itable on earth
·ing pencil drawn.

GREY POOL OF MIST

·rgine it. Your imagination
long enough rest by now. I

See page 152

before – that I don't know what to say. How can I explain? For one thing, to me it is a world of its own, like Jane Austen. Though impossible, it is very fully realized, and all the characters are old friends, we know them so well: you get right away in those forests and somehow to me all the adventures & meetings & dragons seem very real. (I don't beleive that last sentence conveys my meaning a bit) Then too I find in it a rest as you do in Scott: he (M. I mean) is so quiet after our modern writers & thinks of his 'art' so little: he is not self-conscious. Of course he doesn't describe as Morris does, but then he doesn't need to: in the 'Well' you feel it is only a tale suddenly invented and therefore everything has to be described. But the Round Table is different: it *was* a hundred years ago & shall be a hundred years hence. It wasn't just made up like an ordinary tale, it grew. Malory seems to me almost a historian: his world is real to me, his characters are old friends whom you get to know better & better as you go on – he is a companiabl author & good when you're lonely.

I suppose this sounds all rot? But after all when you say it 'doesn't suit you' you strike at the root of the matter. Perhaps you can't enjoy it just as I couldn't enjoy Green's Short History:[1] it is not my fault that I don't like oysters but no reasoning will make me like them. This controversy has proved even more expansive than the other: if you had given me any excuse for going on with the 'exaltation' one I'm afraid I should never get to bed to-night. By the way I suppose at 10 o'clock when I am beginning your letter you are just getting into bed? Remember at 10 next Wednesday night to imagine me just spreading out your one in front of me and starting to jaw. But seriously, do I bore you. I have taken up such reams about 'Boewulf' etc. It is easy to explain a thought, but to explain a feeling is very hard.

Last week-end I spent in reading 'The Professor'. It forms a nice sort of suppliment to Villette – something [like] the same story told from the man's side. I liked the description of Hunsden extremely & also the detestable brother. I do wish she had left out the awful poetry in the proposal scene: they are the worst verses in the language I should think. Its difficult to understand how a woman of Ch. Brontës genius could help seeing how bad they were. But on the whole it is a very enjoyable book, tho' not of course to be compared with her other three. What did you think of it?

Yes, I shall be home for Xmas, rather earlier in fact. This exam.[2]

[1] John Richard Green, *Short History of the English People* (1874).
[2] The scholarship examination for Oxford.

will take place in the first week of December and when it is over I shall come straight home. I am beginning to funk it rather: I wish you were in for it with me (so as to be sure of one, at least, worse than myself). I wish I could see 'The Winter's Tale': it, 'The Midsummer's Nights Dream' & the Tempest are the only things of Shakespeare I really appreciate, except the Sonnets. It is a very sweet, sort of old fairy-tale style of thing. You must certainly see it. As to Bennet's book, if a person was really a book-lover, however ignorant, he wouldn't go and look up a text book to see what to buy, as if literature was a subject to be learned like algebra: one thing would lead him to another & he would go through the usual mistakes & gain experience. I hate this idea of 'forming a taste'. If anyone like the feuilletons in the 'Sketch' better than Spenser, for Heaven's sake let him read them: anything is better than to read things he doesn't really like because they are thought classical. I say, old man, it's beastly kind of you to keep the 'Country of the Blind'[3] till I come. Of course if you hadn't told me I should have thought you would throw it off the top of the tram. Ha-Ha-Ha-Ha, likewise He-He-He! (You do love that sort of writing!) By the way why do you call it your dog if it lives at Glenmachen? I suppose in the same way as you like Shakespeare but I don't like reading him? Can't write more to night, your last letter was very short –

J.

48

[Gastons
8 November 1916]

My dear Arthur,

You certainly have all the luck! I should give anything to be at home for these operas. (Cant get a decent pen so you'll have to do with pencil this week) As I can't see them myself I can only hope & pray devoutly that they will be badly sung & staged, your seat be uncomfortable, yr. neighbours talkative & your escapade deteted by your terrible parent – Amen.

To be serious: if I were going to three of them I should choose Aida & the Zauberflut straight off without hesitation: the latter is of course old fashioned but, to me – tho' of course my views on music are those of an ignoramus – the formal old beauty of old music has something very attractive about it. At all events a thing with an overture like that must be good. As to the libretto, my ideas are

[3] By H. G. Wells (1911).

rather hazy, but an article on it which I read last year in the 'Times' gave me the impression of something rather nice & fantastic. These two then I'd certainly go to: in the third it is more difficult to decide. 'Tales of Hoffman' I thought was a comic opera – at any rate I am sure it's not in the first rank. 'Carmen' & 'the Lily' are out of the question – the latter being an awful hurdy-gurdy, tawdry business by all accounts. Perhaps on the whole you would get more pleasure out of 'Faust' than any: here too you'd have the dramatic interest as well. 'Pagliacci' & 'Cavaleria' you have seen haven't you? – Though of course that's no reason why you shouldn't see them again.

'En passant' I don't exactly 'despise' your opera-book. I think it very useful like a Greek grammar or a time-table, but no more a 'book' in the proper sense than they are. For instance I should never think of getting 'Bradshaw's Railway Guide' printed on hand made paper with illustrations by Rackham, wd you? And talking about Rackham I saw in my French list the other day an edition of Perrault's 'Contes'[1] 'avec gravures en couleurs de Rackham' for 1 fr. 95 (at the present rate of exchange about 1/6, I suppose). If its the same Rackham that wd. be wonderful value, wouldn't it? Though I daresay Perrault himself (the French 'Hans Anderson') would not be up to much, – coming as he did of the most prosaic nation on earth.

It is hardly fair to be sarcastick about my 'controversies' as you deliberately asked for both of them. I am afraid I have not made my views on old literature very clear but it can't be helped. The word 'feuilleton' is French, I suppose, originally but quite naturalized. (By the way can the whole of Bernagh not raise a French dictionary? I might give you one in calf for an Xmas box!) It means the horrible serial stories that run in the daily papers: if you've never happened to glance at one it's worth your while. They are unique! Yes, Sir!, it IS correct to say 'if he like' & not 'if he likes' – tho' a little pedantic.

I thought you would enjoy 'The Antiquary'. The scene on the beach is fine & tho' it hadn't struck me before the whole scenery of 'Fairport' is rather like Portsalon. What I liked best was the description of the antiquary's room at Monkbarns – I wish I could fill up my room with old things like that – also the scene where the doting old woman sings them the ballad at her cottage, but perhaps you haven't come to that yet. Of course the hero – as usual in Scott – is a mere puppet, but there are so many other good characters that it doesn't much matter.

What fiddlesticks about Malory being only a translation: I wish you were here that I could have the pleasure of stripping every shred

---

[1] Charles Perrault, *Histoires et Contes du Temps Passé* (1697).

of skin from your bones and giving your intestines to the birds of the air. What do you mean by saying 'It' is 'an old French legend': the 'Morte' includes a hundred different Arthurian legends & as you know the Arthur myth is Welsh. Of course he didn't invent the legends any more than Morris invented the Jason legends: but his book is an original work all the same. Just as the famous 'Loki Bound' of Lewis is based upon a story in the Edda, but still the poem is original – the materials being re-created by the genius of that incomparable poet. As a matter of fact I am at present reading a real 'old french' romance 'The High History of the Holy Graal' translated in the lovely 'Temple Classics'.[2] If I dared to advise you any longer – . It is absolute heaven: it is more mystic & eerie than the 'Morte' & has [a] more connected plot. I think there are parts of it even you'd like.

I am also reading Chaucer's minor poems ('World's Classics', a scrubby edition but the only one I can find) and am half way thr[ough] 'The House of Fame', a dream poem half funny & half fantastic that I like very much. But the print, tho' clear, is very small. As to 'The Letters of D.O. to W.T.' I suggest you had better have a look at them in my copy before you do anything. There is a lot in them I think you would like but also a good deal that is dull.

I got this morning a letter from His Majesty the King of the Fiji isles expressing his pleasure at your gift. How much he appreciates it may be seen in his own terse and elegant words 'Oor mi dalara bo chorabu platlark pho'.

We have had glorious storms here & a big old elm at the bottom of the garden is down by the roots. There is something majestic about a giant tree lying dead like this.

By the way take care of that weak heart of yours: it seems pretty sure that CONSCRIPTION is coming to Ireland now. I for one shall be jolly glad to see some relations of mine (and some of yours) made to behave like men at last. Goodnight, old man –

Jack

---

[2] *The High History of the Holy Graal* was translated (from the first volume of *Perceval le Gallois*, ed. by C. Potvin) by Sebastian Evans, with illustrations by Edward Burne-Jones (1898).

49

Dear Arthur,

I must begin my letter this week by heartily apologizing for some foolish remarks which I thoughtlessly directed against a book for whose merits your approval should have been to me and to all who enjoy the honour of your friendship a sufficient guarantee. As you very properly remind me, I am profoundly ignorant of the scientific side of music in which you specially excel, while my aesthetic judgements on the subject are modelled upon the sane and temperate example of your own criticism. What amends I can make by studying with diligence the admirable work which you commend, shall immediately be made: for, believe me, I am not insensible of the kindness and indulgence which a man of your education has displayed in such musical discussions to a boy so ill informed as I.

Your verdict upon Macdonald's tale was worthy of so shrewd and serious a gentleman as yourself: I can well understand that the puerilities which attract a schoolboy may indeed seem [a] waste of time to an experienced business man. I am not a little ashamed of my own light-headedness, and am resolved to turn my attention to that excellent study of history with which you beguile your leisure. Here may I take the liberty of expressing my ardent and continued admiration of those qualities which make you the ornament of the society to which you belong: first and foremost the practical nature of your character which enables you to relinquish in a moment those trivial fairy tales and such like useless inventions: then your habits of economy and regularity, your sound knowledge of the Lord's Word, your unaffected piety, your knowledge of modern thought, the perfect control of your temper, the justness of your sentiments and – above all – the elegance of your language.

Well! we'll drop it now, as I want some room left for a chat: but honestly thats the sort of answer your last letter seemed to expect. Goodness!, you gave me an awful dressing down! And all because I dared to make a joke on a book of yours that has been a recognised subject for fooling this year or so. Perhaps, however, you just happened to be in bad form when you wrote, so I needn't take it too seriously. Or, what is more likely, J[anie] M[cNeill] has been annoying you and I come in for the aftermath. Anyway, language such as I have just read is not pleasant, and I was on the point of writing a very rude letter. But I remembered, what I do hope you will remember

old man, that real friendships are very, very rare and one doesn't
want to endanger them by quarelling over trifles. We seem to be
always sparing now a days: I dare say its largely my fault (tho' in this
case I really don't know why you're so angry) but anyway do let us
stop it. Perhaps my nerves are a bit on edge as I get nearer to this
abominable exam., and that makes me irritable. But I'll try to do my
best if you will.

So I may imagine you this evening just about now coming from
dinner at Lily's with Mr. Thompson, with the memory of 'Aida' from
last night and the prospect of the 'Magic Flute' to-morrow! I would
give much to be in your place, and more to be in the same place with
both of us there. I am very interested to hear what you think of the
'Flute', so mind you give me a special account of it – and accounts
of the others also. Aida, of course, if well sung and staged must be
enjoyable. I do hope you found them all three so, for that matter.

It must be lovely to really appreciate music (I am not fooling now).
My taste for it was always that of a philistine and I am afraid even
that is leaving me now. Perhaps it is as well I was not with you, or I
might just have sat eating my heart out because I couldn't enjoy what
I would have enjoyed in those delightful days when we first 'discovered' one another. But even if music fails I still have books!

And talking about books I am surprised that you don't say more
of the 'Golden Key':[1] to me it was absolute heaven from the moment
when Tangle ran into the wood to the glorious end in those mysterious caves. What a lovely idea 'The country from which the
shadows fall'! It is funny that we should both have the same idea
about the Temple Classics. I was almost sure they were out of print
and only wrote on the off chance for the Pilgrims' Progress[2] (did I
mention it? I have read it again and am awfully bucked) and then for
the 'Grael'. I wonder would Mullan's tell you a thing was out of
print just because they didn't think it worth while to get you the few
we'd want? At any rate, for paper etc they are far the prettiest cheap
books I know, and if you still think of getting 'The Compleat
Angler'[3] I should advise you to try this edition. The 'set' of the print
and the notes in the nice broad margin are what I particularly like.
Also the frontispieces – in some. My 'Grael' has a lovely one (in the
extreme mediaeval style of course) in each volume by Burne-Jones &
a title page design that reminds me of the Goodfridaymusic. I envy

[1] George MacDonald, *Short Stories* ('The Light Princess', 'The Giant's
Heart', 'The Golden Key') (1928).
[2] John Bunyan, *The Pilgrim's Progress*, 2 parts (1678–84).
[3] Izaak Walton, *The Compleat Angler* (1653).

you, having your Letters of D.O. to W.T. in the Wayfarers – a very
nice series except for the end leaf if I remember right – mine is only
the 1/- Everyman and rather shop-soiled at that!

Was Mr. Thompson as nice as ever last night? He is a man I should
love to meet again – but here too you have all the luck. Are you still
reading 'The Antiquary' and does it still please you as much as ever?
Here I am at the end of my letter and I had meant to give you a long
jaw about some beautiful frost & mist effects I saw on Saturday
evening (like Oldbuck's article on Castrametation) but you will have
to pine without it. I must say I heartily agree with your remarks
about autumn. There are some lovely colours here, & though I fancy
there are finer 'cold' looking afternoons at home, the woods here are
perhaps even richer.

Time to dry up now. My head is splitting, & my feet are like ice so
I suppose if you were here you'd explain to me how & why I was in
for a cold. Well I'd be glad to have you even on those terms. Goodnight & do be indulgent to my many failings. There's a frost –

J.

50

[Gastons
22 November 1916]

My dear Arthur,

I quite agree with you and hope we shall have no more controversies at any rate for the present: for, as you say, it is too much to
hope that we should live in peace and good will for more than a few
weeks continuously. In passing I must explain that when I said your
'language was not pleasant' I only meant the general tone of what
you said – 'diction' or 'sentiments' as Jane Austin would have
delighted to put it. I wasn't using 'language' in the slang sense of the
word meaning swearing – for of course I don't mind 'language' of
that sort in itself. However, this is only a lesson in English & has
nothing to do with the argument, which we will consign to the
swarthy mere of Acheron!

Which reminds me I am no longer in a position to take your
advice about 'Letters from Hell' as we had a jumble sale for the red
cross or something in 'our village' last week and I contributed this.
A mean enough offering indeed but they tell me it sold for 1/6! I am
at present enjoying the malicious pleasure of expecting that the buyer
will be as dissapointed as I was.

What a pity about the 'Magic Flute': I particularly wanted to hear your impressions of it. I am surprised to learn that it is 'comic' (a horrid word to describe a horrid thing) tho' of course it may only be nice humour of the fantastic kind. Your description of Aida is most tantalizing, and I would love to have been there. Even if I had found that I could no longer enjoy the music – tho' I think I am still up to Verdi – I could always have amused myself by talking to you or coughing loudly in the middle of the best passages! Seriously, did they play that lovely prelude well and did the Belfast boors give you a chance to hear it in peace?

I daresay I am wrong about the 'Wayfarer's Library': but whatever the end-leaves be like I remember that the whole effect is good. Have you looked at 'Dorothy Osborne' yet and do you think you will like her? I am desperately in love with her and have accordingly made arrangements to commit suicide from 10 till 4 to-morrow precisely. I wonder does the 'Wayfarer' series publish my latest discovery – the most glorious novel (almost) that I have ever read. I daresay you have read it already or at any rate you must have hearded it praised too often to need my advice. It is Nathaniel Hawthorne's 'House with the Seven Gables'.[1] I love the idea of a house with a curse! And although there is nothing supernatural in the story itself there is a brooding sense of mystery and fate over the whole thing: Have you read it? See if it is in the 'Wayfarers' as I want to get an edition of my own as soon as possible.

I am afraid I have really no memories! I had clean forgotten your ever speaking to me about the 'Golden Key': tho' I well remember setting off in the cab that grey, early morning and waiting for L. & G.[2] at the station! How funny Gordon was with his stiff back! That sounds a strange thing to say but you know what I mean. But after all has not Hewlett (or is it some one else) told us that the fairies have the shortest memories of all! So short that they cannot even remember their lovers from one new moon till the next.

I must say I admire your pluck in taking back 'The Antiquary' after so many years! But as you say the books we buy or return doesnt make much matter to Macmullans. I was sure you'd like the Antiquary very much. I tried to start 'Guy Mannering' on Saturday but some how it didn't grip me. As to the 'mist scene' I am afraid tho' it was very beautiful at the time it will hardly come to life again,

> 'inimitable on earth
> By modle or by shading pencil drawn.'

---

[1] Nathaniel Hawthorne, *The House of the Seven Gables* (1851).
[2] Gordon and Lily Ewart.

I will leave you to imagine it.

Your imagination by the way has had a long enough rest by now. I have so far purposely refrained from saying anything about further instalments of 'Papillon', for fear, since you seemed to have no inclination to go on with it, that it might only hinder you from starting something new. But apparently this is not coming off. Do let us have something – tale, novel, what you will. I am revolving plans for a sort of fantasy much shorter than Bleheris and – which I hope will be an improvement – in modern English. I don't know exactly when I shall inflict the first instalment upon you, but like the people in Northanger Abbey you may be prepared for something 'really horrible'.

Talking about 'Northanger' I have been condemned during this last week to watch Mrs K. reading it in her own edition – your one. I wish you could have seen it. It is not that she actually dirtied it, but what is almost worse she held it so rudely and so close over the fire that the boards have developed a permanent curve and the whole book has a horrible twist! It went to my heart all the more because it was your copy: at least I couldn't get that idea out of my head[.] Must stop now sorry I was late starting to night.

Jack

51

[Gastons
29 November 1916]

Although by experience I am somewhat shy of recommending books to other people I think I am quite safe in earnestly advising you to make 'the Gables' your next purchase. By the way I shouldn't have said 'mystery', there is really no mystery in the proper sense of the word, but a sort of feeling of fate & inevitable horror as in 'Wuthering Heights'. I really think I have never enjoyed a novel more. There is one lovely scene where the villain – Judge Phycheon – has suddenly died in his chair, all alone in the old house, and it describes the corpse sitting there as the day wears on and the room grows darker – darker – and the ticking of his watch. But that sort of bald description is no use! I must leave you to read that wonderful chapter to yourself. There is also a very good 'story in a story' – curiously resembling the Cosmo one[1] tho' of course not so openly impossible. I intend to read all Hawthorne after this. What a pity such a genius should be a beastly American!

[1] Cosmo von Wehrstahl in MacDonald's *Phantastes*.

have so far purposely refrained from saying anything about further instalments of 'Papillon', for fear, since you seemed to have no inclination to go on with it, that it might only hinder you from starting something new. But apparently this is not coming off. Do let us have something - tale, novel, what you will. I am revolving plans for a sort of fantasy much shorter than Bleheris and - which I hope will be an improvement - in modern English. I don't know exactly when I shall inflict the first instalment upon you, but like the people in Northanger Abbey you may be prepared for something 'really horrible'. Talking about 'Northanger' I have been condemned during this last week to watch Mrs K. reading it in her own edition - your one. I wish you could have seen it. It is not that she actually dirtied it but what is almost worse she held it so rudely and so close over the fire that the boards have developed a permanent curve and the whole book has a horrible twist! It went to my heart all the more because it was your copy: at least I couldn't get that idea out of my head must stop now sorry I was late starting to night

Jack

See page 153

I am sorry to hear of your infatuation (very much inFATuation)* for a certain lady, but you need not despair, nor do I propose to call you out; we will divide mother & daughter between us, and you can have first choice! I really don't know which would be the worse do you?

That is certainly a glorious prelude to Aida. Do you remember that first afternoon last hols! How dissappointed we were at first and yet how we enjoyed ourselves afterwards sitting under those trees in the evening (or rather late afternoon) sunlight & throwing pencils & poems from one to the other? Well, we shall soon be there again if all goes well. I am going up for this damnable exam next Monday, shall be back here not later than Saturday & home on the following Monday if not sooner. So that is all well, but I wish to hell next week was over. Don't you sympathise with me? Pray for me to all your gods and goddesses like a good man!

No the Meagre One was not born with a squint: but long, long, long ago, so long ago that Stonehenge had a roof and walls & was a new built temple, he killed a spider. The good people of his day, outraged at this barbarity, stuck a dagger thro his nerve centre which paralyzed him without making him unconscious, seated him on the altar at St. Henge's temple & locked him up with the spiders son. The latter began to spin a solid mass of cobwebs from the opposite corner. Very very slowly through countless years the web grew while the poor Meagre One – who couldn't die – developed a squint from watching it getting nearer. At last after countless ages Stonehenge dissapeared under an enormous mass of web & remained thus till one day Merlin hapenned to set a match to it and so discover what was inside: hence the myth of Merlin's having 'built' St. Henge's. To this day if you go there at sunrise & run round it 7 times, looking over your shoulder you can see again the wretched prisoner trying to struggle as the horrid sticky strands close round him. Cheap excursion trains are run for those who wish to try it.

The Tales of a Grandfather [see figure] in a rather scrubby but old edition has lived in the study these ten years, so you may try a taste of it before risking your money. I imagine it is in rather a childish style, tho' of course you know more about Scott than I do.

I am sorry to hear that you have not yet begun your novel, and as I am sending you four pages of punishment I trust you will let me have something in your next letter. Which reminds [me] I don't know what my address will be at Oxford so you must just write to Bookham as usual. Do go on with the good work. What about taking that magic story Mr Thompson told us, for instance, toning down the super-

PROBLEM A
To raise the Meagre
One.
A = the student
B = the M.O.

3.

a solid mass) of cobweb from the opposite corner. Very very
slowly through countless years the web grew while the poor
meagre One who couldn't die - developped a squint from watching it getting nearer. At last after countless ages stonehenge
disappeared under an enormous mass of web & remained thus
till one day Merlin Rahenned to set a match to it and so dis
-cover what was inside. Hence the myth of Merlin's having
"built." St. Henge's To this day if you go there at sunrise & run
round it 7 times, looking over your shoulder you can see again
the wretched prisoner trying to struggle as the horrid sticky strands
close round him. Cheap excursion trains are run for those
who wish to try it [SEE FIGURE] The Tales of a Grandfather
in a rather scrubby but old edition has lived in the study
these ten years, so you may try a taste of it before risking
your money. I imagine it is in rather a childish style, tho'
of course you know more about Scott than I do. I am sorry
to hear that you have not yet begun your novel, and as
I am sending you four pages of punishment I trust
you will let me have something in your next letter (which
reminds I don't know what my address will be at O,

See page 155

natural parts a bit & making a Donegal novel of the Bronte type? Or
else working that local idea of the Easelys and all. Remember the
second attempt will be easier & pleasanter than the first, and the
third than the second.

Talking about the Easeleys, whether I read 'Guy Mannering' or
no I shall not take to skimming as Kelsie does – for much as we esteem
our beautiful and accomplished cousin – as Mr Collins[2] would
have said – I don't think I shall follow her in literary matters. I am
quite sure that every thing bad is true of your cousin Florence: she
and her sister are young women who need transportation – as also
my cousins at Bloomfield. But indeed if only those who deserved to
have books had them! – who besides you & me would there be to
support the booksellers?

We have had some glorious frosty mornings here, with the fields
all white & the sun coming up late like a red hot ball behind the bare
woods. How I do *love* winter. We have had a book of Yeats' prose
out of the library, and this has revived my taste for things Gaelic &
mystic. Ask Mullan's if he knows a book called 'The Rosacrutian
Cosmo Conception' or any on that subject. Gute Nacht. I wish I were
dead –

Jack[3]

* Ha! Ha! Poor little Bill, he only tries to be agreeee-able.

[2] The pompous and silly clergyman in *Pride and Prejudice* who was so
obsequious to persons of high social station.

[3] Lewis went up to Oxford for the first time on Monday, 4 December
1916, to sit for a scholarship examination. He described this visit in *Surprised
by Joy* (ch. xii) where he says he found lodgings in the first house 'on the
right as you turn into Mansfield Road out of Holywell'. The examination,
which was given in Oriel College, took place between 5 and 9 December,
after which he returned to Great Bookham. He crossed over to Belfast on
11 December and his rather fearful worries about the examination were laid
to rest when, on 13 December, he heard from the Master of University
College, Reginald W. Macan, informing him that 'This College elects you to
a Scholarship (New College having passed you over)'. An announcement of
this award appeared in *The Times* of 14 December.

52

My dear Galahad,

(If you are still to be Galahad after all) here I am at last, on Sunday evening, once more starting the first letter of a term. Well, I left you on the telephone at four of the clock, and I will go over my adventures, to get you thoroughly bored before we start talking.

The crossing was rough and cold, and we were late getting into Fleetwood; after which the train thought it wd. be best to wait for an hour before starting. We dawdled on to Crewe and there waited for another hour, tho' I didn't mind this as it gave me an opportunity of breaking my fast. So by very slow stages I got to Oxford at 6 o'clock. I took the same rooms as before, had a comfortable night, rose at 9.30, bathed, shaved, breakfasted in great ease and so sallied forth.

After wandering about the place and buying a second-hand copy of the 'Gesta Romanorum' (of which more anon) I took my courage in both hands and knocked up the Master of University. He turned out to be a very, very nice old boy and after settling our business he made me stay to lunch. His wife and niece were there, both very decent, ⟨indeed the latter wouldn't be a bad subject for the lash.⟩ But what pleased me most was the masses upon masses of books in his house: among which I saw, tho' of course I couldn't look at it properly, a volume of that glorious new Malory – the one like my 'Psyche'[2] you know. So you may imagine I left Univ. very much relieved and delighted.

---

[1] Although a Scholar of University College, Lewis was not yet a member of Oxford University as he had still to pass Responsions, the entrance examination. He left Belfast on 25 January 1917, arrived in Oxford on the 26th, and called on the Master of University College on the 27th. The Master promised that if he passed the Responsions to be given on 20–26 March he could come up to Oxford at the beginning of Trinity Term in April. Responsions included elementary mathematics as a compulsory subject, and while Mr Kirkpatrick could assure Albert that Clive was 'the most brilliant translator of Greek plays I have ever met' (16 September 1915) and capable of mastering Italian in seven weeks, it was known that neither the tutor nor the pupil had any head for mathematics. Nevertheless, Lewis returned to Great Bookham on 27 January to prepare for the forthcoming examinations.

[2] The story of 'Cupid and Psyche', which Lewis read over Christmas, is one episode in *The Golden Ass* of Apuleius (b.c. AD 114).

(Here my borrowed fountain pen loses its temper) The 'Gesta Romanorum' (you read about it in Mackail's 'Life of W.M.')[3] is a collection of mediaeval tales with morals attached to them: they are very like the Arabian Nights, tho' of course the characters and setting are chivalric instead of Eastern.[4] It is not a first class book but it only cost me 1/– and helps to while away an hour or so between serious things. I also bought at Oxford a copy of the poet Collins in the same edition as my Gray (you know?) I don't know if you would care for him, but I like him quite well: you can look him up in your History of Literature and see what it says. I also bought a French Book on the Poetry of the middle ages[5] – so you see dear Oxford is a dangerous place for a book lover. Every second shop has something you want. Meanwhile I am going on with the 'Life' and besides Collins have read over the 1st Book of Paradise Lost again. I think I shall go through the whole poem this term, and if you begin it some day soon it would be interestin to keep side by side. About books, don't forget to tell Walter to send hither the Lambs & the Macaulay so soon as they come. The cold here is beyond words.

I can see my way clear to the end of 'Dymer'[6] now and will let you have an instalment next Sunday: three more will finish him, and after that I shall expect something from you. For my own part, I should like to write some short narrative poem if I could – about the length of a Book of 'Jason'.[7] I am tryin to think of some subject, at once romantic, voluptuous and homely. You must excuse (tho' Im sure I don't care a damn if you don't, mon vieux!) this writing, as it is being done across my knee.

⟨'Across my knee' of course makes one think of positions for Whipping: or rather not for whipping (you couldn't get any swing) but for that torture with brushes. This position, with its childish, nursery associations wd. have something beautifully intimate and also very humiliating for the victim.⟩

[3] J. W. Mackail, *The Life of William Morris* (1899).
[4] The *Gesta Romanorum* was compiled in England in the fourteenth century and first printed about 1472.
[5] Gaston Paris, *Littérature Française du Moyen Age* (1912).
[6] Over the Christmas holiday, Lewis began a prose tale called 'Dymer'. Though the prose 'Dymer' is no longer extant, he was to begin a narrative poem about the same hero in 1918, which poem was to go through many revisions till it was eventually published in 1926 under his pseudonym 'Clive Hamilton'. 'Dymer' has most recently been reprinted in his *Narrative Poems*, ed. Walter Hooper (1969), which volume also contains Lewis's chronological account of the writing of the poem.
[7] William Morris, *The Life and Death of Jason* (1867).

Quite enough for a first letter. Good bye, my old Archibald (you are fut a-a-ille) –

Jack

53

My dear Arthur,

I was specially glad to get this letter of yours, both because it is longer than your usual ones (I hope you will keep this up) and because there are several good items in it.

First, I am glad you are starting French: I knew you would find no difficulty if once you began. Dont slack off after the first week or so, but don't read French on ordinary work day evenings when you are tired. Keep it for week ends. I should think 'Les Miserables'[1] pretty tough reading in any language, but then you like that sort of thing. As well, you always have your translation to save you dictionary turning. By the way, whether in French or English, you simply must read this book of Maeterlink's on death.[2] It is full of most interesting stuff, and even where you don't believe his theories they always have a sort of romantic interest. One case he tells of reminds me of 'John Silence'!, it is so wierd: but I mustn't spoil it by an outline.

I was also glad of your adventure in the billiard room. See how the gods lead you on of their own accord! ⟨I am given to understand that the idea of suffering yourself appeals to you more than that of inflicting. It used to be so with me, and perhaps the experienced victim does get a more vivid voluptuous sensation than the operator – at first. But of course once you are really in pain you can't think of anything else while the operator grows keener all the time.⟩

(In passing, can you imagine a horrible book, in paper, illustrations & binding than the 'History'?) Just before supper I finished the 2nd volume of Mackail's 'Life of W.M.'. There is nothing nicer than to lay aside a book with a certain satisfaction at getting it settled with and yet having enjoyed it thoroughly, is there? I certainly know Morris better than I did before, tho' in a way his character is a dissapointment. You can't really think there's any resemblance between him and me? Of course I would give mine eyes to be like

[1] By Victor Hugo (1862).
[2] Maurice Maeterlinck, *La Mort* (1913).

him in some ways, but I don't honestly think my temper is quite so bad.

As to the other point I often think he must have been ⟨a special devotee of the rod.⟩ Do you remember in the 'Well at the World's End' where a man at the Birg of the Four Friths says that the advantage of slave girls as opposed to wives is that we need care nothing for their ill humours ⟨'so long as the twigs smart and the whips sting'? That sentence is dragged in quite unnecessarily and is exquisitely worded.⟩

Item (as Morris says in his letters) the 2nd Vol. of Macaulay[3] is come, in excellent condition. The leaves are all stuck together and lump in ridges and make the right crackly noise. Thanks for sending it, old man: I wish indeed you were coming the same journey. How perfectly happy we could be here, walking and talking together and both doing work we liked.

Your suggestion that I did not want your company in the cab, is purely rhetorical, I hope. You must know that I wanted it very much, although I cant talk about those sort of things the way you do. It seems to me indecent somehow, if you know what I mean.

I am sorry to hear that you're fed up, and, although nobody who gets enough food and clothing in a world where most are hungry and cold has any business to talk about 'misery' I do sympathise with you exceedingly. I wish to goodness (or to Jeshua shall we say?) that you could get out of the office. If only you had work that you liked you'd feel a different being in spite of loneliness and so on. I know I can always turn to pleasant work for comfort as a last resource. But what's the good of telling you this! I think your father and mother should be shot for keepin' you in that hole, ⟨while the only other member of your family whom I am interested in could be punished in an other way – to the general enjoyment of the operator, and to the great good of her soul.⟩

Dear! Dear! How the theme comes back. To change it, I had a lovely walk this afternoon in the snow. As I walked up the village street the ground and house tops were thick, and it was coming fluttering down à la Debussy. But best of all, the blacksmith's place was open, and you could see the red forge glowing inside. Can't you imagine it?

I long to see the picture you have made of that lane in THE wood. Any more designs for the 'Poems'? That first little one is such a success that you must do lots of tail-peaces and such.

No: I didn't see 'La Bohème', and it took from 2–6 to get from

[3] Thomas Babington Macaulay, *History of England*, 5 vols. (1849–61).

Oxford to here. Good night, old sinner, ⟨and imagine yourself the slave of some Eastern queen who whips you – I mean when you next go North.⟩

I am just going to have the first bath since seeing you, as there has been no hot water. –

⟨Philomastix⟩

54

[Gastons
1 February 1917]

Just a scrape to thank you a thousand times for the books[1] which have just come. Can you really spare them? It is most awfully good of you and I am very pleased with them, especially when I think of the other edition which is certainly not so nice, tho' I hope *you* will come to think otherwise.

I wrote to you on Wednesday as usual, which letter will now have reached [you] & will write again next Wednesday after getting your next. You say 'Arethusa'[2] is lovely: have you bought it or got a copy from the library? In any case I am very glad you have started it. Isn't Omobono a lovely character, and also the slave dealer's wife? I think it a very good romance all round. Having finished Morris I am reading a silly book of [F.] Anstey's 'The Talking Horse', before settling down to Macaulay. I never heard you speak of Anstey, but you should read him certainly: this book is fantastic & almost as ridiculous as 'Alice' tho' of course in a more ordinary way.

The snow is nearly gone now, but the country still keeps a wintry look which is lovely & the mornings a wintry nip which is not. You'll be glad to hear that I've started a 'friendly' tobacco-pipe instead of the cigarettes you so object to. Glad your interest in R. is increasing, but more of this elsewhere – Addio,

Jack

55

[Gastons
7 February 1917]

My dear Arthur

I must begin by explaining why there is no instalment with this letter. On Sunday, when I should have written one I spent the

---

[1] Charles Lamb's *Essays of Elia*.
[2] Francis Marion Crawford, *Aresthusa* (1907).

in the usual florid, expensive continental
paper back – still this gives you the exciting task
of getting it bound. Good night for the present

~~[crossed out]~~ a ~~[crossed out]~~, you can learn
My Dear Arthur that amount of Gk. letters to myself
– (by the unlettered!)

I must begin by explaining why
there is no instalment with this letter. On Sunday, when
I should have written one I spent the whole day most
delightfully skating on a lake at a place called Wesley
near here, which you reach by a road through the woods
As it is now thick snow again you can imagine what
a topping walk it is. The winding road covered with snow,
the bare trees with their snow covered branches & the sunlight falling thro' them in bars on the ground also covered with snow. Absolutely lovely, especially as the air is
very dry and the sky clear. To day I have been to the
same place to skate again & tho' the ice is now rather cut
up. I was in pleasant company (NO – not that sort) and
enjoyed it greatly. especially the walk back. The moon
was out, & starting under a clear starry sky we grad
ually walked into a cold white fog. The white of the
ground and the white of the fog became indistinguish
able and you seemed to be floating in a sort of silver
cloud, broken by the red light of a railway signal
at the station. This is a vague description, but I think
you'll understand. How I do love real winter

See pages 162–5

whole day most delightfully skating on a lake at a place called Wisley near here, which you reach by a road through the woods. As it is now thick snow again you can imagine what a topping walk it is. The winding road covered with snow, the bare trees with their snow covered branches & the sunlight falling thro' them in bars on the ground also covered with snow. Absolutely lovely, especially as the air is very dry and the sky clear.

To day I have been to the same place to skate again & the ice is now rather cut up. I was in pleasant company (NO – not that sort) and enjoyed it greatly, especially the walk back. The moon was out, & starting under a clear starry sky we gradually walked into a cold white fog. The white of the ground and the white of the fog became indistinguishable and you seemed to be floating in a sort of silver cloud, broken by the red light of a railway signal at the station. This is a vague description, but I think you'll understand.

How I do love *real* winter like this! The thermometer in the hall stands at 7° to night, the water in my jug is solid to the bottom and all the pipes are frozen up. If you look out for a moment through the willow-pattern of frost on the windows you see this lovely haze of snow & mist & moonlight. What with the general beauty of the world and my lovely hours of skating I have not been so bucked for a long time.

My French is under rather different conditions from yours, as I read from 10–11 every night except on Wednesdays when I write to you. I have really never counted exactly how much I cover and it wd. not be accurate to count by pages, as they vary so in size and in type. I shouldn't read for more than an hour at a time in your case, certainly not for a whole afternoon. I never read Perrault myself but I am sure he is good (A. Lang praises him) and you may remember that there is an edition of him with illustraggers by Arthur Rackham – I forget the details however. What would you say to the 'Contes Fantastiques' of Charles Nodier, in that nice blue Collection Gallia at 1/–? Some of these tales you would like tho' some seemed to me dull. Then again why not get something in that 1/6 Dents edition with the lovely paper, say Voltaire's 'Contes' (very amusing) or the shorter tales of Georges Sand, – you can see the list. I have now made a good start on my second volume of Macaulay, which is admirable. What a nice man James must have been! But before starting this I read in a library copy two of F. W. Bains Indian Tales 'The Descent of the Sun' & 'The Heifer of the Dawn'.[1] They are translations from

[1] Francis William Bain, *The Descent of the Sun* (1903); *A Heifer of the Dawn* (1904).

the Sanskrit and are 'really rather adorable'. A little too weird, perhaps, for your solid tastes; but you should certainly have a look at them in Lily's copies.

It is most exasperating of you to say you have come to a conclusion which will dissapoint me, but you don't want to put it in paper. What tawdry nonsense! If any person did read our letters, he would be an ill-bred cad & therefore we shouldn't mind what he saw. But anyway I will be really annoyed if you don't clear up the mystery in your next letter. My own ⟨Philomastix⟩ is only a harmless piece of Greek affectation: 'philo' is the same word you see in 'philosopher' 'philologist' etc, and means 'fond of' while ⟨'mastix' is the ordinary word for a whip.⟩

I think I can understand your getting tired of Iceland before Morris left it: but didn't you like the Faroe Islands? That part reminded me of our mountain walks at Portsalon, didnot it you? I rather expected some fuller criticism on Arethusa, and would like to know your final verdict when you write. Tho' of course it's not in the rank of 'real books', I have a sentimental affection for it from reading it over ever since I was about ten. I am now through the first two Books of Paradise L. and really love Milton better every time I come back to him, &, what is more to the point, I think his merits are of a [kind] you'd appreciate. However, if Harrap won't let you have a copy till 1919, our plan [of] reading in harness goes 'off'. I can quite understand the interest of the Welsh marches at the time of the Wars of the Roses – especially as it was in that place & that time that our good friend Thomas Malory lived (see introduction to the Morte). I am now reading in French this book on French literature of the Middle Ages which to me at least is very interestin. By the way Maeterlink's book on Death is in the usual horrid, expensive continental paper back – still this gives you the exciting task of getting it bound.

Good night for the present – ⟨Philomastix (*ΦΙΛΟΜΑΣΤΙΞ,*⟩ you can learn that amount of Gk. letters to mystify the unlettered!)

Next morning – colder still! Remember to clear up the mystery when you write & if you like I'll destroy the letter –

J.

56

You begin on this page

Cher Ami,

One of the vertues of snow is that it chiefly teacheth and instructeth us for to loven and cherish the greene grasse – certainly I never appreciated grass until about Teusday the snow began to melt and after so many days whiteness it was nice to see the old homely fields again, all pale and washed looking, with drifts still lying in the hollows.

Your letter, although dated a long while ago (9th) only arrived this morning, Thursday: so that I am afraid this will not come to your hands at its wonted time. Which is your fault, not mine.

⟨If the whole mystery was that you didn't love the Rod as I do – well there's no mystery about that. Very, very few are affected in this strange way and I am only surprised that you can enter into my feelings even so much as you do. As a matter of fact, just as the other – the normal desire has a poignant sensual side and a vague sentimental side, so that has too. I can understand your being able to like the *idea*, and yet not having your physical feelings raised by the thought of the 'mastix' – . . . . Is this at all your state of mind? Yes, that business about stepping on Zoe appeals⟩ strongly to the sentimental or theoretical side of this feeling. But we are getting too sticky. Passez outre!

Item, I am reading such a splendid book in German, by a man called Chamisso 'Peter Schlemichl's Wundersame Geschichte' (The Amazing Adventures of Peter Schlemichl).[1] It is about a man (modern) who sells his shadow to a wizard: his subsequent adventures are treated chiefly in the absurd 'Alice' style but there is a sort of core of horror lurking in it all the time, that is to me very attractive. I see from the introduction to my copy that there are several translations: I should certainly advise you to get it out of the library – except in a specially nice edition it is perhaps hardly worth buying. I am writing to night to see about an edition of 'Undine' in the original. I also have seen in a book on German literature the name of some of Fouqués other books – Thiodolf the Icelander, The Magic

[1] Adelbert Von Chamisso, *Peter Schlemihls Wunderbare Geschichte* (1853.)

Ring etc.[2] Sweet lord! how one does want to read *everything*. I am nearly through Macaulay Vol. II, which I have enjoyed immensely, especially the part about Oxford: I am sorry Obadiah Walker should have been at Univ![3] However, Shelley & I goin there should make up for it.

Cher ami, j'ai a confession to make. I have thee told a lie. A certain operation is NOT called going North at Malvern. I invented this phraze so that you & I might have some convenient & safe way of referring to that thing. It wd. be unpleasant to have to use the ugly expressions which slang has evolved & this one has the advantage of being quite meaningless to an outsider. But I couldn't have stopped and explained all this to you in the middle of that breathless night walk.

I do so hope you will enjoy the opera: and if I could only be at home worrying you & making little plans for going to them (I couldn't leave my father of course) I'd risk being dissapointed. One sort of music still holds me as much, or indeed more than ever – piano music. I suppose the gods are doing this to console me. By the way, here's a bright idea, perhaps the gods have a touch of my disease & that is why the world is tortured so every day. I wonder could that be work[ed] into a mystical story. Which reminds me, when is your novel comin? The Bible (which you don't read) has very hard things to say of people who put their hand to the plough and turn back. There was great promise in poor 'Papillon' – imagination, charm – the technical part you will learn by practice. Buck up!

At any rate I am sending you Dymer's next excursion, and have begun the poem. The subject is 'The childhood of Medea', & it will leave off where the most poems about her begin – shortly after her meeting with Jason. It will describe her lonely, frightened childhood away in a castle with the terrible old king her father & how she is gradually made to learn magic against her will. Of course I'll make a mess of it 'cracked absolutely', but there's a fine subject in all that for someone who knew how to manage it. I wish Morris or Apollonius had made a poem about that. Descriptions of childhoods & gradual growings up are very fascinating I think.

Glad you are coming to like your Lamb, tho I don't think you can love it so well as I do mine. His novel is called 'Rosamund Gray'

[2] Fouqué, Friedrich, Baron de la Motte, *Undine* (1811); *Thiodolf the Icelander* (1815); *The Magic Ring* (1812).

[3] Possibly because Obadiah Walker (1612–99), the Master of University College from 1676 to 1688, had been a Roman Catholic who was imprisoned in the Tower because of his religious beliefs. See the D.N.B.

isn't it?[4] It was published anonymously and some one (someone like poor little Bill, I suppose) said that

> Friends coming up to examine it
> Observe a good deal of Charles Lamb in it.

What is it like. Yes!, isn't the collection Gallia awfully dainty. As soon as I've finished my book on French Literature of the Middle Ages I think I'm going to tackle 'Notre Dame';[5] It is rather in your line & mine too, isn't it? Do you know I believe I shall come to like history kwite as much as u do? What nonsense about the Heiffer of the Dawn; you never told me a syllable. The Silver library is very nice but is the Library Edition (like My Sigurd[6] you know) not worth the difference? I heartily recomend the E[arthly] Paradise (never having read it) and intend to buy a copy myself as soon as I have finished the Paradise Lost. Have been reading Malory, the 'Beaumains' part again & cant understand how anyone can help loving him. But you always were a cross sent to try me, cher ami, so cher ami good night. Is this letter long enough, because it's all your going to get anyway.

⟨*ΦΙΛΟΜΑΣΤΙΞ*⟩

57

[Gastons
20 February 1917]

Cher Ami,

Il y a je ne sais quoi de charme in your style of writing a letter on a number of loose sheets in devil knows what order. It is so nice when you think that the pleasure of reading it is over to suddenly come on half a page more hiding somewhere. I wish I wasn't such friends with you – it takes away from ones independance: I hang on Teusday evenings and Wednesday mornings for your letter just like a schoolgirl and am quite put out if it doesn't turn up.

Item, it is very annoying for a habitual liar like me, when he *does* tell the truth for once to be accused of invention: however, tho' my little confession was quite true, many of my statements are so 'Of imagination all compact' that I can't blame you for disbelieving this one. It is a pity tho' that you always fix on the true ones to suspect and swallow down the lies with avidity!

I am sorry that you don't like Mackail's second volume. I suppose

[4] Charles Lamb, *The Tale of Rosamund Gray and Old Blind Margaret* (1798).

[5] Victor Hugo, *Notre Dame de Paris* (1831).

[6] William Morris, *Sigurd the Volsung* (1877).

I am a bundle of contradictions, but I must say socialism does interest me. When you think of the way labourers in the factory live at home, – men & women slaving from half past five in the morning to six at night at hard, monotonous work in hideous rooms full of shrieking machinery year after year, with never a moments pleasure except when they are drunk (and you can't blame them) it really does make you feel that the whole thing is wrong. Aren't you ashamed to think of us, blessèd prigs, with our books and music and little grumbles about nothing, dawdling along (your office is absolute Paradise & idleness compared with their lives) while half or more than half the people are slaves. As much slaves as ever there were in Rome, their only liberty being liberty to starve when the torture becomes unbearable! However I am not going to afflict my cher ami with a political letter, but I just wanted to explain why I can't help thinking about those things.

By the way, what do you mean by ⟨the whip in music? At any rate the mere sound of a whip doesn't affect me in the least. There's no special virtue in a whip – hundreds of other methods of mild torture are just as good.⟩

I am glad I wasn't there to have the last remnants of my Wagnerian taste murdered by a garbled Tannhaüser. Aye me! how our tastes and feelings have changed since the days when Wagner was the great common ground of talk, when Morris was only a name (perhaps you wish he were still) and I had never read Charlotte Brontë. A propos of which, having finished Macaulay (an admirable book, tho' of course the writer is too much of a whig and puritan for my taste: the old cavaliers were at any rate gentlemen) I am beginning 'Mansfield Park' again, after a futile effort to read 'Vanity Fair'.[1] I waded knee deep into the marish of endless characters, sentimentalism & platitude and then really could not go on. Why is it I can't appreciate Thackeray?

It is difficult to choose between two such perfect flowers as the 'Crock of Gold' & 'Phantastes'. The former has a beautiful sense of nature and open air, and a certain voluptuousness that the other ha'nt, but then there is nothing in it quite so fine as the faery palace or the place where Anodos comes out on the sad sea shore and throws himself into the waves – or the story of Cosmo. You see!, what memories crowd up. Still the homely, Irish beauty of the other is topping: so is the humour both of the philosopher and the policemen. The philosophical parts (I mean the serious philosophical parts at the beginning of some chapters) I don't understand, but they stir me

[1] By William Makepeace Thackeray (1848).

in some strange way that they probably wouldn't if I really could follow them.

⟨By the way, cher ami, you must have a very depraved taste if you like THAT passage best in Dymer tho'⟩ I admit twas pleasant to write. Perhaps it is true what the Greek poet in the Anthology says: 'Sweet is water to the thirsty man, and to the weary mariners sight of land is sweet. But sweeter than all it is when one bed holds twain that love, and the queen of Cypris is praised of both.' Queen of Cypris, you know, is Aphrodite. I have no intention of giving up Dymer, tho' I fear he will dissapoint you.

The childhood of Medea has progressed to some two hundred and twenty lines, in the metre of 'Jason' – tho' I am trying not to imitate Morris too much. The subject of course is far too good for a schoolboy of eighteen to blunder at, but I think I shall try & go on. I write it whenever the fit takes me, in a pocket book, so you will not see it till tis done.

My Responsions exam begins on Tuesday 20th of March and I cast me to be home before the following Monday. You say you hope to have some more 'breathless' walks. I can undertake to manage the 'breathless' part either by strapping a sponge bag onto your head, or by compelling you to advance up the steepest hills at the double.

I have finished my book on French Literature (admirable, excellent, exquisite) and started a very interesting work 'Les Confessions' de Rousseau – ⟨qui avait, lui aussi, un penchant pour la verge qui consacre a ce sujet adorable quatre pages.⟩ Altogether a 'really rather lovely' book. ⟨His taste is altogether for suffering rather than inflicting: which I can feel too, but it is a feeling more proper to the other sex.⟩

The pleasures of spring have been jawed about so often that I am rather shy of saying anything about the lovely weather that has succeeded to the snow here. Do you know what it feels like when you go out for the first time without an overcoat and feel all the nerves funny up the back of your legs and see the clouds blowing about a really blue sky? All the same I know spring too well to really like her. She invariably makes you feel lonely & dissatisfied & long for

> 'The land where I shall never be
> The love that I shall never see.'

You know what I mean?

Yrs.,
J.
⟨Philom.⟩

⟨VERGERS POUR LES VIERGES⟩

58

[Gastons
28 February 1917]

Cher Ami,

Thou art fool: you take tremendous care about putting in anything too ⟨*philomastigian*⟩ for fear it should be seen and then go and stick in a reference to a certain lady of my passion, making it quite clear whom you mean so that it *really would* matter if somebody got hold of it. However, they shan't.

But as to that lady, I remember that you did not agree when I suggested ⟨her as a suitable subject for the lash⟩, on that eventful night. But surely now that you have seen her again you must agree with me. Is she not absolutely perfect from head to heel – and moreover ⟨the necessary part of the body – one of the most beautiful parts anyway – shaped with an almost intolerable grace? The gods⟩ – whom I'm always abusing – certainly produced a masterpiece in her: even to see her walk across the room is a liberal education. Ah me!, ⟨if she had suffered indeed half the stripes that have fallen upon her in imagination she would be well disciplined.⟩ Of course I don't say that it is quite my own ideal type of beauty. But then who ever is? After all 'The love that I shall never see' is better both in body and soul than all the real women on earth.

Which reminds me, that couplet (a beauty isn't it) is NOT by me – I wish it were. Andrew Lang quotes it somewhere, but I have never been able to discover the author. Whoever it be, he deserves immortality for those two lines alone.[1]

Item, I have read nearly all Tacitus, his short works the Agricola & Germania, the Histories & am now at the Annals.[2] At first I absolutely hated him, partly because I had not then learned to appreciate history, partly because his twisted and obscure style (he is called 'the Latin Carlyle' & 'the Latin Meredith', so you can imagine) at first repelled me. Now, however, I am grown to be very fond of him indeed. I have just finished the 14th and am beginning the 15th book of the Annals – all about Nero. Some of N's depravities are so

[1] The lines 'The land where I shall never be, / The love that I shall never see' are by Andrew Lang and they are found in his *History of English Literature* (1912), p. 579, which book Lewis was reading in 1915. Lewis was, however, quoting from memory. Lang's actual lines are 'The love whom I shall never meet, / The land where I shall never be'.

[2] Cornelius Tacitus, *The Life of Agricola* (c. 98); *Germania* (98); *Histories* (c. 116); *Annals* (c. 116).

fearful as to be almost funny, aren't they? I expect that like me, it will especially interest you as being the source of 'Quo Vadis'.[3] The only other author of ancient history I can recommend is the Greek historian Herodotus.[4] He combines the pleasure of real history & the charm of romance: he tells all about Egypt & Persia and the wonder of Babylon & the Hyperboreans who live beyond the North Wind, & the gryphons who guard their gold in the Scythian deserts etc. I am sure a good translation of him would provide you with agreeable reading.

Since writing last I have read for the first time 'The Tenant of Wildfell Hall'[5] In spite of some excellent passages it is a bad book. People who have been brought up as gentlemen don't even when drunk, fight and beat their wives in their hostesse's drawing room. It is all very melodramatic & gives you the impression of being written by a lady's maid. However the beginning and the end, the part outside Helen's own narrative, are topping & I had rather have read it than not. I am now beginning Mrs. Gaskell's 'Life'[6] in the household edition & love it already. The description of Haworth with the moors going up behind it is heavenly — wouldn't you like that sort of country — tho' of course not better than our own. You will be glad to hear that in the introduction to this copy, that ill-bred journalist Clement Shorter gets well slated & is shown to have most maliciously [mis] represented lots of things.

Your description of 'John Inglesant'[7] is not very appetising: as to the subject about Catholics and Protestants, I fear me that my views would only annoy you (comment 'Has that ever prevented you from stating them if you wanted to?' Ah well! . . .) Doesn't it seem ages ago, cher ami, since we sat that day in the library looking down on the street and trying to talk? I *am* looking forward to a return homeward. Responsions is the entrance exam to the University: for you see, tho' I have got a scholarship at one college, I don't belong to the whole show. ·

'The Confessions' of Rousseau (to jump from one subject to another) quite apart from THAT splendid passage, continue very interesting indeed. The description of his wanderings and adventures is rather like that of De Quincey — perhaps even better. It would be

[3] By Henryk Sienkiewicz (1896).
[4] Herodotus (c. 480–c. 425 BC).
[5] By Anne Brontë (1848).
[6] Elizabeth Cleghorn Gaskell, *The Life of Charlotte Brontë* (1857).
[7] By Joseph Henry Shorthouse (1881).

rather long for you at present but you should keep it in your mental list of French books to be got.

I do hope you are really speaking the truth about Dymer in all your flattery. As he draws near his end I am getting quite anxious lest I should not finish him. You will understand with what pleasure I look forward to being able to say 'Well, there is a book written: long or short, good or bad, there it is by itself and done.' How I wish I could make you start writing again so that we could have all these little wheezes in common as we do everything else.

Item, the

'springs voluptuous pantings'

still go on, damn them! It has now got to the stage when real comfort in bed must be given up till next winter. If you keep on the clothes you had last week you will be asphyxiated, if you lay them off you will have, not cold, but a lonely, comfortless sense of thinness. All the same I must admit it is lovely to hear the birds of a morning and feel the sun on your back as you're getting into your bath. Voilà de l'éloquence à propos d'a worn out theme: but honest all the same, and therefore pardonable. Do you know, cher ami, that it is at great cost I write hard like this up to the very moment of going to bed? I never sleep well on the nights of writing – all the ideas buzzing in my head keep me awake.

Which reminds me, you will be releived to hear that 'Medea's Childhood' after struggling on for 300 turgid lines has been quietly made into spills for my 'tobacco pipe' – all those fine landscapes and vigorous speeches, devoted to real use at last! En effet, it is a failure. I can quite share your annoyance about the Essays. There are a hundred things I meant to say in this letter and haven't. My feet are cold & there is a moon. Look at the lady we mentioned & think. Good night old fool: have finished P. Schlemihl.

59

[Gastons
6 March 1917]

Cher Ami,

I think sometimes that we have spoiled everything by starting this subject. For one thing, we always are like the ladies in Jane Austin, who each want to talk about her own concerns and neither to hear the other's. ⟨I mean, you are interested in a brand of *That* which doesn't appeal to me, and I in one that doesn't appeal to you.⟩

But it is not only that: I happened this morning on an old letter of yours from the days of Papillon, full of enthusiasm about books and music and scenery, which somehow made me feel that we were on a much higher level then, much more removed from the common mob. And yet I do not see that it is sensible to pretend that these things don't exist, when we are both really very sensual at heart. Rather, when we first started the subject, I didn't think it would be quite the same: I fancied there was a way of treating such themes with gravity, delicacy and real, honest appreciation of the good things of the world, that could sort of fall into line with our other interest in literature and so on: that we could raise the subject to our level instead of falling to its. Nor can I see exactly how we have failed in that ideal: yet – without blaming you in the very, very, least – when I had read your letter this evening I felt that something was wrong.

Perhaps I was just in a particular kind of mood, but more likely it was the unhappy reference to Catullus that finished me. For Catullus (you saw him in my big Medici volume) though I have only read $\frac{1}{3}$ or so of him, is to me one of the really sacred poets, some of his tiny little things leave me really breathless – in particular one bit about that wander-lust feeling in the Spring, which he describes beautifully; in fact he is one of my gods, I put him on a level with Morris or Keats. You can understand what a sudden shock it gave me ⟨to think of anyone approaching him from your point of view. It was blasphemy⟩: mind, I don't blame you in the very least, still less do I suggest that I wouldn't have felt just the same in your position ⟨(I may remark in passing that in the parts of Catullus I have read there is no allusion to your particular taste).⟩ All the same it set me thinking – and I have just tried to jot down the substance of it. In a way we have spoiled our paradise.

All the same, having gone thus far, there is no good trying to go back – it would be horrible to keep an artificial silence and feel that there was something there all the time. Let us talk of these things when we want, but always keep them on the side that tends to beauty, and avoid everything that tends to sordid-ness ⟨and beastly police court sort of scandal out of grim real life (like the O. Wilde story).⟩ Cher ami, please, please don't think this is preaching. I don't pretend that I have done so any better than you, but I am only suggesting plans for the future: for I am sure you have felt at times as I do now.

You will have gathered that I am in bad form to-night:

'Oh Galahad, my Galahad,
The world is very lone and sad,
The world is old and gray with pain
And all the ways thereof are bad.'

For one thing it is most annoying to think that I shall only have 3 weeks holiday this Easter: for another, as it draws to its close, I begin to regret the very happy time I have spent at Bookham. As well Mrs Gaskell's Life, though a book quite beyond all praise, especially in the description of scenery, has regularly given me the blues, so sad is the story it tells. When God can get hold of a really first rate character like Charlotte Brontë to torture, he's just in his element: cruelty after cruelty without any escape. How little right we have to grumble at any little discomforts of ours.

Cher ami, of course that lady is not my ideal, and I agree with you that she is much too big. I wonder would you think my ideal even pretty if I could produce her in bodily form! I have her very clearly in my mind however & could recognize her at once if such a person came into existance. The girl in the last instalment of Dymer is the one from the witch's house of course: it was dark when they met there, and in the morning Dymer left her still sleeping – so of course he knew her but she had never seen him. But I admit, that was so long ago that you may be pardoned for having forgotten. I am afraid this instalment is a failure. I have made three attempts at it and am not at all satisfied. Both in prose & verse & my everyday work the things I take most pains with are always the poorest. Regardez comme je suis égoiste! Half the time I talk about the state of my soul & the other half of my own book.

Item, 'Peter Schlemihl' is the name of that German 'admirable' book about the man who sold his shadow. I am very pleased to have read it. I am now (in German) at 'Sintram' a tale by Fouqué. It has some good eerie touches in it, but none of the homely beauty of 'Undine' – indeed 'tis rather tawdry as a whole. The edition is so horrible that it ought to emanate from 'Satan & Co.' & sometimes I have a ghastly suspicion that it is 'scripted': for these school editors are absolutely without conscience & wouldn't hesitate to mutilate a book and then publish it without a word of explanation.

By the way, did you know that the 1/– Nelson French series had several other bindings? I have got a 4/– 'half-polished morocco' one at which you will 'fly with delight'. It is Victor Hugo's 'Hans d'Islande' (Islande=Iceland, not island, you know) of which a book on F. literature says 'it is founded on a modern Icelandic tradition of a man-beast who lives among the mountains.' So I hope it will be good. The whole set of Hugo built up in that binding would be splendid.

I have finished 'Paradise Lost' again, enjoying it even more than before. Really you must read it sometime soon. In Milton is everything you get everywhere else, only better. He is as voluptuous as Keats, as romantic as Morris, as grand as Wagner, as wierd as Poe, and a better lover of nature than even the Brontes. A propos of which, there are certainly some true Bronte touches in 'The Tenant of Wildfell (lovely name) Hall', especially in the homely gathering of the first chapter and some fine descriptions of the moors. Those moors must be lovely. Mrs. Gaskell's excellent description has quite fired me – not that any scenery could quite fill the place of our own dear glens and fields. I do hope we shall have some really good rambles among them soon: we must be careful never to talk of '*That*' in the precincts of the Sacred Wood – as well, our vegetable loves, the hazels & brambles, might be jealous. Have your 'Essays' come yet? I wrote to Mullans a long time ago for the 3rd volume of the History which of course has not come. If this goes on I shall get all my books from London both in term and holydays. Yet that would be against all my principles.

'Our azure sister of the Spring' is so annoyed at my praises of winter that she has retired and left the field to snow and slush. And the bare trees are all waving to and fro and sighing, and the drenching rain is blowing sideways out of a gray sky today – altogether a very fine spectacle. I got onto one of the big Roman roads (theres something fine about feeling that a road runs away to Carlisle behind you) and trudged for miles watching the dead leaves floating along the swollen gutters. A most fascinating amusement, have you ever tried it?

I have written for the 'Faithful Shepheardess'[1] in the Temple Dramatists. What are they like? I have also got a Chatto & Windus list with some interesting news in it. My usual smoking nowadays is one of those very long old fashioned clay pipes. The sort that Milton may have smoked. You should try one. It is the cheapest and one of the best ways of smoking & you can understand the 'old world charm' of it. I wish there wasn't a week to wait for your next letter, make it as long as long as long. Good night, mon vieux.

[1] John Fletcher, *The Faithful Shepherdess* (1610).

60

Cher Ami,

I have just been debating whether the pleasure of getting a letter will outweigh the dissapointment of finding a very short one: for without anything from you to provoke argument I don't know how long I can go on gassing. See how concieted I am grown, as if in *my* letters shortness would not be the best recommendation.

Well to proceed (and recite the following verses of the poet) I was delighted to hear of your illness, which I did yesterday from M. mon père and to day from Mme. vôtre mère & your own scrawl. I hope you will be just nicely convalescing when I turn up – well enough to go out, but of course not nearly well enough for Niffleheim (or Frankleheim). Seriously, unless it is [a] very painful or opressive illness I always get some pleasure out of 'keeping my bed'. Especially if you are sick enough to have a fire! There is something beautifully cosy about meals brought up on a tray, and after a frugal but thoroughly enjoyable breakfast I love to pile up my pillows, call for a choice pile of bright volumes and settle down to an endless read: if there be snow falling so much the better.

I say 'bright volumes' advisedly, because all books are not suitable for bed reading. Books of the 'Phantastes' & 'Crock of Gold' type are best; some new ones if possible, several old favourites, a trashy novel from the library (trashy, but not bad, if you know what I mean) AND some picture books of the Rackham & Robinson type. I should find 'Jason' very good company too. By the way don't imagine I'm trotting all this out as sort of 'advice to invalids': its only that the subject naturally came up & I couldn't lose an opportunity of airing **my** own tastes. Expect you wont agree with any of them. I suppose the Titian print is great company: or can you see nothing but reflexions in it's glass from where you sit?

Cher ami, 'Han d'Islande' in its lovely binding is the best book I've read for many a day. It is about Norway in the 16th century, a good historical romance, gets along quicker than Scott tho' without any of the hiccupping style that annoys us in Dumas. Although there is no supernatural element there is a great deal of the terrifying and the 'macabre'. Hans himself, a sort of ugly & ferocious Rob Roy, with a dash of Alberich in his character and appearance is a real treat. There are also excellent descriptions of scenery among the mountains and ruins. Altogether a book I should very heartily recommend you. Amn't I good to write to you instead of readin it at this moment? The III vol. of my Macaulay has come at last in a shocking shop soiled copy, but I suppose I shall have to keep it.

You will see from the tag in this week's Dymer that I have begun Italian, which is the easiest language of the world.[1] I shall be able to shew you one charming edition in that language next hols. My adress after Teusday is,

> C/o Mrs Etheridge,
> 1 Mansfield Road,
> Oxford.

'No more now' as the housemaids say. Goodnight.

P.S. I wonder what you really thought of my last letter

61

> [University College,
> Oxford.
> 28 April 1917][1]

Cher Ami,

I wonder how much description will be tolerable for you to hear and me to write. I am so full of new things that I don't know where to begin, and yet nothing has really happened so far. I will try to tell you at least my first adventures in some detail.

Heavily laden with suitcase, parcels and coats I arrived at the

---

[1] Writing to Clive's father on 18 April 1917, Mr Kirkpatrick said 'I conceived, with the enthusiastic assent of the pupil, of course, the bold conception of mastering the Italian language in half a term. And we did it. None but a quite exceptional student could have attempted it, much less succeeded in it.'

[1] Lewis returned to Oxford on 20 March and lodged in the same digs as before. Responsions began on the 21st and he returned home on 27 March, soon afterwards learning that he had been ploughed in algebra. He was, however, allowed to come into residence in Trinity Term so as to be able to pass into the Army by way of the University Officers' Training Corps. He arrived in Oxford on 26 April – as described in this letter – and Matriculated on the 28th. From an academic point of view he was supposed to be reading for Responsions, and shortly after his arrival he began algebra lessons with J. E. Campbell of Hertford College.

great gate of Univ. at about 5 o'clock. From the porter's lodge a sandy-haired man emerged and shouted 'Jo'. Somewhat timidly I came further in and asked 'Can you tell me where my rooms are, – my name is Lewis.' 'Yes, Sir,' said the man. 'Can't say where you'll be, Sir, the Dean hasn't come up yet – Jo!' Jo now appeared.[2] 'Show Mr Lewis into Mr Crawford's[3] old rooms' said the sandy haired man. Jo took my various baggage and led the way along one side of the quad (I was very relieved to see no one about). Then he led me up three very bare noisy flights of stairs, between stone walls, dark with tiny windows, halted before a room, and throwing open the 'oak' and the inner door said 'Here you are, Sir. Your servant'll be here in arf an hour, and if these aren't the right rooms, he'll tell you Sir.'

You can imagine, ami, with what intense excitement I stepped into the first varsity rooms I'd ever seen. The first thing that struck me with amazement was the size. I had expected something rather less than the little end room at home. What I saw was a very low-roofed, rather uneven-floored room somewhat larger than the study at home. The furniture was of dark oak very richly carved, and valuable I should think. On the floor was a red carpet with great profusion of rugs. Besides the old furniture was a big modern sofa & several very easy chairs. There was also a little bed-room and a cupboard. I was awfully bucked with it and went on sitting down in one chair after another, and opening and shutting the 'oak' after Jo had left me.

I looked down on the quad. and saw a tall youth in spectacles talking to the porter. I began to wonder what I should do. Did one wear a gown for hall? How did one sit in hall? The question of wearing a gown was solved soon, because I heard someone in the opposite room saying to someone else 'Oh no, no gowns.' Presently I went down into the quad to prospect – but be of good cheer, cher ami, I am not going to keep up this detailed description much longer. I must try and give you a general account of the college in shorter terms.

The rooms I am in now are very nice tho' not so magnificent as the first ones (which turned out to be wrong). They really belong to a tremendous blood who is at the front – at least the furniture is all his. Of course this takes away from me the pleasure of choosing the things for myself; but then it is much better done than I could have afforded. There is a grand piano – couldn't we have great times, ami? It is getting to be quite homely to me this room, especially

[2] 'Jo', as he was called, was the college scout Cyril Haggis.
[3] Edward Hugh Martin Crawford.

when I come back to it by firelight and find the kettle boiling. How I love kettles![4]

Dinner is not in Hall now, as there are only 12 men in college, but in a small lecture room, and the dons don't turn up. For all other meals the scout brings you a cover in your rooms; tea etc you make for yourself. So far, I have done absolutely nothing. The Dean[5] refuses to map out any plans for me, on the ground that the Corps will take me all my time. Corps doesn't begin till Monday afternoon.

Now as to the human part of the place. None of the older men (from last or previous terms, I mean) take any notice of us freshmen, except to ask us for the salt and that sort of thing. There are 3 freshmen counting myself. One of them is quite impossible, and I and the other one, a certain Edgell,[6] have lived mostly together so far. He is writing letters in my rooms at the moment. Well what like is he? I can hardly say. First of all, in tastes he is no friend of ours. He doesn't read, and is interested in mechanics – ugh! However, he can talk not without interest on a good many subjects, among which we reached religion, when I was foolish enough to tell him my own views. 'Natheless he so endured.' He is very useful to me, because his father was at Univ. and has told him all the tricks of the trade. He also makes excellent cofee, and so I am sticking to him at present. Later on, as I get to know more people, perhaps I shall find some real friends here also.

The only other thing I can think of that may interest you – in that way – is the Shelley memorial which you would love. I pass it every morning on the way to my bath. On a slab of black marble, carved underneath with weeping muses, lies in white stone the nude figure of Shelley, as he was cast up by the sea – all tossed into curious attitudes with lovely ripples of muscle and strained limbs. He is lovely. ⟨(No – not since I came back. Somehow I haven't even thought of it.)⟩

[4] This lovely set of rooms is number 5 on Staircase 12, and overlooks Radcliffe Quad.

[5] John Clifford Valentine Behan (1881–1957) came to Oxford in 1904 as the first Rhodes Scholar from the State of Victoria, Australia. He became a Fellow of Law at University College in 1909 and was the Dean of the college from 1914–17. He returned to Australia and was the Warden of Trinity College in the University of Melbourne from 1918–46.

[6] Lawrence Fayrer Arnold Edgell (1898–1950) after receiving his B.A. in 1923, read Theology at Wycliffe Hall, Oxford, and was ordained a priest in the Church of England in 1927. After some years with the Church Missionary Society in Persia, he returned home and was the vicar of several churches, his last being in Shalford, Essex, from 1946 until his death.

Well, there you have all my news. Now let us talk about yourself. So write at once and tell me everything, and be of good cheer. We get potatoes every day here. – Addio,

Jack

62

[University College
6 May 1917]

My dear Galahad,

I am afraid this letter is not punctual and I am further afraid that many of my letters this term will not be punctual. We do not do really much here, but somehow the whole day is frittered away in little things. As for going on to my diabolical romance – tis out of the question. Your last letter is lost, so what shall I jaw about?

Well first, let me most earnestly advise you to get Gautier's 'Un Trio de Romans'[1] when you next want a French book. It is really excellent; one story rather reminds me of the Cosmo episode in 'Phantastes'. I am afraid I shall get too many in that edition, it is so very convenient. The 2nd vol. of the Earthly Paradise stands in my bookcase here, but I have progressed only a few pages since coming up. However I am going to make out a regular time-table for each day & try if I cannot get more time like that. When you are not made to work and when there is such a lot to do, it is very hard to get on with things.

It is most glorious weather here now and we spend most of our spare afternoons on the river. Edgell knows something about rowing, so I am gradually learning through many blunders. We ran someone down today (Sunday) greatly to the amusement of the assembled river: but as the other wasn't a varsity man of course it didn't matter!

My chief 'cross' at present is my friend, or rather my companion, Edgell, whose limitless piety I don't think I can endure any longer. He has all your particular faults, cher ami, with none of your merits. He is economical, methodical to the verge of insanity. He is fully convinced of his own moral superiority, and lectures me on my 'weakness of character'. Still, I suppose I must stick to him until I get to know some of the senior men a bit better!

Don't imagine however that I'm grumbling. The place is on the whole absolutely ripping. If only you saw the quad. on these moon-lit nights with the long shadows lying half across the level, perfect grass and the tangle of spires & towers rising beyond in the dark!

[1] Théophile Gautier (1852).

Oh ami, ami, what times we could have here together: you really must come. What talks we could have in the privacy of these rooms by firelight while the kettle was boiling. Item, you must get a ground room if you come, as even I begin to find the dashing up & down stairs rather tiring. I am finding a whole lot of Malvernians here – a new one every day. How lovely the country must be at home now – I hope you are still on half time and are having some nice afternoons ⟨(– in that way?)⟩ in the garden. Which reminds me, I have 'Digestive' biscuits every day for tea, & always wish I was sharing them with you instead of with that six feet of spectacled priggery!

The book shops here are rather adorable, and also our college library. Still better is the Library of the Union Society (a club everyone belongs to) where I spent this morning turning over one book after another and enjoying myself hugely. My books have not finished binding yet, but of course I shall give you a full account so soon as they arrive. The Maeterlink's are to be plain dark blue cloth, and the 'Literature Française au Moyen Age' in green linnen. I'm afraid this [is] all the length of letter I can raise. Do reply soon and at full length.

63

[University College
13 May 1917]

Cher Ami,

As you seem able to bear my boring accounts of life here, I may give you a little more. To-day, for instance, (Sunday) has so far been a very prosperous and a not untypical day. I woke at about 7 o'clock with the pleasing reflection that there was no early parade and read Wm. Morris and Gautier till 8.30. I then went down to the bathroom and had first a hot & then a cold bath – which is 'done' here.

We are gradually getting to know people and a very senior man, Butler,[1] has asked us to 'brekker' (breakfast) this morning. I arrived in his rooms a little too early, and thus had an opportunity of studying his books, which I always consider the best introduction to a new acquaintance. I was pleased to find Keats, Shelley, Oscar Wilde, Dante & Villon, as well as Plutarch & one of the lately executed Sinn

[1] Theobald Richard Fitzwalter Butler (1894–1976), who was to achieve great distinction as a lawyer, was called to the Bar, Inner Temple, in 1921, became Master of the Bench in 1960, and Chancellor of the Diocese of Peterborough in 1962.

Fein poets: for Butler is an Irishman & a nationalist. I was just trying to find out the publisher of the nice Plutarch when Butler arrived with the other guests, Edgell & a certain Edwards[2] & we sat down to brekker. I like Butler exceedingly. Of course he talked a good deal to me about Ireland: it seems that he knows Yeats quite well, & also Gilbert Murray.[3] Otherwise the talk turned on books. Can I confess that I had certain spiteful pleasure in seeing Edgell, who has been lecturing me on morals & motor bykes for the last fortnight, very much out of his element in such a conversation?

After brekker we all decided that a bathe would be a very sound plan. Some kind friend lent me a bycyle and thus we set out. It was a perfectly lovely morning with a deep blue sky, all the towers & pinnacles gleaming in the sun & bells ringing everywhere. We past down through quieter streets among colleges and gardens to the river, & after about quarter of an hour's ride along the bank came to the bathing places. Here, without the tiresome convention of bathing things we enjoyed a swim. The bathing place is a lovely backwater surrounded by those *level* (you know the sort) daisied & buttercuped fields & overhung by those short fluffy trees – named – I don't know.

So about 11.30 we arrived back at college and I am come straight thence to the Union. 'The Union' is a club to which nearly everyone in the varsity belongs. It has a writing room of strictest silence, where I am scribbling this, and an admirable library where I have already passed many happy hours and hope to pass many more. Oh, Galahad, you simply must come up after the war. This at present is only a shadow of the real Oxford, yet even so I never was happier in my life. Do make an effort!

By the way my books have finished binding and are absolutely ripping. In a fit of extravagance I am getting two more done. One is an Apuleius: he as you know wrote the book in which the 'Cupid & Psyche' story occurs. I have found his complete works in the college library and their brooding magic no less than their occasional

---

[2] John Robert Edwards (1897–   ) taught Classics at Chigwell School and Merchant Taylors' School, Crosby, until 1931. He was then appointed Headmaster of Grove Park Grammar School, Wrexham, where he remained until 1935. He went from there to the Liverpool Institute High School as Headmaster where he remained until his retirement in 1961. Writing to me on 6 January 1978, he recalls that Lewis in 1917 'could join in any discussion on any subject and talk fluently and knowledgeably; he was particularly interested in those early days in religion and was particularly challenging in his scepticism'.

[3] Gilbert Murray (1866–1957) was the Regius Professor of Greek at Oxford 1908–36, and the distinguished translator of Greek plays.

voluptuousness & ridiculous passages have made me feel that I must get a copy of my own. What lots I shall have to show you when I come down!

But voila que je suis égoiste! I have done nothing but jaw about myself. However reply by jawing about *your*self & tell me all you are reading & thinking & how things go forward at home.

Jack

64

[University College
20 May 1917]

Cher Ami,

I wonder if we could not arrange our letters so that they don't always cross. I mean, as things at present are, you will not have got this until you have written your own replying to my last. This spoils the 'conversational' effect of letter writing. However, I am afraid Sunday is now my only possible time, and if it is yours too I am afraid there is no help for us.

I am glad to hear that you like Milton: I was sure he would appeal to you. The language is, I admit, not always easily understood: tho' using English words, he often builds his sentences on a Latin framework which makes it almost meaningless to a purely English reader. Some words, too, he uses in very strange ways. For instance, when, at the opening of the 3rd Book you come to the line

'Or hear'st thou rather pure ethereal stream'[1]

remember that 'hear' means in this place 'hight', i.e. 'to be called'. What he wants to say is 'Shall I call thee rather "Pure, ethereal stream." ' Don't you love all the descriptions of Hell? (Item. When reading about the Shetlands in 'The Pirate'[2] I was disconsolate because I thought I should never see them. In reading about the scenery of Hell, I need have no such uneasiness!) You will also love the parts about Eden when you come to them.

The chief event in things of art this week has been my discovery of Albert Dürer. I don't know if you have heard of him before: he was a German engraver of the 16th century, and I have often heard him referred to as the 'most Romantic of engravers', the 'Founder of the Fantastic school in Art' etc. Yesterday I came across some post-card reproductions of his pictures, and bought some. I daresay they

---

[1] *Paradise Lost*, III, 7.

[2] By Sir Walter Scott (1821).

will dissapoint you, but I like them greatly: especially one 'Study of an old Man's Head'. Although not a modern, you can easily see that he is the father of Rackham and all this modern school of fantastic illustrators. But all this must wait for full discussion when I come down, & we can go over them side by side.

Life goes on very pleasantly here. Besides Butler (whom I mentioned in my last letter) the other most interesting person here is a man named Edwards. He is not a very attractive person, and has a rather unpleasant accent (tho' not so bad as some of my friends have!): what interests me about him is that he was an atheist till lately, and is now engaged in becoming a Catholic, or is very near it. He came into my rooms last night, and sat till about 12. We had a long talk about religion, Buddhism, poetry and everything else. How I like talking!

As to the other man, Butler, I like him better the more I know him (Item. He often comes to Portsalon so we may see him sometime). He is, however, not an immaculate character. I had often heard that he was very amusing when drunk, but I had no experience until last night. At about 10, he burst into my room exclaiming 'God bless you, God bless you.' He sank down on my sofa but soon rolled onto the floor, repeating in tragic accents 'I would that I were dead, and lying in the woods with the corpses of the great ones of Erin about me. (This is all out of some nationalist poet) None is unhappier than I, save only the great yellow bittern.' He continued lying on the floor reciting, expressing an ardent deisre to go and kiss the Dean, and calling on the 'Holy Mother of God', until Edwards and a rather pointless man called MacNicholl[3] came in to see the fun. We began to try to get him to bed, but he begged in pathetic tones to be left there on the floor for just ten minutes and swore 'by the Holy Ghost and by Venus Aphrodite' that he would go then. By about 11 we did actually succeed in getting him out. His mood had changed now and instead of wanting to lie 'dead in the wood' he wanted 'To be in the pine forest in the white arms of Aphrodite'. You see how a man of taste & reading preserves his natural character even when dead drunk. He used the most beautiful language. I went for a bathe with him this morning and he seemed almost quite recovered. He is going to lend me a copy of the nationalist poet from whom he was quoting from.

I have finished the 2nd vol. of Wm. Morris, all except the last story

[3] John Milne MacNicoll (1898–   ) matriculated in 1917, but in 1918 enlisted as a 2nd Lieut in the Royal Horse Artillery and served in Palestine. He did not return to Oxford.

of 'Ogier the Dane'. I don't think I shall order the next until I come down, as I have so little time for reading here. By the way – don't ever imagine, as I used to, that access to good libraries is an inducement to reading. Among thousands of interesting books it is impossible to settle down to one. Yes, I did and do think of Papillon on the river – especially when we pass pretty people.

Yours
Jack

65

[University College
27 May 1917]

Cher Ami,

First, lest we forget, I must answer your question. I do not know yet when I shall get down nor for how long: it is certain that we shall not be down for the whole vac., but even so, I think we shall be at home longer than a school holiday. I hope to be able to tell you exactly in my next letter.

You say that your books have come at last from Denny, and then add that you may give up buying books altogether. Am I to gather that this last parcel (consisting of what?) is very dissapointing? Personally I am being rather extravagant. This week's purchases include the poems of Thomson and Renan's 'Vie de Jésus'.[1] The Thomson here mentioned is not the modern but an 18th century man, whose best thing is a poem in Spencerian stanzas called 'The Castle of Indolence'.[2] Tis as good as the title suggests. The other (Nelson's 1/- edition), Renan's 'Vie de Jesus' you will probably have heard of: it is a life of 'Jeshua' written from a free thinker's point of view, and is very beautiful in style. I think you would not care for it, but I like it immensely. I have also ordered a copy of the first volume of Tennyson in a new edition by Macmillan. It is excellent in paper and title page & so on, but the binding is a kind of semi-limp leather that I don't much care for. However, as it is the only tolerable edition of Tennyson that I can hear tell of, I thought it fit to be bought. Dunsany's book was reviewed in the Times Literary Supplement some time ago, where they spoke of him as an experimenter in prose style. I should like to see his 'Tales of Wonder', but I do not think it would be worth 5/-.[3] Another good book I am reading at

---

[1] Joseph Ernest Renan, *La Vie de Jésus* (1863).

[2] James Thomson, *The Castle of Indolence* (1748).

[3] The review of Edward Dunsany's *Tales of Wonder* is found in *The Times Literary Supplement* (12 April 1917), p. 172.

present (from the Union Library) is Andrew Lang's and R. Haggard's 'The World's Desire' of which you have heard Chainie [Janie McNeill] speak very, very, very often. Item, tell Chainie that I am coaching with a friend of hers, Mr Campbell of Hertford.

The other morning I was surprised by Gundrede, (up for the day) Mrs and Cherry Robbins.[4] G. of course has gone but of the other two I have seen a good deal. Cherry is not pretty unfortunately but she is what I call a really ripping kind of person – an awfully good sort, and (greatest recommendation to us) a lover of books.

No – all days are not so pleasant as the Sundays. On week days I am called by my scout at 7.0. I tramp down to the parks for early parade, from which I return to bath and brekker at about 8.45. I then work till 1, have lunch, and set off for another parade from 2 till 4. At 4 I come back, have tea (either in college or at the Union) and go down to the river for a bathe. I get back to college at about 5.30, and then read English until dinner at 7. In the evenings I work mildly or talk or sometimes play cards or even go for a byke ride, getting to bed at about 11. It is on the whole a very pleasant life.

To-day (Sunday) Butler had brekker with me and afterwards we bathed. We had a long talk on the rival merits of Swinburne & Keats, the improbability of God, and Home Rule. Like all Irish people who meet in England we ended by criticisms on the invincible flippancy and dulness of the Anglo-Saxon race. After all, there is no doubt, ami, that the Irish are the only people: with all their faults I would not gladly live or die among another folk.

Edgell – the other fresher of whom I have spoken – gets more and more wearisome every day: he is the most priggish, illiterate and narrow-minded ass I ever met. His chief subject of conversation is his relatives, especially his brother and cousin who have been killed at the front. Well of course I respect them for it, and I sympathise with him for loosing them. At the same time, I don't think they need be dragged into every single conversation, on every opportunity!

The country about here with its two rivers and its tall poplars, though not exciting is now beautifully fresh and green and sleepy. How I look forward to the hills of Down, the little copses and the view over the lough! I am sorry my letters from here cannot be so long as they were from Bookham, but I really have not time. Addio,

yours
Jack

[4] Mrs Kittie Robbins (wife of Col. Herbert E. Robbins) was the sister of Mary, Lady Ewart – and, so, first cousin to Lewis's mother. Her daughter 'Cherry' was with the V.A.D. at a military hospital in Oxford during the war.

66

Cher Ami,

I am delighted to hear that you have at last arriven at 'The Victorians'.[1] The criticism that most of these novels begin with a very interesting part about the childhood and then get more conventional as they go on is only too true – at least for us who are attracted by 'childish things'. In this case I think it is certainly true that the school scenes are the best (very good in every way). But there is no very violent slump in the interest and I for one followed the rest of it very eagerly. She is a most excellent character.

Last Sunday I began reading Blackwood's 'Prisoner in Fairy-land'[2] in the Union Library, & liked it immensely. But I think I shall wait until they publish it in the 7d edition & then get it for myself. My other book 'The Castle of Indolence' goes on excellently: it is quite a good imitation of Spencer, and has a certain shy humour mixed with it, which Spencer himself has not. I am also, in Italian, reading Ariosto's 'Orlando Furioso', from which there are many stories in your Andrew Lang romance book. It is in the same edition as my Tasso which you have probably forgotten: I am just reading a canto here & a canto there, and it is very good, really suggesting 'Phantastes' more than the Faery Queen.

How beautiful Donegal must be now! I often think how lovely twould be if you could take up this city of Oxford bodily and put it down somewhere

'By a northern sea'

between the mountains of Donegal. I am afraid the river would have to go, though!

I hope you are right as to the possibilities of my finding my particular kind of love. ⟨Butler tells me that the person to read on my subject is a Frenchman of the 17th century called the Visconte de sade⟩: his books, however, are very hard to come by.

I cannot understand Denny's behaviour to you, as they never gave me any trouble at all. How you would love the shops here! At home you have to hammer what you want into their thick heads: here

[1] By Netta Syrett (1915).
[2] Algernon Henry Blackwood (1913).

they know all about publishing and literature (Sanskrit or Russian if you want!) & your only effort is to conceal your ignorance.

I do wish you were here: what long and private talks we could have. Somehow the place seems to lend itself to endless conversation. Butler came in and sate till twenty to two last night. The piano too would be a perpetual joy, for Cherry was playing it when she was in here to tea the other day, and says it is quite good. I suppose Cherry has only met you for a few moments, as I have never heard you speak of her. She is a real sportsman, the sort of person I really like. Quel domage que sa figure n'égale pas son ésprit! Yet after all she is plain in rather a pleasing kind of way when you get to know her. Mrs Robbins I also like immensely.

In prose at present I am reading one of those 'Home University Library' books on 'Psychic Research'.[3] It is a subject in which my old interest is awakening: so far the phenomena are certainly extraordinary, tho' I fear they do not actually prove the agency of real spirits – yet. They tell me that Dodds,[4] who is coming up next week is very interested in the subject also, so I shall be able to have a talk about it.

I quite agree with you that cards are the most utter and senseless and losing waste of time ever invented, and I never play them from inclination but only because you can't go on refusing the same people if you have nothing to do. We have had a college group of our 9 surviving undergrads. so I will be able to point out to you all these characters.

Item, somebody pointed me out Bridges[5] in the street the other day. How I should like to meet him! Really cannot spare a second longer, now old man. Write soon & LONG, returning good for evil –

Yours
Jack

[3] William Fletcher Barrett, *Psychical Research* [1911].
[4] Eric Robertson Dodds (1893–   ), a fellow Ulsterman, was Lecturer in Classics at University College, Reading, 1919–24, Professor of Greek in the University of Birmingham 1924–36, and Regius Professor of Greek in Oxford 1936–60. For an interesting picture of his undergraduate years at 'Univ.' see his autobiography *Missing Persons* (1977).
[5] Robert Bridges (1844–1930), the Poet Laureate from 1913 to 1930.

67

[Keble College,
Oxford.
10 June 1917]

My dear Arthur,

I must admit that you have a very reasonable ground of complaint against me. But you must remember that my whole way of life has now completely changed, and that I have practically no time for reading or writing except at week-ends. However I will try to do better in future, tho' I hope that you, who have more time to yourself, will give me longer letters than you get: just as, when I get to the trenches, tho' I may not be able to write to you at all, I shall hope to hear from you at regular intervals. This may seem a one-sided bargain: yet surely it is fair, that when one of us has escaped and the other has got into this military nonsense, the freeman should make some allowances for the slave.

I will only tell you very shortly of the new life as there is not much of interest. It is a great change to leave my own snug room at Univ. for a carpetless room, with beds without sheets or pillows, kept miserably tidy & shared with another cadet, at Keble. However, tho' the work is very hard & not very interesting, I am by now quite reconciled to my lot. It is doing me a lot of good (days of trench digging and route marching under a blazing sun are a fine cure for tendencies in THAT direction) and I have made a number of excellent friends – especially Somerville,[1] a scholar of Eton & King's (Cambridge) who is very well up in books. My room-mate Moore (of Clifton)[2] is quite a good fellow too, tho' a little too childish and virtuous for 'common nature's daily food'. The advantages of being in Oxford are very great, as I can get week end leave (from 1 o'clock Saturday till 11 o'clock p.m. Sunday) and go to Univ. where I enjoy the rare luxury of sheets & a long sleep.

Last week end was a great success. Butler and Dodds (Dodds a Campbellian[3] and Univ. man whom you must have heard of) both

---

[1] Martin Ashworth Somerville (1898–1918) became a member of King's College, Cambridge, in April 1917. During the war he served, as a member of the Rifle Brigade, in Egypt and Palestine and died 21 September 1918 of wounds received in action.

[2] Edward Francis Courtenay ('Paddy') Moore (1898–1918) came into the Oxford OTC from Clifton College, Bristol.

[3] An 'Old Boy' of Campbell College, Belfast.

got 'Firsts' in their Schools and gave a dinner to celebrate the event, at which, for the first time in my life, I was royally drunk. ⟨I am afraid I must have given myself away rather as I went round imploring everyone to let me whip them for the sum of 1*s*. a lash!⟩ All this happened at Exeter in the rooms of an Indian called Gokeldas: but as I was not the only person in that condition, the Dean of Exeter got fed up with the row and sent round a notice that Mr Gokeldas' guests must leave the College at once. I have absolutely no recollection of the walk home, and in fact, tho' I remember leaving Exeter, knew nothing more till I woke up on the floor of my own room at about 9 next morning.[4]

The story that you have a headache after being drunk is apparently quite a lie ⟨(like the other one about going mad from THAT).⟩ But the interesting part is that Butler, having muddled recollections of my last night's ⟨desire to whip,⟩ challenged me on the subject, and we had a long conversation. ⟨He's not himself that way inclined. He has come across the thing in the course of his varied reading. The right name for it is sadism, so called from its great originator of the 16th century, M. Le Vicomte de Sade whose history we looked up in a French 'Dictionaire de la Bibliographie Nationale'.⟩

Butler (and nearly every one else) has now gone down, so that this week end I have lived very quietly, but no less happily in an empty College, sleeping late, and reading my new volume of Maeterlinck's plays. Two of them I have read before in English ('Pelleas & Melisande', 'L'Interieur') but all could be read with pleasure a score of times. They all have a peculiar mystic dreamlike atmosphere about them, and tho' much more possible are somehow much more wierd than 'L'Oiseau Bleu', especially the 'most musical, most melancholy' 'Alladine et Palomides', where Palomides may be the Malory Palomides or may not.

I have also been spending more time than usual in the College Library, dipping here and there. Did I tell you that there was a queer little volume in Latin by Cornelius Agrippa the great magician (mentioned in Cosmo's episode)? Unfortunately the print is so execrable and the worms have done their work so well that I cannot

---

[4] He seems not to have exaggerated the degree of his intoxication as the Indian he calls 'Gokeldas' was Madhavji Dharamsi Morarji Gokuldas (1896–1931) and a member of Brasenose College – and it was, undoubtedly, in that college, rather than in Exeter, that the party was held. The Dean of Brasenose, W. T. S. Stallybrass (1883–1948), was later to become Principal of that college in 1936.

make much of it: but I love to have it in my hands, and think of all the wizards who have centred their hopes on it – perhaps on this very copy, for it is some 300 years old.[5]

I have also read a good deal of Spencer in a big folio and of my favourite Johnson. On taking up my Homer this morning it was shocking to find how strangely the Greek came to me after three weeks soldiering. I do hope I shall not forget all I know, and come back from the war a great empty-headed military prig!

Yesterday afternoon I spent on the river with Cherry Robbins, in whom I am pleased to find an ardent admirer both of Arthur Rackham & of Wagner. She has heard 'Die Walküre' at Covent Garden & has read the Ring in my edition. She says that the stage is a terrible come down to those who have seen Rackham's pictures first and that she listened with her eyes shut most of the time. The 'Wotan' however was splendid, and really terrifying. She is also very keen on Norse mythology, and for this reason praised the Ring above 'Parsifal' or 'Lohengrin'. Although the subject did not arise, I rather think from some phrazes she let fall about Norse & Christian mythology, that I shall find another agnostic here. How sad that so interesting a girl is not beautiful (tho' she is certainly not nearly so plain as I at first imagined) Even sadder that she should like Browning and have a morbid appetite for photography!!

I am in a strangely productive mood at present and spend my few moments of spare time in scribbling verse. When my 4 months course in the cadet battalion is at an end, I shall, supposing I get a commission allright, have a 4 weeks leave before joining my regiment. During it I propose to get together all the stuff I have perpetrated and see if any kind publisher would like to take it. After that, if the fates decide to kill me at the front, I shall enjoy a 9 days immortality while friends who know nothing about poetry imagine that I must have been a genius – what usually happens in such cases. In the meantime my address is

> No 738 Cadet C. S. Lewis
> 'E' Company,
> Keble College
> Oxford.

[5] He is writing about either vol. I or vol. II of the *Opera* (Lugduni: Per Beringos Fratres [1531]) of Henricus Cornelius Agrippa (1486–1535) of Nettesheim. This same, very rare, leather-bound work which Lewis handled is now on permanent loan from University College to the Museum of the History of Science in Broad Street, Oxford.

Write me a nice long letter and help to keep up other interests amid all this damned military show.

Yours as ever
Jack

68

[University College
8 July 1917]

Chèr Ami,

The best, in fact the only really important tale in Gautier's little book was the last one 'Avatar', which I would have had you read first & read the other two or not, as might seem worthwhile afterwards. It was this third one that I compared, not to Phantastes as a whole, but to the Cosmo story – which, you know, has rather a different flavour from the main book. I must admit that the resemblence is rather a vague one: still, I am sure that you will like 'Avatar' if you give it a trial. In French I am going on with this new volume of Maeterlinck's plays. The last one 'La Morte de Tintagiles' is even better than Palomides, and quite one of the eeriest and most overwhelming things I have struck yet – though I am not quite sure if I understand what the author is driving at. You must certainly get this volume, or borrow mine someday.

'From a College Window' is one of the 5 or 6 Benson books that I have read: but as the titles are so vague, I never can remember which is which. I enjoyed them all very much, they are nice companionable reading for lonely men. Perhaps the 'Upton Letters' was the one that pleased me best.[1]

I was sure that you wd. like 'Balder Dead': I used to prefer it to 'Sohrab' tho' I don't now.[2] All the same it is a topping piece of work, especially the journey, as you say, and the description of the ghosts, and the ending with its impressive pause before the glorious line

'At last he sighed & set forth back to Heaven.'[3]

Doesn't it all make you think of the dear old days when we were writing our great opera on Loki & Odin & the rest? Indeed I am recalled to our earlier stage by other things as well: for all morning I

---

[1] Arthur Christopher Benson, *From a College Window* (1906); *The Upton Letters* (1905).

[2] Matthew Arnold, *Balder Dead* (1853); *Sohrab and Rustum* (1853).

[3] *Balder Dead*, III, 566.

T.S.T.–G

have been reading the German text of 'Siegfried'. The splendid first Act has quite stured up my old Wagnerian enthusiasms, & for the first time this twelve months or so I have really felt the want for a gramophone. Of course a great deal of my pleasure in it is owing to Rackham's pictures: still it is lovely wild poetry &, like everything else, much better in its own language. The edition is the same as my one of the Dutchman & I can get the other three parts of the Ring in the same: when I have them all I think I shall bind the 4 thin volumes into one nice book & have a really good addition to my library.

This week end, as you gather, I am again spending in Univ. But the Dean says I can't come any more, as the Scouts are going for the holidays!! Damn him! Do you know, Ami, I am more homesick for this College than ever I was for Little Lea. I love every stone in it: I do wish we could be here together after the war!

Last night, at about nine o'clock I wandered out into the deserted quad. & after 'strolling' for some time went up a staircase where nobody ever goes in these war days into the oldest part of the College. The windows here are all tiny ivy covered & stained so that it was very dark already. I walked up & down long passages with locked rooms on each side, revelling in 'desolation'. The 'oaks' of these rooms were mostly (as I say) locked, but by good luck I found one open & went in. On the inner door the faded name 'Mr Carter' greeted me: inside was a tiny room, smaller than my own at home, very dark & thick with dust. It seemed almost sacrilege to turn on the lights in such a forsaken place, but I simply had to inspect it. The furniture was all just as the owner must have left it & his photos were there on the wall. I also inspected his book (mostly ordinary Everymen) including 'Lavengro', 'Tristram Shandy', [Edmund] Burke's Speeches & 'Tom Jones'.[4] I suppose this sounds trivial to you; but perhaps you can picture the strange poetry of the thing in such a time & place. I wonder who Carter is, and if he has been killed yet, & why he left his pile of music so untidily on the dressing table?[5]

I had another thrill too, when I got up (quite dark by now) into a sort of attic place full of old trunks etc. & heard a strange thumping noise just beside me. I was mystified for a while, till I realized that I

[4] Henry Fielding (1749).
[5] Arthur Norwood Carter (1891–   ), whose rooms Lewis was in, matriculated as a Rhodes Scholar from New Brunswick in 1913. He not only survived the war, but has sent two sons – also Rhodes Scholars – to University College.

was just behind the big college clock & this was the ticking of it. You know how sad & grand a big clock sounds in a lonely place! These are all rather conventional remarks, but I really did get into a great mood among all the cobwebs. When I came back into the quad & saw all the empty windows staring at me all round, I turned a bit creepy & was glad to get back to my own rooms & settle down on the 'Faerie Queene', & another book, which I must tell you about.

This is a book on William Morris in the 'English Men of Letters Series' by Alfred Noyes[6] which I took out of the Library. It is chiefly interesting for its venomous hostility towards Mackail's great 'Life of W.M.' which it loses no opportunity of attacking. This of course is rather petty: but I must admit that the book has some very good points about it, & certainly appreciates 'Jason' far better than Mackail does.

Yes, I must say that the society of some interesting person of the other sex is a great anodyne in a life like this – especially if it is one of the very few people who share our own pet tastes – Wagner, Rackham and the rest. Cherry has been away on leave this last week, and I find this causes quite a gap in my routine. A propos, when is there any prospect of your long expected visit being paid to Oxford. If you were here for a week-end I could come & stay with you somewhere in the town, & I think that the time would pass pleasantly.

It is pouring with rain outside as I write. If I do ever send my stuff to a publisher, I think I shall try Maunsel, those Dublin people, and so tack myself definitely onto the Irish school. What castles in the air – but still better have a cloud castle than no castle at all –

Yours,
Jack

69

University College,
Oxford.
24/7/17

Cher Ami,
How horribly conventional to be writing on ordinary note paper just like other people – why I'll be putting the date at the top soon if I'm not careful. A propos de Maunsel, you say that the patriotic motive could have no influence on me. Well perhaps that may be deserved: tis true that I have no patriotic feeling for anything in

[6] Alfred Noyes, *William Morris* (1908).

England, except Oxford for which I would live and die. But as to
Ireland you know that none loves the hills of Down (or of Donegal)
better than I: and indeed, partly from interest in Yeats and Celtic
mythology, partly from a natural repulsion to noisy drum-beating,
bullying Orange-men and partly from association with Butler, I
begin to have a very warm feeling for Ireland in general. I mean the
real Ireland of Patsy Macan etc, not so much our protestant north.
Indeed, if I ever get interested in politics, I shall probably be a
nationalist (another subject for us to quarrel on, you see). Of course
one sound reason for choosing Maunsel is that they are only a second-
rate house and therefore more likely to give me some attention.

I suppose that by now you are nearly at the end of 'Avatar', and
see what I meant by comparing it to the Cosmo story. It is an
excellent little novel, I think, as voluptuous and magical as only you
and I can appreciate. The titles of Benson's essays which you quote
bring back memories of pleasant mornings over my tea in bed at
home.

Good God, if only I could get back to it all! And yet I am not
nearly so unhappy as I ought to be. This week I have been reading
the works of Bishop Berkely, an eighteenth century country man of
ours, & philosopher. Published under the title of Principles of
Human Knowledge etc'[1] in the Everyman. The part I have been
reading is 3 dialogues written to prove the existence of God – which
he does by dis-proving the existence of matter. The reasoning is very
subtle but not difficult. Look here, oh my Galahad, philosophy is a
subject I am just arriving at, so why shouldn't we start abreast & read
it side by side. After Berkely I shall try Hume or Descartes also in
Everyman. What do you say? Expend 1/- on Berkely and have a go
on those 3 Dialogues!

Your idea of the old wizard, up in the clock-tower, the in dwelling
spirit of this dear college since Alfred's time,[2] is excellent; and when
I am in the mood again I must write on it either in prose or in verse
(outher in verse, as Malory would say).

You must remember a copy of Pater's 'Renaissance' badly stained
with hair oil in my cupboard. I tried to read it some time syne when
I knew even less of liter[ature] and art than I do know now, – I found
it rather stiff. Pater is called a great prose stylist – but except Malory,
Bunyan, Ruskin and the Authorised Version of the Bible, I am afraid
I have not much ear for prose style.

[1] George Berkeley, *Principles of Human Knowledge* (1710).
[2] University College, according to some histories, was founded by
Alfred the Great.

I find that we get 4 days leave in about 3 weeks. Unless they allow me some time for travelling it will mean very little time at home for me, and of that little even less can be devoted to you: though you know my wishes. However I trust we shall have some few hours of happiness together. How I long to see your new books & to shew you mine – especially the ones I got bound, which I hope you will approve. Then too I will choose that present which you have so kindly offered to give me. (And so there will be no sinful waste on postal orders to worry the just.)

I must dry up now. Sorry this letter is late, but I lost it when half finished & have found it again in a pocket only to-day (Teusday).

Yours
Jack

70

University College,
Oxford.
[4 August 1917]

Cher Ami,

Before I go on to anything interesting I must just have one little growl at you about something in your last epistle. You express a fear that my father 'may take into his head' to stay at home during my day or two of leave. Well I resent this 'take into his head' tone. A man is living absolutely alone: both his sons are in the army and one of them – who will soon be 'out' and in the infantry, not the A.S.C. or the Friends' Ambulance Corps – gets the first day's leave he has had since joining. And then you talk about the man 'taking it into his head' to see something of him! I am afraid that my father will most certainly 'take it into his head' to stay at home. But I hope to be able to see something of my Galahad, though I fear not much.

I was interested to hear that you liked Tristram Shandy – I think I told you about seeing a copy of it in one of the deserted rooms of Univ. Personally I have tried in vain to see the good points of it. The absolute disconnection or scrappiness, the abundant coarseness of an utterly vulgar, non-voluptuous sort and the general smoking-room atmosphere of the book were too much for me. In all these points it is the direct opposite of our quiet, balanced & delicately humourous Jane Austen. Tell me more about it in your next letter and try to shew me its merits: one often learns to appreciate a book through one's friends in this way. What edition are you reading it in?

I am delighted to hear that you enjoyed Comus – it is agreed to be one of the most perfect things in English poetry, and if you prefer it to Paradise Lost you have Saintsbury[1] (but not little me) to back you up. Don't you love the opening speech

'Above the smoke & stir of this dim spot . . .'[2]

– which always reminds me of our walks over the clean hills when we look down into the Nibbelheim below. Also the descriptions of the forest and the weird sounds that lonely shepheards have heard on its outskirts are very weird. I think the best thing of all is the last song with its allusions to

"Hesperus and his daughters three
That sing about the golden tree',[3]

– so beautifully lonely and romantic. I hope you won't give up your idea of reading Berkely; he is, I should think, a very good philosopher to begin on: perhaps that little book in the Home University series 'Problems of Philosophy' would help too.

By the way I have forgotten to tell you any news about leave. It was going to be from next Friday till next Teusday, but that has been changed. It is now going to start on Wednesday[4] 9th & go on till that Sunday midnight. A lot depends on whether I can get any extension for travelling, which is still

'in even poise.'[5]

If I can't it will be pretty poor.

You have started the question of prose style in your letter and ask whether it is anything more than the 'literal meaning of the words'. On the contrary it means less – it means the words themselves. For every thought can be expressed in a number of different ways: and style is the art of expressing a given thought in the most beautiful words and rythms of words. For instance a man might say 'When the constellations which appear at early morning joined in musical exercises and the angelic spirits loudly testified to their satisfaction'. Expressing exactly the same thought, the Authorised Version says 'When the morning stars sang together and all the sons of God

---

[1] George Edward Bateman Saintsbury, *Short History of English Literature* (1898).
[2] John Milton, *Comus* (1637), 5.
[3] *ibid.*, 982–3.
[4] A mistake for Thursday.
[5] *Comus*, 410 ('an equal poise').

shouted for joy.'[6] Thus by the power of style what was nonsense becomes ineffably beautiful. See?

Talking about 'Comus', I forgot to mention my new edition of it. The binding is not interesting. The paper is a kind of parchment (like your Omar Khayyam) and it is illustrated by the person who did 'Tchainie's' copy of the 'High History of the Holy Grael'. A thoroughly desirable book of which I hope you will approve.

Have lots to talk about but no time, and too dead tired as we were up till 2 o'clock last night doing 'attack' and then got up at the usual hour of 6.30 again this morning.

Yours
Jack

[Shortly after he was billeted in Keble College, Lewis's room-mate E. F. C. ('Paddy') Moore invited him to meet his mother Mrs Janie King Moore (1872–1951). Mrs Moore was 45 at the time and had for some years been separated from her husband Courtenay Edward Moore (1870–1951). While Mrs Moore's home was nominally in Bristol, she had, during the period of Paddy's training in Oxford, taken rooms there with her daughter Maureen (b. 1906) to be near him. Lewis seems to have taken a great liking to Mrs Moore from the first, and even, as this and subsequent letters show, to have been youthfully infatuated by her. He was on leave in Belfast from 9–11 August, after which he went for a week's training in Warwick. He was on leave again from 18 September–18 October, and much to his father's chagrin he spent the first three weeks with the Moores in Bristol, not arriving home till 12 October. It was probably during this time that he confided to Arthur Greeves his feelings for Mrs Moore. News arrived while he was at home that he had been gazetted into the 3rd Somerset Light Infantry and he joined this regiment in Crown Hill, near Plymouth, on 19 October.]

[6] Job xxxviii. 7.

71

3d Somerset Light Infantry,
Crown Hill,
Plymouth
Sunday [28? October 1917]

Cher Ami,

'At last' you will say, and I admit I should have written long ago. I am the more sorry to have to begin my letter by saying something rather ungracious. Since coming back & meeting a certain person[1] I have begun to realize that it was not at all the right thing for me to tell you so much as I did. I must therefore try to undo my actions as far as possible by asking you to try & forget my various statements & not to refer to the subject. Of course I have perfect trust in you, mon vieux, but still I have no business to go discussing those sort of things with you. So in future that topic must be taboo between us.

And now to tell you all the news. I am quite fairly comfortable here, we are in huts: but I have a room to myself with a fire in it & so am quite snug. The country is glorious – very wild & hilly & we are up a good height ourselves. From the camp I can enjoy a fine land-scape – nice cosy little bits of green country with cottages & water & trees, then woodier hills rising at last into big, open moors that make up the horizon. It is especially lovely in the mists of early morning or of night.

There is very little work to do here, so you will see that I might be worse off. I even manage to get a little reading done. At present I am engaged on Hawthorne's 'Transformation' in the Bohn's 1/– edition. In spite of repeated advice from me I don't think you have ever read this man. This one is very good indeed & has a lot about painting in it & some fine descriptions of Italian scenery. It is better than 'The Scarlet Letter',[2] but, of course, not so good as 'The House with the Seven Gables'. I have also got the 1st 2 volumes of Malory in the Temple Classics. The frontispieces are from designs by Beardsley.[3] They are v. good in the extremest style of mediaevalism – perhaps rather affected. One is of the finding of Excalibur & the other of someone giving Tristam a shield. In the Excalibur one, Merlin is shewn as a not very old clean-shaven but beautifully wizened man.

---

[1] Mrs Moore.

[2] Nathaniel Hawthorne, *Transformation* or *The Marble Faun* (1860); *The Scarlet Letter* (1850).

[3] *Le Morte d'Arthur* (1897).

Not what I'd have imagined him but good all the same. I have also bought in the ordinary Everyman 'Adam Bede' (by George Eliot) because it was the only thing I could find – the bookshops in Plymouth are rotten. I rather like the look of it and it is one of the best kind of Everyman as regards paper & type.

There is a rumour that we are all going to Ireland to quell the Sinn Feiner in a day or two – but the above address is safe to find me. Better not send the MS. book[4] till we're sure where I'll be.

Adieu mon ami, write soon

Jack

72

[Crown Hill,
Plymouth.
4? November 1917]

My dear Arthur,

To your last three letters, which, with all respect, indicate a sad falling under influences which I thought we had killed, I might make a very long reply indeed: but as free criticism is notoriously dangerous, even among friends of our standing, I will content myself with saying 'Don't be a damned fool' and je passerai outre.

I am so sorry that you have never heard before that 'Green'[1] arrived safely, for which many thanks. I rather thought I had told Mrs Moore, but perhaps she forgot to pass the information on, or, which is more likely, I forgot to give it in the first place. I approve most thoroughly of this shelter of yours in the garden, it will make a resort where we can always have privacy, even when everyone else is at home.

I shall certainly be in Ireland, by the way, though when & for how long I don't know. By the way (to descend into practical matters) after your leave, you go to a battalion at home until you are posted 'overseas' again. In my case the 3d Somersets to which I shall go is at Holywood Barracks, so that if I have a short respite before going out again, during *that* time also I shall be able to come up and see you of an afternoon. You will be glad to hear that I have revised my former 'patriotic' views about having a hospital in Craigavon: and I now regard a Tommy whether wounded or not as an abominable sight, especially among the scenes of home.

---

[4] The manuscript volume of his poems, *Metrical Meditations of a Cod*, some of which he hoped to publish.

[1] John Richard Green, *Short History of the English People*.

I am much obliged to you for the suggestion that I am now become 'a cheer-oh young man' (by the way, in my experience, only lodging house landladies etc. refer to people as 'young men') and if I had the energy would take my revenge by playing the part of one: but it would be too fatiguing.

I think the only real change that you will find in me is an increasing tendency towards philosophy; which has grown in the course of many interesting talks with my good friend Johnson, whom I hope to meet after the war as a scholar of Queens at Oxford. I think you would like him for his literary tastes and for a morality as strict as your own, but based on reasonable, not religious grounds: in music you would have many a quarrel with him and perhaps consider him a prig when he pronounces Chopin to be 'sugary' – his severe tastes apparently do not fall below Bach & Wagner. Debussy, strange to relate, he does not know.[2]

Both he and all the other literary people whom I have met since I left home for Oxford, have made me feel how deep is my ignorance of modern, that is to say, *contemporary*, literature, especially poetry. I have often sat in amazed silence amid glib talk of Rupert Brooke, Masefield, Chesterton, Bottomley etc. But after all I suppose our steady nibbling at older works is a safe-guard against 'crazes' – deadly things that arise so easily about a new writer. At the same time I am often surprised to find how utterly ignored Yeats is among the men I have met: perhaps his appeal is purely Irish – if so, then thank the gods that I am Irish.

But philosophy or metaphysics is my great find at present: all other questions really seem irrelevant till its ones are solved. I think you should take it up – its probings would at least save you from the intellectual stagnation that usually awaits a man who has found complete satisfaction in some traditional religious system.

By the way, you never told me what Carpenter's ⟨'The Intermediate Sex'[3]⟩ was like (– or did you? Yes, I think you did). I don't much fancy a book – 'something like the psalms' – it sounds as if it were that detestable thing known as 'prose-poetry' which is usually the cave of Adullam for those who can write NEITHER prose NOR

[2] This good friend was Laurence Bertrand Johnson who was elected a Scholar of Queen's College in the spring of 1917 but, being commissioned a 2nd Lieutenant in the Somerset Light Infantry on 15 April 1917, he was never able to matriculate at the University. Lewis was to see a good deal of him over the next few months, and not only did he like him better upon closer acquaintance, but he was to write a deeply affectionate reminiscence of him many years later in his autobiography, *Surprised by Joy* (ch. XII).

[3] Edward Carpenter, *The Intermediate Sex* (1908).

poetry. But perhaps I have not quite understood you.

Since I have been here I have had one parcel from Denny's containing 'The Ultimate Belief' by Clutton-Brock[4] and 'Eighteenth Century Studies' (in the Wayfarers' Library) by Austin Dobson.[5] Clutton Brock wrote a monograph on Wm. Morris in the 'Home University Series'[6] – that is all I knew about him until this new book of his was on everyone's lips. I expected it to be a fat tome at 12/6 but it turned out to be a mere pamphlet in size (though not in format) published by Constable at 2/6. I should like you to read it: it is partly about education, but is of great general interest and has given me new points of view, especially on the subject of morals. Hitherto I had always thought there were only two possible views of morals: either, if you believed in a religion, that they were a god-imposed law: or, if you did not, that they were merely rules for convenience – 'The rules of our prison-house' as Blake called them. This man gives a third possibility which is very interesting – regarding them as a kind of art, an object to be pursued for its own beauty. He says several other good things – also on aesthetics. The other book is just what I expected – pleasant & chatty & good to read in bed tho' not wildly exciting or original.

In your last letter – the 'neglected' one, written apparently on the model of Mrs Gumadge in one of Dicken's books[7] – as far as I remember you don't tell me much about your reading. I was glad to hear in a former letter that you liked Benvenuto Cellini – of course your knowledge of history would make it even more interesting to you than to me. The references to ⟨'That'⟩ were slightly involved and may easily have escaped you: I could scarcely find them again. I think you *would* like Andrew Lang's translation of the Odyssey: the Iliad is much less pleasing,[8] mind you don't try it.

I wonder have those walks in sun & rain vanished forever? I wonder shall I ever live as I lived then? However we must get on as best we can: I shouldn't drop that romance of yours except to begin something else. Burton's advice to the melancholy you know was 'be not idle, be not solitary'[9] – which has been corrected to 'be not

---

[4] Arthur Clutton-Brock, *The Ultimate Belief* (1916).

[5] Henry Austin Dobson, *Eighteenth-Century Essays* (1914).

[6] Arthur Clutton-Brock, *William Morris: His Work and Influence* (1914).

[7] Mrs Gummidge in Charles Dickens's *David Copperfield* (1850) – a 'lone lorn creetur'.

[8] Andrew Lang (with S. H. Butcher), *The Odyssey* (1879); (with W. Leaf and E. Myers) *The Iliad* (1883).

[9] Robert Burton, *The Anatomy of Melancholy* (1621), part I, sec. 2, mem. 2, subs. 6.

idle when you are solitary'.

Good bye, now, cher ami, write to me soon and tell me all your thoughts and doings.

Yours
Jack

[For weeks Lewis had heard rumours of his battalion's almost certain departure for Ireland to fight either the Sinn Fein or the Germans – which latter were said to have landed there. Suddenly, on Thursday, 15 November, they were ordered to the front following a 48-hour leave. As it was impossible for Lewis to go home, he set out for Mrs Moore's home in Bristol from whence he sent the following telegram to his father: 'Have arrived Bristol on 48 hours leave. Report Southampton Saturday. Can you come Bristol. If so meet at station. Reply Mrs Moore's address 56 Ravenswood Road Redlands Bristol. Jack.' Mr Lewis wired back: 'Don't understand telegram. Please write.' Clive Lewis did write and on 16 November he wired that he must report to Southampton by 4 o'clock on the 17th. His father made no effort to meet him either in Bristol or in Southampton and Lewis crossed to France on 17 November without seeing him. He reached the front line on his nineteenth birthday, 29 November, and it is from there that the next two letters were written.]

73

[France.]
14/12/17

My dear Galahad,

Just the proverbial few lines to answer your letter & to thank you for writing to Mrs Moore – she appreciated it very much and you may perhaps understand how nice & homely it is for me to know that the two people who matter most to me in the world are in touch.

I do get a certain amount of time for reading here, but of course it takes a long time to eat up a whole book in such small mouthfuls. I have just finished 'Adam Bede'. As you know, it is the first of hers I have read, and I earnestly advise you to read it. Of course as in so many of the older novelists there is a feeble happy ending stuck on to a tragedy: but the greater part of it is excellent. I am now reading a book of Balzac's called 'Le Père Goriot'.[1] It is rather a grim, realist production but quite good. I am writing home for Boswell, Milton, and another George Eliott in the Everyman.

[1] Honoré De Balzac, *Le Père Goriot* (1834).

I don't know when I can give you a decent letter but I may manage a note like this fairly often. Write as often & long as you can, mon ami, it's a great comfort –

ever yours
Jack

(Never tell mon père when I write to you – J)

74

[France.]
New Year's Eve [1917]

Cher Ami,

So glad to hear from you again yesterday evening. My last correspondent from Strandtown was 'Chanie' who wrote me a very typical would-be facetious letter – ⟨she certainly is an apalling woman and I shall⟩ never forget her on various occasions profaning our sacred haunts & soaking machines with her chatter. Do you remember the day we heard or thought we heard her in *the* wood and fled through many devious paths. Oh I'd just love to have another of those walks, particularly now in the snow – I suppose there's snow at home too, it is just thawing here. Don't think I've lost the taste for all that life.

I hope I have gained the new without losing the old and if we were all three – you know my meaning – together somewhere I'm sure we could be very happy, without any clash of interests. Apologies for not telling you much 'about myself' in my last letter. You know we always avoided practical details & anyway I assume that you hear all that from another source.

I am delighted to find that you appreciate 'Yeats' – I think the eeriness of that opening conversation in 'The Countess Kathleen' is splendid – rather like 'Christabel'[1] in a way

'What can have made the grey hen flutter so?'[2]

By the way will you send on my MS. book – the Metrical Meditations one – to Ravenswood Rd – I have yielded to oft repeated suggestions that it should go there.

Write as much as you can & as often

Yours
Jack

[1] By Samuel Taylor Coleridge (1816).
[2] William Butler Yeats, *The Countess Cathleen* (1892), scene I, line 1.

75

No 10 British Red Cross Hospital
Le Tréport
France.[1]
2/2/18

My dear Galahad,

Here I am safely ensconced in a bed in hospital, miles away from the line, thank the gods, and therefore at last in a position to write you a more or less respectable letter. The news of my illness will have been given you by Mrs Moore, so there is no need to waste words on that.

I was sorry to hear that you were in trouble over the death of your cousin:[2] I did not think that you had been so attached to him. Your letters are always very sad now. I hope you are not letting yourself 'fall into a melancholy' as Johnson would have said in some severe letter to his Boswell. Now is the time to rally all your interests about you & to paint & write for dear life.

I must admit fate has played strange tricks with me since last winter: I feel that I have definitely got into a new epoch of life and one feels extraordinarily helpless over it. How I should love one of our old afternoons again when we sat in your drawing room and discussed our tea and digestive biscuits: we were usually discontented over something but we had many a good laugh. As for the older days of real walks far away in the hills & journies out of town on the top of the tram – ma foi, that was the golden age infinitely remote 'mais ou sont les neiges d'antan'. Perhaps you don't believe that I want all that again, because other things more important have come in: but after all there is room for other things besides love in a man's life. As well, you should trust in me after I have given you so much confidence.

How rude of me! – to come thus far without thanking you for your parcel. Let me hasten to do so. I am still reading the 'Lavengro' (although I'm sorry to say both books were rather crushed when they arrived) & like it very well though of course I am most violently

[1] After some months on the front line Lewis fell ill with pyrexia, or 'trench fever' as the troops called it. On 1 February he was admitted to this hospital where he was to remain until 28 February.

[2] Thomas Malcolmson 'Malcolm' Greeves, born in 1895, was the son of Alfred Greeves of 'Fernbank', Belfast, and attended Campbell College from 1907–13. During World War I he served as a Flight Sub-Lieut with the Royal Navy, and was killed in action on 23 December 1917.

out of sympathy with the author at times – when he is loudly patriotic (as in the idiotic passage about painters in chapter XXI) or when he indulges in vulgar invective against the parent church. Of course *that* is probably agreeable enough to you – eh?, old puritan. I am also reading Boswell vol. II and enjoy very much renewing my acquaintance with all these great old gentlemen. It is the ideal book to read out here and to keep me in touch with all the quiet literary pleasant things in the world – one feels so cut off at times among all these godless philistines. However I'm having an excellent time here doing nothing – if only it could last.

You are lucky you know; it must be grand to look forward to an endless prospect of regular nights' sleep & comfortable chairs & good meals & books & everything decent & civilized

Well, good bye for the present mon vieux, keep true to the old interests – and don't let your relations influence you too much. You see I begin to fear for you now I can't watch over you & guard you against evil!

Yours
Jack

76

[No. 10 British Red Cross Hospital]
12/2/18

My dear Galahad,

Your letter dated the 24th January 1917 (sic) arrived a few days ago. It has certainly been a famous time, – a year and a month – in coming.

Your account of the various meetings with your friend Mr Thompson reads rather like our Boswell. 'I met him at luncheon at so-and-so: I dined with him at etc.' From which you will gather that I am still reading my 'Bo*zz*-well' (you remember the proper way of pronouncing it?) and enjoying it very much: it is such a rest to come back to after everything else. I also have a confession – to wit that I have given up Lavengro at any rate for the present. I gave up everything, of course, during a bad spell with high temperature which I have had since I last wrote to you: and now I feel no inclination to return to him. I don't object to the scheme of the book; in fact I think that in other hands, say A. C. Benson's, it might be charming. But my lack of sympathy with, nay by now my violent hostility to the author, prevents me from enjoying it. I expect you will think me rather foolish over this.

How do you like the tour to the Hebrides?[1] That book follows naturally after one has read the Life. I remember taking up the Everyman copy of it in a shop in Oxford (oh! for those bookshops in 'The Broad' – how we could ramble there!) & liking the paper and type.

I am sorry 'Tommy' has gone as he must have brightened up your 'circle' a good deal. ⟨Are you still bound to him by the chains of desire as well as by 'pure' friendship?⟩ I consider your reasons for not going to stay with him seem to me, with all due respect to be rot. A person with a weak heart may need quiet & may have to take care not to tire himself etc but Lord-a-mercy, short of actual hardships, why should he be more uncomfortable than other people? Of course you know best, but I must say if I ever thought you were refusing to come and stay with me for like cause I should think pretty poorly of your excuses – and your friendship. Not that I think you would, old man: I flatter myself that you could endure a few discomforts if we were together again.

'Shall we ever be the same again' Oh, how far we have travelled, you and I. To think of the things we've done: do you remember that day we walked up the glen in the rain, & everything was soaking? Or the evening up in Tiglath's field at dusk – the only real evening walk we ever had? Or the days of scheming over Loki when I first shewed you any work of mine, and you used to play over bits from the un-born opera? And the night when we first broached the 'nameless secrets of Aphrodite' and walked up and down that bit of road in the dark? And now – well, umph However, we may have good times yet, although I have been at a war and although I love someone.

You talk about the days of our book-discussing as being far off, but indeed I think they're the only thing that has survived, I still want to hear all you are reading & I am still buying books. Apropos I have written home (London, I mean) for 'The Autobiography of Benvenuto Cellini' (Everyman)[2] which I'll talk about some other time. Fancy you beginning to care for old books! I was beginning to love some of the old books in the college library at Univ. Of course London is the place, I suppose, for rumaging second hand shops.

You don't tell me what you are reading: always remember that it keeps us in touch. I'm afraid you'll be on very stodgy stuff – but then I'm getting stodgy too. After Benvenuto I'm thinking of reading Lockhart's 'Life of Scott' or else a life of 'G. Eliot'. Hers ought to be

[1] James Boswell, *The Journal of a Tour to the Hebrides* (1785).
[2] The Everyman edition was called *The Memoirs of Benvenuto Cellini written by Himself*, trans. Anne Macdonell (1913).

interesting. She had an affair with De Musset.[3] Is there any other edition of Green's Short History than the one that both our fathers have? Please answer this.

Good bye now, old man, try to keep in touch and feel to me as you used to –

Yours
Jack

77

[No. 10 British Red Cross Hospital.]
21/2/18

My dear Galahad,

Your last letter would have been answered earlier but for two reasons. 1 that as my last apparently crossed yours I thought you had something to go on with; 2 when I had actually started writing to you the other day, duty suddenly called to me and made me write to M. mon père instead. So you see your good precepts have stood in your own way!

I will dispose of the immensely uninteresting subject of my own health shortly – I am up again now and was out for the first time yesterday. Indeed I am beginning to tremble as to how long I shall be left here – but of course I may have the good luck of another relapse: but I doubt it, the gods hate me – and naturally enough considering my usual attitude towards them.

The country round, so far as I could see in yesterday's walk, quite comes up to expectation. I in vain tried to get onto a road leading to the cliffs and the sea, but, like the house in 'Alice in Wonderland'[1] they evaded me. I struck a very pretty little village however: the houses are mostly clay walled, which gives them a lovely colour, and are very ramshakle. The roofs are all of old old tiles and there are lots of old stone crucifixes, with their little offerings of grass & beads & things on them. Catholic Christianity is certainly more picturesque than puritanism. But what pleased me most was an old granary with little kinds of arrow slits under the eaves through which you could see oats or corn or whatever it was projecting: it gave you the impression of the place being filled to bursting and was somehow very homely, snug and comfortable. There are also pigeons all over the place, lodged in dovecots of the real old type that you see in pictures.

[3] He is probably thinking of Alfred De Musset's affair with the French novelist, George Sand.
[1] Lewis Carroll, *Alice's Adventures in Wonderland* (1865).

3

little kinds of arrow slits under the
eaves through which you could see oats
or corn or whatever it was projecting : it
gave you the impression of the place
being filled to bursting and was
somehow very homely, snug and comf
-ortable. There are also pigeons all over
the place, lodged in dovecots
of the real old type that you
see in pictures. Another nice things
was the orchards, where you could look
along the bright grass among the tree
stems — very like our wood at home
just above and beyond the vicious
dog. Wandering about the sleepy country
reminded me of Bookham days - what
a paradise of peace and quiet interest
that was with our weekly letters so
full of life & always following up

See pages 209–11

Another nice thing was the orchards, where you could look along the bright grass among the tree stems – very like our wood at home just above and beyond the vicious dog. Wandering about the sleepy country reminded me of Bookham days – what a paradise of peace and quiet interests that was with our weekly letters so full of life & always following up some new idea.

I hardly realized till your last letter that of course from your present liesure you must look back with a kind of horror to the days when you had to go into town. Yet we had a few minutes of 'good talk' sometimes in that sordid old office – which, by the way, if I had a bunk in one corner, I should now regard as an almost incredibly luxurious billet – actually windows and a fireplace.

I am longing to see those old English romances of yours: I think that *is* the kind of book I had rather hunt out second hand than buy brand new and obvious in a shop. If, as I imagine from your account they suffer from being too thin, could you not have them bound together in some good solemn half leather & strong boards. The girl in Ovenell's, Broad St., Oxford assured me they could make a good job of binding books together like that. I am sure your cautious soul would never risk it, but I think you'd be quite safe in sending them to Ovenell's with instructions. She would understand & a good shop like that would certainly do it with taste. If it suits the style of the book you could have a guilt top as well.

I wait anxiously for your answer as to there being any other edition of Green's Short History – but I'm afraid there is NOT. I feel inclined to read history somehow. By the way I must recommend the 'Autobiography' of Benvenuto Cellini which I am now three quarters way through. I expect you know who he was – a Florentine designer born in 1500. The book professes to be a sober 'life' but seems to me most impossible. He lives like a character in a Dumas novel: he is often attacked in the street by five or six men, all of whom he kills wounds, or puts to flight: he is shut up in a castle (with a 'castellan' who is mad & imagines himself to be a bat), and makes a most wonderful escape – letting himself down by a rope of sheets *of course*. He goes with a magician to practice sorcery in the ruins of the Colisseum, and after the magician had 'conjured for more than two hours many thousands of spirits began to appear' so that the whole amphitheatre was full of them threatening to come inside the magic circle. And perhaps what would appeal to you most is the background of great historical figures by whom he is patronized – two popes, cardinals both of France and Italy, Lorenzo & Cosimo de' Medici, the King of France and his powerful & spiteful mistress Madame d'Etampes, the Emperor. It is like a grand historical romance, with the added pleasure that it is, at least for the most part, true: how I look forward to reading it in the Italian when (and if) I get back to real life. It is also a good Everyman speciman: the paper is thin & crisp, the print just a comfortable size & the margins larger than usual – making a very pretty page. But I could talk forever about it. I should very, very strongly recommend you to get it as in the historical way it may appeal to you even more than to me. ⟨It touches in one place tho' very briefly on your penchant, and is from time to time interesting in 'that way'.⟩ I expect you are now heartily sick of the subject!

The 1st volume of Johnson has arrived and I am now started on it: I also discovered among the piles of trash of the hospital Blackwood's 'Incredible Adventures'[2] and a ragged copy containing some of Tennyson. Of the former I have read 2 stories, excellent of his style but I feel it a waste of time in these precious days. Tennyson, too, never raises any great enthusiasm in me. I am starting G. Eliot's 'Middlemarch' [1871–2] to night. So, you see I am in clover.

Do write soon again or I shall begin to feel neglected –

Yours
Jack

[The following must be one of the most bookish and unlikely letters to be written by a soldier. Lewis lay in hospital seriously wounded from his part in the final German attack on the Western Front. Indeed, it was not until some 37 years later that Lewis was to say much about the war. It was to come in his autobiography, *Surprised by Joy* (ch. xii), and even what he says there is mainly an overall impression of what it was like in the trenches. Some years later, when for him it didn't matter any more, he told me how he had captured a small party of German soldiers; but he seemed to dismiss any notion of bravery on his part by adding that they were not really afraid of him but 'just walked out with their hands up'.

The facts, however, are that Lewis returned to duty on 28 February and was among those who were wounded on Mount Bernenchon during the Battle of Arras on 15 April from an English shell which burst behind him. He was taken to the Liverpool Merchants Mobile Hospital, and there he was to remain till he could be moved to a hospital in London on 25 May. While it is unlikely that Lewis ever read it, or even saw a copy of it, those who are interested in following the Battle of Arras in detail should read Everard Wyrall's *History of the Somerset Light Infantry (Prince Albert's) 1914–1919* (1927). The author says in chapter xxxiii, p. 295, that 'The casualties of the 1st

[2] Algernon Henry Blackwood, *Incredible Adventures* (1914).

Battalion between the 14th and 16th April [1918] were: 2/Lieut. L. B. Johnson died of wounds (15/4/18) and 2/Lieuts. C. S. Lewis, A. G. Rawlence, J. R. Hill and C. S. Dowding wounded: in other ranks the estimated losses were 210 killed, wounded and missing.' As they were in the same battle it is possible that Lewis knew at the time that his friend Laurence Johnson had been killed.

Lewis's father could not be fobbed off as easily as Arthur, and he demanded to know what actual wounds his son suffered. Writing to Albert on 4 May 1918, Lewis told him that he had been 'hit in the back of the left hand, on the left leg from behind and just under the knee, and in the left side just under the arm'. On 14 May he wrote again to say that 'In one respect I was wrong in my last account of my wounds: the one under my arm is worse than a flesh wound, as the bit of metal which went in there is now in my chest, high up under my "pigeon chest" as shown: this however is nothing to worry about as it is doing no harm. They will leave it there and I am told that I can carry it about for the rest of my life without any evil results.']

78

> [Liverpool Merchants Mobile Hospital,
> Etaples,
> France.
> 23 May 1918]

My dear Arthur,

I was so glad to get your answer to day as it is the first 'answer' I've had for a long time – thro' my own neglect I admit.

I think your criticisms on my 'Literary Supplement' letter[1] were quite just, but I must give two reasons why I was led to write in such a style. In the first place I was rather stung by your gratuitous supposition that I had become a 'cheer-oh young man', and this naturally urged me into the opposite extreme of being what somebody calls 'a university prize prig'. Of course I don't mean to say that I didn't write throughout of things that really interested me and which I expected to interest you: but the general tone was probably influenced by that feeling. The second reason is this. The personal element naturally found a large field in my letters from Bookham and Univ. where all my life and surroundings were of interest to us both: but here, where everything I do & suffer is dull and repulsive, I don't turn to description and details which would bore me to write and – probably – you to read. If you think that I look to you only for abstract interests and no longer yearn for the old intimacy, the teas, the laughter the walks and the comparing of books – you are very

[1] So called because of his lengthy comments on Cellini's *Memoirs*.

much mistaken, mon ami.

(Talking about comparing of books, if you are still minded to sell your Trollope you will now find a purchaser in me. A chance copy of 'Barchester Towers'[2] has quite converted me and I am now all a-gog to read his others, so that I will certainly take your whole set if I may. By the way, this is an advantage – the only one – of being in the army: I have always plenty of money for anything I want. To any one in my irresponsible position the despised pay of a second lieutenant is a never-empty purse, unless he chooses to waste it on prostitutes, restaurants and tailors, as the gentiles do.)

When I see you face to face I will tell you any war impressions quite freely *at your request* – and not otherwise: for it is very proper that you should make use of me if you ever happen to want to know how certain things feel – but on the other hand there is no reason why I should bore you with a subject that we have always disliked, if you do *not* want.

Congratulations old man. I am delighted that you have had the moral courage to form your own opinion, ⟨independently,⟩ in defiance of the old taboos. I am not sure that I agree with you: but, as you hint in your letter, ⟨this penchant is a sort of mystery only to be fully understood by those who are made that way – and my views on it can be at best but emotion.⟩

You will be surprised and I expect, not a little amused to hear that my views at present are getting almost monastic about all the lusts of the flesh. They seem to me to extend the dominion of matter over us: and, out here, where I see spirit continually dodging matter (shells, bullets, animal fears, animal pains) I have formulated my equation Matter=Nature=Satan. And on the other side Beauty, the only spiritual & not-natural thing that I have yet found. Does all this bore you?

I think my stilted style must be due to the fact that I read 'Old Mortality'[3] a short time ago and am at present in the midst of 'Guy Mannering'. The former I thought very disappointing but am quite pleased with the latter, tho', truth to tell, I enjoyed 'Barchester Towers' much more. I have got here but not yet begun Blackwood's new book 'The Promise of the Air':[4] perhaps you read the verdict of the Times L.S. that this is his first really serious book.[5] I hope it may be true.

[2] Anthony Trollope (1857).
[3] Sir Walter Scott (1816).
[4] Algernon Henry Blackwood, *The Promise of Air* (1918).
[5] *The Times Literary Supplement* (9 May 1918), p. 219.

Strange! how wrongly one can read the simplest sentence: just reading over part of your letter I have realised for the first time that when you say you were 'driven' to town you mean driven in the car: I thought you meant 'driven' by circumstances of some sort. Now theres one of those little things which are useless on paper but would have made us roar with laughter if we were together.

By the way, are you allowed to go up & downstairs freely these days? If so, it occurs to me that it would be a very good idea for you to act as a sort of librarian to the little-end-room when I return to my penance. I mean, the key would be left in the bookcase and I should like you to go there frequently & see that they were alright, and borrow or examine anything you wanted & put in suitable places any new volumes I sent you. This would keep me in touch with my books to some extent and save the room from looking disused when I come back. What do you say?

I have only come across a few references to the Dorian customs: I hope Carpenter does not fall into the error common to enthusiasts, of reading into ancient institutions more than is really there. However, of course I have never studied the subject and can't give an opinion.

I was to have been sent across to England last night, but we were heavily bombed, so of course all traffic stopped. It is interesting to note that an air-raid here frightened me much more than anything I encountered at the front: you feel so helpless in bed, knowing you can't walk or anything even if you get out of it. Unless the same things happen again I shall probably go, or at least the night after. I suppose it would be out of the question for you to come and see me in hospital in England for a few days? It would be a great something to look forward to & it would give you an opportunity to meet Mrs Moore.

I am tired now, old man, after a very disturbed night & a stifling day so I will dry up & just enclose a little song I wrote the other day, which I hope you will approve –

Yours ever
Jack

SONG

Faeries must be in the woods
Or the satyr's merry broods,
Tritons in the summer sea,
Else how could the dead things be
Half so lovely as they are?
How could wreathèd star on star
Dusted o'er the wintry night,

Fill thy spirit with delight
And lead thee from this care of thine
Through a land of dreams divine
To the dearest heart's-desire,
Unless each pale & drifting fire
Were indeed a happy isle
Where eternal gardens smile
And golden globes of fruit are seen
Twinkling thro' the orchards green
Where the Other People go
On the soft sward to and fro?
Atoms dead could never thus
Wake the human heart of us,
Unless the beauty that we see
Part of endless beauty be,
Thronged with spirits that have trod
Where the bright foot-prints of God
Lie fresh upon the heavenly sod.[6]

79

[Endsleigh Palace Hospital,
Endsleigh Gardens,
London.
29 May 1918]

Cher Ami,

I am sitting up in bed in the middle of a red sunset to answer this evening's letter straightaway. Your letters set me thinking of so many old interests that I cannot go on with my book.

First a word or two as to my present estate: I am in a vastly comfortable hospital, where we are in separate rooms & have tea in the morning & big broad beds & everything the heart of man could desire and best of all, in close communication with all the bookshops of London. Of course you can easily understand what other and greater reasons there are for me to be happy. There are still two pieces of shrapnel in my chest, but they give me no discomfort: ⟨Mrs Moore and⟩ I are always hoping that it *will* start to give some trouble and thus secure me a longer illness (This is quite like the Malvern days again, isn't it?).

The thing in your last letter with which I most want to disagree is the remark about Beauty and nature: apparently I did not make

[6] This poem was later to appear under the same name, but with considerable alterations, in Lewis's *Spirits in Bondage* (1919), pp. 73–4.

myself very clear. You say that nature is beautiful, and that is the view we all start with. But let us see what we mean. If you take a tree, for instance, you call it beautiful because of its shape, colour and motions, and perhaps a little because of association. Now these colours etc are sensations in my eye, produced by vibrations on the aether between me and the tree: the real tree is something quite different – a combination of colourless, shapeless, invisible atoms. It follows then that neither the tree, nor any other material object can be beautiful in itself: I can never see them as they are, and if I could it would give me no delight. The beauty therefore is not in matter at all, but is something purely spiritual, arising mysteriously out of the relation between me & the tree: or perhaps as I suggest in my Song, out of some indwelling spirit behind the matter of the tree – the Dryad in fact.

You see the conviction is gaining ground on me that after all Spirit does exist; and that we come in contact with the spiritual element by means of these 'thrills'. I fancy that there is Something right outside time & place, which did not create matter, as the Christians say, but is matter's great enemy: and that Beauty is the call of the spirit in that something to the spirit in us. You see how frankly I admit that my views have changed: I hope I don't bore you.

⟨I admit the associations of the word paederasty are unfortunate but you should rise above that. As well what does 'Uranian' mean – it ought to mean 'Heavenly' as far as my knowledge goes, and I will stick to the word that I understand in preference.⟩

I don't agree with you about Trollope's being mamby pamby: in fact the sentimental part seems to me very slightly sketched and only to serve as a turning point for all the delightful 'Austinesque' work about the Mrs Proudie's etc. I have now read the 'Warden' and am more than half way through 'Dr Thorne'.[1] I cannot understand why you got tired of him, I should have thought he was so very much in your line: but indeed one can never really say what will please another person.

I told you I was reading Blackwood's new one 'The Promise of Air': it is very disappointing, being merely a long & tedious expansion of a theory that could have been explained in a single essay. Although it is in story form nothing ever happens: I'm afraid if he goes on being 'serious' after this fashion we shall have lost a good romancer for a bad mystic.

Can you imagine how I enjoyed my journey to London? First of

[1] Anthony Trollope, *The Warden* (1855); *Doctor Thorne* (1858).

all the sight and smell of the sea, that I have missed for so many long and weary months, and then the beautiful green country seen from the train: I suppose its because I've been shut up in a hut so long, but I think I never enjoyed anything so much as that scenery – all the white in the hedges, and the fields so full of buttercups that in the distance they seemed to be of solid gold: and everything such a bright, bright green. I am sure our hills look lovely now and the wood must be full of life and sweet smells.

Yes, after all our old conversations I *can* feel otherwise about the lusts of the flesh: is not desire merely a kind of sugar-plum that nature gives us to make us breed, as she does the beetles and toads so that both we and they may beget more creatures to struggle in the same net: Nature, or the common order of things, has really pro-duced in man a sort of Frankenstein who is learning to shake her off. For man alone of all things can master his instincts.

From my window I see a big flat plain of houses and beyond that actually a green hill with trees on it, which I am told is the aristo-cratic district of High Hampstead. In the foreground is the Euston station hotel – bringing old, old memories. 'Mais ou sont les neiges.'

Your quotation from Pater expresses my attitude to philosophy exactly: I don't really think it will teach me the truth, but I do think it will supply me with thoughts & feelings that I may be able to turn into poetry. As you turn all kinds of nourishment into blood.

I was glad to see Willie (I suppose 'Bill' since his marriage)[2] he seems in good form.

Good bye, old man, write by return.

Yours ever
Jack

80

[Endsleigh Palace Hospital
3 June 1918]

My dear Arthur,

Your letter of the 1st arrived this morning. I am very sorry that you are getting bored with our 'tree' argument (the Dry Tree as it might well be called from the nature of the discussions to which it gives rise) for I am afraid I cannot let the subject drop without refuting the heresies which you started in to-day's letter.

First, as to the colour of the atom, I would remind you that atoms

[2] Arthur's brother, William Edward Greeves, who married Marion Janet Cadbury on 14 February 1918.

are regarded as all identically the same – as the original world-stuff, and if therefore they had colour all things would be coloured the same. And to analyse colour: ninety-two million miles away the action of certain vibrations in the sun sets up a wave on the ether which travels to the atom under your consideration: this sets up certain other vibrations in the atom which again sends off another wave along the ether towards your eye. When this reaches the tissue of your eye it sets up more action which travels along a nerve and produces in your brain a sensation which we call greenness. Here for the first time we reach the colour – in your brain, not in all these vibrations of atoms. Magnify your atom to infinity, and still your consciousness has no *direct* communion with it. All you can ever say is that certain sensations arise in your brain: you suppose (which in itself was doubted by Berkeley and other idealists) that there is some exterior cause for these: but what that exterior cause is like in itself you do not know and never can know. Suppose this vibration from the atom never happened to strike an eye, but went on for ever into space – where then is your greenness? No – the whole exterior world can only make itself known to us by certain sensations which it produces on our brain in a complicated manner, and it is simply a habit of mind which makes us call these impressions (colour, shape, sound etc) the thing-in-itself. Hence as I said before, beauty cannot be in the material thing.

Of course there is another simpler argument, without going into abstruse regions. If beauty were really in the tree, then two people who both had normal eyes would be bound to see the same beauty. But nothing is easier than to find two people one of whom would see beauty and the other see no beauty in the same tree. Therefore the beauty cannot be in the tree but in some obscure and non-material point of view or relation between the mind of the perciever and the sensations which the tree – very indirectly – causes in that mind. I have done: are you bored beyond endurance?

Perhaps you feel that we are wandering away from the grounds that supplied our earlier interests in common and first brought us together. I hope not: I like to think of our interests as a circle which may increase in size but whose centre is always the same. For myself I think I am true to the old cannons – romantic beauty, eeriness, terror, homeliness, solidity – & absurdity. These were the gods we worshipped in the golden age, were they not mon vieux?

By the same token, I have been reading since this morning an incomparably homely book, of which I am having a copy sent to you – 'The Private Papers of Henry Ryecroft' by G. Gissing (Constable

1/-).[1] Gissing's name I have often heard, but I have no idea what else he wrote. This is a collection of very loose, spontaneous essays, about books and other quiet interests – including food. He has some splendid things to say about the glory of 'tea', so homely & cheery after a long walk. There is hardly a bad piece in the whole book, and it is a very companionable volume to fill up the spaces of serious reading with, or to read over a lonely meal.

Are you lonely these days, or are you over-much oppressed with visitors? I should like to hear from you a fuller account of your cousin Gribbon: I remember him – with a shudder – at Campbell. I hear he is enormously clever and knows all things: I expect he will pulverize me – rusted as I am with a year's barbarity – if I should ever meet him.[2] But I mustn't talk thus or you will perhaps think, like somebody in a French play 'que je vous fasse l'honneur d'être jaloux'.

Spenser, I am sure, would be greatly surprised to hear that Britomart was a type of [illegible] – considering she is represented as loving Artegall the knight of Justice; I don't remember her being described as having a 'man's heart' in the real Faerie Queene, and the book which you mention probably uses that phrase in the conventional sense as 'having a man's courage'. But how I love to hear you say 'I came across so-and-so in a book this morning': it conjures up such visions of those old happy hours when I sat surrounded by my little library and browsed from book to book. You, who have never lost that life, cannot understand the longing with which I look back to it.

By the way, haven't you got a reddy-brown MS. book of mine containing 'Lullaby' and several other of my later poems? I wish you would send it here, as I have decided to copy out all my work of which I approve and get it typed as a step towards possible publishing. Even if nobody will have them a complete typed copy would be a great convenience.

Wouldn't it be glorious if I were writing you the last letter of a term at Bookham, perhaps with an 'instalment', with all the rich harvest of the pleasant term behind me and the glorious liesure of the long summer holidays (with after dinner walks to the shrine of

[1] George Robert Gissing (1903).

[2] Arthur's cousin Charles Edward Gribbon (1898–1938) was the son of R. W. Gribbon of 'Ardvarna', Strandtown, Belfast. He had been a pupil at Campbell College between 1904–14, and became a professional artist. Some of his pictures were bought by the Friends of the National Collection of Ireland.

Tigliath-Pileser) before me. I knew then that those were good days, but I think now that I didn't prize them enough. Ahem!, the sunset appears to be making me sentimental: & yet its not sentiment at all but very certain truth. Doesn't the word 'ahem' breathe of old-fashioned novels?

You accuse me of talking, 'as your own father might talk': and perhaps that is one thing you may find in me now – a vein of asceticism, almost of puritan practice without the puritan dogma. I believe in no God, least of all in one that would punish me for the 'lusts of the flesh': but I do believe that I have in me a spirit, a chip, shall we say, of universal spirit; and that, since all good & joyful things are spiritual & non-material, I must be careful not to let matter (=nature=Satan, remember) get too great a hold on me, & dull the one spark I have.

Yours ever
Jack

81

[Endsleigh Palace Hospital]
Monday [17 June 1918]

My dear Galahad,

Now will I make you envious. On Friday night I went to Drury Lane to hear 'The Valkyrie'.[1] The dream of years has been realised, and without disillusionment: I have had thrills and delights of the real old sort, I have felt as I felt five years ago.

We had difficulty in getting seats, and from those which we had we could only see one side of the stage. I was also much worried by the people that sat near us. Not that they were philistines and talked, but their very enthusiasm made them a nuisance. One little man in front of me was so moved that at several interesting points he stood up, until at last I became so exasperated that I caught him by his coat tails and pulled him into his seat. Another, who was following the score, kept on giving vent to quite audible criticisms such as 'Louder, Louder!' or 'No, no, no' whenever the conductor's design differed from his own.

But the performance was beyond all words. The first act as you remember is in Hunding's hut with the tree growing in it: and towards the end you remember how Siegmund draws the sword and

---

[1] *The Valkyrie* (1870) is the second part of Richard Wagner's *Nibelung's Ring*. The performance on 14 June was conducted by Sir Thomas Beecham and there is a notice about it in *The Times* (15 June 1918), p. 3.

how they throw open the great doors at the back. This showed us a most beautiful scene of distant snow covered peaks and a wild valley. The lighting gave a really unusual impression of spring moon-light, and that combined with the glorious love-music of the orchestra (you remember the spring song?) simply swept you away – and then all the time creeping in under this the faint horn blown motive of the sword and the far-off tinkling hammers to remind you of the Niblungs – oh, ami, it was simply heaven! But the next act which opens in 'A wild rocky place' – represented not conventionally but with real sympathy – and Brünhilde singing 'Moi-a-a-hei' (you know) was even better. She, it is true, was a trifle full-breasted and operatic, but as the interest of the scene went on, one forgot that. Wotan was magnificent whenever he came on, and all his music is splendid – there are whole hours of music just as wonderful as the little bits we know: the singing was in English, and so clear and un-strained that with my knowledge of the story, I could follow nearly all the dialogue, and so all the poetic and romantic pleasure came to help the musical. As a spectacle the third act was the best, where Brünhilde is hiding from Wotan. The stage is almost dark, lit only from time to time by flashes of lightening, as the angry god draws nearer and nearer and at last enters in a glare of red light, glinting on the huge raven-wings of his helmet and the rings of his mail – one gleaming figure in that sinister gloom – and the music, I cannot describe it. Most unfortunately it was so late that I had to come away before the end, and miss the fire music: but I was so full of delights that I could hardly find it in my heart to grumble.

Looking back, what pleases me most was the training of all the singers together and the entire absence of strain: none of your Italian screaming and contortions. There was no famous name in the caste, and no-one except Brünhilde had a voice of any unusual power: but the beauty was that they never tried to sing louder than they could, and were content to sacrifice power to real beauty – playing into each other's hands and making it all musical dialogue NOT mere duets. You felt that they all loved the Ring and took it seriously not merely as an opportunity for noise. Sieglindë particularly, with a sweet voice and clear enunciation, *acted* very well, quietly & naturally not in the usual operatic style. And oh! the blessèd absence of a chorus! So you have my verdict that if the Ring is all like this it quite comes up to our old dreams, and that all Italian opera is merely a passtime compared with the great music-drama of Wagner. In spite of all our efforts we could not get a programme and so I cannot send you one.

To descend from the windswept eerie's of the swan-maidens to a further argument about the Dry Tree may seem bathos: but as you have agreed to go on with it, let us do so. The subject is of great interest too.

Of course we all start with the idea that our senses put us in direct contact with reality – you think that your eyes are windows by which your brain 'sees' the world. But science teaches you that your eye, or rather the nerve of your eye, is merely a telegraph wire. It's vibration produces a feeling in your brain which we call colour etc.: but what the Something at the other end which starts the vibration may be, of this no human being can have any conception. No increase of our sensory keenness, no microscope or teloscope can put us in any direct relation with the Thing: we still remain dependant on this long chain of communications, travelling by vibration from atom to atom: and we can never have any proof that the sensation which it produces in our brain conveys any true idea of the external Thing. Nay the thing *must* be quite different from our conception of it: for we necessarily concieve it in terms of the senses – we think of any object as having a certain size, shape, colour and feel. But all these are only the names of our own sensations: take size, which may seem at first to be outside ourselves. On the table lies my pipe: if I wish to have an idea of the size of this I naturally handle it: in other words I send out a *will* from my brain (which I call 'moving my hand') and presently a set of impressions come back to me – smoothness, hardness, width and the rest. It is true that at the same time as these come along my touch-nerves another set of brown-ness, shininess, rotundity etc come along my visual-nerves. And if I repeat the action ten times I find that the same set of sight-impressions always accompanies the same set of touch-ones: in other words what looks a pipe, always feels a pipe too. But this brings me no nearer to the real pipe: I can only think of it as long, brown, smooth, hard and rounded: therefore think of it wrongly, since length, smoothness, brown-ness, hardness and rotundity are feelings in my brain, and cannot belong to the real pipe at all. (Shape, which was bothering you, is of course on the same footing as colour or hardness: it can only be apprehended thro' the same chain of communication, by the senses of touch or sight, and therefore is in me not in the external Thing). Hence you see we are driven to the conclusion that we have no knowledge of the external world: that it is concievable that there IS no external world at all, and that if it does exist it must be quite different from our usual ideas of it. A good many modern scientists think that 'matter' consists of atoms which are not (as we used to think) small solid bodies but merely points of force and that all the phenomena of matter can be attributed to the inter-action of these forces. If you are still interested in these subjects I will talk in another letter about the various conclusions which philosophers have drawn from this ignorance which we are forced to acknowledge, and the ways by which they have tried to escape from it.

I have sent you two books from Hatchards' of Picadilly: whether you have them already or would care to have them, I can't say, but you will have no difficulty in changing them. I finished my last letter in rather a hurry, and can't remember whether I referred to your drawing in them: I am glad you are going on with it. The absence of models, as far as hands, limbs, folds of clothes, etc go could be helped by the looking-glass, which I imagine is an excellent teacher. How fine it will be when you can get me up in your room again and show me all your new work and all your new treasures. I too shall have plenty for you to see: I have sent home a fine edition of Yeats which I have been wanting for ages, and have bought hear Dent's Malory with designs by Beardesly. It is a beautiful book, with a handsome binding, good paper and a fair page: there are lovely chapter headings and decorations, and somehow a great big book suits Malory, doesn't it? In that same shop, Bain's, where I got this they showed me some of Morris's Kelmscott Press books, including the Chaucer, very rare and now at £82. I suppose it is bad taste on my part, but I don't care for Morris's type, it is much too ornate and difficult to read. Ordinary old black-letter I should much prefer.

By the way, ⟨if you have alone established 'Uranianism' in your own mind as something virtuous and natural, I must remind you that for men in ordinary sexual arrangements, a promiscuous desire for every beautiful person you meet is usually disapproved of. Your talk about continually meeting people and having to conceal your feelings suggests that you have no intention of confining yourself to one love: but perhaps I have misunderstood you.⟩

On Sunday we were down at Bookham and I called at Gastons.[2] You can imagine how strange it was to go back now among those old scenes and people.

I think I have talked enough now. Addio, write by return.

Yours
Jack

---

[2] For an account, which Lewis wrote to his father, of this visit to Mr Kirkpatrick on 16 June see *Letters of C. S. Lewis*, ed. W. H. Lewis (1966), pp. 42–3.

82

[Ashton Court,
Long Ashton,
Clifton,
Bristol.
17? July 1918][1]

My dear Arthur,

I am truly sorry to have left you so long without a letter. My best
excuse is that already 'my hand aches and my eyes grow weary' with
writing, for I am at present busily engaged in copying out the final
version of my poems: in a few days the new MS. will be ready for the
typist and when it returns thence it will begin the round of the publishers. I shall start with the famous houses and go on until I have
exhausted all that I can hear of: even if it is unsuccessful all round, I
may pick up some useful criticisms, and at any rate it will be well to
have a typed copy.

Of course the book now is very different from the one you have,
by the insertion of several new pieces and the alteration or omission
of some of the old. The arrangement I find particularly difficult and
besides I am beginning to grow nervy and distrust my own judge-

[1] Since he arrived back in England, Lewis had been begging his father to
visit him in hospital. We do not know how his father justified this neglect,
but his son remained unvisited. When Lewis learned that he was being sent
to a convalescent home out of London, he asked to be sent to one in Ireland
so as to be near his father. This proved to be impossible and he chose
Ashton Court (arriving there on 25 June) in order to be close to Mrs Moore
who already believed her son 'Paddy' to be dead and whose death was to be
confirmed in September 1918. The story of 'Paddy's' part in the war was
summarized, from information supplied by his mother, in his school magazine *The Cliftonian*, No. CCXCV (May 1918), p. 225: '2nd-Lieutenant
E. F. C. Moore. He joined the Rifle Brigade after the usual training, and was
in action in France in the great German attack which began on March 21st.
He was reported missing on March 24th, and it is now feared that he cannot
have escaped with his life. The Adjutant of his battalion writes: "I have to
tell you that your very gallant son was reported missing on the 24th of last
month. He was last seen on the morning of that day with a few men defending a position on a river bank against infinitely superior numbers of the
enemy. All the other officers and most of the men of his company have
become casualties, and I fear it is impossible to obtain more definite information. He did really fine work on the previous night in beating off a
party of Germans who had succeeded in rushing a bridgehead in our lines.
We all feel his loss very deeply, and I cannot express too strongly our
sympathy with you." '

T.S.T.–H

ment. It is so hard to know whether you are improving or spoiling a thing.

This will partly explain my silence, tho' of course I know I should have written. But, ami, you must never suppose when I don't write that this means any change in my feelings or any loss of touch with the old life – put it down to laziness or forgetfulness or other occupations rather than to that. When I have got the MS. off (it used to be my love but is now becoming more my tyrant!) I will write you a longer and better letter. In the meantime I will just run over my news up to date and then say good-bye.

My last adventures before leaving town were a visit to 'Faust' and to 'Tosca'.[2] With the former I was disgusted: the crowded stage, the conventionality, the noisy comic-opera scenes of drinking, the choruses etc were really too much after the 'Valkyrie'. The church scene was very well done I admit: but on the whole I got very little pleasure out of it. Of course if I were a real musician like you I should appreciate this kind of music too 'in its own way' and get a sort of critical & historical interest out of it to make up for the sheer ecstasy of modern music: but then literature is my province, and in music I can only afford to enjoy the music that really suits me. By the way they had the whole ballet, which is very rarely done now I suppose, as a separate scene. The dancing was very uninspired and I didn't care for the music, but you would have agreed with me in praising the setting – which was a wild open place done in the style of Heath Robinson: in the back ground was a typical absurdly beautiful mountain of his, and steep little vallies, and big masses of pink cloud. The whole was lighted to represent early summer morning and gave a fine impression of loneliness.

'Tosca' I revelled in: from beginning to end I enjoyed it, and it seemed to my untutored ears to be very well sung – tho' not of course with the solemnity of the 'Valkyrie' (you see I cannot help harking back to that, it was immeasurably beyond anything I had seen or hoped to see so gloriously un-operatic – in the silly sense). Puccini certainly has a wonderful richness of orchestration and a sort of continuity – hasn't he? None of those nasty gaps that you have in 'Faust' where one 'number' (loathsome word) has ended and the other begins, like pieces in a concert: 'E lucevan le stelle' was quite up to expectations.

The books which you returned did not arrive until I had left London – but don't bother about that: I have decided to keep

[2] Giacomo Puccini, *La Tosca* (1900). The production which Lewis saw on 21 June is reviewed in *The Times* (22 June 1918), p. 3.

'Peacock Pie'[3] and can easily dispose of the others. As it seems impossible to get what would suit you 'by the light of nature' I am sending you the wherewithal to choose for yourself at Mullan's. This is an unconventional way of giving a present, but you are too sensible to mind that. I will tell you all my details in my next letter. Bear with me.

Yours ever
Jack

83

[Ashton Court,
Bristol.]
Wednesday [7 August 1918]

My dear Arthur,

The fact of trying to publish a book at once makes you regard publishers in quite a new light. When you sit down to consider where you will send it first, you immediately realize the enormous prestige of Macmillan – when you come to think of it, everyone who is published by them gains a certain importance from that very fact. I looked upon acceptance by them as a goal almost beyond hope, and sent my MS. to them first. Needless to say it has come back, accompanied by the following note: – 'Dear Sir, We duly received your manuscript entitled "Spirits in Prison: A cycle of lyrical poems", by Clive Staples, and regret to say that we do not see our way to undertake its publication. Some of the shorter nature poems seem to us to have no little charm, but we do not feel that the collection as a whole would be likely to appeal to any considerable public. We beg therefore to return the MS. with thanks. We are, yours faithfully, Macmillan and Co. Ltd.'

This is at any rate courteous and I suppose not very discouraging: perhaps, however, they always sweeten their refusals with some little complement. However that may be, I am determined not to lose heart until I have tried all the houses I can hear of. I am sending it to Heinneman next – they seem to publish a far amount of new poetry. From the title which I have given my collection, you will gather that it differs in many ways from the one which you possess.

I find I am getting very slack and idle. My serious reading at present is Burton's Anatomy of Melancholy, as published in one big volume by Chatto & Windus at 7/–. The paper and type are of a good, plain quality, but the binding is not attractive. I get on with it

[3] Walter de la Mare, *Peacock Pie: A Book of Rhymes* (1913).

very slowly, and have intermixed with it a new book called 'A Schoolmaster's Diary',[1] which interest me being mainly on education and literature. I also read a good deal of Wordsworth in my Everyman. You remember perhaps how violent my criticisms on him once were, but I am becoming a reformed character. I feel very weak and tired these days and inclined to lose interest in anything that needs continued attention. If only I could get my book accepted it would give me a tremendous fillip and take my mind off the future. In my present mood few things have pleased me more than Macdonald's 'The Goblin and the Princess',[2] which I borrowed from Maureen Moore. This child has a well stocked library of fairy tales which form her continual reading – an excellent taste at her age, I think, which will lead her in later life to romance and poetry and not to the twaddling novels that make up the diet of most educated women apparently. I am getting the Life of Thomas More in the Temple Classics.

Forgive me if I don't write any more, I don't feel like it to day. It is terribly hot, which you know I hate.

Yours
Jack

84

[Ashton Court,
Bristol.
31 August 1918]

My dear Arthur,

In spite of the loneliness and melancholy of which you complain I must begin by congratulating you on the excellent time which you had in Dublin and the interesting people whom you met. Indeed I think you are as much to be envied as anyone I know: you live in comfort, surrounded by interests, in pleasant society, and are not a slave of the state and do not have the menace of France hanging over your head. When you were toiling in the office how you would have looked forward to this time if you had known it was coming! How many men to-day, living in holes and mud heaps, driven, hunted, terrified, verminous, starved for sleep, hopeless, would give their very souls to change places with you even for twenty four hours. And yet of course we can all be discontented in any circumstances, and I dare say I should be just the same in your place.

[1] By S. P. B. Mais (1918).
[2] George MacDonald, *The Princess and the Goblin* (1871).

So you are inclining to the New Ireland school are you? I remember you used rather to laugh at my Irish enthusiasm in the old days when you were still an orthodox Ulsterman. I am glad you begin to think otherwise: a poetry bookshop for Ireland, in Dublin, would be a most praiseworthy undertaking: it might also bring out some monthly journal on Irish literature, containing reviews of contemporary books, articles on classical Gaelic literature and language, and a few poems and sketches. The idea is fascinating: if you could get some big man to take it up.

I should like very much indeed to meet your friend Parker: it is a grand idea to build a house after a dream. What talks you all must have had. Were they purely literary or did they talk anything about religion and philosophy? I suppose that set are mostly mystics, rosacrutians and the like. Here I must indulge my love of preaching by warning you not to get too much bound up in a cult. Between your other penchant . . . . and the Irish school you might get into a sort of little by-way of the intellectual world, off the main track and loose yourself there. Remember that the great minds, Milton, Scott, Mozart and so on, are always sane before all and keep in the broad highway of thought and feel what can be felt by all men, not only by a few. Attractive as they are these side-tracks are always a little decadent if one lives wholly in them. But I suppose your good solid old faith in history and 'stodge' will keep you from that danger.

It is partly through this feeling that I have not begun by sending my MS. to Maunsels: it would associate me too definitely with a cult and partly because their paper and binding are rather poor. I suppose none of your friends have any influence at Maunsels that might be of use to me?

I have just finished reading a very pleasant book called 'The Four Men', by Hillaire Belloc.[1] I always imagined that his books were of a very different kind but this is rather in the style of Lavengro, only, it seems to me, more homely and humorous: in one or two places where the four wanderers sit in a little forest hut smoking and telling tales it rather reminds me of the 'Crock of Gold'. I began to read the 'Egoist'[2] and after five pages came to the conclusion that it was one of the worst books I had ever seen or heard of. I don't know how you can stand Meredith's affectation. By the bye, 'The Four Men' is in the 1/– Nelson blue edition with quite nice pen and ink sketches. I should not advise you to try Burton. I have got stuck with him and I think he would be less in your line than in mine. Oh don't you some-

[1] Hilaire Belloc, *The Four Men: A Farrago* [1912].
[2] George Meredith, *The Egoist* (1879).

times feel that everything is dead? I feel, and apparently you feel, a sort of impossibility in getting on solidly with any serious book in the way we used to do.

Yours
Jack

85

56 Ravenswood Rd.,
Redland,
Bristol.
[12 September 1918]

My dear Arthur,

The best of news! After keeping my MS. for ages Heinemann has actually accepted it. 'Wm. Heinemann' – apparently there is a real Mr Heinnemann – writes to say that he 'will be pleased to become its publisher'. He adds that it may be well to re-consider the in-clusion of some of the pieces 'which are not perhaps on a level with my best work'. I wrote back thanking him and telling him there were a few new pieces that he might care to use as substitutions for ones he omits. An answer came back this time from a man called Evans, the managing director asking me to send the new pieces and saying that Heinemann himself was out of town for a week or so.[1] I sent him 5 new poems by return – and so things are going on very well although I'm afraid Heinemann's holiday will cause some delay. You can imagine how pleased I am, and how eagerly I now look at all Heinemann's books and wonder what mine will be like. I'm afraid the paper will be poor as it always is now in new books.

It is going to be called 'Spirits in Prison'[2] by Clive Staples & is mainly strung round the idea that I mentioned to you before – that nature is wholly diabolical & malevolent and that God, if he exists, is outside of and in opposition to the cosmic arrangements. I'm afraid you will find a good many of your favourite ones left out: I thought very carefully over them but I think we all have to follow our own judgement in the end.

On no account tell my father that you know anything about it, as he might be hurt at not having been taken into my confidence: I

---

[1] These letters from William Heinemann (1863–1920) and Charles Sheldon Evans (1883–1944) of 3 and 5 September respectively are found in the *Lewis Papers*, vol. VI, pp. 31–2.

[2] Which title Lewis admits having taken from I Peter iii. 19 (Christ 'went and preached unto the spirits in prison').

will let him know myself when I next write (I have written to him since at your instance) and you must hear it from him as news or else pretend that you have just heard. *Of course* don't say anything to the Strandtown fraternity.

I am glad to see that you are more cheerful in your last letter. I don't think I shall follow your advice to try George Meredith again. There is so much good stuff to read that it is wasteful to spend time on affectations. You are quite right about Emerson.[3] I often pick him up here for an odd quarter of an hour, and go away full of new ideas. Every sentence is weighty: he puts into paragraphs what others, seeking charm, expand into whole essays or chapters. At the same time his tense concentration makes him painful reading, he gives you no rest. I don't know why you object to his style – it seems to me admirable. Quel dommage that such a man should be an American.

I have read (in a borrowed copy) 'King Lear's Wife' and also 'The End of the World' which is in the same volume.[4] Bottomley's play seems very closely copied from Yeats, but very good. I prefer the other on the whole – tho' I think better of humanity and believe that quite ordinary folk would face 'The fire that was before the world was made' with less hysteria than Huff and his circle.[5]

Must stop now – good bye –

Yours
Jack

P.S. Board is overdue & may it continue so.[6]

---

[3] Ralph Waldo Emerson (1803–82).

[4] *Georgian Poetry 1913–1915*, ed. E[dward] M[arsh] (1915). 'King Lear's Wife' is by Gordon Bottomley (pp. 3–47) and 'The End of the World' by Lascelles Abercrombie (pp. 195–239).

[5] A line from Act I of 'The End of the World' (p. 205). Huff is a character in that play.

[6] The Army Medical Board who would decide whether or not Lewis should return to active duty.

86

No 3 Officers' Mess,
Perham Downs Camp,
Ludgershall,
Hants.[1]
[6? October 1918]

My dear Arthur,

No, you were wrong, I have not gone on my leave; I was only out for a night at Mrs Moore's. I have now however had my board, over a month late I'm glad to say, and been sent for further convalescence to a camp here. This is Salisbury Plain, a place much cursed by most army people who are sent there because it is in the heart of the country and cannot therefore afford them the only pleasures of which they are capable. Personally I quite like it: it consists of long low hills, grassy and rather grey looking except in bright sun and very few trees. Of course it is rather spoilt by the city of wooden huts that is called a camp, but even these look quite well towards dusk when there are rows of light in the windows.

By this time you have probably got a parcel containing Beardesly's Malory and the Works of Corneille, which I have sent to you for safe keeping. Be sure and let me know what you think of both. Even if you don't care for the designs (and they are a little decadent and 'genre') I think you will like the general get up of the Malory. The Corneille is in a sort of good, solid old fashioned style, which I have grown to like: the plates of course *as* illustrations are idiotic but there is something solid and grand about them. Corneille is not half such a dull author as some people might imagine – don't take him at Tchaine's valuation. Down here I am reading Dante's 'Purgatorio' in the Temple Classics edition with a crib on the opposite page.[2] So 'ave the mighty fallen.

I told you that Wm. Heinemann was away for a fortnight, but he should be back now and I am expecting to hear from him any day now. I had a shock a short while ago when I saw a book of poems 'Counter-Attack' by Siegfried Sassoon[3] (a horrid man) published by him at 2/6 in a red paper cover and horrid type. I do hope they will give me something better than that.

---

[1] Lewis was moved here about 4 October.

[2] *The Purgatorio of Dante Alighieri*, the text with a translation by Thomas Okey, edited by H. Oelsner (1900).

[3] *Counterattack* (1918).

I have also been reading here the 1916–1917 books of Georgian Verse,[4] in which I liked particularly the bits from Robert Nichol's 'Faun's Holiday'. How a man who wrote them could also write such howling gibberish as 'The Assault' must remain a mystery. I believe you have his 'Ardours and Endurances'[5] haven't you? If so you might give me the details as to publisher, price and edition.

Mrs Moore has managed to get rooms in a tiny cottage here, where they keep rabbits and pigs. It is all very rural but not very sanitary. Write soon.

Yours
Jack

P.S. Don't say anything about my being moved, as I don't want my father to start trying to get me moved again.

87

No 3 Officers Mess,
Perham Downs Camp,
Ludgershall,
Hants.
Sunday [13 October 1918]

My dear Arthur,

'Savernake Woods', doesn't that breathe of romance? It is the sort of name one would expect to find in Maurice Hewlett or Geoffrey Farnol, but as a matter of fact it is not invention at all – I have been in Savernake Woods this morning.

You get clear of the village, cross a couple of fields and then a sunken chalky road leads you right into the wood. It is full of beech and oak but also of those little bushy things that grow out of the earth in four or five different trunks – vide Rackham's woodland scenes in the 'Siegfried' illustrations. In places, too, there has been a good deal of cutting down: some people think this spoils a wood but I find it delightful to come out of the thickets suddenly to a half bare patch full of stumps and stacks of piled wood with the sun glinting thro' the survivors. Green walks of grass with thick wood on either side led off the road and we followed one of these down and found our way back by long détours, tho' not before a comfortable 'soaking machine' had been discovered and enjoyed.

[4] *Georgian Poetry 1916–1917*, ed. E[dward] M[arsh] (1917).
[5] Robert Nichols, *Assault and other War Poems* (1918); *Ardours and Endurances* (1917).

By the way, talking about Siegfried, is it not an abomination the way the Germans have named their trench systems after the heroes of the Ring? The other day they were defending the 'Alberich line' and now they have been driven back to 'Brünnhilde'. Anything more vulgar than the application of that grand old cycle to the wearisome ugliness of modern war I can't imagine.

It was strange the way not only our letters but our thoughts crossed about 'the good old style' of the Corneille: the binding was of my own choice. How had both books stood their journey? As long as our views agree to this extent you need not be afraid of that 'getting farther and farther away' of which you always complain. We shall of course have a great many new subjects to talk of when we meet again, and a good many old ones to talk of quite differently, but that is an advantage.

I only wish I *was* busy 'correcting my proof-sheets': I have heard nothing more from Heinnemann although he must be back from his holiday by now. I have horrid fears sometimes that he may have changed his mind and be getting ready to return them – but then it would have been so easy for him to have done that in the first place.[1] *Of course* there is none of the fighting element in my book, but I suppose it has some indirect bearing on the war.

Funnily enough I had been reading a little handbook on Schopenhauer last week:[2] though I have never read him seriously I have often dipped into him at Kirk's and the old man's talk was saturated with Shopenhauer-esque quotations and ideas. There is certainly much worth reading in him: his views on love, for instance, though they are far from being the whole truth, give nevertheless an excellent account of the actual origin of love – what he forgets is that it is man's peculiar glory to make out of something which nature created for her own biological purposes something else which is spiritual and which nature would have no interest in. That is our triumph. Of course he is not really a philosopher at all in the technical sense.

Am still going on slowly with the Purgatorio. Write soon a good long screed

Yours
Jack

[1] Mr Heinemann's enthusiastic letter of 8 October (found in the *Lewis Papers*, vol. VI, p. 49) was sent to Ashton Court and had not yet caught up with him.

[2] Arthur Schopenhauer (1788–1860). Lewis was probably reading *The Wisdom of Schopenhauer*, ed. W. Jekyll (1911).

88

Teusday [15 October 1918]
Same place.

My dear Arthur,

Many thanks for the book,[1] it was most unexpected and delightful. It is nicely got up, but has suffered a little from tight strings on the journey. I haven't begun to read it seriously yet but all that I have seen pleases me. I at once looked up the poem 'The Gift of Song' which you mentioned, and I thoroughly agree with you. It has a beautiful dreamy movement and the sound follows the sense exactly; also, what is more it has that depth and mystery which a lyric should have if you are to read it again and again. I liked too the 'Canticle' in Danaë and indeed all the Danaë pieces, and there are fine passages in the verses on somebody's death – the ones where the last lines all rhyme to 'Despair'. Didn't you like that description of the snow outside the firelit window at Oxford. The war poetry is, at least, no worse than the rest of its kind. Nichols is very different from that great mass of modern poets, who copy the faults but not the merits of Rupert Brooke, and who are so intolerably clumsy and ugly in form. He stands quite apart and seems to me the best of the younger lot whom I have come across – much better than Brooke himself for instance. I'm afraid I shall never be an orthodox modern – I like lines that will scan and do not care for descriptions of sea-sickness.

Now for a little growl: if you realised what I'd got to go back to you wouldn't be so damned keen on my having another board. And you should understand that the longer it is before you see me the longer that evil day is put off.

Talking about Schopenhauer have you read anything about his views on music? He regards the arts in general as the only escape from the Will, and music in particular as the supreme escape and perhaps in itself the fundamental Reality. It is rather finely worked out and should appeal to you.

I am so glad you have got into that school at last: I hope they will do you good and lead you on to a proper development of your natural bent. After all interesting and arduous work is about the one thing to save us from melancholy – your besetting disease (I had almost written 'sin').

The Purgatorio, or even the whole Divine Comedy with the Inferno and Paradiso, is much shorter than the Faerie Queene.

[1] Robert Nichols, *Ardours and Endurances* (1917).

Without Latin I am not sure that even your knowledge of French &
the crib would carry you through: but if you would care for a translation remember that Cary's version in blank verse is supposed to be
the best piece of verse-translation ever written.[2] Don't get Long-
fellow's or any of the modern ones, they are all (I'm told) bad.
Gilbert Murray is a very sound man, and his translations should be
good – I have never more than glanced at them, not being fond of
Euripides myself.[3]

I got Mrs Moore's sister in town to call on Heinemanns, which
she did on Wednesday last and they said they'd written the day before,
but it must have been lost. That of course accounts for the delay and
I hope to hear some day soon.

The hills and all our favourite walks should be lovely just now –
Hadn't heard about K.'s arm.

Yours
Jack

89

[Perham Downs Camp,
Ludgershall.]
Saturday [2 November 1918]

My dear Arthur,

Many thanks for your letter (what a conventional opening!)
which shows you much more cheerful and contented than you were
in the last. I am delighted about these classes at the technical, and I
am sure, tho' it may be tiring at times, that you will feel much the
better for them both in your painting and spirits. What sort of
people do you meet there? I suppose they are of all ages, sexes and
classes, but you ought with luck to find plenty of interesting folk in a
place of that sort.

I suppose I *was* the last person to whom the bramble spoke. Your
reference to her does carry one back to the old days that were so
happy although one hardly realized how happy at the time (another
frightfully conventional remark, but you can't help feeling that it's
true). It is terrible to think how quickly an old order changes and
how impossible it is to build it up again exactly the same.

I wonder will there be many changes when we meet again?

---

[2] *The Vision; or Hell, Purgatory and Paradise of Dante*, trans. H. F. Cary
(1814).

[3] *Hippolytus and The Bacchae of Euripides, and the Frogs of Aristophanes*,
trans. Gilbert Murray (1902).

Maureen told me the other day that I was greatly changed since she first knew me, but, with the impenetrable reticence of a child, declined to say in what way. Personally I don't feel very different. I suppose I am a bit broader – more tolerant of people different from ourselves and readier to see the good points in a well-meaning philistine – but I think my interests and ambitions are pretty much the same. You, I imagine from your letters, are a good deal broader, and have developed considerably, especially in your taste for poetry: your dip into the slightly decadent but charming 'celtic' circle at Dublin has certainly made you less of a Northerner. You were once a trifle bigoted about catholicism: that has passed. I suppose we are each of us different from being away from the other: we had perhaps learned to think & even read too much with an eye on the other's criticism. However we shall have enough to talk about for years, when once we get going.

By the way these rather stuffy reflections are holding up all my real news. Last Friday, or rather last Friday week, I made a journey to London to see Heinemanns.[1] You will understand well how pleasant it was to walk in under a doorway, adorned with the 'windmill' we have so often seen, feeling that I had some right to be there. I offered a card to a young woman who said that she thought Mr H. was out, would I see the manager? I was led through innumerable corridors, thro' all sorts of offices, past armies of typists and shown into a rather dingy room. C. S. Evans, the manager, was a young man, pale and fair &, I think, a gentleman. He was very nice to me and quite enthusiastic about the book and especially about one piece. John Galsworthy, he said, had read the MS. and wanted to put this piece in a new Quarterly which he is bringing out for disabled soldiers & sailors called Reveille: of course I consented.[2] While we were talking he was interrupted to speak on the telephone. I listened to quite a long technical conversation (if you can call *one* end of a telephone conversation) apparently with a female interlocutor on 'some designs for endleaves' – all of which, as you would heartily agree with me, was very interesting.

Later on H. himself came in. He was a little, fat bald man, very agreeable and fussy, but, as far as one could see, a really literary not a

---

[1] On 25 October.

[2] When it was discovered that Robert Hitchens had published a book under the title *Spirit in Prison* in 1908, Lewis (who altered his pseudonym to 'Clive Hamilton') changed the title of his to *Spirits in Bondage*, which phrase he borrowed from Milton's *Paradise Lost*, I, 658. His poem 'Death in Battle' appeared in *Reveille*, No. 3 (February 1919), p. 508.

mere business man. We fixed up all the formalities about terms and he hopes to let me have the proofs in about three weeks.

I returned home treading on air and bought a copy of Reveille – the August number & the first. It included only one poem, by Kipling so I suppose I should be satisfied with the company. So at last dreams come to pass and I have sat in the sanctum of a publisher discussing my own book (Notice the hideous vulgarity of success already growing in me). Yet – though it is very pleasant – you will understand me when I say that it has not the utter romance which the promise of it had a year ago. Once a dream has become a fact I suppose it loses something. This isn't affectation: we long & long for a thing and when it comes it turns out to be just a pleasant incident, very much like others.

The country is gorgeous, it is so still that hardly a leaf has fallen & I have never seen such autumn colours anywhere. They are lovely beech woods down beyond Savernake with winding roads thro' them and some fine old houses hidden away. They are all like a big yellow flame now – and a lovely autumn smell.

Am sending you a new photo to-morrow

Yours
Jack

90

Officers' Command Depôt,
Eastbourne.[1]
Monday 2nd [December 1918]

My dear Arthur,

Many thanks for your letter. I am sorry to have left you so long without anything; the chief reason was the bustle of being moved here. At first I thought it abominable – it is [a] much worse camp than the Ludgershall one – but now that the others have come down of course I spend most of my time out.

You are wrong in supposing that I am doing no reading, indeed I don't know why I have not kept you up to date. I have just finished the life of Browning (Everyman) by Dowden[2] which was a most interesting book – just what the life of a writer should be in my opinion, i.e. mainly about his work, not all futile personal details & dates. Moved by this I read his (B's) 'Paracelsus'[3] which I liked much

---

[1] Lewis was moved here about the middle of November.
[2] Edward Dowden, *Robert Browning* (1915).
[3] Robert Browning, *Paracelsus* (1835).

better than I expected. Of course a good deal of it is not what we used to call poetry in the good old days, but there are some bits of the real stuff and it is all full of interest.

But the great event is that I have learned to enjoy Shakespeare. I bought an Everyman copy of the Comedies[4] and am just finishing 'Measure for Measure'. Isn't it funny the way you come round to things you used to hate? I think the characterisation is excellent & there are fine passages of poetry. Don't you like Claudio's piece about,

> 'worse than worst
> Of those that wayward & uncertain thought
> Imagines howling'?[5]

I am also reading Virgil & Euripides 'Alcestis'.[6]

At the same time I am doing a lot of writing again. I have just finished a short narrative, which is a verse version of our old friend 'Dymer', greatly reduced & altered to my new ideas. The main idea is that of development by self-destruction, both of individuals & species (as nature produces man only to conquer her [*sic*], & man produces a future & higher generation to conquer the ideals of the last, or again as an individual produces a nobler mood to undo all that to-day's has done). The background proceeds on the old assumption of good *outside* & *opposed to* the cosmic order. It is written in the metre of Venus & Adonis:[7] 'Dymer' is changed to 'Ask' (you remember Ask & Embla in the Norse myths) & it is in the 3rd person under the title of 'The Redemption of Ask'. I am wondering what you will think of it. I am also at work on a short blank verse scene (you can hardly call it a play) between Tristram & King Mark & a poem on Ion, which is a failure so far.

By the way have you thought of getting the Xmas Bookman? I suppose not & I am in despair because it has all been bought up in advance. It is a thing I always want to get & it will be especially desirable this year as it may have a review of my book in it. Item, the proofs have NOT come yet but we live in hopes.

It is almost incredible that the war is over, isn't it – not to have that 'going-back' hanging over my head all the time. This time last year I was in the trenches, & now – but, come!, the tendency to

---

[4] *Shakespeare's Comedies*, with Biographical Introduction by Oliphant Smeaton and Prefatory Notes by D. C. Browning (1906).

[5] *Measure for Measure*, III, i, 124 (slightly misquoted).

[6] Euripides (480–406 BC) *Alcestis*.

[7] William Shakespeare, *Venus and Adonis* (1593).

moralize is getting the better of me.

The child is writing another fairy tale – rather the plan of 'Puck of Pook's Hill'[8] I fancy.

Yours
Jack

91

[University College,
Oxford.
26 January 1919][1]

My dear Arthur,

I was agreeably surprised to hear from you so soon: perhaps you will be equally surprised to hear that I have already performed your commissions if not to your satisfaction at any rate vastly to my own. I found two complete editions of the Larger Temple Sh.,[2] one new and the other second hand at 36/-. In neither case would they sell separate volumes and I therefore got the 36/- one myself with malicious glee! It is a little bit battered in some volumes but absolutely clean inside and has the real pre-war guilding, and good edges. Slowly as I can afford [it] I must get them re-bound.

As to the Gibbon they showed me specimen volumes of two editions both by Methuen: the larger one at 10/6 a volume was about the size of your 'British Empire' book & very similar in paper and type: the binding was a somewhat unpleasant ribbed blue cloth with elaborate gilding on the back – not unlike my Benedetto Croce. The smaller was the one which my father has, beautifully fresh & clean: I have therefore asked them to order this,[3] explaining that it would be no use unless they could get you the complete set – which they seem

[8] Rudyard Kipling, *Puck of Pook's Hill* (1906). The 'child' is probably Maureen Moore.

[1] After wiring his father that he would be home in January on a twelve-day leave, Lewis suddenly found himself demobilized from the Army and he arrived home on 27 December. His brother Warren (now a Captain in the Army Service Corps) was on leave and it was the first time the family had been together since Lewis went to France. Lewis returned to Oxford on 13 January 1919 to embark on the 'Honour Mods' course in Greek and Latin literature. He took up residence in University College, and Mrs Moore and Maureen found rooms nearby in the home of Miss Featherstone in 28 Warneford Road.

[2] *The Works of Shakespeare*, ed. Israel Gollancz, 12 vols., 'The Larger Temple Shakespeare' (1899).

[3] Edward Gibbon, *The History of the Decline and Fall of the Roman Empire*, ed. J. B. Bury, 7 vols., 'Methuen's Standard Library' (1905–6).

fairly confident of doing. I suppose this is what you would like done?
I certainly envy you such a nice book if they *do* get a complete set:
where will you put it? I am very pleased indeed with my Shakespeare.

Now for some account of myself and my doings. My day is as
follows: called at 7.30, bath, chapel and breakfast – in Hall.* Owing
to the lack of coal and servants we are having all our meals in Hall
this term. Next term we hope to go back to the traditional and much
more pleasant arrangement of having breakfast and lunch in our own
rooms. After breakfast I work (in the library or a lecture-room which
are both warm) or attend lectures until 1 o'clock when I bycycle out
to Mrs Moore's.

They are installed in our 'own hired house' (like St Paul only not
daily preaching & teaching). The owner of the house has not yet
cleared out & we pay a little less than the whole for her still having a
room. She is an elderly maiden lady and – I am not joking – a saint.
She gets up early every morning and goes to church – very high
Anglican – through the bitter frost. In spite of protests she brings
Mrs Moore a cup of tea in the morning: she can hardly be persuaded
to use her own kitchen, which by the arrangement should be common
to us both. Altogether a most remarkable character – and very given
to good works. At another house we tried we met a Miss Tennyson,
niece of the poet.

After lunch I work until tea, then work again till dinner. After that
a little more work, talk and laziness & sometimes bridge then bycycle
back to College at 11. I then light my fire and work or read till 12
o'clock when I retire to sleep the sleep of the just. At this little end
of the day I have read three Acts of King John which I like immensely. At that time of life he wrote much more simply: the verse has
a more correct flow and the characters are easily understood. Don't
you like Constance, especially her speech about death & the scene
between Pandulph & the Dauphin just afterwards?[4] Also, whether
working or not I always end the day by looking into Bridges. He is so
quiet and has something for every mood.

(From this [point] on you may read the letter to my father if you
want.) The place is more beautiful than ever in this weather: every
morning when I am called I see a lovely picture out of my window: a
battlemented tower and three bare trees against the cold, cold red of
the morning: then looking out you see the grass of the quad. powdered
in white and all the old stone of the roofs white too and pinched with
cold. However one can get quite warm in the library or the Junior

[4] William Shakespeare, *King John*, III, i, 29 *et seq.*

Common Room: of course it is in the former I work – if only you could smoke there, it would be ideal: the temptation to spend all your time rambling over the interesting modern books & the great old worm-eaten folios has to be sternly resisted!

Now for a piece of good luck – I go to lectures by Gilbert Murray twice a week, on Euripides 'Bacchae'. Luckily I have read the play before and can therefore give him a freeër attention: it is a very wierd play (you have read his translation, have you not?) and he is a real inspiration, – quite as good as his best books, if only he didn't dress so horribly, worse even than most dons. I go to Christchurch to hear him and to Balliol to hear a man called Bailey on Lucretius, who is very amusing.[5] He began by saying 'I hope none of you gentlemen have got my edition of this book[6] as it was written in my unregenerate days.'

One of the things that worries me is that every lecturer you go to tells you of about 5 books 'you should all have access to', which comes expensive. Some, of course, can be got second hand: my regular book-monger keeps his second-hand stock downstairs in a 12th century crypt, at one period haunted by Guy Faulkes.[7] Some of the best bits of Oxford seem to be underground – hidden away beneath prosaic grocers, hotels and tobacconists. Another thing that bothers me is the terrible independence with which you have to work here: I only see my tutor once a week and at other times it is very trying to reflect after a long day's work that you may have been simply wasting your time ever since you got up. On the whole, however, I get on fairly well & the amount of reading I've done stands me in good stead. Of course there is *very* little time for ordinary reading, which has to be confined to the week-end as it was at Kirk's. At present I am still at the Philosopher book which is excellent.

I have found one old friend, Edwards, who was here when I was last up and as an 'unfit' has been here all the time. It *is* good to be back and doing something one is interested in. I bless my good fortune every night when I hear the hours strike, lying in my bed. One chime takes it from another with varying notes, getting fainter & fainter, as though the whole great city were turning over and settling

[5] Cyril Bailey (1871–1957) was Classical Tutor at Balliol College.

[6] *Lucreti De Rerum Natura Libri Sex. Recognovit brevique adnotatione critica instruxit C. Bailey* [1899].

[7] This was Mr H. G. Gadney's bookshop at 2 and 3 Turl Street. It later became the 'Turl Cash Bookshop' – taking its name from the fact that Mr Gadney never gave credit. The twelfth-century crypt, haunted by Guy Fawkes, is now a pub called 'The Monks' Retreat'.

itself to sleep in the cold, cold night. That Debussy thing keeps on running in my head.

I hope the biliousness is gone, & that you are getting on with your varying works: anything in the writing line?

Yours
Jack

* I mean breakfast only in hall – not bath & chapel as well.

92

[University College.
9 February 1919]

My dear Arthur,

I am really sorry that I did not write you your letter as I should last week. At present I am working at such high pressure that if anything unexpected turns up it must swallow something else. So long as nothing interrupts my routine I get on just comfortably, with a little time to spare at week ends for reading: when something does, I am stranded. However I hope to be more regular in future. Last Sunday I had to go out to tea with a don here called Poynton who is my tutor.[1]

The place has been looking just lovely in the snow. As you come out of our college gate you see All Souls and just beyond it the grey spire of St Mary's Church: you know what real Gothic is like: all little pinaccles with every kind of ornament on them and in the snow they look like a wintry forest hung up against the dark sky, and always associated in ones mind with the sound of bells. Just beyond St Marys you come into a solemn silent square with the great dome of the Bodleian in the middle: you can imagine how fine it looks with the white carpet underfoot. But I must send you some penny postcards.

I expected my father read you about the 'Martlets', a literary club I have joined:[2] I only hope it won't absorb valuable time. The great

---

[1] Arthur Blackburne Poynton (1867–1944) of whom Lewis was very fond and with whom he had tea at his home in 3 Fyfield Road on 2 February, had been a Fellow of University College since 1894. He was Master of University College 1935–7 and, sadly, was killed by a motor car as he was crossing the High Street in front of his college on 8 October 1944.

[2] The 'Martlets Society' minute-books are preserved in the Bodleian Library under the shelfmark MS. Top. Oxon. d. 95/1–5. There is a general article about 'The Martlets' by P. C. Bayley in the *University College Record* (1949–50). My essay entitled 'To the Martlets' in *C. S. Lewis: Speaker and Teacher*, ed. Carolyn Keefe (1971) contains all the minutes of the papers Lewis read to the Martlets between 1919 and 1940.

treat is the prospect of whistling John Masefield up from his villa in the suburbs of Oxford to read us a paper. I must really get some of his books when I have any time. I see from this week's Supplement that he has just published another volume of narrative poems.[3] Judging by the quotations it is execrably bad.

Tea at the Poynton's was quite amusing by the way: he is a very humorous old man who says the funniest things in a monotonous, melancholy voice. He showed us some books of Russian fairy tales – he is learning the language. They were badly printed on poor paper but exquisitely illustrated and illuminated: the designs were all 'flat' of course but very effective, and in one or two cases very simple colouring produced the best impressions of evening or cold or so forth.

The only man of much interest whom I have met in College is Blunt.[4] His father is a don at Christ Church,[5] and he was at Winchester where he acted a minor part in a production of Yeat's 'On Baile's Strand' [1904] with the young Asquith[6] as 'The Fool' – some wd. say an appropriate part! He has also met Kipling and Bergson, neither of whom impressed him in talk tho' he professes to admire the latter. Of course he is a trifle affected and omniscient like all these people who stayed out the whole numbing time at 'one of our great public schools' but he is really appreciative of some kinds of literature, especially Morris, Yeats and Maeterlinck which of course pleases me. I also find that another man in college called Paisley[7] has written some poems which that man Mais (who wrote 'Diary of a

[3] John Masefield's *A Poem and Two Plays* (1919) was reviewed in *The Times Literary Supplement* (30 January 1919), p. 54.

[4] Henry Pyot Blunt (1898–1955) took his B.A. in 1922. He was with the Bombay Burma Trading Corporation, Rangoon 1922–6; an Assistant Master in the Upper Canada College, Toronto 1927; with the John Lewis Partnership in 1936; Minister of Food in 1939; the Commercial Corporation in 1942; and Minister of Food from 1947 to 1952.

[5] Herbert William Blunt (1864–1940) who was Tutor in Philosophy and Librarian of Christ Church from 1888 to 1928.

[6] The Hon. Anthony Asquith (1902–68), fifth son of the 1st Earl of Oxford and Asquith.

[7] Sir Rodney Marshall Sabine Pasley (1899–   ) was educated at Sherborne School, after which he served as a 2nd Lieut in the Royal Field Artillery during 1914–18. He took his B.A. from University College in 1921, after which he became an Asst Master at Alleyn's School, 1921–5; Vice-Principal of Rajkumar College at Rajkot, India, 1926–8; Asst Master at Alleyn's School, 1931–6; Headmaster of Barnstaple Grammar School, 1936–43; and he was Headmaster of Central Grammar School, Birmingham, from 1943 until his retirement in 1959.

Schoolmaster' and an introduction to 'The Loom of Youth'[8]) is 'trying to get published'. The thing rather sniffs of modernism, of general Alec-Waugh-ishness. I don't know Paisley very well but I shall be interested to see the book when and if it comes out. I wish I could hear anything of my own: I am sure I shall be white haired before it sees daylight!

In reading I am still at the philosopher book, have finished King John and am reading Troilus & Cressida – a very good play. I progress so slowly that I shall have little to chronicle in this way for a long time. The Gibbon for you has not turned up yet but I shall order them to send it immediately.

'The family' has been greatly taken with your photo: they didn't expect you to be so good-looking! & Mrs Moore asks me to ask you for one for herself and sends her love.

I wonder are you right about George Elliot not living? Perhaps so, for even already one hears less of her than of the Brontes: but there is a sort of balance and sanity, a good-breeding even about them & especially 'Middlemarch' that you don't get in the Brontes. You said you *had* read Gilbert Murray's translation of the Bacchae didn't you? I think I shall write one myself some day: his doesn't satisfy me at all!

I am glad to hear you are still working. Do get on with the writing: as you said yourself it at least needs no physical energy and I am sure you only need to stick at it. The cold here is simply awful – thats not a conventional remark, because it *is*. Oh, by the way, somebody else *did* ask me who wrote the librettos of Wagner's operas – I nearly expired. Two such ignorami in one world is *too* much.

Yours
Jack

P.S. Nearly all this is fit for 'publication' except one sentence.[9]

---

[8] By Alec Waugh (1917).
[9] He did not wish his father to see the reference to Mrs Moore.

93

My dear Arthur,

Many thanks for your letter. Your account of strike life at home was very amusing – rather trying to have your model eaten! Only why were you painting those sort of things? 'Faute de mieux' I suppose!

About the Gibbon, Blackwell's have at last heard: you can get only three volumes and there is no talk of a reprint. Would you like me to try and get a complete set of that larger edition by the same publisher? I think I described it to you before, but I can't say I should advise it myself: the type is a little bit larger but it has no other advantage & is certainly not worth the difference in price.

I have bought two copies of drawings by Albrecht Dürer. You will find a good article about him in the Encyclopedia Brittanica. I have always looked upon [him] as the founder of the fantastic & illustrative school now represented by Rackham and Heath Robinson. This view is probably quite wrong historically but I am sure you would recognize the similarity in the very lines and shadows. These two are 'S. Jerome' and the 'Prodigal Son'. The first is very dark, and shows a heavy Gothic chamber: in the light of the single window sits an old wizardy figure pouring over a monstrous book. The room contains the typical insignia of mediaeval sorcery – a crocodile hung on the wall. At the saint's feet sleep together a lion and a dog. I do wish Dürer had illustrated 'The Faerie Queene'. The best thing about the 'Prodigal Son' is the drawing of the swine, which are really like great, wild boars, shaggy and tusked, and recalling somehow in their fantastic strength the dwarfs in Rackham. The background containing the thatched buildings of the sty and the 'tangled spires' of a house is – le Romance même. I haven't had time to study the prodigal himself and so don't describe him. I hope they will be framed by Teusday. There are several others in a shop here – from 2/6 each and a few shillings more for framing. I wonder would you like them? There are a lot I would like to get but some of his best backgrounds are spoilt by nude female figures of the most brutal and deliberate ugliness I've ever seen. I can't think what he is trying to do in these cases -- whether they are done in malice or whether that seemed beautiful in his day.

I am still reading the philosopher book: there is something to be said for reading so little, you take it in better. Of course in work I am reading as fast [as] I can & am more than half way through the Iliad. I have to read all Homer, all Virgil, all Demosthenes & all Cicero, besides four Greek plays and a special subject instead of verse. I think in my case it will be Logic, but am not quite sure.

By the way when are you going to get Lang's translation of Homer? I suggest you should get 'The World's Desire' [1891] the romance about Helen that he wrote in collaboration with Rider Haggard (a good blend!) and then his Oddyssey after that. 'World's Desire' is so Homeric that you would pass from one to the other insensibly. By the way people from Christ Church tell me they have a don there who tells you to translate Homer in the style of Pope and sternly quells anything like Morris or Chaucer. Can you believe that such barbarism survives in the 20th century, such an absolute lack of historical sense?

Did I describe to you our meeting of the 'Martlets' on Yeats,[1] I think I did. I have got to read a paper on Morris at the next but one. I fought hard against undertaking this extra time devouring job, but had to in the end. Luckily I shall have no difficulty in finding things to say, and I really have read nearly all his important works – which is a very rare qualification in people that read papers at college societies.

Winter has broken up here and it is quite warm. Once or twice in the mornings I have been able to sit in my own rooms without a fire and the window open. One of the annual joys is the first day you go out without an overcoat.

I have been talking to Pasely, the man whose poems Mais is trying to get published. He says he is of an old-fashioned type, not at all a modernist and has promised to show me his things. He was at the same school with Alec Waugh and confirms the story of his getting the order of the boot.

You don't say anything about your own writing: mine of course is compulsorily 'off'. I think it would do you [a] lot of good to start something and perhaps send me instalments in the old way.

Many thanks for the photo.

Yours
Jack

---

[1] The minutes of this meeting, held on 12 February, are found in the Bodleian: MS. Top. Oxon. d. 95/3, fos. 64–6.

94

My dear Arthur,

I was rather under the impression that I *had* kept to the weekly arrangement this last time. At any rate you will observe that I am answering your last at once for it only came yesterday.

You seem to be lucky in your theatrical fates at home. I should very much like to have seen 'The Importance of Being Ernest',[1] tho' perhaps some of it would be lost on the stage. So far as I can remember I don't agree with you about the feeble ending. The beauty of it is that it entirely rejects probability or sentiment – would that all our society farces did the same – and gives itself up to a sort of glittering and classic nonsense that reminds me strongly of 'Alice in Wonderland'.

I have Layamon's Brut and Wace's translated in the one Everyman volume[2] – or rather the parts of them about the Arthurian period. Wace you remember was 'a french clerke, well could he write' who copied Layamon's poem in French rhyming couplets, with more style but less vigour. Wace is famous for his 'rationalising' remarks about a magic fountain he went to see in Broceliande, and, being the wrong sort of man, of course did not find the marvels 'A fool I went, a fool I returned.' Layamon I quite liked tho' I didn't finish it. Of course his battles are fatiguing, but the whole thing is very 'heroic' – much more like Boewulf than Malory. Arthur cleaves the Dane Skallagrim to the teeth and exults over him just like the warriors in the Iliad. On the other hand the passing of Arthur is really more romantic than in Malory, who, you remember, makes Avalon a really existing valley where the great king is buried. Brut, however, knows better 'They say he abideth in Avalon with Argante the fairest of all elves: but ever the Britons think that he will come again to help them at their need' – a great deal of which I copied in a poem rejected by Heinemann – on whom ten thousand maledictions. Every week nearly in the Times Supplement I see a new book of poems published by him, but never mine. I can't think why he took it at all at this rate. I shall probably write to Evans to day – with the usual result.

---

[1] Oscar Wilde, *The Importance of Being Earnest* (1895).

[2] *Arthurian Chronicles, Represented by Wace and Layamon*, trans. by Eugene Mason, with an Introduction by Lucy Allen Paton, 'Everyman Library' [1912].

As your letter arrived yesterday afternoon (Saturday) I couldn't follow your commands about going for the Gibbon-hunt at once. I am still at the philosopher book, tho' nearly finished. The later & more modern chapters are pretty difficult – Spencer and William James etc, who do not so easily fit into formulae as simple minded gentlemen of the Locke or Paley type. I thought you would like 'The Private Papers of Henry Ryecroft'. I don't know that the 'soothing qualities' were what struck me most, but no! – I'm thinking of 'The Corner of Harley Street'.[3] Now I remember: don't you like his remarks about cooking? Also on spiritualism he expresses a feeling I have sometimes experienced – mechanical reaction I suppose. We do get quite good things at the theatre but when should I have time to go? The only one I regret was Maeterlinck's 'Burgomaster of Stilmonde': but it was only two nights, and the waste of an evening and the rush there would have been to get seats put me off.

To go back 'to the last remark but one' for a minute, as Alice says, that book of mine on Epic and Heroic Poetry gives a very good account of Layamon: reading it I have often wished you could get a complete crib instead of only the Arthutian bit. Geoffrey of Monmouth is in the Everyman is he not? I am waiting to try and get a copy of him in the Latin[4] – perhaps there is one in the College Library. If only one had time to read a little more: we either get shallow & broad or narrow and deep.

At our last meeting of the Martlets a man called Wyllie read a paper on Newbolt.[5] I hadn't thought the subject *very* promising but he quoted a great many good things I hadn't known – especially a very queer little song about grasshoppers that you must read if you can get hold of it: so different from the usual patriotic business, tho' that is good too, until you've ready sixty odd pieces on exactly the same lines. I have had a most interesting talk with Pasely and seen his poems. I mentioned him before, didn't I? Mais is trying to get him published. He has written one long piece that I envy him very much, and a number of pretty enough things – no stuff in them, the sort of things that are as common and not quite as good as wild-flowers. But the one piece was really extraordinarily good. I wonder will he do the same again? At the meeting, by the way, some bright

[3] By Peter Harding (1911).

[4] Geoffrey of Monmouth (d. 1154), *Historia Regum Britanniae* (Paris, 1508). Or *Histories of the Kings of Britain*, trans. Sebastian Evans, 'Everyman' [1912].

[5] Basil Platel Wyllie's paper, read at the meeting on 26 February, was entitled 'The Poetry of Henry Newbolt'. Bodleian: MS. Top. Oxon. d. 95/3, fos. 67–9.

person was found to make a defence of vers libre.[6]

I got a letter the other day from an unknown member of the female sex – an undergraduate apparently – asking me to play my part in National Reconstruction by joining the Oxford University Socialist Society. As it was a printed circular I didn't 'feel called upon' to answer it.

I think the ugly figures in Dürer go beyond your suggestion – there is spite in every line: they were probably fancy portraits of ladies who didn't ask him to dinner. But it would be unfair to judge him by these explosions of ill temper. By 'verse' in exams I mean the composition of Latin & Greek verses, which is the usual subject to take: if you don't do them, you do something else. Of course it is nothing to do with the verse or prose that you read.

We are having some lovely days here now, and it must be just glorious in the country: thank goodness there is plenty of greenery in Oxford.

There is no decent edition of Chaucer except the fabulously expensive Medici press one and even that only gives the Canterbury Tales – except of course the Everyman Canterbury Tales which is garbled and modernised: by a ridiculous arrangement whenever they come to an obscene passage they slip back into the real language.[7] Chaucer was very like Dickens – a virtuous, bourgeois story teller fond of highly moral vulgarity & indecency for its own sake, incapable (at the Tales period not in his early life) of appreciating romance.

Yours
Jack

95

[University College.]
Monday [5 May 1919][1]

My dear Arthur,

Many thanks for your letter. I had meant to write to you yesterday whether I heard or not, but when the time came I was not feeling well and so it got put off till to-day.

[6] 'An interesting discussion on "Vers Libre", arising out of one poem quoted by Mr Wyllie, then followed. Mr Pasley maintained that this school was not entirely free from a certain charlatanism, but the Society was interested to find in Mr [Geoffrey Odell] Vinter an enthusiastic defender of this kind of composition.' MS. Top. Oxon. d. 95/3, fo. 69.

[7] Charles Cowden Clarke, Tales from Chaucer, 'Everyman' [1911].

[1] Lewis's first book, Spirits in Bondage: A Cycle of Lyrics, was published the last week in March, and he was on vacation in Belfast from 2–24 April.

My first news I'm afraid will plunge you into despair. The copy of Morris's Odyssey which I had seen last term is gone and they could produce only a rather dirty one in its place! I felt I had better not order a copy, as you [are] rather afraid of doing that – tho' I think it is a case of 'nothing venture, nothing win', you'll *have to* order a book sometime again.

I was in some anxiety to see my new rooms, having left them in a ghastly state from my luckless attempt at distempering, and having heard nothing from the man whom I had told to paper them. Of course he hadn't done it, but by way of compensation the distemper had dried out excellently – all my splotches and thick & thin variations had disappeared. It is a nice quiet greyish blue: of course it is rather untidy and splashed about the woodwork a bit, but you don't notice that very much. It suits the two Dürers very well and also the Venus. There is also *one* good piece of furniture, a small bookcase of dark oak. You would agree with me in liking the beam in the ceiling and the deep windows and the old tree that taps against them, recalling Phantastes and Wuthering Heights. When it gets into leaf I shall look out into a mass of greenery with glimpses of the old walls across and of the grass below – such a scene as the redoubtable Heath Robinson did in your 12th night.[2]

But all this you shall see for yourself. I shall go to the dean as my tutor to-morrow and ask him then about the 'guest-room'. By the way I was annoyed to find that I had left behind all the pictures you gave me. Will you please send them as soon as possible: you can understand my desire to get fixed in and see all my household gods around me. How is the Rackham-esque drawing of the hills going on? I hope it will be a great success: it was certainly a splendid idea to do that particular bit in that style.

I have nearly finished the Venus poem and am full of ideas for another, which Gilbert Murray gave me the hint of in a lecture – a very curious legend about Helen, whom Simon Magus, a gnostic magician mentioned in the Acts,[3] found living as a very earthly person in Antioch and gradually recalled to her who she was and took her up to Zeus again, reborn: on their way they had to fight 'the Dynasties' or planets – the evil powers that hold the heaven, between us and something really friendly beyond. I have written some of it, but of course I get hardly any time either for reading or writing.

I have not quite finished the third volume of Gibbon, and it still pleases me as much as ever it did, in fact all the more as I go on. The

[2] Shakespeare's *Twelfth Night*. See letter of 18 July 1916.
[3] Acts, ch. viii.

only attitude you can adopt towards my father's underhand and contemptible efforts to get information out of you (he apparently judges
your character by his own) is the one you rightly do already – as you
say, ignore it; and if he becomes unbearable, go away. You throw out
merely a hint about the Glenmachonians' remarks on my book: tell
me all they say when you write, you can easily understand how
interested I am. I am glad you liked the Patriotism book, many parts
of it sounded attractive: the Masefield one I hope to get one of these
days.

We have had one meeting of the Martlets at which a very dull
looking youth read a surprisingly good paper on Synge:[4] it has really
quite encouraged me to try him again, tho' I feel some grains of
prejudice against what I remember of him – perhaps because he has
become a cult, which few writers escape now a days. I am afraid I
have not got to know any of the Balliol poets yet, and am not sure
that I shall be able to manage it – I don't see very many people and I
don't think Pasely himself meets them very often.

I hope by this time you're sailing the seas of Gibbon (the new
counterpart to the old 'Have you read your Swinburne?') and not
feeling too depressed with the world in general – that 'The thing's
not becoming intolerable!' in fact.

We are having lovely weather here and I shall soon begin to bathe.
Don't forget the pictures.

Yours
Jack

96

[University College]
Monday [2 June 1919]

My dear Arthur,

I really was ashamed of myself when I got your letter: I had put off
my weekly one to you from day to day, hoping to work it in 'some day
soon' and hardly realized how long I'd let it go. My letter-writing
time last week was rather upset by a long standing debt to Aunt
Lily,[1] which simply *had* to be done and an unexpected letter from
W.[2]

<hr>

[4] Edward Fairchild Watling (1899–   ) read his paper on 'The Plays
of J. M. Synge' at the 192nd meeting of the Martlets on 30 April. Bodleian:
MS. Top. Oxon. d. 95/3, fos. 71–2.

[1] Lily Hamilton Suffern (1860–1934) was Lewis's mother's sister, and an
ardent suffragette. She moved about a good deal and, being very fond of
Lewis, visited him often in Oxford.

[2] Lewis's brother Warren (or 'Warnie') is usually referred to as 'W.' in

Now as to all the important questions (1) Come whenever is convenient and let me know beforehand when I may expect you (2) I am afraid you can only get a guests [room] for one or two nights in College, therefore (3) You had better stay in 'The Mitre' in High Street which is the best and also the nearest to College (4) Would you like me to book you a room there.

Thanks very much for the pictures: the two best, the garden one and the tree in the new Soaking Machine are better than I remembered. I am having them both framed. The little Rackhamesque one I am not sure yet how I will treat. It gives me pleasure and has indeed a *special* appeal that the ordinary kind of drawing has not, but I can't find any place I think it would suit. We shall see.

It is perfectly lovely now both in town and country – there are such masses of fruit trees, all white. One big cherry tree stands in the Master's garden just below my windows and a brisk wind this morning had shaken down masses of leaves that lay like snow flakes on the bright smooth grass. Then beyond the lawn you see the gable end of the chapel.

I usually go and bathe before breakfast now at a very nice little place up the Cherwell called 'Parson's Pleasure'. I always swim (on chest) down to a bend, straight towards the sun, see some hills in the distance across the water, then turn and come again to land going on my back and looking up at the willow trees above me. It is a most romantic bathe and rather like William Morris – as one of his characters would 'wash the night off'. I have been reading at breakfast lately 'The Water of the Wondrous Isles',[3] which is more romantic tho' not so well-constructed as 'The Well at the World's End': all the same I have enjoyed it immensely with quite the old thrill, his witches and wanderers I can usually rely on. He is so inexhaustible!

How very funny about Bob, and how typical of Kelsie! Is it that she hides her opinions – I mean on other subjects as well as this – or that she has none.

I have NOT 'woken up and found myself famous' yet but I have slunk into a modicum of notoriety it would seem. At the last meeting of the Martlets I was asked by a man called Hartman[4] whether I was 'the famous Lewis' jokingly of course. It appears that some of the

this correspondence.
[3] William Morris (1897).
[4] Cyril Augustus Hughes Hartmann (1896–   ) was educated at Charterhouse and matriculated at Oxford in 1914. He received his B.A. in 1921 and a B.Litt. in 1922.

extreme literary set at Balliol and Exeter, the writers of 'vers libre' etc, who run the yearly Books of Oxford Poetry had got the book and asked Hartman if he knew a Lewis at Univ. and if that was the man. The result is that several people are going to buy it who might not have otherwise done so. On Wednesday I am to meet at Hartman's rooms a man called Childe who edits these books of Oxford Poetry[5] & tho' I am sure I shall disapprove of him and his views it will possibly be useful. Hartman himself is rather an interesting character: his mother was a member of the set that included Oscar Wilde and Whistler[6] and would have included Swinburne if it could. He said he had once met Wilde but did not remember much about it. Lucky man, he was in Spain all thro' the war!

I am afraid I shall never get on with the Gibbon as I go now; although I still like it as much as ever it is awfully hard to keep the connection in my head with so many other irons in the fire. If I once give it up I shall be lost!

Hardly writing anything at all except a few lines yesterday for the Helen poem, and bits for a short one I thought of doing on 'Nimue'. What are the possibilities of the subject?

Awfully sorry to hear you've been laid up again: you mustn't do too much when you're here.[7]

Yours
Jack

P.S. Haven't heard from my esteemed parent for some time; has he committed suicide yet?

97

[University College.
14 July 1919]

My dear Arthur,

I suppose you have already decided about my remissness as a correspondent that 'The thing is intolerable': and perhaps I have been more ready even than usual because I have to convey to you a

[5] Wilfred Rowland Childe (1890–1952) was the editor (with T. W. Earp and A. L. Huxley) of *Oxford Poetry 1916* (1917) and (with T. W. Earp and Dorothy L. Sayers) of *Oxford Poetry 1917* (1918).

[6] James Abbott McNeill Whistler (1834–1903).

[7] Arthur visited Lewis in Oxford from about 20 to 28 June, during which time he met the Moores. From Oxford he went to London to consult a heart specialist.

piece of information which as Miss Austin[1] says may produce 'the cruelest sense of mortification'. It is about the song: on the more technical side of the question Miss Plowman will write to you but I can give you some outline.[2] It appears, to speak frankly, that you will have to learn a great deal more about composition, and even about more elementary points of technique before you can hope to do yourself justice. It is not merely a question of embellishing or pruning what you have done to suit arbitrary rules. As far as I can gather, the real trouble is that your weakness on these points leads you, so to speak, to run your ideas into moulds already prepared by compositions which you unconsciously remember, and therefore appear to be less original than you are. Do I make it clear?

It seems to me the inevitable result of a lack of formal knowledge: it is like an essay by a schoolboy who gives you a sentence of his own here and there and then ends up the sentence with a remeniscense of Macaulay. I don't think myself that in any art this argues a real lack of originality: it merely shows that he is 'groping about in worlds not realised' and his thought clutches at any ready-made clothing which seems fairly suitable. But Miss Plowman's letter will make all clear.

Now I do hope you won't let yourself be discouraged by what her friends have said. If without any knowledge you *had* succeeded in giving yourself a chance it would have been very wonderful: that you have not, was only to be expected, and I certainly think you have no reason to give it up. When I was at Bookham I twice went in for the lyric competition in the Bookman, once with 'Night! black Night' and again with the piece which appears as 'Ad Astra' in the MS. & 'Victory' in the printed book.[3] Both were complete failures – failed of the first prize, failed of the second, failed even of a mention. This was much worse than what has now happened to you! Besides you could not be in a better position than you are for going on: you have absolutely unbounded liesure – you don't have to work at odd moments stolen from your 'work' in the other sense like the rest of us: according to this specialist your heart is not so bad as you have supposed: good feeding and a little more exercise which good feeding will enable you to take will set you up. A course of solid but

[1] Jane Austen.

[2] Mary Plowman was the elocution mistress as well as a teacher of music at Headington School, where Maureen was a pupil. In time she became friends with Maureen's mother and Lewis and was a frequent visitor at their house. Her opinion had been sought about a piece of music Arthur had just written.

[3] *Spirits in Bondage*, p. 16.

agreeable work with hopes and dreams ever in view would be the best thing for your nerves & spirits. That is, of course, unless you decide to take up painting or writing *really* seriously instead. Now that you have made a sort of landmark in your routine by coming to England, do try not to slip back into the old ways: do not give in to depression – and give everything up as soon as difficulties arise. Remember all we dreamed and did in the golden age of Bookham. I think I have nearly talked myself out now, & it is a wonder if you have put up with it.

Since you left I have read the 'Talisman',[4] merely because Maureen happens to be 'doing it' at school and it was lying about. Of course it is one of his poorest: the rapid episodes and impossible disguises remind us of what monstrosities the Romantic movement could and did commit in its infancy. I imagine Walpole's 'Castle of Otranto' [1764] and the 'really horrid' Gothic romances of Mrs Whats-her-Name[5] were something in this style. The subject however is fascinating, and Saladin is a great figure. I wonder where one could read something else about the Crusaders & the Saracens – do you know of anything? I suppose for the next six years or so I shall have no time to get thro' Tasso[6] in the original! I am now reading an Everyman crib to 'Marco Polo'.[7] The descriptions of innumerable Eastern towns would probably bore you, not having my appetite for collecting useless information: but I think you would like it once he reaches China and describes the wonderful court of the great Khan Khublai (Coleridge's Khubla Khan): the royal park with its palaces & pavilions and lakes 'full of all kinds of birds' and bridges reminds one of a willow pattern plate. There is also an excellent introduction by John Masefield and as a book this copy is a very favourable specimen of Everyman. This and the Talisman have begun to revive my interest in the East which was swept aside by Morris and Malory about the time I first knew you.

I hope you are avoiding my father as much as possible. Keep me posted however in all that may occur. I wired to him the other day to ask if W. had come home, and as he calls the latter 'Warren' in his reply I conclude he is in a temper about something or other.

The 'Medea' is very nearly finished, and will be about twelve hundred lines. The main interest hangs on the family relations of the

[4] Sir Walter Scott, *The Talisman* (1825).
[5] Mrs Ann Radcliffe who wrote *The Mysteries of Udolpho* (1794).
[6] Torquato Tasso, *Gerusalemme Liberata* (1581).
[7] *The Travels of Marco Polo the Venetian*, with an Introduction by John Masefield, 'Everyman' [1908].

horrible old king and his daughter, whom I imagine as a sort of Emily Brontë, only more of a wolf – some of her father's bad blood coming out. The defect of the poem as a whole will be – heaven help us! – dulness.

I picture to myself your pleasure in arranging all your new books and getting settled down again: I do hope you will keep well and do something – perhaps I might get an instalment some day. Give me a full account of what you saw in town, especially about Cyrano.[8] The Minto[9] sends her love & says she is very pleased with the doctor's report on you: she also tells me to add that she has been expecting a letter from you by every post, and her 'face falls' three times a day. The hot weather comes back. Cheer up & write soon & don't shoot yourself yet.

Yours
Jack

[The rather acid references to Albert Lewis in the last two letters are evidence of an estrangement which had been building up between father and son – and which was soon to get much worse. Besides the friction caused by their very different dispositions and the fact that Albert had not visited him in hospital, Clive resented being away from his new 'family' in Oxford. And Albert, for his part, was deeply troubled about his son's mysterious involvement with Mrs Moore. While Albert absolutely refused to discuss the matter with his relations in Belfast, he opened his mind to Warren (now stationed in Belgium) who was not only worried by Clive's increasing coolness towards himself but, likewise, piqued by his brother's preference for Mrs Moore's company. Warren was shortly to come home on leave and Clive long hesitated to say whether or not he would spend part of his summer vacation with his family.

Eventually, Clive wrote to his brother on 9 June 1919 saying: 'Would the early part of September do for your leave: one doesn't get any chance of fine weather or of endurably warm sea water any earlier in Donegal. I quite agree with you that we could have quite an excellent time together at Portsalon – if we were "both" there; if, as you suggest, we were "all" there, I suppose we could endure as we always have endured. You ask me what is wrong with P[apy] which he describes as exceedingly painful and horribly depressing . . . What the difficulties of life with him always were, you know: but I never found it as bad as when I was last at home. I needn't describe the continual fussing, the

---

[8] Presumably the play *Cyrano de Bergerac* (1898) by Edmond Rostand which Greeves could have seen in London.
[9] The nickname used by Lewis and Greeves for Mrs Moore.

T.S.T.–I

sulks, the demand to know all one's affairs.' (*Lewis Papers*, vol. VI, pp. 133–4.)

Clive continued to delay giving his father a clear answer as to whether he would come home, and Albert, feeling profoundly hurt by the neglect, wrote to Warren on 25 June explaining what he thought might be the cause of his younger son's behaviour. 'I am afraid I understand the situation too well,' he said. 'He has never once since he went to Oxford come straight home to me when he got leave. Always Mrs Moore first. On one occasion he had six weeks leave and he spent five of them with her. I am afraid therefore that he has kept silence because he does not wish to bind himself for the earlier part of his holidays. I am not "grousing" exactly. I am rather explaining that if you have to take your leave early in July we may not have the pleasure of the "young'uns" society. After all perhaps there is some excuse for his not running home at once when I am alone, and if I were sure that mischief were not afoot, I should not feel as keenly about it as I do. I haven't anything very attractive to offer, and I suppose Arthur's constant society palls. But I would rather he was kept from me by some other cause.' (*Lewis Papers*, vol. VI, p. 145.)

Torn between his desire to remain in Oxford and the wish not to disappoint his father, Clive wrote to Albert on 29 June making the following proposal. 'Where could you pass your holiday better than in Oxford?' he asked. 'The three of us could certainly spend our afternoons in a punt under the willows at least as comfortably as we did at Dunbar, and the Mitre, honoured with so many famous ghosts would be an improvement on the Railway Hotel! Let me know in your next letter what you propose to do.' (*Lewis Papers*, vol. VI, p.151.) This proved to be too complicated, and in the end Clive met Warren in Oxford on 23 July and they travelled together to Belfast arriving there on the 27th. The holidays passed peacefully enough until there occurred the following event which Albert recorded in his diary of 6 August: 'Sitting in the study after dinner I began to talk to Jacks about money matters and the cost of maintaining himself at the University. I asked him if he had any money to his credit, and he said about £15. I happened to go up to the little end room and lying on his table was a piece of paper. I took it up and it proved to be a letter from Cox and Co stating that his a/c was overdrawn £12 odd. I came down and told him what I had seen. He then admitted that he had told me a deliberate lie. As a reason, he said that he had tried to give me his confidence, but I had never given him mine etc., etc. He referred to incidents of his childhood where I had treated them badly. In further conversation he sd. he had no respect for me – nor confidence in me.' (*Lewis Papers*, vol. VI, p. 161.)

The quarrel, which was to rankle for some months, explains the bitter remarks Lewis was later to make about his father ('Excellenz') in his letters to Greeves. Judging from his diary, Albert Lewis bitterly lamented his 'estrangement from Jacks', and though Lewis continued to write respectful and newsy letters to his father, it was some years before they were perfectly reconciled. Meanwhile, the brothers departed Belfast on 22 August and journeyed to Dublin whither they visited a friend of Warren's, Dr Horace Stratford Collins, who was house surgeon at Doctor Steeven's Hospital, Dublin. Clive returned to Oxford on 24 August to find that Mrs Moore had left 28 Warneford Road and taken a flat in the home of Mr and Mrs Albert Morris in 76 Windmill Road.]

98

Sunday [24 August 1919]
'Hill View'
Windmill Rd.
Highfield
[Oxford]

My dear Arthur,

Just a line to let you know of my arrival and of this change of address – the Minto having left Uplands and come here. Our land-lady is a funny old woman, the wife of an Indian engine driver: I sleep on the sofa which quite satisfies my moderate demands on the world's comfort though it would hardly do for you.

We had quite a pleasant day in Dublin. I liked W's friend, who is house-surgeon in Steeven's hospital where he has a very pleasing little set of rooms. Have you ever been in Steeven's? There is a fine little library – despite some shocking portraits – containing some letters of Swift's. This letter begins to read like a guide book, so I will pass on.

Pass on to what? We are all well here and the Minto sends her love and tells me to thank you for all your labours on our behalf in the matter of letters etc[1] and also for the butter which we are still eating. She expects to go to France in a week or so now, which is rather horrible. What a pity you couldn't come over and bear me company in the solitudes of Highfield. By the way there is a thing I want you to do. No sooner had we got outside the gate on Friday than I remem-bered I had left the Reviews of my book[2] behind, which I particularly wanted to bring. Would you please go across some morning when his Excellenz is out and get them: they are in the bottom shelf of the

[1] Lewis and Mrs Moore exchanged daily letters whenever he was in Ireland, and to avoid Albert Lewis knowing about this (though he did, in fact, know) Mrs Moore addressed hers to Arthur's home.
[2] The reviews of *Spirits in Bondage*.

miniature roller-top desk thing that stands on the table of the little end room nearest the window. They are in a white envelope – please see about it, will you, and send them on.

Have not been doing much in the way of reading so far but the Hell-story is nearly finished. Write soon and tell me all developments.

Yours

Jack

99

[University College]
Thursday [18 September 1919]

My dear Arthur,

Your first letter, to quote Dr Johnson, 'was in such a strain of peevish discontent and unmanly resolution as could afford little comfort to a friend or satisfaction to a philosopher.' Hem! Well, perhaps it wasn't so bad as all that: but I hope that the bad spirits which seem to have resulted from mountains, sea and pleasant society have been banished by the charms of Bernagh.

You seem to have had some adventures in rescuing my reviews from the jaws of Excellenz! How fortunate that you had really borrowed some books to carry off the scene with. 'De Profundis'[1] is hardly more than a memory to me. I seem to remember that it had considerable beauties, but of course in his serious work one always wonders how much is real and how much is artistic convention. He must have suffered terribly in prison, more perhaps than many a better man. I believe 'The Ballad of Reading Gaol' [1898] was written just after he came out, and before he had had time to smelt down his experiences into artificiality, and that *it* rather than 'De Profundis' represents the real effect on his mind. In other words the grim bitterness is true: the resignation not quite so true. Of course one gets very real bitterness in D.P. too – as in the passage where he waited at the railway junction. Hartman's mother was a member of the Wilde set, and Hartman knows the person (refferred to in the book by initials) who waited to take off his hat – but I've forgotten who it was. 'The Ideal Husband'[2] is not, I think, one of the best.

I have written to and had an answer from Excellenz. He observes that he was pleased to get my letter and would have been more pleased to see in it 'some expression of regret for the terrible things I had said to him'. You see, he still insists on occupying the position of

---

[1] Oscar Wilde (1905).

[2] Oscar Wilde, *An Ideal Husband* (1899).

joint judge, jury and accuser, while relegating me to that of prisoner at the bar. So long as he refuses to acknowledge any faults on his side or to attribute the whole business to anything but my original sin, I do not see how he can expect a real or permanent reconciliation.

The Minto has returned from France: on which subject you will probably hear from her own pen. Since then we have moved into the flat which is very comfortable. Of course there has been a tremendous amount of work settling in but we begin to see daylight now.

On getting back to England I had the pleasure of looking over my 'Medea' of which I told you and finding that it was all hopeless and only fit for the fire! Nothing daunted however I bade it a long farewell – poor still-born – and consoled myself by turning the 'Nimue' from a monologue into a narrative, in which form it may do. It appears in 'stanzas' of my own invention and is rather indebted to 'St Agnes' Eve' with touches of Christabel and some references to contemporary politics – by way of showing how much better I could manage the country if they made me Prime Minister. Sounds promising, DON'T it? It relates the events of a single evening – Merlin coming back & catching Nimue at last. This is the first stanza, do you think it any good?

> 'There was none stirring in the hall that night,
> The dogs slept in the ashes, and the guard
> Drowsily nodded in the warm fire-light,
> Lulled by the rain and wearied of his ward,
> Till, hearing one that knocked without full hard,
> Half-dazed he started up in aged fear
> And rubbed his eyes and took his tarnished spear
> And hobbled to the doorway and unbarred.'

You will perhaps be surprised to hear that I am reading 'The Prelude' by way of graduating in Wordsworth-ism. What's even funnier, I rather like it! I'm coming to the conclusion that there are two orders of poetry – real poetry and the sort you read while smoking a pipe. 'The Prelude' nearly always on the second level but very comfortable and interesting all the same – better than Rousseau's Confessions in something the same style. You read it, didn't you? I expect like me you recognised lots of the early parts from recollections of your own childhood. I fancy the first Book is the best.

I sent 'Hippolytus' to the Odds & Ends Magazine[3] but I haven't

---

[3] I have been unable to discover any copies of the *Odds & Ends Magazine*. However, among the literary fragments preserved in the *Lewis Papers* (VIII, pp. 165–57) is a portion of the 'Hippolytus' poem no doubt referred to here. The poem was to go through various transformations, from 'Hip-

seen it yet. I shall be interested in trying to pick out Mrs Pomeroy's contribution. Does she write prose or verse?

The country is just beginning to think about Autumn. We have had some lovely walks. There are delightful 'rights of way' about here through fields and wood, all over styles made of single old stones – rather Druidical looking.

Write soon again. The family sends their love.

Yours
Jack

100

University College.
[18 October 1919]

My dear Arthur,

I am sorry to have left your last letter so long without an answer: of course the beginning of the term is accompanied with a lot of business which fills up my time. And I am afraid there is another cause which operates against you – namely that the idea of writing to you is inevitably associated with that of writing to Excellenz, a task for which I have so little relish that, in my cowardly way, I keep it as much out of my mind as possible.

I should have spared my 'sarcasm' if I had known that it would 'cut you to the heart': that susceptible and sorely-tried organ of yours should not offer itself so readily to the knife: and, as you see, Johnson was much *more* severe. Not of course that I consider myself entitled to the great man's privilege of colossal rudeness. But we follow as we may.

I am not very fond of Euripides' Medea: but as regards the under-working of the possibilities which you mention, you must remember that the translation has to be rather stiff – tied by the double chains of fidelity to the original and the demands of its own metres, it cannot have the freedom and therefore cannot have the passion of the real thing. As well, even in reading the Greek we must miss a lot. We call it 'statuesque' and 'restrained' because at the distance of 2500 years we cannot catch the subtler points – the associations of a word, the homeliness of some phrazes and the unexpected strangeness of others. All this we, as foreigners, don't see – and are therefore inclined to assume that it wasn't there.

polytus' to 'Wild Hunt' to 'The King of Drum' till it finally became 'The Queen of Drum' which is found in Lewis's *Narrative Poems* (1969).

I quite see the humour of your idea about Excellenz's double life and clandestine marriage. I don't think it *has* evaporated on paper. But, oh ye gods, what fun there would have been if he had been at home when Mrs Pomeroy arrived! What mysteries and suspicions he would have spun.

Yeats has taken up his residence in Oxford,[1] and some of us are going to beard the lion in his den one of these days. Perhaps we shall get him to read a paper to the Martlets: perhaps we shall be kicked out. But I think his vanity is sufficient to secure us a good reception if we come with the obvious purpose of worshipping devoutly.

I finished the Prelude and liked it. It is about as bad as a poem could be in some ways but one considers the great passages not too dearly bought at the price of the rest. Since then I have read Geoffrey of Monmouth's 'History of the Kings of Britain'. I don't think you would care much for it, there are a good many dull battles and his Arthur is merely contemptible. Where he really is good is in the early part. Who would not hear about the first coming of Brut, and Bladud (our first aeronaut, the British counterpart of Daedalus), and the birth of Merlin and the building of Stonehenge (its delightful alternative name being The Dance of Giants) and Vortigern and Lear and Locrine? One learns a little too. 'Kaer' apparently is British for 'city'. Hence Leil builds Kaer-Leil (Carlyle) and Kaer-leon is the city of legions. 'Kaerleon of the legions' (as I call it in Nimue) what a name! Also I have been looking into Macdonald's poems in book-shops lately: now-a-days I am too poor to buy anything without long consideration. They look much better than I thought before. I have been so long with Wordsworth and philosophers that I want something mystical – pure unadulterated imagination.

One gets lovely autumn bits even in town now. The other day I was sitting under the tower of Magdalen on a bus. The big bells were just chiming five and the tower was turning paler and paler every minute. The trees were getting ghostly and everything had just one word 'frost'. I do love to feel the winter coming on.

The Minto is frightfully busy and hasn't written to a creature except her sister since she came back, but when she has time you will be among the first claimants. We are both delighted to hear that you are coming to London[2] at last and shall expect to see you here for a week end whenever you can come. I do hope the London idea will set you up & start a new 'era' (hideous word) in your life. I am

---

[1] No. 4 Broad Street.
[2] Greeves was thinking of going there to study art.

writing to Excellenz tomorrow (Sunday). Owing to the darned strike
I have had no copy of Odds and Ends yet but am living in hopes.

Yours

Jack

101

[University College]
Teusday [3? February 1920][1]

My dear Arthur,

I shall expect to hear from you soon that your plans are settled: I
suppose it is useless to hope that you have still any intention of going
to Harrogate, though you may tell your advisers, for their comfort,
that it is absolutely warm and springlike in England.

You will be surprised when you hear how I employed the return
journey – by reading an H. G. Wells novel called 'Marriage' [1912],
and perhaps more surprised when I say that I thoroughly enjoyed it;
one thing you can say for the man is that he really is interested in all
the big, outside questions – and the characters are intensely real,
especially a Mr Pope who reminds me of Excellenz. It opens new
landscapes to me – how one felt that on finding that a new kind of
book was waiting for one, in the old days – and I have decided to read
some more of his serious books. It is funny that I – and perhaps you –
read the old books for pleasure and always turn to contemporaries
with the notion of 'improving my mind'. With most, I fancy, the
direct opposite is so.

But I must work like ten devils this term and bid good-bye to
general reading except for an odd hour on Sundays. I read the
Bacchae over yesterday – for the last time before the exam: to rush
through great poetry at top speed is not, of course, the right way to
appreciate it, but one gets a peculiar value out of such a flying survey
now and then. I realized, for one thing, how very quickly the terrible
story happens: in the morning the old men with the magic youth in
them are going out to the mountains, and before evening you have
the stupid anger of Pentheus, the capture of the God and his quiet,
ominous words to his captor, his escape, the swift madness of
Pentheus, the catastrophe, and then it is all over and the long years of
misery follow the one fatal mistake when mortal wisdom met im-

[1] The *Lewis Papers* supply no hint as to how long Lewis spent with his
father over Christmas. The only proof of his having been at home is a
photograph of Lewis in vol. VI, p. 175, taken in the 'little end room' of
Little Lea in December 1919.

mortal passion. You did like it didn't you?

I was in Baker's[2] rooms with Pasley last night: Pasley departed early and the conversation between us two fell on shadowy subjects – ghosts and spirits and Gods. You may or may not disbelieve what followed. Baker began to tell me about himself: how he had seen things ever since he was a child, and had played about with hypnotism and automatic writing: how he had finally given it all up, till now 'things' were coming back of their own accord. 'At one time' he said 'I was afraid to look round the room for fear of what I might see.' He also stated confidently that anyone could compel a ghost to appear, that there were definite ways of doing it: though of course the thing you 'fished up' might not be what you wanted – indeed *quite* the contrary. The greater part of his views I will reserve for our next meeting: what I wanted to tell you was the effect on me. I got, as it were, dazed and drunk in all he said: then I noticed his eyes: presently I could hardly see anything else: and everything he said was real – incredibly real. When I came away, I moved my eyes off his, with a jerk, so to speak, and suddenly found that I had a splitting headache and was tired and nervous and pulled to pieces. I fancy I was a bit hypnotised. At any rate I had such a fit of superstitious terror as I have never known since childhood and have consequently conceived, for the present, a violent distaste for mysteries and all that kind of business. Perhaps he is a bit mad.

The Minto was so pleased with your bag and so was Maureen with her box which I think is quite charming. I have decided to come out and 'dig' at Headington altogether next term.[3] Hope you're alright.

Yours
Jack

---

[2] Leo Kingsley Baker (1898–   ) matriculated at Wadham College in 1917. He served as a Flight Lieut in the 80th Squadron of the RAF and was awarded the Distinguished Flying Cross in 1918, returning to Oxford in 1919. After receiving his B.A. in 1922, he enjoyed a career on the London stage.

[3] Undergraduates were normally required to spend three terms in College, after which they were allowed to move into University-approved 'digs' or lodgings. About the time this letter was written the Moores moved from 76 Windmill Road, Headington, into the house of Mrs John Jeffrey, a butcher by occupation, in 58 Windmill Road.

102

My dear Arthur,

I was very glad to see from your letter that you have at last escaped from Ireland. New scenery, pleasant society, books to read and an empty hotel to read them in – what could be nicer? I hope you have got over your usual 'unsettlement' at leaving home: certainly it is good that you have left: it is not the disadvantages of home but its comforts that kill – lazy comfort gets hold on one like spiders-web, doesn't it? I hope you told Mrs P[omeroy] that it was 'lack of time' decided me to give up 'Odds & Ends', not that I thought it pretty bad? You are so tactful you know!

You will be glad to hear that I have started Lavengro again (at breakfast) and though I still dislike the anti-Catholic propaganda and the rhetorical passages where the inspiration failed him and he filled up with the usual style of the period, I feel the charm as I did not feel it before and find the book hard to put down. I think with authors as with people we meet, when one finds an objectional feature the best thing is to trace it back to some central point of character from which it originates. When a thing is explained it loses half its nastiness, 'tout comprende c'est tout pardonner'. I have therefore found an explanation which might account for Borrow's rampant protestantism – it lies in the extreme Northernness or Saxon-ism of his nature. He thrilled, as we once did, to everything Norse, even the skull of Dane. I am glad to see that he knew the Kalevala. Hence, of course, a thoroughly Southern, Latin & Mediterranean thing like the Church was antipathetic and he worked up reasonable explanations to support the feeling which was really independent of them. I think the descriptions of the walk thro' the snow and the fairy-smith are admirable.

Did you see the Times Review of a new poem 'Mansoul' by Charles Doughty?[1] Doughty is an old poet and traveller whom I have heard mentioned now & then by the 'people who really know', always with a profound if distant respect. The review persuaded me to buy Mansoul, which is the strangest thing to be written in 1920 – an epic poem in 6 books, of which I have read two and a half so far. Now, mark, for this is important if I'm right – I think it was one of

[1] Charles Montagu Doughty, *Mansoul, or the Riddle of the World* (1920). Reviewed in *The Times Literary Supplement* (22 January 1920), p. 49.

the *really* great things that will stand out like Dante or Milton, and, if so, isn't it wonderful to be alive when it has come out. It is very, very difficult, being written in a curious grammar which leaves out nearly all the pronouns: this is wicked, but even through it you can see the signs of a great work. It is a sort of journey into the under-world, where various ancient sages are interviewed on the meaning of life: we have a glimpse of hell, too, and some fine well-at-the-worlds-end kind of scenery in the first book: later on, I see, there are very learned & very English fairy passages. On the whole its more like Spenser than Milton.

Damn Tchaine's impudence for thinking I am to be a critic: the only thing in the world I could criticize really well is her wonderful self.

It is frosty here again, and there has been beautiful twilight to-day with the cold red light behind the black trees. All of us and chiefly the Minto find this place[2] more and more intolerable as time goes on: but all our hopes of a change seem to become will o' the wisps (do you remember that song – at Portsalon – ye gods!!) when we are hottest on the trail.

I have decided to send you some spelling-notes every time I write until you improve. To day I suggest 'digging' and 'asthma' as pre-ferable to 'diging' and 'asma'.

Yours
Jack

103

22 Old Cleeve
Washford,
Somerset.
[2 April 1920]

My dear Arthur,

I don't know what you must think of me by now. Sometimes I try to console myself by saying that you would have written again your-self unless you had been sufficiently occupied in the interval. All the same I know the fault is mine – but hear my tale.

First of all came some weeks of hard work before the exam. Then the exam, itself for eight days,[1] on the first day of which this swollen

[2] Mrs Jeffrey's house in 58 Windmill Road.

[1] These were the examinations for Honour Mods which began on 4 March. The results were already known and, curiously, Lewis failed to tell his friend that he took a First, an announcement of which appeared in *The Times* (1 April 1920), p. 18.

gland in my throat appeared again, much larger this time and more painful. I had a night with practically no sleep and could hardly eat anything – I think sanatogen saved me in the end. After the exam, I had a few cheery days packing up all my books etc (heart-breaking task!) preparatory to living at Headington next term. Then when I got out there, relations with our landlady had become so intolerable – the Minto will describe it to you some day – that we had to leave at once – and as the place we are going next term was not ready we had no other alternative but to decamp and leave our effects with various friends. More days of packing, pulling & hawling cases, arranging and re-arranging in boiling weather. We had seen an advertisement of a cottage here for a month and taken it on chance, so desperate were we. Thus finally, after the most loathsome and degrading scenes with our landlady and landlord, who nearly became violent, we departed – all of us pretty nearly done. The Minto and I still dream of the Jeffreys. I shall never get the taste of that woman out of my mind – 'not uglier follow the night-hag'.[2] But now that we are here, to quote Milton again, 'This turn hath made amends.'[3]

You do not, of course, know where old Cleeve is: nor did I till a week ago. It is not far from the end of the world: from a delightful thatched cottage with big low rooms *and* modern arrangements we look out on a sea of fruit trees. The village is so small as hardly to deserve the name: and all round there is not a single straight line in the landscape. From the sea which is about a mile to our right to the black mountains on our left the hills are piled together like eggs in a basket, with the most charming villages nestling between them and orchards and streams everywhere and primroses as thick as the lights from the town at home on every bank. Across the water is the hazy outline of Wales – the Arthurian country round Kaerleon and the Usk, I believe. Those same 'Black Hills' on the extreme left of our landscape I have been trying to reach for some time and succeeded this morning (Good Friday). They are rather of the same type as Divis[4] – very black and grim. On one side I looked down into our own homely and rolling valley, on the other to more and more hills with deep gorges between where fir woods sometimes straggled up the sides. Then I went half way down a deep fold in the hill where a stream ran under queer gray trees and there were rocks to sit on, for the bracken and heather were wet. There I rested in an enormous silence and gradually the old feeling came into my mind. You know

[2] *Paradise Lost*, II, 662 ('Nor uglier . . .').
[3] *ibid.*, VIII, 491.
[4] Mount Divis in Co. Antrim.

what I mean – a feeling associated with Wagner and the Well at the Worlds End, which I haven't had for over a year now. I wish I had my copy of The Lore of Proserpine here – it is just the place to read it in.

You can't imagine what a relief it is to be down here, away from work and exams and rows and packing and luggage! I am writing a good deal and also reading. Before we left Oxford I read Romola.[5] Certainly there is great comfort in these old-fashioned historical novels with a slow but not languid movement and plenty of work in them. I have forgotten whether you have read it or not. Since then followed Washington Irving's Life of Mahomet [1850], a silly and scanty book on an interesting subject and Lowes Dickinson's 'The Meaning of Good' [1901]. You should read the latter if you get hold of it – it introduces you to a good many points of view in philosophy without being at all technical or pedantic. I am now at 'Waverley'[6] which I like very much so far and 'Prometheus Unbound'.[7]

I am writing to my father on Monday to tell him that I shall not be home this Vac. – I really can't face him on top of everything else – but you had better pose as having heard nothing about me or my movements if you should be compelled to meet him.[8]

The Minto has a nasty cold but I think the place is doing her good – she sends her love and hopes that your stay in England has done you good. And now, don't be fed up with me for my long silence: write and tell me how your world goes on – I only hope you are having as good a time as I at present have without the purgatory through which I passed to reach it.

Yours
Jack

---

5 By George Eliot (1863).
6 By Sir Walter Scott (1814).
7 By Percy Bysshe Shelley (1820).
8 Lewis wrote to his father on 4 April saying '. . . as this is the shortest vac., and also as I felt in need of some "refresher" I thought it a good opportunity of paying off an engagement with a man who has been asking me for some time to go and "walk" with him. We are at present at this tiny little village in a perfectly ideal cottage . . . from which as a base we shall set out when the weather clears.' *Letters*, p. 50.

104

22 Old Cleeve,
Washford,
Somerset.
Sunday [11 April 1920]

My dear Arthur,

Your letter gave me great pleasure both because it was the first after a long pause (for which I was responsible) and also because it had a cheerfulness and resolution which have long been strangers to you. If the mind really reflects the body you must be enormously better. Is it possible that the good days are at last dawning again? I can't say how pleased I should be to see you strong and able to do things and doing them: above all don't get a relapse either mental or physical, and incidentally excuse what may sound a patronising tone and put it down to the best motives. As we cannot have that 'long talk' you mention, we must try to discuss things as well as possible on paper.

One thing I should take as data – whatever you do, let it be something that will take you from Belfast. Absence cured you: nothing, I fancy, is more likely to un-cure you than a long period at Bernagh. I can't put into words the effect which surroundings familiar even to staleness and the sort of heavy impetus of all that has passed are likely to have. And Ireland itself – much as I love and 'desire it all my days' as Homer says, if other things were equal – I think there is some truth in my own 'Irish Nocturne'.[1] Look it up, not as a poem but as a theory and tell me if you agree.

It would please me beyond everything if you could realize your plan of coming to Oxford. Though of course I could not see you so often nor so regularly as at home we should be constantly meeting, and once you get 'settled' – which you would in time – I think the life would be splendid for you. You would find an enormous choice of congenial friends, and you can have no idea how the constant friction with other and different minds improves one. You would have none of the reasons (either of circumstance or temperament) which make my circle small and would, I hope, soon 'know everybody'. The difficulty is to find an ostensible pretext for Oxford.

---

[1] *Spirits in Bondage*, pp. 18–19:

> . . . I know that the colourless skies
> And the blurred horizons breed
> Lonely desire and many words and brooding and never a deed.

What the exact conditions of entering are since Greek has been withdrawn I do not know: but perhaps merely to be here, *not* as an undergraduate, would leave you freer to develop on your own lines – though of course a degree is useful in itself and gives you, as you say, some object in life. You might come up to study some particular period of history – not as an undergraduate – and to use the old documents etc in the Bodleian: always provided you can trust yourself to be busy and happy without a definite task and exams. Your father could easily afford it: would he approve. Of course you can frankly use my presence as a reason for wanting to be here!

Except for my own pleasure the Slade[2] is undoubtedly the best plan, and I suppose it is that you really have in view. I don't see on what principle the doctor could veto it and yet allow any of the other plans.

I suppose you are not really serious about the poultry farming? The Minto has plenty of experience in that line and says that IF you could get the ground and house at Headington you could run a partnership with her and she would undertake to make it pay! You know best whether you could really be happy in what is called an outdoor life.

In fact if the doctor forbids the Slade, I suppose it comes down to pursuing something definite in private – but I hope NOT at home. I do most strongly fear the effects of another dull, empty winter at Bernagh. I know you don't like to apply to your father again very soon but if nothing else turns up you should make an effort at all costs to be away, here or anywhere, for as long as possible. You wouldn't care to turn your attention to philosophy – seriously, I mean, not just as ordinary reading? I am just starting it soon for my next exam. and we could keep each other up by letter.

I didn't at all agree with you about the difficulty of 'getting into' Waverley. I personally would not have a sentence of those early chapters curtailed: they showed me Scott in quite a new light, describing the childhood and development of the hero in his world of imagination. I can't help feeling that when he wrote this Scott had a higher sense of responsibility to his own characters – took them more seriously and worked out their natural growth more thoroughly – than in his later novels. Isn't the scene at the end where Waverley finds the old Baron of Bradwardine by the guidance of the idiot David Gellatley simply typical Scott – and delightful.

I saw a scene the other day that was typical Scott too – the Castle of Dunster. It stands on a little wooded hill just at the mouth of a

[2] The Slade School of **Fine Art**, University College, London.

scene at the end where Waverley finds the old Baron of ...
wardine by the guidance of the idiot David Gellatting, simply
typical Scott — and delightful. I saw a scene the other
day that was typical Scott too — the Castle of Dunster
It stands on a little wooded hill just at the mouth
of a long valley with very steep sides
half covered by fir-woods. and just
from its gates downwards straggles the
single broad street of a drowsy village with
an old fountain: and the upper storeys of the cottages
project in Elizabethan style. But it can only be described
in language of Scott's period. I am glad you saw
"Dear Brutus". "Don't go into the wood!" — how well that
first act works up to the supernatural of the second. I hope
the "Dream-child" was good— everything depends on her and
that reminds me, the best news of all in your letter was
that you are writing again. I won't repeat all my old
wishes on the subject: but I still think it most unlikely
that all the romance and imagination which are in you
should evaporate in nothing more than appreciation of other
people's work. Of course the thing's always difficult for a
man who begins after his own critical faculties are fully
grown. A child, if easily discouraged, is also easily satis-
-fied and his powers grow with his ideals. But I hope
you will make up your mind to go through with a
good deal of trouble. Look at me — I am still working

See pages 271–3

long valley with very steep sides half-covered by fir-woods and just from its gates downwards straggles the single broad street of a drowsy village[3] with an old fountain: and the upper storeys of the cottages project in Elizabethan style. But it can only be described in language of Scott's period.

I am glad you saw 'Dear Brutus'.[4] 'Don't go into the wood!' – how well that first act works up to the supernatural of the second. I hope the 'Dream-child'[5] was good – everything depends on her. And that reminds me, the best news of all in your letter was that you are writing again. I won't repeat all my old wishes on the subject: but I still think it most unlikely that all the romance and imagination which are in you should evaporate in nothing more than appreciation of other people's work. Of course the thing's always difficult for a man who begins after his own critical faculties are fully grown. A child, if easily discouraged, is also easily satisfied and his powers grow with his ideals. But I hope you will make up your mind to go through with a good deal of trouble.

Look at me – I am still working at my poem on Merlin and Nimue. It has been in succession – rhymed monologue – rhymed dialogue – blank verse dialogue – long narrative in stanzas – short narrative in couplets – and I am at present at work on a blank verse narrative version. I hope I am not wasting my time: but there must be some good in a subject which drags me back to itself so often. You see, as Chaucer says,

> We toilen ever and poren in the fire
> And for all that we fail in our desire.[6]

Since finishing Waverley I have started Heroes and Hero-Worship[7] and finished the first lecture, which I read long, long ago when I first knew you, in the days when everything to do with the Norse lore was honey to me. Even now, when I have found so much better, I can't help regretting the extraordinary keenness and singleness of *wish* that one had then.

Write soon and I will really try to keep up a regular interchange in

[3] Dunster, Somerset.
[4] Sir James Matthew Barrie (1917).
[5] Found in Oliphant Down's *Three One-Act Plays* (1923).
[6] *The Canon Yeoman's Tale*, 670–1:

> We blondren evere and pouren in the fir,
> And for al that we faille of oure desire.

[7] Thomas Carlyle, *On Heroes, Hero-Worship, and the Heroic in History* (1841).

the 'good, old' style. I hope that you will go on as you now are: remember how others have kept themselves full of hope and life in worse predicaments – and excuse my ever preaching.

Yours
Jack

P.S. I never got the last letter you mention. If you can please say *when* it was sent, for we are afraid those damned Jeffreys are keeping our letters. Love from all.

105

[University College]
Monday [3? May 1920]

My dear Arthur,

Your last letter reached me the day after my return here and this is positively the first opportunity I have had of answering it. I must deal first of all with your definite questions. Ist As far as I can make out (for, indeed, the whole subject is still very uncertain) Greek will still be compulsory for Responsions in June but *not* for those in October and after. IInd I do not consider the choice of a college very important, much less so than that of a house at school. There are one or two you should avoid, as Christchurch and Magdalen for their expense, or Keble and Jesus for their vulgarity. Wadham is a very nice, quiet place and not too big. My great friend Baker is there and finds a great many pleasant people. There is no reason why Univ. should be 'out of the question', tho there is equally no reason why you should prefer it, especially now that I am living out. IIId I do not think that most colleges have entrance exams. in addition to Responsions. But on that and on the question of coming up before you take Responsions you had better write to the Bursar of the college you decide on and get definite information. It is much better to open such a correspondence than to rely on unofficial snippets like mine. I should say that you hoped to come up to So-and-So and ask I. for a syllabus of the Responsions subjects, II. whether you must take them before you come up – and any other questions that may occur to you. I do not think that anyone can fail in 'Smalls' after the removal of Greek, unless, like myself, he is incapable of elementary mathematics!

I do not quite gather if your going to Oxford is still only a pis-aller for the Slade or whether you now mean to come in any case. I most sincerely hope you will, for I can imagine nothing that would do you more good. I feel rather nervous, lest, if it disappoint you, the responsibility may rest with me. It is a pity Caesar is such a dull book, but I suppose you'll have to stick it. With care and going slowly at first you should easily pick up your Latin again. Perhaps indeed the historian in you may find interest where most of us cannot: of course it is mainly military history but if you once see it in perspective as an important step in the evolution of Europe you may not be too hopelessly bored.

How splendid to hear of you on the hills again: I can imagine what you felt in reaching at last that Mecca of ours after being exiled so long. There is much better scenery elsewhere no doubt, but as long as I live those little bits of wood and field will be an enchanted country to me. I think you touch on the great problem of writing when you put off describing your walk because the feeling of it is already past. If only the moment of inspiration cd. be identical with that of composition! As Chénier says 'Le Coeur seul est poète'[1] – only the heart, not the poor intellect trying to recapture it with his words and craft. Have you tried anything more in the writing line since? but I daresay your mind and your time are fully occupied in other ways.

We find our new quarters much more to our liking (so far) than we expected, though very expensive. It is a great relief to be living here and not trailing back in every night. Our landlady is a strange character – with a mystery about her: but that needs a whole letter if not an Algernon Blackwood story to describe.

Our Anthology[2] (you know what I mean) goes to the publishers finally to-morrow and will be out for the Autumn sales. I am not just too satisfied with it, but Blackwell seems to think it will pay its way and even leave a little profit with its five authors.

I am very sorry to find that my friend Baker is leaving at the end of this term: he is in every way the best person I have met in Oxford. I wonder what you will think of his poems. I say nothing of reading as I have been busy working and seeing people ever since I came up. The Minto sends her love and is like me delighted to hear of the revolution in your plans.

Just one more thing – if you really believe that painting is your job

[1] André Chénier (1762–94), *Les Élegies*, viii, 2.
[2] This anthology, to be called *The Way's the Way*, contained poems by Lewis, Leo Baker, R. M. S. Pasley, Carola Oman and Margaret Gidding and had been accepted for publication by Mr (now Sir) Basil Blackwell of B. H. Blackwell's Bookshop, Oxford.

rather than a life of letters, don't let this obscure that object. There is plenty of time for both, I suppose, but the real thing must always be the background of ones mind, mustn't it? Hoping that nothing will occur to set you back in anyway – how conventional the words are, but I do most intensely mean them.

Yours
Jack

P.S. Your other letter has turned up.

106

[University College]
Sunday [6? June 1920]

My dear Arthur,

You certainly seem to be working with a vengeance now, and I daresay you find a great deal of effort necessary. I shouldn't do too hard at the beginning: certainly I should not advise work on walks. I am a great believer in having your periods of rest, complete rest, however short they may be: ten minutes absolute 'slack' is far more useful than an hour of the half in between business.

The Latin Constructions did at one time seem rather a 'slough', I remember. The great thing is to pin them onto the nearest English equivalent constructions. Thus, for instance, if you have 'He said I was a fool', instead of thinking mechanically for the Accus. & Inf. rule, remember simply to say in English 'He declared me to be a fool' – then you get it at once $\left. \begin{array}{l} \text{'dixit} \\ \text{declaravit} \end{array} \right\}$ me stultum esse'. Always make the verb of saying 'declare' in English. Similarly the Ablative Absolute has a parallel in the Irish idiom: as you might have *'He kept on talking while I waited'* which in the language of Meehawl Mac-Murrahu would [be] 'He kept on talking, so he did, and me waiting' – there you have it (leaving out the 'and' of course) 'mê expectante'. I am afraid I don't know the difference between a final and consecutive clause in English *or* Latin! – I always do what sounds right in either, but of course you can't begin that way. 'That I may get a copy' would certainly be Pres. Subj. 'ut librum procurem'. I shouldn't kill myself trying to get ready for 'Smalls' by any particular time, though, of course, the sooner the better.

You will be interested to hear that I met your friend Robert Nicholls the other day. He is much less beautiful than the frontis-

'Smalls' by any particular time, though, of course, the sooner the better. You will be interested to hear that I met your friend Robert Nicholls the other day. He is much less beautiful than the frontispiece to "Ardours & Endurances" would lead you to suppose: as the particular grin which makes that big mouth tolerable in the photo cannot be kept up in conversation! He also sees fit to wear enormous goggle spectacles rimmed with thick, dark horn which cover most of his cheeks. He is a pleasant fellow, though rather overpowering and Tchaine-like (could a suitable match be arranged? I have no doubt the "ardours" could be found on her side, but would the "endurances" on his be forthcoming?) He went over the "Wild Hunt" with me, suggesting several emendations, most of which I (and Baker) thought definitely bad — or rather he goes on a peculiar theory which may be good for him, but is not good for me. Certainly the little trivial things such as shaving, cooking, eating and the like run away with a lot of time. I have had some days in bed with flue and been generally very lazy, reading "Kim" and Trollope's "Small House at Alington". I am also, in the evenings, reading Virgil through again: I do hope you will someday be able to read Latin with enjoyment — tho' perhaps that seems to you at present a contradiction in terms. I saw "Romance" in Oxford in 1917 before I went into the army (antequam militiam suscepi) and liked it pretty well, though there is really only one character in it - the woman. If she is good, parts of it are really very

See pages 276–8

piece to 'Ardours & Endurances' would lead you to suppose: as the particular grin which makes that big mouth tolerable in the photo cannot be kept up in conversation! He also sees fit to wear enormous goggle spectacles rimmed with thick, dark horn which covers most of his cheeks. He is a pleasant fellow, though rather overpowering and Tchanie-like (could a suitable match be arranged? I have no doubt the 'ardours' could be found on her side, but would the 'endurances' on his be forthcoming?) He went over the 'Wild Hunt' with me, suggesting several emendations, most of which I (and Baker) thought definitely bad – or rather he goes on a peculiar theory which may be good for him, but is not good for me.

Certainly the little trivial things such as shaving, cooking, eating and the like run away with a lot of time. I have had some days in bed with flu and been generally very lazy, reading 'Kim'[1] and Trollope's 'Small House at Alington'.[2] I am also, in the evening, reading Virgil through again: I do hope you will someday be able to read Latin with enjoyment – tho' perhaps that seems to you at present a contradiction in terms.

I saw 'Romance'[3] in Oxford in 1917 before I went into the army (antequam militiam suscepi!) and liked it pretty well, though there is really only one character in it – the woman. If she is good, parts of it are really very fine – and oh!, I forgot the other character, Tomaso, the monkey. I expect you will see in it the same people whom I saw (censeo te in illâ fabulâ visurum esse eosdem histriones quos ego!!)

I hope this last bout of hot weather has not set you back. You really shouldn't grudge any time spent on walks: now that you feel better able to get about it must be delightful to visit the old haunts. By the bye, I hope you keep the week-ends quite free from work: what can be better than to get out a book on Saturday afternoon and thrust all mundane considerations away till next week. You never get the same pleasure out of books as when you come back to them from these periodical exiles. I doubt if the amount of history you'd require for Smalls would really be much use to you afterwards: and I am quite sure that it would for the moment be more troublesome than the literature.

Wonderful to relate W. has been home and back again without giving us the honour of a visit.[4] Miss Plowman was here the other

[1] Rudyard Kipling (1901).

[2] Anthony Trollope, *The Small House at Allington* (1864).

[3] Edward Brewster Sheldon (1914).

[4] Warren, who was now stationed at Aldershot in Hampshire, was in Belfast on leave from 23 to 29 May.

fine — and oh!, I forgot the other character, *Tirreno*, the number I expect you will see in it the same people whom I saw (*censeo te in illa fabula mecum esse eosdem histriones quos ego!!*) I hope this last bout of hot weather has not set you back. You really shouldn't grudge any time spent on walks now that you feel better able to get about it must be delightful to visit the old haunts. By the bye, I hope you keep the week ends quite free from work what can be better than to get out a book on Saturday afternoon and thrust all mundane considerations away till next week You never get the same pleasure out of books as when you come back to them from these periodical cycles. I doubt if the amount of history you'd *[?]* for Smalls would really be much use to you afterwards and I am quite sure that it would for the moment be more troublesome than the literature. Wonderful to relate W. has been home and back again without giving us the honour of a visit Miss Plowman was here the other night Mr. Nimle sends her love and hopes to see you soon "flusht with victory — yrs Jack.

P.S. "~~Really~~" "Realize" not "reallige" How is Gundred's portrait getting on

Jane.

How well you'll look in a commonaire's gown!

See pages 278–80

night. The Minto sends her love and hopes to see you soon 'flusht with victory'.

Yrs
Jack

P.S. 'Realize' not 'reallize'. How is Gundred's portrait getting on.

107

[University College]
Saturday [19 June 1920]

My dear Arthur,

The new syllabus for 'Smalls' certainly looks attractive. Quite putting aside the question of interest, I should advise you to take the literature. There is a lot of work in making up even a short period of history: but, for a person who has acquired the habit of reading, it should be really very easy to pass on the plays and the Milton and even on the Bacon. Of course you will have to read the books several times and make yourself master of all the biographical details etc: since you do not naturally remember things 'to quote' you must simply (as many another) learn by heart the 'pivot' passages which illustrate important qualities. Thus in Milton I you would quote 'That to the height of this great argument / I may assert eternal Providence / And justify the ways of God to Man'[1] to illustrate the moral purpose, as a commentator would say, and the passage about 'Faery-elves'[2] (near the end) for his Romanticism: and find out from the notes where he is imitating the classics or the Italians etc. Never having done this kind of thing I can't say what are the best annotated editions of these books: but doubtless any 'English master' at Campbell could tell you. I scarcely think that you ought to need any tuition for the English: nor would I recommend Helen – ⟨the unspeakable Helen⟩. Can you get hold of any old papers on the subjects to give you an idea of the sort of questions they ask? That is a very great help. The one and only method in reading Latin is to go slowly and scientifically at first, looking for the verb etc in the old childish way: to rush like a bull in a china shop is fatal. As for the composition, it must be taught. Whether you enjoy it or not, the mere working for this exam. will do you an enormous amount of good: you have no idea how routine work and exactness improve the

---

[1] *Paradise Lost,* I, 24–6 (slightly misquoted).
[2] *ibid.,* I, 781.

brain. I, for instance, have gained enormously in clearness and honesty of thought from my last year's work. I am reading Bergson now and find all sorts of things plain sailing which were baffling a year ago.

Without a scholarship I do not think you can manage on less than £300 a year: £250 might be just possible, but most uncomfortable and your attention would be everlastingly settled on money matters. (Some colleges, by the way, have musical scholarships: would you have any chance for one of those?).

I hope you won't mind my calling your attention to one other necessity – that of a drastic revision in your methods of spelling, which are at present a trifle too eccentric for general acceptance. I am afraid if the first page of your English paper contained such peculiarities as 'unprepaired', 'Hellen', 'reallized', 'overate' (over-rate?) it might prejudice an examiner! (It has just struck [me] that of course 'overate' would be the past tense of 'over-eat' but that can't be what you mean – I never over-eat your abilities.) This, of course, is a matter which can easily be put right: and I know that you are not bothering about it in a letter to me, as indeed there is no reason why you should.

Our anthology 'The Way's the Way' is to come out in autumn. The contributors are Carola Oman[3] (the daughter of the historian),[4] Margaret Gidding (a friend of Pasley's), Pasley, Baker and myself. My own pieces are 6 in number, one of which is the longish 'Wild Hunt' which I think you saw: it was sent, in a slightly different form to 'Odds & Ends'. Most of the others I think you have seen, but you would not remember them by their names. Blackwell has the audacity to talk of 'five or six shillings' as a price for the book and seems to hope for a profit: I suppose he ought to know, but I feel dubious.

You ask about Baker, and I hardly know how to describe him. He was at a mixed school of a very modern type, where everyone seems to have written, painted and composed. He is so clairvoyant that in childhood 'he was afraid to look round the room for fear of what he might see'. He got a decoration in France for doing some work in an aeroplane over the lines under very deadly fire: but he maintains that he did nothing, for he was 'out of his body' and could see his own machine with 'someone' in it, 'roaring with laughter'. He has a bad heart. He was a conscientious objector, but went to the war 'because this degradation and sin might be just the very sacrifice which was

[3] Carola Mary Anima Oman (Lady Lenanton) (1897–   ).
[4] Sir Charles William Chadwick Oman (1860–1946) who had been a Fellow of All Souls College, Oxford, since 1883.

demanded of him'. He maintains that everything in Algernon Black-wood is quite possible: and though the particular cases may be fictitious, 'things of that sort' are quite common. He is engaged to be married. In appearance, he is about my height, with very fair hair, glasses, remarkable eyes and according to the Minto, rather like you. I like and admire him very much, though at times I have doubts on his sanity. He is almost exactly my own age. He is quite different from Pasley, who represents rather the best type of the average English, 'nice boy' and combines literature and athletics.

It is really quite delightful here. I walk into Oxford every morning down a green lane[5] and across the bridges and islands of the Cherwell: they are all white with may[6] and quite deserted at that time. I have had one bathe. The Minto and I 'drank a dish of tea' with Miss Plowman the other day, and came away a trifle 'bethumped with words'. I should like to see her and Tchanie together.

I am trying to imagine what your life is like these days, and always hoping that nothing will turn up to change your mind. What hours do you work? and do you find time to go for walks? You *must* begin to write something now, whether good or bad, in order to acquire a faculty of expression: for of course, whatever you take up here, you will do a lot of essay writing. It is simply splendid to think of all the difference between now and a few months back: perhaps you are hardly enjoying the change yet, but I have no doubt there is a good time coming. If you can pass a year or two here with success, learning what you want to know and making friends, you will still be able to go back to the painting. The loss of time is serious: but more, far more than compensated by the extra power and brain you would take to your work. Write soon or I shall augur a relapse.

Yours
Jack

108

[University College]
Sunday [27? June 1920]

My dear Arthur,

Do you think Davis is a good teacher?[1] I should be sorry to weaken your confidence in him, but I don't like his just passing over the

[5] Cuckoo Lane which runs parallel to Headington Hill.

[6] Hawthorn blossom.

[1] Robert Furley Davis (1866–1937), who took his B.A. from St John's College, Cambridge, in 1888 and his M.A. in 1896, was the Senior Classical Master at Campbell College from 1902 until his retirement in 1931.

Oratio-Obliqua and saying you won't get anything as hard in Smalls. I think with care and patience – but so few schoolmasters have any patience – anyone could be led to master a reported speech in Caesar: and it is just possible you might get an equally difficult Unseen. My Unseen was the passage from Statius (Davis will show it you) beginning 'Crimine quo merui juvenis, placidissime divum'[2]: it is a lovely little poem; have a look at it and see if you can make it out.

I have had a delightful windfall: £5 worth of books as a prize from College for getting a First. Oh ye gods, if this had come four or five years ago, what raptures and debatings, what making and re-making of lists had been! As it is was I had great difficulty in making them out at all, being perpetually haunted by the fear that I should after-wards find out that I had got all the things I really did NOT want. It is a dismal sign of breaking up and old age that I look forward to their arrival with very luke warm pleasure. The nicest among them all will be Hall's 'Ancient History of the Nearer East'[3] – which bears to some extent on my work in Herodotus, but goes beyond it.

This subject of ancient history is now one of my absorbing interests: Herodotus is pure delight, and so are the modern writers who comment on [him]. Isn't the magic of mere names wonderful? Babylon, Nineveh, Darius, the Pharaohs – I revel in every trace of them – and to see things piecing together: a story in Herodotus and a story in the Book of Kings, backed up by an inscription newly un-earthed in Mesopotamia or a scrap of Persian legend! However, this may not interest you.

'Abraham Lincoln'[4] came here last term and all the world except me went to see it: I have heard it praised by everyone. It is very cheering to see these 'literary' plays with verse in them like the Dynasts[5] and Drinkwater's one, on the stage at all. Fifty years ago I don't suppose they'd have got a hearing.

My imagination boggles at the idea of you – or myself – on a motor byke. When you come up here I suppose you will become one of the young men who toot-toot-toot up and down the High clad in over-alls: and instead of the Muses it will be spanners and magnetos and intermezzos and cut-outs and petrol that will fill our conversation. Ah well!, I must move with the times. I can't quite rise to a motor-byke but perhaps I could get a scooter (Picture – Excellenz and my-

---

[2] *Silvae*, V, iv, 1.
[3] H. R. H. Hall, *The Ancient History of the Near East* (1913).
[4] John Drinkwater, *Abraham Lincoln* (1919).
[5] Thomas Hardy, *The Dynasts* (1904–8).

self going to Church on scooters 'Ah – these scooters are r-r-r-otten tools: the thing's intolerable')

This letter was begun I don't know how long ago. 'Sunday' is all I can find at the top: but whether it was a week or a fortnight ago I can't say. I'm sorry: a mood of laziness has been upon me. It has been one of those periods when we do nothing because we always feel tired and feel tired because [we] do nothing. Also – Tchanie is here: I have chust returned from lunching with her and her amiable mother, with the usual exhausting effect.[6] Mrs McNeil has made several exquisitely ridiculous remarks in her solemn style, but they would be spoiled on paper. Tchanie has been strongly urging the advantages which would result from your having Helen as a tutor: and, though you may fancy that I have been talked over, I would advise you to think of it. When I said before that you didn't need a tutor for English, I am afraid I was thinking rather of the mere 'getting up' of the books: for essays etc you really do need someone to put you up to those little tricks of vocabulary and rounding off sentences which may seem trivial but which examiners demand. Whether Helen is the best person you can get, is, of course, quite a different story: if you had any authority outside Tchanie's for believing her to be good, I should not let any personal dislike stand in the way. Who are the alternatives? The divine mother & daughter have mentioned some other McNeil at Wadham who appears to be a friend of yours:[7] did you ever speak to me of him? – you know I can never remember names.

The publication of our Anthology has been put off to an indefinite date because of a printing strike: I shall improve the interval by correcting my contributions out of recognition.[8]

[6] Jane ('Tchanie') McNeill and her mother Margaret McNeill arrived in Oxford on 22 June.

[7] William Martin McNeill who matriculated in 1919.

[8] *The Way's the Way* was never published. In an undated [September 1920] letter to Leo Baker, Lewis said 'Now, to get this damned anthology of my chest: it has been sent back to Basil [Blackwell] who has now kept it in silence for a fortnight. He talked about being able "to meet us in some way": I pointed out on behalf of the Big Three [Lewis, Baker, Pasley] that we could meet him to precisely the extent of £0-0s-0d. In spite of this he still wanted to see the MS again, but I am quite sure he will never publish it.' In another undated [23 December 1920] letter Lewis informed Baker that 'The Way's the Way to bankruptcy, paying cash down and heavy loss: and for this reason Edmund Gosse those lovely lines will never see. And oh! to think with what a shock we crush the hopes of Clutton Brock; and luckless G. K. Chesterton is fated not to look thereon. The blow has fallen: Basil refuses to publish the dam' thing unless we raise some money – I forget how much.

The only book I have read with satisfaction lately is Mackail's 'Lectures on Poetry' [1911]: I think he is one of my favourite moderns – he always has just the right point of view and deals with the right subject: he has sent me back to 'Endymion' which I read for some time in a church porch yesterday afternoon. Otherwise books have been absorbed in the general inertia of this time. I I hope you are having exactly opposite experiences.

Yours
Jack[9]

109

[University College.
June 1921]

My dear Arthur,

I am ashamed that this has been so long delayed. Now that you have been caught, though late, in the snares and cares of this wicked world you will be able to understand how the time rushes past, how you have scarcely time to notice a new week beginning before it is Saturday again, and thence at a single stride into the middle of the next. And always like a mountain piles up the list of things that you must put off, books you want to read, people to see, letters to write.

So many things have happened since we last met that it is no use to attempt chronology: I may as well begin with what is, I must admit, uppermost in my mind – this Chancellor's prize, that you ask about. It is set every year for the whole university and decided by seven judges chosen in rotation. The subject this year was 'Optimism'. Suitable to my family, as you probably guess! The actual prize is £20 in money (that is in strict secrecy – I don't want the fact disclosed at home until it has to be) but of course it is much more valuable as a means of self advertisement and may help me towards a job one of these days: it serves a little to mark you out from the crowd. I liked the subject and took a lot of trouble and am consequently very pleased. The essay may possibly be published – I don't know yet: in

but more than we thought possible. Please find enclosed our own babes from the ruined crêche.'

[9] It is possible that Arthur lost some of Lewis's letters, but this was probably the last 'regular' letter for some time. Arthur gave up the idea of going to Oxford when he was finally permitted to enrol in the Slade School of Fine Art in London. He entered the Slade in January 1921 and took lessons three days a week till he left in December 1923. His address while in London was 66 Torrington Square and, later, 49 Leinster Gardens. During Arthur's years in England the friends met often in Oxford.

any case I don't think anyone at home will care much for it – its rather dull and metaphysical.[1]

The other thing which I suppose you would be most interested to hear about will be my two visits to Yeats.[2] I really cannot do this justice in the space of a letter, but will give you something to go on with. His house is in Broad Street: you go up a long staircase lined with pictures by Blake – chiefly the 'Book of Job' and the 'Paradise Lost' ones, which thus, en masse, have a somewhat diabolical appearance. The first time I came I found a priest called Father Martindale,[3] his wife and a little man with a grey beard who never spoke, sitting with him. It was a very funny room: the light was supplied by candles, two of them in those 6-ft. candle-sticks that you see before the altar in some English churches. There were flame-coloured curtains, a great many pictures, and some strange foreign-looking ornaments that I can't describe. The company sat on very hard, straight, antique chairs: except Mrs Yeats who lay on a kind of very broad divan, with bright cushions, in the window.

Yeats himself is a very big man – very tall, very fat and very broad: his face also gives one the impression of vast size. There would have been no mistaking which was THE man we had come to see, however many people had been in the room. Grey haired: about sixty years of age: clean shaven: glasses with a thick tape. His voice sounded rather French, I thought, at first, but the Irish shows through after a bit. I have seldom felt less at my ease before anyone than I did before him: I understand the Dr Johnson atmosphere for the first time – it was just like that, you know, we all sitting round,

---

[1] Lewis won the Chancellor's English Essay Prize on 24 May 1921 and, as is traditional, he read portions of his essay at the ceremony of Encaenia in the Sheldonian Theatre on 22 June. The essay on 'Optimism' was not published and, unhappily, no copy of it has yet been discovered.

[2] The visits occurred on 14 and 21 March 1921, a more detailed account of which is found in Lewis's serial letter to Warren written on the days Lewis saw Yeats (see *Letters*, pp. 56–8). Lewis was taken to the poet's house in 4 Broad Street by his friend William Force Stead (1884–1967) who is signified as 'X' in the *Letters*. Stead was born in Washington, DC, and attended the University of Virginia before he came to England. He was ordained a priest in the Church of England in 1917, took a degree from Oxford in 1925, was Chaplain of Worcester College from 1927 to 1933, and will doubtless be remembered for having baptized his friend T. S. Eliot into the Church of England in 1927. Stead, who published a number of volumes of verse, married an American, Miss Goldsworthy, whose sister was the wife of Mrs Moore's brother Dr John Hawkins Askins.

[3] Fr Cyril Charlie Martindale SJ (1879–1963) who wrote a number of biographies, and whose lectures Lewis had attended in the University.

putting in judicious questions while the great man played with some old seals on his watch chain and talked.[4]

The subjects of his talk, of course, were the very reverse of Johnsonian: it was all of magic and apparitions. That room and that voice would make you believe anything. He talks very well and not unlike his own printed prose: one sentence came almost directly out of 'Per Amica Silentia Lunae' [1918]. The priest was guardedly sceptical but allowed himself to be argued down. One gets the impression (as I have sometimes got it from others) of a tremendous amount of this sort of thing going on all round us. Yeats 'learnt magic from Bergson's sister' – 'for a long time I wondered what this dream meant till I came across some Hermetic students in London, who showed me a picture of the same thing I had seen' – 'ah yes – So-and-so: he went in for magic too, but his brain wasn't strong enough and he went mad' – 'at that time I was going through what are known as Lunar meditations etc, etc'. You'll think I'm inventing all this but it's really dead, sober truth. The last two or three years have taught me that all the things we used to like as mere fantasy are held as facts at this moment by lots of people in Europe: perhaps, however, you have run across it in town.

The second time I went to see Yeats, the talk ran more on literature: it also was very interesting, better in some ways than the other, but I haven't time to describe it – beyond recording the fact that he is an enthusiastic admirer of Morris prose romances: which shd. give us confidence.

That constitutes about all my real news: otherwise it has been all the usual thing. I walk and ride out into the country, sometimes with the family, sometimes alone. I work: I wash up and water the peas and beans in our little garden: I try to write: I meet my friends and go to lectures. In other words I combine the life of an Oxford undergraduate with that of a country householder: a feat which I imagine is seldom performed. Such energies as I have left for general reading go almost entirely on poetry – and little enough of that.

If my letters fail by their rarity, yours tell me very little about yourself. I have had no news yet, save very indirect snippets, as to how you are getting on with the Slade. Have you met any interesting people? What is your day made up of? I await with interest the results

---

[4] In the Preface to his poem *Dymer* (1950 edition), p. xiv, Lewis wrote 'The physical appearance of the Magician in vi. 6–9 owes something to Yeats as I saw him. If he were now alive I would ask his pardon with shame for having repaid his hospitality by such a freedom. It was not done in malice, and the likeness is not, I think, in itself, uncomplimentary.'

garden: I try to write: I meet my friends and go to lectures.. In other words I combine the life of an Oxford undergraduate with that of a country householder — a feat which I imagine is seldom performed. Such energies as I have left for general reading go almost entirely on poetry — and little enough of that.

If my letters fail by their rarity, yours tell me very little about yourself. I have had no news yet, save a few indirect snippets, as to how you are getting on with the studio. Have you met any interesting people? What is your day made up of? I await with interest the results of this "re-arrangement of your face". Have you become infected with futurism and do you intend to practice it on yourself? Will something of this sort be the re- result? Seriously, I hope you won't have too bad a time. Like you, I am too hard up to think of leaving Oxford except for a compulsory tête-a-tête with ___ellery. There is an awful suggestion of his coming over to England on a motor tour with the Hamiltons, calling of course at Oxford. What on earth that might lead to I daren't even begin to imagine: my only consolation is that the difficulty of removing him from Little Lea will probably

See pages 287–9

of this 're-arrangement of your face'. Have you become infected with futurism and do you intend to practice it on yourself? Will something of this sort be the result? Seriously, I hope you won't have too bad a time.

Like you, I am too hard up to think of leaving Oxford except for a compulsory tête-a-tête with Excellenz. There is an awful suggestion of his coming over to England on a motor tour with the Hamiltons, calling of course at Oxford. What on earth that might lead to I daren't even begin to imagine: my only consolation is that the difficulty of removing him from Little Lea will probably prove insurmountable.[5]

Kelsie and Cousin Mary[6] have been here for a few days & are going to-morrow: I think they intend to 'look you up' in London. Just between ourselves I have been bored to death with them: I came in a thunderously hot evening to find them sitting in a private room at the Mitre with a big fire blazing – then an ample meal of tea & cakes an hour after their dinner. Well I don't know: they have been very kind to me all my life and are in many ways excellent people: but just seeing them here suddenly, out of their setting, the main impression is of provincialism, narrow Ulster bigotry and a certain sleek unreality – so hardly will a rich woman enter into the Kingdom.

Try to let me have an answer to this & I'll try to answer *that*. Let me know *between what dates* you'll be at Bernagh: I must try to get my compulsory visit coinciding with you.[7] The Minto sends her love and sympathises for the nursing home.

> Yours
> Jack

---

[5] Albert arrived in Oxford on 24 July 1921. Lewis's description of his motor tour with his father and uncle and aunt, Mr and Mrs Augustus Warren Hamilton, is found in a letter to his brother of 7 August (*Letters*, pp. 65–71).

[6] Isabella Kelso Ewart and her mother Mary, Lady Ewart (1849–1929).

[7] Lewis went to Belfast in mid-September for a three-weeks holiday with his father.

T.S.T.–K

110

28 Warneford Rd.,
Oxford
[25 July 1922][1]

My dear Arthur,

We were all glad to get your letter and not only for the enclosure as you might maliciously say! Although we may seem to you at times ribald spectators we really feel the greatest sympathy for your present restoration to the paternal roof tree.

We all miss you very much and so, no doubt, do our neighbours. Veronica[2] is so heart broken that she has not sent us any word since! We duly delivered your message to Miss Wibelin[3] who has her exam. to morrow and is in an awful state of nerves. Baker is rehearsing for his play but is out nearly every day: it is going to be perfectly absurd and we are trying to arrange for Miss W., Maureen and me to go to it together.[4] The Doc is not very well and is going to Brittany in a few weeks.[5] Baker, by the bye, met an American woman in London who has devoted the last twenty years of her life to astrology. Without the least knowledge of his intended career she told him that he

[1] Lewis and the Moores were, again, installed in Miss Featherstone's house. Arthur had always got on very well with Mrs Moore, and he had been a visitor at 28 Warneford Road from 28 June to 19 July, during which time he met for the first time most of the others mentioned in this letter. He was now visiting his family in Strandtown. Lewis, who had taken Schools in June, was awarded a First in Greats on 4 August.

[2] Veronica FitzGerald Hinkley was a native of Oxford and a member of Lady Margaret Hall. She, too, had only just finished Schools and she took her B.A. in 1922.

[3] Lewis always misspelled the name of Miss Vida Mary Wiblin who matriculated at the Society of Oxford Home-Students (later to become St Anne's College) in 1920 and received her Bachelor of Music in 1924. She was a close friend of the 'family', and in return for giving Maureen violin lessons Lewis was tutoring her in Latin.

[4] Leo Baker was admitted to hospital, suffering from nervous exhaustion, after finishing Schools. On discovering this, Mrs Moore arranged for him to come and convalesce at 28 Warneford Road where he was to remain for some weeks. The play *Glorious England* (published this same year) was by Baker's friend Bernice de Bergerac. It was performed in the Priory gardens of Christ Church on 31 July.

[5] 'The Doc' was Mrs Moore's brother Dr John Hawkins Askins (born 1877) who was a psychoanalyst. He was in poor health and he and his wife, the former Mary Goldsworthy, had taken a cottage in Iffley, a few miles from Oxford.

was going on the stage and prophesied early success.[6] I fancy this is telepathy and that the 'astrology' is all rot. I don't and won't see what stars have to do with it.

Ever since you left, it has been beastly weather, but to day was beautiful. We have the french window open in the dining room and a glorious night outside – there was a fine sunset awhile ago over the church tower.

Such a tragedy! On Friday we found the poor 'dam' Vee' lying dead in the hall, poisoned apparently. Before we were out of mourning for him a tiny fluffy black kitten from across the way began to visit us – and we really believe it is his son, for Vee led the devil of a life.

Do you remember my mentioning the Chanson de Roland in the old days? It is the Norman epic about Charlemagne etc, written in the eleventh century: I have been reading a copy with the Norman on one page and the French translation opposite.[7] It is exceedingly fine.

You have made a mistake about the cheque which should have been only £4–10s., and Minto remembers she owed you 2/1 so I enclose the balance of 12/2 with many thanks. Minto was most distressed at forgetting the 2/1 when you were going & we both hope you were not short for the journey.

Everyone sends best love (except Tibbie who is in a bad temper because of the intrusions of 'Vee's' son who ate all her supper and you should have seen her face). Minto specially asks me to say how much we enjoyed your being here & to add both our hopes that you will soon repeat your visit.

Yrs. ever
Jack

P.S. Miss Wibelin says she's going to write to you. Lucky Choseph! Maureen has finally decided to leave school & devote her time entirely to music.

---

[6] It had for some time been Leo Baker's intention to go on the stage. In his diary for 28 August 1922 (*Lewis Papers*, VII, p. 218) Lewis describes his visit to London to see Baker in his first professionl role – that of Westmoreland in Shakespeare's *Henry IV* at the Old Vic.

[7] He was reading this twelfth-century poem in Léon Gautier's edition, *Le Chanson de Roland: Texte critique, accompagné d'une traduction nouvelle, et précédé d'une introduction historique par L. Gautier* (Tours, 1872).

III

28 Warneford Rd.
April 22nd [1923][1]

My dear Arthur,

Your letter was very welcome. We have been through very deep waters. Mrs Moore's brother – the Doc – came here and had a sudden attack of war neurasthenia. He was here for nearly three weeks,[2] and endured awful mental tortures. Anyone who didn't know would have mistaken it for lunacy – we did at first: he had horrible maniacal fits – had to be held down. We were up two whole nights at the beginning and two, three or four times a night afterwards, all the time. You have no idea what it is like. He had the delusion that he was going to Hell. Can you imagine what he went through and what we went through?

Arthur, whatever you do never allow yourself to get a neurosis. You and I are both qualified for it, because we both were afraid of our fathers as children. The Doctor who came to see the poor Doc (a psychoanalist and neurological specialist) said that every neurotic case went back to the childish fear of the father. But it can be avoided. Keep clear of introspection, of brooding, of spiritualism, of everything eccentric. Keep to work and sanity and open air – to the cheerful & the matter of fact side of things. We hold our mental health by a thread: & nothing is worth risking it for. Above all beware of excessive day dreaming, of seeing yourself in the centre of a drama, of self pity, and, as far as possible, of fears.

After three weeks of Hell the Doc. was admitted to a pensions hospital at Richmond: and at first we had hopeful accounts of him. But the poor man had worn his body out with these horrors. Quite suddenly heart failure set in and he died – unconscious at the end, thank God.[3] Of course I cannot pretend to have the same share in it

---

[1] Lewis having decided to embark on an academic career, but being unable to secure a Fellowship in any of the Oxford colleges, University College agreed to continue his scholarship for another year if he would stay up and take another school. At the time this was written he was reading English Literature preparatory to taking Schools in June 1923. Lewis and Greeves had not seen one another since they met in Belfast in September 1922 when Lewis wrote in his diary 'I saw Arthur frequently. Whether it was his [ill] health or my absorption in other things I don't know, but we found practically nothing to say to each other' (*Lewis Papers*, VII, p. 230).

[2] Between 23 February and 12 March.

[3] Dr John Askins died on 5 April and was buried at Clevedon on 10 April.

as poor Minto, but I am very, very sorry – tho to me the horrors he suffered here were much more heartrending than his death could ever be.[4] As you will understand we are all rather run down and dead tired, in mind at any rate. Isn't it a damned world – and we once thought we could be happy with books and music! We are at present engaged in moving to another house.[5]

Your letter is rather cryptic. I gather you objected to your Irish visit more than ever – and so we shall every time till the bitter end. One thing in your letter however is excellent – I mean what you say you feel about your work. Thats the stuff! As you say, work is the only thing (except people of course, the very few people one cares about) that is worth caring about. I find it hard to imagine your way of thinking in painting – the technical side counts for so much more with you than with poets. One thing I take it is sure for all the arts – that the 'noble thoughts' and 'beautiful ideas' and 'vision' and all the other rot that appeals to amateurs is just what does *NOT* count for twopence: its the man who sees *how* to do something, that matters. I am glad you read Strachey's Victoria[6] – a capital book.

In the intervals of packing etc I am working away at routine work for exams – chiefly the dull mechanical parts for wh. alone I am fit just at present. If you can make your visit to Oxford later than May you will be more likely to see something of us, for we're in the devil of a muddle at present.[7] With love and good wishes from all the family.

Yrs ever
Jack

[After taking his Certificate from the Slade School of Fine Art, Arthur set up a studio at 119 Westbourne Terrace in London where he was to

[4] It would be difficult to exaggerate the effect of this experience on Lewis. Though he did not reveal Dr Askins's name in his autobiography, Lewis was years later to cite his friend's madness as one reason for 'a retreat, almost a panic-stricken flight, from all that sort of romanticism which had hitherto been the chief concern of my life' (*Surprised by Joy*, ch. XIII, pp. 191–2).

[5] Lewis sometimes spelled it 'Hillsborough', but the name of the house they moved into on 30 April 1923, and where they were to remain until they bought 'The Kilns' in 1930, is 'Hillsboro House'. Up until they left in 1930 the address was Western Road, but the name of the road was later altered to Holyoake so that the present address of 'Hillsboro House' is 14 Holyoake Road, Headington.

[6] Lytton Strachey, *Queen Victoria* (1921).

[7] Greeves arrived in Oxford on 11 July and stopped at 'Hillsboro' for a fortnight.

spend much of his time for the next few years. It is likely that their proximity to one another caused Lewis and Arthur to write less frequently. That they corresponded occasionally is certain, but it remains a mystery as to what happened to the letters written between April 1923 and December 1926. Arthur travelled a good deal during these years, and with no permanent 'home', such as Bernagh, I assume that whatever letters he had from Lewis were lost.

There also appears to have been a temporary 'cooling-off' in the relationship as each found himself surrounded by new friends and different ideas. It is evident from various entries in Lewis's diary that Arthur was never quite comfortable with Lewis's companions in Oxford, and Lewis seems to have spent little time, if any, in the company of Arthur's London friends. *Alone* they usually found much to say, but Lewis's diary makes it clear that he was often embarrassed *for* Arthur when others were about.

When Greeves arrived in Oxford (from London) on 11 July 1923 for his fortnight's stay, Lewis met him at the station and was to write in his diary: 'We took, or rather he took a taxi out, stopping for some shopping of mine at Eaglestone's. I was delighted to see him: we renewed our earlier youths and laughed together like two schoolgirls.' A few days later Lewis was writing with obvious disappointment that 'He is great changed . . . someone has put into his head the ideal of "being himself" and "following nature". I tried on one occasion to point out to him the ambiguity of that kind of maxim: but he seems to attach a very clear meaning to it – namely that the whole duty of man is to swim with the tide and obey his desires . . . He has taken over from psychoanalysis the doctrine that repression in the technical sense is something quite different from self-control. I tried to put him on to [Leo] Baker's distinction between will-men and desire-men but he took no interest in it. I argued that immortality – which he believes in – was not likely to fall to the lot of everyone, since "gift is contrary to the nature of the universe". He on the other hand is confident that we should all be immortal anyway: he gave me the impression of believing in heaven but not in hell, nor in any conditions attaching to heaven. On mora l he thought that our whole duty consisted in being kind to others. I pointed out that a man who was "natural" could not be kind except by accident. I soon introduced him to Parson's Pleasure and after that he spent a good deal of his time bathing and sketching . . . His only besetting sin of greed came out several times at our table. Like other poor families, we usually eat margarine with jam – except Dorothy [Vaughn] who "CAN'T" eat margarine. Arthur soon made his position plain, stretching across to the butter and remarking that he much preferred it. Another good example of "nature" occurred in the first two days of his visit when we had tropical weather. [Minto], bring the most free and easy of mortals, had made no objection to Arthur wearing pyjamas till lunch time. It was left to Arthur to take the one step further from freedom to beastly familiarity by taking off his slippers in the dining room and laying his bare feet on the table. His feet are very long, and he perspires freely' (*Lewis Papers*, vol. VIII, pp. 140, 141–2).

The touch of astringency in Lewis's diary – and there is little else about Arthur in it – is almost certainly owing to the worries and pressures of his life during the year preceeding this visit. On 16 July 1923 he learned that he had taken a First in the English School, and commenting on it in the *Lewis Papers*, vol. VIII, p. 140, Warren wrote: 'Six Firsts were awarded this year. When we reflect on the circumstances of Clive's life during the time he was reading this School – the shortness of the period at his disposal, his ill health, the constant anxiety inseparable from supporting a family out of an undergraduate's allowance, his fears for the future, the unceasing domestic drudgery, the hideous episode of Dr John Askin's final illness, and the move to Hillsboro – we are astounded at the extent of an achievement which must rank as easily the most brilliant of his academic career.'

Still, outstanding as his academic career had been – with three 'Firsts' to his credit – a position in one of the Oxford colleges eluded him. Nevertheless, his ambition was to acquire a Fellowship in Philosophy, and while his father was still ignorant of the close tie with the Moores, he increased his son's termly allowance from £67 to £85. After his First in English his supervisor suggested that Lewis work towards a B. Litt. or perhaps a D. Phil., but the need to earn enough money to keep his establishment at Hillsboro going prevented Lewis from following up either of these proposals. He corrected Higher School Certificates to earn a little money and generally carried on the best he could till in May 1924 he was offered a temporary post at Univ. – taking over E. F. Carritt's work as a Philosophy tutor during the academic year Carritt was to spend in America – the emolument being £200 which Lewis accepted gratefully.

Before the academic year (1924–5) was over Lewis had applied for every Fellowship in Philosophy going, and, for extra measure, a Fellowship in English Language and Literature at Magdalen College. By a remarkable – and certainly fortuitous – irony, the only one offered him was the Fellowship at Magdalen. He accepted, his appointment was announced on 20 May 1925, and the long prologue was at last over. Thereafter, Lewis was to spend his nights in College and his week-ends and vacations 'at home' in Headington.]

112

My dear Arthur,

I was on the point of writing to find out where you were, when your letter arrived.[1] Of course I am sorry that we shall not meet at Christmas, but I quite understand that after your long spell of home you are not eager to return.

About the play[2] – of course I ought not really to speak without knowing more details of your new ideas than I do: but I can not help thinking that the introduction of incest is a mistake. I think it is quite legitimate for a man to take incest as his main theme, if he is really interested in a tragedy of it or the various moral and psychological problems which it raises. And in that case I shd. regard any moral objection to his work as invalid. But it is a very different thing for him simply to throw it in as a makeweight in a play whose real purpose and interest lie elsewhere. *That*, I think, might be legitimately objected to. At any rate it would irritate the best kind of spectator by diverting his attention from your real theme into the realm of mere pathology, and attract the wrong kind who will always find sexuality (specially abnormal sexuality) more interesting than anything else. Besides, you bring it in only to make things 'more so'. Wasn't it just that desire for the 'more so' which spoiled so many Elizabethan plays – piling horror on horror and death on death till the thing turns ridiculous? It's quality not quantity that counts. If you can't make tragedy out of the story as it was, you won't be any the more able to do so by the help of the unnatural. I think, myself, the whole feeling about incest is very obscure – almost a savage taboo, and not really moral at all: that makes it, to me, rather external and superficial. Again, won't it force you to load your play with improbabilities & long explanatory dialogues? I don't know if Gribbon is in your confidence about the play. If he is, you should discuss my view with him and try to reach a conclusion. The Banshee may be a good idea enough – it all depends, as you know, on the way it is introduced.

Minto and Maureen are well and send their love. I have had rather a nasty term with a cough wh. has kept me awake at nights and a good

[1] From Paris, where Greeves had gone for a visit.
[2] Greeves's play, *Trees*, which was never published.

deal of work. I don't know how Dymer is selling, if at all. One thing
is most annoying: you remember that the T.L.S. reviewer wrote a
very kind letter, promising a good review. It has not yet appeared.
No doubt it will in time, but it is too late now to give a lead to other
papers – wh. wd. have been its chief value.[3] I am learning Old Norse
and thus beginning to read in the original things I have dreamed of
since before I really knew you. Dreams come true in unexpected
ways.

Yrs
Jack

P.S. I don't know the French for C/O. Is it 'chez' or 'au son soin
de'?

113

[Magdalen College
26 June 1927]

My dear Arthur,
   Knowing the state of your finances I couldn't find it in my conscience to keep the whole of your extremely kind and unexpected
present, and herewith return £1. The other I retain with very many
thanks, and shall devote it to a pleasant edition of Thomas Browne
in three volumes which I saw lately: or perhaps I shall get Dryden's
plays in a folio wh. I think sells for about that amount. De la Mare's
poems I have had for a long time and I read them more often than
any other book. I put him above Yeats and all the other moderns, and
in spite of his fantasy find him nearer than any one else to the
essential truth of life.

[3] Lewis's poem *Dymer* was published on 18 September 1926 under his
pseudonym 'Clive Hamilton'. Hugh l'Anson Fausset (1895–1965) wrote to
him on 29 September saying 'I have just read and reviewed your Dymer for
the Times Literary Supplement, but as some weeks will probably elapse
before the review gets printed, I wish to send you a line to say what a remarkable achievement I consider your poem to be. I have not read any poem
recently which has so impressed me by its inevitability of expression and by
the profundity of its metaphysic. I use the word "metaphysic", unpleasant
as it is, because it is by its metaphysical reach that your poem stands head
and shoulders above most modern verse. But it is a metaphysic which is
wholly and quite incalculably translated into terms of image and symbolism,
and this seems to me the final test of greatness in poetry . . .' (*Lewis Papers*,
IX, pp. 130–1). Fausset's review appeared in *The Times Literary Supplement*
(13 January 1927), p. 27.

I was sorry to hear such a poor account of my father from you. Of course three weeks in an English hotel with him would for me have all the disadvantages of my usual spell at home without any of the advantages: but I feel bound not only to make the suggestion but to try and bring it to reality. This by itself would give me unhappy anticipations of this summer, but I am much more bothered by the possibility of Minto's having to have an operation – not, thank heavens, a very serious one, but her bad veins make even a slight one unpleasant. At present things seem more hopeful than they did a few weeks ago, and it may not be necessary: but you can imagine that we are all pretty uneasy.

I am glad to hear that you are still working on the play, and think that the new idea you have of the Trees is a great advance. I haven't read the essay of Clutton Brock's which you mention, but the theory – that out of the deep reservoirs of nature (the caverns of Erda) we draw power and inspiration which *we* make good or evil – is a familiar and favourite one of my own. If you will re-read what I make the girl say in Canto VIII of Dymer you will get my view on that subject better expressed than I can hope to put it in a letter, and summed up in the line 'With incorruptibles the mortal Will corrupts itself.'[1] But I will read the Clutton Brock as soon as I come across it and see what he says. I like and agree with most of his work.

I am realising a number of very old dreams in the way of books – reading Sir Gawain in the original[2] (you remember my translation of it in a companion volume to my translation of Beowulf) and, above all, learning Old Icelandic. We have a little Icelandic Club in Oxford called the 'Kólbitar': which means (literally) 'coal-biters', i.e. an Icelandic word for old cronies who sit round the fire so close that they look as if they were biting the coals. We have so far read the Younger Edda and the Volsung Saga: next term we shall read the Laxdale Saga. *You* will be able to imagine what a delight this is to me, and how, even in turning over the pages of my Icelandic Dictionary, the mere name of god or giant catching my eye will sometimes throw me back fifteen years into a wild dream of northern skies and Valkyrie music: only they are now even more beautiful seen thro' a haze of memory – you know that awfully *poignant* effect there is about impression *recovered* from ones past.

I feel great sympathy with your situation at home and can just imagine it this wet Sunday morning on which I write – with St

---

[1] *Dymer*, VIII, xv, 5–6.
[2] He had recently acquired *Sir Gawain and the Green Knight*, ed. J. R. R. Tolkien and E. V. Gordon (1925).

Mark's bell ringing in the distance and 'the O'Mulligan' trotting off
to Church.[3] Talking about home, have you seen Helen Wadell's book.
I am sure Tchanie is never tired of talking of it. It is specially interesting to us because when you have read it you see what an enormous
influence H.W. has had on Tchanie: the book is full of passages that
Tchanie wd. have written herself if she could. I know now where
Tchanie's dreadful serious moments (when she recites!) come from.[4]
Alas poor Tchanie! 'I was chust saying to Chanie.' So Gundred is
married.[5] Tout change! I hope you will keep me informed as to what
my father is *really* thinking of doing. As I said before, I shall press
the English trip: but I have a secret conviction that it will not come
off, and we shall probably meet this summer as usual.[6] With many
thanks again, and with love from all here.

Yours
Jack

[3] Miss Lizzie Mulligan and her sister who lived on Glenfarlough Road,
about 200 yards from Little Lea, had been friends of Lewis's mother.
Albert and his sons referred to her affectionately as 'the O'Mulligan' as she
passed Little Lea and Bernagh on her way to St Mark's.

[4] The reference is to Helen Jane Waddell (1889–1965) the translator and
interpreter of the Middle Ages whose book *The Wandering Scholars* was
published in April of this year. Though born in Tokyo, Miss Waddell spent
most of her early life in Co. Down. She attended the Queen's University,
Belfast, and was a close friend of Jane ('Tchanie') McNeill. Writing to his
father on 16 February 1921, Lewis said 'I met a friend of the said Tchanie's
the other night at the Carlyles, a girl called Helen Waddell whom you may
have heard of. When last I saw her she was lying face downwards on the
floor of Mrs McNeill's drawing-room, saying rather good things in a quaint
Belfast drawl' (*Lewis Papers*, VI, p. 243).

[5] Lewis's cousin Gundreda Ewart was married on 15 June to Colonel
John Forrest, formerly of the Royal Army Medical Corps, who had just
become the Secretary of the Royal Victoria Hospital, Belfast.

[6] Lewis tried hard to get his father to come over, but in the end Albert
was prevented by a bout of rheumatism and his usual disinclination to leave
home.

114

The Folly,
Perranporth,
Cornwall.
Aug 24th [1927]

My dear Arthur,

A thousand apologies. We have come down here for a bit to set us all up, specially Minto, and you can imagine that the almost nomadic grandeur of family packing and family travelling, combined with the pleasant, yet crowding, picnic life we are now leading, has left me little liesure for writing. Still, I certainly ought to have let you have a line if only to acknowledge the cheque, and am very sorry that I did not. Very many thanks: but I still protest that it is an excessive gift from poor you to me. However, if you are going to challenge me to a duel in case I return it again, I will see what I can do towards spending it. Again, many many thanks.

As to showing my father the play. I think his criticism, tho' formal, is valuable on questions of *style* for a speech or essay or the narrative parts of a novel. Whether it wd. be much use for *dialogue*, I am hardly prepared to say. The general philosophy and meaning and all that, would not, I think, interest him, nor would he take very much trouble to understand it. He would assure you that he knew exactly what you meant and then substitute something of his own: probably identifying your view with some very superficially similar view expressed in some book he had read, in the words 'Sure this is the old business of so-and-so.' I fancy, however, he wd. have a pretty good eye for theatrical effect, specially on the humorous side. I am afraid I cannot be much more conclusive, and you must decide for yourself. After all you know his literary conversation nearly as well as I do. One thing you must be warned of. If he thinks the whole thing bosh he will be much too kind to tell you so: and at the same time he is habitually *rather* contemptuous of local literary endeavours. It would be hard for you to excite his admiration, and yet he will be determined not to hurt you.

I expect to be home on the 5th of September[1] – leaving the others here. The doctor thought Minto ought to get away – she is much better and really (but touch wood!) has made a remarkable escape from the trouble that threatened her. We are having a delightful time

---

[1] In his diary for 6 September Albert wrote 'Jacks arrived in time for breakfast. Bright and cheerful and amusing as ever.' He was to remain at home with his father till 5 October.

and the best surf bathing I've had since our old days at Portsalon. As I write I look out on a deep blue sea and a golden sand, divided by twenty yards of pure white foam. *Of course you won't mention at home that I am not in Oxford.*

I am busy all morning at rather dull and mechanical work, and fit in more at odd times when I can. Looking forward to seeing you again, & with many thanks.

Yrs
Jack

115

[Magdalen College
March 1929]¹

My dear Arthur

I am very sorry your message has been so long delayed. If you remember my way of life, you will know that I am kept in by pupils all morning, that I then have to go out to Headington, that I then return to pupils again after tea – after which the shops are shut. It really is with the greatest difficulty that I ever get free in the streets of Oxford to visit shops. I ought, I confess, to have *made* the occasion, but I want to plead in my defence that it is not, as you, forgetting, probably suppose, a question of just walking out any old day and doing it. Term ends soon (don't say so at Leeboro) and I will really try to get it done.

I admit freely that I was in the wrong and apologise. I wish you could avoid writing things like ⟨'Am I so soon forgotten.'⟩ You had a right to be annoyed: but you certainly did not really think that my failure to do an errand for you betokened any change in a friendship that has now lasted the greater part of our lives: and if you *had* thought so, this was hardly a manly or a sensible way of opening the subject ⟨(If I had left the letter lying about anyone wd. have supposed it was from a girl whom I had deserted and who was just going to have a baby!)⟩ I am sorry to have inconvenienced you, but hope the matter is not mortal.

Yrs
Jack

¹ Though their correspondence had lapsed since they met in September–October 1927, Lewis and Greeves saw one another regularly during Lewis's visits home. Warren had been ordered to China in April 1927 and during his three years away Lewis's relationship with his father was as close and as comfortable as it ever had been. He was at home from 21 December 1927 until 11 January 1928, from 5 August until 5 September 1928, and again from 21 December 1928 until about 11 January 1929.

116

My dear Arthur,

I have had ten days in bed with flu', four days walking tour from Salisbury to Lyme Regis and a week with Minto and family in a Sussex farmhouse – of which items only the walking tour had better be communicated to the P'daitabird[1] – but before all this I visited Blackwells and looked up their Lamb. After investigating such copies as I could lay my hands on (viz. two) in private and finding that neither of them contained the missing letters I consulted the man who thought they might have some second hand old sets in stock, but thought wrongly. I am sorry if it has been my dilatoriness that led to this negative result, but trust that even when you have learned by heart all the remaining letters (and, dear me, what a convenience that will be to *me*!) the lack of those ten will not drive you to desperation (Of course, perhaps, the most sensible thing would be for both of us to blow our brains out).

I am also, and more seriously sorry that I wrote you rather a snarky[2] letter when we last communicated, and tried to turn an apology into an accusation, which was a very unhandsome thing to do. I hope you will allow for end of term feeling and frayed nerves.

We arrived back from Sussex to day and travelled within a couple of miles of Bookham, all up the Dorking valley which I know so well. It very nearly made me weep, I got such a rich poignant whiff of memory from the old days – Phantastes, Bleheris, Dymer, Papillon, T. Edens Osborne all jumbled up. But as you know, one has the secret of these memories now and knows how to extract the spiritual sweet without falling into mere desire and regret.

While ill, I re-read both *Sense & Sensibility* and *The Antiquary* and most strongly advise you to read the latter again, and specially notice the effect of Elspeth in her earlier scenes.

Yrs
Jack

[1] The Lewis brothers' nickname for their father.
[2] 'For the Snark's a peculiar creature, that won't / Be caught in a commonplace way.' Lewis Carroll, *The Hunting of the Snark* (1876), Fit IV, p. 40.

117

> Magdalen College,
> Oxford.
> May 19th [1929]

My dear Arthur,

I enclose a letter wh. I have been waiting to send you for ages.[1] Of course I am delighted to hear of your coming to Oxford to-morrow, but hope that you will stay in College with me. You will remember that last time you found the hardships of Collegiate life worse in anticipation than in experience. If you insist on going to a Hotel try the Eastgate which is cheap & quiet & just beside Magdalen. Let me have a line or wire at once. I am looking forward tremendously to meeting again

> Yrs
> Jack

118

> Magdalen College,
> Oxford.
> [16 July 1929]

My dear Arthur

It is only to-day that we have made up our minds about our arrangements for the summer. As far as I can see, I shall be in Ireland from the 12th of August onward, for three to four weeks. I very much hope that this will fit in with your plans, as it will be impossible for me to fit it in either later or earlier. I will make a note of the *Rebel Passion*.[1]

Bryson[2] told me you were going to visit these parts? Is that untrue? And, by the way, could you let me know whether there is any difficulty about bringing dogs into Northern Ireland? Can you let me have an answer.

> Yrs
> Jack

[1] Presumably the letter of 22 April.
[1] By Katharine Burdekin (1929).
[2] John Norman Bryson (1896–1976) was born in Portadown, Co. Armagh, and was educated at the Queen's University, Belfast, and at Merton College, Oxford, taking his B.A. from Oxford in 1922. He was a lecturer at Balliol, Merton and Oriel Colleges from 1923 to 1940, and a Fellow and Tutor in English Literature of Balliol from 1940 to 1963.

119

[Magdalen College
18? July 1929]

My dear Arthur,

Good man. I shall book for the 12th and look forward to our journey together as a very bright spot.[1] I had of course thought of the possibility of my father & you and I going away together, but don't want to raise false hopes in you or me in case it doesn't come off. It would be just as good for him & of course infinitely better for me.

If you are wondering where to go for a few days out of London, I shall be at Cambridge from the 8th to the 10th.[2] I shall be working all day till 6 p.m., so it wd. be absurd for you to come *to see me*: but if on other grounds you cared to visit that ancient city we might have a couple of evenings together. I shall have a sitting room to myself in Queens. However, that's as it may be.

Thanks again & again for coming home – my faithful Arthur! I'm dead tired examining all day.

Yours
Jack

120

Hillsboro,
Western Rd.,
Headington
July 25th [1929]

My dear Arthur,

I have had bad news from home. First a letter from my Scotch uncle[1] commenting on my father's poor state of health, saying that he is losing wait and that they suspect 'something internal', and urging me to get him away for a holiday. Second, a letter from my cousin Joey[2] to say that they are putting him into a nursing home for

[1] Greeves was residing in London and, as his time was very much his own, Lewis hoped he would accompany him to Belfast on 12 August.

[2] 8 to 10 August when he would be examining in English Literature at Cambridge.

[1] Albert's brother, Richard Lewis (b. 1861) who was living at 'Westdene' in Helensburgh, Scotland, and who visited Albert from 4 to 9 July.

[2] Dr Joseph Lewis (b. 1898), the son of Albert's eldest brother Joseph (1856–1908), who was appointed bacteriologist to the Belfast Infirmary in 1928, and later to become one of the leading blood specialists in Northern Ireland.

inspection to-day (the 25th) but, thank goodness, saying that they don't suspect any growth, though they do suspect some inflammation.

The way in which this concerns you and me in common is this (a) I shall have to spend a good deal longer with him this summer than usual (b) I shall have to do my best to get him away for part of that time and as long a part as possible, and it will probably have to be to our relations in Scotland. As far as my selfish wishes go this, of course, is the last thing on earth: but you will easily see that I've got to try and bring it about. I shall go home on the 11th or 12th of August. Now it is extremely likely that with all my efforts *either* I shall not be able to get him away at all *or* I shall be able to do so only after hammering away at persuasion for some considerable time. In the first event I need hardly say how glad I should be if you and I cd. both have together in Ireland this longer-than-usual spell. In the second event (which is more probable and which, probable or not, it is my duty to try to bring about) I hope I shall not have the chagrin of being at home *alone* for a fortnight or so and then setting off for the loathsome Scotch relations just as *you* arrive in Ireland and thus missing our time together for the year.

Poor Arthur, I have so B-g--red you about that you will hardly know whether you are on your head or your heels! I only lay this before you because you suggested in your last letter that you wd. have been coming home earlier if *I* had not proposed coming later. You will not feel hardly if you remember from your own experience how horrible one feels when the people whom one ought to love, but doesn't very much, are ill and in need of your help & sympathy;[3] when you have to *behave* as love wd. dictate and yet feel all the time as if you were doing nothing – because you can't give what's really wanted. Among other things I have to face the prospect that it may be my duty to get him permanently over here – with God knows what upsets & difficulties for everyone I care about – you, Minto, Warnie, myself, everyone.

Do let me have a line as soon as you possibly can: at best, to say you will come home (with me) on the 12th: at worst a word of good cheer. Isn't it all beastly. Poor, poor, old Pdaitabird, I cd. cry over the whole thing

Yrs
Jack

[Albert Lewis was seized with pain on 20 July and entered Miss Bradshaw's Nursing Home on 25 July for a series of X-rays. Immediately

[3] Arthur's father, Joseph Greeves, had died on 19 February 1925.

the Cambridge examining was over, Lewis set off for home, arriving there on 13 August. On 25 August he wrote to his brother Warren, who was stationed in Shanghai, giving him a full account of their father's illness the cause of which was believed to be a 'narrowing of the passage in one of the bowels' (*Lewis Papers*, X, p. 182). This was to be one of the most exhausting periods of Lewis's life as his father was often in terrible agony; and, being in his own home, the chief share of nursing fell upon Lewis who was up most nights with his father and served him with touching devotion. Lewis and his father were lonely for the third member of their family and on 29 August Lewis wrote to his brother saying 'I would give a pint of blood – nay, what's more a tooth (stipulating for a general anaesthetic) if you would throw a pebble at the window and announce your unexpected return' (*Lewis Papers*, X, p. 186).

In September Albert was removed to hospital, and an operation discovered cancer. As the doctors thought Albert might still live for some years, and as Lewis's work for the next term was becoming desperate, the doctors advised him to return to England. He arrived in Oxford on 22 September, only to learn by wire on the morning of 25 September that his father was worse. He caught the train an hour later, and on arriving in Belfast the next morning, he discovered his father had died on the afternoon of the 25th.

Warren first learned of his father's death from a wire Lewis sent on 27 September, none of the letters about Albert's illness reaching him till some time in October. Warren having now no home, as it was decided they would sell Little Lea, both Lewis and Mrs Moore wrote urging him to come and live with them in Oxford. Meanwhile, it was decided to leave Little Lea as it was till Warren's arrival in England – which was not until 16 April 1930.]

121

> Magdalen College,
> Oxford.
> Monday [28 October 1929]

My dear Arthur,

A straggling letter in diary form is in process of composition and will be posted in due course:[1] the present is written for practical purposes and contains a proposal wh. I make with some diffidence. However I must take my courage in both hands: here goes.

Warnie is not coming home till April.[2] Therefore the proposed

---

[1] Portions of the 'letter in diary form' which he writes about here were composed before this and the next two letters, but all are given in the order in which the individual items were received by Greeves.

[2] This news reached him on 26 October.

visit by him and me to Leeborough to clear it out at Christmas will not take place. But unless a purchaser turns up I am disposed to leave the house as it stands until his return. The danger is that if I do not do something this vac. a purchaser may suddenly spring on me next term wanting immediate possession, when I could only run across for a week end at the most, and it wd. be almost impossible to do the whole job in the time. I have therefore decided at least to make a start at the end of the present term. I want to have Minto with me and she v. much wants to come: partly that she may have a look at household things of whose value W. and I are ignorant, partly because we shd. both like her to have seen my old home before it goes. But I cannot (and she agrees) take her to Leeborough. There are ghosts there who wd. not be happy to see her nor anxious to make her happy. Also, it wd. look like the traditional insolence of an heir, trampling on the old king's laws before the crown is warm on his head. But I could take her to Bernagh as a mutual friend of yours and mine.

So what I want to know is could you possibly put the pair of us up (only us two – no Maureen, no cats & no dogs) for a week from Dec. 7th to Dec. 15th. This is the cheekiest proposal I have ever made to any one in my life: but – well, my want is urgent, you are my oldest friend, and I think I can count your mother such too. If it is inconvenient, don't be afraid to say so. I wait for an answer v. eagerly.

Yrs
Jack

122

Magdalen College,
Oxford.
[4? November 1929]

My dear Arthur,

A thousand thanks! I was 'all in a flutter of spirits' when I got your letter for my proposal seemed to me & still seems extraordinarily cool. I am now trying to prevent my anticipations from running so high as to ensure their own disappointment.

Lovely sunrise through tall elms twinkling over the frosty grass this morning.

Yours
Jack

123

Magdalen College,
Oxford.
[11? November 1929]

My dear Arthur,

Yes, it is *Sunday*[1] morning we shall arrive on, all being well. If you arrive by 9.30 I expect we shall have breakfasted on board, being then hungry, wh. will be no harm as we can then be washing and changing etc while you are at breakfast. I *have* primed Minto I presume you have primed your mother. Provided they don't hurt one another their cross purposes & misunderstandings will be very funny. Selah!

Yours
Jack

[Long before they appeared in these letters Lewis had met and introduced Arthur to two Oxford contemporaries who were to become Lewis's life-long friends. They are Arthur Owen Barfield (1898–   ) who met Arthur on 7 July 1922 and Alfred Cecil Harwood (1898–1975) who met Arthur on 29 June 1922. Barfield and Harwood had known one another since 1909 and both came up to Oxford in Michaelmas Term 1919, Barfield having been elected to a Classical Scholarship at Wadham and Harwood to one at Christ Church. They met Lewis through Leo Baker during their first term in Oxford. While neither of them was to know Arthur well, they heard a good deal about one another. Barfield, specially, has achieved great fame through his own books, but a particularly fine description of them is found in Lewis's *Surprised by Joy* (ch. xiii, pp. 189–90): 'There is a sense in which Arthur and Barfield are the types of every man's First Friend and Second Friend. The First is the *alter ego*, the man who first reveals to you that you are not alone in the world by turning out (beyond hope) to share all your most secret delights. There is nothing to be overcome in making him your friend; he and you join like rain-drops on a window. But the Second Friend is the man who disagrees with you about everything. He is not so much the *alter ego* as the anti-self. Of course he shares your interests; otherwise he would not become your friend at all. But he has approached them all at a different angle. He has read all the right books but has got the wrong thing out of every one. It is as if he spoke your language but mispronounced it. How can he be so nearly right and yet, invariably, just not right? He is as fascinating (and infuriating) as a woman. When

[1] Sunday, 8 December – when Lewis and Mrs Moore arrived in Belfast and where they remained till 20 December.

you set out to correct his heresies, you find that he forsooth has decided
to correct yours! And then you go at it, hammer and tongs, far into the
night, night after night, or walking through fine country that neither
gives a glance to, each learning the weight of the other's punches, and
often more like mutually respectful enemies than friends. Actually
(though it never seems so at the time) you modify one another's thought;
out of this perpetual dog-fight a community of mind and a deep affection emerge. But I think he changed me a good deal more than I him.
Much of the thought which he afterwards put into *Poetic Diction* had
already become mine before that important little book appeared. It
would be strange if it had not. He was of course not so learned then as
he has since become; but the genius was already there.

'Closely linked with Barfield of Wadham was his friend (and soon
mine), A. C. Harwood of The House, later a pillar of Michael Hall, the
Steinerite school at Kidbrooke. He was different from either of us; a
wholly imperturbable man. Though poor (like most of us) and wholly
without "prospects", he wore the expression of a nineteenth-century
gentleman with something in the Funds. On a walking tour when the
last light of a wet evening had just revealed some ghastly error in map-
reading (probably his own) and the best hope was "Five miles to Mud-
ham (if we could find it) and we *might* get beds there", he still wore that
expression. In the heat of argument he wore it still. You would think that
he, if anyone, would have been told to "take that look off his face". But
I don't believe he ever was. It was no mask and came from no stupidity.
He has been tried since by all the usual sorrows and anxieties. He is the
sole Horatio known to me in this age of Hamlets; no "stop for Fortunes'
finger".']

124

[Hillsboro,
Western Road,
Headington,
Oxford.]
Thursday Oct 3rd [1929]

My dear Arthur,

I have decided to write a snippet to you every odd time when I
have a moment and thus gradually to fill up a letter. This is the first
snippet.

I am feeling better. Oh how delicious the gradual recovery from a
time of horror is. There is a good description in *The Ring & the Book*
of this: where a man speaks of beginning to feel again 'the comfort-

able feel of clothes And taste of food'.[1] Remember also Herbert's poem – *The Flower* I think – 'I once more feel the sun and rain And relish versing.'[2]

It is much colder here and from my window I see the lawn covered with yellow leaves: the long drought had shrivelled them so that they drop early this year at the first touch of cold. I am sleeping solid and it is a delight to wake up each morning with the sense of peace and safety and home. Then I sing in my bath & take Mr Papworth[3] for a run before breakfast, eating my apple the while. Unfortunately the morning has to be given to uninteresting work done as fast as I can manage to get through it – a process which would rob even voluntary work of its interest. How thankful you should be that you never have tasks which are not chosen by yourself. And yet I don't know. So many things have now become interesting to me because at first I had to do them whether I liked them or not, and thus one is kicked into conquering new countries where one is afterwards at home.

Oct 4th

Yesterday Barfield[4] came to lunch and afterwards took me out for a drive-and-walk – you see you are not the only friend I sponge on. We walked in the flat fields by the Thames near Iffley. I wonder if you remember Iffley, where the Norman church is. I sat on the bridge at Iffley lock with you and Minto's doctor brother, Johnnie, (the one who died) and we talked about sailing up the Amazon.[5] It was a luminous grey day yesterday with a fresh wind that curled the river into crisp waves. A fleet of ducks that passed us were going up and down about as much (in proportion to their size) as fishing smacks in a real swell. We also saw two swans and their cygnets. As often happens with the best of friends we were not in a very good talking mood – only that pleasant sense of security that comes from being

---

[1] Robert Browning, *The Ring and the Book* (1868–9), X, 1710:
    'The healthy taste of food and feel of clothes.'
[2] George Herbert, *The Flower*, 38–9:
    'I once more smell the dew and rain
      And relish versing . . .'
[3] Their dog. See *Biography* (ch. V), p. 123.
[4] Owen Barfield and his wife were living at Long Crendon.
[5] On 18 July 1922, when Lewis wrote in his diary 'The Doc. gave us a vivid description of his sail 1500 miles up the Amazon. Speaking of exploring central Brazil, Arthur said "That's the sort of thing I'd like to do!!"' (*Lewis Papers*, VII, p. 181.)

with those who understand you.

Last night I told Minto about your nursery rime book, and we went all through 'The dog began to bite the pig' together, and then the House that Jack built. She said she so wished to be a grand-mother so as to tell them to her grand-children. I said that now that she has big spectacles and her eyes look very big through them she could do it most impressively.

To day I worked in the morning and afternoon and walked into town by Cuckoo Lane and Mesopotamia[6] after tea. The real autumn tang in the air had begun. There was one of those almost white skies with a touch of frosty red over the town, and the beginnings of lovely colouring in the college garden. I love the big kitchen garden there. There is something very attractive about rows of pots – and an old man potting – and greenhouses and celery trenches. I suspect that 'trench' was a delicious earthy word (like 'ditch') before it was spoiled by the war associations. I saw both a squirrel and a fat old rat in Addison's walk, and had glimpses of 'it'.[7]

I think almost more every year in autumn I get the sense, just as the mere nature and voluptuous life of the world is dying, of some-thing else coming awake. You know the feeling, of course, as well as I do. I wonder is it significant – in stories nymphs slip out of the tree just as the ordinary life of the wood is settling down for the night. Does the death of the natural always mean the birth of the spiritual? Does one thing never sleep except to let something else wake. Milton found that his genius was never in full tide except in autumn and winter.

We have our first fire to night. Mr Papworth is asleep in his basket and Minto is listening-in[8] and mending on the sofa.

Oct. 6th

I have nothing to tell you about books these days. The mornings and afternoons are occupied with making notes on *Loves Labour's Lost*, the last of those four plays which I have been making up all this summer & which will also be associated with this time in my mind.

[6] That area, just north-east of Magdalen College, which lies between the two branches of the River Cherwell. Its name is derived, of course, from the ancient country between the Tigris and Euphrates.

[7] The special name he gave to the experience of poignant longing, later to be described as 'Joy' in *Surprised by Joy*.

[8] i.e., to the radio.

The evenings so far have been nearly always occupied in answering letters of condolence or business correspondence from Condlin.[9] Last night was an exception and I read a short new book, Foligno's *Latin Thought in the Middle Ages*,[10] which I strongly suspect of being Fascist propaganda. When a man is very anxious to emphasise (what everyone admitted before), the greatness and influence of Rome, and to suggest that even yet we have not fully appreciated it, my suspicions are awakened – perhaps unjustly. I also glanced through A. E. Houseman's *Shropshire Lad*[11] for the hundredth time. What a terrible little book it is – perfect and deadly, the beauty of the gorgon. I think you know it.

I have not yet started meditation again. The difficulty is to find a suitable time. These are not suitable days for sitting out of doors: indoor times are occupied with work or conversation. In bed at night – well work and Headington make me so sleepy that I have never yet mustered the resolution to tackle such a difficult job when the pillow and the sheet and the rain on the window are wooing me to glide away into drowsiness. (By the way I don't ever remember a time when the coming of sleep was such a positive pleasure to me as it has been since I left Ireland: and by the way there is a fine passage on that subject in Barfield's novel.)[12] Then in bed in the morning, at early-tea time, I am still sleepier. When I go back into College perhaps I shall be able to fit in five minutes after breakfast. (Memo: can meditation be combined with emptying of the bowels? What a saving of time, specially for a constipated man like you.)

To-day, Sunday, I worked till lunch. After lunch, dug up the hen-run and worked again till tea. All this time it was raining hard. After tea it cleared and I sallied forth for a v. good walk. There was a very high wind, the trees were waving, and a lot of tattered rain clouds were scudding across the sky, unusually low. I walked down Cuckoo Lane and into the Private Road[13] where I had a magnificent view of Oxford below me all gleaming in a sudden dazzling gold break in the cloud. I came home through the fields to old Headington, where the colouring in the hedgerows was rich. But these winds are bringing the leaves down too quickly.

[9] J. W. A. Condlin had been Albert Lewis's managing clerk since 1917.
[10] Cesare Carolo Foligno, *Latin Thought During the Middle Ages* (1929). Foligno (1878–1963) was at this time the Serena Professor of Italian Studies, and a Fellow of Magdalen.
[11] A. E. Housman, *A Shropshire Lad* (1896).
[12] The novel is called *English People*, and has not yet been published.
[13] Pullens Lane.

Oct 10th

We haven't been having a very nice time for the last day or so as Mr Papworth has been seriously ill, which bothers me not only for the poor beast's sake, but also for Minto's, who takes it so to heart and gives herself so much extra work about it. I am also very busy getting ready for term. You can well imagine how I dislike all these preparations because they are always associated with leaving my homely timeless days at Hillsboro and going back to the solitude of my college bedroom and the routine of a time-table. Of course college and ones own rooms & books have their charm: but you know what I mean – especially late at night when people go away and you find that you have let the fire [go] out.

I am slowly reading a book that we have known *about*, but not known, for many a long day – Macdonald's *Diary of an Old Soul*.[14] How I would have scorned it once! I strongly advise you to try it. He seems to know everything and I find my own experience in it constantly: as regards the literary quality, I am coming to like even his clumsiness. There is a delicious home-spun, earthy flavour about it, as in George Herbert. Indeed *for me* he is better than Herbert.

Oct 15th?

I have been back in College for about a week and find I can't go on with this very well. I may try to start another on a more purely diary model. The return to College and its regular routine has done me good: the lag ends of recent horrors have begun to fade in my mind. I am very busy this term, but the beautiful weather over-rides everything.

Yrs
Jack

[14] Though it may not have been the copy he was reading at the time, Lewis owned the 'New Edition' of *The Diary of an Old Soul* (1885) which contains the inscription in MacDonald's hand 'Charlotte Kolle with kindest regards from George & Louisa MacDonald. April 27, 1885.' It contains, as well, an inscription in Lewis's hand 'Later: from C. S. Lewis to Joy Davidman, Christmas 1952.' Following his wife's death, Lewis gave it to me.

125

[Magdalen College]
Thursday Oct. 17th [1929]

Altho I had not gone to bed till one and had then been kept awake by the brilliant moonlight in my room (after walking a half hour in the same moonlight thro' the grove with Griffiths[1]) I woke perfectly refreshed after one of those sleeps deeper than usual which sometimes comes to us in a short night. Went round the walks with Griffiths after breakfast and both enjoyed the bright yellow leaves floating on the water. He packed off and set out to bicycle home to Newbury at 10.

From 10 to 1 pupils. Out home for lunch. Dug the hen run, dug worms for the hens, and took Tykes[2] for the short walk which is all he can manage at present: then at 3.30 walked v. quickly up Shotover getting back about 4.15 for tea. Left home at 5 and got back for pupil at 5.30.

My new book on Marlow[3] had come which I read after dinner. It is chiefly concerned with the appalling career of Poole, who was one of those present when Marlow was murdered: an incredible person who was receiving pay from the Papists for carrying letters to Mary Queen of Scots and also from the govt. for spying on the Papists and Mary: at the same time engaged in litigation with the husband of a woman who visited him while in prison for debt.

Dropped in on Christie[4] for half an hour and was in bed by 11.15 after reading my daily verse from The Diary of an Old Soul.

Mon. Nov. 4th – After breakfast returned to College from home where I had been spending the week end in the hope of getting rid of my flu'ey cold. I had foolishly taken last week end out there in bed, had

---

[1] Alan Richard Griffiths (now Dom Bede Griffiths O.S.B.) who matriculated at Magdalen in 1925 and read English under Lewis. In *Surprised by Joy*, ch. XV, p. 221 Lewis speaks of him as his 'chief companion' on the road to Christianity, and Griffiths has told his own story in *The Golden String* (1954).

[2] Another name for 'Mr Papworth'.

[3] Frederick Samuel Boas, *Marlowe and His Circle* (1929).

[4] John Traill Christie (1899–   ) who was Fellow and Classical Tutor of Magdalen, 1928–32; Headmaster of Repton School, 1932–7; Headmaster of Westminster School, 1937–49; and Principal of Jesus College, Oxford, 1950–67.

to get up too soon, and consequently felt v. poorly all week. No pupils on Monday morning. Spent the whole time till lunch answering letters and setting examination papers. A dull job, rewarded by those sudden gleams of fugitive association that have the habit of starting up only when the intellect is fully engaged on something else.

Home for lunch. Dug the hen run and dug for worms. Worms are a case in which the extension of a name has altered a physical feeling for me. From reading Beowulf and the Edda the word 'Worm' in the sense of 'dragon' has become so familiar to me that I always think of these humble twisters as poor relations of Fafner and Jormungander; their kinship with the monstrous has taken from them the merely disgusting and I can now lift them in my fingers without a shudder. Even if I could not, earth is such a lovely thing that it reconciles one to all its contents. As Minto always says 'There's comfort in the clay.' Took Mr Papworth for his walk. The leaves on the ground are now very thick in Cuckoo Lane. A white liquid sky with horizontal bands of darker grey and a white sun behind them. Not a breath of wind. I had hoped to go and see old Foord-Kelsie[5] after the walk but I am still rather groggy and was tired & sweating when I came back so I did not.

Into college after tea. I intended to write a page or so for you before dinner, but answering letters to Condlin filled up the whole time. After dinner the Michaelmas Club met in my rooms. (An undergraduate society wh. McFarlane[6] and I were instrumental in founding a year ago.) Acton,[7] a funny little chap with a cockney accent but the best philosopher as well as the most earnest and *real* thinker in College – nothing blasé about him – read an excellent paper on *Pessimism*. It had the touch of reality about it – quite unlike most young men's pessimism. A fairly good discussion afterwards till about 11.45 when the Club broke up. McFarlane stayed with me till 12.30 talking by the fire, to the accompaniment of the stags grunting in the grove outside. V. tired.

Tue. Nov. 5th – One of *our* days. Woke to a great roaring wind that kept the trees in the grove rising and falling with the motion and

[5] The Rev. Edward Foord-Kelcey (1859–1934), a retired priest who entered Pembroke College, Oxford, in 1884 and whose last preferment before moving to Oxford was Great Kimble in Buckinghamshire. There is a short biography of him by Lewis in the *Lewis Papers*, XI, pp. 24–5.

[6] Kenneth Bruce McFarlane (1903–66), a distinguished medieval historian, was Tutor in Modern History at Magdalen.

[7] Harry Burrows Acton matriculated in 1927 and took his B.A. in 1930.

noise of seas all morning while the leaves fell in showers. Work all morning and home at 1 o'clock, where the Barfields, a pleasant surprise, turned up after lunch. Mrs B. stayed with Minto while he and I took a short walk. Talked chiefly about his novel (this seems to be a practice of my friends!). He said among other things that he thought the idea of the spiritual world as *home* – the discovery of homeliness in that wh. is otherwise so remote – the feeling that you are coming *back* tho' to a place you have never yet reached – was peculiar to the British, and thought that Macdonald, Chesterton, and I, had this more than anyone else. He doesn't know you of course[8] – who, with Minto, have taught me so much in that way ⟨(in *that* way? No, no.).⟩

Had to be back in Oxford by 5 to attend Simpson's[9] class on Textual Criticism (no, no, Arthur – *T*extual) which I am learning this year in order to teach next. After dinner read with Ker (a pupil)[10] some of the fragments of Anglo-Saxon poetry. Immensely fine. There's one begins with a man going to the window & looking out and saying 'No. This light is not the day breaking, nor a fiery dragon, nor is the house on fire. Take your shields & swords.'[11] Ker shares to the full my enthusiasm for the saga world & we had a pleasant evening – with the wind still roaring outside.

Wed. Nov. 6. – A nasty day. Work all morning. Then lunch in college, which I hate, as there was a college meeting at 2: at which everything went the way I didn't want it to go. I had just time to rush out home, take Mr Papworth for a run and have tea, returning to give my lecture at 5, take a pupil at 6, dine at 7.15, and receive a visit from a pupil with a terrible stutter at 8.30. Fortunately McFarlane came in at about ten wh. encouraged this poor fellow – to his own relief as much as mine – to take himself off. We then made cocoa and chatted till eleven. V. tired and – the old phraze – v. much 'entangled in the world' & v. far in spirit from where I would be.

---

[8] He means they didn't know one another well. They met for the first time at 28 Warneford Road on 7 July 1922 on which occasion Greeves drew a pencil sketch of Barfield.

[9] Percy Simpson (1865–1962), the editor of Ben Jonson, besides lecturing on Textual Criticism was the Librarian of the English School from 1914 to 1934.

[10] Neil Ripley Ker matriculated in 1928, and was a Fellow of Magdalen and Reader in Palaeography from 1946 to 1968.

[11] The opening lines of *Finnsburg*, ed. George Hickes (1705).

Thurs. Nov. 7th. – Got an unexpected free evening off owing to a pupil's having another engagement and like a fool wasted it lounging about in the smoking room till after 10 talking to various people whom I don't greatly care for of subjects I'm not greatly interested in. Such fools we are.

Dec. 3rd. – I tried hard to keep this up but it wouldn't do. Awful business correspondence with Condlin filled up any spare hours I had of an evening. I have also got rather into a whirl as I always do in the latter part of the term. I have too many irons in the fire – the Michaelmas Club, the Linguistic Society, the Icelandic Society, and this and that. One week I was up till 2.30 on Monday (talking to the Anglo Saxon professor Tolkien[12] who came back with me to College from a society and sat discoursing of the gods & giants & Asgard for three hours, then departing in the wind & rain – who cd. turn him out, for the fire was bright and the talk good?), next night till 1 talking to someone else, & on Wednesday till 12 with the Icelandics. It is very hard to keep ones feet in this sea of engagements and very bad for me spiritually.

I am trying not to look forward too much to next week. How odd it will be to sleep in Bernagh – and to walk into Leeborough with Minto. I wonder does the future hold for us things as strange to our present point of view as *this* is to our old one? Barfield's novel[13] is finished and already refused by one publisher. To day there is a fog, and all the trees quite bare now.

In spite of the failure so far I intend to keep up the effort of continuing a journal letter to you. In the Vac. it shd. be easier than in the term, and perhaps habit will at last teach me to fit a portion however small into my day's routine. But you must do the same. Think how we shall enjoy the product when we are old.

Yrs
Jack

P.S. Give my love to your mother and v. many thanks for having us.

---

[12] John Ronald Reuel Tolkien (1892–1973) whom Lewis first met on 11 May 1926 shortly after Tolkien was elected the Rawlinson and Bosworth Professor of Anglo-Saxon at Oxford. For details of their long and close friendship see *Surprised by Joy* and the *Biography*.

[13] *English People.*

126

Hillsborough,
Headington,
Oxford.
[27 December 1929]

My dear Arthur,

The perfect guest again! An awful thing has happened: I find that I have not got with me my three most valuable keys. I have wired to the Ulster Monarch[1] & had an answer to say that they cannot be found. My last hope is that they are in the study. Will you please look and then let me know, but do *not* send them till further notice. There are three tied together with string, two ordinary looking keys and one very short & shiny one. They may be in the key hole of my father's desk – i.e. the small one in the key hole & the other two hanging from it – or on the top of the same desk. As one of the keys is my college key which will cost me £100 if I lose it, I am rather in a stew & shall be glad to have a line as soon as possible. Just like me, you will say.

Many thanks & much love from us both. Minto is writing in a few days.

Yrs
Jack

P.S. Of course have a look elsewhere, but if they're not in the study I expect they're a gonner. If you get them please take them home with you (after making sure that the desk is locked) & guard them carefully till further notice. Shall write as soon as I can.[2]

127

[Hillsboro.
1929]

Dec. 21st – Although if I had had my choice I should have preferred some real talk between you and me alone, still I think it worth while to say that I felt something very pleasant in our final chat with John[1]

---

[1] The cross-channel boat on which Lewis and Mrs Moore returned from Ireland on 20 December.

[2] Greeves wired on 28 December to say he had found the keys.

[1] Arthur's brother, John Greeves.

and our drinking on board the Ulster Monarch. On occasions that are rather melancholy a plunge into the cheery and homely world of 'good fellows' and women has something of the same wholesome effect as a romp with dogs or children; it was specially appropriate to this visit too, since the main thing that I bring away with me is a new view of John. Besides, as Barfield said when Christie interrupted us one night that he was staying in College, it is rather important that friends should occasionally share together their experience of a third person.

Dec. 22nd – I think the L.N.W.R.[2] mainline must run through the dullest country in the British Isles – tho' of course no country is without some charm. I read *Grace Abounding* in Everyman, having (you remember) read *Mr Badman* in the same volume on the way over. *Grace Abounding* is incomparably the better of the two. Some of the sentences in it reach right down. 'But the milk and honey is beyond this wilderness'[3] – 'I thought I could have spoken of his love and his mercy even to the very crows that sat upon the ploughed lands before me'[4] – 'I could not find that with all my soul I did *desire* deliverance.'[5] Of course a great part of it paints the horrors of religion and sometimes almost of insanity. What do you make of the curious temptation that assailed him just after he had been converted and felt himself united to Christ; when a voice kept saying 'Sell Him, sell Him': sometimes for hours at a stretch, until in mere weariness Bunyan blurted out 'Let Him go if he will'[6] – which afterwards led him into despair, believing he had committed the unpardonable sin?

I suppose this is the same mental disease of which you and I have felt a trace in the impulse to throw ones new book in the fire – some strange twist that impels you to do a thing because it is precisely the one thing of all others that you *don't* want to do.

I should like to know, too, in general, what you think of all the darker side of religion as we find it in old books. Formerly I regarded it as mere devil worship based on horrible superstitions. Now that I have found, and am still finding more and more, the element of truth

[2] London and North Western Railway.

[3] John Bunyan, *Grace Abounding and The Life and Death of Mr Badman*, with an Introduction by G. M. Harrison (Everyman's Library) [1928], Preface, p. 6.

[4] *ibid*., para. 92, p. 31.

[5] *ibid*., para. 104, p. 34.

[6] *ibid*., para. 139, p. 44.

in the old beliefs, I feel I cannot dismiss even their dreadful side so cavalierly. There must be something in it: only what?

Dec. 23rd – Delighted to get back to my books again and did a good morning's work on Chaucer, mostly textual problems. Too wet for anything but a short walk after lunch. In the evening wrote part of a long letter to Warnie. I find I am (so far) surprisingly little upset about the affair of my keys.

Dec. 24th – Into town in the morning to get my hair cut, and then, before lunch, began indexing my Bunyan. I had a lovely walk in the afternoon – a perfect winter day with mellow sunlight slanting through a half frosty mist on the grey fields, the cosy farms, and the tall leafless elms, absolutely unmoving in the air. On my way back the sun was down and it was cold. I passed two men engaged in penning sheep and walked just by the baa-ing crowd, whose breath looked like smoke.

At seven in to College to dine, which I didn't much enjoy as I got an awful bore called Parker[7] on my left and on my right the Italian professor[8] whose English is so bad that I can't understand *him*, and who is so deaf that he can't understand *me*.

At 9 o'clock we went up into hall for the Christmas Eve revels, which of course I have never seen before. The hall looks very noble with its green branches, and a roaring fire and the centre cleared, and a Christmas tree. Female guests, including, of course, Minto and Maureen, were in the musicians gallery. From 9 to 10 the choir gave us the first part of the *Messiah*: a great mistake, I thought, with only a piano at our disposal for accompaniment. Then came an interval during which those who had no guests remained in hall for supper and to watch the choir boys having *their* Christmas supper, which is the best sight of all: I, and others in the same plight, went down to common room to feed our ladies on sandwiches and hot negus and talk small talk. We returned to hall to find lights out and candles lit on the tree and to hear carols: all the really good ones like the Coventry Carol and *In dulci jubilo* and one by Byrd that I never heard before. This last comes just on the stroke of midnight after the

[7] Henry Michael Denne Parker (1894–1972), Fellow and Tutor in Ancient History. Lewis usually referred to him as the 'Wounded Buffalo' or 'Wounded Bison'.

[8] Professor Cesare Foligno.

Vice President has sent a message to the ringers to begin the peals. I had been rather bored with the proceedings earlier in the evening but at this moment the glorious windy noise of the bells overhead, the firelight & candlelight, and the beautiful music of unaccompanied boys' voices, really carried me out of myself. We then have sack passed round in a loving cup and pledge one another and so break up: home by taxi at about 12.30.

Taking it all in all, with the walk and the evening, and the blessed sense of charity, so rare in me, – the feeling, natural at such a moment, that even my worst enemies in college were really funny and odd rather than detestable, while my friends were 'the many men so beautiful' – this was as good a day as I could wish to have. If only it wasn't for those damned keys!

Dec. 25th – A slack day. All up very late after our debauch of the night before. Went for several short strolls with Mr Papworth, but no real walk. My afternoon one, about five o'clock was the best: an evening of bitter wind with the trees lashing one another across a steel coloured sunset. Afterwards – as a Christmas treat! – I read a modern novel, H. G. Wells' *Meanwhile* [1927] which deals chiefly with the General Strike, and contains very good comic elements. You and I ought to read, think and talk of these things more than we do.

Dec. 26th – Another lazy day. Went in to College at about 10.30, by arrangement, to go for a walk with McFarlane. We were on the road by about eleven. Neither of us was at first disposed for more than desultory chat. The trudge out of Oxford was tedious (as always) and I did not really begin to enjoy myself till we had climbed Cumnor Hill. Once through the beautiful grey and mossy village of Cumnor, I became extremely pleased with everything. Walking on unfrequented paths, we hardly met a soul: the sky was palest blue, without a cloud or a breeze, and the weak sun laid a lovely unity of pale colour over the ploughed fields, the haystacks and the church towers in each village. 'Unity of colour' is not just a phrase – I mean that everything, except the woods (which of course were brownish-black) and the crows, was almost the same colour of chilly greenish grey.

As we dropped down the far side of the hill the floods began to spread themselves out wider and wider below us. Where the Thames

T.S.T.–L

should have been there was a sheet of water about a mile broad, intersected with the tops of hedges and polled willows. We began to wonder whether we could reach the ferry at Bablock Hythe. I was in favour of taking off shoes & stockings, not, of course, to wade the river, but to wade the shallow flood to the real river bank where the ferry begins. McFarlane however couldn't as one of his feet was bandaged under the sock as the result of wearing a tight shoe yesterday. However, when we got there, and called, the man at the pub brought a punt not only across the river but across the floods to where we stood. Once over, we feasted in the pub on bread & cheese, beer, and a following cup of tea – my invariable walking lunch. It left us in that delightful state which (I remember) Harwood once described – 'One is neither full nor hungry and goes on like a ship.' As it was boxing day, no one was working in the fields, and all was so still that the wheeling starlings made quite a noticeable noise.

You know how it sometimes is when you are out for a day's jaunt – as it has so often happened to you and me – that there comes a period when things are getting better and better every moment till suddenly one says 'Oh!' or 'By God!' and that is IT – the centre of the whole day, the thing one will remember it by. Such was the moment when the old man came over the gate in the frost-mist up by *our* wood: or when we saw the fire that night near the house of the sinister old man who sold lemonade: or when we were shown into the postmistress's cottage above the glens of Antrim. To day was of course totally different from all these. It happened by luck that two things came at the same moment.

We came round a turn into the village of Stanton Harcourt and suddenly got a view of the towered manor house and the church, across a farmyard, where a very fine old horse with a white star on his forehead was looking at us across a half gate. That was the first thing. And at the very same moment – this is the second thing – the ringers in the church began practicing their peal. It sounds poor on paper, but the thing about it was the sense of absolute peace and safety: the utter homeliness, the Englishness, the Christendom of it. And then I thought of Antrim only a week or so ago, and what you said (in the rainbow and sleet scene on Divis – itself another instance of this *apex* in the day's outing) about the 'broad-mindedness' of the infinite – Antrim that's desolate and keen in July, Stanton Harcourt and all the sleepy Cumnor country (isn't the very name Cumnor good?) which is snug and dreamy and like cotton wool even in winter.

Perhaps it is less strange that the Absolute should make both than that we should be able to love both. Bacon says 'The whole world cannot fill, much less distend the mind of man.'[9] (By the way, that is the answer to those who argue that the universe cannot be spiritual because it is so vast and inhuman and alarming. On the contrary, nothing less would do for us. At our best, we can stand it, and could not stand anything smaller or snugger. Anything less than the terrifyingly big would, at some moments, be cramping and 'homely' in the bad sense – as one speaks of a 'homely' face. You can't have elbow room for things like men except in endless time and space and staggering multiplicity.[10])

A few miles beyond Stanton Harcourt – in the tower of that manor house, by the way, Mr Pope translated 'his Iliads'[11] – the peace of the afternoon was broken by brutes in the distance firing guns. The only good result of this was that it started a pair of white owls to blunder across our road, stupid with the daylight, poor chaps, and very grotesque to see. We had tea at Eynsham, and sitting over the fire in the pub there we fell (at last) into serious conversation – about the rival claims of reason and instinct. We continued this on the homeward journey – a long stretch of road (we dared not try the towpath in the floods) which would have been dull by daylight. Now that the stars were out it was good enough. The remains of the sunset was before us, and all between us and it seemed to be water. McFarlane observed that it was one of the rare occasions on which night seemed a tangible thing: and looking back I saw what he meant, for the darkness and stars did seem to come up at our backs and then stop just over our heads, while in front was twilight.

We got back to Oxford, very happy but very footsore and tired, at about 6.30, and I was home (by bus) at about 7. Finished *Meanwhile* after supper and took a hot bath to cure my stiffness – this being the first real exercise I have had for ages. It only needed a more perfectly receptive companion – such as you – to have made it one of the really great days: not that McFarlane is half bad, and one ought to learn to like more, and more different, people.

[9] A conflation of several lines in Francis Bacon's *The Advancement of Learning* (1605), First Book, I, 3.

[10] cf. 'Dogma and the Universe' in Lewis's *Undeceptions*, ed. Walter Hooper (1971), pp. 20–1, where he says 'What sort of universe do we demand? If it were small enough to be cosy, it would not be big enough to be sublime. If it is large enough for us to stretch our spiritual limbs in, it must be large enough to baffle us . . . It is to be expected that His creation should be, in the main, unintelligible to us.'

[11] Alexander Pope, *The Iliad*, 6 vols. (1715–20).

Dec 27th – Worked at Chaucer all morning. After lunch as I was carrying a plate into the scullery I suddenly got one of those vivid mental pictures that memory sometimes throws up for no apparent reason – a picture of the deep stony and brambly vallies on the side of Scrabo, wet and grey as they were one day when you and I came down that way. 'Jesus, the times this knight and I have had!'[12] (That's from Henry IV. Read it all, but specially the scene where Falstaff meets his old acquaintance Shallow in the country – one of the best 'Do you remember' conversations in any book that I know.)

After lunch Maureen took Mr Papworth for a walk, which always gives me a blessed liberation to go where I choose: for much as I like Mr P., his presence is a considerable restraint. You can't go *that* way because there is a dog that fights: and you can't go *that* way because there are sheep and you have to keep him on the lead. In fact it is rather like Dick Swiveller's walks in London.[13]

I bussed into College, took out the second chapter of my book[14] & left it at the house of a Professor in Marston who had promised to give me his views on it. Thence home up the hill under grey and windy skies with a little rain. I tried my practice of keeping myself free from thought – a mere sponge to sense impressions – for a certain part of the way. Later I hope to resume the higher stage of meditation proper. Went on with Chaucer before supper: afterwards wrote to Condlin, Aunt Annie, Uncle Bill,[15] Uncle Dick and you.

Dec. 28th – Went to Barfield's to day for my stay. Thanks awfully about the keys – your wire was a great relief. When will *your* big letter arrive? –

Yours

J.

---

[12] A conflation of lines 228–9 and lines 236–7 in Shakespeare's *II Henry IV*, III, ii.
[13] A character in Charles Dickens's *The Old Curiosity Shop* (1841).
[14] *The Allegory of Love: A Study in Medieval Tradition* (1936), which Lewis began writing in 1928.
[15] Another of Albert's brothers, William Lewis (1859–1946), who was living near Glasgow.

128

My dear Arthur,

By now I hope you have my long letter and are well advanced with your *long* reply. You shall have another gripping instalment, D.V., in the course of the next ten days. We both enjoyed your description of your visit to the witches den,[1] most of which I read aloud to Minto. I am now, as you will already have guessed, going to give you the opportunity of paying her another one! This time it is my cheque book (Bank of Ireland) – which is unlikely to be in my Father's desk – tho' it may be, my dear fellow, it may be – and may be in the study or at Bernagh. If found it could be sent by post: and any odd collars or handkerchiefs left at Bernagh would be convenient packing. Don't hate me for ever!

Yours
Jack

129

[Hillsboro
1930]

My dear Arthur: –

Thurs Jan 2 – Got home to day from four day's stay with Barfield.[1] For the first two days his wife and adopted baby[2] were away, so we had the house to ourselves – alas that you and I never have such an uninterrupted feast of each other's society.

We had promised ourselves some solid reading together, and in spite of the temptations of conversation and walking, we stuck to it: Aristotle's *Ethics* all morning, walk after lunch, and then Dante's *Paradiso* for the rest of the day.

The latter has really opened a new world to me. I don't know whether it is really very different from the *Inferno* (B. says its as different as chalk from cheese – heaven from hell, would be more appropriate!) or whether I was specially receptive, but it certainly

---

[1] The home of Mary Cullen, or the 'Witch of Endor' as she was sometimes called, who was the cook-housekeeper at Little Lea from 1917 till the Lewis brothers took their final leave of it in 1930.

[1] The Barfields were living in Long Crendon, Buckinghamshire.

[2] Alexander Barfield (b. 1928).

seemed to me that I had never seen at all what Dante was like before. Unfortunately the impression is one so unlike anything else that I can hardly describe it for your benefit – a sort of mixture of intense, even crabbed, complexity in language and thought with (what seems impossible) *at the very same time* a feeling of spacious gliding movement, like a slow dance, or like flying. It is like the stars – endless mathematical subtlety of orb, cycle, epicycle and ecliptic, unthinkable & unpicturable, & yet at the same time the freedom and liquidity of empty space and the triumphant certainty of movement. I should describe it as feeling more *important* than any poetry I have ever read. Whether it has the things *you* specially like is another question. It is seldom homely: perhaps not *holy* is our sense – it is too Catholic for that: and of course its blend of complexity and beauty is very like Catholic theology – wheel within wheel, but wheels of glory, and the One radiated through the Many.

One night we sat up till four, and heard the cock's crowing as we went to bed: a very good moment, and who shall I ever find to share it with me fully? For *you* would be too sleepy, and Barfield doesn't really taste a thing like that as keenly as you and I. They have a most delightful house, an ex-farmhouse with many outbuildings and an orchard: in one of the most beautiful villages I know. We had one very good walk among the floods, and one very good sky.

Frid. Jan 3 – In the Bodleian all morning. Back after lunch, arriving there at 3 o'clock to find it shutting! Bought the new book on Malory by Vinaver[3] at 15/–, which is necessary for work, but not worth the price.

Sunday Jan 5th – I spent the morning finishing a long letter on philosophical subjects which I had carried about with me all the time in Ireland, to my friend and former pupil, Griffiths. It was owing to this that you have no Saturday's instalment from me: and if you knew how long Griffiths had waited for an answer you would not grudge it to him.

In the afternoon I had a most delicious walk, in that rarified afternoon sunlight which I have tried to describe so often. It is the peculiar glory of the English winter. Apart from a period of meditation – mind-emptying, I mean – which was fairly successful, I was

[3] Eugène Vinaver. *Malory* (1929).

on the whole as free from thought and fancies as I have been for a long time. Two moments are worth preserving.

One, when I suddenly paused, as we do for no reason known to consciousness, and gazed down into a little ditch beneath a grey hedge, where there was a pleasant mixture of ivies and low plants and mosses, and thought of herbalists and their art, and what a private, retired wisdom it would be to go groping along such hedges and the eaves of woods for some herb of virtuous powers, insignificant to the ordinary observer, but well known to the trained eye – and having at the same time a stronger sense of the mysteries of living stuff than usual, specially the mysteries twining at our feet, where homeliness and magic embrace one another.

The second was a stiffish five minutes up-hill towards a hedge of small trees and bushes, behind wh. the sun was setting. A keen frosty wind in my face: all beyond me flaming yellow, and on that yellow, in perfect black, the rich and varied pattern of the hedge, looking quite flat, so that the whole had a Chinese or Japanese appearance.

In the evening I started to read the Everyman volume of Jacob Boehme[4] which I had ordered sometime ago. The Dialogue at the end, called the Supersensual Life, was fairly easy going, and I should advise you to get and read it at once. Then I turned back and began the longer work, the Signatura Rerum. I could see at once that I was reading the most serious attempt I had ever met to describe (not to explain, for he speaks as one who has seen and his description *is* his explanation) – to describe the very mystery of creation and to show you the differences actually coming into being out of the original One and making a world and souls and good and evil. Almost at the same time, I saw, alas, that it was hopelessly beyond me: yet tantalising for I could just grasp enough to be quite sure that he was talking about something tremendously real, and not merely mystifying you.

I had two quite distinct experiences in reading it. (a) Certain sentences moved and excited me although I couldn't understand them – as the mysterious words in the Crock of Gold, which Aengus told the Philosopher. In case they may have the same effect on you I quote two of them: 'That the nothing is become an eternal life and has found itself, which cannot be, in the Stillness.'[5] – 'The wrath extinguishes and the turning orb stands still, and instead of the turn-

---

[4] Jacob Boehme, *The Signature of all Things, with Other Writings* [translated by John Ellistone], Introduction by Clifford Bax, Everyman's Library [1912].

[5] *ibid.* (ch. II, para. 18), p. 16.

ing a sound is caused in the essence.'[6] (b) At certain points a feeling of distress, and even of horror. I had always assumed, in my way, that if I could reach the things Boehme is here talking about, I should *like* them! There is something really very dreadful in this second chapter of the Signatura. (You'll think I'm putting this on *just a little bit*. Honestly, I'm not.) I intend to try and get hold of some good commentator on this book, if there is one, and worrey out the meaning.

In the meantime, I wish to record that it has been about the biggest shaking up I've got from a book, since I first read *Phantastes*. It is not such a pleasant experience as Phantastes, and if it continues to give me the same feeling when I understand more I shall give it up. No fooling about for me: and I keep one hand firmly gripped round the homely & simple things. But it is a real book: i.e. it's not like a book at all, but like a thunderclap. Heaven defend us – what things there are knocking about the world!

Monday [Jan. 6] – Morning's work in town as usual and to the station at 12.30 to see the Harwoods whose train was stopping there for ten minutes. I shall always think of you in connection with him, as through your imitations of his manner, he has become one of our stock characters. It was a silly and useless tryst – nothing can be less like conversation than chatter at a carriage door with a man in the presence of his wife and two babies – and I only kept it to return a pair of skates wh. he left in my rooms last winter.

I walked as usual after lunch, dropping in on the way to see if old Foord-Kelsie would accompany me. I think I have mentioned him to you – a retired country parson of 80, who drives his own car, carpenters, and mends everyone's wireless. He is an irreplaceable character – a great reader, specially of *Tristram Shandy*, Boswell, & *Pickwick* – and as redolent of English country life as an old apple in a barn. He is deliciously limited: cares for no poetry but Shakespeare, distrusts all mysticism and imagination, and all overstrained moods. Yet you could not wish him to be otherwise: and inside this almost defiantly human and mundane framework there is such tenderness of heart that one never feels it bleak. He was in his workshop when I arrived, with shavings all about his ankles, making a cover for the font of old Headington Church. He would not come out, and I stayed to shout conversation for fifteen minutes above the thudding

[6] *ibid.* (ch. II, para. 19), p. 16.

and singing of his circular saw. We had a bit of everything: an outburst against Shaw, a broad story, and then, as always, onto Tristram
Shandy. 'Wonderful book – oh a wonderful book. You feel *snug*
when you read that – you get in among them all in that little parlour.
And my uncle Toby – ah (a *very* parsonical, long-drawn, almost
devotional *a-a-ah*) ah, a beautiful character. And the jokes – I'm sure
I don't know how the rascal thought of it all – the rascal!' I wish you
could have seen him saying all this, bending down as he shoved a
beam of wood against the saw, with one dear old wrinkled eye
screwed up and held close to the work. You must hurry up and come
and see me before he dies, for he of all people should be added to our
stock characters.

Wed. January 8th – I have just got your excellent letter. I find I am
getting great pleasure out of this correspondence – both the writing
and the reading. It recalls old times. I quite agree with what you say
about letters being haphazard and informal – in their choice of
subject. Things ought to come up just as they do in conversation.
The actual expression is a different matter. There is such a thing as
being unnaturally natural – I mean it doesn't really come naturally
to most of us to write exactly as we speak. I say this in self defence,
lest you should think I am sometimes trying to be literary. (There's a
good example. I should never say *lest* in conversation, but it comes
naturally to me in writing: perhaps because *lest* is four letters and *for
fear* is seven.) My only attempt is to get across the picture in my
mind: and in order to do that one *has* to choose ones words, because
there is no chance of correcting a wrong impression as we shd. in
conversation. As for the diary form, that is not much more than a
framework, to keep one going from evening to evening.

I agree about the not looking forward to the time when we shall re-
read them. But one's between the devil and the deep sea. That
pleasure in the future is the chief spur to diary-writing: and yet to
think of it makes the thing artificial. Still, I suppose one can play
hide and seek with ones own mind in that way: e.g. in playing a game.
You've got to hoodwink yourself into thinking that winning is
important, or else it is no fun: and at the same time you've got to
remember that it is not important, or else it ceases to be a game.

I liked your description of your second visit to Leeborough – like
Arthur at Orgoglio's castle. And I'm glad you have the Smaller
Temple. That smell will always carry you back to the old days.

Chevasse[7] really has a *talent* for evil, hasn't he? I've had a very busy day, and lots more to do, so good-night. (Tidying up I came across the old prose Dymer the other day. Emotions and comments can be supplied to taste!)

Thurs 9th – Another day all on Chaucer. What I am actually doing is going thro the parts of the Canterbury Tales which I know least with the aid of several commentators, making copious notes and trying to get really 'sound' on them. You see there has been a new edition since my undergraduate days, so that most of my knowledge – it was never very exact – on Chaucer, is out of date. This sounds dull, but as a matter of fact I take great pleasure in it.

What a glory-hole is the commentary of an old author. One minute you are puzzling out a quotation from a French medieval romance: the next, you are being carried back to Plato: then a scrap of medieval law: then something about geomancy: and manuscripts, and the signs of the Zodiac, and a modern proverb 'reported by Mr Snooks to be common in Derbyshire', and the precession of the equinoxes, and an Arabian optician (born at Balk in 1030), five smoking room stories, the origins of the doctrine of immaculate conception, and why St Cecilia is the patroness of organists. So one is swept from East to West, and from century to century, equally immersed in each oddity as it comes up, and equally sudden in ones flight to the next: like the glimpses (oh how I hate the word *vignette*) that you get from an express train, when the cart going under the bridge seems to be a little world in itself, until it is replaced – instantaneously – by the horses running away from the line in the next field.

About Bunyan – I had forgotten the passage you mention in which a share in judging the damned is held out as one of the pleasures of the saint. I quite agree that it is horrid. As to whether it is contrary to the spirit of Christ – it is certainly not contrary to the letter: for he himself in the Gospels (if I remember rightly) does hold out that very reward to the disciples – 'And ye shall sit on twelve thrones judging the twelve tribes of Israel.'[8] In spite of all my recent changes of view, I am still inclined to think that you can only get what *you* call 'Christ'

[7] The Rev. Claude Lionel Chavasse (1897–   ) was Curate of St Mark's Church, Dundela, from 1928 to 1931. For information about his early life see his essay 'An Irish Setting' in *To Nevill Coghill from Friends*, collected by John Lawlor and W. H. Auden (1966).

[8] Luke xxii. 30. 'That ye may eat and drink at my table in my kingdom, and sit on thrones judging the twelve tribes of Israel.'

out of the Gospels by picking & choosing, & slurring over a good deal. However that's as may be. Of course in Bunyan's case, one must remember the persecution he had undergone – which makes his vindictiveness more pardonable than the intolerance of those you speak of who have never suffered anything at the hands of the 'ungodly'.

To day has been a day of howling wind and low, fast-driving clouds, but no rain. On my afternoon walk my 'NO THINKING' period was rather more successful than usual. I find as I go on that one becomes more conscious of ones thought by trying to stop. After shoving out the obvious loud thought, one listens to the whispered thought underneath. When one has checked that, I suppose there will be another layer underneath! Perhaps it is thought all the way down. Anyway, it is not a bad thing to get even this far: to step out of the thinking and listen to it going on. Perhaps it will teach you to control it better when you step back into the stream. Of course the trouble of writing about it is that the words inevitably mean more than one intends: as these, for instance, sound as if I'd got far further than I really have – wh. wasn't the effect I wanted to produce. Oh! my hand is tired. I've been writing on and off nearly all day.

Frid 10th – It will probably be short commons to night for I have been pretty hard at work all day, except for walk, and I feel rather tired. My life tends to go in spurts. When I am interested in a subject, my interest drives me like a daemon, and for a few days the time at meals (or the time spent in digging the hen run and rinsing plates and talking) seems as if it would never be done and let me back to work. And for the first few days I feel as if I could never be tired. Then suddenly, one evening, (tho the interest remains) virtue has gone out of me, and my legs ache and I feel as if I could do nothing. So I shall do slightly different work to morrow. Another lovely day. I think January, when it is fine, is one of the most exquisite months in the year. I love these skies with level alternate bars of pale yellow and of grey, exactly the grey of a grey horse. Also one seems to hear almost as many birds as in spring.

The others were out for tea, and I had another go at Boehme. Much the same effect. I must try him again in different circumstances and at a different time of the year, to see if it is some trick of my health or of the weather that makes this book have such an astonishing effect on me. On the whole, this time there was a little less of the sinking feeling, and a little more understanding. But there is no question that it is full of the most lovely sentences: 'That many a twig withers on the tree is not the tree's fault, for it withdraws its sap from no twig, only the twig gives forth itself too eagerly with the desire: it runs on in self will, it is taken by the inflammation of the sun and the fire, before it can draw sap again in its mother and refresh itself'[9] – 'He breaks self-hood as a vessel wherein he lies captive, and buds forth continually in God's will-spirit, with his desire regained in God, as a fair blossom springs out of the earth'[10] – 'If the soul did but truly know that all beings were its mothers, which brought it forth, and did not hold the mother's substance for its own, but for common.'[11]

I suppose by now you are at, or finished, Henry IV. Isn't Hotspur a wonderful picture of the kind of 'hearty' public school 'no nonsense' type?

I am afraid this correspondence is sure to languish on my side after the end of next week when term begins: it will be *your* turn then to put your back into it. A letter a day keeps the apples away. (Why not a new slogan – 'Daily castration Prevents Master Bation' – 'Who goes daily to Wadham, he Need have no fear of sodomy' – 'Decapitation each night Teaches you to spell right' – 'Tchanie each afternoon Cures heresy soon.') By the way, I am saddened about the McNeills.

Sunday [*Jan. 12*] – I have had a letter from Warnie, in which he says that he particularly wants to keep *Mother Goose's Fairy Tales* 'the first book of my own which I ever had – this is written in the front of it'.[12] I find something very pathetic in this sudden streak of sentiment in so unsentimental a character, and I expect you will feel the same, and therefore will not mind facing the Witch again and transferring this book (it is probably on the landing or the room opposite my father's) to the study. At the same time would you (wū-ū-ū-d) you please send me the MS. book catalogue that Minto made. It is shoved in on top of the books in one of the shelves of the big bookcase on the north wall of the study – i.e. it is probably now

[9] Jacob Boehme, *op. cit.* (ch. XVI, para. 36), p. 219.

[10] *ibid.* (ch. XV, para. 31), p. 203.

[11] *ibid.* (ch. XV, para. 8), p. 198.

[12] The actual title is *Mother Goose's Nursery Rhymes, Tales and Jingles* (London: Frederick Warne and Co. [1890]). Inscribed in it is a note from Albert to Warren: 'Badgie, his first book from his Papy. Novr. '96.' It is now in my possession.

behind one of the grandfathers' portraits. I am sorry to keep on sending you on these errands. You must feel rather like Crusoe rowing out to the wreck every few days to bring off a bag of tools or a tin of biskets (That is, by the way, an old and good way of spelling *biscuits*) I expect a good long letter from you any day now –

Yours
Jack

130

[Hillsboro]
Jan 26th Sunday [1930]

My dear Arthur,

Thanks very much for sending on the lists: but I was genuinely disappointed not to find a letter inside. Now that term is upon us I shall not be able to keep up letters of my vacation size, but I had certainly hoped that we might manage a short weekly letter as we did in the Bookham days: and I think we both had a good deal of pleasure from them.

Of course there is one possibility that must be frankly taken into account – i.e. that my present letters, dealing necessarily so much with a life you don't share and only rarely touching on common reading – may be, if not tedious to you, (note the vanity of the 'if not'), at any rate too little interesting to repay you for the labour of keeping up your side. I shan't be in the least offended if this is so: tho' even then I would like a line occasionally. However, one good result of growing up is that one learns how small accidents everyone's conduct depend on. I do not assume that you have foresworn my acquaintance forever, nor will I 'fly into a passion'.

This you will notice is a very dignified, magnanimous letter on my part: it will look very well to posterity! (As a matter of fact, to write private letters with an eye on posterity is a lovable fault, springing from honest vanity: to try to forestall criticism by parodying ones own mood, as I did in the last sentence, is a beastly modern sophisticated kind of vanity)

And now, for my first week of term. All private reading has ceased, except for 20 minutes before bed (if alone) when I drink a cup of cocoa and try to wash the day off with Macdonalds Diary of an Old Soul. I shall soon have finished it and must look round for another book. Luckily the world is full of books of that general type: that is another of the beauties of coming, I won't say, to religion but to an attempt at religion – one finds oneself on the main road with all humanity, and can compare notes with an endless succession of previous travellers. It is emphatically coming home: as Chaucer says 'Returneth *home* from worldly vanitee.'[1]

I am called at 7.30 (as you remember to your cost) and rise about 8. Monday morning I have no pupils and can devote to my own work or to preparation. Out home at 12, lunch, dig the hen run, walk (on Mondays with Foord-Kelsie) back to home for tea, then into college for a pupil at 5.30. After dinner a meeting of a society. Tuesday, pupils from 10 to 1, then again at 5: and similarly on Wednesday. Thursday differs by pupils beginning at 9, and by an Anglo Saxon class after dinner, which usually develops into informal talk till midnight. Friday and Saturday are like the other days except that there is no pupil after tea. So far, until things close in on me as they presently will, I have five evenings free a week after dinner. For the first week they have mostly been occupied in correcting what we call 'Collection papers' – i.e. exams one sets the young men on what they have done or neglected to do in the Vac.

On Friday Christie came in from about 11 till 12.45: mostly stood on the fender eating biscuits, and talked on a variety of subjects. I never can make up my mind whether I most like or dislike this man. Perhaps his hard, insistant voice is really what prevents him from being nicer. He is genuinely religious: he has a real love of poetry and nature, – real enthusiasm, quite different from the usual blasé, côterie, critical, twaddle wh. is in fashion here: he even likes Macdonald – a bit. But then suddenly a whiff of the schoolmaster comes reeking out of him: you know he is not thinking whether your view is *true*, but what it signifies in relation to your character: he's not thinking what will be true for him to reply, but what will be best for you, what will rouse least opposition and yet do you most good. All this, damn him!, *very* charitably & making full allowances, internally, for all your antecedents and previous history. It is a habit schoolmasters have got from 'understanding' boys. In fact you might say Christie is so taken up with 'understanding' me, that he has no time to understand what I say. 'Yes' he will say 'I quite understand how you can come to think that, and I quite sympathise: but – ' and all the time he hasn't really taken in what I said. But on the whole I think his good points out-number his bad: and as you are always rightly telling me one mustn't demand to[o] much. (So is he, by the way. He is particularly strong on charity. Now what follows isn't a sneer, for I am really trying to become more charitable, and I think I can at least admire charity in another. But I

[1] *Troilus and Criseyde*, V, 1837.

don't think Christie's is of the right brand. He always seems to select the really evil people to defend: and the next moment you find him being extraordinarily hard on some harmless old man because he is a bore. I suppose there is such a thing as imagining you have got beyond the stage of hating bad men, when in reality you haven't got *as far* as hating them. Divine charity must be very different from human *truckling* to bullies, or human indulgence for rotters because they are amusing: I doubt if Christie knows this difference.)

Just before term began I had to go and call on Farquharson in Univ. He is the senior tutor there, and of course I have known him since my undergraduate days.[2] On the strength of having done some office work at Whitehall during the war, and having been in the Territorials before, he has called himself Lieutenant Colonel ever since. He lives in a tall, narrow house, cheek by jowl with Univ. Library which itself is like a mortuary chapel. The space between them is about six feet across; into the Fark's house daylight never comes. I have never been beyond the ground floor: here in broad low rooms, lined with books, he works by artificial light most of the day. Somewhere, upstairs, is a wife one never meets. He came gliding towards me in the dusk, about five feet four inches high, his face exactly like an egg in shape, with sandy-hair fringing a bald patch, a little military moustache, and eyebrows so far up his forehead that it gives him a perpetual air of astonishment. On this occasion, as on every other on which I have met him, he came towards me with an *air* (not a gesture, an air) that would have suggested an embrace rather than a handshake: then, laying one hand on my shoulder, he wrung my hand with the other, cooing in refined military voice 'My *dear* fellow, this is very good of you.' (He knew perfectly well that I had come on business and hadn't any choice but to come.) No underlining can convey the emphasis on the word *dear*: it was as if he had said 'darling'. At the same time, however, the eyebrows moved a good deal higher up the forehead and while his voice gave the *darling* effect, his face gave the effect of 'Well what a pair of fools we are, to be sure.'

Waiving the matter in hand, he began to consult me on an incredibly obscure point of Greek – he is one of the people producing the new Lexicon. He knows perfectly well that he knows twenty times more Greek than I do, but every word and tone suggested that

[2] Arthur Spenser Loat Farquharson (1871–1942), who had been a Fellow of Univ. since 1898, held the position of Senior Tutor, Praelector in Logic, and Dean of Degrees. Loving the College as he did, it is pleasing to see him commemorated by a plaque in the Hall.

I was the one man in Oxford, if not in Europe, who could help him out of his scrape: but every *look* said just as plainly, 'Isn't this fun? Or course you don't know anything about it, and nobody really knows much about this question, and it doesn't really matter anyway, but you won't mind my pulling your leg a bit, will you?' And I didn't. Then every now and then, his manner would become if possible a little more serious, and a little more insanely deferential, and out would come some extremely indecent story: without a tremor of his gravity: but perhaps a minute later the egg would suddenly crack and he would go off into great solid chunks of laughter – the sort of 'Ha – Ha – Ha' with long intervals between which one imagines Johnson laughing. When I left he told me how much I'd helped him. I said I hadn't known anything at all about the points he'd raised. He said 'It was the stimulus of my presence' (same contradictory effect of voice & face) and left me wondering whether he went back to chuckle at me, or to forget the whole visit as instantly and irrevocably as we sometimes forget a dream. Either seems equally probable. It is an old subject of controversy just how mad the Fark is. (He has put himself down on the list as lecturing on Heraclitus every summer term for years. I am the only person who ever volunteered to go, and he said it was off *that* year: also the surviving fragments of Heraclitus occupy about two pages!)

Well, I have made a big hole in my Sunday time for reading, and I'm glad I have. Tho' you don't reply, I have a friendly feeling from writing and a sort of homeliness: and I enjoy and like the Fark better for having tried to describe him. Try this recipe yourself, and after writing the letter you will go to bed happier.

Minto sends her love to all, & thanks for your mother's letter. A dead still night.

Yours
Jack

131

[Magdalen College]
Jan 30th 1930

My dear Arthur,

Yesterday I was not out to home at all, since morning tutoring ended at one only to be succeeded by a College meeting at 2, which lasted till 5: then evening pupil from 5.30 to 6.30, and a dinner engagement at 7. Consequently I did not get your letter till to-day. Not even to-day did I read it at once, as I had orange cutting for marmalade with Minto to do after lunch – (this sounds a nice homely job, but is as a matter of fact rather unpleasant as the bitter juice always finds little cracks in ones skin and smarts like the devil) which lasted till 3 when I sallied forth taking your unopened letter with me.

I cannot remember that I ever took your letters to read on a walk at Bookham – indeed, funnily enough, I can't remember at what time of day they used to arrive and be read. I wonder did they come at breakfast – and did I read them on my little after breakfast walk? Anyhow, whatever the cause, taking it out to read as I walked like that gave me a remeniscent feeling. I'm afraid (almost) to say much for fear after all we can't keep it up – but at the moment I feel like asking 'Why have we missed this pleasure all these years?' I enjoyed your letter extremely: specially your sight of the

> Hebrid isles
> Set far amid the melancholy main[1]

or at least of their light. I quite agree about the value of the word Hebrides. What you can hardly feel as I do is the value of such words as 'Causeway' and (even) 'Portrush'. Not that I care or know about the places: but they are places to which people in my Irish life have always 'gone' – they call up the feeling of antedeluvian holiday arrangements and put me back for the moment in a world where Castlerock & Newcastle seemed as far away as Edinburgh and Paris do now.

It was in the Italian that we read Dante and I have been wondering rather hard whether it would be a good thing for you to try in Cary. If you do, I think the great point is to *give up any idea* of reading it in long stretches (with one's feet on the fender) for the general atmosphere and conduct of the story, and, instead, read a small daily portion, in rather a liturgical manner, letting the *images* and the purely intellectual conceptions sink well into the mind. i.e. I think what is important (or most important) here is to remember say 'The figures stand in these positions, coloured thus, and he is explaining about free will' – rather as if one was remembering a philosophical ceremony. It is not really like any of the things we know.

I quite agree that the new Everyman backs are a great improvement. There, by the way, is the plague of these letters. *That*, in conversation would be a perfectly natural thing not only for me to say to you, but for any booky man to say to another: but in a letter I can't help feeling 'How like our old letters', and thus it has the air of

[1] James Thomson, *The Castle of Indolence* (1748), xxx, 1–2.

a *revival*. The cure, clearly, is to go boldly on. Let us look forward to the time when instead of feeling 'We have started the old letters again', we shall feel 'Ah yes' – and remember before this long period of correspondence there was that early two years at Bookham that one always forgets. Yet that can never be, perhaps. *Two years* at that age was so enormous. And one can't regret it, for it means that I cannot think of you without thinking of all that: so that you have the aroma of the magical past.

Now I come to a more serious problem. What I feel like saying, if I am to give you my news, is 'Things are going very, very well with me (spiritually).' On the other hand, one knows from bitter experience that he who standeth should take heed lest he fall, and that anything remotely like pride is certain to bring an awful crash. The old doctrine is quite true you know – that one must attribute everything to the grace of God, and nothing to oneself. Yet as long as one *is* a conceited ass, there is no good pretending not to be. My self satisfaction cannot be hidden from God, whether I express it to you or not: rather the little bit of self-satisfaction which I (probably wrongly) beleive myself to be fighting against, is probably merely a drop in the bottomless ocean of vanity and self-approval which the Great Eye (or Great I) sees in me. So I will say it after all: that I seem to have been supported in respect to chastity and anger more continuously, and with less struggle, for the last ten days or so than I often remember to have been: and have had the most delicious moments of *It*. Indeed to day – another of those days which I seem to have described so often lately, the same winter sunshine, the same gilt and grey skies shining thro bare shock-headed bushes, the same restful pale ploughland and grass, and more than usual of the birds darting out their sudden, amost cruelly poignant songs – to-day I got such a sudden intense feeling of delight that it sort of stopped me in my walk and spun me round. Indeed the sweetness was so great, & seemed so to affect the whole body as well as the mind, that it gave me pause – it was so very like sex.

One knows what a psychoanalyst would say – it is sublimated lust, a kind of defecated masturbation which fancy gives one to compensate for external chastity. Yet after all, why should that be the right way of looking at it? If he can say that *It* is sublimated sex, why is it not open to me to say that sex is undeveloped *It*? – as Plato would have said. And if as Plato thought, the material world is a copy or mirror of the spiritual, then the central feature of the material life (=sex), must be a copy of something in the Spirit: and when you get a faint glimpse of the latter, of course you find it like the former: an Original *is* like its copy: a man *is* like his portrait. It occurs to me one might have a myth about the psychoanalyst – the story of a man who was always insisting that real people were only fanciful substitutions for the *real* things (as he thought them) in the mirror. However, one cannot be too careful: one must try to hold fast to ones duties (I wish I did) which are the prose of the spiritual life and not learn to depend too much on these delightful moments.

What worries me much more is *Pride* – my besetting sin, as yours is *indolence*. During my afternoon 'meditations, – which I at least *attempt* quite regularly now – I have found out ludicrous and terrible things about my own character. Sitting by, watching the rising thoughts to break their necks as they pop up, one learns to know the sort of thoughts that do come. And, will you believe it, one out of every three is a thought of self-admiration: when everything else fails, having had its neck broken, up comes the thought 'What an admirable fellow I am to have broken their necks!' I catch myself posturing before the mirror, so to speak, all day long. I pretend I am carefully thinking out what to say to the next pupil (for *his* good, of course) and then suddenly realise I am really thinking how frightfully clever I'm going to be and how he will admire me. I pretend I am remembering an evening of good fellowship in a really friendly and charitable spirit – and all the time I'm really remembering how good a fellow I am and how well I talked. And then when you force yourself to stop it, you admire yourself for doing *that*. Its like fighting the hydra (you remember, when you cut off one head another grew). There seems to be no end to it. Depth under depth of self-love and self admiration. Closely connected with this is the difficulty I find in making even the faintest approach to giving up my own will: which as everyone has told us is the only thing to do.

As to my outer news for the past week or so, let me see. On Monday last but one I had to read a paper before the *Junior Linguistic* Society, which led me into strange haunts very typical of one side of Oxford: for the *Junior Linguistic* has hired the rooms belonging to the *Oxford Broadsheet Club*. These are situated in a very small alley on whose right stands the door into the cheap seats at a Cinema, and on whose left – with its lights gleaming out on to the wet cobbles – stood the sinister public house in which the notorious *Shove Halfpenny* Club meets, or used to meet until it was broken up by the interference of the Proctors.[2]

---

[2] Lewis read a paper entitled 'Some Problems of Metaphor' to the Oxford University Junior Linguistic Society on Monday 27 January. The

Beyond this after three flights of narrow stairs I found myself at my destination, in a crowd of about thirty young men packed into a tiny room whose furniture seemed all to have been specially made for it by people with 'stunt' ideas of furniture. As soon as my eyes had grown accustomed to the sea of tobacco smoke so as to allow me to take in the decorations etc I discovered that the *Broadside* Club might with much more propriety have been called the Oxford Pornographical Society. The walls were adorned with drawings of singularly powerfully-built female nudes whose bellies and genital organs showed a remarkable degree of development, while, in compensation they usually lacked both head and feet. I speculated on the artistic pretext of this omission, until one of the Junior Linguists suggested to me the very obvious consideration that feet and faces are hard to draw: and the bad execution of the hands led to the conclusion that this was the real reason. On the table were several brochures advertising the work of various private presses, of which they themselves were specimens. I must confess that the printing was in most really beautiful: the works advertised were largely translations of the more indecent classical authors. It really does seem a pity that the cause of good printing should have got itself thus intangled with the cause of obscenity – specially as the catalogue betrayed their real ignorance of the classics. One specimen page offered a translation from Catullus – the poem beginning *Vivamus mea Lesbia*[3] – Come, my Lesbia, let us love. Lesbia, of course, is simply the girl's name, or rather pseudonym. The blockheads, however, with the idea of Lesbianism snivelling round their muddy little minds, had jumped to the wrong conclusion and decorated the poem with a woodcut representing two more of the same beefy female nudes sprawling on a bed.

But what really completed the piquancy of the whole scene was the contrast between the Junior Linguists themselves and the surroundings which they had borrowed: for the Junior Linguists is a society consisting entirely of undergraduates of just the opposite type – hardworking eccentrics of all ages and social classes as far removed from the conventional games playing mob in one direction as the Broadsheet decadents are in the opposite direction. It gave me a pleasant sense of the real variety of the society in which I live. Later on at about ten, when my paper had been read I got into a long

meeting was held in the rooms of the Broadside (not 'Broadsheet') Club in No. 19 Friars Entry. This house, nearly in ruins now, stands across the alley and almost opposite the 'Gloucester Arms' public house.

[3] Catullus, *Poems*, No. 5.

philosophical discussion with a total stranger who appeared to be a lunatic.

By the way, one of the results of my having left my keys at home is that I can't let myself into College and therefore always have to be back by 12: which didn't matter on Monday but did matter at the Icelandic Society (the Kolbítar) (pronounced Coal-béet-are) when I had to leave Tolkien, Bryson, Dawkins[4] just as we were getting comfortable. However, I hope to reap the benefits of the earlier hours I am thus forced to keep. Bryson you know: Tolkien is the man I spoke of when we were last together – the author of the voluminous un-published metrical romances and of the maps, companions to them, showing the mountains of Dread and Nargothrond the city of the Orcs.[5] In fact he *is*, in one part of him, what we were.

Monday 10th [February] – I had intended to give you a sketch of Dawkins, the fourth Kólbíti (and very well worth describing) but am carried away once more to nature by the heavenly walk I had yester-day. I had gone out to home after breakfast and had to spend the whole day till tea time working on textual criticism – a beastly job involving no interest & continual minute attention, & abominably tiring to the eyes. After tea I went out, thro' old Headington and over the fields towards Forest Hill – i.e. to that spot where (on your last visit to Oxford) you and I saw the low blue bit of distance framed between the two trees which you always say you remember. The evening was wildly cold. Mark what I say: not *intensely* cold, but wildly: i.e. tho there was little movement in the air the cold gave the feeling of *wildness* to the world – a raging silence. I walked out over the big fields and behind me there was the flaming orange colour that you often get at frosty sunset, but only a thin strip, and above that – green: then above that silver: above my head – at the zenith – stars: before me the moon, at present dead & lightless tho' white, a little above the horizon. I walked faster and faster as one does in sympathy with such 'wildness' until – when I had come out of the big fields and was going up among the pines to where you and I sat, rather a funny experience happened. I had not noticed any change in the light: moon rising and sun setting had so evenly divided the sky that there

---

[4] Richard MacGillivray Dawkins (1871–1955) was the Bywater and Sotheby Professor of Byzantine and Modern Greek Language and Liter-ature at Oxford University from 1922 to 1939. See the D.N.B.

[5] He is referring to Professor Tolkien's vast, invented world of Middle-earth which we can now read about in *The Hobbit* (1937), *The Lord of the Rings* (1954–5) and *The Silmarillion* (1977).

was no break, and I still attributed the light in which I walked to the sunset behind me. Imagine then what it was like when with a quiet shock I saw my shadow *following* me over the turf and thus *in the shadow* first perceived how bright the moonlight must be. I'm afraid I can hardly express it in [a] letter. At any rate the whole walk was wonderful, and that bit in particular ghostly – ghostly in the good sense, not in the spookikal.

Barfield came and had a walk with me on Saturday with tea en route in a pub at Stanton St. John. Splendid talk and splendid evening. I also had Griffiths to stay with me for a night last week. Griffiths was a pupil of mine. He was all mucked up with naturalism, D. H. Lawrence, and so on, but has come right and is I do believe really one of 'us' now: and is even tending on the rebound to a high degree of asceticism. Tobacco and meat he never used ⟨more than he could help⟩: he now half humorously suggests that hot baths must go the same way, as voluptuous, enervating, and leading to an effeminate love of the clean. He is a magnificent looking creature – a dark Celt, but very big.

I think this is enough now.

Yrs
Jack

P.S. When I said that your besetting sin was Indolence and mine Pride I was thinking of the old classification of the seven deadly sins: They are *Gula* (Gluttony), *Luxuria* (Unchastity), *Accidia* (Indolence), *Ira* (Anger), *Superbia* (Pride), *Invidia* (Envy), *Avaricia* (Avarice). *Accidia*, which is sometimes called *Tristicia* (despondence) is the kind of indolence which comes from indifference to the good – the mood in which though it tries to play on us we have no string to respond. *Pride*, on the other hand, is the mother of *all* sins, and the original sin of Lucifer – so you are rather better off than I am. You at your worst are an instrument unstrung: I am an instrument strung but preferring to play itself because it thinks it knows the tune better than the Musician.

GULA J.A.G.
LUXURIA J. A. G., C.S.L.
ACCIDIA J.A.G.
IRA C.S.L.
SUPERBIA C.S.L.
INVIDIA C.S.L.
AVARICIA (neither, I hope)

132

Magdalen College,
Oxford.
Feb 24th 1930.

My dear Arthur,

I also have been ill but, more fortunate than you, have contrived to enjoy my illness on the whole – re-reading among other things *Middlemarch*, & reading Pascal (who seems to me pretty poor stuff). I hope to start another real letter to you soon.

In the meantime can you please let us have the following information.

(1) Was it Cushendall or Cushendun[1] that we lunched at on the day of our last drive together?

(2) What was the name of the hotel?

(3) Do you know anything of De Largy's Hotel either at Cushendall or Cushendun?

Lucky devil to come on a deposit of Geo. Macdonalds. I will buy any you don't like – at any rate don't let any go till I've seen them.

Yrs
C. S. Lewis

133

Magdalen College,
Oxford.
[26 February 1930]

My dear A

In great haste – the ending up C. S. Lewis must have been due to the fact that I had just written *nine* letters all ending in that way. Other things, reply later

Yours
Jack

---

[1] Both in Co. Antrim.

134

My dear Arthur,

I am sorry for my mistake about the signature of my last letter but one, but I hope this has now been set right by my note – was it legible? – yesterday. The overwhelming majority of the letters I write (and I seldom get through a day in term without writing a letter) are naturally signed with my surname and initials, so that to add these at the end is almost as mechanical as to turn the envelope over and lick the flap. On this particular occasion, as I said, your letter was the last of nine which I had had to write, and so I inadvertently followed on – or so I now learn, for, of course, until I heard from you I was quite unaware of what I had done. It is the sort of slip [of] the pen that must, I imagine, be not very uncommon with writers in haste – so be prepared for it happening again!

Now as to our plans. My request to you for information was not so much the result of any decision as an attempt to get data for deciding on. I thought you knew that I, at any rate, would be at home in the Easter Vac? For the rest we are in a state of great indecision. The *basic facts* (as the Newspapers say: and by the way, isn't this new party 'The prosperity Party' a portent and a sign: commercialism more *naked* that it has yet dared to show itself in politics. Just imagine the sort of people who are joining it!) the basic facts are as follows. My term ends on March 15th. Maureen's term ends on March 29th. Warnie is expected to be home about April 10th. The idea was that we should all go to stay somewhere in Northern Ireland for about four weeks beginning from March 29th: but that after W's return he and I should spend a week or so together at Leeboro' for the last time and 'break it up'. I was surprised to hear of your proposed trip as I don't think you had mentioned it. I need hardly say that I had looked forward to seeing you both while W. and I were at home, & also I thought you might run down & see us occasionally while we were at the other place – whether Rostrevor, Cushendall, or elsewhere finally proves best (By the way can you recommend *cheap rooms* at any nice place where you are catered for? If you cd., you wd. do us a *very great service*.) But if you are coming to England, *do* try & arrange it so that you can come & spend a few nights with me in College before I leave it on the 15th. The week 9th–15th March is free: next week is pretty full. Do consider this: I have the pleasantest memories of our joint collegiate life on your last visit.

I am sorry if I failed to make clear to you when we last met that I shd. be in Ireland at Easter – I certainly thought I had done so, but I may not, & confess I am in the habit of forgetting what I have said & what I have merely thought. As to the other matter – the signature (not *Of All Things*, but of my last letter) I hope you now realise that it was quite unintentional and also see how the accident happened.

I can't possibly manage a letter for some days. By the way I said that *I* couldn't understand Boehme in my first letter on the subject. As for Macdonalds, no need to urge me to read any I can get hold of. The faults are obvious but somehow they don't seem to matter. I hope you are better, now.

Yours
Jack (I v. nearly did it again!!)

135

Magdalen College,
Oxford.
March 5th [1930]

My dear Arthur,

Just a line to tell you that the stay (*en famille*) at Rostrevor or else-where is off. This of course does not affect W's and my visit to Leeborough – still less the proposal of your coming to Magdalen next week, which I *do* hope can be managed.

Yrs
Jack

136

Magdalen College,
Oxford.
March 15th 1930

My dear Arthur

(1) Our plans are now fairly settled. We shall be at Oxford till about the 4th of April when the others will go to Southbourne (Hampshire) and I for a four days walking tour after which I shall rejoin them where they are. Any time between the 10th & the 14th I expect to hear of W's arrival upon which he and I will instantly go to Ireland. I leave College to day.

(2) It is a great bore your not being able to come and see me before, as now that Maureen has a separate room instead of the little

annex off Minto's we have no spare bedroom when I am at Headington & I therefore can't offer to put you up. If in spite of this in-
hospitality you still care to come & put up elsewhere I needn't say
what a delight it would be. I always lay in a store of real tranquil
receptivity for the country when I'm with you, and it is now beginning to wear thin again & needs reviving.

(3) When you leave Bernagh please leave the *keys* with Mrs
Greeves so that I can get 'em when I come home.

(4) Now that term is over I hope to begin a proper letter to you
again & finish it in the course of a week. Till then good bye

Yours
Jack

P.S. I am very sorry to hear that you have to think of seeing a
specialist & hope the result will be good. After that do try to stick to
one doctor's advice – don't you think you have been rather blown
about between different doctors' views. Yet what is one to do. Best of
luck!

137

Hillsboro.
April 3rd [1930]

My dear Arthur,

I am very sorry that our correspondence has languished so of
late. My plans now are as follows. (1) Leave to morrow for a walking
tour on Exmoor, with Barfield and Co. (2) Rejoin the others at The
Rest, Hengestbury Rd., Southbourne, Hants on the 8th. (3) Cross
to Ireland with W. on the 12th or 14th. (4) Return to Oxford on the
25th. There's glory for you.

As for a visit from you at Southbourne, I hope you will believe me
when I say that there are no times or places at which I should not like
a walk and talk with you. But there are other factors in the case.
Minto has very generously invited W. to make his home with us
henceforward when he is on leave. They like one another and I hope,
as W. gets broken in to domestic life, they may come to do so still
more: but in the interval there is a ticklish time ahead and in any case
it is a big sacrifice of our

[Greeves, in a pencilled note at the top of this letter, states that it is 'very
private' and 'to be burnt'. What he did, however, before passing the

letters on was to destroy half the first page and the whole of pages 2 and 3. What follows is page 4.]

. . . have fallen so far below – MYSELF!!! Which is rather like a man repenting of being drunk because it was unworthy of his career as a forger.

I hadn't meant to give you such a dose of myself – but there is hardly any of it that I can say to any one but you and it is a relief to let it out. Don't imagine that I'm always like this.

I was, on the whole, glad to hear that all your disorders have been traced to the bowels (what a glorious sentence!) Does that mean that the heart is now judged to be alright? As you know, I think there is a great danger of your being buffeted to & fro between the opinions of varying doctors: but heaven knows it is easier to say that than to see how you can avoid it. Does your silence about Harrogate mean that the surrounding country and the people are unworthy of notice or only that you weren't in the mood for a long letter?

I have been nailed down ever since term ended to a very hard, tho' quite interesting, task: a study of the different versions of *Comus*.[1] You know that Milton's MS is extant & we can trace all his corrections. I am sure you, as an author, will be interested to learn that he often crossed out a phrase, put something else, crossed that out, & then returned to the original phrase. Just like ourselves in fact! Or like our brother in law Mr Suckling.[2] (By the way I read her unfinished novel 'The Watsons'[3] the other night & wished there was more of it – a splendid beginning.)

I have had v. little time for general reading. I began *Moby Dick* on the week end when term ended, and thought, despite its obvious defects of rhetoric & un-dramatic dialogue, that I liked it: but somehow I feel no inclination to go on. Have you ever tried it? I have had a few notable walks.

Shall I be seeing you in Ireland. At any rate *write*. You are my only real Father Confessor so you owe me a line

Yours
Jack

---

[1] See the result of this study, Lewis's essay 'A Note on *Comus*', *The Review of English Studies*, vol. VIII, No. 30 (1932). It is reprinted in Lewis's *Studies in Medieval and Renaissance Literature*, ed. Walter Hooper (1966).

[2] A character in Jane Austen's *Emma* (1816).

[3] A fragment of a novel by Jane Austen, written about 1805 and appended by J. E. Austen-Leigh to his *Memoir of Jane Austen* (1871).

138

My dear Arthur,

Many thanks for both your letters. You mustn't think of mucking up your arrangements on my account. Of course it would make my impending time in Ireland v. much nicer if you were there, but it would be quite monstrous to expect you to come back from London – especially as the latest news is that W. will not reach Liverpool until Wednesday, so that I shall have only a week at home. ('At home' – an awful feeling comes over me at those words. It is impossible to get accustomed to change.) So don't think of altering your arrangements on my account: accept instead my hearty thanks for your second letter, which was one of the nicest I have ever had, and set out on your trip with a clear conscience. You are doing perfectly right and I should be a most exacting & selfish person to demand for a moment that you should do otherwise. I hope you will do yourself and your Pole good.

Beware of holidays, though. The old puritans were wrong but they had something real at the back of their minds when they denied pleasures because 'it would only unsettle the boy'. I speak feelingly, for, having felt it my duty to drop work here and devote myself entirely to holidaying with the others (heavens knows I did it for the best) I am at present suffering from all the spiritual consequences of idleness.

I am reading Virginia Wolfe's *Orlando*[1] to Minto at present. Have you read it? And if so what do you make of it? I think there is a quite astonishing power of rendering the feel both of landscapes and moods, rising sometimes to real loveliness, and a total absence of any matter on which to use the power. Also the usual stale cynicism – the nineteenth century guyed as usual – in fact all the tricks of the clevers.

I note what you say about your George Macdonalds and will certainly borrow one for my stay. Think of me at your bookcase a few days hence. Ah Arthur – aren't things odd? Many thanks & good bye

Yours
Jack

[1] Virginia Woolf, *Orlando* (1928).

139

[Magdalen College.]
April 29th [1930]

My dear Arthur,

I will write to Mary[1] about the commode. Meanwhile I am tearing my hair and dancing with rage so that the books are rattling on my table and the eyes of the undergraduate in the room beneath have dropped out, and all because in the collection of your letters which I have looked over I cannot find the one in which you went to the door on the evening when you were first read[ing] *Phantastes*. It will be maddening if any are lost. Have you got any of them? Did you bring them all back at the end of that time? Be sure to reply to this.

And by the way how that time has already become a remote memory. During my recent flying visit[2] I saw the summer seat out in the middle of the lawn and had such a vivid recollection of sitting there with you and watching that strange illusion of shadowy people creeping up to the hall door and always vanishing just as we set eyes on them – and avoiding Chevasse. I met him for a moment, with W., just outside our back gate, showing his teeth as ever.

The two days and one night were very queer. I found that even with W. there the memory of *our* Ireland was stronger than the memory of his and mine. At least I don't know that 'stronger' is the right word: 'larger' wd. be better. The Ireland I shared with him seemed to be a strictly limited and rather thirsty land: yours was like dewy hills and woods fading into a mist where I felt that one could wander forever. This is not flattery, nor contempt of him. If I have so lived with him as to call forth mainly the sensual, the trivial, & the conspiratorial part of my nature in his society, then *I* have done *him* as great an injury as one man can do to another, but he has done me none, poor chap. I also feel very strongly – as I fancy you do with John – that so many things are innocent in him when the very same things are wrong in me.

Mary was an old dear as ever. I spent the night, no doubt my last in that house, appropriately enough, lying awake with a stomach ache. About three o'clock, getting up to drink water & eat aspirin, I

---

[1] Mary Cullen, the housekeeper at Little Lea.

[2] Warren arrived in England on 16 April and he and his brother crossed over to Belfast on the 22nd, arriving there on the 23rd and returning to Oxford on 24 April. Warren was to visit Little Lea once more (in June 1930) but this was the last time Clive was to be in his old home before it was sold.

looked out of the window. A thick white mist gleaming from the lamps in the road, and a dripping from the leaves. How many miserable nights have I looked from that window – terror of rows, terror of ghosts, worrey about Minto, toothache, quarrels with W. away back in early boyhood when he was my only home so to speak. V. odd that at such a moment it was entirely that side of Leeborough that came back to me: pain, fear, loneliness. I suppose it is steeped in my father's long years of loneliness – and pain & fear too, for all I know. Shall we add to the advertisement (boards are ordered to be put up) 'This house has been well suffered in'? Really I think Leeboro' looks best to me seen from Bernagh.

As to what you say in your letter about introspection & scruples, I think you are right in general: but you must remember how much bigger than itself a thing becomes by being put in writing. A very small dose of self-examination, so small as to be quite wholesome, looks a positive jorum in a letter. You must not imagine that I spend all or most of my time thinking the sort of things I have lately written to you: but in the act of writing to you those things naturally come uppermost which I can only imperfectly share with anyone else.

I wish you could have been with me on my walking tour.[3] We motored from Oxford to Dunster, three of us leaving the car about five miles before it & the fourth driving on. It was about six when we did so and we therefore had a delightful evening 'prologue' to the whole walk over moors with a ragged sunset ahead of us lighting up the pools: very like an illustration to Scott: then down into a steep valley, over a swift stream as broad as Connswater but only an inch or so deep above its rattling pebbles and so into the broad, empty, practically dark street of Dunster wh. stretches up to the castle.

Next morning there was a thick fog. Some of the others were inclined to swear at it, but I (and I soon converted Barfield) rejoiced to meet the moor at its grimmest. Imagine a wonderful morning following a narrow path along the side of a steep hill with gaunt fir trees looming up suddenly out of the greyness: and sometimes a thinning of the mist that revealed perhaps a corner of a field with drystone wall unexpectedly far beneath us, or a rushing brook, or a horse grazing. Then down into greener country and hedges for lunch at the village of Luccombe. In the afternoon the fog thickened but we continued in spite of it to ascend Dunkery Beacon as we had originally intended. There was of course not a particle of view to be

[3] His companions on the walking tour, from 4–8 April, were Owen Barfield, Cecil Harwood and Walter Field.

seen, and we knew when we had reached the top only by the fact that we could find nothing higher and by the cairn of stones over which the wind was hurrying the fog like smoke from a chimney on a stormy day. The descent, largely guided by compass, was even more exciting: specially the suddenness with which a valley broke upon us – one moment nothing but moor and fog: then ghosts of trees all round us: then a roaring of invisible water beneath, and next moment the sight of the stream itself, the blackness of its pools and the whiteness of its rapids seeming to tear holes (as it were) in the neutral grey of the mist. We drank tea at the tiny hamlet of Stoke Pero where there is a little grey church without a tower that holds only about twenty people. Here, according to an excellent custom of our walks, one of the party read us a chapter of Scripture from the lectern while the rest of us sat heavily in the pews and spread out our mackintoshes to let the linings steam off. Then after a leisurely walk through woods we reached Wilmersham Farm where we found our car parked in the farmyard and Field looking out of a window to assure us that there were beds and suppers for all. We had a little parlour with a wood stove to ourselves, an excellent hot meal, and the bedrooms, – two in a room – were beautifully clean. We had only made about 16 miles but were tired enough as it had been v. rough country.

Next morning when I woke I was delighted to find the sun streaming through the window. Looking out I found a blue sky: the farmyard, with hens scratching and a cat padding stealthily among them, was bright with sunlight: beyond the long blue-grey horizons of the moor rolled up to the sky in every direction. This day we made about ten miles by paths across the open moor to a place where we met a road & there Field met us in the car with lunch. A cold wind was blowing by that time so we had our meal (as you and I have often done) in the closed car with all windows up and had the sensation of snugness. About $2\frac{1}{2}$ hours after lunch, having done a very tricky walk across heather by pure map reading (no paths) we were relieved to strike the valley of a river called Badgworthy Water (pronounced Badgerry). A glorious comb[e], deepening of course as it proceeds, steep sided, with many rocks in it, and soon with dotted trees that thicken later into woods: not of fir but of stunted oaks, so gnarled that they give the impression of being in a subterranean forest of sea weed, & the branches often coated with moss to the top. We had to ford the Badgworthy: not v. easy as (like all mountain streams) it will be 6 inches deep in one place and 5 feet the next: ice cold and the bottom slippery.

Barfield created great amusement by putting his socks in his boots and trying to throw them across a narrow place so that he shd. not have that encumbrance while wading: instead they lit in the middle and, after sailing a few yards like high-pooped galleons, lit on the top of a fall where they stuck, rocking with the current and threatening every second to go sailing down into a whirlpool beneath. I, who was already safe on the farther shore, ran down in my bare feet and hoiked them to land with a stick. We sat down for about half an hour with our backs against a little cliff of rock, in the sun and out of the wind, to eat chocolate and dry & warm our numbed legs. The first bumble bee buzzed by us. The colours of the stream, broken by a series of falls above us, and floored with green, brown, golden, & red stones, were indescribable. When we were dry we worked our way down the valley to Cloud Farm where billets had been secured by Field. Minto, Maureen and I had stayed here about five years before, so I had a great welcome from the farm people. This evening all four of us had a kind of formal philosophical discussion on The Good. I shared a room with Barfield. Lay awake a little while, listening to the noise of the stream which is only about twenty feet from the farm house: and under that noise a profound silence. These Exmoor farms are the loveliest habitations you can imagine.

Next day we walked down the valley of the Lynn and lunched at Lynmouth. The valley is very deep – about 800 ft. – and the woods on the sides almost deserve to be called forest. The river – which again we had to wade – is much bigger than the Badgworthy and so agonisingly cold that at the first shock it is almost the same feeling as stepping into a bath much too hot for you. Lynmouth you know. After lunch our route lay along the cliffs and through the Valley of Rocks which I had not greatly admired: a place of enormous crags *without water* is a little bit horrible: one needs a stream to give these huge carcases a soul, don't you think? Best of all was after tea when we struck inland again over the moor in one of those golden evening lights that pours a dreamlike *mildness* over the world: light seemed to be a liquid that you could drink, and the surrounding peace was, if anything, deepened by the noise and bustle of a fussy little narrow gauge railway, the only living thing, which had a train puffing slowly along it, all its windows turned to gold in the light of the sunset. We saw several herons this day. That night we slept at Challacombe and composed ex-tempore poetry: telling the story of the Fall between us in the metre of Hiawatha. We had done well over twenty miles and felt immortal.

The next day was grey with occasional rain. We got badly lost on some rather forbidding hills & failed to meet Field for lunch: got a lift along a dull stretch of road in a lorry: had tea at South Molton and motored to Exeter. Here, seeing the cathedral all lit up and notices outside it about a performance of the Messiah, we had supper in great haste and rushed off only to find that the Messiah was next week and that the lights were on for an ordinary evening service. It was horrid to be in a city again. As Field said 'After training ourselves for the last few days to notice *everything* we have now to train ourselves to notice nothing.'

Next morning the party broke up, Barfield & Harwood motoring back North, while Field and I trained to Bournemouth where I rejoined Minto & Maureen at Southbourne. I will describe Field, whom you don't yet know, in another letter.

I shall post this as soon as I hear your address, when I hope also to hear your news. You must have plenty to write of. I enclose my latest: I think you understand the experience – when we fall not because That is so attractive but because it makes everything else seem so drab.

Yours

J.

> When Lilith means to draw me
> Within her hungry bower
> She does not overawe me
> With beauty's pomp and power,
> Nor with angelic grace
> Of courtesy and the pace
> Of gliding ship comes veil'd at evening hour.
>
> Eager, unmasked, she lingers,
> Heart shaken and heartsore: –
> With hot, dry, jewelled fingers
> Outstretched, beside her door,
> Offers, with gnawing haste,
> Her cup, whereof who taste
> (She promises no better) thirst far more.
>
> What moves, you ask, to drink it?
> Her charms, that all around
> So change the world, we think it
> A great waste, where a sound
> Of wind like tales twice-told
> Blusters, and cloud is rolled
> Always above, yet no rain falls to ground.

T.S.T.–M

Across drab iteration
Of gaunt hills line on line
The dull road's sinuation
Creeps: and the witche's wine,
Tho' promising nothing, seems,
In that land of no streams,
To promise best – the unrelish'd anodyne.[4]

140

[Magdalen College]
June 1st 1930

My dear Arthur,

I have decided to return to the old regulation four page letter once a week as in Bookham days. The long screeds I have been sending you lately will certainly languish some time or other and then there will be an end of the correspondence: but this I think I shall be able to keep up. I hope to get your first letter on Tuesday at latest.

And now let me see (it already seems so long ago since you were here). On the day you left I went our usual walk, through Old Headington, past that little isolated house wh. you admired, across the brook, and then over two fields to our soaking machine. It was just such another glorious summer day with a kind of mist that made the grass and buttercups look watery. I felt that sort of melancholy (you probably know it) wh. comes from going through the same scenes through which you walked with a friend a few hours ago, when he has gone. Now that I come to think of it, you must have had this experience much more often than I: so often in your old letters do I find you describing how you went this or that old walk just after my return to Bookham. Mixed with this melancholy, however, (you will not be offended) there was the freshness of solitude which itself, on such occasions, feels like a friend revisited, and what between the two I fell into an extremely receptive state of mind – a sort of impersonal tenderness, which is the reason why I am mentioning this walk, as one of my good ones wh. was valuable in itself and will, I hope, become even more so in memory.

Just to give you the other side of the picture (I shall not often tell you these things) – I have 'fallen' ⟨twice⟩ since you left after a long period of quite untroubled peace in that respect. Serves me right, for I was beginning to pat myself on the back and even (idiotically)

[4] This poem, considerably revised, was later to appear in Lewis's *The Pilgrim's Regress* (1933).

beginning to fancy that I had really escaped, if not for good, at any rate for an indefinite time. The interesting thing was that on both occasions the temptation arose ⟨when I was almost asleep,⟩ quite suddenly, and carried me by storm ⟨before I really had my waking mind fully about me.⟩ I don't mean to disclaim responsibility on this account: but I feel grateful that the enemy has been driven to resor to *strategems* (not by me, but by God) whereas he used to walk boldly up to me for a frontal attack in the face of all my guns. I hope I don't delude myself in thinking that this is an improvement.

My rooms are quite settled down now and having worked in them for a week I find the novelty falling into the background. The slow business of transferring Headington books to Headington[1] – a little brief-bag full a day – is going regularly forward. Last night I began the business of going through the records, and sorting out those which are such rotten things or so badly worn that I will give them away. I lay on the sofa and played through *The People that Walked,*[2] *Overture & Intermezzo from Carmen,*[3] *Fire Music from the Valkyrie,*[4] *The Laughing Song from the Starlight Express.*[5]

Lying on the study sofa and hearing these old favourites I had sensations which you can imagine. And at once (here is the advantage of growing older) I knew that the enemy would take advantage of the vague longings and tendernesses to try & make me believe later on that *he* had the fulfilment which I really wanted: so I baulked him by letting the longings go even deeper and turning my mind to the One, the real object of all desire, which (you know my view) is what we are *really* wanting in all wants.

At this point it occurred to me that the noise might be disturbing J.A.[6] above and went up to ask him: rather to my disappointment he was so far from being disturbed that he volunteered to come down with me and listen. Still there was something nice and even homely about having the old man there. We went through the *March of the Dwarfs*[7] & *Danse Macabre*[8] (which I thought rubbish) & Delibes

[1] He was unpacking the books and phonograph records from Little Lea, keeping some in his Magdalen rooms and transferring others to Hillsboro.

[2] 'The People that Walked in Darkness' from Handel's *Messiah* (1742).

[3] Georges Bizet's *Carmen* (1875).

[4] From Richard Wagner's *Nibelung's Ring* (1853–70).

[5] Edward Elgar, *The Starlight Express* (1915).

[6] John Alexander Smith (1863–1939), a former Scholar of Balliol College, was the Waynflete Professor of Moral and Metaphysical Philosophy and a Fellow of Magdalen from 1910 till his retirement in 1936. See the D.N.B.

[7] From Edvard Grieg's *Lyric Suite* (1898).

[8] By Camille Saint-Saëns (1875).

Cortège de Bacchus from the *Aprez-midi d'un Faune*.[9] How on earth can we ever have liked this latter? It seemed to me the merest music-hall patriotic song rhetoric on the brass pretending to be something better. Then, as I had anticipated, J.A. became talkative and we drank together and drifted into philosophical conversation.

In reading I have of course little to record, and never shall have much in term time. I read in two evenings a little book that came from Leeborough called *The Practice of the Presence of God*[10] which I picked up & put in the study when I was there last because it seemed to me a promising title. It is by a Seventeenth century monk. It is full of truth but somehow I didn't like it: it seemed to me a little unctious. That sort of stuff, when it is not splendid beyond words, is terribly repulsive, or can be, can't it? No doubt it depends v. largely on ones mood. I had just finished the fourth Gospel in Greek (as I think you know) before you came, and after that most other things are a come down. Not that I liked *that* in all respects either. I have also read an essay on Death, in typescript, which Barfield sent me, which is to my mind one of the finest things there is. He handles death as you would expect it to be handled by a pupil & lover of *Lilith* & *Phantastes*.

Talking of which, I hope you will not be disagreeably surprised to find with this letter the first instalment of a new romance. I don't know how long I shall keep it up, but it occurred to me that I could fit in four pages most weeks and that if I persevered I should thus get quite a lot written. Please criticize freely as it goes on. Of course if I get no answers I shall drop it: on the ground that if you are so changed that you can't write to me, you may also be so changed that you can't be trusted not to use my story for spills. When it is done (if ever) I shall ask you to get it typed in Belfast & sent to me. Is it possible that when you get the novel off your chest you might think of doing *your* next work in instalments? I think there are distinct advantages in that method of writing. But, whatever you do, let me have your weekly letter.

Yours
. Jack

[9] The *Cortège de Bacchus* is from Léo Délibes's *Sylvia* (1875). *Après-midi d'un Faune* is the work of Debussy.
[10] By Brother Lawrence.

141

My dear Arthur,

I was delighted to get your prompt letter. Don't you enjoy the feeling of getting back into our old rhythm again? To me there is another pleasure which you, without a regular routine of work to distinguish the days from one another, will hardly feel: I mean the pleasure of adding another *pivotal* point to my week – so that in addition to Wednesday (interesting pupil) Thursday (Times Literary Supplement) etc I shall now have your letter. I enjoyed the description of your walk through our woods with Gribbon, and wish I could see them again.

As to what you say about instalments & the difficulty of seeing the story as a whole: (1) If you mean the *author's* difficulty, then I reply that I have so little time for writing that this is the only way to get a story done: and that benefit compensates for the disadvantages (Benefit to whom, you may ask!) (2) If you mean the *reader's* difficulty, then you may easily remedy that by *not* reading them until you have about ten (or better still, not reading them at all! As I wrote this I had such a vivid imagination of your voice as you might have said that). As regards your criticism, I was conscious of the fault you refer to while I was writing: specially in the sentence ending 'anxiety for the future'. It is not that I am trying to be complex, but a habit that sticks to my pen from years of writing on subjects that almost inevitably lure one into a rather un-simple style. I am glad you noticed it and will try to simplify: though I should say from the outset that the matters this story deals with *can't* beyond a certain point be put into the absolutely plain narrative style.

I have managed to get a few evenings free this week and have read two new books. The first was Kingsley's *Water Babies*.[1] It was one of the books belonging to my mother which my father had locked up at her death and I only recovered at the recent clearance. It was strange – after the first few pages the most incredibly faint memories began to come about me: she must have read it, or started to read it, to me when I was very small indeed. I had even a curious sense of bringing my mother to life – as if she were reading it through me. The feeling was impressive, but not entirely pleasant. (I don't mean that it was at all unpleasant in the commonplace ghostie sense.) The

[1] Charles Kingsley, *The Water-Babies* (1863).

book itself seems to me not very good. There is some fancy, and I don't object to the preaching: but after Macdonald it is tasteless. Put the two side by side and see how imagination differs from mere fancy, and holiness from mere morality. Have you ever read it? As I say it is not *very* good: but well worth reading.

The other was Coventry Patmore's *Angel in the House*. As you know, it is a long poem in a very strict & even monotonous metre, describing a very simple story of love & marriage, interspersed with half philosophic, half religious odes on the author's theory of marriage as a mystical image of & approach to divine love. The story parts are deliberately prosaic & hum-drum, & would be very easy to parody: e.g. such lines as the following (put in the mouth of the housemaid)

> 'The Dean
> Is out, Sir, but Miss Honor's in'[2]

though it is surprising how one feels less and less inclined to sneer as you go on. But the bits in between are really often sublime. Isn't this good, of Love (=God on his view)

> To praise the thing whose praise it is
> That all which can be praised is it.[3]

He is extremely down on people who take the ascetic view. These will be shut without the fold as 'too good' for God. The whole poem has raised a lot of difficulties in my mind. Even if it were true that marriage is what he says, what help does this give as regards the sexual problem for the innumerable people who can't marry? Surely for them asceticism remains the only path? And if, as he suggests, marriage & romantic love is the real ascent to Spirit, how are we to account for a world in which it is inaccessible to so many, and are we to regard the old saints as simply deluded in thinking it specially denied to them? As a matter of fact he does seem to suggest in one passage that romantic love is *one* ascent, and imagination the other – At all events the book has left me with an extraordinary renewal of my appetite for poetry.

I had an interesting & humiliating experience to-day (Saturday). I had to go out to tea on Boars' Hill and a man I had been lunching with, Lawson,[4] offered to drive me. I used to know him at Univ. and

---

[2] Coventry Patmore, *The Angel in the House* (1863), Book II, Canto I, 'Accepted', stanza 2, ll. 12–14.

[3] *ibid.*, Book I, Canto VIII, 'The Praise of Love', stanza 5.

[4] Frederick Henry Lawson (1897–   ) was Lecturer in Law at Univer-

I lunch wth him & Keir[5] once a week for old sakes sake, though Lawson is a most terrible bore. As soon as he got me in the car he decided that we had a good deal of spare time & said he wd. drive me first to see his old father, recently widowed, whom he has just set up in a little house at the neighbouring village of Holton. On the way I bitterly regretted having been let in for this. Lawson is a tiny little man with puffed out cheeks, a pursed in mouth, and a bristly moustache: v. bright staring eyes: and rolls the eyes, jerking his head this way & that, like a ventriloquists dummy, while he talks, talks, talks, all about himself: or else talks big of university politics, retailing opinions which I know not to be his own and wh. in any case I despise. I thought 'Now he is going to show me over this house and tell me how he arranged this and why he did that – reams of it.'

When we arrived we found a lovely wild garden with a little red cottage in it. We met an old man speaking wth a broad Yorkshire accent & plainly in the technical sense 'not a gentleman'. Point No. 1 in favour of Lawson – he is not ashamed of his origins: he rose enormously in my eyes. Then Lawson shut up completely and let the old man talk, which he did, describing all he was doing in the garden. He was just like Lawson, only in an old man it was different: and the courage of him setting to work to build up a new life here in his old age was impressive. When we had been round the whole place and into the house, & when I saw so many things out of Lawson's rooms in Merton brought out here, and saw the affection between them, and realised how Lawson had busied himself about the whole – and then remembered how abominably I had treated *my* father – and worst of all how I had dared to despise Lawson, I was, as I said, humiliated. Yet I wouldn't have missed it for anything. It does one good to see the fine side of people we've always seen the worst of. It reminded me v. much of the clerk in *Bleak Ho.* (or is it *Great Expectations*) who takes the hero out to see his father & has a cannon on the roof.[6] Do you remember?

I am glad to hear that Gribbon was really appreciative on your

sity College 1924–5, at Christ Church 1925–6, Junior Research Fellow of Merton College 1925–30 and official Fellow and Tutor in Law 1930–48. He was the Professor of Comparative Law and a Fellow of Brasenose College from 1948 till his retirement in 1964.

[5] David Lindsay Keir (1895–1973) was a Fellow of New College 1921–39, President and Vice-Chancellor of The Queen's College, Belfast, 1939–49, and the Master of Balliol College from 1949 till he retired in 1965.

[6] It is in Dickens's *Great Expectations* that Wemmick takes Pip to meet 'the aged P'.

walk: I always feel he may become much nicer yet in time – at present, for me, he is spoiled by that cynical & coarse-grained side to his character.

Yrs

J.

142

[Magdalen College]

June 15th 1930

My dear Arthur,

I spoke too soon about the pleasures of adding Tuesday to my list of regular bright spots in the week! My disappointment was aggravated by the fact that for the rest of the week whenever the post came in and I thought 'Ah! This will be it' I actually got (on five several occasions) a beastly business letter from Condlin involving hours of tedious work. I had already mentally resolved (a) Not to write again (b) To write a letter full of such cutting sarcasms as wd. make you die of mortification (c) To write a letter in such a strain of solemn, manly pathos that you would expire in an ecstasy of repentance (d) To show my magnanimity by writing as if I hadn't noticed the omission – when on getting back to college at 10 o'clock last night I was delighted to find your letter.

I fully appreciate what you say about the Clandeboye woods and think that I too notice smaller things much more than I did: which is a great advantage since, in what we ordinarily call dull country, a flower or the turn of a stream can now make up for the lack of mountains and woods. As for your other point – any comparison between Spring & Autumn – as between youth & age or man and woman – is, I think, hopeless. One becomes less & less inclined to pick & choose, or to pit one part of reality against another. It is all the one thing working itself out in orderly rhythms & branchings which could not be better or other than they are.

'Sentimental stodge' is exactly what one would think of Coventry Patmore, or certain parts of him, if you read them in the wrong mood – though even then, I think, there is a kind of scholarly keenness and cleanness in language and metre which makes stodge hardly the right word. (I don't know if you get my meaning. Can you imagine a picture in which the subject is extremely sentimental, and even the colouring rather bad, but in wh. the *fine firm* lines reveal that it is a master after all?)

I envy you your shelf of Macdonalds and long to look over them wth your guidance. I have read both *The Princess & the Goblins* & *The Princess & Curdie*.[1] In fact I read the former (the other is a sequel to it) for about the third time when I was ill this spring. Read it at once if you have it, it is the better of the two. There is the fine part about the princess discovering her godmother in the attic spinning (This reminds me at once of Mrs McNeill, wh. reminds me I recently discovered a letter written by her to my mother at the time of old McNeill's death in wh. she said 'He always said you were his best pupil and when you came to call I always sent to tell him because I knew he loved to see you' – a fact wh. she has told me a hundred times, with solemn shake of the head, and wh. I can hear her saying at this moment. Never omit to say that I have asked for them, when you meet, and that I send my love: and plead my cause when you can. I don't want it to be by any fault of mine if that old link is broken). Another fine thing in *The Pr. & the Goblin* is where Curdie, in a dream, keeps on *dreaming* that he has waked up and then finding that he is still in bed. This means the same as the passage where Adam says to Lilith 'Unless you unclose your hand you will never die & therefore never wake. *You may think you have died and even that you have risen again*: but both will be a dream.'[2]

This has a terrible meaning, specially for imaginative people. We read of spiritual efforts, and our imagination makes us believe that, because we enjoy the idea of doing them, we have done them. I am appalled to see how much of the change wh. I thought I had undergone lately was only imaginary. The real work seems still to be done. It is so fatally easy to confuse an aesthetic appreciation of the spiritual life with the life itself – to dream that you have waked, washed, and dressed, & then to find yourself still in bed.

I was glad to hear that you had had a long talk with Reid,[3] because I argue from this that the anger wh. Bryson attributed to him has turned out to be all a mare's nest, or at least has blown over. Give him my compliments. As I write I have a vivid memory of that day with you and him in the woods beyond Hannah's Town [Hannahstown] – what wd. I not give to see them this minute. Tho' I believe

[1] George MacDonald, *The Princess and the Goblin* (1871); *The Princess and Curdie* (1882).

[2] George MacDonald, *Lilith* (1895), ch. XL, p. 302.

[3] Forrest Reid (1875–1947), the novelist, who was living in Belfast at this time. His own story is told in his two autobiographies, *Apostate* (1926) and *Private Road* (1940). There are several references to Arthur Greeves and J. N. Bryson in Russell Burlingham's *Forrest Reid: A Portrait and a Study* (1953). A portrait of Reid, painted by Greeves, is in the possession of the Royal Academical Institution, Belfast.

that longing for them is as good, for if I were there what could they (or any other beautiful object) give me but more longing.

The period of bright green meadows golden wth buttercups is over here and they are mowing the hay. One hardly *walks*, it is too hot – in spite of a temporary cooling yesterday after a magnificent thunderstorm the night before; but I have had some delightful 'soaks' amid the smell (almost *maddeningly* remeniscent) of the mowing and the sound of the mowers.

This afternoon I have lounged in the garden & began Mary Webb's *Precious Bane*.[4] I can't remember whether you recommended it to me or not. If it goes on as well as it has begun I shall put it very high indeed. In fact I hardly know a book which has given me such a delicious feeling of *country* – homely yet full of eeriness, as in real life. I have it in the *Travellers' Library* edition. The language – tho some people will call it 'pastiche' – seems to me delicious. Why after all should one always write the speech of ones own time & class?

Isn't it an exciting moment when the whole of a work is typed? Be sure to report further progress.

Yrs
Jack

143

Hillsboro,
Western Rd.,
Headington,
Oxford
June 22nd 1930

My dear Arthur,

Your last letter is mysterious. What is the meaning of the cryptic word 'Pharoh' (*sic*) added to the sentence 'I think I told you this before'? After cudgelling my brains I can make neither head nor tail of it. Again, why should *my* leaving a margin shorten your weekly allowance? I'm afraid I must be getting very dense. Then why the last page of your letter should be called 'the Jacobean MS of 1930' I cannot remotely conjecture. If your jokes continue to be [as] profound as this you will probably find me in an asylum when you next visit England.

By the way, please note that I moved out to Headington last night and am now to be addressed there. It is delightful to have term over and I can feel it so though to-day has been a most exasperating one. It is terrible to find how little progress ones philosophy and charity

[4] Mary Webb, *Precious Bane* (1924; Travellers' Library, 1928).

have made when they are brought to the test of domestic life. However I think I got over most of my fusses fairly quickly and (I hope)
without letting them hurt anyone else.

Did I tell you in my last that a former pupil of mine, Griffiths, had
been to spend a night with me? I mention him now because his name
deserves to be honoured. I happened to tell him that Barfield (he has
only met him once but then he has read *Poetic Diction*[1] so often
that he knows him well) was hoping to edit the unpublished works
of Coleridge if an American university, which was at present toying
with the idea, made up its mind to finance him: but that if they did
not he would go into his father's business. A few days later a letter
came from Griffiths to say that he and the two friends[2] he lived
with had £800 a year between the three of them: that it was impossible morally to spend this on themselves, and that the surplus, on
any right view, was not justly their own: did I therefore think that
Barfield could be prevailed on to accept £100 a year for the next few
years. This is the sort of thing that really makes one feel fit. Of
course I hope he will not accept it, but that doesn't alter the merit of
the proposers – specially the other two who don't even know him.
They must be a remarkable trio.

They have pooled their money – Griffiths by the way had none –
and live together in a Cotswold cottage doing their own work and
pursuing their studies. Their aim is, as far as possible, to use nothing
which is a product of the factory system or of modern industry in
general: for they think these things so iniquitous that every one is
more or less party to a crime in using them.[3] I can't help wondering
where their own income comes from, and suspect an inconsistency
here. Indeed whether the whole thing is folly or not I haven't made up
my mind. What do you think? There is certainly something attractive
about the idea of living as far as may be on the produce of the land
about you: to see in every walk the pastures where your mutton
grazed when it was sheep, the gardens where your vegetables grew,
the mill where your flour was ground, and the workshop where your
chairs were sawn – and to feel that bit of country actually and
literally in your veins.

Tolkien once remarked to me that the feeling about home must
have been quite different in the days when a family had fed on the

[1] Owen Barfield, *Poetic Diction: A Study in Meaning* (1928).
[2] The two friends, both of whom were at Magdalen with Dom Bede
Griffiths, are Hugh Waterman and the poet Martyn Skinner. The correspondence between these three men is in the Bodleian.
[3] Their story is told in Griffiths's *The Golden String*, ch. 4.

produce of the same few miles of country for six generations, and that perhaps this was why they saw nymphs in the fountains and dryads in the wood – they were not mistaken for there was in a sense a *real* (not metaphorical) connection between them and the country-side. What had been earth and air & later corn, and later still bread, really was *in* them. We of course who live on a standardised inter-national diet (you may have had Canadian flour, English meat, Scotch oatmeal, African oranges, & Australian wine to day) are really artificial beings and have no connection (save in sentiment) with any place on earth. We are synthetic men, uprooted. The strength of the hills is not ours. My pen has run away with me on this subject.

I am delighted to hear that you have taken to Johnson. Yes, isn't it a magnificent style – the very essence of manliness and condensation. I find Johnson very *bracing* when I am in my slack, self pitying mood. The amazing thing is his power of stating platitudes – or what in anyone else wd. be platitudes – so that we really believe them at last and realise their importance. Doesn't it remind you a bit of Handel? As to his critical judgement I think he is always sensible and nearly always wrong. He has no ear for metre and little imagination. I personally get more pleasure from the *Rambler*[4] than from anything else of his & at one time I used to read a Rambler every evening as a nightcap. They are so *quieting* in their brave, sensible dignity.

I know the feeling you describe – of talking far into the night wth one friend while the rest of the house sleeps. (I notice it is a feeling you have never given me occasion to indulge in *your* society.)

By the way, about the 'Moving Image' I should warn you that there is going to be a great deal of conversation: in fact it is to be almost a Platonic dialogue in a fantastic setting wth story inter-mixed. If you take *The Symposium, Phantastes, Tristram Shandy* and stir them up all together you will about have the recipe. So now you are prepared for the worst!

I am reading the *Politics* of Aristotle which contains one of the few reasoned defences of slavery in ancient literature – most of the ancients taking it for granted and therefore feeling no need to defend it. Very subtle, but I think I see his weak point. I have finished *Precious Bane* and think I have enjoyed it more than any novel since the Brontë's. Why do women write such good novels. Mens novels, except Scott, seem to me on the same level as womens' poetry.

Yours

J.

[4] Samuel Johnson, *The Rambler* (1752).

144

[Long Crendon,
Bucks.]
June 31st 1930
[1 July 1930]

My dear Arthur,

As your letter did not reach me till yesterday (that is Monday) – and I had before then passed through all the stages of disappointment, you can hardly complain if this comes late. My excuse is that Warnie came up on Saturday and was with me the whole of Sunday, and on Monday I journeyed to Long Crendon to stay wth Barfield where I now am – amid thatched roofs and the crooning of hens, with a pony & a donkey in the orchard and honeysuckle over the door.

The great event of the last week, in one sense, has been in my library. I have effected the exchange of my Bombay Kipling[1] for the big Morris,[2] with the pleasant surprise that they allowed me £50 for the Kipling and charged only 18 guineas for the Morris so that I have a credit balance of £30 odd at Blackwells. Oh what a feast this would have been in the old days! Have you any advice as to the best way of using it? In the meantime I am delighted with the Morris, tho it seems to be rather carelessly printed – i.e. I have already found readings in it wh. must be mistakes. However this is only a trifle.

The real point is that it has made me read *Love is Enough* wh. I never did before, and I most strongly advise you to do so at the first opportunity. You know that it is a play – you will find a very illuminating account of it in Mackail's life. The story is *in one way* a typical Morris story, that of a King who dreams of a fair woman in a distant land and finally abandons his kingdom to go and find her. He does so. Returns and finds his kingdom taken by another, but departs again without bitterness because 'love is enough'. But although this sounds so typical it is extremely different from the usual Morris.

In the first place, his long wanderings, such as you found too long drawn out in the *Well at the Worlds End*, instead of being given in full, are just hinted at in the dialogue, and for this reason gain enormously in suggestiveness. In the second place – I hardly know

---

[1] *The Bombay Edition of the Works of Rudyard Kipling*, 31 vols. (1913–38).
[2] *The Collected Works of William Morris*, ed. May Morris, 24 vols. (1910–15).

how to put it. You know I always thought Morris the most essentially *pagan* of all poets. The beauty of the actual world, the vague longings wh. it excites, the inevitable failure to satisfy these longings, and over all the haunting sense of time & change making the world heart breakingly beautiful just because it slips away ('Oh death that makest life so sweet' as he says) all this, I thought, he gave to perfection: but of what this longing really pointed to, of the reason why beauty made us homesick, of the reality *behind*, I thought he had no inkling. And for that reason his poetry always seemed to me dangerous and apt to lead to sensuality – for it is the frustrated longing that drives us to the *pis aller*, and as we lose hope of our real immortal mistress we turn to harlots.

Now in *Love is Enough* he raises himself right out of his own world. He suddenly shows that he is at bottom aware of the real symbolical import of all the longing and even of earthly love itself. In the speeches of Love (who is the most important character) there is clear statement of eternal values (coupled with a refusal to offer you crudely personal immortality) and also, best of all, a full understanding that there is something beyond pleasure & pain. For the first (and last?) time the light of *holiness* shines through Morris' romanticism, not destroying but perfecting it. Reading this has been a great experience to me: and coming on top of the *Angel in the House* has shown me that in my fear of the sensual cheat wh. lurked at the back of my old romantic days (see Dymer VII) I have aimed at too much austerity and even dishonoured love altogether. I have become a dry prig. I do hope I am not being mocked – that this is not merely the masked vanguard of a new sensuality. But I verily believe not. In this light I shall come back to Morris and all that world. I have the key now and perhaps can stand the sweetness safely. For this too is a feature of life that becomes gradually clearer: namely that the road is always turning round and going back to places we seemed to have left – but they are *different* (yet in a way the same) when you come to them the second time.

I don't remember your *Lives of the Poets*[3] – what is the new Johnson like?

As to the business about being 'rooted' or 'at home everywhere', I wonder are they really the opposite, or are they the same thing. I mean, don't you enjoy the Alps more precisely because you began by first learning to love in an intimate and homely way our own hills and woods? While the mere globe-trotter, starting not from a home

[3] Samuel Johnson, *Lives of the English Poets* (1779–81).

feeling but from guide books & aesthetic chatter, feels *equally* at home everywhere only in the sense that he is really at home nowhere? It is just like the difference between vague general philanthropy (wh. is all balls) and learning first to love your own friends and neighbours wh. makes you *more*, not less, able to love the next stranger who comes along. If a man loveth not his brother whom he hath seen – etc. In other words doesn't one get to the universal (either in people or in inanimate nature) *thro'* the individual – not by going off into a mere generalised mash. I don't know if I make myself clear.

Your description of the empty rooms at home gave me a terrible thought – supposing my father had died when I was sixteen and all that had been lost before I found anything else – and you and I wd. probably never have met again. This week's instalment has been written alright but I forgot to bring it here with me, so you will probably have two next week.

The Barfields have been making wine from the vine that grows on their cottage and next year when it is ready to drink we think of having a Bacchic festival. The adopted baby is to be the infant Bacchus. Harwood with his fat shiny face, on the donkey, will be Silenus. B. and I Corybantes. Mrs B. a Maenad. B. and I will write the poetry & she will compose a dance. You ought to come.

Yrs

J.

145

[Hillsboro]
July 8th 1930

My dear Arthur,

Your letters get later and later every week. If you write on Monday the first week, on Tuesday the second week, and so on, then in seven weeks you will be writing on Monday again: but you will have written one letter less than you should. In a year you will have written eight letters less, that is thirty six pages. Assuming that we both live thirty years more you will in that time have cheated me out of one thousand and eighty pages. *Why*, oh why, do you do these things?

My examining begins on the 17th and for about ten days I shall be at it from morning till night, so that you must look for no instalments or letters during that time: but I hope you will continue to write to me – as your letters, if they arrive, will be about the only pleasure that remains.

I am interested to hear that you have a new friend. Is he really one of us? – not that I don't think dozens of people v. well worth having as friends without their sharing the things we specially like – indeed in *some* ways better worth having on that account.

You have I think misunderstood what I said about the return from austerity. I never meant for a moment that I was beginning to doubt whether absolute chastity was the true goal – of that I am certain. What I meant was that I began to think that I was mistaken in aiming at this goal by the means of a stern repression and even a contemptuous distrust of all that emotional & imaginative experience wh. seems to border on the voluptuous: whether it was well to see in certain romances and certain music nothing but one more wile of the enemy: whether perhaps the right way was not to keep always alive in ones soul a certain tenderness & luxuriousness always reaching out to *that of which* (on my view) sex must be the copy. In other words, whether, while I was right in seeing that a copy must be different from an original, I ought not to have remembered that it must also be *like* it – else how wd. it be a copy? In the second place, what I feared was *not* lest this mood should be temporary but lest it should turn out to be another wile. What I also ought to have said in my last letter but didn't is that the whole thing has made me feel that I have never given half enough importance to love in the sense of the *affections*.

One passage in your letter – in which you corrected *bare* to *bear* amused me v. much, as the original wd. have read 'I find it more difficult to *bare* myself lovingly towards my neighbours & my relation.' The picture of you *baring* yourself 'lovingly' to a long row of neighbours (the O'Mulligan etc) & relations – so remeniscent of a notorious passage in Rousseau – is not easily surpassed!

Almost ever since the Vac. began I have been reading a little every evening in Traherne's *Centuries of Meditations* (Dobell. About 7/–. Lovely paper). I forget whether we have talked of it or not. I think he suffers by making out everything much too easy and really shirking the problem of evil in all its forms: at least, as far as I have got, for it is unfair to say this of a book not yet finished. But apart from this he has extraordinary merits. What do you think of the following; – 'The world . . . is the beautiful frontispiece to Eternity'[1] – 'You never enjoy the world aright till the sea itself floweth in your veins,

[1] Thomas Traherne, *Centuries of Meditations*, ed. Bertram Dobell (1927), 'The First Century', No. 20, p. 13.

till you are clothed with the heavens and crowned with the stars . . . till you can sing and rejoice and delight in God as misers do in gold'[2] – 'I must lead you out of this into another world to *learn your wants*. For till you find them you will never be happy'[3] – 'They (i.e. Souls) were made to love and are dark and vain and comfortless till they do it. Till they love they are idle or misemployed. Till they love they are desolate.'[4] But I could go on quoting from this book forever.

A complete Coventry Patmore wh. I ordered shortly after reading the *Angel in the House* has arrived – Bell & Sons, 7/6, quite a pleasant volume – and I have just dipped into it. I don't remember for many years to have felt so disposed for new reading as I do now, and specially poetry. Everything seems – you know the feeling – to be beginning again and one has the sense of immortality.

Barfield and I finished the *Paradiso* when I was with him. I think it reaches heights of poetry which you get nowhere else: an ether almost too fine to breathe. It is a pity that I can give you no notion what it is like. Can you imagine Shelley at his most ecstatic combined with Milton at his most solemn & rigid? It sounds impossible I know, but that is what Dante has done.

We also read some Beowulf with a very remarkable young woman. She was a farmer's daughter who got a county scholarship and went up to London getting a good degree in English. Then – and here's the marvel – she settled down at home again and divides her time between milking the cows & taking occasional pupils, apparently contented in both. Thats what we want, isn't it? *Emigration* from the uneducated class into ours only swells the intellectual unemployed: but to have education transforming people & yet leaving them wth their roots in the earth (which *then* they will be able to appreciate) is the way to make class disappear altogether. She is 'remarkable' only in this: otherwise the adjective does her gross injustice for she is exquisitely ordinary – and not at all pretty except with the bonny open air plumpness of her age & class.

I also had some lovely bathes wth Barfield in a reach of the little river Thame. Picture us lounging naked under the pollards on a flat field: mowers in the next field: and tiny young dragon flies – too small to be frightful yet – darting among the lilies. Here I learned to dive wh. is a great change in my life & has important (religious) connections. I'll explain that later. They are still v. ungraceful dives but I do get in head first.

[2] *ibid.*, No. 29, p. 19.
[3] *ibid.*, No. 43, p. 28.
[4] *ibid.*, 'The Second Century', No. 48, p. 112.

This is the last letter you'll get till the infernal (but profitable) examining is over – but like a good chap (!) (old man!) do keep on writing to me. So glad you approve of precious bane. Isn't Wizard Beguildy a lovely character: also the scene of Prue Sarn alone in the attic.

Yrs

J.

146

[Hillsboro]
July 29th 1930

My dear Arthur,

Harrah! Examining is over. As to your question why I dislike it, it is not the jaunt to Cambridge (by the bye I am not going this year) wh. I dislike·but the fortnight or so of actually marking the papers that precedes it. I had fewer than usual this time, but even so it means working absolutely solidly from after breakfast till supper: often it means going on after supper as well. As the work has no interest whatever & yet demands unsleeping attention, one gets very tired.

Thank you for writing – I enjoyed your two letters enormously. Do stop apologising for them and wondering archly (à la Tchanie!) how I can read them. Surely it needs no great imagination for you to realise that every mention of things at home now comes to me with the sweetness that belongs only to what is irrevocable. Secondly, there are a great many subjects on which you are the only person whom I can write to or be written to by with full understanding. Thirdly our common ground represents what is really (I think) the deepest stratum in my life, the thing in me that, if there should be another personal life, is most likely to survive the dissolution of my brain. Certainly when I come to die I am more likely to remember certain things that you and I have explored or suffered or enjoyed together than anything else.

It is an interesting and rather grim enquiry – how much of our present selves we cd. hope to take with us if there were another life. I take it that whatever is *merely* intellectual, *mere* theory, must go, since we probably hold it only by memory habit, wh. may depend on the matter of the brain. Only what has gone far deeper, what has been incorporated into the unconscious depths, can hope to survive. This often comes over me when I think of religion: and it is a shock to realise that the mere *thinking* it may be nothing, and that only the tiny bit which we really practice is likely to be ours in any sense of which death can not make hay.

I think you must be mistaken about having shown me Traherne. Surely it is much more likely that *you* are talking balls. Anyway I am glad you like him.

Your question about the difference of writing between my instalments and my letters I don't understand. If you mean handwriting, of course the answer is that in the letter I just scribble as hard as I can lick, while in the instalments[1] I stop to think. If you mean language, the answer is (I shd. have thought) obvious.

Oh you can't imagine the poignancy with wh. your account of the sunny windy day near the dry tree fell across a dreary, dusty afternoon of those sordid papers, when my head was aching and the boys' horrid handwriting seemed to jump on the page.

I don't know quite what I feel about your assistance at the accouchement of our sister the cow. I know what I ought to feel – simply the same thrill that I feel at the first coming up of a flower. Physical disgust is a sensation wh. I have very often and of which I am always ashamed. If one lets it grow upon one it will in the end cut one out from all delighted participation in the life of nature. For God is gross and never heard of decency and cares nothing for refinement: nor do children, nor most women, nor any of the beasts, nor men either except in certain sophisticated classes. And yet its hard to feel that the faculty of disgust is a sheer evil from beginning to end. I don't know what to make of it. (Perhaps in one way it is, in another, it isn't!) At any rate there can be no two opinions about the delightfulness of seeing the other cows coming round to inspect the infant. Did they show any signs of congratulating the mother? for I notice that when *one* of our hens lays an egg, *all* join in the noise – whether that is congratulation or simply that they regard themselves as a single individual and annouce '*We* have laid an egg.'

Talking about hens, have you read the Nonne Prestes Tale in Chaucer – its *delicious*: homely & ridiculous in the best possible way. Which reminds me, did you ever in your 'pink book' stage read any version of Reynard the Fox? It is one of the great medieval creations, and I want someday to get it: the English version is by Caxton,[2] I am afraid from a rather late French version, but probably quite good.

[1] This was to be his last reference to *The Moving Image*. Unluckily, no copy of it has survived.

[2] *Reynart the Foxe* (Caxton, 1481).

Since writing the last sentence I have come into College to entertain two people to dinner & spend the night. As they did not leave till 3 o'clock (it is now 10) I am feeling rather morning-after-ish! One of them is a man called Dyson[3] who teaches English at Reading. He is only in Oxford for a few weeks and having met him once I liked him so well that I determined to get to know him better. My feeling was apparently reciprocated and I think we sat up so late with the feeling that heaven knew when we might meet again and the new friendship had to be freed past its youth and into maturity in a single evening. Although my head aches this morning I do not regret it. Such things come rarely and are worth a higher price than this. He is a man who really loves truth: a philosopher and a religious man: who makes his critical & literary activities depend on the former – none of your damned dilettanti. In appearance he is like a plumper edition of Uncle Gussie & has something the same vivacity & quickness of speech, but a much more honestly merry laugh. Have you observed that it is the most serious conversations which produce in their course the best laughter? How we roared and fooled at times in the silence of last night – but always in a few minutes buckled to again with renewed seriousness. Then, as always here, the close of the whole thing is the journey through pitch black cloisters to let them out by the little gate with my key, where after the dark one suddenly sees the tower far above, in the light cast up from the street lamps. How I shall remember all this some day!

The other man was Coghill[4] of Exeter, a friend of Chevasse, who talks v. like Chevasse (in voice I mean) but is a far better fellow.

I am looking forward to reading *Desert Islands*[5] & am glad to have your judgment of it. Oh, by the way, I forgot to thank you for your offer of the Macdonalds. *Pro tanto quid retribuamus?* as the tramcars say – what can I give you in return? About Johnson & Milton –

[3] Henry Victor Dyson Dyson (1896–1975) was an undergraduate at Exeter College, taking his B.A. in 1921. He was a Lecturer and Tutor in the University of Reading from 1921 to 1945, and a Fellow and Tutor in English Literature of Merton College from 1945 to 1963. For details of his long friendship with Lewis see *Surprised by Joy* and the *Biography*.

[4] Nevill Coghill (1899–   ) first met Lewis in 1923 when they were reading English together. Coghill was a Fellow and Tutor in English Literature of Exeter College from 1925 to 1957, and afterwards the Merton Professor of English Literature in the University of Oxford from 1957 to 1966. For details see *Surprised by Joy*, the *Biography*, and Professor Coghill's essay 'The Approach to English' in *Light on C. S. Lewis*, ed. Jocelyn Gibb (1965).

[5] Walter de la Mare, *Desert Islands* (1930).

wasn't it M's politics that made J. so unfair?[6] The old die-hard Tory could never forgive the puritan, republican & regicide.

Yrs

Jack

147

[Hillsboro]

Aug. 3rd 1930

My dear Arthur,

Your account of your novel is certainly v. obscure. I thought the whole was already typed – or was that only a draught? I am sorry that I cannot be present at the accouchement, however 'painful and disgusting'.

I have been wondering why these days of rain & wind in the summer have such a charm for me. Is it simply an offshoot of my general love of winter, and these days please me as a foretaste of winter – as if the wind shook Summer and he buttoned his coat and said 'Dear me. I'm beginning to get old.' I walked in the fields beyond Barton after tea to day and sat under a hedge – the sort of hedge that is nearly all trees. The wind tossed it and tumbled it: and from the field – which was full of stacks of corn – straws kept on blowing up to me. Endless rain clouds went overhead. Somehow I was very happy in it – snug, you know. And yet one ought to feel snugger in a warm ditch in winter. Or is it that such days fall outside ones conventional categories of the seasons, being neither typical summer days nor typical autumn days, nor typical anything, and therefore, thwarting ones *derivative* reactions and all that has been already stereotyped by literature and painting, they force one to wake up and see the thing as it really is? Or is it part of the same general law which makes the landscape look more exciting upside down? However a fool can ask more questions in an hour than a wise man can answer in a life time.

The other thing I was thinking on my walk was this: I had just begun M. Arnold's *Studies In Celtic Literature*[1] and looking on to the end I saw that he said that German Romanticism (he particularly mentioned Novalis) was a kind of clumsy attempt at the 'natural magic' of the Celts. Now I was perfectly certain that whatever else was true, *that* was not: but this set me puzzling as to what the real difference between the two was. I found that when I tried to get the

---

[6] In his treatment of Milton in his *Lives of the English Poets*.

[1] Matthew Arnold, *On the Study of Celtic Literature* (1867).

spirit of German romance I got the idea of smiths, gold, dwarfs, forests, mountains, cottages and castles: while the other gave me the idea of water and rushes and clouds. Then I noted that the Celtic was much more sensuous; also less *homely*: also, entirely lacking in *reverence*, of which the Germanic was full. Then again that the Germanic *glowed* in a sense with rich sombre colours, while the Celtic was all transparent and full of nuances – evanescent – but very bright. One sees that Celtic is essentially Pagan, not merely in the sense of being heathen (not-Christian), as the Germanic may be, but in the sense of being irredeemably Pagan, frivolous under all its melancholy, incapable of growing into religion, and – I think – a little heartless. In fact, add Roman civilisation to it and you get – France. I'm not running it down: before it gets Romanised it is delicious and refreshing. I don't want to give up either: they are almost ones male and female soul. Do you feel at all in sympathy with what I have been saying? And do you agree that the Germanic – gold & smiths – runs peculiarly to mineral images, i.e. the Earth – while Celtic runs to the elements. I think in the *Tempest* Caliban is almost a picture of the Germanic at its lowest, and Ariel the Celtic: but look at the lovely earthy poetry put into Caliban's mouth on two occasions.

To be frank I was rather prepared for *Desert Islands* turning out a disappointment, tho' my hopes had been temporarily resurrected by what you said of it. *De La Mare* has fallen infinitely below himself. I was looking at the *Connoisseur* again not long ago. Of course it is good – he can't write anything that isn't that. But isn't there just a touch of the dilettante about it? – certainly a lack of the real spirituality one finds in the *Veil*? My idea is that he really bade good bye to the best part of himself in the lovely poem 'Be not too wildly amorous of the far'.[2] The peculiar kind of vision he had was of a strangely piercing quality and probably almost unbearable to the possessor: only a man of great solidity, of real character, sound at the bases of his mind & braced with philosophy, could have carried it safely. But De La Mare was not such a man. It was quite likely really leading him to madness, & he knew it. Hardly knowing what he did, and yet just knowing, he *sent* it away. I am told he lives in the midst of the silly London literary sets. His real day is over. Do you think this a possible theory?

Yes. The Witch is gone. Do you ever go into Leeborough garden? How strange it would be for you to sit on that summer seat now: it

[2] The opening line of 'The Imagination's Pride' from de la Mare's *The Veil and Other Poems* (1921).

almost makes me shudder. Do you know it sometimes comes to me as a shock to realise that all the *rest* of Strandtown is going on just the same.

As to when we shall meet: we are moving house in September (I'm going to tell you nothing about this so that it will be a surprise when you see it) so I am afraid I shall not be able to come to Ireland this summer. As to your coming here, it wd. be obviously a bad time to choose the move! (I hear[d] your views on this after your last experience!) I think October would be the best, and will keep you informed. Of course if you *are* in England at the end of August let me know. How I long for one of our walks & talks together: and how I would like to see you peering into the pages of my Ellis' *Metrical Romances*[3] wh. at last I have got: not to mention the Morris. A propos of which (& this is what my whole letter *should* have been about) what with Morris & other things I really seem to have had youth given back to me lately. But I must try to describe this another time, as I am spoiling the margin wh. you demand!

Yrs

J.

148

[Hillsboro]

Aug 13. 1930

My dear Arthur,

I wonder what has happened. Are you ill – or away – or simply lazy? However, as you wrote to me so perseveringly during *my* silence (tho' you must allow that mine was foretold and unavoidable) I will continue to write during yours: and also to prevent a bad habit of silence setting in on both sides.

It is a curious thing that as I look back I can remember no breaks in the regular course of letters during the Bookham period. Breaks I suppose there must have been and my failure to recollect them is part of the same delusion (but not all delusion either) of memory, wh. makes the past summers always fine and the past winters always frosty. Yet on the whole I do really think that we were very regular, and am very anxious to keep it up now without a break – at least until the habit is so fully formed that it is sure to survive a short intermission. This is becoming rather prosy!

Talking about the breaking of resolutions – you see how skilfully I glide away from my prosing to something really gay and brilliant

[3] George Ellis, *Specimens of Early English Metrical Romances* (1805).

and witty and novel – in fact 'much more rational but much less like a ball'[1] – talking then of resolutions (but we weren't talking. Yes, but we are now!) – talking of resolutions, one of the worst things about a moral relapse – to me – is that it throws such a shadow back on the time before during which you thought you were getting on quite well. Having found oneself – for the hundredth time – back where one started, it seems so obvious that one has never really moved at all: and that what seemed progress was only [a] dream, or even the irrelevant result of circumstances or physical condition.

I have again begun my German and do half an hour every morning before beginning my other work. I am still at Novalis – you will wonder how I have not finished it long ago, and even to myself I seem to have been reading it almost all my life. As I go at about the pace of a schoolboy translating Caesar I expect it will last me for the rest of my days. (I am like the man in the story. 'Why not buy a book?' 'Oh I have one already.') This certainly leads to economy. It has better results too. As you know, 'Heinrich Von Ofterdingen'[2] wh. I am reading is a very Macdonaldy book – indeed Novalis is perhaps the greatest single influence on Macdonald – full of 'holiness', gloriously German-romantic (i.e. a delicious mingling of earthy homeliness and magic, also of a sort of spiritual voluptuousness with innocence) and to be compelled to spell out such stuff word by word instead of galloping greedily thro' it as I certainly should if I could find a translation really forces me to get the most out of it. There is *no* translation either into French or English: so you will have to rely on what I tell you. However I have probably said all this before.

Last night I slept very little owing to a pain I sometimes have wh. Joey says is the kidneys: so I have gone a walk longer than usual to day in the hope of tiring myself out. In spite of the heavy green August foliage it really might be October: the wailing wind and the clouds are sheer Autumn. How unfortunate it is that you cannot follow my walks as I can yours. It would convey nothing to you if I said that I went thro' the Eatons (Wood Eaton and Water Eaton). The first half of the walk is all in a road, absolutely flat, with a clear stream behind it: through every break in the high hedges you get specimens of that sort of beauty that flat country has: i.e. that you never see further than across the first field, and beyond its further hedge the big elms – tho really scattered – look like a continuous forest. Nearer, of course, are the wild flowers and the cows whisking

[1] Jane Austen, *Pride and Prejudice*, ch. 11.
[2] Novalis (the pseudonym of Friedrich Leopold von Hardenberg), *Heinrich von Ofterdingen* (1802).

their tails. Wood Eaton itself is an almost ideal village. There is a great house (Georgian),[3] severe in outline, but mellowed with yellow moss, in a park where there are some fine cedars: about sixteen cottages round a pond and green, all of grey stone and nearly all thatched: a church: and in every direction very high walls of flat stones without mortar, and inside them the invariable rows of huge elms – greatly improved this afternoon by the wind.

Thence my walk led out into open fields, where the flatness made the sky enormous and the cows seemed to go on forever and ever. Do you know the strange sort of contrast there is in such a place on such a day between the utter placidity of the landscape and the hurry and scurry of the clouds – at least of the clouds immediately overhead, for away on the horizon, with the absent sun shining on *them*, one always sees remote, clear, shining clouds that look almost calmer than anything else in the world. The only adventure on the ground was the sudden discovery of a field almost black with crows, which, of course dashed up cawing into the air as I approached them and then were blown about. 'The untidy crows' as Sackville West says in *The Land*[4] (a poem you should read) speaking of their flight on a windy day.

Did I tell you I have been reading a lot of Matthew Arnold's prose (I've got to for tutorial purposes). Oh, I remember, I talked about him in my last letter. I don't know that I recommend him. How do you get on with your Johnson? And how does your ac-couchement proceed. Perhaps it is that which has hindered you from writing.

I had a most horrible dream the other night, which I retail in case you would like to make use of it. Mrs Lovell was a poor old woman whom Minto used to give odd jobs to: she has now disappeared. I dreamed that I went to a cupboard in the kitchen to look for some-thing. A heavy thing in brown paper dropped out at my feet. Picking it up and unwinding it I found – Mrs Lovel's HEAD! (I think it might be worked in along with the hairy gums, 'Your grandmother etc etc' into the super-shocker that so often flits about our minds.)

There will, I think, be no shortage of hedgehogs in our new garden.

Do write

Yours
Jack

[3] Wood Eaton Hall.
[4] Victoria Sackville-West, *The Land* (1926), 'Autumn', line 94.

149

My dear Arthur,

The first thing, when one is being worried as to whether one will have to have an operation or whether one is a literary failure, is *to assume absolutely mercilessly that the worst is true*, and to ask *What Then?* If it turns out in the end that the worst is not true, so much the better: but for the meantime the question must be resolutely put out of mind. Otherwise your thoughts merely go round and round a wearisome circle, now hopeful, now despondent, then hopeful again – that way madness lies. Having settled then that the worst is true, one can proceed to consider the situation: and I will talk to you as one in that situation.

Now the worst of all the things we usually say to a man who is suffering is that they inevitably provoke him to retort, in feeling, if not in words, 'Yes. It's all very well for *you*. It isn't *your* tooth that is aching.' So as soon as I read your letter I bethought me of myself on the evening when the MS of *Dymer* came back from Heinemanns rejected without a word of criticism or encouragement: and I remembered that after a very miserable night I sat down to assume the worst, as I advise you to do, and *on that basis* to come to terms with the situation. Only I did it in writing. I have been in to College this morning and found the document wh. I enclose. It is perfectly genuine and unaltered except for the marginal notes wh. I have now added in explanation of one or two expressions you might not have come across. I don't know whether it will be any help to you: it was of the greatest to me. You will be tempted to say that my situation was quite different from yours: for I succeeded in the end. To this I answer (1) That when I wrote this document I did not know I should succeed in publishing. (2) That when I did finally publish, the book was a complete failure.

To you, no doubt, at the moment it seems that to read your own book in print and to have it liked by a few friends would be ample bliss, whether any one bought it or not. Believe me, Arthur, this is an *absolute delusion*. It might satisfy you for a moment: but very soon, if it didn't sell, you would find yourself just as disappointed as you are now. So that in this sense I am *still* as disappointed an author as you. From the age of sixteen onwards I had one single ambition, from which I never wavered, in the prosecution of which I spent every ounce I could, on wh. I really & deliberately staked my whole contentment: and I recognise myself as having unmistakably failed in it. So that not only in my enclosed document, but now, in this letter, I feel that I have some right to talk to you as a man in the same boat.

Suffering of the sort that you are now feeling is my special subject, my profession, my long suit, the thing I claim to be an expert in: and if I were not writing to a man still smarting under the novelty of the blow I should point out at length how absurd it is to dignify such disappointment with the name of suffering in a world like this. (There is a woman lives in our road who is sinking into creeping paralysis and going blind: and for the last three nights she has been awake, and crying, all night, with neuritis. She says 'I feel as if my blood was boiling in my arms.') This side of the question you cannot yet be ready to feel: it wd. be more than human if you did. I only mention it because otherwise I wd. be ashamed, in speaking of myself, to use the noble word 'suffering'. However, whether you call it 'suffering' or not, I claim to be a dab at it.

The worst of it is that all the mental habits contracted during the work, go on after hope is dead. You see a tree waving in the wind and you think 'I'll put that in.' You notice some psychological fact in yourself and think 'By Jove! I'll use that in such a scene.' You read in some review a statement about contemporary literature and think 'I wonder if his opinion will be modified when he reads – ' and then *bang*! it comes back again: ALL THAT IS OVER. And yet one has to go through with it: and little by little the real consolations come. Read what Bunyan says about the valley of humiliation. Read about Anodos at the low island where the old woman lived.

For its quite true what my document says. The side of me which longs, not to write, for no one can stop us doing that, but to be approved as a writer, is not the side of us that is really worth much. And depend upon it, unless God has abandoned us, he will find means to cauterise that side somehow or other. If we can take the pain well and truly now and by it *forever* get over the wish to be distinguished beyond our fellows, well: if not we shall get it again in some other form. And honestly, the being cured, with all the pain, has pleasure too: one creeps home, tired and bruised, into a state of mind that is really restful, when all ones ambitions have been given up. Then one can really for the first time say 'Thy Kingdom come': for in that Kingdom there will be no pre-eminences and a man must have reached the stage of not caring two straws about his own status before he can enter it.

Think how difficult that would be if one *succeeded* as a writer: how bitter this necessary purgation at the age of sixty, when literary success had made your whole life and you had *then* got to begin to go through the stage of seeing it all as dust and ashes. Perhaps God has been specially kind to us in forcing us to get over it at the beginning. At all events, whether we like it or not, we have got to take the shock. As you know so well, we have got to *die*. Cry, kick, swear, we may: only like Lilith to come in the end and die far more painfully and later. Does it sound like priggery if I say 'I implore you'? Heaven knows I do it as a friend not as a preacher: do it only because you stand very high among the half-dozen people whom I love. I implore you, then, seriously, to regard your present trouble as an opportunity for carrying the dying process a stage further. If necessary, go back to the Puritan language you were brought up in and think of your literary ambitions as an 'idol' you have to give up, as a sacrifice demanded. I 'implore' because such disappointments, if *accepted* as death, and therefore the beginning of new life, are infinitely valuable: but if not, are terrible dangers. Once let self-pity come uppermost and you know where you are sure to turn for consolation. In other words they are bound to leave a man (permanently perhaps) very much better or very much worse than they found him.

So far I have said nothing about Reid's judgement, nor about your going on with the attempt. I am afraid, human nature being what it is, you must have glanced eagerly thro' this letter for some word on those very subjects: even have wondered dismally when I wd. have done moralising and get to business. Perhaps even when you so strongly urged me to write, you had always the hope that my letter would restore your confidence in yourself as a literary man. Perhaps all this time what you are asking yourself is 'Does this letter mean that Jack thinks Reid is probably right and doesn't like to say so?' Poor Arthur! You must – it is only nature – be simply starving for some word of *literary* encouragement instead of all this moral encouragement. But don't you also see that I mustn't give it? For as long as you are still thinking about *that*, still wondering whether Reid is right, you haven't taken the *first step*. Whether you are going to be a writer or not, *in either case*, you must so far die as to get over putting that question first. The other thing is so very much more important. For be sure, until we learn better, we shall get this kind of suffering again and again. Better take it now: better learn the trick that makes you free for the future. It sounds merely brutal, I expect: but do remember I'm in the same boat. I would have given almost *anything* – I shudder to think what I would have given if I had been allowed – to be a successful writer. So don't think I am writing this

in order to avoid giving my own opinion about your possibilities of
success. I couldn't give an opinion in any case without seeing the
book: but I am writing as I do simply & solely because I think the
only thing for you to do is absolutely to *kill* the part of you that wants
success. It's like in Phantastes where the voice said 'Ride at him or
be a slave *forever*.'[1]

At present (1) Maureen is away (2) Minto is bad with indigestion
(3) We are going to move on Sept. 25th (4) There is a possible visitor
in the next three weeks.* In these distressing conditions I can
neither go to you nor ask you to come to me. But I could (I am pretty
sure) get you quite nice rooms in Old Headington and we cd. meet
every day. I am *dying* to show you the new place & to have a walk &
talk with you. Wd. you think of this while your mother is away. Do.
It wd. honestly give me more pleasure than any (possible) thing at
the moment. I am sorry to seem so inhospitable – and I would *love*
to come to you for a week if I could.

Write soon. If you eat this you will grow into a unicorn. I hope you
won't loathe this letter

Yours
Jack

* *which* unspecified!

[The entry from Lewis's diary of 1926, with notes added 18 August
1930.]

Saturday March 6th 1926.

Last night Heinemann's returned the MS. of Dymer on which I
have been at work for several years. Though I intend to try all the
publishers, it seems good, in the event of a complete failure, to find
out by the analysis of my present disappointment what exactly it is I
hope to gain by poetical success: and what the abandonment of the
hope would mean. To understand is the safest resource.

1. A certain part of my disappointment is clearly special to the
present case. Heinemann's had treated me well before. I had allowed
myself to think of them as οἰκείους(1) and flattered myself on
being admitted to the rank of the number of good poets whose work
they publish. I had also hoped that rejection, if it came, wd. come
signed by Evans with some personal expression of regret or kindness.
This is an element in my feelings at the moment wh. cannot occur

[1] *Phantastes*, ch. 22.

when another house returns it. It may therefore be eliminated.

2. I may clearly also eliminate the desire for money, as I never seriously hoped that Dymer would pay. Or if, in more sanguine moods, I sometimes dreamed of having a few pounds of extra pocket money by it, this is something that counts for a negligible quantity in my disappointment.

3. I can also rule out, tho' not entirely, the desire for Fame, if this means the desire to be known as the author of an approved poem, the *monstrari digito*.(²) It is true that I should like and like greatly to be known (and praised) by one or two friends and good judges: but I hold this as a refinement of pleasure easily foregone. If it went by another's name, so long as it was read and liked, I should be quite content.

4. But I cannot say simply that I desire not my fame but that of the poem. In the impossible case of an exactly similar poem written by someone else and winning success I should be very far from content. Though no one else need know that the approved poem is mine, I at least must know it. The feeling is not, therefore, a disinterested love for Dymer simply as a poem I happen to like.

5. It is then a desire that something which I recognize as my own should be publicly found good: whether it is known by others to be mine is of comparatively little importance. Is it then what Aristotle says? I desire public praise as a proof that it really is good: i.e. I wish to be able to think that I am a good poet and desire applause (tho not paid to my name) as a means to that end.

6. This is the most probable account yet suggested. One objection occurs. If an archangel or a mystical intuition admitting of no doubt, assured me that Dymer was the greatest poem ever written by man, but added that it would never be read, I should be hardly more contented that I am now. The supposition, however, raises many difficulties. (a) Is the reason of my dissatisfaction that a poem unread is not a poem at all, and that there is therefore no sense in calling it great? (b) Does the disinterested wish that, if it were great, humanity should enjoy it, count for anything? (c) Is my acquiescence in not being known (or thought) great by others, not quite what it seemed to be in Para. 3?

7. (b) is very attractive but I cannot find that it is what I feel. No poem is indispensible. In my worst moods I never supposed that the 'spirit of man' would be the worse for not having Dymer. Let it be as good as you like: they will get the same thing out of other books sooner or later. For in a larger sense and in the long run we do get the same thing out of different books.

8. (a) certainly seems to be true. The greatness of a poem can mean only the good that particular readers do actually get from it. And it is certain that no acknowledgement, however public, of my claims as a poet would make up for Dymer's not being read and enjoyed. If my archangel promised that the human race wd. go about ever after lamenting a great lost work of mine, and pay me the highest honours: no doubt this wd. give me some kind of pleasure, but not the kind I am really concerned about at present

9. (c) This seems to have some truth in it. I shall be forced to admit that tho I do not want public praise for 'someone called Lewis' I do want it for 'the author of Dymer'. In fact the suggestion in Para. 5 is not true. I do not desire the praise *simply* as a proof. I desire that my value as a poet should be acknowledged by others as well as myself, even if they do not know where to find 'this great poet' or what he looks like etc. Perhaps some dream of being sooner or later discovered mixes still with my acquiescence in such anonymous success. I honestly don't know: tho I might know if I cd. be perfectly honest. *That* problem I leave open for the present

10. My desire then contains two elements. (a) The desire for some proof to myself that I am a poet. (b) The desire that my poet-hood should be acknowledged even if no one knows that it is mine. (b) is a means to (a) but it is not valued only as a means.

11. As far as I can see both these are manifestations of the single desire for what may be called mental or spiritual rank. I have flattered myself with the idea of being among my own people when I was reading the poets and it is unpleasing to have to stand down and take my place in the crowd. Such a desire is contrary to my own settled principles: the very principles which I expressed in Dymer. It is fair to say that I had already gone some way towards repressing it – the writing of Dymer was a purgation – when the completion of the poem, Coghill's praise of it, and the sending off to a publishers (after so many years) threw me back into a tumult of self-love that I thought I had escaped. This must be recognised as pure retrogression. The desire will not bear examination. To stand above ὁ τύχωα([3]) is a wish that cannot be universalised.([4]) Worst of all I have used the belief in such secret pre-eminence as a compensation for things that wearied or humiliated me in real life: Thomas Browne's insidious nonsense about 'they that look upon my outside etc.'([5])

12. The cure of this disease is not easy to find – except the sort of violent, surgical cure which Reality itself may be preparing for me. I was free from it at times when writing Dymer. Then I was interested in the object, not in my own privileged position of seer of the

object. But whenever I stopped writing or thought of publication or showed the MS. to friends I contemplated not that of which I had been writing, but my writing about it: I passed from looking at the macrocosm([6]) to looking at a little historical event inside the 'Me'.

The only healthy or happy or eternal life is to look so steadily on the World that the representation 'Me' fades away. Its appearance at all in the field of consciousness is a mark of inferiority in the state where it appears. Its claiming a central position is disease.

13. Is self-consciousness, the possibility of contemplating the object Me, a pure mistake? It may be, rather, that this power of objectifying myself has its value as a necessary preliminary to being rid of it.

([1]) 'My ain folk'.

([2]) Being pointed at with the finger (i.e. pointed out as the 'great man' in the streets).

([3]) The ordinary man.

([4]) Kant says that you should desire nothing wh. you can't 'universalise', i.e. desire for every one else as well as for yourself. Now clearly I can't desire that every one shd. be pre-eminent above the ordinary run of people, for there wd. then be no ordinary run, & therefore no pre-eminence.

([5]) i.e. used it to console myself by saying 'Ah! I mayn't cut a great figure externally: but if only you knew what a poet I was!'

([6]) The great world.

150

[Hillsboro]
Aug 28th 1930

My dear Arthur,

I was delighted to get your cheering letter. Do not thank me, much less admire me. The splendid *talking* has, as usual, fallen to my share: what had to be done and lived fell to yours. All men can give excellent advice!

I quite agree by the bye with your rejection of Forrest's consolatory remark that you may write as a hobby. It reminds me of that romantic saying of R. L. Stevenson's 'It is better to travel hopefully than to arrive'[1]: against whose abuse Barfield is always protesting. For as he says, how can you travel hopefully except in the hope of

[1] *El Dorado*, vi.

arriving? And if a person, having taken away your hope of arriving, still tells you to travel hopefully, he is talking nonsense. (It's like saying 'What a bore. I see we shant be able to go to the opera after all. However we can still enjoy *looking forward* to going!' or 'It's true that I am going to get nothing to eat. But then what a splendid appetite I have!') If this sort of thing is consolatory, certainly no human evil can lack consolation.

As for the real motives for writing after one has 'got over' the desire for acknowledgement: – in the first place, I found and find, that precisely at the moment when you have really put all that out of your mind and decided not to write again – or if you do, to do it with the clear consciousness that you are only playing yourself – precisely then the ideas – which came so rarely in the days when you regarded yourself officially as an author – begin to bubble and simmer, and sooner or later you will *have* to write: and the question *why* won't really enter your mind. In my own case it is a very remarkable thing that in the few religious lyrics which I have written during the last year, in which I had no idea of publication & at first very little idea even of showing them to friends, I have found myself impelled to take infinitely more pains, less ready to be contented with the fairly good and more determined to reach the best attainable, than ever I was in the days when I never wrote without the ardent hope of successful publication.[2]

The truth is, I think, that 'our deeds are ours: their ends none of our own'. Who knows – why should we know? – what will in the end reach the ear of humanity? The successes of our own age may be speedily forgotten: some poem scribbled in pencil on the fly leaf of a schoolbook may survive and be read and be an influence when English is a dead language. Who knows, even, whether to reach the ears of other men is the purpose for which this impulse is really implanted in us? Perhaps in the eyes of the gods the true use of a book lies in its effects upon the author. You remember what Ibsen said, that every play he wrote had been written for the purgation of his own heart. And in my own humbler way I feel quite certain that I could not have certain good things now if I had not gone through the writing of Dymer. Or if a book has an audience of one – surely we must not assume that this may not be, from some superhuman point of view, as much justification as an audience of thousands. I am sure that some are born to write as trees are born to bear leaves: for these,

[2] These religious lyrics were later to appear in Lewis's *The Pilgrim's Regress: An Allegorical Apology for Christianity, Reason and Romanticism* (1933; new and revised edition, 1943).

writing is a necessary mode of their own development. If the impulse to write survives the hope of success, then one is among these. If not, then the impulse was at best only pardonable vanity, and it will certainly disappear when the hope is withdrawn. So that whether the necessity and duty of writing is laid on a man or not can soon be discovered by his own feelings. With remote consequences we have no concern. We never know enough.

I think the thing is to obey the ordinary rules of morality: subject to them, to be guided by those impulses which *feel* the most serious and innocent as opposed to those that *feel* trivial and shamefaced: but for ultimate justifications & results to trust to God. The bee builds its cell and the bird its nest, probably with no knowledge of what purpose they will serve: another sees to that. Nobody knows what the result of your writing, or mine, (or Masefield's) will be. But I think we may depend upon it that endless and devoted work on an object to which a man feels seriously impelled will *tell* somewhere or other: himself or others, in this world or others, will reap a harvest exactly proportional to the output. The accounts of this universe are probably very well kept: everything finds its place in the long run. As Von Hügel (an author you shd. read – remind me about him some other time) says 'No effort will ever be as if it had not been'. The situation may be just the reverse of the nightingale in *Endymion*, who

> 'Sings but to her mate, nor e'er conceives
> How tiptoe night holds back her dark grey hood.'[3]

Unsuccessful writers like us thought that night would stand tiptoe to hear us: perhaps we really are singing to some mysterious mate within. Remember too what Traherne says that our appreciation of this world – and *this* becomes fully conscious only as we express it in art – is a real link in the universal chain. Beauty descends from God into nature: but there it would perish and does except when a Man appreciates it with worship and thus as it were *sends it back* to God: so that through his consciousness what descended ascends again and the perfect circle is made.

Dear oh dear! I never meant to fill this whole letter with the subject: and my pen has been running away with me. I suppose it is natural on a subject that touches both of us so near. In fact my experience at this moment is not a bad example in little of my whole argument. For I started aiming at you and thinking that the value of my words lay in the effect they might have on *you*: but now I have drawn out of my own letter so much unexpected matter for my own

[3] John Keats, *Endymion*, I, 830–1.

needs that if it should be lost in the post, I at least will remain a gainer.

Unfortunately it has crowded out a lot of other things. I wanted to tell you about De Quincey's *Autobiography*[4] which I have just finished the first volume of. Not the *Opium Eater* – tho it covers some of the same ground. It is really splendid reading, but I'm too tired to try and explain why. I wanted to tell you all about the bonfire I spent most of yesterday in stoking – and so on. By next week perhaps I shall be finding room for other things. It has been a most terribly hot day here to day and I am *dripping*! I'm glad to hear that *Desert Islands* has bucked up again & shall certainly try it at the first opportunity. Good night

Yours
Jack

151

[Hillsboro]
Aug 31st 1930

My dear Arthur,

I have had two delightful moments since I last wrote. The first was the arrival of the Macdonalds. Thank you over and over again! Perhaps the best way I can thank you at the moment is by trying to give you a share in my delight.

Imagine me, then, seated in a shady, but even so sweltering, corner of the garden with a shade temperature of 88°, in the middle of the afternoon. Imagine the sound of Mr Papworth barking and my rising wearily, as at the 100th interruption, to investigate. I took in the bulky parcel carelessly enough and looked at it without hope of interest, till suddenly your handwriting transformed the whole situation and in a minute I had it opened. Three distinguishable waves of pleasure went over me. The first was a welling up of all that Macdonald himself stands for: the second an added delight as this present, coming so appropriately from you, linked itself up with all our joint life and old times (I begin to see that it is not all rot – tho' it often is – when people say they will value a gift more for the sake of the giver): the third a pleased surprise at finding three, at least, of the books respectably bound, and clean pages of decent type and paper within – for I had always taken it for granted that they would be hideous.

If I followed my inclinations I would have read them all by now:

---

[4] Thomas De Quincey, *Autobiographic Sketches*, 2 vols. (1853-4).

but fortunately work forbids me such a dangerous orgy. I have however finished *Wilfrid Cumbermede* – I took it down with me after tea that same afternoon to Parson's Pleasure and read naked under the willows. I shall not venture on my next Macdonald, tho' tempted, for some time, for fear of spoiling my own delights.

As you said in one of your letters, his novels have great and almost intolerable faults. His only real form is the symbolical fantasy like *Phantastes* or *Lilith*. This is what he always writes: but unfortunately, for financial reasons, he sometimes has to *disguise* it as ordinary Victorian fiction. Hence what you get is a certain amount of the real Macdonald linked (as Mezentius[1] linked live men to corpses) – linked onto a mass of quite worthless 'plot': and as his *real* parts have to involve strange happenings, the plot is usually improbable, obscure, and melodramatic. Thus Wilfrid's dream of Athanasia, his waking to find Mary (transfigured) by his side, and the sword between them, is pure vision. It is in fact closely connected in *that* world with the sword-divided sleep of Sigurd and Brynhild, and also with Dymer's adventure (For we don't individually invent these things, perhaps. Look how the 'empty castle' theme is present in *Phantastes*, *Wilfrid*, & *Dymer*. No doubt it passed into *Dymer* from *Phantastes*: but then, from it, in Dymer, I passed on to the mysterious bedfellow without any guidance from Macdonald – and only *now* find that he has got that bit of the story too, only in another book. Don't you get the feeling of something waiting there and slowly being recovered in fragments by different human minds according to their abilities, and partially spoiled in each writer by the admixture of his own mere individual invention?) This is pure vision, as I say: unfortunately, in order to keep up the pretence that he is writing a novel, he has to explain it all away – hence all the impossible rigmarole about Clara's putting the sword there and Mary's getting into the wrong bed. Yet the gold is so good that it carries off the dross and I hope to read this book many times again. Things that particularly affected me were the grass plain round the old farm (I don't know why this gives such a magical air), the storm raised by the pendulum and the sudden appearance of the horseman, the chapter called '*On the Leads*', the scene of Wilfrid lost on the Alps, and the dream of Charley (*what* a name!) and Wilfrid dead, and perching on the bushes. I don't think as a whole it is so good as *Sir Gibbie* which seems of all G.M.'s novels so far as I've read to avoid best the mere deadweight of 'plot' that I have complained of. Thanks, Arthur,

[1] A mythical Etruscan king who bound living men to corpses and left them to die of starvation. See Virgil's *Aeneid*, VIII, 485–8.

again and again. I know nothing that gives me such a feeling of spiritual healing, of being washed, as to read G. Macdonald.

My second delightful moment was of a different kind, and takes a little arrangement to describe. Imagine first a pure rosy pink sunset: in the extreme distance a sky covered with thin 'mackerel' as delicate as the veins in a shell, & all pink: in the foreground, blackly outlined against this, huge crags and castles and Valkyrie-shapes of cloud. Got that? Now; – imagine that all this existed only for a fraction of [a] second, the pink light being in fact no sunset but a vast flood of summer lightening: so that all those beetling cliffs and tottering cities of the gods, together with the rosy flush behind which made them visible, had leaped out of pure star-set darkness an instant before, and vanished into it instantaneously again – and so times without number. Later in the night it developed into a real thunderstorm: but for a long while it was very distant and I heard thunder at a greater distance (it seemed) than I had ever heard it before. It was *tinkly* – like the crushing of very delicate tumblers by a giant millions of miles away. The comparison is not very good: at any rate it had the most extreme beauty, and the most unlike the grandeur of ordinary thunder, that you can imagine.

I have also had some splendid bathes in the last few days and have suffered, along with the exhaustion of extreme heat, something of a trance-like condition that exhaustion sometimes brings.

We have an old maid, Miss Walsh, staying with us, who, on a very small income, seems to have travelled nearly everywhere. She talks too much of her travels, but there is an old-maidish torrent of details about trunks and trains and an American I met in Corsica (quite *un*like Kelsie – no attempt at humour) which somehow I rather like. A little pinched face with pince-nez. She surprised me by having read the *Crock of Gold* and saying she loved fairy tales: so I have lent her *Phantastes* and await results.

I am now in the second volume of de Quincy's *Autobiography* which continues excellent. We expect to move on Sept. 29th. I suppose I shd. end up 'again thanking you v. much' as we used to do in replying to Christmas boxes! –

Yrs
Jack

P.S. This is a very mortuary letter 🕱 be prepared for the worst!

Sept 15th 1930.

My dear Arthur – Apologies for delay! I was feeling rather seedy on Sunday besides having a weary right arm, whether this was neuritis or writers cramp from making notes all day long: as I am v. busy making notes for an extremely dull subject wh. I have to take next term. I was glad to get your letter from Cush -endun. Did you visit our old friend at the Post-Office? And how did the new friend turn out on closer acquaintance? Miss Walsh, by the way, did not get through Phantastes and I now strongly suspect that her alleged love of fantasy was merely a bye-product of her fanatical love of everything Irish. This, wh. in any case cd. only be a respectable weakness, took in her case the degraded form of endless chit-chat about about all the famous Irish literary people she had met. She referred to Yeats as "W.B." – "for short" – until I asked her how four syllables could be a shortened form of one. The last five minutes of her, while I was seeing her off at the bus, led to the horrible discovery that I was learning Icelandic, and not learning Irish: for which I was soundly scolded. In fact she behaved about Ireland as Americans behave about America – and finally went off with her head in the air as who shd. say Hoity-Toity! The most interesting thing since I last wrote is a dream I had about my father. As a rule dreams about the dead fall into two distinct classes. (a) Rare in wh. one simply forgets that the person has died (b) Those in which the dead

See page 391

152

P.S. This is a very mortuary letter, be prepared for the worst!

[Hillsboro]
Sept. 15th 1930

My dear Arthur,

Apologies for delay! I was feeling rather seedy on Sunday besides having a weary right arm, whether this was neuritis or writer's cramp from making notes all day long: as I am v. busy making notes for an extremely dull subject wh. I have to take next term.

I was glad to get your letter from Cushendun. Did you visit our old friend at the Post-Office? And how did the new friend turn out on closer acquaintance?

Miss Walsh, by the way, did *not* get through *Phantastes* and I now strongly suspect that her alleged love of fantasy was merely a bye-product of her fanatical love of everything Irish. This, wh. in any case cd. only be a respectable weakness, took in her case the degraded form of endless chit-chat about all the famous Irish literary poeple she had met. She referred to Yeats as 'W.B.' – 'for short' – until I asked her how four syllables could be a shortened form of one. The last five minutes of her, while I was seeing her off at the bus, led to the horrible discovery that I was learning Icelandic, and not learning Irish: for which I was soundly scolded. In fact she behaved about Ireland as Americans behave about America, and finally went off with her head in the air as who shd. say Hoity-Toity!

The most interesting thing since I last wrote is a dream I had about my father. As a rule dreams about the dead fall into two distinct classes. (a) Those in wh. one simply forgets that the person has died (b) Those in which the dead appears as a bogey. My dream belonged to neither. I was in the dining room in Little Lea, with all the gasses lit, and talking to my father. I knew perfectly well that he had died, and presently put out my hand and touched him. He felt warm and solid. I said 'But of course this body must be only an appearance. You can't really have a body now.' He explained that it *was* only an appearance, and our conversation, which was cheerful and friendly, but not solemn or emotional, drifted off onto other topics. I then went over to fetch you and we came across together in a closed car. As we drove I told you of his return in order to prepare you for meeting him: and I think (tho' this may be a waking invention) that at that point I was looking forward to seeing him come to the door and say 'Well, Arthur' and offer you your drink. We were exactly at that place where an increased crushing under the wheels tells you that you have passed off the cinders onto the gravel at the study corner: when you, in a voice of suppressed anxiety, said 'Oh no, Jack. Its just that you've been thinking about him and you've *imagined* he's there.' Till that moment everything had been pleasant and homely: but suddenly, as your words made me see the whole adventure *from outside*, as I realised how it would sound if repeated that I had been TALKING TO A DEAD MAN, the thing wh. had been so normal in the experiencing it, rose up with such retrospective horror that the nightmare feeling flared up and I woke in terror. The dream seems to me a good idea of what might v. probably happen if one really met a ghost. At least I sometimes hope so.

Have I propounded before to you my theory that the *corpse* and the *ghost* each owe all their terrors to the other? The corpse, tho so horribly different, is yet so like a man that you can't help thinking it has a life of its own – i.e. you put a ghost in it. But for the idea that this un-man may still live, it wd. not be horrible. Conversely, when you think of the spirit, tho you know it to be unpicturable, you can't help picturing it, and yet you feel you must make it different from the man as he was: then in comes the horrible association of the corpse. In each case you are trying to think of a thing as living and dead at the same time, and from the impossible conception comes the horror.

Certainly ones own death wd. be a much pleasanter idea if one cd. be quite rid of the lingering idea that the corpse is alive. I thought I had got over this years ago: but every now and then some old strain of savage materialism starts up and tries to make me believe that it is *me* they will nail in a box and bury. The same sort of confusion explains why the idea of being buried alive, with a hearse & a coffin etc, is so much worse than the idea of being smothered, say, in a landslip, or by getting on your face in sleep, – wh. latter of course are just the same mode of death really. The secret is that what one fears is *not* smothering – wh, tho' bad enough, is probably much nicer than the 'natural' deaths which most of us are going to die.* It is that the funeral accompaniments give you the idea of entering alive into the normal and regular *status* of a corpse – i.e. of being alive and dead at the same time. It can't really be worse than drowning. So the next time you're buried alive, Arthur, be sure and remember that its no worse than drowning. Trust an old hand, my boy. It pays! Heigh-ho! If we were talking instead of writing letter I shd. begin to fool now ('Beshrew me, the knight's in excellent fooling')

What put you onto the Priestly novel? It may be excellent, but it somehow never occurred to me to try. Perhaps I will after your recommendation.

I think you must have misunderstood me about the Macdonald. I never meant the novels wd. be better without a *story*, nor that the good parts consisted of anything other than story. All I meant was that a really valuable story of the Phantastes kind was constantly being interrupted by a story of a quite inferior kind, and even an inferior specimen of that kind. Also, I agree that the first few chapters of *S. Gibbie* are nothing like as good as the first few chapters of *W. Cumbermede*. But by now you will have got to the good parts. Don't you love 'sleep was scattered all over the world'[1] – and the lovely homeliness of the farm kitchen – and the apparition of Sir Gibbie when the old woman mistakes him for Christ. I hope for your views on it on Saturday – also for a final account of your time at Cushendun.

Yours
Jack

* One might almost leave directions in ones will that one was to be buried alive.

153

[Hillsboro]
Oct. 6th 1930

My dear Arthur,

I had hoped to get off not a letter (that was out of the question) but a line of apology on Sunday: but Sunday when it came was wholly occupied with packing jam. You will excuse my silence when you hear that I am (all at the same time) (a) Having a perfectly stupifying cold, almost 'flu. (b) Packing for a move on Saturday. (c) Preparing for term on Saturday. (d) Finishing a course of lectures. (e) Setting papers for next summer's Exams.

Oh Arthur – do you know how lucky you are to be able to say any evening 'I may take a day in bed to-morrow' – the luck of one in a million.

This is just to explain my silence.

Yours
Jack

[1] George MacDonald, *Sir Gibbie* (1879), vol. I, ch. ix, p. 138.

Magdalen College,
Oxford.
Oct. 29th 1930

My dear Arthur,

Things are no better and I don't know when I shall have time to write to you properly again. I really am at it from morning till night at present, Sundays included. Thanks so much for your letter. Try to give me another as soon as may be and don't abandon me to my fate. You mustn't think that I am having a specially *nasty* time – in some ways quite a good one, in every respect except leisure. My days are filled with pupils in college and settling in in the new house at Headington: and I am enjoying both. I have made a vow not to tell you anything about our new residence, because if I do you will certainly be disappointed when you actually see it. But oh – ! I never hoped for the like[1]

About Geo. Macdonald, I am afraid we must agree to a real difference. The exciting story in Wilfrid Cumbermede seems to me a pure drag and Sir Gibbie seems to me much better because the excitement in it is of the *real* sort and not interrupted by the mere machinery of the old melodramatic 3-vol. novel. I bought two others in London, *Adela Cathcart* & *What's Mine's Mine* just before term began (By the way the bookseller told me that there was a small but steady demand for Macdonalds – wh. is interesting and encouraging) *Adela* I'm afraid I think definitely bad, tho it begins well: and *The Seaboard Parish* the same. The real holiness is, in them both, degenerating into mere flat moralising and sometimes it is hard to feel that you're reading the author of *Phantastes*.

Have you been having lovely autumn? We have. Woods all speckled with yellow, drifts of leaves at the roadside, and the most exquisite pale skies. The other morning on some gorse bushes I saw a wonderful display of cobwebs – like a thick bridal veil, unbroken, extending for many yards. The smells are delicious. I also had the experience lately of walking under an avenue of trees after a shower, and saw that

---

[1] This is 'The Kilns' in Headington Quarry which Lewis, Warren and Mrs Moore bought and moved into on 11 October, and which was to be their home for the rest of their lives. The house at that time was situated within eight acres of gardens and woodland, and beside the house were two brick-kilns from which the house took its name. See Warren's description of it in the *Biography*, ch. III.

tho all the rest was still, a kind of wave-motion was passing over the branches on one side, followed by a patter of drops. Coming nearer I found it was a squirrel leaping from branch to branch and sending a wake of tiny showers to earth as they bent under him.

Had tea the other day with the Provost of Worcester[2] who is a wonderful old man and has a huge garden which he has converted into a real country farm in the middle of Oxford. He introduced me to two alderneys – lovely creatures, as delicately made as deer: you wd. hardly believe that cows cd. be so dainty – and their sweet breath.

I have started going to morning Chapel at 8, wh. means going to bed earlier: and indeed I live such vigorous days that I am usually glad to go. My moral history of late has been deplorable. More and more clearly one sees how much of one's philosophy & religion is mere talk: the boldest hope is that concealed somewhere within it there is some seed however small of the real thing

Yrs
J.

155

'This is the only paper I can find!'

[The Kilns,
Kiln Lane,
Headington Quarry,
Oxford.]
Dec 24th 1930

My dear Arthur,

I take no blame for the long silence. In the latter half of term writing became quite impossible and then when term was over I had to waste the first fortnight of my Vac. examining – which, as you know, means work from morning till night. I am now free at last – hungry to get back to my *real* work, and ordinary life: in which I include the resumption of my correspondence with you.

By this time you should have a book which I sent you[1] (a) Because I have been asked to help the author by drawing peoples attention to it – he is a friend of mine. (b) Because he is the same man who wrote *Harvest in Poland*, that v. dubious book lent me by the sinister

---

[2] The Rev. Francis John Lys (1863–1947) took his degree from Worcester College, Oxford, in 1886, and was an assistant master at Radley College from 1887–8, and, returning to Oxford, became a Lecturer at Worcester in 1889, and then Fellow, Tutor, Senior Tutor, Bursar and Provost of Worcester, all at the same time, from 1919 to 1946.

[1] Geoffrey Dennis, *The End of the World* (1930).

The Kilns. Headington
Quarry. Ox. Dec. 24th 1930

My dear Arthur — I take no blame for the long silence. In the latter half of term writing became quite impossible and then when term was over I had to waste the first fortnight of my Vac. examining — which, as you know, means work from morning till night. I am now free at last — hungry to get back to my real work, and ordinary life: in which I include the resumption of my correspondence with you. By this time you should have a book which I sent you ⓐ because I have been asked to help the author by drawing people's attention to it — he is a friend of a friend of mine. ⓑ Because he is the same man who wrote Harvest in Poland, that v. dubious book lent me by the sinister Clevacé ⓒ Because I have myself enjoyed it and think — tho' with some doubts — that you will enjoy it too. The get-up is rather what we should once have liked than what we like now: but the picture on the wrapper is worth having for its own sake. I envy you your stay at Ballycastle: even the name gives me a faint pleasant twinge. But there is one odd thing I have been noticing since we came to our new house, which is much more in the country, and it is this. Hitherto there has always been something not so much in the landscape as in every single visual impression (say a cloud, a robbin, a a ditch) in Ireland, which I lacked in England: something for which homeliness is an inadequate word. This something I find I am now getting in England — the feeling of connectedness, of being part of it. I suppose I have been growing into the soil here much more since the move. You would be surprised how few walks I have taken. My afternoon hours of exercise have been almost wholly occupied with sawing and axing for firewood, or clearing the lines of future paths with shears, with feeding birds, and messing about in an old punt on a small lake or large pond which is a stone's throw from our house. You have tenan no idea what horrid work sawing is for the first week, and how delightful after that, when your muscles have got used to it and your hands are hardened. Almost every afternoon as I stand at my sawing block looking as I work at the sun going down beyond a line of bare pollards. Nearly always a red cannon ball sun, for we have had gloriously winter weather. I also love the sound of the saw and the flying of the sawdust. Then after sawing the log into lengths comes the splitting of each of them with an axe. It is absurd how remote all simple human activities have been from me all my life: so much so that when I heave up my axe I still always see myself as an illustration in Robinson Crusoe. There is something in country work of this sort which you can't get out of walks. Silently clipping (silent except for the noise of the clipping itself) among thick branches in the depth of winter afternoon — when the day takes on its friendl hue — I am continually watched by bright eyed robbins which come surprisingly close. More than once I have seen a pair of squirrels among the fir trees, and rabbits in our own garden: and up at the top (for our bit runs up the side of a hill) there is a burrow too big for rabbits which Foord ke'tus (the old booky carpentering parson — you remember) avers to be that of a badger. Now to meet a badger on your own land, if such chance ever befell me — would be almost the crown of one kind of earthly bliss! At night owls are very plentiful: and one thing I have noticed since the very first night I slept here, is that this house has a good night

Chevasse. (c) Because I have myself enjoyed it and think – tho' with some doubts – that you will enjoy it too. The get-up is rather what we should once have liked than what we like now: but the Dürer on the wrapper is worth having for its own sake.

I envy you your stay at Ballycastle: even the name gives me a faint pleasant twinge. But there is one odd thing I have been noticing since we came to our new house, which is much more in the country, and it is this. Hitherto there has always been something not so much in the landscape as in every single visual impression (say a cloud, a robbin, or a ditch) in Ireland, which I lacked in England: something for which homeliness is an inadequate word. This something I find I am now getting in England – the feeling of connectedness, of being part of it. I suppose I have been growing into the soil here much more since the move.

You would be surprised how few walks I have taken. My afternoon hours of exercise have been almost wholly occupied with sawing and axing for firewood, or cleaning the lines of future paths with shears, with feeding birds, and messing about in an old punt on a small lake or large pond which is a stone's throw from our house. You have no idea what horrid work sawing is for the first week, and how delightful after that when your muscles have got used to it and your hands are hardened. Almost every afternoon as I stand at my sawing block looking as I work at the sun going down beyond a line of bare pollards. Nearly always a red cannon ball sun, for we have had gloriously winter weather. I also love the sound of the saw and the flying of the sawdust. Then after sawing the log into lengths comes the splitting of each of these with an axe.

It is absurd how remote all simple human activities have been from me all my life: so much so that when I heave up my axe I still always see myself as an illustration in Robinson Crusoe. There is something in country work of this sort which you can't get out of walks. Silently clipping (silent except for the noise of the clipping itself) among thick brambles in the depth of winter afternoon – when the day takes on its *Grendel* hue – I am continually watched by bright-eyed robbins which come surprisingly close. More than once I have seen a pair of squirrels among the fir trees, and rabbits in our own garden: and up at the top (for our bit runs up the side of a hill) there is a burrow too big for rabbits which Foord-Kelsie (the old booky carpenting parson – you remember) avers to be that of a badger. Now to meet a badger on your own land, if such chance ever befell me – would be almost the crown of one kind of earthly bliss!

At night owls are very plentiful: and one thing I have noticed since the very first night I slept here, is that this house has a good night atmosphere about it: in the sense that I have never been in a place where one was *less* likely to get the creeps: a place *less* sinister. Good life must have been lived here before us. If it is haunted, it is haunted by good spirits. Perhaps such things are the result of fantasy: yet the feelings are real. Even if they signify nothing more than the state of ones organs, yet are not ones organs real, and is not their state also a fact of spiritual significance? For if anything is spiritual, everything is.

I have of course read very little apart from work. One more Macdonald 'Annals of a Quiet Neighbourhood', which went far to restore my faith in him: badly shaken by an unsuccessful attempt to read the *Seaboard Parish*. Yesterday I picked up for 4/6 *Alec Forbes* in three half leather volumes. Do you know it? One reason I enjoyed the Quiet Neighbourhood so much was that I read it immediately after Trollope's *Belton Estate*: quite a good book, but all the time one was making excuses for the author on the moral side: saying that this bit of uncharitableness and that bit of unconscious cynicism, and, throughout, the bottomless *worldliness* (not knowing itself for such) belonged to the period. Then you turned to Macdonald, also a Victorian, and after a few pages were ashamed to have spent even an hour in a world so inferior as that of Trollope's.

Have you had glorious fogs – frost-fogs? We have had some of the finest I have ever seen. In fact we have had all sorts of beauty – outside. Inside myself the situation has been quite the reverse. I seem to go steadily downhill and backwards. I am certainly further from self control and charity and light than I was last spring. Now that W. is with us[2] I don't get enough solitude: or so I say to myself in excuse, knowing all the time that what God demands is our solution of the problem set, not of some other problem which we think he ought to have set: and that what we call *hindrances* are really the raw material of spiritual life. As if the fire should call the coal a hindrance! (One can imagine a little young fire, which had been getting on nicely with the sticks and paper, regarding it as a mere cruelty when the big lumps were put on: never dreaming what a huge steady glow, how far surpassing its present crackling infancy, the Tender of the Fire designed when he stoked it)

I think the trouble with me is *lack of faith*. I have no *rational* ground for going back on the arguments that convinced me of God's existence: but the irrational deadweight of my old sceptical habits,

[2] Warren, who had been stationed at Bulford in Wiltshire since his return from China, was temporarily retired from the Army.

and the spirit of this age, and the cares of the day, steal away all my lively feeling of the truth, and often when I pray I wonder if I am not posting letters to a non-existent address. Mind you I don't *think* so – the whole of my reasonable mind is convinced: but I often *feel* so. However, there is nothing to do but to peg away. One falls so often that it hardly seems worth while picking oneself up and going through the farce of starting over again as if you could ever hope to walk. Still, this seeming absurdity is the only sensible thing I do, so I must continue it. And all the time, on the other side, the imaginative side, (the fairy angel) I get such glimpses and vanishing memories as often take my breath away: as if they said 'Look what you're losing' – as if they were there just to deprive one of all excuse.

How well I *talk* about it: how little else I do. I wonder would it be better not to speak to one another of these things at all? Is the talking a substitute for the doing?

Yrs
Jack

156

The Kilns,
Headington Quarry,
Oxford
Jan 10th 1931

My dear Arthur,

I am writing this in the principle sitting room of the new house, which we call the common room, at my Mother's desk which you remember in the drawing room at Little Lea. I wonder when last it was written at? The others are all out: I have come in from my walk – a beautiful pearl grey winter sky – and it is now half past three.

I was delighted to get your letter. Next term, which begins next week, promises to be not quite so hectic as last, so I will do my very level best to get back to our weekly interchange: but you know what my difficulties are in term time and you will not be surprised if I have to give up.

As regards my giving all the reasons but the right one for sending a book – I suppose the right one is friendship. But that can only be a reason for gifts in general: what I was explaining was my reasons for sending *this particular* book at *this particular* time. As regards the latter, I gave special reasons because I did not want it to be a Christmas present since you and I don't give them. Your complaint therefore, my dear Sir, is as if a man said 'We'd better lunch here, because it will be too late when we get to London, and they give you an excellent meal here for 2/6' and you had replied 'Ah but those are not the right reasons for eating lunch. The right reason is that the vital processes are attended by a wastage of the tissues and certain organic substances if introduced into the stomach have the power of repairing this wastage.' In other words, for any action there is usually *a*. A general reason for doing it *at all*. *b*. A particular reason for selecting to do it at such and such a time and place and in such and such a way. We usually take *a*. for granted, and explain *b*. You are the sort of man who would try to persuade a girl to marry you by reading her all the general reasons for marriage out of the prayer book ('procreation of children & prevention of sin' etc) Again, the actual presence of a W.–C. cd. never to you be a reason for emptying your bladder: for you deal only in generalities: and as the general reason for this operation (i.e. the fact that the bladder is finite in size) always holds good, you on your principles, I suppose, think it a matter of indifference where and when it is performed. But come – my pen runs away with me (I am afraid I can never resist a ludicrous piece of logic) and I shall have wasted my whole letter on foolery.

The most important thing since I last wrote is a three days walking tour wh. Warnie and I took.[1] We trained to Chepstow, breaking our journey at Gloucester for a couple of hours to see the cathedral. Got to Chepstow that evening & went out for a stroll after dinner. It was brilliant moonlight and freezing hard. Having reached a bridge over the Wye – the cliffs of the far bank shining in front of us and the little huddled town behind – we looked back and saw on our left, rising above a grassy sweep of hill, the ruins of a big castle. We came back with only a very faint hope of getting near it, when as if by magic a lane led us out of the main street into fields and up without hindrance to the great gate of the castle itself. The doors were shut, but through the chinks and under them a bright light seemed to be streaming. 'What is this?' said I. 'A witches' Sabbath' said he. We looked through the key hole and saw nothing but moonlight. The whole thing was an optical delusion: we had been in the shadow of the castle as we came up and the moonlight within, thro the cracks, had somehow looked exactly like artificial light. We then walked all round it. The space is empty for a long way from the walls – just grass and a few seats – and you can walk in the bottom of the former moat wh. is very deep. I never saw so huge a castle. The circuit is not much smaller than the town hall at home: tower after tower, and

[1] The tour began on New Year's Day, Lewis and his brother returning home on 4 January.

battlements with ivy falling over them like a cascade, and even little wild bushes growing out of crannies, and above them all the roofless gables of what must have been the great hall, not much smaller than a cathedral. Imagine all this under a cloudless moon and the grass, stiff with frost, crunching under our feet.

Next day we walked to Monmouth, passing Tintern about eleven A.M. Have you see it? It is an abbey practically intact except that the roof is gone, and the glass out of the windows, and the floor, instead of a pavement, is a trim green lawn. Anything like the *sweetness* & peace of the long shafts of sunlight falling through the windows on this grass cannot be imagined. All churches should be roofless. A holier place I never saw. We lunched at St Briavels where there is another castle: inhabited by the Aunt of a pupil of mine who is 'worreyed' by 'the ghosts', but won't 'do anything' about them because she doesn't like 'to be unkind'[2] (This is the pupils account. A *very* queer fellow indeed: it was he who put me onto the *End of the World*). That night to Monmouth, after a lovely walk: not on *roads* more than half an hour all day. Next day to Ross, and then next to Hereford. I can't describe it all. We had two days of pure winter sunlight, and one of mist: the latter luckily was spent almost entirely in woods whose delicious feeling of confusion it served only to increase.

This was W's first experience of a walking tour. I had been a little nervous as to whether he would really care for it, & whether his selfish habits wd. really accomodate themselves to the inevitable occasional difficulties. My fears however were quite unfounded. He has been with us all the month here and everyone says how greatly he is improved. He and I even went together to Church twice: and – will you believe it – he said to me in conversation that he was beginning to think the religious view of things was after all true. Mind you (like me, at first) he didn't *want* it to be, nor like it: but his intellect is beginning to revolt from the semi-scientific assumptions we all grew up in, and the other explanation of the world seems to him daily more probable. Of course I have not had and probably never shall have any *real* talks on the heart of the subject with him. But it is delightful to feel the whole lot of us gradually beginning to move in that direction. It has done me good to be with him: because while his idea of the good is much lower than mine, he is in so many ways better than I am. I keep on crawling up to the heights & slipping back to the depths: he seems to do neither. There always have been these two types.

[2] St Briavels Castle, which was built during the reign of Henry I, was inhabited at this time by the Hon. Mrs Ronald Campbell.

About [Geoffrey] Dennis: I doubt whether the kind of effects he aims at could be attained by a simpler style, tho' an effect you and I prefer probably could be. Still, one mustn't be dogmatic about simplicity. It may be our favourite style – but the pomps and sonorities are good in their different way none the less.

I have read Alec Forbes – good things in it, but not by any means a good book. The more I read his novels the more I rage at the tragedy of his being forced to write for money and thus diverted from his true sphere, so that we get only as much of the real Macdonald as he can smuggle in *by the way*. It is, I really think, a loss as irreparable as the early death of Keats.

Glad to hear you are at *Tristram Shandy*. What good company! Isn't Uncle Toby, seriously and morally, one of the loveliest characters ever created.

Must stop now. When are you coming to see me? I have no chance of visiting you till the summer at earliest.

Yours
Jack

At present reading the Autobiography of Keat's friend the painter Haydon[3] – quite good. W. has finished Lockhart's *Scott* & pronounces it excellent.

157

[The Kilns]
Jan 17, 1931

My dear Arthur,

I am much divided in my mind as to whether I should devote this after tea hour – the first free one of the day – to starting a new book or to writing you a letter. The fact that you are in my debt is strong for the first alternative: on the other hand when I hear from you during the week (as I hope I shall) I shall probably be too busy to reply. Then again I have been in a bad temper to day over trifles: and it is too much to face bedtime with the added knowledge of having neglected you as well – so here goes. Perhaps this sounds unflattering, and you may retort that you wd. rather not have a letter on these

---

[3] *The Life of Benjamin Robert Haydon from his Autobiography and Journals*, ed. Tom Taylor (1853).

terms. However, I am sure you understand how a momentary dis-inclination to begin is quite compatible with a real interest in going on.

I have read a new Macdonald since I last wrote, which I think the very best of the novels. I would put it immediately below Phantastes, Lilith, the Fairy Tales, & the Diary of an Old Soul. It is called *What's Mine's Mine*. It has very little of the bad plot interest, and quite frankly subordinates story to doctrine. But such doctrine. Some of the conversations in this book I hope to re-read many times. The scene and the characters are Highland Celtic, as opposed to the Low-land Scots of most of the novels: highly idealised. Yet somehow they convince me. Or if they don't quite convince me as real people, they differ from most ideal characters in this, that I wish they *were* real. A young chief of a decaying clan is the hero: and the chief contrast is between the clansmen and a vulgar rich Glasgow family who have come to live in the neighbourhood. These are, like most of Mac-donald's worshippers of Mammon, over-drawn. I venture to think that there was some *moral*, as well as some literary, weakness in this. I mean in characters like the baronet in *Sir Gibbie* etc. I observe that M. is constantly praying against anger

> Keep me from wrath, let it seem never so right.

I wonder did he indulge (day-dreamily) an otherwise repressed fund of indignation by putting up in his novels bogeys to whom his heroes could make the stunning retorts and deliver the stunning blows which he himself neither could nor would deliver in real life. I am certain that this is morally as well as artistically dangerous and I'll tell you why. The *pleasure* of anger – the gnawing attraction which makes one return again and again to its theme – lies, I believe, in the fact that one feels entirely righteous oneself only when one is angry. *Then* the other person is pure black, and you are pure white. But in real life sanity always returns to break the dream. In fiction you can put absolutely *all* the right, with no snags or reservations, on the side of the hero (with whom you identify yourself) and all the wrong on the side of the villain. You thus revel in unearned self-righteousness, which wd. be vicious even if it were earned.

Haven't you noticed how people with a fixed hatred, say, of Ger-mans or Bolshevists, *resent* anything wh. is pleaded in extenuation, however small, of their supposed crimes. The enemy must be un-redeemed black. While all the time one *does* nothing and enjoys the feeling of perfect superiority over the faults one is never tempted to commit:

> 'Compound for sins we *are* inclined to
> By damning those we have no mind to.'[1]

I suppose that when one hears a tale of hideous cruelty anger is quite the wrong reaction, and merely wastes the energy that ought to go in a different direction: perhaps merely dulls the conscience wh., if it were awake, would ask us 'Well? What are you *doing* about it? How much of your life have you spent in really combatting this? In helping to produce social conditions in which these sort of things will not occur!?

Term began yesterday. Yesterday afternoon & evening and this morning I spent in correcting papers: not only a hard but a depressing job, for ones pupils always seem to do worse than you expect. That, by the way, is the angle from which to understand (instead of being self-righteous about) the cruelty of schoolmasters. One can't gauge the temptation to cruelty for a man who is trying to keep his wife and family on the profits of a decaying private school, and who sees the boys getting fewer & fewer scholarships each year and can never, even if honest, be quite sure that it is not the boys fault. 'God help everyone' as you say.

The night before last (my last night of Vac) we had the most glorious storm: trees plunging like terrified but tethered horses, leaves eddying, chimneys howling, and under all the lesser and lighter noises a great solid roar above the house. I lay in bed and revelled in it – tho' it is partly spoiled for me by the fact that Minto hates it and hears in it only a sound of death and desolation. Odd, what different notes we different souls draw from the organ of nature. Some people hate the cry of an owl at night: I love it.

Oh, by the bye, our new maid says she has been kept awake at night this week by the squirrels! Asked what kind of noise they make she replied 'I don't know' – wh. I think is her way of saying 'I can't describe it.' But what a lovely idea. And what a lovely sentence for the Witch of Endor – 'Please, Mr Lewis, the squirrels – '

You say Reid is reading his new book[2] to 'some of us'. Who are the others? Give him my kind regards.

I find this cold weather desperately trying to the bladder.

Yrs

Jack

---

[1] Samuel Butler, *Hudibras* (1663–78), Pt. I, Canto I, 1. 213.
[2] Probably Forrest Reid's *Uncle Stephen* which was published in October 1931.

158

My dear Arthur,

This will probably be a short, and certainly a dull letter, for I am tired. Minto has been in bed all week with flu' which means a good deal of bustle and extra work: I am recovering from a baddish cold myself: and have had a pretty tough week. I was glad to get your letter.

I haven't read Jeans' book[1] and it is unlikely I will – there are so many things I want to read more. One of the blessings of your life is that you ought to be able to read fairly well nearly everything that interests you. As a matter of fact – apart from time – I am not now greatly attracted to that kind of book: though you will remember that astronomy, fed on H. G. Wells' romances, was almost my earliest love. I don't know why it has not lasted, nor why it now interests me much less than I should expect. Partly I think, because one knows that all the really interesting things about other planets and systems can't be found out: partly, too, I suspect that philosophy and religion (in a person of my limited range) rather take the shine out of curiosity about the material universe. It seems like having new bits of a curtain described to one, when one is all agog for hints of what lies behind the curtain. Now that I come to think of it, it is not quite true to say that I don't feel any interest in these things now: rather they rouse a very intense, impatient interest for a very short time, which quite suddenly leaves one at once sated & dissatisfied. Mind I am not *recomending* this state of mind – only recording it.

I liked very much your account of the party who meet to hear Reid's novel. It reminded me of Tristram Shandy – just such an ideally inappropriate conjunction of minds as he delights to bring together. Don't you think the great beauty of that book is its picture of affection existing across unbridgeable gulfs of intellect? My Father & Uncle Toby never understand one another at all, and always love one another. It is the true picture of home life: far better than the modern nonsense in wh. affection (friendship is a different thing) is made to depend on mental affinities.

I am almost shocked to find from more than one passage that Geo. Macdonald hated Sterne. The coarseness apparently revolted him: but I cannot understand how he was not attracted by the over-

[1] Sir James Jeans, *The Mysterious Universe* (1930).

flowing goodness at the heart of the book. One must remember that the wayward Highland temperament, with its reserve and delicacy, may find coarseness a greater trial than our rougher Saxon grain.

I had a lovely ten minutes the afternoon before last in a wood of fir trees in the snow. The wood comes down to within a few yards of the top of a small cliff, from which direction the snow was coming. Just as the flakes got near this edge, some current of air caught them and whirled them upwards so that in the wood they were flying skywards as if the earth was snowing. I am often in this bit of wood, and have seen a great many fine winter sunsets – very pale, you know – through (first) the tall straight firs and then some twisted beechtrees which form the border of the wood. I have also had some fine hours of storm in it when all the trees were groaning and swaying.

I hope you won't be disappointed by What's Mine's Mine. Of course it has not the fantastic charm of Phantastes: nor the plot excitement of Wilfrid Cumbermede. It is just the spiritual quality with some beautiful landscape – nothing more.

I wonder how your tea with the McNeils went off. Give them my love when next you meet.

The O.U.D.S.[2] are doing *Hassan*[3] this term and I think I shall go to it. I can't remember whether we have talked of this play or not, but I imagine you know it. However badly the O.U.D.S. do it, at least they will not turn it into a Chu Chin Chow as (I am told) the London actors did. Which reminds me of Kismet (one of my early thrills) which reminds me of lying on the beech at Donaghadee reading to each other out of the Arabian Nights.

Do or die for it – I *must* manage to get over to Ireland in the summer and revisit some of the old haunts with you. Once more to spend one of our delightful banjo evenings with Jimmy Thompson – to have another of our old rousing evenings at the Hippodrome – once more to dance the Black Bottom at midnight with Sir Robert Ewart & the Witch of Endor – whether-her-mother-will-let-her-or-no – I'm too tired for anything but foolery. Bryson is to marry the Princess Elizabeth: poor chap, it is a pity he was castrated by the Vice Chancellor and Proctors last week for riding a bicycle in St Mary's. I suppose you have heard about Warnie's peerage – for gallantry during the recent manoeuvres. I have grown a beard – Good night

Yrs
Jack

[2] Oxford University Dramatic Society.
[3] James Elroy Flecker, *Hassan* (1922).

P.S. In that fir wood I suddenly got a terrific return the other day of my earliest Wagner mood – the purely Nibelung, Mime, mood before the Valkyries rose on my horizon. You know – very earthy, and smith-y, and Teutonic. How *inexhaustible* these things are. You think you have done with a thing and – whoop! – it's all back again, strong as ever.

159

[The Kilns]
Feb 23rd 1931

My dear Arthur,

I was glad to hear from you again, despite the fact that your letter, specially towards the end, appears to have been written in a state of intoxication.

I was almost relieved to hear that you shared my views of *What's Mine's Mine*. Yes, you are right in saying that it is good not despite, but because of, its preaching – or rather (preaching is a bad word) its spiritual knowledge. So many cleverer writers strike one as quite *childish* after Macdonald: they seem not even to have begun to understand so many things.

On Saturday I went to the matinee of Flecker's *Hassan* done by the O.U.D.S. I can't remember whether you saw it in London, but I suppose you read it. It was not very well done, but well enough for me: indeed to see it really well acted would be too much for me. In reading it the cruelty is just about balanced by the extreme beauty of the lyrics and much of the dialogue, so that the total effect, tho' sinister, like a too-bright dream which is sure to turn into nightmare before the end, yet is bearable. On the stage, where one has less time to dwell on the cadence or suggestion of the individual words, the cruelty is unendurable. Warnie went out half way through. I felt quite sick but thought it almost a duty ⟨for one afflicted in my way to remain, saying to myself 'Oh you like cruelty do you? Well now stew in it!'⟩ – the same principle on which one trains a puppy to be clean – 'rub their noses in it'. It has haunted me ever since.

On its merits as a work of art I am very undecided. The intense effect which it produces is not, in itself, proof of greatness, for it is easy to produce an effect by the suggestion of physical pain: and such an effect, reaching the spectator through his nerves rather than his imagination, is perhaps as much outside art in one direction, as pornography is in another. On the other hand, the whole of the ending seems to me amost great. You remember how Ishak finds Hassan fainting after being compelled to witness the torture of the lovers, and how, when Hassan begins to stammer out some of the horrible details, Ishak says 'You are still full of devils. Wake up! STOP DREAMING!!' – and that, flashing ones mind back to what Pervaneh says in the Diwan scene about this world's being an illusion, and leading straight on to the caravan for Samarkand – the broad moonlit desert stretching away and swallowing up the nightmare city in its clean solitude – all that does give one the true tragic feeling of having been brought, thro horrors, right out of the ordinary illusion of life into some higher world. Another thing that is good is the scene in which all the adventures begin – where they are taken up in the basket into the house with no doors whence they heard the sounds of dancing. This is the only place which strikes the note of the real Arabian nights – the midnight possibilities of an Eastern city full of magicians. It is a pity he didn't work it out on those lines. As it stands it is too morbid: and one sees Flecker in places not feeling it as tragic at all but licking his lips (you remember his horrible face – it is the frontispiece of the *Poems*)[1] and gloating. Still, his powers were extraordinary and one is sorry that he didn't live to grow out of consumption and Parnassianism and decadence: he would have been a great writer in the end I believe.

As a contrast to my nightmare afternoon at the theatre I spent most of Sunday with W. and Dorothea Vaughan[2] (did you meet her?) digging holes for planting trees for what W. calls 'the Kilns Afforestation Scheme'. A lovely afternoon of early spring sunlight – the distance very pale blue, primroses out, and birds trilling and chuckling in abundance. All the better for the contrast with Hassan.

Did I tell you I was reading Ruskin's *Praeterita*[3] i.e. his autobiography? Contains an account of his boyhood which wd. particularly interest you, R's mother having had a great deal in common with your father. The good thing about it is that while not disguising the narrowness & pride at all, the final impression he leaves with you is one of peace & homeliness: the dateless, timeless peace of childhood in a really regular household. Later on there is some of the best description of travel wh. I have ever read.

I had had a baddish cold but am otherwise well. Any sign of the

[1] James Elroy Flecker, *Forty-Two Poems* (1911).

[2] Dorothea Vaughan, who had been a day pupil at Headington School with Maureen, was a frequent visitor at Hillsboro and the Kilns.

[3] John Ruskin, *Praeterita*, 28 parts (1885–9).

new people moving into Little Lea? How strange it will be to you. Try to reply in less time than last!

Yours
Jack
I was just going to put
C. S. Lewis again

160

The Kilns,
Kiln Road,
Headington Quarry,
Headington, Oxford
Sunday, March 29th 1931

My dear Arthur,

I am afraid I am badly behind hand with this letter. I am afraid I cannot honestly plead that I have been too busy to write. The trouble is rather that when once the end of term has set me free from my compulsory work, I am so hungry for my real, private work,[1] that I grudge every moment from my books. This is a bad, selfish reason for not writing and I only give it because it happens to be true.

By the bye – I spoke some time ago about coming to visit you for a week in the summer, and you suggested fixing a date. If you still want to have me, how would the second or third week in August do? I should like it because I shall have finished my examining then wh. usually leaves me rather knocked up, and a holiday with you would be just the right tonic. Let me know how it would suit you. If this won't do, I should then – as a second choice – take my week with you as a *preparation* for examining instead of a cure, and come about the second week of July. But of course it is nicer to take the medicine first and the sweet after, than vice-versa. I try not to spoil this visit by thinking too much about it, but every now and then it comes over me with a delicious whiff of anticipation.

The most interesting thing that has happened to me since I last wrote is reading *War and Peace*[2] – at least I am now in the middle of the 4th and last volume so I think, bar accidents, I am pretty sure to finish it. It has completely changed my view of novels.

Hitherto I had always looked on them as rather a *dangerous* form –

[1] He means *The Allegory of Love: A Study in Medieval Tradition* (1936), which he had been at work on since 1928.
[2] Leo Tolstoy, *War and Peace* (1865–72).

I mean dangerous to the health of literature as a whole. I thought that the strong 'narrative lust' – the passionate itch to 'see what happened in the end' – which novels aroused, necessarily injured the taste for other, better, but less irresistible, forms of literary pleasure: and that the growth of novel reading largely explained the deplorable division of readers into low-brow and high-brow – the low being simply those who had learned to expect from books this 'narrative lust', from the time they began to read, and who had thus destroyed in advance their possible taste for better things. I also thought that the intense desire which novels rouse in us for the 'happiness' of the chief characters (no one feels that way about Hamlet or Othello) and the selfishness with which this happiness is concerned, were thoroughly bad (I mean, if the hero and heroine marry, that is felt to be a happy ending, tho every one else in the story is left miserable: if they don't that is an unhappy ending, tho it may mean a much greater good in some other way). Of course I knew there were tragic novels like Hardy's – but somehow they were quite on a different plane from real tragedies.

Tolstoy, in this book, has changed all that. I have felt everywhere – in a sense – you will know what I mean – that sublime *indifference* to the life or death, success or failure, of the chief characters, which is not a *blank* indifference at all, but almost like submission to the will of God. Then the variety of it. The war parts are just the best descriptions of war ever written: all the modern war books are milk and water to this: then the rural parts – lovely pictures of village life and of religious festivals in wh. the relations between the peasants and the nobles almost make you forgive feudalism: the society parts, in which I was astonished to find so much humour – there is a great hostess who always separates two guests when she sees them getting really interested in conversation, who is almost a Jane Austen character. There are love-passages that have the same sort of intoxicating quality you get in Meredith: and passages about soldiers chatting over fires which remind one of Patsy Macan: and a drive in a sledge by moonlight which is better than Hans Andersen. And behind all these, and uniting them, is the profound, religious conception of life and history wh. is beyond J. Stephens and Andersen, and beside which Meredith's worldly wisdom – well just *stinks*, there's no other word.

I go on writing all this because my pen runs away with me: meanwhile perhaps you have read the book long ago and even advised *me* to read it! If you have not, I strongly advise you to try it. Its length,

which deters some people, will not frighten you: you will only
rejoice, when the right time comes, – say after tea some day next
autumn when fires are still a novelty – at that old, delicious feeling of
embarkation on a long voyage, which one seldom gets now. For it takes
a book nearly as long as *War and Peace* to *seem* as long now as a Scott
did in boyhood.

And talking of boyhood – I recently re-read (being out-of-sorts)
both *She* and the sequel *Ayesha*,[3] and found the story good in both:
what troubles one is the v. silly talk put into She's mouth, which is
meant to be profound. You feel that she has made very ill use of her
opportunities. In re-reading them I re-visited one of the very few
parts of my past which is not associated with you – tho' if I remember
rightly we once discussed together the pictures in my editn. of
Ayesha.

About Flecker's face – I don't think it is just sensuality that's the
trouble. There is a sort of slyness and knowingness, tipping-the-
wink-ness with it. Some sensuality one pities: other kinds one admires
– full, Pagan magnificence. But there is a kind at once furtive and
self-satisfied, at once secret and defiant that seems peculiar to very
highly educated people in very big cities, which makes me shudder.
You know – the atmosphere of the whispered confidence and the leer
– one eye always watching to see how you take it and the whole face
ready, at a moment's notice, *either* to take you into full conspiratorial confidence (if the man sees you like it) *or else* to turn up his
nose and sneer at you (if you don't). In Barfield's long poem it is well
described: the man who tells stories

> Purring with female, strutting in the puddle
> Of his great naughtiness.

We had a fine burst of spring last week and I have sat and worked
in the garden: one morning I saw a rabbit come out and wash its face
not fifteen yards away from me. To-day I was only just warm enough
while sawing wood in the shed in a gale that sent the sawdust whirling
round me and covered Mr Papworth like snow.

You wd. have been so amused if you'd been here last week end.
Mrs Armitage is a sort of blend of Kelsie and Tchanie and often
comes to call. I had had a pupil to tea and took him out for a walk
after. Coming back at 7 I found Mrs A. *still there*, seated on the same
sofa with Warnie, and conducting a feverish conversation with him

[3] Sir Henry Rider Haggard, *She* (1887); *Ayesha, or the Return of She*
(1905).

about married life, women, and kindred subjects, and under the impression (she is a widow) that she was making great headway. I wish she cd. have seen W., a few minutes later when she had left (for of course my return broke up the party), coming out of the front door into the twilit garden, drawing his hand across his brow, and remarking with great solemnity 'I'm going down to "the Checkers" to have a LARGE whisky and soda.'

Perhaps this doesn't sound funny as I tell it: at the time it reminded me so of the lady and the man (both of whose names I've forgotten) in your '*Trees*'. Let me hear soon. How delightful our old hills will be in a week or two now.

Yrs
Jack

161

The Kilns,
Kiln Rd.,
Headington Quarry,
Oxford.
[April 1931]

My dear Arthur,

No time for a proper letter. Minto is laid up with pleurisy. She is past the worst and I hope all is now on the right path: but tho' our anxiety is less, of course we are still very busy and tired. I had hoped to be giving you an account of my usual spring walking tour, but of course that's off.

I don't think I shall be able to come for more than a week in the summer – and in a way, wouldn't it be rather a waste to spend any time of our precious holiday except in the old haunts? You can hardly imagine how I pine for our wood, and our new wood, and the shepherds hut, and Divis. I can hardly look forward to it without dancing.

I don't think Barton[1] is insincere – at any rate as far as you are concerned. Maureen met him last summer while staying with her uncle[2] in Cavan and said 'He seemed to think a great deal of Arthur.' The worst of a Parson's life is that the duty of being pleasant to

[1] Arthur William Barton, who was Rector of St Mark's, Dundela from 1914 to 1925, was consecrated Bishop of Kilmore, Elphin and Ardagh in 1930.

[2] Mrs Moore's brother, the Very Rev. William James Askins (1879-1955), was Dean of Kilmore Cathedral.

people is bound to give a certain taint of insincerity to the *manner*.

I see this is too late for your address.[3] If they don't forward it, let me know at once.

Yrs
Jack

P.S. I *do* hope you will come and see us on your way back. I'm dying to show you some of my new haunts.

162

The Kilns,
Kiln Rd.,
Headington Quarry,
Oxford.
May 18th (Monday) [1931]

My dear A,

Come on the day you suggest rather than not coming at all – a thousand times rather, but this week is a bad one. I am staying out here recovering from flu: therefore I can't have you in College. We are threatened with two week end visitors: therefore I can't have you here. So there is hardly any week when I should miss so much of your society – specially those odd evening hours which are good for talking. What I should like would be for you to come on *Monday* next – if you can amuse yourself in London till then. In that case we could be in college together.

I shall not book the room without hearing from you again.

I am longing to see you. Reply at once.

Yours
Jack

P.S. Yes I have read Wm. Law[1] – a v. severe but wholesome draught! It may save *trouble* if you bring a dinner jacket, but not absolutely essential. (But a razor and clean handkerchief you *must* bring)

---

[3] Arthur had just left for a holiday in London.
[1] He refers to William Law's *A Serious Call to a Devout and Holy Life* (1728).

163

The Kilns,
Kiln Rd.,
Headington Quarry,
Oxford.
Wednesday. [20 May 1931]

My dear Arthur,

I have just got your letter and am rather disappointed. Do you mean that you may possibly not come *at all*? I should be very sorry if that were so. At the same time I am acutely conscious that I have not much to offer in my busy life and chaotic days to such a lover of tranquility as you: and I certainly don't wish to press a visit on you as a duty. All the same – (I don't think this is making a duty of it) I would remind you that there is a good case for coming to see me even at the cost of some discomfort; because it is important to the continuance of a friendship that each should have some experience of the other's life. I have always specially prized those few pleasant walks we had last time you were here, on that ground. Our sitting in the little thicket by that stream is an important addition to our stock of memories shared. And now that I am in quite new surroundings I shall never feel at ease till you have shared them with me. How can I write to you about places you have never seen?

As to your doubt whether you can stay in London till Monday – I quite realise that it is a bore to you just to mark time there for my convenience, when your mind is beginning to turn pleasantly towards books and home. You will admit that I (on whom your letter fell without warning very late in the day) could hardly have made plans to avoid this. And then, is there not perhaps a special reasonableness in asking *you* to do this? I mean being one of the very, very few who can live without a profession and having therefore so few demands on your time, ought you not to yield the more readily to such rare demands as do turn up?

As to staying in College, I take it the real objection is the early rising. I can offer you breakfast at 8.45; not later, for I have a pupil at 9 most mornings. But you will remember that last time, after trying it, you became a complete convert and swore always to be an early bird in future – so little terrible did it prove in actual practice. Of course you must please yourself: but I feel v. strongly that to spend our evenings hanging about in public rooms or in a bedroom at a hotel will be, as it always has been, a miserable makeshift. Surely last time was much the most successful time we've had? Surely our snug evenings together (you can go to bed as early as you like) are worth having. The other arrangement is not only inconvenient, but (I find) rather depressing. Conversation does not flow in those conditions, and neither of us is himself.

Well, I have trotted out all my arguments. I wish I could believe they wd. all seem as strong to you as to me: but, as I say, I haven't much to offer. I can only moralise and plead the claims of friendship: but perhaps these will weigh as heavily with you as the more solid claims of comfort and convenience wd. weigh with a more selfish man. I await your reply eagerly

Yrs
Jack

164

[Swiss Cottage,
16 Buckland Crescent,
London.]
26th(?) June 1931

My dear Arthur,

My conscience accuses me of laziness. I have done *nothing* since term ended but sit in deck chairs in the shade, bathe twice a day in the pond, and talk. A little pottering about with Donne and Beowulf which I have done hardly deserves the name of work. The truth is that I am not only lazy but tired. I still can't walk a mile without aching legs. Whether I can write a page without aching hand is an experiment now to be tried. I am writing this in London where I am spending a day or two with Barfield – splendid talks and reading of Dante, but of course our nights tend to be late so that perhaps it is not a very judicious kind of holiday. However, it is short.

During this spell of hot weather the Kilns has been delightful. I know the pond looks dirty, but as a matter of fact one comes out perfectly clean. I wish you could join me as I board the punt in the before-breakfast solitude and push out from under the dark shadow of the trees onto the full glare of the open water, usually sending the moor hens and their chicks scudding away into the reeds, half flying and half swimming, with a delicious flurry of silver drops. Then I tie up to the projecting stump in the middle and dive off the stern of the punt. There is one thing in which fresh water bathing surpasses the sea – the beauty of broken ground and trees and flowers seen from an unfamiliar angle as you swim.

Thanks for your account of the fox. I don't see why a fox shouldn't be as happy as a dog in captivity if he is properly treated – but I certainly shudder for one whose owners contemplate such drastic dental treatment!

No – I didn't feel the earthquake and am rather sorry to have missed what must have been (and what we hope will *remain*) so rare a sensation.

You cannot have enjoyed your time in Oxford more than I did – it seemed to me quite one of the best times we have ever had together. Our stroll on the roof, our window seat at the bonfire, our good long talks on one or two evenings, are still in my mind – though of course memory has not yet done its real work in transfiguring them.

It is a long time since I read Peacock: I remember him as having something of the whimsical charm of Lewis Carroll's minor works, and have always meant to go back to him.

Warton's *History of Poetry*[1] marks the beginning of our modern interest in mediaeval literature. Being pioneer work, it is quite unreliable and some of the theories he develops are grotesque: but what it lacks in accuracy it amply makes up in enthusiasm. He is discovering all the charm of the old writers for the first time, and infects you with his feeling, and sends you back to the feelings you had yourself as a boy. In fact, though not a great authority, it is a great book: and its very plentiful quotations will supply you with thousands of lines of old poetry which you will probably never meet elsewhere. If it is a nice edition it would make a really sound purchase for your library: and, besides being a great, it is an eminently 'dippable' book.

I am reading Inge's 'Personal Religion and the Life of Devotion' (Longmans) – one of the best books of the kind I have yet struck.

I am at Hampstead which gives me quite a new idea of the suburbs of London. There is a little quiet court of Georgian houses here which might come out of any beautiful English country town – besides immense views from the Heath. Distant '*town*scapes' have a peculiar *dreamy* beauty of their own which makes one feel it ungrateful to blame them for not being landscapes.

Forgive me for a short letter – even this much has been done with some effort. I hope I shall wake up properly in a week or so.

Yours
Jack

---

[1] Thomas Warton, *The History of English Poetry from the Eleventh to the Eighteenth Century*, 3 vols. (1774–81).

165

The Kilns,
Headington Quarry,
Oxford.
26th [July 1931]

My dear Arthur,

I am in the midst of the annual examining. I propose to cross to Ireland on Saturday night August the 8th and stay with you till Saturday morning August 15th when I will join W. for breakfast on the Liverpool boat. If I can possibly get away from Cambridge on the Friday I will do so, but it is not likely. If any of these arrangements don't suit please let me have a line *at once*. I am looking forward to it almost *unbearably*!

Yours
Jack

P.S. In the event of a hitch about W's times can I come the following week instead? i.e. *from* the 15th.

166

[The Kilns
30? July 1931]

My dear Arthur,

Why do you do (or rather leave undone) these things? Owing to a variety of circumstances I now choose the *second* of the two periods you offer in your wire – i.e. from the 18th. That will be Tuesday and I shall come to you in the evening at about 9. The advantage of the second period is that I can give you a full week (Perhaps this may not seem advantageous to you?)

I shall turn up (D.V) on that evening unless I hear to the contrary – unless you'd like to come in and fetch me from the Liverpool boat where I shall be seeing W. off.

Yours
Jack

167

Queen's College,
Cambridge.
Aug 6th [1931]

My dear Arthur,

I have your letter of the second August. I don't quite understand, as in my wire I said the 2nd period – 19th–26th was preferred (or didn't I?) At any rate I now intend to come to Bernagh on the evening of the 20th (Thursday) and stay till the 27 (following Thursday). If you cared to come in and meet me at the Liverpool boat (where I shall be seeing W. off) at about 8 and bring me out, that would be admirable. Have you and I ever brought off a scheme without these intense complications. However I have some excuse. I now *shall* arrive on the 20th *whatever* you say, so there's no good trying to prevent me!

I am here examining but having quite a good time – a lot of nice people, and I think this College the most beautiful in either University

Yours
C.S.L.

168

Golf Hotel,
Castlerock,
Co. Derry.[1]
Aug. 19th [1931]

My dear Arthur,

Thanks for letter. W. says he would love to come and dine on Thursday night. We want, for sentimental reasons, to make the railway journey from town to Sydenham, so if you wd. meet us at Sydenham that would be capital. As I don't know the exact times of the rail motors I will ring you up from the Co. Down Ry. station at about 6.45 to 7. Isn't this going to be great! I still feel a great fear of something happening to prevent it: perhaps the world will end before to-morrow night!

Yours
Jack

[1] i.e. Co. Londonderry, where Lewis and his brother spent a few days before travelling to Sydenham (a suburb of Belfast) where they were met by Greeves on 20 August.

169

[The Kilns]
Sept 5th 1931

My dear Arthur,

How long ago it seems since I left you. I had a delightful evening, though tinged with melancholy, on the Liverpool boat, watching first the gantries and then the Down coast slipping past and picking out, more by imagination than sight, our favourite woods. I did not go to bed till we were off the Copelands. I felt and still feel that I was returning from one of the very best holidays I have ever had. Please thank your Mother (who was in one sense my hostess) and tell her how I enjoyed myself. I probably enjoyed the time more than you did, for the hills cannot have quite the same feeling for you who have never left them. What sticks in my mind most of all is the walk on which we visited Mrs McNeil. We were both in exactly the right mood. In another kind I have very fine memories of Croob and our session on top of it: as also of our homely and familiar evenings.

Meanwhile, as tangible mementoes of your almost excessive hospitality I have Hooker[1] and Taylor.[2] I did not thank you nearly enough for them at the time. The Taylor has been to the binders and returned very neatly mended yesterday. I started him after church this morning. He is severe and has little of the joyous side of religion in him: and some of his incentives (e.g. where he reminds you that there will be different degrees of glory in Heaven and would have you aim at getting as high a degree as possible) seem to me unspiritual or at least highly dangerous. But his painstaking, practical attitude has the charm of an old family doctor: beautifully homely and sincere. I have dipped into Hooker again and re-read some of my favourite passages.

On Thursday W. motored me over to Bulford (his station) on Salisbury plain, where he wanted to get some of his things, and we visited the village of Boscombe where Hooker was vicar and saw (from without) the parsonage in which he wrote most of his book. The church is the smallest one I have ever been in and contains some of the old square pews. It is very primitive and lit by oil lamps and

[1] Richard Hooker (1554?–1600), the famous Anglican theologian and apologist of the Elizabethan Settlement of 1559 whose doctrines are developed in his *Treatise on the Laws of Ecclesiastical Polity* (1594–1662).

[2] Jeremy Taylor (1613–67), an Anglican bishop and writer, best known for his *Rule and Exercise of Holy Living* (1650) and *Rule and Exercise of Holy Dying* (1651), which works Greeves gave his friend in one volume.

candles. It has not much real architectural beauty, but being honestly and unaffectedly built and now having the charm of antiquity it is very pleasant. I love these little old parish churches more and more: even the stuffiness delights me, and a sort of cosiness and friendliness in which the dead under their brasses seem to share. It all speaks of a life in which everyone knew every one else, and of real neighbourliness. What a nice word neighbour is – don't you like 'Well, neighbour So-and-So' in Bunyan. I forget whether you know Salisbury plain or not? I love it – all chalky downs and little beech woods and fir woods: a most excellent air.

As for reading – in the train I bought and read Yeats-Brown's 'Bengal Lancer'.[3] Unless you remember the reviews of it (which were what made me buy it) you will wonder at my opening a book with such a title. It is the autobiography of a man who began as an ordinary Cavalry officer in the Indian army and ended up by becoming a Yogi – a mystic on the Hindu pattern. A strange story and in its latter stages told with real beauty. One can't help feeling that if he had been more educated be could have found what he wanted in traditions more hereditary to him than that of the Yogis – but judge not.

I have also been studying the Winters Tale. You remember the last scene – where Hermione is introduced as a statue and then comes to life.[4] Hitherto I had thought it rather silly: this time, seeing that the absurdity of the plot doesn't matter, and is merely the scaffolding whereby Shakespeare (probably unconsciously) is able to give us an image of the whole idea of resurrection, I was simply overwhelmed. You will say that I am here doing to Shakespeare just what I did to Macdonald over Wilfrid Cumbermede. Perhaps I am. I must confess that more and more the value of plays and novels becomes for me dependent on the moments when, by whatever artifice, they succeed in expressing the great *myths*.

This afternoon W. and I have been at work in the wood clipping the undergrowth, he with shears and I with a sickle. I hope you can see the whole scene – the light slanting through the fir trees, the long elder branches swaying and then swooping down with a rustle of leaves, the click-click of the shears, and the heavy odour of crushed vegetation. *What* pleasures there are in the world. I seem to have more than anyone could deserve – a fortnight ago with you on our own hills, and now woodcutting on a fine autumn day in this delightful place.

[3] Francis Yeats-Brown, *Bengal Lancer* (1930).
[4] *The Winter's Tale*, Act V, Scene iii.

Minto is well and sends her love. I met Baxter, the professor of English at Belfast,[5] last night. The only common acquaintance we discovered was – Dr Leslie!![6]

Yours
Jack

170

[The Kilns]
Sept 22nd /31

My dear Arthur,

Thanks for your letter of the 11th. I couldn't write to you last Sunday because I had a week end guest – a man called Dyson who teaches English at Reading University. I meet him I suppose about four or five times a year and am beginning to regard him as one of my friends of the 2nd class – i.e. not in the same rank as yourself or Barfield, but on a level with Tolkien or Macfarlane.

He stayed the night with me in College – I sleeping in in order to be able to talk far into the night as one cd. hardly do out here. Tolkien came too, and did not leave till 3 in the morning: and after seeing him out by the little postern on Magdalen bridge Dyson and I found still more to say to one another, strolling up and down the cloister of New Building, so that we did not get to bed till 4. It was really a memorable talk. We began (in Addison's walk just after dinner) on metaphor and myth – interrupted by a rush of wind which came so suddenly on the still, warm evening and sent so many leaves pattering down that we thought it was raining. We all held our breath, the other two appreciating the ecstasy of such a thing almost as you would. We continued (in my room) on Christianity: a good long satisfying talk in which I learned a lot: then discussed the difference between love and friendship – than finally drifted back to poetry and books.[1]

On Sunday he came out here for lunch and Maureen and Minto and I (and Tykes) all motored him to Reading – a very delightful

[5] Frederick William Baxter (1897–   ) was Professor of English Literature in the Queen's University of Belfast from 1930 to 1949, and Professor of English Language and Literature in that same university from 1949 to 1958.

[6] Richard Whytock Leslie (1862–1931) was the Lewis family doctor. In addition to his private practice he held a number of medical appointments, one of which was Physician to Campbell College. There is a short biography of him by Warren Lewis in *Lewis Papers*, vol. III, pp. 309–10.

[1] Further details of this 'memorable talk' with Hugo Dyson and J. R. R. Tolkien on 19 September are found in the next two letters.

drive with some lovely villages, and the autumn colours are here now.

I am so glad you have really enjoyed a Morris again. I had the same feeling about it as you, in a way, with this proviso – that I don't think Morris was conscious of the meaning either here or in any of his works, except *Love is Enough* where the flame actually breaks through the smoke so to speak. I feel more and more that Morris has taught me things he did not understand himself. These hauntingly beautiful lands which somehow never satisfy, – this passion to escape from death *plus* the certainty that life owes all its charm to mortality – these push you on to the real thing because they fill you with desire and yet prove absolutely clearly that in Morris's world that desire cannot be satisfied.

The Macdonald conception of death – or, to speak more correctly, St Paul's – is really the answer to Morris: but I don't think I should have understood it without going through Morris. He is an unwilling witness to the truth. He shows you *just how far* you can go without knowing God, and that is far enough to force you (tho' not poor Morris himself) to go further. If ever you feel inclined to relapse into the mundane point of view – to feel that your book and pipe and chair are enough for happiness – it only needs a page or two of Morris to sting you wide awake into uncontrollable longing and to make you feel that everything is worthless except the hope of finding one of his countries. But if you read any of his romances through you will find the country dull before the end. All he has done is to rouse the desire: but so strongly that you *must* find the real satisfaction. And then you realise that *death* is at the root of the whole matter, and why he chose the subject of the Earthly Paradise, and how the true solution is one he never saw.

I have finished the Taylor, and enjoyed it much from the purely literary point of view. As a religious writer I put him low and still think as I did when I last wrote.

I have been studying Hamlet very intensively, and never enjoyed it more. I have been reading all the innumerable theories about him, and don't despise that sort of thing in the least: but each time I turn back to the play itself I am more delighted than ever with the mere atmosphere of it – an atmosphere hard to describe and made up equally of the prevalent sense of death, solitude, & horror and of the extraordinary graciousness and lovableness of H. himself. Have you read it at all lately? If not, do: and just surrender yourself to the magic, regarding it as a poem or a romance.

I don't *think* I left any pyjamas at Bernagh, but I'm afraid I want you to send me something else. W. is editing (i.e. arranging and typing) all the letters we brought from home (*don't* mention this to any one) so as to give a continuous history of the family.[2] We have just got to 1915 and it is maddening to have all my Bookham letters to my father (wh. tell nothing) and to know that all my Bookham letters to you are eating their heads off at Bernagh. Also, once I had them in type, I could renew those glorious years whenever I read them. Would it be a great bother to you to let me have the lot. If you want, you can have them back when they have been edited: and I promise faithfully that he will see nothing wh. gives you away in any respect, for I will go through them all first by myself.[3] If you wd. let me have them *as soon as possible* and tell me what I owe you for registered postage, I shd. be very much obliged.

It is perfect autumn here – splashes of yellow on every other tree and delicious smells. We have been up in the wood clipping all afternoon.

I think I know the walk at the back of Stormont and may have done it oftener than you. This is a bad business about the rum. Give my love to your Mother. Tell Forrest I ask every one I meet about the human tendency to represent oneself as a daring sinner (untruly) and have met no one yet who doesn't regard it as being too obvious to be worth talking about

Yrs
Jack

171

[The Kilns]
Oct. 1st /31

My dear Arthur,

Very many thanks for the letter and enclosure that arrived this morning. Now, as to their return. I confess that I had not supposed you often read them, and had in view merely an *ultimate* return when W. had finished his editing, that is, in about 4 years' time.[1] If however you want them at once, they are of course your property and will be returned by registered post whenever you wish. I shall follow absolutely your directions. In the meantime you can feel quite confident about their safe keeping. I have spent this morning on them

---

[2] What was later to become the *Lewis Papers: Memoirs of the Lewis Family 1850–1930*.

[3] See the Introduction to this volume for a list of those Warren was allowed to include in the *Lewis Papers*.

[1] Warren, having re-enlisted for a tour of duty in China, had only a few more weeks at home.

and established a pretty good order for all except about eight. (How maddening my habit of not dating them now becomes! And how ridiculous the arguments by wh. I defended it!)

All the ones that deal with what we used to call 'It' I am suppressing and will return to you in a day or two. I am surprised to find what a very large percentage of the whole they are. I am now inclined to agree with you in *not* regretting that we confided in each other even on this subject, because it has done no harm in the long run – and how could young adolescents really be friends without it? At the same time, the letters give away some of your secrets as well as mine: and I do not wish to recall things of that sort to W's mind, so that in every way they had better be kept out of the final collection. I am also sending back some others in which my replies to you imply that you have said foolish things – you will see what I mean when I return them. Finally, I am suppressing (i.e. sending back at once and keeping from W. – that is what the word 'suppressing' means throughout) all letters that refer to my pretended assignation with the Belgian.[2] I am not at all sure that if J. Taylor were at my elbow he would not tell me that my repentance for that folly was incomplete if I did not submit to the 'mortification' of having them typed and laid open to posterity. I hope, however, this is not really necessary in the case of a sin so old and (I hope) so fully abandoned.

Thanks for all you say about the letters in general. You see mine with too friendly eyes. To me, as I re-read them, the most striking thing is their egotism: sometimes in the form of priggery, intellectual and even social: often in the form of downright affectation (I seem to be posturing and showing off in every letter): and always in the form of complete absorption in ourselves. I have you to thank that it was at least 'ourselves' and not wholly 'myself'. I can now honestly say that I envy you the much more artless letters you were writing me in those days: they all had at least the grace of humility and of affection. How ironical that the very things wh. I was proud of in my letters then should make the reading of them a humiliation to me now!

Don't suppose from this that I have not enjoyed the other aspect of them – the glorious memories they call up. I think I have got over *wishing* for the past back again. I look at it this way. The delights of those days were given to lure us into the world of the Spirit, as sexual rapture is there to lead to offspring and family life. They were nuptial ardours. To ask that they should return, or should remain, is like wishing to prolong the honeymoon at an age when a man should rather be interested in the careers of his growing sons. They have

[2] See Letter 11 *et seq.*

done their work, those days and led on to better things. All the 'homeliness' (wh. was your chief lesson to me) was the introduction to the Christian virtue of charity or love. I sometimes manage now to get into a state in wh. I think of all my enemies and can honestly say that I find something lovable (even if it is only an oddity) in them all: and your conception of 'homeliness' is largely the route by wh. I have reached this. On the other hand, all the 'strangeness' (wh. was my lesson to you) has turned out to be only the first step in far deeper mysteries.

How deep I am just now beginning to see: for I have just passed on from believing in God to definitely believing in Christ – in Christianity. I will try to explain this another time. My long night talk with Dyson and Tolkien had a good deal to do with it.

I am so glad you liked the *Seasons*.[3] I agree with you that some parts are frankly boring, and some (e.g. the bathing episode in *Summer*) are in a false taste. I don't myself think that any of it is as good as the opening of *The Castle of Indolence*: the second canto everyone gives up as hopeless. It is delightful to hear of your thinking of having another try at Spenser. I have read nothing that would interest you since my last letter and am engaged on the Poetical Works of [John] Skelton (XVIth century) – a very bad poet except for the half dozen good things I knew already.

W. and I are busy still clearing the undergrowth in the top wood. This place gets more beautiful every day at present, with yellow leaves and crimson leaves and a more and more autumnal smell. I do hope you will some time make an opportunity of visiting it in winter.

Did it strike you in reading those letters how completely *both* of us were wrong in most of our controversies, or rather in the great standing controversy about 'sentiment' wh. was the root of most of our quarrels? If anyone had said 'There is good feeling and bad: you can't have too much of the first, and you can't have too little of the second' it wd. have blown the gaff on the whole argument. But we blundered along – my indiscriminate hardness only provoking you into a more profound self pity (wh. is the root of all bad sentiment) and that bad sentiment in return making me harder and more willing to hurt.

Term begins next Friday.

Yours
Jack

P.S. I have just finished *The Epistle to the Romans*, the first Pauline

[3] James Thomson, *The Seasons* (1730).

epistle I have ever seriously read through. It contains many difficult and some horrible things, but the essential idea of Death (the Macdonald idea) is there alright. What I meant about the Earthly Paradise was simply that the whole story turns on a number of people setting out to look for a country where you don't die.

172

[The Kilns]
Oct. 18th 1931

My dear Arthur,

I must have expressed myself rather confusedly about the letters. When I asked you for them I did not think that you would want them back except 'ultimately' – that is, the question of *time* was not seriously in my mind at all. Besides this, as people usually do in such circumstances, I was half consciously fooling myself about the length of time W. had still here. You know how 'He's not going just yet' leads one to plan and feel as if there was a month more when there is really 10 days. Then came your letter, showing your wish (a very flattering one to me) to have the letters back quite soon: and on top of that the *fact* (now unconcealable) that W. was actually packing and wd. be off in a day to two. It was therefore impossible that he should finish his editing of the family letters and get them all typed before he went: if I had known that you wanted them back soon, and if I had faced the real date of his departure, I would not have raised the question of the letters with you till after his return, 3 years hence. That indeed is what I ought to have done.

As things are, the four years I mentioned consist of 1 year's editing preceded by 3 years during wh. W. will be in China and the letters will be lying neatly in a drawer – safe, but idle. You see what a fool I have made of myself! The matter is now entirely in your hands, for of course they are your property not mine. If you want them seriously I will send them back: if you don't, they will be perfectly safe where they are, and safer indeed without the risk of a second postal journey. Still, the next move is to you and I will obey any orders you give.

This has filled up nearly a page so that I don't know whether I should now start to try and explain what I meant about Christianity. For one thing, reading your reply, I began to feel that perhaps I had said too much in my previous letter, that perhaps I was not nearly as clear on the subject as I had led you to think. But I certainly have moved *a bit*, even if it turns out to be a less bit than I thought.

What has been holding me back (at any rate for the last year or so) has not been so much a difficulty in believing as a difficulty in knowing what the doctrine *meant*: you can't believe a thing while you are ignorant *what* the thing is. My puzzle was the whole doctrine of Redemption: in what sense the life and death of Christ 'saved' or 'opened salvation to' the world. I could see how miraculous salvation might be necessary: one could see from ordinary experience how sin (e.g. the case of a drunkard) could get a man to such a point that he was bound to reach Hell (i.e. complete degradation and misery) in this life unless something quite beyond mere natural help or effort stepped in. And I could well imagine a whole world being in the same state and similarly in need of miracle. What I couldn't see was how the life and death of Someone Else (whoever he was) 2000 years ago could help us here and now – except in so far as his *example* helped us. And the example business, tho' true and important, is not Christianity: right in the centre of Christianity, in the Gospels and St Paul, you keep on getting something quite different and very mysterious expressed in those phrases I have so often ridiculed ('propitiation' – 'sacrifice' – 'the blood of the Lamb') – expressions wh. I cd. only interpret in senses that seemed to me either silly or shocking.

Now what Dyson and Tolkien showed me was this: that if I met the idea of sacrifice in a Pagan story I didn't mind it at all: again, that if I met the idea of a god sacrificing himself to himself (cf. the quotation opposite the title page of *Dymer*)[1] I liked it very much and was mysteriously moved by it: again, that the idea of the dying and reviving god (Balder, Adonis, Bacchus) similarly moved me provided I met it anywhere *except* in the Gospels. The reason was that in Pagan stories I was prepared to feel the myth as profound and suggestive of meanings beyond my grasp even tho' I could not say in cold prose 'what it meant'.

Now the story of Christ is simply a true myth: a myth working on us in the same way as the others, but with this tremendous difference that *it really happened*: and one must be content to accept it in the same way, remembering that it is God's myth where the others are men's myths: i.e. the Pagan stories are God expressing Himself through the minds of poets, using such images as He found there, while Christianity is God expressing Himself through what we call 'real things'. Therefore it is *true*, not in the sense of being a 'description' of God (that no finite mind could take in) but in the sense of being the way in which God chooses to (or can) appear to our facul-

[1] 'Nine nights I hung upon the Tree, wounded with the spear as an offering to Odin, myself sacrificed to myself.' *Hávamál*.

ties. The 'doctrines' we get *out of* the true myth are of course *less* true: they are translations into our *concepts* and *ideas* of that wh. God has already expressed in a language more adequate, namely the actual incarnation, crucifixion, and resurrection. Does this amount to a belief in Christianity? At any rate I am now certain (a) That this Christian story is to be approached, in a sense, as I approach the other myths. (b) That it is the most important and full of meaning. I am also *nearly* certain that it really happened.[2]

No time for more now. I hope to have some literary chat in my next letter.

Yours
Jack

[2] By a most fortunate coincidence, Tolkien was so interested in the conversation he and Hugo Dyson had with Lewis on the night of 19 September that he set down his own account of it in a long poem called 'Mythopoeia', a copy of which he sent to Lewis. The only portion of it which has been published is found in Tolkien's essay 'On Fairy-Stories' (*Essays Presented to Charles Williams*, 1947, pp. 71–2) where he says: 'I once wrote to a man [Lewis] who described myth and fairy-story as "lies"; though to do him justice he was kind enough and confused enough to call fairy-story making "Breathing a lie through Silver".

> "Dear Sir," I said – "Although now long estranged,
> Man is not wholly lost nor wholly changed.
> Dis-graced he may be, yet is not de-throned,
> and keeps the rags of lordship once he owned:
> Man, Sub-creator, the refracted Light
> through whom is splintered from a single White
> to many hues, and endlessly combined
> in living shapes that move from mind to mind.
> Though all the crannies of the world we filled
> with Elves and Goblins, though we dared to build
> Gods and their houses out of dark and light,
> and sowed the seed of dragons – 'twas our right
> (used or misused). That right has not decayed:
> we make still by the law in which we're made." '

A paraphrase of 'Mythopoeia' can be found in Humphrey Carpenter's *J. R. R. Tolkien: A Biography* (1977), ch. 4, where he points out that 'In expounding this belief in the inherent *truth* of mythology, Tolkien laid bare the centre of his philosophy as a writer' (p. 147).

For the different – but not contradictory – emphasis Lewis was to put upon the Christian implications of myth, one should read what he says about it in *The Pilgrim's Regress* (Bk. VIII, ch. 8), the essay 'Myth Became Fact', and *Miracles* (1947) where in chapter XV, footnote 1 is found the best and most crystallised explanation of how 'the truth first appears in mythical form and then by a long process of condensing or focusing finally becomes incarnate as History'.

173

My dear Arthur,

I was sorry to hear of your cold and of your musical disappointment, though I must confess that your beginning your letter with an (unfavourable) account of a concert was pleasantly remeniscent of old times.

It is delightful to hear of your reading *Endymion*. Funnily enough I had been re-dipping into it the last week end too. I don't think you can say that either it or Hyperion is the better for they are different in kind. The one is a sweet, the other a dry, flavour. It is like comparing Spenser & Milton, or Wagner (at his richest) with Bach (at his most classical). People will tell you that Hyperion is more Greek, but I doubt if that is a good description. As to *why* the goddess takes on the form of a mortal at the end, he may mean that the mystical love does not complete itself until it has appeared as a human love also, and that the soul, when this happens, may dread as an infidelity to the spiritual what is really its completion. But I am inclined to think that when Keats wrote Endymion he was not v. certain of his own intention: that he faltered between the myth as his imagination set it before him (full of meaning, but not meaning necessarily decipherable by Keats' intellect) and between various ideas of conscious meanings of his own invention, wh., considering his age and education, were possibly confused and even shallow. There is thus some confusion throughout: and this, along with another fault, prevents it from being a perfect poem.

The other fault is the lack of spiritual experience. He knows about the hunting for 'it' and longing and wandering: but he has, as yet, no real idea of what it wd. be if you found it. Hence while Endymion's description to Peona of his unrest, and Endymion's journeying under earth and sea, are wonderful, his actual meetings with Cynthia are (to me) failures: not because they are erotic but because they are erotic in a rather commonplace way – all gasps and exclamations and a sort of suburban flirtatious air. It is horrible to use such words of Keats, but I think he would be the first to agree.

My memories of the *Phaedrus*[1] are vague – mainly of the beautiful scene in which the discussion takes place and of the procession of the

---

[1] This is one of Plato's Dialogues, and is about Persuasion and Eros and their part in our perception of the eternal Forms.

gods round the sky. You must be enjoying yourself no end. I don't know any greater pleasure than returning to a world of the imagination which one has long forsaken and feeling 'After all this is my own.' Be careful of Reid. I am sure he is in danger of stopping at the purely sensuous side of the Greek stories and of encouraging you to do the same. You, on the other hand, if you are in for a new Greek period, will be able to do him some good.

I, like you, am worried by the fact that the *spontaneous* appeal of the Christian story is so much less to me than that of Paganism. Both the things you suggest (unfavourable associations from early upbringing and the corruption of one's nature) probably are causes: but I have a sort of feeling that *the* cause must be elsewhere, and I have not yet discovered it. I think the thrill of the Pagan stories and of romance may be due to the fact that they are mere beginnings – the first, faint whisper of the wind from beyond the world – while Christianity is the thing itself: and no thing, when you have really started on it, can have for you then and there just the same thrill as the first hint. For example, the experience of being married and bringing up a family, cannot have the old bittersweet of first falling in love. But it is futile (and, I think, wicked) to go on trying to get the old thrill again: you must go forward and not backward. Any *real* advance will in its turn be ushered in by a new thrill, different from the old: doomed in its turn to disappear and to become in its turn a temptation to retrogression. Delight is a bell that rings as you set your foot on the first step of a new flight of stairs leading upwards. Once you have started climbing you will notice only the hard work: it is when you have reached the landing and catch sight of the new stair that you may expect the bell again. This is only an idea, and may be all rot: but it seems to fit in pretty well with the general law (thrills also must die to live) of autumn & spring, sleep and waking, death and resurrection, and 'Whosoever loseth his life, shall save it.'[2] On the other hand, it may be simply part of our probation – one needs the sweetness to *start* one on the spiritual life but, once started, one must learn to obey God for his own sake, not for the pleasure. Perhaps we are in the stage Endymion went through on the bottom of the sea.

I saw a most attractive review of *Uncle Stephen* in the T.L.S.[3] I am glad he stuck to that name after all, though surprised, for I thought he had definitely turned it down.

Did I tell you I had bought the complete works of Jeremy Taylor

[2] Luke ix.24.
[3] *The Times Literary Supplement* (29 October 1931), p. 838.

in 15 volumes – half leather (not v. nice – the rather pimply, nearly black, office-looking type of leather but excellent paper and print) for 20/–.[4] I have also been presented by an old pupil with what I think must be a first editn of Law's Appeal:[5] much better than the *Serious Call*, but it will need a letter to itself.

I wish you could see the Kilns at present in the autumn colours

Yours
Jack

P.S. Minto says I must have left a suit of pyjamas at Bernagh, and I seem to remember your saying something about it (wh. I didn't heed) in a previous letter. If so 'woooo-d' you please send them. Really Arthur, I am awfully sorry, honestly, really

Yrs
J.

P.P.S. I chust wanted to say, Arthur, how very sorry I am.

174

[The Kilns]
Dec 6th 1931

My dear Arthur,

Hurrah! I was beginning to feel the want of a word from you. I envy you your stay at Ballycastle, or rather I wish I had been there: I feel I can do so without selfishness because I should have enjoyed the storms better than Reid who doubtless lost through them most of the pleasure he expected to get out of his jaunt.

That is a thing you and I have to be thankful for – the fact that we do not only don't dislike but positively enjoy almost every kind of weather. We had about three days of dense fog here lately. That was enough to tax even my powers of doing without the sun, but though it became oppressive in the end I felt that it was a cheap price to pay [for] its beauties. There was one evening of mist about three feet deep lying on the fields under the moon – like the mist in the first chapter of Phantastes. There was a morning (up in the top wood) of

---

[4] *The Whole Works of . . . Jeremy Taylor . . . With a Life of the Author, and a Critical Examination of His Writings*, by Reginald Heber, 15 vols. (1822).

[5] On 19 October his former pupil Dom Bede Griffiths gave him William Law's *An Appeal to all that Doubt* (1742), which book was first published in 1740.

mist pouring *along the ground* through the fir trees, so thick and visible that it looked tangible as treacle. Then there were afternoons of fairly thin, but universal fog, blotting out colour but leaving shapes distinct enough to become generalised – silhouettes revealing (owing to the suppression of detail) all sorts of beauties of grouping that one does not notice on a coloured day. Finally there were days of *real* fog: days of chaos come again: specially fine at the pond, when the water was only a darker tinge in the fog and the wood on the far side only the ghostliest suggestion: and to *hear* the skurry of the waterfowl but not to see them. Not only was it an exciting time in itself but by the contrast has made to day even more beautiful than it would have been – a clear, stinging, winter sunshine.

As to Lucius[1] about the atonement not being in the Gospels, I think he is very probably right. But then nearly everyone seems to think that the Gospels are much later than the Epistles, written for people who had already accepted the *doctrines* and naturally wanted the *story*. I certainly don't think it is historical to regard the Gospels as the *original* and the rest of the New Testament as later elaboration or accretion – though I constantly find myself doing so. But really I feel more and more of a child in the whole matter.

I begin to see how much Puritanism counts in your make up – that both the revulsion from it and the attraction back to it are strong elements. I hardly feel either myself and perhaps am apt to forget in talking to you how different your experience and therefore your feeling is. All I feel that I can say with absolute certainty is this: that if you ever feel that the *whole spirit and system* in which you were brought up was, after all, right and good, then you may be quite sure that that feeling is a mistake (tho' of course it might, at a given moment – say, of temptation, be present as the alternative to some far bigger mistake).

My reasons for this are *1.* That the system denied pleasures *to others* as well as to the votaries themselves: whatever the merits of *self*-denial, this is unpardonable interference. *2.* It inconsistently kept *some* worldly pleasures, and always selected the worst ones – gluttony, avarice, etc. *3.* It was ignorant. It could give no '*reason* for the faith that was in it'.[2] Your relations have been found very ill

---

[1] Sir (then Mr) Frederick Lucius O'Brien (1896–1974) was Arthur's cousin on his mother's side. He was educated at the Friends' School, Lisburn, and Bootham School in York. He was the first Chairman of the Northern Ireland Housing Trust, 1945–60, and during his life he held many civil and governmental positions in Belfast. He and Arthur frequently travelled together.

[2] I Peter iii.15.

grounded in the Bible itself and as ignorant as savages of the historical and theological reading needed to make the Bible more than a superstition. 4. 'By their fruits ye shall know them.'[3] Have they the *marks* of peace, love, wisdom and humility on their faces or in their conversation?[4] Really, you need not *bother* about that kind of Puritanism. It is simply the form which the *memory* of Christianity takes just before it finally dies away altogether, in a commercial community: just as extreme emotional ritualism is the form it takes on just before it dies in a fashionable community.

Like you I can get very little out of the *Imitation*.[5] Since last writing I have read Carlyle's *Past and Present*. One gets rather tired of a certain monotonous stridency, as in *Sartor*[6] but more so, but it is tremendously exciting (often wrong-headed) and very well worth reading, specially the mediaeval part in the middle.

I also read the *Dream of John Ball*, perhaps the most *serious* of W. Morris's works, except *Love is Enough* and the fullest exposition of his whole philosophy of life: and *The Wood Beyond the World* wh. is neither better nor worse than any other of the prose romances. What an achievement his treatment of love is: so undisguisedly physical and yet so perfectly sane and healthy – *real* paganism at its best, which is the next best thing to Christianity, and so utterly different from the nonsense that passes under the name of paganism in, say, Swinburne or Aldous Huxley.

I wish you knew my two pupils, Lings[7] and Paterson.[8] Both are poets (quite promising I think) and fast friends of each other. They

[3] Matthew vii.20.

[4] See Galatians v. 22–3.

[5] Thomas à Kempis, *The Imitation of Christ*, a manual of spiritual devotion first put into circulation in 1418.

[6] Thomas Carlyle, *Past and Present* (1843); *Sartor Resartus* (1836).

[7] Martin Lings (1909–   ), after taking his B.A. in 1932, lectured in the University of Kaunas (in Lithuania) on Anglo-Saxon and Middle English, 1935–9. From 1940 to 1951 he held a lectureship in English Literature at Cairo University where he lectured mainly on Shakespeare. In 1952 he returned to England and took a degree in Arabic from the University of London. He was the Assistant Keeper in the Department of Oriental Printed Books and Manuscripts of the British Museum from 1955–70, the Deputy Keeper in 1970, and was made Keeper in 1971. Besides his many scholarly books, he has published *The Elements and Other Poems* (1967), the Preface to which contains some interesting facts about his friendship with Lewis.

[8] Adrian Hugh Patterson, who was born in 1909, lectured on English at the University of Hong Kong, 1934–8, and was a lecturer at Cairo University from 1938 till he died in July 1940 as the result of an accident while he and his friend Lings were riding together in the desert.

are just in the state you and I remember so well – the whole world of beauty opening upon them – and as they share the same digs they must have a glorious time. One or other of them often accompanies me on my afternoon walk. Paterson is the wild, and Lings the steady one. Paterson looks very southern, almost an Italian face, and is all moods, and a little effeminate, and is at present in the throes of a terrific quarrel with his father which he poured into my sympathetic ear the other day. Lings is about five feet nothing, very ugly, very dark, and looks a hundred years old, and moves and sits as stiffly as an old man. Paterson truly says that Lings hurrying noiselessly along the cloisters is like nothing so much as a furtive mouse. This doesn't sound like a poet, does it? But he is the better poet and the better man of the two. What times you and I could have had if we had been up here together as undergraduates! Neither of them knows many other people in College and they only discovered each other after they had been up some time. Paterson spent most of his first two terms sitting in his rooms listening to the feet of people on the staircase, always hoping that it was someone coming to call on him, but it never was. You can imagine how I enjoy them both. Indeed this is the best part of my job. In every given year the pupils I really like are in a minority; but there is hardly a year in which I do not make some real friend. I am glad to find that people become more and more one of the sources of pleasure as I grow older.

Not that I agree for a moment about books & music being 'vanity and vexation'. Really imaginative (or intellectual) pleasure is neither the one or the other: the *bad* element is the miserly pleasure of *possession*, the delight in this book because it is *mine*.

Of course it was entirely my own fault about the pyjamas – I only hope that your mother was not worried when you asked about them. Give her my love and if her mind needs setting at rest on the subject – why Sir, set it.

Try to write soon again.

Yours
Jack

175

[The Kilns]
Jan 10th 1932

My dear Arthur,

I was glad to hear from you again, and sorry you are so dull. Perhaps you are suffering from too much turkey and 'plumb' pudding – or too many late nights and dances! How did you manage to get your mother's consent to the introduction of a dog – I thought she was the insuperable difficulty?

I quite understand the *mood* in wh. you fall back upon detective stories, though I have never been able to understand how that mood could lead to detective stories. I mean, I know well from experience that state of mind in which one wants immediate and certain pleasure from a book, for nothing – i.e. without paying the price of that slight persistence, that almost imperceptible tendency *not* to go on, which, to be honest, nearly always accompanies the reading of [a] good book. Not only accompanies by the way, but (do you agree) actually makes part of the pleasure. A *little* sense of labour is necessary to all perfect pleasures I think: just as (to my palate at least) there is no really delicious taste without a touch of astringency – the 'bite' in alcoholic drinks, the resistance to the teeth in nuts or meat, the tartness of fruit, the bitterness of mint sauce. The apple must not be *too* sweet, the cheese must not be *too* mild. Still, I know the other mood, when one wants a book of sheer pleasure.

In fact I have been going through such a mood lately. I have had to work v. hard all day this Vac. and in the evenings I have wanted relaxation. I have accordingly read *The Wood Beyond the World*, Rider Haggard's *The People of the Mist*, and am now at Kingsley's *Hereward the Wake*. In fact when I am in that state of mind I want not so much a grown-up 'light' book (to me usually the hardest of all kinds of reading) as a boy's book; – distant lands, strange adventures, mysteries not of the American but of the Egyptian kind. Of course what makes detective stories appeal to you is that they were one of your first loves in the days when you used to come round and borrow *Sherlock Holmes* from my father, and therefore in reading them now you have the sense of *return*, you step back as into an old easy shoe – and that certainly is one of the essentials for this kind of reading. One would never read a new *type* of book for pure relaxation: and perhaps *re-reading* of an old friend – a Scott with much skipping – is the best of all. I don't think you re-read enough – I know I do it too much. Is it since I last wrote to you that I re-read *Wuthering House?*[1] I thought it very great. Isn't it (despite the improbability) an excellent stroke of art to tell it all through the mouth of a very homely, prosaic old servant, whose sanity and mother-wit thus provides a cooling medium through which the wild, horrible story becomes tolerable? I have also re-read Burke's *Reflections on the French Revolution*[2] and find that I had forgotten it nearly all. It is, in the famous words, 'too long drawn out' and becomes mere scolding in the end.

What wd. perhaps interest you more is Pater's *Marius the Epicurean*[3] which I had twice before tried to read without success, but have this time reached the end of – and reached it before my desire to punch Marius' head had become *quite* unbearable. Do you know it? It is very well worth reading. You must give up all idea of reading a *story* and treat it simply as a vaguely narrative essay. It interests me as showing just how far the purely aesthetic attitude to life can go, in the hands of a master, and it certainly goes a good deal further than one would suppose from reading the inferior aesthetes like Oscar Wilde and George Moore. In Pater it seems almost to *include* the rest of the spiritual life: he has to bring in chastity, he nearly has to bring in Christianity, because they are so beautiful. And yet somehow there is a faint flavour of decay over it all. Perhaps it is his *patronage* of great things which is so offensive – condescending to *add* the Christian religion to his nosegay of spiritual flowers because it has a colour or a scent that he thinks would just give a finishing touch to the rest. It is all balls anyway – because one sees at a glance that if he *really* added it it would break up the whole nosegay view of life. In fact that is the refutation of aestheticism: for perfect beauty you need to include things which will at once show that mere beauty is not the sole end of life. If you don't include them, you *have* given up aestheticism: if you do, you *must* give it up Q.E.D. But Pater is valuable just because, being a perfectly honest aesthete, he really tries to follow its theory to the bitter end, and therefore betrays its weakness. I didn't mean to make this letter a mere catalogue of books read, but one thing has led on to another.

About Lucius' argument that the evangelists would have put the doctrine of the atonement into the Gospel if they had had the slightest excuse, and, since they didn't, therefore Our Lord didn't teach it: surely, since we know from the Epistles that the Apostles (who had actually known him) *did* teach this doctrine in his name

[1] Emily Brontë, *Wuthering Heights* (1847).
[2] Edmund Burke, *Reflections on the Revolution in France* (1790).
[3] Walter Pater, *Marius the Epicurean* (1885).

immediately after his death, it is clear that he *did* teach it: or else, that they allowed themselves a very free hand. But if people shortly after his death were so very free in interpreting his doctrine, why should people who wrote much later (when such freedom wd. be more excusable from lapse of memory in an honest writer, and more likely to escape detection in a dishonest one) become so very much more accurate? The accounts of a thing don't usually get more and more accurate as time goes on. Anyway, if you take the sacrificial idea out of Christianity you deprive both Judaism and Paganism of all significance. Can one believe that there was just *nothing* in that persistent *motif* of blood, death, and resurrection, which runs like a black and scarlet cord through all the greater myths – thro' Balder & Dionysus & Adonis and the Graal too? Surely the history of the human mind hangs together better if you suppose that all this was the first shadowy approach of something whose reality came with Christ – even if we can't at present fully understand that something.

Try and write soon.

Yrs

Jack

176

[The Kilns]

Feb 1932

My dear Arthur,

I have been laid up with flu' for over a fortnight or I shd. have answered you before. As you preferred my last letter to my previous ones, and also took longer to answer it than ever, I suppose if I want a speedy answer to this I had better write a letter you *don't* like! Let me see – I must first select all the subjects which are least likely to interest you, and then consider how to treat them in the most unattractive manner. I have half a mind to do it – but on second thoughts it would be almost as big a bore for me to write it as for you to read it. How exasperating to think of you being at Ballycastle with an unappreciative companion, in bad weather, and a lethargic mood: it seems such a waste.

I thought we had talked about Naomi Mitchison before. I have only read one (*Black Sparta*) and I certainly agree that it 'holds' one: indeed I don't know any historical fiction that is so astonishingly vivid and, on the whole, so true. I also thought it astonishing how, despite the grimness, she got such an air of beauty – almost dazzling beauty – into it. As to the cruelties, I think her obvious relish is morally wicked, but hardly an *artistic* fault for she cd. hardly get some of her effects without it. But it is, in *Black Sparta*, a historical falsehood: not that the things she describes did not probably happen in Greece, but that they were not typical – the Greeks being, no doubt, cruel by modern standards, but, by the standards of that age, extremely humane. She gives you the impression that the cruelty was essentially Greek, whereas it was precisely the opposite. That is, she is unfair as I should be unfair if I wrote a book about some man whose chief characteristic was that he was the tallest of the pigmies, and kept on reminding the reader that he was very short. I should be telling the truth (for of course he would be short by our standards) but missing the real point about the man – *viz*: that he was, by the standards of his own race, a giant. Still, she is a wonderful writer and I fully intend to read more of her when I have a chance.

I am so glad to hear you have started Froissart.[1] If I had the book here (I am out at the Kilns – only got up yesterday) we could compare passages. What I chiefly remember from the first part is the Scotch wars and the odd way in which just a very few words gave me the impression of the scenery – the long wet valleys and the moors. How interesting too, to find how much of the chivalry in the romances was really practised in the wars of the period – e.g. the scene where Sir Thing-um-a-bob (you see you are not the only one who forgets things) espouses the cause of the lady of Hainault. Or again, at the siege of Hennebont (?) where you actually have a lady-knight fighting, just like Britomart in the *Faerie Queene*.

To enjoy a book like that thoroughly I find I have to treat it as a sort of hobby and set about it seriously. I begin by making a map on one of the end leafs: then I put in a genealogical tree or two. Then I put a running headline at the top of each page: finally I index at the end all the passages I have for any reason underlined. I often wonder – considering how people enjoy themselves developing photos or making scrap-books – why so few people make a hobby of their reading in this way. Many an otherwise dull book which I had to read have I enjoyed in this way, with a fine-nibbed pen in my hand: one is *making* something all the time and a book so read acquires the charm of a toy without losing that of a book.

By the way, when you ask me to 'pray for you' (in connection with

---

[1] Jean Froissart's *Chroniques* (c. 1373–1400) is a lively, though sometimes inaccurate, record of Europe in the fourteenth century with particular emphasis on the first half of the Hundred Years' War between France and England. The best-known translation is that by Lord Berners which was published 1523–5.

Froissart) I don't know if you are serious, but, the answer is, I do. It may not do you any good, but it does me a lot, for I cannot ask for any change to be made in you without finding that the very same needs to be made in me; which pulls me up and also by putting us all in the same boat checks any tendency to priggishness.

While I have been in bed I have had an orgy of Scott – *The Monastery, The Abbot, The Antiquary* and the *Heart of Midlothian* which I am at present in the middle of. The *Monastery* and *Abbot* I have read only once before – long, long ago, long before you and I were friends – so that they were the same as new ground to me. Neither of them is Scott at his best – the *Monastery* indeed is about the worst I have yet read – but both are worth reading. *The Antiquary* I have read over and over again, and old Oldbuck is almost as familiar to me as Johnson. What a *relish* there is about him and his folios and his tapestry room and his paper on Castrametation and his 'never taking supper: but trusting that a mouthful of ale with a toast and haddock, to close the orifice of the stomach, does not come under that denomination' (How like my father and his 'little drop of the whiskey').

I think re-reading old favourites is one of the things we differ on, isn't it, and you do it very rarely. I probably do it too much. It is one of my greatest pleasures: indeed I can't imagine a man really enjoying a book and reading it only once. *Do* try one of the old Scotts again. It will do admirably as a rest in the intervals of something that needs working at, like Froissart.

There has been a good deal of snow during my illness. Where I lay in bed I could see it through two windows, and a bit of the wooded hill gradually whitening in the distance. What could be snugger or nicer? Indeed my flu' this year would have been delightful if I hadn't been worried about Warnie, who is in Shanghai.[2] When there is something like this wh. forces one to read the papers, how one loathes their flippancy and their sensational exploitation of things that mean life and death. I wish to goodness he had never gone out there.

Do try and let me know when you are coming to London and when there is a chance of your coming here. Otherwise you know what it will be: you will turn up unexpectedly on some day when I have 15 hours' work to do, and I shall be angry with you and you will be angry with me, and we shall meet for a comfortless half hour in a teashop and snap and sulk at each other and part both feeling miser-

[2] Warren was possibly in danger by reason of the Japanese attack on the Chinese part of that city.

able. Surely it is worth while trying to avoid this.

Give my love to your mother: and to the dog. I hope we shall have some famous walks with him

Yours
Jack

177

[The Kilns]
Easter Sunday [27 March] 1932

My dear Arthur,

We are about 'quits' this time in lateness of answering. I had to get off a letter to Warnie before I wrote to you, as he had been longer in my debt, and that of course had to be a long one. (By the bye the trouble in China seems to be over, I am glad to see.) And now I find that your last letter is in College, while I am out here at the Kilns, so that I shan't be able to *answer* it very definitely.

Almost the only thing I remember about it is that you are writing a detective story. After I have spent so much of my life in writing things of the kind that don't appeal to *you*, I suppose I should not be surprised at you writing in one of the kinds that doesn't appeal to me – gradually more of your letter begins to come back to me. You have given up Naomi Mitchison because you find the characters unreal. I *didn't* feel that myself. Of course one does not feel the same intimacy in detail with characters from the far past as with those in a novel of contemporary life. I don't think I mind that. Hamlet or, say, the Baron of Bradwardine – of course one doesn't in *one* way know them as well as Soames Forsyte or Kipps:[1] in another way I feel I know them better. In fact 'in one way it is, in another way it isn't'. But then, I think one of the differences between us [is] that you appreciate much more than I do the 'close-up' detail – superficial detail I often think – of modern character drawing.

There I go in my usual way – expressing an opinion on modern fiction when the real state of the case is that I have read so little of it, and that so carelessly, that I ought to have no opinion on it at all. I must rely mainly on you. Perhaps as time goes on you will drift more to the present and I more to the past and we shall be useful to each other in that way. Fortunately, there is a solid something, neither of the present or of the past, which we shall always have in common.

[1] The Baron of Bradwardine is a character in Sir Walter Scott's *Waverley* (1814), Soames Forsyte a character in John Galsworthy's *Forsyte Saga* (1922), and Arthur Kipps is a character in H. G. Wells's *Kipps* (1905).

Talking of the past, I had a really delightful experience some weeks ago. An old pupil of mine, one Wood, came to spent a night with me. When I was his tutor he had been a curiously naif, almost neurotic youth, who was always in love and other troubles, and so childish that he once asked me (as if I were his father!) whether one fell in love less often as one grew older, because he hoped so. Altogether an appealing, but somewhat ridiculous young man.[2] When he went down he was compelled against his will to go into his father's business: and for a year [or] so I got letters from him, and accounts of him from common friends, which seemed to show that he was settling down into a permanent state of self-pity.

You can imagine how pleased I was to find that he had got over this: but above all – that is why I am telling the story – to find that his whole support is romantic reading in those precious evening hours 'after business' which you remember so well. He quoted bits of Middle English poems which he had read with me for the exam. They were mere drudgery to him at the time, but now, in memory, they delight him. He has just re-read the whole of Malory with more delight than ever, and has bought, but not yet begun, *The High History of the Holy Graal*. He also writes a bit – in those same precious evenings, and Saturday afternoons.

In fact as I sat talking to him, hearing his not very articulate, but unmistakable, attempts to express his pleasure, I really felt as if I were meeting *our* former selves. He is just in the stage that we were in when you worked with Tom and I was at Bookham. Of course there was an element of vanity on my side – one liked to feel that one had been the means of starting him on things that now are standing him in such good stead. There was also a less contemptible, and, so to speak, professional, pleasure in thus seeing a proof that the English School here does really do some good. But in the main the pleasure was a spiritual one – a kind of love. It is difficult, without being sentimental, to say how extraordinarily *beautiful* – ravishing – I found the sight of some one just at that point which you and I remember so well. I suppose it is this pleasure which fathers always are hoping to get, and very seldom do get, from their sons.

Do you think a good deal of parental cruelty results from the dis-

[2] Arthur Denis Wood (1907–   ), after taking his B.A. in 1929, joined the family firm of William Wood & Son Ltd., landscape gardeners, in Taplow. He served with the RAF between 1941–5, and he has published *Terrace and Courtyard Gardens for Modern Homes* (1965) and *Practical Garden Design* (1976). Mr Wood has commented, upon being shown this letter, that he was 'engaged in *one*, continuing, happy love-affair' as an undergraduate. He thinks Lewis may have confused him with someone else.

appointment of this hope? I mean, it takes a man of some tolerance to resign himself to the fact that his sons are *not* going to follow the paths that he followed and *not* going to give him this pleasure. What it all comes to, anyway, is that this pleasure, like everything else worth having, must not be reckoned on, or demanded as a right. If I had thought of it for a moment in the old days when I was teaching Wood, this pleasant evening would probably never have happened.

By the way he left a book with me, as a result of which I have lately read, or partially read, *one* modern novel – *The Fountain* [1932], by Charles Morgan. It is about a mystic, or would-be mystic, who was interned in Holland. I thought I was going to like it very much, but soon got disappointed. I was just going to say 'it soon degenerates into an ordinary novel', but realised only just in time that this wd. show an absurd point of view – as if one blamed an egg for degenerating into a chicken, forgetting that nature intended it for precisely that purpose. Still the fact remains that I personally enjoy a novel only in so far as it fails to be a novel pure and simple and escapes from the eternal love business into some philosophical, religious, fantastic, or farcical region.

By the way how did the Macdonald historical novel turn out? I shd. imagine it might suit him better than his modern ones.

I had meant to tell you all about my work in the wood these days, and how nice it looked and smelled and sounded: but I am suffering from a disease, rare with me, but deserving *your* sympathy – namely an extreme reluctance to write, even to my oldest friend about the things I like best. You see I have struggled with this reluctance for three pages. It is your turn now to reply soon and wake me from my lethargy as I have often tried to do you

Yrs
Jack

P.S. I think being up very late last night and up for the early 'cele-brrrration' this morning may be the cause of my dulness.

178

> The Kilns,
> Headington Quarry,
> Oxford
> July 29th 1932

My dear Arthur,

Thank heavens – *at last* I have finished examining. I am much too tired to write a letter: and also hungry to get to a morning's reading – my first since the beginning of last term 18 weeks ago. This is merely to ask whether it will suit you if I come from Aug. 15th to 29th? I am looking forward to it immensely. Thanks for your letter of June 12th.

> Yrs
> Jack

179

> The Kilns,
> Headington Quarry,
> Oxford.
> Aug 11th 1932

My dear Arthur,

I have written to book a berth[1] for the night of Monday the 15th (which, by the bye, they have not yet acknowledged) and am at present in a fever of pleasing anticipation. I am so tired that our old rôles will be reversed: you will be the one who wants to walk further and sit up later and talk more. The latter probably sounds too good to be true!

> Yours
> Jack

---

[1] On a cross-channel boat. As planned, Lewis did in fact cross over to Ireland on 15 August and remained there as Greeves's guest until the 29th of that month.

180

2 Princess Villas,
Bayview Park,
Kilkeel.
[30 August 1932][1]

My dear Arthur,

I am very sorry you did not come down but I quite see your point of view. I don't think the idea of a meeting half way would be much good. I can't drive: it would have to be a party of three at least – perhaps a mass meeting – and what should we all do when we had met? There would certainly be no opportunity for walk or talk on our own. Dotty sends profuse thanks for your exertions about her luggage, which has since turned up. I hope your cold will soon be better. I am alright now and have done some good mountain climbs.

I quite understand about the cheque – it was quite absurd suggesting such a roundabout method. We shall be crossing (D.V.) on Thursday Sept. 1st. and I shall tell you my train later.

I don't think the meeting half way *would* be any good: do *you*?

Yours
Jack

181

[The Kilns]
Dec 4th 1932

My dear Arthur,

Thank you very much for your list of suggestions.[1] I am **really** grateful for the trouble and interest you have taken. As for the future, I think I cannot ask you to sweat through the rest of the book in quite

---

[1] The dating of this letter is suspect, but if Lewis's mention of 'Thursday Sept. 1st' is correct it must have been written in 1932. Besides that, the peculiarities of his handwriting in this letter compare exactly with others written at this time. Probably, after his visit with Arthur, Lewis came here to join the Moores and their friend 'Dotty' Vaughan for a few days before returning to England.

[1] For some time Lewis had been trying, unsuccessfully, to write the story of his conversion to Christianity, and, while he probably had no intention of attempting anything like this on his holiday, he was nevertheless moved to write his spiritual autobiography *The Pilgrim's Regress* during his fortnight at Bernagh. The manuscript had been sent to Greeves for criticism. For details of his earlier attempts to tell this story, see the *Biography*, ch. V.

such detail. What I had in mind was not so much criticisms on *style* (in the narrower sense) as on things like confusion, bad taste, unsuccessful jokes, contradictions etc., and for a few of these I should be very much obliged. These would be less trouble to you than minute verbal points: and also, if anything, *more* useful to me. I have not had a free day yet to work through your notes, but from a cursory glance I anticipate that on the purely *language* side of writing our aims and ideals are very far apart – too far apart for either of us to be of very much help to the other. I think I see, from your criticisms, that you like a much more correct, classical, and elaborate manner than I. I aim chiefly at being idiomatic and racy, basing myself on Malory, Bunyan, and Morris, tho' without archaisms: and would usually prefer to use ten words, provided they are honest native words and idiomatically ordered, than one 'literary word'. To put the thing in a nutshell you want 'The man of whom I told you' and I want 'The man I told you of'. But, no doubt, there are many sentences in the P[ilgrim's] R[egress] which are bad by *any* theory of style.

I have just finished the 2nd volume of Lockhart and it fully justifies all the recommendations both of you and of Warnie. After Boswell it is much the best biography I have read: and the subject is in some ways, or at least in some moods, more attractive. Didn't you enjoy the account of his ballad-hunting journey in Liddesdale? It will send me back to the Dandie Dinmont parts of *Guy Mannering* with renewed appetite.

It is a very consoling fact that so many books about real lives – biographies, autobiographies, letters etc. – give one such an impression of *happiness*, in spite of the tragedies they all contain. What could be more tragic than the main outlines of Lamb's or Cowper's lives?[2] But as soon as you open the letters of either, and see what they were writing from day to day and what a relish they got out of it, you almost begin to envy them. Perhaps the tragedies of real life contain more consolation and fun and gusto than the comedies of literature?

I wish you could see this place at present. The birch wood is a black bristly mass with here and there a last red leaf. The lake is cold, cold lead colour. The new moon comes out over the fir trees at the top and a glorious wail of wind comes down from them. I certainly like my garden better at winter than any other time.

I hope I shall soon have a letter from you. This, by the bye, is not a letter, but a note of acknowledgement. And I hope you will not think me any less grateful for your criticisms because of what I have

[2] Charles Lamb (1775–1834) and William Cowper (1731–1800).

said. I *do* appreciate your pains most deeply.

Do you ever take a run down to your cottage in winter. It would be 'rather lovely'.

Yours
Jack

182

[The Kilns
17 December 1932]

My dear Arthur,

You really must forgive me for being a slack correspondent in term time. I think we have talked of this before! However, I was much to blame for not at least letting you have a line about W. who, thank God, turned out to be well though he *had* been ill, and had had a worreying summer in various ways. He had also warned us, he said, (wh. was quite true, though we all forgot it) that he might not keep up his regular correspondence during the hot weather. We were all greatly relieved.

I am sorry to hear about the flu' – one of the few ailments of which I can speak with as large an experience as your own. We have both talked of it and agreed often enough about its pleasures and pains. I hope you are quite set up by now.

It was, in any case, almost worth having for its throwing you back on the old favourites. I will make a point of telling Foord-Kelsie – how pleased he will be. I wish I had your early associations with Pickwick: and yet I often feel as if I had. So many scenes come to me with the *feel* of a long since familiar atmosphere returning after absence – I suppose because even without having read it as a boy one has drunk in so much of the Dickensy world indirectly through quotation and talk and other orders. Certainly what I enjoy is *not* the jokes simply as jokes – indeed the earlier and more farcical parts like the military review and Mrs Leo Hunter's party are rather unpleasant to me – but something festive and friendly about D's whole world. A great deal of it (in a way how different from Macdonald's!) the charm of goodness – the goodness of Pickwick himself, and Wardle, and both Wellers.

Thanks for your criticisms on P[ilgrim's] R[egress]. The detailed criticisms (the 'passages where one word less wd. make all the difference') are what I should like best and could profit by most. Perhaps when you sent the MS back (there is no special hurry) you wd. mark on the blank opposite pages any bits that you think specially in need of improvement and add a note or two in pencil – but don't let it be a bother to you. As to your major criticisms

1. *Quotations.* I hadn't realised that they were so numerous as you apparently found them. Mr Sensible, as you rightly saw, is in a separate position: the shower of quotations is part of the character and it wd. be a waste of time to translate them, since the dialogue (I hope) makes it clear that his quotations were always silly and he always missed the point of the authors he quoted. The other ones may be too numerous, and perhaps can be reduced & translated. But not beyond a certain point: for one of the contentions of the book is that the decay of our old classical learning is a contributary cause of atheism (see the chapter on Ignorantia). The quotations at the beginnings of the Books are of course never looked at at all by most readers, so I don't think they matter much.

2. *Simplicity.* I expect your dissatisfaction on this score points to some real, perhaps v. deep seated, fault: but I am sure it cannot be remedied – least of all in a book of controversy. Also there may be some real difference of conception between you and me. You remember we discussed last summer how much more sympathy you had than I with the Puritan simplicity. I doubt if I interpret Our Lord's words[1] quite in the same way as you. I think they mean that the *spirit* of man must become humble and trustful like a child and, like a child, *simple in motive*, i.e. disinterested, not scheming and 'on the look out'. I don't think He meant that adult Christians must *think* like children: still less that the processes of thought by wh. people *become* Christians must be childish processes. At any rate the *intellectual* side of my conversion was *not* simple and I can describe only what I know. Of course it is only too likely that much of the thought in P.R. offends against simplicity simply by being confused or clumsy! And where so, I wd. gladly emend it if I knew how.

We have had a most glorious autumn here – still, windless days, red sunsets, and all the yellow leaves still on the trees. I wish you could have seen it. This is a Saturday evening after a hard week, so you will excuse me if I close. I will *try* and write again soon but can't promise. It was *very* nice to see your hand again. Your peculier spellinge is indeerd bi long associashuns!*

* I had to make them violent mistakes for feer you wldn't notis them

Yours,
Jack

[1] Matthew xviii.3–6; Mark x.15; Luke xviii.16–17.

183

My dear Arthur,

I am really penitent for having left you so long without a letter. The reasons are the usual ones – term and its demands, coupled this time with a good deal of laziness: for I have been rather less busy than usual and have been in excellent health and form.

Warnie has been home since before Christmas and is now *retired* (Read Lamb's Essay on The Superannuated Man). He has become a permanent member of our household and I hope we shall pass the rest of our lives together. He has settled down as easily as a man settles into a chair, and what between his reading and working in the garden finds himself busy from morning till night. He and I are making a path through the lower wood – first along the shore of the pond and then turning away from it up through the birch trees and rejoining at the top the ordinary track up the hill. It is very odd and delightful to be engaged on this sort of thing together: the last time we tried to make a path together was in the field at Little Lea when he was at Malvern and I was at Cherbourg. We both have a feeling that 'the wheel has come full circuit', that the period of wanderings is over, and that everything which has happened between 1914 and 1932 was an interruption: tho' not without a consciousness that it is dangerous for mere mortals to expect anything of the future with confidence. We make a very contented family together.

I have had some fine solitary moments too when we have been working in different parts of the wood. You know how intensely silent it is in a thicket on a warm winter afternoon: and how if you are digging sooner or later a robin comes up and hops about for worms – both his eye and his breast looking unnaturally bright among the prevailing greys and greyish greens. I say *warm* days, for the warm weather has just arrived with a rush: but we had the frost alright. The pond was frozen and we had two days skating. You can imagine how lovely the smooth flow of ice looked as the sun came down onto it through the steep little wood.

In the way of reading Lockhart kept me going through the whole vac. and I am still only at Vol. 8. What an *excellent* book it is, isn't it? – and what a nice addition. I think Scott is the one of all my favourite authors whom I admire most as a man – though of course there is a side of him that you and I would not have got on with, the rather insolent Tory country-gentleman side with the coursing, hard riding and hard drinking. Also perhaps as a father he was a little heavy – how sententious (and how unlike all his other letters) the letters to young Walter are.

Since term began I have had a delightful time reading a children's story which Tolkien has just written.[1] I have told of him before: the one man absolutely fitted, if fate had allowed, to be a third in our friendship in the old days, for he also grew up on W. Morris and George Macdonald. Reading his fairy tale has been uncanny – it is so exactly like what we wd. both have longed to write (or read) in 1916: so that one feels he is not making it up but merely describing the same world into which all three of us have the entry. Whether it is really *good* (I think it is until the end) is of course another question: still more, whether it will succeed with modern children.

And, talking of this sort of thing, would you believe it – I am actually officially supervising a young woman who is writing a thesis on G. Macdonald.[2] It is very odd – and curiously difficult – to approach *as work* something so old and intimate. The girl is, unfortunately, quite unworthy of her subject: apart from everything else, she is an American.

Dent's has accepted the *Pilgrim's Regress* with a number of conditions – shortening, alteration of title etc – which I intend to make some resistance to.[3]

I have no right to expect a letter after my long silence, but of course I shd. like one. How does the detective story go? It will soon be getting suitable weather for your cottage again: although, as you see, I am having a good time, the memory of the Mournes is still very poignant. Give my love to Mrs Greeves, and to the McNeills (all *three* – the one on the hill included) if you see them.

Yours,
Jack

Warnie send you his greetings and hopes we shall see you this year.

[1] This was J. R. R. Tolkien's *The Hobbit: or There and Back Again*, parts of which were probably re-written before it was published in 1937.

[2] *The Fairy Tales and Fantasies of George MacDonald* (1934) by Mary McQueen McEldowney. A copy is in the Bodleian Library (Mss B.Litt. d.257).

[3] Lewis's *The Pilgrim's Regress: An Allegorical Apology for Christianity, Reason and Romanticism* was published in May 1933.

T.S.T.–P

184

The Kilns,
Headington Quarry,
Oxford.
March 25th. 1933.

My dear Arthur,

I wonder how you have been getting on this many a day. I am certain I was the last to write, but whoever began it we have both been wrong to keep such a silence. We ought to be ashamed when we remember the weekly letters of the Bookham period. Fortunately each feels sure that the cause of this decline, whatever else it may be, is no diminution of the friendship. I think you pointed out to me once that it was natural we should write more easily in the old days, when everything was new and our correspondence was really like two explorers signalling to one another in a new country. Also – neither of us had any other outlet: we still thought that we were the only two people in the world who were interested in the right kind of things in the right kind of way.

I think I mentioned the skating in my last letter. Since then life has gone on in a pretty smooth way. Warnie sinks deeper and deeper into the family life: it is hard to believe he was not always here. What a mercy that the change in his views (I mean as regards religion) should have happened in time to meet mine – it would be awkward if one of us were still in the old state of mind. He has an excellent gramophone and is building up a complete set of the Beethoven symphonies, one of which (complete) he often plays us on a Sunday evening. I have quite foresworn the old method of hearing one's favourite bits played separately, and I am sure one gains enormously by always hearing one symphony as a whole and nothing else. By the way which is the one that contains the beautiful slow movement you played me – the one whose quality you defined as 'compassion'? I have been waiting for it eagerly but so far W. has not produced it. I am getting back more of my old pleasure in music all the time.

I saw Bryson last night. We were having a little supper for some of the English tutors, at the 'Golden Cross', which Bryson ought to have attended and as we knew he was in Oxford we went round to his digs to root him out. We found him sitting nursing a terrific black eye (the result of a very mild motor accident – better not mention this at home) and refusing to join us. I suspect that these little suppers are not really much to his taste: the fare is fried fish, ham and eggs, bread and cheese, and beer, and the whole thing is too homely, too rowdy, and too unluxurious for Bryson. This sounds like malice, but it isn't. Between ourselves, Bryson's beautiful clothes and general daintiness are a perfectly friendly and well established joke among some of his colleagues. There must be some real good in him; for though many laugh at his foppery and grumble at his laziness, I have never met any one, even in this hotbed of squabbles, who seriously dislikes him.

I had to abandon Lockhart at the beginning of last term and have not yet resumed it. It is most annoying when the last few volumes of a long book have to be left over like that. One somehow feels a disinclination to begin them again and to find how many names and facts one has forgotten: yet it is uncomfortable not to polish the book off. You will have the laugh of me this time.

While having a few days in bed recently I tried, at W's earnest recommendation, to read the *Three Musketeers*,[1] but not only got tired of it but also found it disgusting. All these swaggering bullies, living on the money of their mistresses – faugh! One never knows how good Scott is till one tries to read Dumas. Have you noticed how completely Dumas lacks any background? In Scott, behind the adventures of the hero, you have the whole society of the age, with all the interplay of town and country, Puritan and Cavalier, Saxon and Norman, or what not, and all the racy humour of the minor characters: and behind that again you have the eternal things – the actual countryside, the mountains, the weather, the very *feel* of travelling. In Dumas, if you try to look even an inch behind the immediate intrigue, you find just nothing at all. You are in an abstract world of gallantry and adventure which has no *roots* – no connection with human nature or mother earth. When the scene shifts from Paris to London there is no sense that you have reached a new country, no change of atmosphere. And I don't think there is a single passage to show that Dumas had ever seen a cloud, a road, or a tree. In a word, if you were asked to explain what you and I meant by 'the homely' in literature, you could almost reply, 'It means the opposite of *The Three Musketeers*.' But perhaps I am being too hard on what after all was written only for amusement. I suppose there must be a merit in the speed and verve of the plot, even if I don't like that kind of thing.

I was talking about this to Tolkien who, you know, grew up on Morris and Macdonald and shares my taste in literature to a fault. We remarked how odd it was that the word *romance* should be used

[1] By Alexandre Dumas (1844).

to cover things so different as Morris on the one hand and Dumas or Rafael Sabatini on the other – things not only different but so different that it is hard to imagine the same person liking both. We agreed that for what *we* meant by romance there must be at least the hint of another world – one must 'hear the horns of elfland'.

For fear you shd. think I am going too much off the deep end, let me add that I have just read a real modern thriller (Buchan's *Three Hostages*)[2] and enjoyed it thoroughly. So perhaps I shall be able to enjoy yours. Is it finished, by the way, and am I to see it? I have also read a war book (*Landlocked Lake* by Hanbury Sparrow)[3] – but that was because Barfield is introducing him as a new member of our Easter walking party. A 'regular' colonel seems an odd fish to come on a walk with my friends and me – I wonder if I shall quarrel with him!

Do try to write me a long letter soon. You are constantly in my mind even when I don't write, and to lose touch with you would be like losing a limb.

Dents say they will have *Pilgrim's Regress* out by the end of May. I have successfully resisted a foolish idea they had of an illustrated edition – whose price wd. of course have killed any sale it might hope for. But it *is* going to be decorated by a map on the end leaf which I had great fun in drawing the sketch for. I suppose you have no objection to my dedicating the book to you? It is yours by every right – written in your house, read to you as it was written, and celebrating (at least in the most important parts) an experience which I have more in common with you than anyone else. By the bye, you will be interested to hear that in finally revising the MS I did adopt many of your corrections, or at least made alterations where you objected. So if the book is a ghastly failure I shall always say 'Ah it's this Arthur business'

Do write. W. in bed with flu' (mild) but otherwise all well here

Yours

Jack

Give my love to your mother: I hope she is well.

[2] John Buchan, *The Three Hostages* [1924].
[3] Arthur Alan Hanbury-Sparrow, *The Landlocked Lake* (1932).

185

Magdalen College,
Oxford.
June 13th. 1933

My dear Arthur,

You ought to have had a copy of *Pilgrim's Regress* from me before now and a letter long before. My six complementary copies turned out to have so many unexpected claimants that I had exhausted them before I knew where I was: some new ones are now on order and I will send you one as soon as they arrive.

As for letters, they have been rather out of the question. I have never had a busier term – 9 to 1 and 5 to 7 every week day and two Sundays completely filled with extra work in the middle of the term: not to mention exams which have now set in and which will keep my nose to the grindstone till the end of July. However I have kept very well and have therefore nothing to complain of – except that I am rather hungry for reading and don't know when I shall get a few uninterrupted hours again.

'Invigilating' in exams last week I did manage to read *one* novel (I find that anything harder than novels is too much for me in the Schools) which I can recommend – *Tom's a-cold* by John Collier. The theme is one not uncommon now-a-days: that of a barbaric 'heroic' society growing up on the ruins of the present civilisation. But it has two great advantages over most such books. *1*. It doesn't waste time telling you how civilisation collapsed but starts a 100 years on. *2*. It lays the scene in the South of England and is very topographical, so that you can actually see the Berkshire downs and Savernake Forest turning into the fortresses, the greenwoods, and the valley communities of a world at about the same stage of development as that in *The Roots of the Mountains*. One gets v. well the idea of how much *larger* England would seem under those conditions.

I must announce with regret that I shall not be paying you a visit this summer (Perhaps this is premature as I have not yet been asked!) I have come to the decision with considerable doubt, but I think on the whole I am right. Warnie and I want to go and see the Scotch uncles and as they are getting on it ought to be done this year. This will sound an odd programme to you. It is not all 'duty' – curiosity, desire to revive childish memories, and the anticipation of an amused yet affectionate pleasure in seeing our father in them, all come in to it. We shall then go back from Glasgow by the Clyde Shipping Company boat – and I admit I shall be such a rag by the time exams are over that I rather look forward to some lazy days at sea as the best, if not the only, holiday I shall be capable of. I am sorry to disappoint you (if I may flatter myself that it is a disappointment). At any rate don't think that this is a precedent or that it means the end of my appearances at Belfast!

I was up to London for the *Rheingold*, which I enjoyed less than *Siegfried* – chiefly I think because we had very bad seats (*We* is Barfield and I).[1] MacFarlane – who has had a nervous breakdown since, poor chap – says he saw you* at one of the other operas: what a pity we hadn't known and gone together.

I had an extremely kind letter from Reid about the book. I think it is going to be at least as big a failure as *Dymer*, and am consequently trying to take to heart all the things I wrote you when you were bowled over by Reid's decision on your first novel – not entirely without success. How goes the detective story?

I hardly deserve a letter, but hope you will treat me better than my deserts

Yours
Jack

* Sounds as if this were the *cause* of the breakdown!

186

The Kilns,
Headington Quarry,
Oxford.
Aug. 17th. 1933.

My dear Arthur,

I have been silent for a terribly long time, I know, but it has not really been my fault. I had a solid month's examining after term ended, and then I went away for my sea holiday. I had pictured myself writing to you on the boat, but this turned out to be practically impossible: so that I am really writing if not on the first possible day, at any rate on the second or third. Before I go on to anything else I must answer one point in your last letter: – you comment on my saying nothing about your having come so near me without visiting me. The fact is I deliberately said nothing about it because I feared that, if I

[1] He saw *Das Rheingold* at Covent Garden on 2 May. See the report of this performance in *The Times* (3 May 1933), p. 12.

did, it might seem that *my* intention of not visiting *you* this year was a kind of tit-for-tat – that I was offended and was thus taking my revenge, or, at least, was excusing my intention by your action. I would have liked you to come and see me, of course: but I never thought that England ought to be forbidden ground to you if you were not seeing me for any reason. I have no wish to reduce you to stealing past Oxford with a false beard on – like you and me stealing past Leeborough from Bernagh in the old days.

I did not enjoy the *Rheingold* this year *nearly* as much as I enjoyed *Siegfried* last year – neither at the time nor in memory. Oddly enough the hammer passage which you mention I actually disliked. I had enjoyed it on your gramophone, but at Covent Garden it seemed to me so much cruder and, before it ended (and I thought it would never end) nearly ridiculous. You must not think that my loyalty to the *Ring* is wavering. The main causes of my disliking the *Rheingold* were (a) Our having very bad seats (b) My not liking the man who sang Alberich [Eduard Habich]. I admit that Alberich must sometimes shout instead of singing – but that man seemed to shout unnecessarily. Next year I hope to go to the *Valkyrie*.

While I am on these things, I might add that I have actually been to the films to-day! – to see *Cavalcade*!![1] This is one of the most disgraceful confessions I have ever made to you. I thought it would be interesting historically, and so I suppose it was: and certainly very clever. But there is not an idea in the whole thing from beginning to end: it is a mere brutal assault on one's emotions, using material which one can't help feeling intensely. It appeals entirely to that part of you which lives in the throat and chest, leaving the spirit untouched. I have come away feeling as if I had been at a debauch.

The sea holiday was a success. We went first by train to Arrochar where we slept a night [4 August] and had one glorious day's walking on the shores of Loch Long and Loch Lomond and across the mountains between them. I forget if you have been in those parts. They seemed to me to excell all other mountains in one respect – the curiously fantastic, yet heavy shapes of rock into which the summits are formed. They realise one's idea of mountains as the fastnesses of the giants. The actual *beach* of Loch Lomond also pleased me very much – an ordinary pebbly beach such as you might find at the sea

[1] The stage play *Cavalcade*, which was about contemporary British history, was written by Noël Coward and first acted in 1932. It was made into a film by Frank Lloyd in 1933, and was so popular that a command performance was given at Windsor Castle before King George V and Queen Mary on 2 May 1933.

with the unusual addition that it had trees on it and that you could drink the water. Up in the mountains we had a glorious hour at a stream – a golden brown stream, with cataracts and deep pools. We spread out all our clothes (sweat-sodden) to dry on the flat stones, and lay down in a pool just under a little waterfall, and let the foam come down the back of our heads and round our necks. Then when we were cool, we came out and sat naked to eat our sandwiches, with our feet still in the rushing water. Why have you and I never done this? (Answer – because we never came to a suitable stream at a suitable time)

This glorious day was followed by a very tiring and trying, but extremely *interesting*, week end *chez l'oncle* at Helensburgh.[2] It was uncannily like being at home again – specially when Uncle Bill announced on the Sunday evening 'I won't be going into town to-morrow', and we with well-feigned enthusiasm replied 'Good!'. But to describe the whole thing would take a book.

On the Monday afternoon [7 August] we sailed from Glasgow. The journey down the Clyde was beautiful, despite some rain, and tho' there were more passengers on board than I would have chosen, there was usually a quiet corner to read in. I liked – you would probably not – the homely feeling on these boats, with dinner at 1 and 'High Tea' at 6. It was very strange coming into Belfast next morning. I had made up my mind that it was no good trying to arrange a meeting with you. The time – we were sailing again at one o'clock – was much too long for a three-handed talk of you and W. and me, and too short for sending *him* off anywhere so that I could have you tête-à-tête. Our programme was simple. We trammed to Cambell and thence walked up the hills round the Shepherd's hut. The sight of all those woods and fields made me regret very much that I was not having an Irish holiday with you: and the new house (near Kelsie's new house) made me wonder how much more might be altered by next year. We walked down by the ordinary, poignantly familiar, route, stopped to look at Leeborough – how the trees are growing! – and then went down the Circular Rd. to St Marks to see the window which W. had never yet seen.[3] He was delighted with it. Here we had a conversation with the verger – who referred to Gordon

[2] The uncles were Albert's brothers, William and Richard Lewis, who moved to Scotland in 1883 and entered into a partnership selling rope and felt. Their business was located in Glasgow, but the brothers had their homes at Helensburgh, on the north bank of the Clyde, some fifteen miles from the city.

[3] This was a stained-glass window the Lewis brothers placed there in memory of their parents.

me wonder how much more might be altered by real years. We walked down by the ordinary, poignantly familiar, route, stopped to look at Leeborough – how the trees are growing! – and then went down the Circular Rd. to St Marks to see the window which W. had never yet seen. He was delighted with it. Here we had a conversation with the verger – who referred to Gordon as "Gordon"! Then, after a drink in the reformed pub at Gelson's corner, we got back into town.

The rest of the tour I shall not describe in detail. The bit I should most like to have shared with you was the departure from Waterford. The sail down the river, peppered with v. early Norman castles, was good, but what was better was the next three hours out to sea. Imagine a flat F. grey sea, and a sky of almost the same colour: between these a long fish-shaped streak of pure crimson, about 20 miles long, and lasting, unchanged or changing imperceptibly, for hours. Then add three or four perfectly transparent mountains, so extraordinarily spiritualised that they absolutely realised the old idea of Ireland as the "isle of the saints". Like this —

I do not remember that I have ever seen anything more calm and spacious and celestial. Not but what we had some wonderful sunsets at other times in the voyage. You with your dislike of the sea will hardly admit it, but from a boat out of sight of land one does get effects hardly to be got elsewhere. For one thing the sky is so huge and

See pages 456–8

as 'Gordon'! Then, after a drink in the reformed pub at Gelson's corner, we got back into town.

The rest of the tour I shall not describe in detail. The bit I should most like to have shared with you was the departure from Waterford. The sail down the river, peppered with v. early Norman castles, was good, but what was better was the next three hours out to sea. Imagine a flat French grey sea, and a sky of almost the same colour: between these a long fish-shaped streak of pure crimson, about 20 miles long, and lasting, unchanged or changing imperceptibly, for hours. Then add three or four perfectly *transparent* mountains, so extraordinarily spiritualised that they absolutely realised the old idea of Ireland as the 'isle of the saints'. Like this –

I do not remember that I have ever seen anything more calm and spacious and celestial. Not but what we had some wonderful sunsets at other times in the voyage. You with your dislike of the sea will hardly admit it, but from a boat out of sight of land one does get effects hardly to be got elsewhere. For one thing the sky is so huge and the horizon is uninterrupted in every direction, so that the mere *scale* of the sky-scenery is beyond anything you get ashore: and for another, the extreme simplicity of the design – flat disk and arched dome and nothing else – produces a kind of concentration. And then again to turn suddenly from these huge sublimities as one passes a staircase head and hear the sound of plates being laid or the laugh of a boy coming up on the warmer air from below, gives that delicious contrast of the homely and familiar in the midst of the remote, which is the master-stroke of the whole thing.

I am re-reading Malory, and am astonished to find how much more connected, more of a unity, it is than we used to see. I no longer lose myself in the 'brasting'. There is still too much of it, to be sure, but I am sustained by the beauty of the sentiment, and also the actual turns of phrase. How could one miss 'He commanded his trumpets to blow that all the earth trembled and *dindled* of the sound.'[4] Clearly one must read every good book at least once every ten years. It now seems to me that my Bookham reading of Malory was almost worthless. Did you ever realise that it is full of *pathos*? I never did until a pupil pointed it out to me a few months ago – wh. is what set me re-reading it.

I hope I shall be able to be a fairly regular correspondent again for the rest of the summer. Bad luck about the book!

Yours,
Jack

[4] Sir Thomas Malory, *Morte d'Arthur*, Bk. V, ch. 8.

187

[The Kilns]
Sept 1st. 1933

My dear Arthur,

I have no right to complain that I have not yet heard from you. Nor have I much to say on my own account: but I think I will write a little just to feel that we are keeping the channel open.

W. and I are heartily sick of the summer, the others not. The pond is sinking lower and lower and all sorts of stones and roots that ought to be covered are projecting – it seems almost an indecency. The water is getting dirtier and warmer and bathing has been abandoned. Flowers and vegetables are withering and the ground is so hard that a short walk leaves you footsore as if you had been walking on pavements. This morning we woke to coolness and thick mist and spangled cobwebs. I thought it was the first day of autumn and felt the old excitement. But it was all a cheat and by the time we came out of church it was another blazing day – pitiless blue sky, sun hammering bleached white grass, wasps buzzing, dragon flies darting, and Mr Papworth panting in the shade with his tongue out.

Which reminds me – I am so sorry to hear about your Paddy. I couldn't lay my hands on your letter when I was writing last – I knew there was something in it I hadn't dealt with but couldn't remember what. How heartless you must have thought me. I now have your letter and can fully sympathise. It is always hard luck when you feel that other people have hidden facts from you till it is too late. I don't now agree – how heartily I once would have – with any idea of 'trying to forget' things and people we have lost, or indeed with trying always and on principle to exclude any kind of distressing thought from one's mind. I don't mean one ought to sentimentalize a sorrow, or (often) scratch a shame till it is raw. But I had better not go on with the subject as I find my ideas are all in disorder. I know I feel very strongly that when in a wakeful night some idea which one 'can't stand' – some painful memory or mean act of ones own or vivid image of physical pain – thrusts itself upon you, that you ought not to thrust it away but look it squarely in the face for some appreciable time: giving it of course an explicitly devotional context. But I don't fully know why and am not prepared to work the thing out. Anyway, this only very faintly arises out of what you said – and it won't bring the poor beast back to life!

I have just re-read *Lilith* and am much clearer about the meaning.

The first thing to get out of the way is all Greville Macdonald's nonsense about 'dimensions' and 'elements' – if you have his preface in your edition.[1] That is just the sort of *mechanical* 'mysticism' which is worlds away from Geo. Macdonald. The main lesson of the book is against secular philanthropy – against the belief that you can effectively obey the 2nd command about loving your neighbour without first trying to love God.

The story runs like this. The human soul exploring its own house (the Mind) finds itself on the verge of unexpected worlds which at first dismay it (Chap. I–V). The first utterance of these worlds is an unconditional demand for absolute surrender of the Soul to the will of God, or, if you like, for Death (Chap. VI). To this demand the soul cannot at first face up (VI). But attempting to return to normal consciousness finds by education that its experiences are not abnormal or trivial but are vouched for by all the great poets and philosophers (VII *My Father's MS*). It repents and tries to face the demand, but its original refusal has now rendered real submission temporarily impossible (IX). It has to face instead the impulses of the subconscious (X) and the slightly spurious loyalties to purely human 'causes' – political, theological etc (XI). It now becomes conscious of its fellow men: and finds them divided into 'Lovers' (='Hearts' in our old classification) and 'Bags' or 'Giants' (='Spades'). But because it is an unconverted soul, has not yet died, it cannot really help the Lovers and becomes the slave of the Bags. In other words the young man, however amiably disposed towards the sweet and simple people of the world, gets a job or draws a dividend, and becomes in fact the servant of the economic machine (XII–XIII) But he is too good to go on like this, and so becomes a 'Reformer', a 'friend of humanity' – a Shelley, Ruskin, Lenin (XIV). Here follows a digression on Purgatory (XV–XVII).

With the next section we enter on the deepest part of the book which I still only v. dimly understand. Why do so many purely secular reformers and philanthropists fail and in the end leave men more wretched and wicked than they found them? Apparently the unconverted soul, doing its very best for the Lovers, only succeeds first in *waking* (at the price of its own blood) and then in becoming the tool of, *Lilith*. Lilith is still quite beyond me. One can trace in her specially the Will to Power – which here fits in quite well – but there is a great deal more than that. She is also the real ideal somehow

---

[1] *Lilith: A Romance*. With Introductory Key, a paraphrase of an earlier manuscript version, and explanation of notes by Greville MacDonald (1924).

spoiled: she is not primarily a sexual symbol, but includes the characteristic *female* abuse of sex, which is love of Power, as the characteristic male abuse is sensuality (XVIII–XXIX). After a long and stormy attempt to do God's work in Lilith's way or Lilith's work in God's way, the soul comes to itself again, realises that its previous proceedings are 'cracked absolutely' and in fact has a sort of half-conversion. But the new powers of will and imagination which even this half conversion inspires (symbolised in the horse) are so exhilarating that the soul thinks *these* will do instead of 'death' and again shoots off on its own. This passage is v. true and important. Macdonald is aware how *religion itself* supplies new temptations (XXX–XXXI). This again leads to another attempt to help the Lovers in his own way, with consequent partial disaster in the death of Lona (XXXII–XXXVII). He finds himself the *jailer* of Lilith: i.e. he is now living in the state of tension with the evil thing inside him only just held down, and at a terrible cost – until he (or Lilith – the Lilith-part of him) at last repents (Mara) and consents to die (XXXVIII–end)

I hope this has not bored you. I am so excited about it myself that for the moment I can hardly imagine anyone else being bored: but probably I have done it so badly that in the result nothing survives to be excited about. For one thing, I have emphasised the external side too much. Correct everything above by remembering that it is not only helping the Lovers outside against the Bags, but equally the Lover in himself against the Bag in himself.

You will be surprised to hear that I have been at the Cinema again! Don't be alarmed, it will not become a habit. I was persuaded into going to *King Kong* because it sounded the sort of Rider Haggardish thing that has always exercised a spell over me. What else I have done I hardly know. Read Plato's *Gorgias*, and am reading a long *Histoire de la Science Politique* (!!) by Janet ——[2] surprisingly interesting. Almost everything is, I find, as one goes on.

You say nothing about Harrogate – was it nice? I have missed our annual meeting a good deal. I remember you at least once a day whatever happens and often in between, and wish we could see more of one another. I wonder if the time will ever come when we shall? And would it work if we did? I often feel that you are the one who has changed. This seems absurd when I have changed from atheism to Christianity and from *The Crock of Gold* to, say, the history of political science! But I feel all my changes to be natural developments

[2] Paul-Alexandre Janet, *Histoire de la Science Politique dans ses Rapports avec la Morale* (1872).

of the original thing we had in common, and forget that *of course* they seem natural to me because they are mine, while yours, doubtless equally natural, can never seem so to me to the same extent. I don't know how I come to be writing about this and writing it so badly. I had better stop.

Any news of your MS yet? I have tried to keep myself this time from getting too wrapped up in my own book's success and think I have partially succeeded – just as well, too!

Yours
Jack

188

Hotel Victoria,
Milford-on-Sea,
Hants.
Sept 12 1933

My dear Arthur,

It was a delightful surprise to get your long and interesting letter: certainly the longest and one of the most interesting letters I have ever had from you.

I have been thinking all morning over your question about God and evil which is very far from being 'elementary' to me – or for that matter, I suppose, to the angels. If I understand you rightly you are not *primarily* concerned with the sort of logical problem as how the All-Good can produce evil, or produce a world in which there is evil, but with a more personal, practical, and intimate problem as to how far God can sympathise with our evil will as well as with our good – or, to draw it milder, *whether* he does.

I should begin, I think, by objecting to an expression you use: 'God must have a potentiality of His opposite – evil.' For this I would substitute the idea which someone had in the Middle Ages who defined God as '*That which has no opposite*' i.e. we live in a world of clashes, good and evil, true and false, pleasant and painful, body and spirit, time and eternity etc, but God is not simply (so to speak) *one* of the two clashes but the ultimate thing beyond them all – just as in our constitution the King is neither the Prime Minister nor the Leader of the Opposition, but the thing behind them which alone enables these to be a lawful government and an opposition – or just as space is neither bigness or smallness but that in which the distinctions of big and small arise. This then is my first point. That Evil is not something outside and '*over against*' God, but *in some way* included under Him.

My second point seems to be in direct contradiction to this first one, and is (in scriptural language) as follows: that God 'is the Father of Lights and in Him is *no darkness at all*'.[1] *In some way* there is no evil whatever in God. He is pure Light. All the *heat* that in us is lust or anger in Him is cool light – eternal morning, eternal freshness, eternal springtime: never disturbed, never strained. Go out on any perfect morning in early summer before the world is awake and see, not the thing itself, but the material symbol of it.

Well, these are our two starting points. *In one way* (our old phrase!) God includes evil, in another way he does not. What are we to do next? My beginning of the 'next' will be to deny another re-mark of yours – where you say 'no good without evil'. This on my view is absolutely untrue: but the opposite 'no evil without good' is absolutely true. I will try to explain what I mean by an analogy.

Supposing you are taking a dog on a lead through a turnstile or past a post. You know what happens (apart from his usual ceremonies in passing a post!). He tries to go the wrong side and gets his lead looped round the post. *You* see that he can't do it, and therefore pull him back. You pull him *back* because you want to enable him to go *forward*. He wants exactly the same thing – namely to go *forward*: for that very reason he resists your pull *back*, or, if he is an obedient dog, yields to it reluctantly as a matter of duty which seems to him to be quite in opposition to his own will: tho' *in fact* it is only by yielding to you that he will ever succeed in getting where he wants.

Now if the dog were a theologian he would regard his own will as a *sin* to which he was tempted, and therefore an *evil*: and he might go on to ask whether you understand and 'contained' his evil. If he did you cd. only reply 'My dear dog, if by your will you mean what you really want to do, viz. to get forward along the road, I not only understand this desire but *share* it. Forward is exactly where I want you to go. If by your will, on the other hand, you mean your will to pull against the collar and try to force yourself forward in a direction which is no use – why I *understand* it of course: but just because I understand it (and the whole situation, which you *don't* understand) I cannot possibly share it. In fact the more I sympathise with your *real* wish – that is, the wish to get on – the less can I sympathise (in the sense of 'share' or 'agree with') your resistance to the collar: for I see that this is actually rendering the attainment of your real wish impossible.'

I don't know if you will agree at once that this is a parallel to the

John i.5.

situation between God and man: but I will work it out on the assumption that you do. Let us go back to the original question – whether and, if so, in what sense God contains, say, my evil will – or 'understands' it. The answer is God not only understands but *shares* the desire which is at the root of all my evil: the desire for complete and ecstatic happiness. He made me for no other purpose than to enjoy it. But He knows, and I do not, how it can be really and permanently attained. He knows that most of *my* personal attempts to reach it are actually putting it further and further out of my reach. With these therefore He cannot sympathise or 'agree': His sympathy with my *real* will makes that impossible. (He may *pity* my mis-directed struggles, but that is another matter.) The practical results seem to be two.

1. I may always feel looking back on any past sin that in the very heart of my evil passion there was something that God approves and wants me to feel not less but more. Take a sin of Lust. The over-whelming thirst for *rapture* was good and even divine: it has not go to be unsaid (so to speak) and recanted. But it will never be quenched as I tried to quench it. If I refrain – if I submit to the collar and come round the right side of the lamp-post – God will be guiding me as quickly as He can to where I shall get what I really wanted all the time. It will not be very like what I now think I want: but it will be more like it than some suppose. In any case it will be the real thing, not a consolation prize or substitute. If I had it I should not need to fight against sensuality as something impure: rather I should spon-taneously turn away from it as something dull, cold, abstract, and artificial. This, I think, is how the doctrine applies to past sins.

2. On the other hand, when we are thinking of a sin in the future, i.e. when we are tempted, we must remember that *just because* God wants for us what we really want and knows the only way to get it, therefore He must, in a sense, be quite ruthless towards sin. He is not like a human authority who can be begged off or caught in an in-dulgent mood. The more He loves you the more determined He must be to pull you back from your way which leads nowhere into His way which leads where you want to go. Hence Macdonald's words 'The *all-punishing, all-pardoning* Father'. You may go the wrong way again, and again He may forgive you: as the dog's master may extricate the dog after he has tied the whole lead round the lamp-post. But there is no hope *in the end* of getting where you want to go except by going God's way. And what does '*in the end*' mean? This is a terrible question. If endless time will really help us to go the right way, I believe we shall be given endless time. But perhaps

God knows that time makes no difference. Perhaps He knows that if you can't learn the way in 60 or 70 years on this planet (a place probably constructed by Divine skill for the very purpose of teaching you) then you will never learn it anywhere. There may be nothing left for Him but to destroy you (the kindest thing): *if He can.*

I think one may be quite rid of the old haunting suspicion – which raises its head in every temptation – that there is something *else* than God – some other country (Mary Rose . . . Mary Rose)[2] into which He forbids us to trespass – some kind of delight wh. He 'doesn't appreciate' or just chooses to forbid, but which wd. be real delight if only we were allowed to get it. The thing *just isn't there.* Whatever we desire is either what God is trying to give us as quickly as He can, or else a false picture of what He is trying to give us – a false picture wh. would not attract us for a moment if we saw the real thing. Therefore God does really in a sense contain evil – i.e. contains what is the real motive power behind all our evil desires. He knows what we want, even in our vilest acts: He is longing to give it to us. He is not looking on from the outside at some new 'taste' or 'separate desire of our own'. Only because he has laid up *real* goods for us to desire are we able to go wrong by snatching at them in greedy, mis-directed ways. The truth is that evil is not a real *thing* at all, like God. It is simply good *spoiled.* That is why I say there can be good without evil, but no evil without good. You know what the biologists mean by a parasite – an animal that lives on another animal. Evil is a *parasite.* It is there only because good is there for it to spoil and confuse.

Thus you may well feel that God understands our temptations – understands them a great deal more than we do. But don't forget Macdonald again – '*Only God understands evil and hates it.*' Only the dog's master knows how useless it is to try to get on with the lead knotted round the lamp-post. This is why we must be prepared to find God implacably and immovably forbidding what may seem to us very small and trivial things. But He knows whether they are really small and trivial. How small some of the things that doctors forbid would seem to an ignoramus.

I expect I have said all these things before: if so, I hope they have not wasted a letter. Alas! they are so (comparatively) easy to say: so hard, so *all but* impossible to go on *feeling* when the strain comes.

I have not time left for the rest of your letter. It was bad luck getting ill at the cottage: an illness at home has its pleasures, but on a holiday it is – well 'disconsolate' is the word that best fits my feeling

[2] See J. M. Barrie's *Mary Rose* (1920).

about it. We have had a spate of unwanted and mostly uninvited visitors all summer and have (all four of us) come down here to give Minto a rest. It is opposite the Isle of Wight, and quite pleasant. We went to Beaulieu Abbey this afternoon – which would well deserve a letter in itself. I have since I came down read Voltaire's *Candide*, and Gore's *Jesus of Nazareth* (Home University Library) which I most strongly advise you to get at once. It is perhaps the best book about religion I have yet read – I mean of the theological kind – not counting books like *Lilith*. I am particularly pleased at having at last found out what Sadducees and Pharisees really were: tho' it is an alarming bit of knowledge because most of the religious people I know are either one or the other. (Warnie is a bit of a Sadducee, and I am a good bit of a Pharisee.) I am now going to tackle a John Buchan.

When I suggested that you had changed, I didn't mean that you had changed towards me. I meant that I thought the centre of your *interests* might have shifted more than mine. This leads on to what you say about being a mere mirror for other people on which each friend can cast his reflection in turn. That certainly is what you *might* become, just as a hardened bigot shouting every one down till he had no friends left is what I am in danger of becoming. In other words *sympathy* is your strong point, as *stability* is mine – if I have a strong point at all, which is doubtful: or *weakness* is your danger, as *Pride* is mine. (You have no idea how much of my time I spend just *hating* people whom I disagree with – tho' I know them only from their books – and inventing conversations in which I score off them.) In other words, we all have our own burdens, and must do the best we can. I do not know which is the worse, nor do we need to: if each of us could imitate the other.

The woods are just beginning to turn here – the drive was exquisite this afternoon. Love from all.

Yours,
Jack

189

[The Kilns]
Nov 5th. 1933

My dear Arthur,

I was glad to see your hand again. In spite of the remarks at the beginning of your letter, which tempt me to further discussion, I must try to prevent this also from becoming an essay in amateur Theology.

I am glad to hear that Tchainie is once more sufficiently my friend to ask about my mediaeval book. You can tell her that it is not finished yet, though it might have been if I had not been made English Examiner which has devoured a good deal of my last two long Vacs. As one holds the job only for two years I am now free again and hope to get on with it. By the way has she read the *Regress* – I don't mean '*Ask her* if she has read the *Regress*'!

To answer the next point in your letter, MacFarlane is back at work again and seems alright: but that perhaps does not count for much as he seemed alright to me up to the moment when he went sick. I have no eye for health. 'How much better he is looking' – 'How ill he is looking' people say to me as a visitor leaves the room, and I have never noticed any difference. I hope mere selfishness is not the cause.

The news of your learning to ride was surprising, amusing (as you foresaw!) and on the whole good. Perhaps you will be a 'huntin' man' when I next meet you, slapping your leggings with a crop, and drinking whiskies with the county families' fast daughters and hard-riding sons. What a fine sight it would be to see Bob, Janie, and you, altogether and all in full hunting kit (Janie wd. look fine in a tall hat and breeches) taking a fence together. What would attract me most about riding, viz. the unity of man and beast, is, I suppose, largely spoiled by having to use hired horses. But if you find you like it I suppose you could easily afford a horse of your own, if Lea knows anything about the care of a horse. Certainly I should enjoy very much strolling round with you to visit it in its stable.

I haven't read the new De La Mare,[1] but probably shall. Galsworthy, though I fully acknowledge his merits, I somehow never feel any desire to return to. Warnie feels quite differently and the original *Saga* is one of his old favourites which he can always read again. I forget whether I mentioned to you Collier's *Poor Tom's A-cold*[2] as the new book I have enjoyed most for a long time.

Did I (also) tell you that Warnie has complete sets of all the Beethoven symphonies, and that we have a whole symphony each Sunday evening? This is one of the best hours of the week. Maureen who is (to be frank) the difficult one of the household has by then returned to Monmouth from her week end at home: the rush and crowd of visitors and continual flurry of the week end subsides and after a quiet supper Minto, Warnie, Mr Papworth and myself sit down in the study and have our music. In this way we have worked

[1] Walter de la Mare, *The Fleeting, and Other Poems* (1933).
[2] John Collier, *Tom's a-cold* (1933).

through the first Seven, and it was my recollections of the Seventh (last Sunday) which made me mention the matter – just to let you know that I had once more been enjoying what I still think the best slow movement there is, and, of course, enjoying it all the more because of the associations. I don't however think the Seventh quite satisfactory as a whole: the final movement is by no means one of the best, and still less is it fit to follow the other. So far I think the Fifth quite easily the best, thus agreeing with the orthodox view: tho' I differ from it in finding the Eroica the poorest of the lot. The Eroica (the connection is Napoleon) leads me to what you say about Germany.

I might agree that the Allies are partly to blame, but nothing can fully excuse the iniquity of Hitler's persecution of the Jews, or the absurdity of his theoretical position. Did you see that he said 'The Jews have made *no contribution to human culture* and in crushing them I am doing the *will of the Lord*.' Now as the whole idea of the 'Will of the Lord' is precisely what the world owes to the Jews, the blaspheming tyrant has just fixed his absurdity for all to see in a single sentence, and shown that he is as contemptible for his stupidity as he is detestable for his cruelty. For the German people as a whole we ought to have charity: but for dictators, 'Nordic' tyrants and so on – well, read the chapter about Mr Savage in the *Regress*[3] and you have my views.

I wish you didn't always choose summer for your visits here. The place is to day at its best: the pond a smooth almost black sheet, sprinkled, or rather *paved* with bright leaves: the little birch wood flaming on the far side, and the hill and fir wood beyond fading into mist. Yes – the weather is alright *now* and I am getting all those fine feelings of revival – beginning to take longer walks again, remembering how much mere branch and sky and hedge ought to mean to one, and noticing suddenly for how long one has been only half awake.

Write again soon. Love to Mrs Greeves.

Yours,
Jack

[3] *The Pilgrim's Regress*, Bk. VI, ch. 6.

190

[The Kilns]
Oct 1st. 1934

My dear Arthur,

I am sending you back Pope Hadrian.[1] Warnie and I have both read it with a good deal of amusement and enjoyment. The latter is due, I suppose, entirely to the subject – for everyone likes to imagine what a man could do if he were a dictator, or Pope, or Caliph –; the amusement is mainly at the author's expence. The style is one of the most preposterous I have ever read, and I doubt if I ever saw so much pedantry combined with so much ignorance. Almost every one of his numerous and unnecessary Greek quotations contains some mistake: and in English he seems to think that *euphuism* means *euphemism* and that *verisimilar* means *very similar*. He is a queer fish – a man with a grievance, obviously: a sincere Catholic who hates almost everything and everybody with which Catholicism is associated: specially France and Ireland. He must have been a most disagreeable man.

We had a most interesting journey back.[2] We drove from Heysham across the back of England to Lincoln. A great deal of this route was spoiled by big industrial towns, but the first stages were lovely: very big, pale hills with many cliffs of that silvery-white rock – it is limestone. It is very different when you get down into Lincolnshire, which is as flat as a pancake. Lincoln itself is quite the best cathedral city I have ever seen. The centre of the town, where the cathedral stands, is on the only hill for miles, and the cathedral consequently dominates the whole countryside. The surroundings of the cathedral are magnificent – a beautiful close, a castle, and a Roman wall. What would specially have appealed to you was that after dinner as we strolled round it, we had the accompaniment of a little summer lightning and very distant *gentle* thunder. Do you know the kind of thunder which has almost a tinkle in it, like a musical sound?

I don't know that much has happened since we got back. My reading has been of a most miscellaneous order – Rider Haggard, Thomas Aquinas, Trollope, the Old Testament. Do you remember the passage in the latter where Moses sends spies into Canaan and

[1] Frederick Rolfe ('Baron Corvo'), *Hadrian the Seventh* (1904).
[2] In April 1934 Lewis, Mrs Moore and Maureen took a motor tour (Maureen driving) through parts of Ireland, stopping to visit Arthur, and returning home through the country described here.

they come back and say 'We have seen the giants, the sons of Anak; and we were in our own eyes as grasshoppers.'[3] Isn't that perfect? It brings out the monstrosity of the giants so well, because one thinks of the grasshopper as being not only small, but fragile, light and even flimsy. 'Beetles', for example, would not have done nearly so well.

Summer still drags on – far outstaying its welcome with me – and the pond shows no sign of rising to its normal level, though we have had a fairish amount of rain. Everyone is well – that is to say, we have all recovered from our holiday and are nearly as fit as if we had never been away. Of how few holidays can this be said!

Give my love to your mother, and – write soon.

Yours,
Jack

191

[The Kilns]
Dec. 26th. 1934

My dear Arthur,

I have carried your letter about in a pocket all this term with the intention of answering it, and here goes at last! I wonder how much of its news is still up to date. For example, if I had replied when the letter came I should have said 'I am so glad to hear that you have settled down in a comfortable routine' – but I can't do so now because you may have got unsettled since!

I wish you had told me a little more about Voyage to Arcturus.[1] Even if you can't describe it, you could at least give me some idea what it is about: at least whether it is about a voyage to Arcturus or not. I haven't come across the book yet, but will certainly read it if I do.

Which reminds me have *you* read 'Gape Row' by Agnes Romilly White? Gape Row is the name of a village which turns out with absolute certainty to be Dundonald, if you work out all the geographical indications. It is not a very good novel – indeed I am not sure it isn't a definitely bad novel (tho' several reviewers seem to have thought otherwise), but fancy reading of characters in a book looking down on the Lough from above Holywood Barracks, or, again, nearer Dundonald, looking over to the Castlereagh Hills! The scenery is quite well described, and it is probably the only chance you and I will ever have of seeing that landscape described in fiction – except

---

[3] Numbers xiii.33.
[1] David Lindsay, *A Voyage to Arcturus* (1920).

our own fiction, of course! The characters [are] all of the cottage class, and the dialect is well done – not that that kind of thing interests me after a few pages. If you want a New Year's Gift for any one like Gundrede or Janie (I mean like them in love of dialect) this would do admirably. Now I come to think of it, is Janie the author? (Don't let this raise false expectations in your mind. I don't mean what you mean.)

We had this term a concert which I enjoyed more than any I have ever heard.[2] Beecham conducted and the bill of fare was Beethoven's Fifth Symphony, A Debussy suite, Sibelius' *Tapiola* (forest-god of the Finns) and Elgar's Enigma Variations. For one thing, I have hardly ever before been at a concert where I liked *all* the items. The Elgar (do you know it?) I had never heard before and did not fully understand, but I understood enough to admire it greatly. For another thing, the playing was marvellous. I thought I knew the symphony from Warnie's records, but Beecham brought things out of it that I'd never dreamed of.

Apart from this, very little has happened to me. I have addressed societies at Manchester and Birmingham and am doing one at Cambridge next term, which, I suppose, is a step in one's career. I have had lunch and spent the afternoon at a monastery in the Cotswolds, where a former pupil of mine is a monk.[3] Funny to have a silent lunch (except that a book is read aloud) amidst rows of white robed figures and then to file out behind them – chanting – down the long, dark corridor. One of them was a fine old man with a white beard, which just added the last touch. Don't be alarmed: the effect on me was purely aesthetic, not religious, and during the afternoon my host talked nonsense enough to put me off the conventual life for ever and a day.

Give my love to your mother and let me have a letter when you can.

Yours
Jack

[2] This concert by the London Philharmonic Orchestra, under the direction of Sir Thomas Beecham, was performed in the Sheldonian Theatre on 15 November 1934.

[3] Lewis had been the guest of Dom Bede Griffiths at Prinknash Priory in Gloucester.

192

The Kilns,
Headington Quarry,
Oxford.
April 23^d 1935

My dear Arthur

It is a weary time since I heard from you and I ought to have answered you before: but though I am in your debt I doubt if my silences are longer than yours. The immediate object of this letter is to ask if I can come and stay a week with you this summer, please. As at present advised any date between July 1st and Oct. 5th will suit me. Now if you could within the next few weeks fix on any date between these two (preferably quand tu seras seul!) it would be a great advantage: for though all that period is at present free I do not know when engagements may begin to creep in. Of course it may not be convenient to have me at all, but I am assuming you would have no scruple about telling me if that were so. I am only anxious that if you are able and willing to have me we shd. not let the thing slip through our fingers as we did last year. If you can't arrange so far ahead, of course you can't (what it is to have a brain!) and there we are: but no doubt you see the advantage of so doing if it is possible.

I had seen the reviews of the Powys book and also heard (by an accident) what you hint about its contents: therefore I shall not read it. I do not always win even when the enemy attacks me in my own lines, but the one thing I can do is to make sure that at least I never go out of my way to seek him. What an extraordinary profile Powys has – I suppose you saw the pictures in several papers. I take it he is almost a lunatic?[1] The most interesting story I have read recently is *Land Under England* by one [Joseph] O'Neill: you should try it.

I am just back from my Easter walking tour with Barfield and co., this year in Derbyshire. Have you been there? It is appreciably more like my ideal country than any I have yet been. It is limestone moun-

---

[1] Arthur wrote 'T. F. Powys' at the top of the page. But of the three brothers, Theodore Francis, John Cowper and Llewelyn Powys, all of whom wrote many books, it is quite certain that Lewis was talking about Llewelyn who seemed the most wildly atheistic. He did not single out Lewis by name, but in his *Damnable Opinions*, published in April 1935, he attacked orthodox Christianity, and specially as it was practised and written about in Oxford, with maniacal fervour, claiming that for him 'the true religion is simple – it is to worship life, to bow down before life, beating our heads upon the grass in jubilant acquiescence' (p. 5).

tains: which means, from the practical point of view, that it has the jagg'd sky lines and deep vallies of ordinary mountainous country, but with this important difference, that owing to the paleness of the rock and the extreme clarity of the rivers, it is *light* instead of sombre – sublime yet smiling – like the delectable mountains. It gives you something the same sensation as Blake's songs.

This place is being ruined by building and what was Kiln Lane is turning into a street of council houses. Where will it end? If we live to be old there will hardly be any real country left in the South of England.

Give my love to your mother and any other of my friends whom you may meet: and let me have an answer as soon as possible to my question.

Yours
Jack

193

Magdalen College,
Oxford.
June 17th. 1935

My dear Arthur,

'Will you come Sunday or Monday?' says the host. 'No, I'll come Saturday,' says the guest. 'Oh Lord,' says the host (as it might be my father) or '*Why* do you do these things?' (as it might be another). On second thoughts I am booking a berth for Monday night, July 1st by Liverpool – leaving you Mon 8th.

There is just one cloud on the horizon. Minto's sister is seriously ill (in Dublin) and if Minto has to go over for a funeral she may want me to stay and run the house. Let us hope this won't happen. If it does, I suppose we shall be able to fix on a week that will suit both you and me later. In the meantime I thought it better to let the arrangement stand, and hope for the best – I hate putting off anything so nice.

Give my love to your mother and many, many thanks.

Yours,
Jack

194

My dear Arthur,

I am sorry you have had to haul this letter out of me by the scruff of its neck. It's not that I have nothing to say to you and don't want to hear what you have to say. I believe I could still make a fair attempt at a *regular* correspondence, but you yourself vetoed that, and odd letters, like odd bills, I do find it hard to meet when I'm busy.

Minto told you about our present bother. The guests are still here, and will be, so far as I can see, until the end of January.[1] Oh Arthur, what a snag it is that the people who are *pitiable* are not necessarily *likeable*. Molly Askins is emphatically one of those people of whom old Foord-Kelsie said 'We must learn to love those whom we can't like.' She's what you would call an encroaching person – do you know the type of small, dark woman with big gentle eyes and soft voice, who just gently and softly and even pathetically gets her own way in everything and really treats the house as a hotel? However, the thing's a duty and there's an end of it: tho', by the bye, as W. and I were saying the other day, the New Testament tells us to *visit* the widows, not to let them visit us!

I have finished my book, which is called *The Allegorical Love Poem*, and is dedicated to Barfield. The Clarendon Press have accepted it and hope to have it out by May. As I am to get 12 free copies (Dents only give one 6) you and Tchanie shall each have one and save your siller: and whatever you think of the matter, I hope, from experience of the Clarendon Press, that binding, paper etc will be – in our old formula – excellent, exquisite, and admirable. In other words, if you can't read it, you will enjoy looking at it, smelling it, and stroking it. If not a good book, it will be a good pet! It will be about 400 pp, they say. (It will be very funny, after this, if they do it in double columns and a paper cover.)

My other bit of literary news is that Sheed and Ward have bought the *Regress* from Dent. I didn't much like having a book of mine, and specially a religious book, brought out by a Papist publisher: but as they seemed to think they could sell it, and Dents clearly couldn't, I

---

[1] The guests were Molly Askins and her son Michael. Molly was, I think, the widowed daughter-in-law of Mrs Moore's brother, the Rev. William James Askins, at this time Rector of a church in Cavan, Co. Cavan.

gave in. I have been well punished: for Sheed, without any authority from me, has put a blurb on the inside of the jacket which says 'This story begins in Puritania (Mr Lewis was brought up in Ulster)' – thus implying that the book is an attack on my own country and my own religion. If you ever come across any one who might be interested, explain as loudly as you can that I was not consulted & that the blurb is a damnable lie told to try and make Dublin riff-raff buy the book. I didn't mean to spend so much of this letter on egoism.

I have tried in vain to buy *Voyage to Arcturus* but it is out of print. For reading, lately, I have re-read the *Faerie Queene* with enormous enjoyment. It must be a really great book because one can read it as a boy in one way, and then re-read it in middle life and get something very different out of it – and that to my mind is one of the best tests. I am at present engaged with Sir Thomas More's English works (i.e. everything except the Utopia) which are necessary to a job I'm doing. They are quite interesting, and sometimes really helpful in religious aspects, but not so good as they have lately been made out to be.

The worst of these letters at long intervals is that I can never remember how much has happened since I wrote last. e.g. did I tell you how much I was moved by seeing *A Winter's Tale*? I can't have told you about the magnificent philharmonic performance of the Ninth Symphony we were at a few weeks ago.[2] You know I used to dislike the choral part of it. I was completely converted and have seldom enjoyed anything more. How *tonic* Beethoven is, and how festal – one has the feeling of having taken part in the revelry of giants. By the way, the Siegfried Idyll, which we had in the same programme seems to me the dullest thing Wagner ever wrote: do you agree? The only successor to Wagner (since we've got onto that subject), the only man who has exercised the same enchantment over me since the old days, is Sibelius. This bent to 'Northern' things is quite real and one can't get over it – not that I ever thought of trying!

You would like this day. Behind the hill there is yellow early morning light and small clouds racing. Then, the bit of wood, bare and brown, and furiously agitated. Then, the pond half skinned with ice – the swans both ashore. And round the house a terrific wind is roaring – 'Arthur o'Bower has broken his band.' In fact I have en-

[2] This concert, conducted by Malcolm Sargent, was given by the London Philharmonic Orchestra in the Sheldonian Theatre on 28 November 1935. For details see *The Oxford Magazine*, vol. LIV (5 December 1935), pp. 244, 246.

joyed the whole of this winter – especially after the really tropical summers.

The only member of the visiting family whose society we like is the boy, Michael, about 5. You will be interested to hear that W. gets on with him much better than I do. That is, I theoretically hold that one ought to like children, but am shy with them in practice: he theoretically dislikes them, but is actually the best of friends. (So many new sides to his character have appeared in the last few years.)

Minto reads him the Peter Rabbit books every evening, and it is a lovely sight. She reads very slowly and he gazes up into her eyes which look enormous through her spectacles – what a pity she has no grandchildren. Would you believe it, that child had never been read to nor told a story by his mother in his life? Not that he is neglected. He has a whole time Nurse (an insufferable semi-lady scientific woman with a diploma from some Tom-fool nursing college), a hundred patent foods, is spoiled, and far too expensively dressed: but his poor imagination has been left without any natural food at all. I often wonder what the present generation of children will grow up like (how many middle aged men in all generations have said this). They have been treated with so much indulgence yet so little affection, with so much science and so little mother-wit. Not a fairy tale nor a nursery rhyme!

Please thank your mother for her kind and forgiving letter; I was very rude to her. I should like to be at home in these gales. I am sure there are waves in the Lough, and the firs are lifting the earth in our old wood. I must stop now and do a little work. A happy Christmas to you all, and from all.

Yours,
Jack

195

[The Kilns]
29th. Dec. 1935

My dear Arthur,

I am staying at home from Church this morning with a cold on the chest, so it seems a good occasion to answer your letter.

As regards your news – sympathy and congratulations. Sympathy on the wrench of parting and the gap it will leave: congratulations on having done the right thing and made a sacrifice. The chief consolation at such times, I think, is that the result, however unpleasant, must be a kind of relief after the period of saying 'Shall I really have to – no I won't – and yet perhaps I'd better.' There is always *some* peace in having submitted to the right. Don't spoil it by worrying about the *results*, if you can help it. It is not your business to succeed (no one can be sure of that) but to do right: when you have done so, the rest lies with God – and Will!

I don't think you exaggerate at all in your account of how it feels. After all – tho' our novels now ignore it – friendship is the greatest of worldly goods. Certainly to me it is the chief happiness of life. If I had to give a piece of advice to a young man about a place to live, I think I shd. say, 'sacrifice almost everything to live where you can be near your friends.' I know I am v. fortunate in that respect, and you much less so. But even for me, it wd. make a great difference if you (and one or two others) lived in Oxford.

I am correcting the first bunch of proofs for my book[1] and am (as we wd. have said in the old days) tearing my hair because it doesn't look at all the size of page I expected. It will not be as *tall* a book as I had pictured – and what is the good of a scholarly work if it does not rise like a tower at the end of a shelf?! I fear it may even be thickish and stumpy. Mon Dieu! quel douleur, o rage, o desespoir! (What on earth would we have done if either of us had succeeded in publishing a book in the old days – I imagine we might have gone literally out of our minds with horrors and ecstasies.)

I'm sorry you didn't have our weather. We had about a week of snow with frost on top of it – and then rime coming out of the air and making thick *woolly* formations on every branch. The little wood was indescribably beautiful. I used to go and crunch about on the crusted snow in it every evening – for the snow kept it light long after sunset. It was a labyrinth of white – the smallest twigs looking thick as seaweed and building up a kind of cathedral vault overhead. One thing the snow showed me was the amazingly high population of rabbits – usually concealed among the greens and greys. On the snow one cd. see them scuttling. W. and I have been much puzzled by some of the footprints. There seem to be a great many more and larger animals than we had supposed. Bears, Arthur, bears – at least it looks like it. I wish you cd. have had a couple of strolls with me round this place in the snow: it would have charmed away all your sorrows.

No, no, I never meant that Sibelius had the *tonic* quality of Beethoven. Do you remember our once talking about B. and Wagner & agreeing that B. was Olympian, W. titanic – B spiritual, W. natural? Well Sibelius is definitely like W. not like B. in that respect. He is not *noble* like Beethoven: he is inarticulate, intimate, en-

[1] *The Allegory of Love.*

thralling, and close to one, like Nature itself. Very, very *Northern*: he makes me think of birch forests & moss and salt-marshes and cranes and gulls. I mean the symphonies. You needn't be busied for music while you have a gramophone. Set aside a portion of your money for buying big works (symphonies etc): never play them except in their entirety – but perhaps I've given you all this good advice before.

I never finished *Gape Row*. But the descriptions of our own walks & hills were v. interesting. I thinkk yourr neww methodd of sspellingg bby ddoubbllingg alll cconnssonnanntts ssavvess a ggreatt ddeall off ttroubblle!

Please give my love to Mrs Greeves and remember me to all our friends.

Yours,
Jack
or JJacckk

When I said you had vetoed the idea of regular correspondence, I meant that you had vetoed the idea of *your* taking part in it. I didn't mean you had actually *forbidden* me to write to you!!

196

Magdalen College,
Oxford.
Feb 26th 1936

My dear Arthur,

I see to my consternation that it is over a month since your letter came. It certainly deserved an earlier answer but you must forgive me.

I was very sorry indeed to hear about 'Tommy'. I am particularly sorry for John.[1] You know I crossed with the pair of them last time I left home: and I should like to say as impressively as I can – and you to take note – that I was very much impressed by seeing them together and by the fire, almost the spiritual atmosphere of their whole world of mountain climbing. It gave me a new and most favourable sidelight on John: and I am afraid it is most unlikely that he will find any one to take Tommy's place. I am very sorry for him. Try to be as nice to him as you can – but I have no doubt you are doing that already.

For yourself I expect days are pretty dim at present. Do you hear

---

[1] 'Tommy' and 'John' were Arthur's dogs.

good news of the boy? As I said before, I am sure you have done the right thing, and I'm afraid that is all the comfort I can offer.

I quite understand what you say about the comfort derived from all a dog's 'little affairs', and enjoyed reading that passage as much as any in your letter. They are a *busy* folk. And talking of dogs, poor old Mr Papworth has been gathered to his fathers. He had been ailing for some time and finally got a bad ulcer on his chin. He was given a strong sleeping draught. When I went to bed he was asleep in his basket and breathing as gently as a child: in the morning he was dead. Minto has been very badly upset – almost as if for a human being. I don't feel it as badly as that myself and would discourage the feeling (I think) if I had it. But it is a parting, and one sometimes remembers his old happy days, especially his puppyhood, with an ache.

I have just read what I think a really great book, 'The Place of the Lion' by Charles Williams. It is based on the Platonic theory of the other world in which the archtypes of all earthly qualities exist: and in the novel, owing to a bit of machinery which doesn't matter, these archtypes start sucking our world back. The lion of strength appears in the world & the strength starts going out of houses and things into him. The archtypal butterfly (enormous) appears and all the butterflies of the world fly back into him. But man contains and ought to be able to rule all these forces: and there is one man in the book who does, and the story ends with him as a second Adam 'naming the beasts' and establishing dominion over them.

It is not only a most exciting fantasy, but a deeply religious and (unobtrusively) a profoundly learned book. The reading of it has been a good preparation for Lent as far as I am concerned: for it shows me (through the heroine) the special sin of abuse of intellect to which all my profession are liable, more clearly than I ever saw it before. I have learned more than I ever knew yet about humility. In fact it has been a big experience. Do get it, and don't mind if you don't understand everything the first time. It deserves reading over and over again. It isn't often now-a-days you get a *Christian* fantasy.

My own book will be 15/–, so if you can sell it it will be 15/– clear! I am sick of proof correcting which has had to go on concurrently with all my other work this whole term.[2]

[2] Unbeknown to Lewis at this time, the proofs of *The Allegorical Love Poem* were being read by the author of *The Place of the Lion* who was on the editorial staff of the Oxford University Press and indeed responsible for altering the name of Lewis's book (published on 21 May 1936) to *The Allegory of Love*. Lewis and Charles Williams were to meet shortly after-

Our visitors, thank God, are gone. They have left Minto very worn out but not, so far as I can see, actually ill.

We have had such a severe winter than even I, with all my polar bear instincts am tired of it. But the snow drops are up now and we have had one or two of those very early fine days which excite me more than the real spring. You know – that thin, tingling, virginal weather.

Most of Sibelius' symphonies are recorded and are glorious. I agree with you about the *Old Curiosity Shop* – one of the most homely and friendly of all Dickens. With love to you all.

Yours
Jack

197

Magdalen College,
Oxford.
May 1st 1936

My dear Arthur,

I must confess it would *not* have been a good time for you to turn up. *Why* will you insist on coming to England in vacations and summers? If you would only come in the Autumn term (Oct 11th– Dec. 5th) I would try to make you comfortable in college: and I don't need to breakfast so early now. About the Kilns, I am sorry: I know that for many reasons it can never be a comfortable house for you to stay in.

I shall be free on and after June 27th and would come any time you suggested. I look forward to it with enormous pleasure – tho' rather ashamed that I can make so little return. I trust you won't be packing all the time I'm with you!

Oddly enough I read *Aerial*[1] too, and in the same edition a few weeks ago – good fun. I don't know how far it is reliable.

No time to write now. Please let me have a line saying which dates after the 27th wd. suit you. Is the enclosed good? – I can't help hoping *not*.

I shall be sending you my book in a week or so. Love to all

Yours,
Jack

wards, and thus began one of the most cherished friendships of Lewis's life. Among the many tributes Lewis was to pay Williams was his Preface to *Essays Presented to Charles Williams* (1947). See as well the references to Charles Williams in the *Biography*, particularly chapter V.

[1] John H. Bone, *The Aerial: A Comedy in One Act* (1932).

198

The Kilns
Easter Sunday [28 March] 1937

My dear Arthur,

I have been meaning to write to you for some time, and had partly excused myself because I was waiting to send you a story of Tolkien's which is to be published soon and which I think you may like:[1] but Uncle Gussie[2] turned up on Thursday (the coolest and most characteristic visit – merely a wire to announce his arrival!) and jogged my conscience with a message from you.

Thanks for your letter. I suppose I shall hear more from you about America when we meet. Am I right in concluding from your mere list of towns that on the aesthetic side – as regards mountains, rivers and woods etc. – it made no impression? I am glad to hear that you think of risking another visit to us and will do my best to make you less uncomfortable than you usually are.[3] I suppose it *must* be in the

[1] *The Hobbit* was published on 21 September 1937.

[2] Lewis's mother's brother, Augustus Warren Hamilton (1866–1945).

[3] Arthur's trip to America was at the invitation of William Moncrief McClurg (1907–   ). The young men met in the 1920s and, though unlike in many ways, they delighted in one another's company and took a number of trips together. After some science courses in Belfast, McClurg set his heart on becoming an osteopath. However, being unable to afford the training, he received enough financial help from Arthur and Arthur's four aunts to pursue his studies at the Kirksville College of Osteopathy and Surgery in Kirksville, Missouri. The visit to America, presumably in the summer of 1936, has been described to me by Dr McClurg in a letter of 25 April 1978 (now in the Bodleian). 'Arthur,' wrote William McClurg, 'came out for my second years summer vacation and we bought a second hand car in New York . . . We drove up to the Adirondack Mountains in New York state and stayed in Hurricane Lodge, a delightful place – chalets with balcony and main building and dining room: the air was so fresh after the City. We made friends at the Lodge and went to Long Island to stay with them for a long week-end. We drove through Vermont state and visited some friends there, then we started on our trip to Cape Cod . . . There is quite an artists colony there and of interest to Arthur to see some paintings by the local artists. We went to see a Ballet performed by Ted Shawn and his dancers – a small male company and very athletic and exciting it was . . . We were both well content, Arthur having made and enjoyed the trip and the knowledge that he had helped me towards the only profession I could ever want and I so fortunate and grateful to have such a good friend.'

Dr McClurg, now an osteopathic physician, has had a practice in London since World War II, and besides owning a number of his friend's paintings, entertained Arthur whenever he visited in England.

T.S.T.–Q

summer term? I have often told you that this is an injudicious (lovely adjective!) time to choose, but I know you are not entirely free. By the bye, I should warn you that you will find the Kilns changed much for the worse – which you might have thought impossible – by a horrible rash of small houses which has sprung up all round us. All thanks to Lord Nuffield, I suppose: it would take a good deal more than a million pounds to undo the harm he has done to Oxford.[4]

We have had rather an unfortunate spring. First of all a maid got flu' just before she was leaving and had to be kept on as a patient for several weeks. Then I got flu'. Then as I was getting better Paxford (that is our indespensable fac-totum, like your Lea, you know) got flu'.[5] Then I had a grand week end doing as much as I could of his work and the maid's until I got flu' again. Then Minto's varicose ankles broke down. Then Warnie got flu' and was rather bad. However, we have come through it all and seem pretty cheery now. The 'dreadful weather' I have been rather enjoying: I quite like seeing the primroses one day and the snow the next.

I have not read anything you would be likely to care for lately except a *Vie de Jésus* by a Frenchman called Mauriac, which I strongly recommend: it is papist, of course, and contains what English and Protestant taste would call lapses, but it is very good in spite of them. I suppose you noticed about Christmas time that someone has re-published the complete *Adventures of Tim Pippin* by Roland Quiz.[6] I half thought of getting it, but have satisfied myself with assuming that you have done so. I hope you have not satisfied yourself with a similar assumption about me!

I have been progressing all this lent through the first volume of a v. nice edition of St Augustine's *City of God* only to find that the other volume has been so wrongly bound that it begins and ends in the middle of sentences. What a tragedy this would once have been!

We have got (*vice* Mr Papworth, now gathered to his fathers) a

---

[4] William Richard Morris (1877–1963) was created 1st Baron Nuffield in 1934 and 1st Viscount Nuffield in 1938. From his simple beginnings as a maker of bicycles, he became the chairman of his own automobile factory, Morris Motors Ltd., which he built at Cowley, a few miles from Oxford and about a mile from the Kilns.

[5] While this is the first time he has been mentioned in this correspondence, Fred W. Paxford (1899–   ) had been with Lewis since the move to the Kilns and was to serve him faithfully for the rest of Lewis's life. For a description of his duties and his engaging personality see the *Biography*, ch. V.

[6] Roland Quiz, *Giant-Land: or the Wonderful Adventures of Tim Pippin* [1874].

golden retriever puppy who is about the size of a calf and as strong as a horse: has the appetite of a lion, the manners of a hurricane, the morals of a gangster, and an over salivated mouth.

Please give my love to your mother, and remember me to Reid. I saw Bryson about a fortnight ago and I think he said he was going home this Vac. Will you be able to have me this summer? It is a very bright spot in the year, but don't hesitate to say if it is inconvenient.

Yours
Jack

199

Magdalen College.
Oxford.
June 10th 1937

My dear Arthur,

In my diary I have down 'cross to Arthur' for July 12th not July 5th and as I have arranged everything on this basis I trust it will be alright.

Your suspicion that I was fuming with wrath during the lunch is a sad commentary on my previous character, and coming from one who knows me so well, it must (I fear) be correct. This time, however, tho' of course I would have preferred to see you alone, I quite liked it.

Stamps . . . I can't understand the attraction: but I send all I have.*

Yours
Jack

* Of course there are many more in number, but only duplicating what I enclose

200

Magdalen College,
Oxford.
June 15th 1938

My dear Arthur,

I agree that it's risky to put it off till September, specially if you may be going to America.

I propose therefore, if I may, to cross on Monday July 18th and leave you on Monday July 25th. Thanks very much, and please convey my thanks and love to Mrs Greeves. I look forward to it immensely.

Yours
Jack

[Before this could be posted Lewis had a letter from Arthur and, beginning with the following pastiche of Jane Austen's *Emma*, he went on to make further suggestions for his Irish jaunt.]

'Oh my dear Miss Woodhouse, what *do* you think? Such a singular thing has happened – Jane Fairfax's letter to my mother has crossed my mother's letter to Jane Fairfax. As soon as I began reading Jane's letter to my mother, I had to lay it down. "My dear Madam", I said "You will never believe it. Such a singular thing has happened. I protest our letters have crossed." '

Well, what shall we do. You see my fixtures are not in favour of any date before July 12th. Can I come in September – or in the latter part of July and lump your not being so free?

201

The Kilns,
Headington Quarry,
Oxford.
Sept. 15th 1939

My dear Arthur,

My position is that I am 41 on Nov. 29th so that till then I am within the ages liable to military service 'if and when called up'. Unless things go *very* ill with the allies I don't think I am very likely to be required, the less so as they want some dons to teach the people between 18 and 20 (they're not calling up boys under 20 at present) and others in govt. departments. We are having a university term and I shall probably, for a bit, continue in my own job.

In fact so far this household has nothing to complain of. Warnie has, of course, had to rejoin, being on the reserve, and is pretty miserable, tho' safe & physically comfortable, at Catterick.[1] We have three evacuated children in the house, but all really nice girls.[2] Minto

---

[1] Warren, who had remained in the Army Reserve, had been called into active service. From Catterick, in Yorkshire, he was posted in November to the Base Supply Depot at Le Havre.

[2] During the course of the war a number of evacuated girls, usually from the blitzed areas of London, and not always the same three or four children,

is bearing up wonderfully. We have had *one* air raid warning but it was a false alarm. So we mustn't cry out before we're hurt.

I'm very sorry to hear you have been ill and very sorry too that we are not to meet this year. You are very often in my mind.

The next few years will be ghastly, but though my *nerves* are often staggered, my faith and reason are alright. I have no doubt that all this suffering will be for our ultimate good if we use it rightly . . . but I can't help wishing one could *hibernate* till it's all over! As W. said in his last letter what makes it worse is the ghostly feeling that it has all happened before – that one fell asleep during the last war and had a delightful dream and has now waked up again.

I daresay for me, personally, it has come in the nick of time: I was just beginning to get too well settled in my profession, too successful, and probably self complacent.

Write when you can. Give my love to your mother and to F. Reid.

Yours
Jack

202

Magdalen College,
Oxford.
May 9th 1940

My dear Arthur,

I was very nice to hear from you. I also missed our annual meeting last year very much.

At present, tho' part of my income has disappeared for the duration, I have as little to complain of as anyone in England. My job still exists and is in one way even nicer for some of those whom I liked least in college have gone away to work in Govt. departments and one to America. Two of the things that worry most civilians – lack of petrol and the blackout – to me (as, I expect, to you) are no grievance at all, rather the reverse. Indeed the blackout has given me so many beautiful sights of Oxford in moonlight that, for purely selfish reasons, I shouldn't mind if it continued for ever. Warnie is on leave at the moment; his first since he went out. He is so wholly confident about the war and so different from the people here in that respect

were billeted at the Kilns. Lewis very much enjoyed their company as can be seen from his letters to his brother, and one of the girls, now Mrs Margaret Leyland, who lived at the Kilns between January–July 1940 has written of her experiences in *The Lamp-Post of The Southern California C. S. Lewis Society*, I, No. 3 (July 1977), pp. 1–2.

that his presence is like a breath of fresh air.

Don't you find it quite extraordinarily different from last time? When you were in Tom's office and I was at Bookham I can't remember that either of us gave a fig for the whole business or even felt the slightest anxiety about the ultimate issue: and certainly, after I was in the army, I never thought about the war in general at all. Is it just the difference between a man in the 20's and a man in the 40's – or am I forgetting what we really did think & feel in those days?

The other Mrs Moore died:[1] I think your aunts will have heard this by now. I'm sorry to hear you have been ill. I got through last winter (a magnificent winter it was – the pond frozen for about 12 weeks on end) without flu'. Minto has a touch of rheumatism, but not too bad.

I'm interested in what you tell me about Marjorie Bowen. (Is that the same one who writes historical romances?) Did you read my tale about Mars 'Out of the Silent Planet':[2] if not, shall I send you a copy? But I can make a v. good guess what your criticism wd. be.

Give my love to your Mother and to both the McNeills. I don't think I shall be able to get over this summer, much as I should like to.

Why doesn't the world end?

Yours
Jack

203

The Kilns,
Headington Quarry,
Oxford.
Dec. 27th 1940

My dear Arthur,

I'm afraid I am in your debt this long time and I don't even remember how up to date with our news you will be. The main items are (1) That W. is back ever since August i.e. they decided they didn't need officers of his seniority in the R.A.S.C. and put him

---

[1] The 'other Mrs Moore', who died on 2 November 1939, was the widow Alice Hamilton Moore, formerly of Bayview Park, Kilkeel, Co. Down, Northern Ireland. She was not related to Mrs Janie King Moore, but because of her reduced circumstances and because she was a fellow Ulster-woman, she had been allowed to occupy a bungalow which stood on the Kilns property east of the tennis court. She was buried in the churchyard of Holy Trinity Church, Headington Quarry.

[2] Lewis's *Out of the Silent Planet* was published in 1938.

back on the retired list, greatly, of course, to his delight and ours.

(2) Maureen got married in August to a music master called Blake,[1] a very small, dark, ugly, silent man who hardly ever utters a word – wh. is perhaps just as well for anyone married to such a chatterbox as Maureen! You will laugh at the idea of her being married, and indeed so do I, for she is as childish as ever.

(3) We have not so far had any bombs in Oxford, though we get a good many alerts. At first we used to go out to the dug out and sit and freeze in the dark and the cold, but we now take no notice of them.

(4) I am, save the mark!, a Home Guard and spend one night in nine mouching about the most depressing and malodorous parts of Oxford with a rifle. Otherwise I am living a normal life. I think a great deal of nonsense is talked about the food shortage: at least I have never yet had a meal from wh. I rose unsatisfied.

(5) I have published another book, only a little thing called the *Problem of Pain*. At least I thought it little, but I expect you'd find it 'too long drawn out'!

I had a long and most interesting letter from Janie McNeill: please thank her and tell her I will reply in the next few days. I quite agree with the contrast you drew in your last letter between our complete indifference during the last war (parts of wh. were probably among the happiest days in our lives) and our present hanging on the news. Is it because this is so much more serious, or because we are older? Janie says you are not very well – nothing serious, I hope? I often picture you going the old walks and living the old life (But I suppose you are now usually to be found splitting a bottle or having a game of billiards with the present master of Glenmachan. He must be a great addition to the neighbourhood – quite carries on the fine old roistering tradition of Bob!)[2] Minto bears up pretty well, tho'

---

[1] Maureen married Leonard James Blake (1907–   ) on 27 August 1940. Mr Blake had been the Director of Music at Worksop College since 1935, and in 1945 he became the Director of Music at Malvern College. While they were somewhat slow in getting acquainted, in after years the Lewis brothers were frequent and enthusiastic visitors to the Blakes' home in Malvern.

[2] There was some confusion at this time as to who was the master of Glenmachan. Sir Robert ('Bob') Ewart had died on 12 August 1939 to be succeeded in the baronetcy by his cousin Sir Lavens Mathewson Algernon Ewart who himself died on 21 September 1939. He, in turn, was succeeded by an American cousin Sir Talbot Ewart of New York who died without issue in 1959 to be succeeded by the present baronet Sir Ivan Ewart. Thus, while the title moved out of Sir Robert's immediate family, Glenmachan itself was inherited by Sir Robert's sister Gundreda who lived there till her death in 1978.

terribly overworked.

I don't know that I've read anything you wd. care about lately except (what I started yesterday) Charlotte M. Yonge's *Heir of Redclyffe* wh. is a good old fashioned novel about large families in nice houses in the good old settled, pious, comfortable days. Oh Arthur, why didn't we live a century earlier? Still we must console ourselves by being glad that we didn't live any later, that we had at least acquired our habits of mind before everything went bust. How is Reid? I was re-reading *Apostate* not long ago, with real enjoyment.

It is an exquisite frosty morning. Please remember me to your Mother and Chahn.

Yours
Jack

204

[The Kilns]
May 25th 1941

My dear Arthur,

I've been meaning, in a vague sort of way to write to you ever since we heard that Belfast had been blitzed,[1] but I had no notion until we got a letter from Ruth[2] to day that anything had been dropped out our end of town. She says that all my friends are alright so I suppose she wd. have mentioned you if you weren't. It's like the end of the world to think of bombs near Schomberg. Can you let me have a line in the near future? You said in your last letter that this war was in one way so different from the last (e.g. you and I actually follow the news now! nay, you have seen and heard the news happening) but in other ways brought the old time back. I feel both points very strongly.

[1] From *The Times* of 17 April 1941, page 2: 'Belfast bore the brunt of the indiscriminate enemy air attacks carried out against Northern Ireland on Tuesday night [15 April]. Shortly after the alert had been sounded high explosives and incendiary bombs were dropped at random over the city. A considerable number fell in residential and shopping areas, causing numerous casualities, many of which it is feared are fatal. Other bombs caused damage to industrial and commercial premises. While the enemy was being met by the spirited defence from the anti-aircraft guns, the various A.R.P., A.F.S., and other civil defence units were carrying out their duty with courage and devotion under conditions of difficulty and danger. In other areas in Northern Ireland the intensity of the attack was not so severe and the casualties were on a correspondingly smaller scale.

[2] Ruth Hamilton (1900–   ), now Mrs Desmond Parker, is the daughter of Lewis's uncle, Augustus Hamilton.

Yesterday evening I got a telephone call from a lady who introduced herself as 'a friend of Arthur Greeves' and turned out to be Mrs Pomeroy. I went round to her hotel after dinner and had about an hour and a half of most interesting conversation. She wasn't in the least like what I remembered either in appearance or in mind. I had thought of her as rather vague and perhaps theosophical, but she turns out to be very definitely Christian. The talk was all on that subject and I liked her.

About 3 weeks ago I had to make a gramophone record (not a song!) and heard it played through afterwards. Tho' warned to expect a surprise, I was unprepared for the total unfamiliarity of the voice; not a trace, not a hint, of anything one could identify with oneself – one couldn't possibly guess who it was. I realise (an awful moment) that certain imitations of my voice wh. I've heard in Bernagh are much nearer the reality than I supposed. But don't any of you crow; wait till you hear yourselves and then talk if you dare![3]

Minto is pretty poorly and has a game heart. We are sometimes rather a sad household and then at other times rather better – wh., I suppose, is what the plain truth about any house wd. come down to now-a-days, or indeed in any days. Warnie has not been recalled to the Army I'm glad to say and is living in his motor boat a few miles away as part of the Upper Thames Patrol. He's painted the boat battleship-grey and bought a blue peaked cap so as to emphasise the fact that he's now part of the navy! Dear Warnie – he's one of the simplest souls I know in a way: certainly one of the best at getting simple pleasures.

I'd love news of everyone at home. How are the McNeills? and Kelsie? and Gundred? and Reid? and your nice friends out at Conber? and I'd like news of *things*. I hope they didn't drop a bomb on the Shepherds Hut or Africa or our own wood. Was it prophetic when we used to walk about those parts talking about the 'giant knocking on the door of the world'? He's knocked now. And mixed up with all this come the irresistible, inexcusable, comedy pictures of if-it-had-happened-then, as (a) The Witch of Endor entering the study and saying *very* fast 'If-you-please-Sir-there's-an-incendiary-bomb-in-the-water-closet.' P.B.[4] What's that Mary? W of E (much faster and

---

[3] Earlier in the year Lewis had been invited to give some talks by the BBC. The visit to London mentioned here was for the purpose of taking a 'voice test'. The actual broadcasts, of which there were four, were given 'live' over the air every Wednesday evening during August 1941 under the title *Right and Wrong: A Clue to the meaning of the Universe?*

[4] 'P.B.' or 'P'daitabird' was Lewis's nickname for his father.

an octave higher) P.B. Speak up, Mary, speak up etc. (b) Bob *sniffing* to detect gas (c) *Very* allusive and cryptic lecture on the *moral* dangers of public shelters from – well, I cd. select more than one candidate to deliver this.

I'm tremendously busy at present and get hardly any reading done. I have at last read a book by an author we often joked about Phyllis Bottome, called *Private Worlds*, and am about half way through Moberley's *Atonement and Personality* – v. good argument very badly written. I've also read some Peacock, and occasionally refresh myself with a dip into the *Prelude*.[5] I read the *Imitation* [*of Christ*] pretty nearly every day, but it's rather like creatures without wings reading about the stratosphere. Oh, and I re-read *Woodstock*[6] and found I'd quite forgotten how good it was. Full of ridiculous improbabilities, but how little that matters when a book has got atmosphere and gusto.

So far our mutual positions are exactly the reverse of those we occupied in the last war: you are seeing it, and I am in a back area. While it lasts, Oxford is really nicer than ever at present. I am feasted on friendship and good talk (ranging from religion to bawdy) and kindness and cheeriness all day long. I don't know what you think but I think a great deal of nonsense is talked about rationing. I've never been hungry yet – in fact the only way it affects me is to plunge me back into the pleasures of early boyhood: I mean food is a subject infinitely interesting and every meal a high light.

I've just been interrupted to go and hear the 6 o'clock news (wh. seems a shade better). I do wish people wouldn't turn it on. Once they've done so you can't help listening, but why submit to this nerve-racking more than *once* a day?

How is Mrs Greeves? Give her my love. I wish we could meet. I never pass a day without remembering you and the Glenmachonians and the McNeills.

Isn't sleep lovely these times? It always was of course, but more so now. And by the way, I wonder how much of the excessive love of sleep in boyhood is due to the outward circumstances being so unkindly?

Yours
Jack

---

[5] William Wordsworth (1850).
[6] Sir Walter Scott (1826).

205

The Kilns,
Headington Quarry,
Oxford.
Dec 23d 1941

My dear Arthur,

I've had a letter from Tchanie in which she says you say I owe you a letter. I thought your last was in answer to one of mine telling you about Mrs Pomeroy so that the next move lay with you! In fact I still think so. But I had in fact been meaning to write to you for some time in answer to your cheerful and encouraging letter about the Belfast Blitz. (By the way Tchanie praises you to the skies for your 'courage and *decisiveness*' as a Warden. Don't tell her I repeated this to you, because, as Miss Bates[1] says 'It would be so very.' But I thought it right to pass it on. Johnson says in Boswell, if you remember, that one always should pass such things on because 'Sir, it increases benevolence.'[2] Anyway, congratulation. The courage I always knew about – from many hair-raising occasions in your car.) I have had a very busy time all this year.

I was made Vice President in College and the real President then got ill so that I had all his work to do as well – office work, which as you know is not in my line. I have become quite a dab hand at dictating letters to a secretary. But there were still a great many to be written by my own hand, and committees, telephone calls, and interviews innumerable.

In the second place, all through the Vacation I was going round lecturing to the R.A.F. – aways for 2 or 3 days at a time and then home for 2 or 3 days. I had never realised how tiring perpetual travelling is (specially in crowded trains). One felt all the time as if one had just played a game of football – aching all over. None the less I had some interesting times and saw some beautiful country. Perthshire, and all the country between Aberystwyth and Shrewsbury, and Cumberland, are what chiefly stuck in my mind. It also gave me the chance in many places to see and smell the sea and hear the sound of gulls again, which otherwise I wd. have been pining for.[3]

---

[1] A character in Jane Austen's *Emma*.

[2] Boswell's *Life of Johnson* (conversation on 4 April 1778). Actually, it is Boswell who says it to Johnson.

[3] It had been mainly Lewis's success as a broadcaster that had led the Chaplain-in-Chief of the RAF to ask him to give these lectures. The first

In the third place as the aftermath of those Broadcast Talks I gave early last summer I had an enormous pile of letters from strangers to answer. One gets funny letters after broadcasting – some from lunatics who sign themselves 'Jehovah' or begin 'Dear Mr Lewis, I was married at the age of 20 to a man I didn't love' – but many from serious inquirers whom it was a duty to answer fully. So letter writing has loomed pretty large!

Warnie is still at home. As I think I told you he spent the summer as part of the floating H.[ome] G.[uard] in his motor boat, but is now in winter quarters at the Kilns. Maureen you know is married – to a most uninteresting little man but she seems to like it! Minto suffers a good deal with arthritis and overwork. Mrs Pomeroy has been in Oxford again but most unfortunately on a day when I couldn't see her.

I've managed in spite of other work to do a little writing. I'm engaged on a sequel to *The Silent Planet* in wh. the same man goes to Venus. The idea is that Venus is at the Adam-and-Eve stage: i.e. the first two rational creatures have just appeared and are still innocent. My hero arrives in time to prevent their 'falling' as *our* first pair did.[4] You will also soon see another book by me called *The Screwtape Letters*, but that was written last year and has been appearing weekly in *The Guardian*. It consists in letters from an old devil to a young devil on the art of temptation – you see the sort of thing.[5]

There seems to be little time for reading: and anyway we know now that any book I recommend to you will be one you find unreadable! By the bye, I cherish a hope that the novels of John Galt which I mentioned fairly recently will have proved an exception. At present I'm re-reading Traherne's *Centuries of Meditations* which I think almost the most beautiful book (in prose, I mean, excluding poets) in English. I also read on journies in the summer Graves' *I Claudius*, wh. is quite interesting, but so close to Tacitus and Suetonius that perhaps he doesn't deserve very much credit for it. Dorothy Sayers *The Mind of the Maker* I thought good on the whole: good enough to induce me to try one of her novels – *Gaudy Night* – wh. I didn't like

talks were given at the RAF base at Abingdon in April 1941, and thereafter, during the whole of the war, Lewis travelled to bases all over the country explaining the essentials of the Faith. For further details see the *Biography*, ch. IX.

[4] The sequel, *Perelandra*, was published in 1943.

[5] The 31 'letters' comprising *The Screwtape Letters* appeared one at a time in weekly instalments in the *Guardian* between 2 May and 28 November 1941, and the book, still one of Lewis's most popular, was first published in February 1942.

at all. But then, as you know, detective stories aren't my taste, so that proves nothing. I re-read the *Fair Maid of Perth* when I went to Perthshire, and enjoyed it tho' it's by no means one of the best.

I'd give a lot to be able to see you again. I'd like to see how you look in a tin (or Bakerlite) hat. How is Mrs Greeves? Give her my love. To think of Mrs McNeil under fire is almost as strange and unearthly (tho' less pleasant) as an old idea of meeting her in heaven. Do you ever see the other Mrs McNeil now? But I imagine everything is so different under present conditions (including petrol rationing) that all that has gone by the board.

How little you and I guessed when we first knew one another what life had in store for us! And how little we guessed that in this war you were going to see (up to date) so much more of it than I. But I'm beginning to twaddle – why is it that things one feels and thinks extremely deeply sound so platitudinous when they are written down. All good wishes.

Yours
Jack

P.S. I'm giving 5 more BBC talks in Jan. & Feb. at 4.40 on Sunday afternoons, beginning on Jan. 11th.[6]

206

[Magdalen College]
Dec. 10th 42

My dear Arthur,

It was nice to hear from you again. If you see Tchanie thank her for her letter (received to-day) and tell her I hope to answer it soon. She praises you to the skies, by the way. I sent a copy of my Milton book[1] to her but not to you because you once told me not to send you my books, not for the obvious reason ('I don't know what to do with all these books; the house is R-R-R-otten with books') but because you kindly wanted to buy them!

I begin to see both from her letter and yours what a difference lack of petrol must make; in fact it has, I suppose, pretty well broken up

[6] This second series, called *What Christians Believe*, were read over the air on 11 and 18 January and 1, 8 and 15 February 1942, and they were published with the first series on *Right and Wrong* as *Broadcast Talks* (1942).

[1] *A Preface to 'Paradise Lost'* (1942).

your life by putting nearly all walks and all friends out of bounds. *You* don't complain, but *I* sympathise. (Odd that you and I must often be thinking about our favourite haunts with an *equal* sense of exile – the fact that you're 6 miles from them and I a couple of hundred making no practical difference.) And when we can both re-visit them together again, as I dearly hope we shall, will they be the same? or shall we be the same?

By the way it's all balls about my coming to lecture at Belfast; I'd come hopping if I were asked but I haven't been. It would be lovely.

I was going to say 'I can just picture your room upstairs with me on the sofa in the window and you in your "made to measure" chair' – but suddenly realise I can't quite picture the room. Only one picture comes to mind – the one of the corn field; and, absurdly, the *bed* keeps on creeping in from the days when it was a bedroom. (It wd. be amusing if a bed kept *literally* 'creeping into' a room! Which reminds me, do you object to my using in a story your idea of the dead man coming back into the clothes?)[2]

All pretty well, here. Minto has one of her recurrent varicose ulcers but is surprisingly well in spirits. W. is at home. I have had neuralgia to-day but am otherwise alright – except for rheumatism which has prevented me from sleeping on my right side for nearly a year now. (What a series of rediscoveries life is. All the things which one used to regard as simply the nonsense grown-ups talk have one by one come true – draughts, rheumatism, Christianity. The best one of all remains to be verified . . .)

I have introduced such a lot of people to Macdonald this year: in nearly every case with success. On my innumerable journeys I've re-read *Lavengro*. Yes, I did read Ld. Elton's book:[3] quite good, I expect, but I'm no judge of that kind of thing.

Did I tell you in my last letter that I'd struck up quite an acquaint-ance (almost a friendship) with a rabbit in Magdalen Grove who used to come and eat leaves from my hand? Alas, I must have given something that disagreed with him, for he disappeared for about 10 days, and since his reappearance has refused to look at me.

It's a grand day, to day, of low racing clouds and strong wind: you and I cd. enjoy a good walk among whirling dead leaves. Well, 'I

[2] If Lewis used the idea in a story it has not, I think, survived. Perhaps it became fused with his idea of having Merlin wake after 1500 years' sleep, in *That Hideous Strength*.

[3] Possibly Lord Elton's *St George or the Dragon* (1942).

must be getting along now' as so many visitors say and then *don't* get along for half an hour or more. Blessings, and here's to our next meeting

Yours ever
Jack

207

The Kilns,
Headington Quarry,
Oxford
[January 1943]

My dear Arthur,

For the first time in my life I find myself writing you a business letter. I have to assist someone in writing an academic thesis on A.E. (– Russell, you know) and he says Forrest Reid knew him and knows a lot about him. Incidentally, my pupil, though his name is Budd, admires Reid 'consumedly'. Can you (a) Let me have Reid's address, and (b) By judicious conversation put him in the frame of mind in which he will think letters (requiring answers) from an unknown man (called Budd) will be flattering and not boring. This is untrue, of course: that's why it will need such judicious conversation to convince him of it.[1]

Well, how are you? Minto is laid up with one of her terrible varicose ulcers, but W. and I are alright. But it's a weary world, isn't it? My wish for a walk and talk with you is at some times acute ('And what is it at the other times?' said Alice. 'Oh when it's not acute, it is grave,' said the White Knight). As you will have noticed I've been having great luck with my books lately, and it wd. be affectation to pretend I hadn't got much pleasure out of it: but the catch is it increases the amount of letters one has to write almost beyond endurance. I'm pretty well: sometimes sad, other times not. How are the McNeils? – my love and duty to them, and the Glen-machonians.

Except in bed and in trains I get v. little reading done now. Re-

---

[1] Kenneth George Budd, referred to here, was a member of Exeter College, and wrote a B.Litt. thesis on 'A.E.' (the pseudonym of George William Russell) called *A Study of the Poetry of 'A.E.' George Russell and 'A.E.'s' Essays on the Nature of Poetic Inspiration*. Budd was examined for the B.Litt. in 1945 but, unfortunately, failed, so the thesis was never accepted by Oxford.

read *Middlemarch* in trains last Vac. with great enjoyment, only the marrying Dorothea to Ladislaw at the end is an anticlimax. Also recently read J. Austen's *Sanditon* for the first time: not very good, except for the fat pale man with his basin of cocoa – a little like Bob, one pictures. Am at present browsing in Lamb's letters. The 2 vols of *Elia* wh. I so often use and wh. bear the inscription 'From J. A. Greeves. Xmas 1916' are so faded you can hardly recognise the colour now, but fresh as ever inside. Those illustrations still please me as much as ever. (How you must regret having parted with it? Still, you've got *Lore of Proserpine* back, rot you!).

Warnie has grown thin. It's quite interesting seeing the shape of the face coming out: like unpacking a parcel. I'm as bulgy as ever. Let me have a line. It would be a really cheering thing for me – honest! I never met Mrs Pomeroy again. My love to your mother. Well, I must be getting on. Writing, writing, writing – letters, notes, exam papers, books, lectures. I've enough rheumatism in my right hand now to prevent me from sleeping on that side.

Yours

C. S. Lew

(Nearly did it wrong!)

Jack

208

[Magdalen College]
June 1st 43

My dear Arthur,

The time stretches out longer and longer and I become more hungry for a chat and a walk with you. You may be unrecognisable now! Whenever one meets a friend after long absence these days the first thing one notices is how *thin* he's got.

Things with me are pretty much as usual. Minto still has her nasty varicose ulcer and suffers a great deal with it. Warnie is still with us and is a great help to me as a secretary – he types all my non-personal letters now. Maureen as you know is married.

We are keeping rabbits at the Kilns now, in addition to the hens! But they are very much nicer. As I passed the enclosure in which all the young ones are the other evening, I saw they had all got into a box wh. happened to be lying there. They were all standing (or sitting) up on their hind legs and all facing in the same direction: so that they looked exactly as if they were conducting some kind of evening service – the box looked just like a pew.

It is nice in college at present: as I think I said before, much nicer than in peacetime, for the stormy spirits are away. (Talking of 'stormy', do you know the novels of a woman called Storm Jameson? I had to write to her about a quite different matter the other day and would *like* to have said something nice about her books, but have never read any. Wd. I like them?)

I seem to get v. little reading done these days. One thing I *have* read recently is D. Sayers' *The Man Born to be King* wh. I thought excellent, indeed most moving. The objections to it seem to me as silly as the similar ones to *Green Pastures*, wh. I think you and I agreed about.[1]

(By the bye I *did* write and answer your query about L. P. Jacks[2] didn't I . . . in the long run? Anyway, I'm not going to do so here. Let it be relegated to the world of 'Have you read your Swinburne?' and the controversy about souterains.)

Bryson tells me you have become quite a man of business. Wouldn't it be awful if when I met [you] again you'd become a really practical man in a blue suit and a bowler hat talking rather as my Uncle Gussie did in his prime! There are of course equally awful changes that may occur in me. Perhaps you'll find that I've become a golfer, or a bridge player, or a politician. I sometimes like to think in optimistic moments that you may find me better tempered – heaven knows you well might!

Hatton (do you remember Hatton, my nice quiet college servant?) has been put in a factory and I now have a most awful man who never stops talking. He's told to call me at 7.15 and nearly always wakes me by saying triumphantly 'It's only just five past seven' and

[1] Dorothy L. Sayers's *The Man Born to be King: A Play-Cycle on the Life of our Lord and Saviour Jesus Christ* (1943) was read over the BBC in twelve instalments between December 1941 and October 1942. Though perfectly orthodox and beautifully written, there was at the time a frantic outburst against the plays by the Lord's Day Observance Society and others who vilified them as 'irreverent', 'blasphemous' and 'vulgar' because an actor was allowed to impersonate Our Lord, but mainly, it seems, because of Miss Sayers's talent for making real things seem real.

Marcus Cook Connelly's stage-play *The Green Pastures* (1930) was written in Negro dialect.

[2] Lawrence Pearsall Jacks (1860–1955) became the Professor of Philosophy at Manchester College (the only Unitarian college in Oxford) in 1903 and was the Principal of Manchester College between 1915–31. At this time Arthur was moving gradually towards something like Unitarianism, and he may have been interested in Jacks because he not only published *The Life and Letters of Stopford Brooke* (1917), but was the son-in-law of Brooke as well.

giving me a report on the weather which lasts about 10 minutes. Warnie came in dripping wet the other day and said 'It's a bit of luck I met Martin on the stairs' – 'Why?' – 'Because if he hadn't told me I might not have known it was raining.' A good character to put in a book.[3]

Give my love to your Mother and very specially to the McNeills. My handwriting has gone to pot – partly rheumatism.

Yours
Jack

209

[The Kilns]
Dec 20th 43

My dear Arthur,

I've found it at last! It was in the Union Library, a large green book called *Giant-Land* which on being opened revealed the sub-title *Or the Adventures of Tim Pippin*: by Roland Quiz. This goes back to an earlier stage than the stories I (and probably you) knew as a boy. *Our* Tim Pippin was in fact the son of the one whose life is here narrated, and this explains certain mysterious allusions to the Granite City and the Subterranean City which used to fascinate me in the ones we knew. It is also rather better. What is very much better is the pictures. These, in our little green books, were the grossest crudities as you no doubt remember, bad pen and ink. In *Giant-Land* you have engravings, some really in the best tradition of that Nineteenth Century school of fairy-tale illustration. Forrest Reid might not disdain some of them. They are better than the text which is pretty poor stuff written in a kind of gim-crack glossy style – though there are one or two (not many) traces of true imagination in the episodes.

The one really good idea is that nearly all the giants are *asleep* in an enchanted wood at the beginning. Tim, tho' warned 'Do not wake the giants', foolishly does so. That has the right thrill, hasn't it? But Quiz doesn't seem to know how good it is and wastes it. Some of the semi-comic giants have good names – 'Uncle Two-Heads' and 'Giant Safe-sides'. But on the whole it's poor stuff – though I naturally enjoyed reading it. I find a giant still has a queer fascination for me.

[3] W. K. Hatton joined the staff at Magdalen in September 1923 and became a scout in January 1926 and stayed there until September 1941 when he was forced, by the war, to work in a local factory. He died on 25 November 1943. P. W. Martin was employed as Hatton's replacement in October 1941 and remained with the College until May 1944.

Each of those fairy tale dangers has a different flavour, hasn't it? I mean a dragon is quite a different feeling from a giant, and a witch from either. I read *Giant-Land* while invigilating at an exam, and was interested to find that my fellow invigilator had a small son who was interested in almost *nothing* but giants.

My only other adventure of the same sort lately has been reading a lot of Grimm's tales in German. There seem to be about five times as many in the original as there were in any of the translations: many of them v. sinister or harrowingly pathetic. What a lot of *real* peasant suffering and crime must lie behind the repeated stories of cruel stepmothers and of parents who, being unable to feed their children any longer, try to get rid of them and *leave* them in a lonely part of the forest. In the end, after about fifty stories, I find the *predominant* effect is one of depression.

Things are pretty bad here. Minto's varicose ulcer gets worse and worse, domestic help harder and harder to come by. Sometimes I am very unhappy, but less so than I have often been in what were (by external standards) better times.

The great thing, if one can, is to stop regarding all the unpleasant things as interruptions of one's 'own', or 'real' life. The truth is of course that what one calls the interruptions are precisely one's real life – the life God is sending one day by day: what one calls one's 'real life' is a phantom of one's own imagination. This at least is what I see at moments of insight: but it's hard to remember it all the time . . . I know your problems must be much the same as mine (with the important difference that mine are of my own making, a very appropriate punishment and, like all God's punishments, a chance for expiation.[)]

Isn't it hard to *go on* being patient, to go on supplying sympathy? One's stock of love turns out, when the testing time comes, to be so very inadequate: I suppose it is well that one should be forced to discover the fact! I find too (do you?) that hard days drive one back on Nature. I don't mean walks (there is nowhere to walk to here, the whole neighbourhood is ruined)[1] but little sights and sounds seen at windows in odd moments.

I had a most vivid, tranquil dream about you the other night, just chatting in the old way. Let's hope it will happen sometime. For the rest, I've no news.

I've finished another story which I think of dedicating to Tchanie.[2]

---

[1] Because of the 'horrible rash of small houses' mentioned in his letter of 28 March 1937.

[2] *That Hideous Strength* published in 1945.

Do you think it matters that the heroine's name is also Jane? (In one way it'd be rather fun because she would say *Chain* every time she mentioned the book.)

I also (for a special reason) had to re-read *Guy Mannering* the other day, which I enjoyed enormously. It is one of the few Scotts (*Rob Roy* & *Midlothian* are the other two) in which there's a heroine with some life in her.

I've had a lot of examining work and been pretty busy. I have a cold of course but none of us has flu' so far, thank God. Warnie is flourishing. My old 'scout' Hatton whom you may remember has died.

We've had hard frosts – very beautiful on moonlit nights in Oxford now that there are no lighted windows or street lamps to spoil it. The black out is certainly one of the *pleasanter* results of the war as far as I'm concerned.

Give my love to your mother. Write when you can. All best wishes.

Yours
Jack

210

[The Kilns]
Jan 30th/ 44

My dear Arthur,

(1) I'm afraid I don't know anything about theatrical agencies, nor indeed agencies of any kind. Nor do I know any theatrical people.

(2) Probably the best *single* book of modern comment on the Bible is *A New Commentary on Holy Scripture* edited by Gore, Goudge and Guillaume, and published by the S.P.C.K. [1928] (Northumberland Avenue, W.C.2.) – a very fat, ugly volume in double columns, but quite readable print. Of course for separate commentaries on particular books of the Bible, their name is legion. The Clarendon Bible (Clarendon Press) is not bad.

(3) The starting point for interpreting Chas. Williams is *He Came Down from Heaven* (Methuen) where Florence will find some of his main ideas explained directly – i.e. not in imaginative form. If either Florence or you wd. like a copy of his book on Dante (*The Figure of Beatrice*) I have a spare copy wh. I wd. gladly give. It might help.

As for the man: he is about 52, of humble origin (there are still traces of cockney in his voice), ugly as a chimpanzee but so radiant (he emanates more *love* than any man I have ever known) that as soon as he begins talking whether in private or in a lecture he is transfigured and looks like an angel. He sweeps some people quite off their feet and has many disciples. Women find him so attractive that if he were a bad man he cd. do what he liked either as a Don Juan or a charlatan. He works in the Oxford University Press. In spite of his 'angelic' quality he is also quite an earthy person and when Warnie, Tolkien, he and I meet for our pint in a pub[1] in Broad Street, the fun is often so fast and furious that the company probably thinks we're talking bawdy when in fact we're v. likely talking Theology. He is married and, I think, youthfully in love with his wife still. That's about all I can think of.[2]

You needn't ask me to pray for you, Arthur – I have done so daily ever since I began to pray, and am sure you do for me.

Yours
Jack Lewis

211

Magdalen College
Oxford
22 Feb./ 44

My dear Arthur,

I wonder does your cousin[1] differ from me as much as she thinks? I don't want to deny the sense in wh. Heaven enters wherever Xt enters, even in this life: and I don't suppose she wants to deny the resurrection of the dead and the full & final 'redemption of the body' wh. so obviously has not yet occurred.

About *unselfishness*, whatever dictionaries say, *you* know perfectly well what I mean, and I expect we've often talked about it – people going about making martyrs of themselves and annoying everyone else by doing things nobody wants under pretext of 'unselfishness'.

[1] The Kings Arms.
[2] A fuller assessment of Williams's character is found in Lewis's Preface to *Essays Presented to Charles Williams* (1947).
[1] Arthur's cousin and close friend Lisbeth Greeves (1897–   ) was born Lizzie Snowden Demaine in Melbourne, Australia. In 1926 she married Arthur's first cousin Mr (now Lt-Colonel) John Ronald Howard Greeves and moved to Crawfordsburn, Co. Down. Lisbeth Greeves has described herself as a 'rebel' against some of the beliefs of the Church, and in 1955 she became a member of the Baha'i Faith.

But we cd. explain it better in conversation.

Yes, I will indeed pray for 'yours' as well as you.

All best wishes.

Yours

Jack

212

[Magdalen College]

Dec. 11th 1944

My dear Arthur,

I was delighted to hear from you. The statement you read in the papers about the Cambridge professorship was untrue; so far from having accepted it, I haven't even been offered it! Which just shows what newspapers are.

Your view about the divinity of Christ was an old bone of contention between us, wasn't it?[1] But I thought when we last met you had come down on the same side as me. I don't think I can agree that the Churches are empty because they teach that Jesus is God. If so, the ones that teach the opposite, i.e. the Unitarians, would be full wouldn't they? Are they? It seems to me that the ones which teach the fullest and most dogmatic theology are precisely the ones that retain their people and make converts, while the liberalising and modernising ones lose ground every day. Thus the R.C.'s are flourishing and growing, and in the C. of E. the 'high' churches are fuller than the 'low'. Not of course that I wd. accept popularity as a test of truth: only since you introduced it, I must say that as far as it is evidence at all it points the other way. And in history too. *Your*

[1] There had been a third series of talks over the BBC on eight consecutive Sundays between 20 September and 8 November 1942, later to be published in April 1943 as *Christian Behaviour*. Lewis consented to write one more series for the BBC, but instead of being read 'live' over the radio these seven talks were recorded and played over the air on consecutive Tuesday evenings between 22 February and 4 April 1944. Arthur probably heard all the talks. However, this final series was published as *Beyond Personality: The Christian Idea of God* on 9 October 1944, and it is the contents of this book which Lewis is defending in this letter. Arthur seems not to have been persuaded by Lewis's argument that God was fully revealed in Christ, for at the top of this letter he wrote 'Not a good argument'.

The published versions of all four series differed slightly from the talks as given over the BBC, and Lewis made even further revisions before they were collected and published in a single volume called *Mere Christianity* (1952).

doctrine, under its old name of Arianism, was given a chance: in fact a v. full run for its money for it *officially* dominated the Roman Empire at one time. But it didn't last.

I think the great difficulty is this: if He was *not* God, who or what was He? In *Mat.* 28.19 you already get the baptismal formula 'In the name of the Father, the Son, & the Holy Ghost'. Who is this 'Son'? Is the Holy Ghost a man? If not does a man 'send' Him (see *John* 15.26)? In *Col.* 1.12 Christ is 'before all things and by Him all things consist'. What sort of a man is this? I leave out the obvious place at the beginning of St John's Gospel. Take something much less obvious. When He weeps over Jerusalem (Mat. 23) why does He suddenly say (v. 34) '*I* send unto you prophets and wise men'? *Who* cd. say this except either God or a lunatic? Who is this man who goes about forgiving sins? Or what about *Mark* 2.18–19. What *man* can announce that simply because *he* is present acts of penitence, such as fasting, are 'off'? Who can give the school a half holiday except the Headmaster?

The doctrine of Christ's divinity seems to me not something stuck on which you can unstick but something that peeps out at every point so that you'd have to unravel the whole web to get rid of it. Of course you may reject some of these passages as unauthentic, but then I cd. do the same to yours if I cared to play that game! When it says God can't be tempted I take this to be an obvious truth. God, as God, can't, any more than He can die. He became man precisely to do and suffer what as God he cd. not do and suffer. And if you take away the Godhead of Christ, what is Xtianity all *about*? How can the death of one *man* have this effect for all men which is proclaimed throughout the New Testament?

And don't you think we shd. allow *any* weight to the fruits of these doctrines? Where are the shining examples of human holiness wh. ought to come from Unitarianism if it is true? Where are the Unitarian 'opposite numbers' to St Francis, George Herbert, Bunyan, Geo. Macdonald, and even burly old Dr Johnson? Where are the great Unitarian books of devotion? Where among them shall I find 'the words of life'? Where have they helped, comforted, & strengthened us?

I'm glad our prayers have been answered and things are a bit better with you. They're pretty bad with us. Minto had a v. slight stroke some months ago. Maureen (her husband teaches at Worksop) is going to have a baby[2] and is staying with us. I long to see you again.

[2] Their son Richard Francis Blake (now Richard Dunbar of Hempriggs) was born on 8 January 1945.

Remember me to all our friends: tell Jane *her* book[3] is in the printer's hands but prob. won't appear till June. All good wishes.

Yours

Jack

213

Magdalen College,
Oxford.
Feb 5. 1945

My dear Arthur

Your position, as re-stated in your last letter, is one I entirely agree with. What puzzles me is that you originally brought it forward as a *disagreement* with my *Beyond Personality*. As about half of that book is taken up with the very doctrine you are now arguing (viz: that all men can become sons of God) I am completely bewildered! I must be a less lucid writer than I thought.

About too much 'emphasis on material things', if you mean on 'What shall we eat and drink and wherewithal shall we be clothed',[1] I agree. But if you mean sacramentalism, I don't think I do. Isn't Xtianity separated from the other religions just by the fact that it does *not* allow one to exclude or reject *matter*? But the whole question is too big to go into by letter.

I've re-read *Shirley* for the first time almost.[2] In one way C. Bronte seems to me a worse novelist than one wd. have thought possible: such preposterous dialogue, such tawdry rhetoric, such ridiculous devices (like L. Moore's notebook!) and such false scents – all the scenes in the Yorke family lead nowhere. Yet through it all the character of Shirley herself triumphs.

Things are a bit better with us, after an orgy of frozen pipes etc. Some of the beauties not so much of the snow as of the heavy frost wh. preceded it were exquisite. But as you say we are all almost perilously fortunate by modern European standards.

I am hoping for proofs of the new novel, the one dedicated to Janie, any day now and shall be interested to see what you think of it. I have also finished the book on Miracles[3] wh. I've been working at for 'several years'.

---

[3] *That Hideous Strength* which was dedicated to 'J. McNeill'.

[1] Matthew vi.31.

[2] This probably means that he had not re-read the whole of *Shirley* since he first wrote to Arthur about it on 4 May 1915.

[3] His *Miracles: A Preliminary Study* was not to be published until 1947.

It is bitter cold this morning but lovely to see the green earth after all the snow and to hear the birds singing. I have just seen the first celandines in Addison's Walk.

I long to meet again. I imagine each will find the other so *old-looking* as to be almost unrecognisable. God bless you.

Yours
Jack

214

[The Kilns]
Boxing Day [26 Dec.] 1945

My dear Arthur,

I am sorry to see that it was October last when you wrote to me. But real correspondence (i.e. with my personal friends) is almost impossible in term time now.

You ask me a question about something on p. 323 of *That Hideous Strength*,[1] saying 'Surely God has always been the same loving and heavenly Father and it was the *interpretation* of God that Christ revealed.' I see what you mean but the question is to me v. difficult to answer. On the one hand something really *new* did happen at Bethlehem: not an interpretation but an *event*. God became Man. On the other hand there must be a sense in which God, being outside time, is changeless and nothing ever 'happens' to Him. I think I should reply that the event at Bethlehem was a novelty, a change to the maximum extent to which any event is a novelty or change: but that *all* time and *all* events in it, if we cd. see them all at once and fully understand them, are a definition or diagram of what God eternally is. But that is quite different from saying that the incarnation was simply an interpretation, or a change in *our* knowledge. When Pythagoras discovered that the square on the hypotenuse was equal to the sum of the squares on the other two sides he was discovering what had been just as true the day before though no one knew it. But in 50 B.C. the proposition 'God is Man' wd. *not* have been true in the same sense in wh. it was true in 10 A.D. because tho' the union of God and Man in Christ is a timeless fact, in 50 B.C. we hadn't yet got to that bit of time which defines it. I don't know if I make myself clear.

[1] Where Lewis has Dr Ransom say 'Angels in general are not good company for men in general – even when they are good angels and good men. It's all in St Paul. But as for Maleldil [God] himself, all that has changed: it was changed by what happened at Bethlehem' (XII, v).

Warnie has just been playing me Holst's *Planets* on the gramophone. Have you got them? I distrust my own musical judgements more and more the more I hear really musical people talking and suspect that most of my enjoyment is emotion produced out of my own imagination at rather slight hints (it may even be *accidental* hints) from the music. I therefore don't think it is any very real commendation of the *Planets* to say that I was greatly moved by it. I should be glad to hear your views, if you have got the work. I thought the three last (Saturn, Uranus, Neptune) the best and Jupiter the weakest. Mars, of course, bowls one over but I suppose there is an element of trick in it.

I had great hopes a while ago of getting over to Belfast to give a lecture at Queen's (without some official pretext it seems almost impossible to get allowed onto the Liverpool boat) but dates wouldn't fit and it all fell through, much to my disappointment. I long to see you and the place again. Though I also dread seeing the place. How much has it been spoiled? – I don't mean by the war but by the peace. Is there a building estate all round the Shepherd's Hut by now? or a factory half way up Cabra?

We got news of Uncle Gussie's death yesterday. A difficult man to think of from that point of view. He was, as far as one can see, a very selfish man who yet succeeded in avoiding all the usual consequences of selfishness: that is, he was not at all a bore, had no self-pity, was not jealous, and seemed to be as happy as the day was long. I think he illustrates the enormous difference between selfishness and self-centredness. He had plenty of the first: he pursued his own interests with v. little regard to other people. But he had none of the second. I mean, he loved outside himself. His mind was not occupied with himself but with science, music, yachting etc. That was the good element and it was (as I think all good elements are) richly rewarded in this life. Let's hope and pray that it will carry him through where he is now. It may be the little spark of innocence and disinterestedness from which the whole man can be reconstructed. There's all the difference in the world between a fire that has gone out and one that is *nearly* out. The latter, with skilful treatment, can always be coaxed back to life. It is rather a terrible thing that some people who try really hard to be unselfish yet have in them that terrible self-centredness which he was free from.

I've got a v. rheumaticy shoulder wh. partly explains the bad handwriting and am threatened with a second small operation on my throat: but nothing to be alarmed about. Minto is only so-so in health, and often v. unhappy in mind. She is supposed not to get up till lunch time now and hates the inactivity. Luckily she has taken to reading, however, and to my great surprise got through & enjoyed the whole of *War & Peace*. She sends her love and asks if you have any hair left! (I have practically none.) I hope your mother keeps fairly well. Give her my warmest love . . . dear, dear, I wonder what you and I will be like when we're old? Shall we do any better?

I suppose I advised you before to get E. R. Eddison's *The Worm Ouroboros* if you ever come across it? But the book famine is very bad: it is one of my difficulties as a tutor that my pupils simply can't get any of the books I want them to read. You and I were immensely fortunate in growing up during a period when the supply of good books in cheap editions was practically inexhaustible. Indeed we were fortunate in many ways: in finding one another, in delightful country, in having enough money but not too much

Well, all good wishes

Yours
Jack

215

[Magdalen College]
May 13th 46

My dear Arthur,

It was more than usually nice to get your letter because I have been for the last few weeks especially haunted by a desire for your society. The picture of some place on a hill beside a wood and you and me talking there floats before me, and I constantly pray that we may meet again in the not-too-far future. But I cannot leave home for more than a night, or two at the outside, now. And this seems likely to be so as long as poor Minto lives.

Oddly enough I had been thinking of Forrest Reid: and indeed in an article (one of two wh. I have just written for *Time & Tide*) I have referred to him as a neglected artist.[1]

The Macdonald anthology,[2] as you see, is not of his verse, wh. I still consider greatly inferior to his prose. In the novels the three things I like are (a) The parts that have something of a fairy tale quality, like the terror of the trees and wind at the beginning of *W. Cumbermede* or the lovely journey 'up Gaunside' in *Sir Gibbie*.

[1] 'Notes on the Way', *Time and Tide*, XXVII (1 June 1946), pp. 510–11.
[2] Lewis's *George MacDonald: An Anthology* had just been published.

(b) (Like you) the melodrama. The older critics are v. unjust to melodrama (c) The *direct* preaching. What I can't stand is the *in*-direct preaching – I mean Connie on her sofa in *The Seaboard Parish*. What between him and Scott and an Ulster upbringing I now find no difficulty with the Scotch dialect parts, indeed I like them. They enable him to make characters say strongly and racily things he wd. spoil in English. I *have* read *The Disciple*, but long ago and don't remember it.

Surely you must be mistaken about hearing *The Planets* on the old gramophone. I cd. take my oath we never had it and I doubt if it was even recorded. Was it even *written*?

About Hell. All I have ever said is that the N.T. plainly implies the possibility of some being finally left in 'the outer darkness'.[3] Whether this means (horror of horror) being left to a purely *mental* existence, left with nothing at all but one's own envy, prurience, resentment, loneliness & self conceit, or whether there is still some sort of environment, something you cd. call a world or a reality, I wd. never pretend to know. But I wouldn't put the question in the form 'do I believe in an *actual* Hell'. One's own mind is actual enough. If it doesn't seem fully actual *now* that is because you can always escape from it a bit into the physical world – look out of the window, smoke a cigarette, go to sleep. But when there is nothing for you *but* your own mind (no body to go to sleep, no books or landscape, nor sounds, no drugs) it will be as actual as – as – well, as a coffin is actual to a man buried alive.

I suppose, like me, you often catch yourself grumbling about 'this rotten government' and realise we are talking just as our fathers talked. My love to your mother, Janie, and the Glenmachonians. God bless you.

Yours
Jack

216

Magdalen
Jan 5/ 47

My dear Arthur,

I had heard of dear old Mrs McNeill's death and written to Tchanie before I got your letter: and I have just heard to-night of Forrest Reid's. This must be bad for you. He has been daily in my prayers

[3] Matthew viii.12; xxii.13; xxv.30.

for a long time and will be. He wasn't a real part of my life, of course, as he was of yours but I liked the man very much – liked him, indeed, better than I cd. find it easy to explain – something about his voice and face and manner.

As for Mrs McNeill – well, what could you and I *say* about it even if we were together? It's just a flood of queer, absurd, adorable memories, isn't it? – something that you and I cd. both respond to, and in exactly the same way as long as we remained ourselves. I did very much hope to have seen her again. By the way, I told Tchanie in my letter how you and I once, talking about the next world, said how lovely it wd. be if, after all sorts of strange and perhaps terrible adventures, one suddenly (perhaps in a clearing in a huge wood) suddenly heard a voice saying 'Well, Arthur!' and turned round and there the old lady was. Do you remember?

And all this greatly increases my longing to see you again. You know why I can't! I envy you having that 'nurse companion'. The same thing is really needed here but the mere suggestion would almost kill her. And I'm glad to hear of your house too. If only you and I (or you *or* I) doesn't go and die before we have a chance to meet! And yet, if we did no doubt there wd. be some good and loving reason for it. I am (except in bad moods) more convinced of that all the time. We shall meet and be happy together if it is good for us: otherwise not (e.g. I might after all be disappointed in a hope I sometimes cherish that you wd. find me a little less aggressive and dictatorial and arrogant than I have often been in the old days. But who knows? The first argument might shatter all these good resolutions!)

Funny to think we're both elderly, isn't it? And what a sham this business of age is. Do you (except physically) *feel* any older than when we saw the hedge pig and played gramophone records to one another? I don't a bit. My own pupils still seem to me in many ways older than I. Indeed (nice men as many of them are) I am a little worried by the fact that so few of them seem ever to have had youth as we had it. They have all read all the correct, 'important' books: they seem to have no private & erratic imaginative adventures of their own. (I suppose the explanation is that I am the last person who is likely to hear of such things even where they exist. I mean, with me they're all talking 'grown-up' as hard as they can. Yet I don't know: the modern world is so desparately serious. They have a taste for 'books of information' wh. wd. have done credit to your father!)

There's thick snow on the ground and moonlight to-night. God bless you.

Yours
Jack

Do you read *Punch*. The poems signed N.W. wh. sometimes appear there are by me. This is a secret.[1]

[It seems likely that Lewis wrote one or more letters between the one of 5 January 1947 and the one which follows, making arrangements for his visit to Belfast. If so, they have been lost. However, Lewis was in Ireland for a short holiday with Arthur during June 1947, the first time the friends had met since the summer of 1938.]

217

Magdalen
July 4/ 47

My dear Arthur,
There was no need to apologise about the money. As you antici-pated, I got it without difficulty from the hospital – indeed only my nervousness and fussiness cd. ever have made me suppose there'd be any difficulty in doing so. Our meeting was a lovely refreshment but too short.
No more now: the daily letter writing without W. to help me is appalling – an hour and a half or two hours every morning before I can get to my own work.
God bless you.

Yrs
Jack

218

Magdalen
Aug 19/ 47

My dear Arthur,
I agree that we don't know what a spiritual body is.[1] But I don't like *contrasting* it with (your words) 'an actual, physical body'. This

[1] Between 1946 and 1954 Lewis published 24 poems over the initials 'N.W.' in *Punch*, all of which are now reprinted in his *Poems*, ed. Walter Hooper (1964).
[1] Lewis is answering Arthur's criticism of ch. XVI of his *Miracles: A Preliminary Study* published in May 1947.

suggests that the spiritual body wd. be the opposite of 'actual' – i.e. some kind of vision or imagination. And I do think most people imagine it as something that *looks* like the present body and isn't really there. Our Lord's eating the boiled fish seems to put the boots on that idea, don't you think? I suspect the distinction is the other way round – that it is something compared with which our present bodies are half real and phantasmal.

When I say that certain graces are 'offered' us only through certain physical acts[2] I mean that is the ordinary public offer certified by scripture & supported by unbroken Xtian experience. I don't of course (heaven forbid!) mean to limit what God may please to do in secret & special ways. In fact 'offer' is the operative word. No doubt He gives more than He offers: but the offer was as I describe.

I feel the better for our meeting still.

Yours
Jack

219

[Magdalen College]
Jan 20/ 49

My dear Arthur,

I hope you have not thought badly of me for not writing sooner. The news[1] reached me (from Kelsie, as well as Janie) just as term was starting and I have hardly had a moment to myself till now. But I've been thinking of you in plenty and trying to imagine how you might be feeling. I know you have long dreaded this final break up. And I suppose you now find that you miss your Mother more than you expected. But it's really such a mix up of sensations at such times: 'comfortless excitement' is how I wd. describe it. My *reason* tells me that you will now be freer and there is perhaps more chance of seeing you in England: but I *feel* something quite different – as if a new gap had opened between us, as if this somehow cut us off from the happy past. (Not that it was very happy, really: you know what I mean.) For you, of course, the wrench will be v. big, all the bigger because the same home life in wh. you grew up has gone on so very long without a real break. I am glad you – and she – were not harrowed with a long or painful illness.

What happens now? Where will John go?[2] Poor John. And poor

---

[2] *ibid.*, p. 194.
[1] Arthur's mother, aged 87, died on 1 January 1949.
[2] John Greeves was unmarried and lived at Bernagh with his mother.

Mrs Greeves: she was always kind to me. I expect you are writing innumerable letters at present, so of course I look for no answer.

God bless you, my oldest friend: you, and she, will be in my prayers

Yours
Jack

Warnie of course sends his sympathies: what rot it all sounds between you and me!

220

As from Magdalen
June 21st 1949

My dear A,

I have not your address and fear that a letter W. sent some days ago to Bernagh may not have reached you. I have been ill and am ordered a real change. I'm coming home (Belfast) for a month. I aim at crossing about July 4th – it depends on when I can get a sailing ticket. And of course I want to be with you as much as possible. Can you find me a nice little hotel (or decent rooms) near your cottage? If you wd. care for us to go somewhere else for part of the time together (e.g. Ballycastle or Hilltown or what not) I'm your man. I shall be free for once. The sooner you reply the happier I shall be. It seems too good to be true.

Yours
Jack

I am assuming that you wd. like to be with me as much as I wd. like to be with you! – I hope this is not vanity

221

Magdalen etc
June 23/ 49

My dear Arthur,

Hurrah! I was beginning (with all the morbid anxiety of a convalescent) to wonder if you were away or ill. Now for plans. The *Inn* wd. suit me down to the ground. Thanks for asking me to the cottage[1] but I think the relation of guest & host prevents friends from

[1] Arthur's cottage at Silver Hill, Crawfordsburn, Co. Down.

getting the most out of one another. The one feels responsible & the other feels grateful and the old *camaraderie* is lost. So make it the Inn please.

I cross by Heysham on the night of Mon. July 4th and leave Ireland on the night of Thurs. Aug. 4th. And now, do you think of booking me a room for that whole time or should you and I go away together to some Ulster sea-side place or mountain place for a week or so during my stay? I shall be equally content either way, so just do what you prefer. It all seems too good to be true.

I suppose there's a Ry. Station at Crawfordsburn? I always prefer train to bus with luggage.

God bless you.

Yours (all of a dither)
Jack

P.S. Have you ever had injections every 3 hours.
P.P.S. I much prefer *inns* to *hotels*. Cheaper too, I expect

222

Magdalen College
Oxford
July 2d 1949

My dear Arthur,

Thanks for your most kind and comforting letter – like a touch of a friend's hand in a dark place. For it is much darker than I feared. W's trouble is to be called 'nervous insomnia' in speaking to Janie and others: but in reality (this for yr. private ear) it is Drink. This bout started about ten days ago. Last Sunday the Doctor and I begged him to go into a Nursing Home (this has always effectively ended previous bouts) and he refused. Yesterday we succeeded in getting him in: but alas, too late. The Nursing Home has announced this morning that he is out of control and they refuse to keep him.[1] To day a mental specialist is to see him and he will be transferred, I hope for a *short* stay, to what is called a hospital but is really an asylum.[2] Naturally there is no question of a later Irish jaunt for me

---

[1] This was the Acland Nursing Home in 25 Banbury Road. One of the drawbacks of looking after an alcoholic is that the rear exit of the Acland Home opens on to Woodstock Road and a few yards from the Royal Oak public house.
[2] The Warneford Hospital in Warneford Lane.

T.S.T.–R

this year. A few odd days here & there in England is the best I can hope for.

Don't imagine I doubt for a moment that what God sends us must be sent in love and will all be for the best if we have grace to use it so. My *mind* doesn't waver on that point: my *feelings* sometimes do. That's why it does me good to hear what I believe repeated in your voice – it being the rule of the universe that others can do for us what we cannot do for ourselves and one can paddle every canoe *except* one's own. That is why Christ's suffering *for us* is not a mere theological dodge but the supreme case of the law that governs the whole world: and when they mocked him by saying 'He saved others, himself he cannot save'[3] they were really uttering, little as they knew it, the ultimate law of the spiritual world.

God bless you.

Yours
Jack

223

Magdalen College
Oxford
6/ 7/ 49

My dear Arthur,

I think the view you express in your letter is the same as I hold, and indeed I fancy I have stated it in print.[1] I do *not* hold that God 'sends' sickness or war in the sense in which He sends us all good things. Hence in Luke xiii. 16 Our Lord clearly attributes a disease not to the action of His Father but to that of Satan. I think you are quite right. All suffering arises from sin.

The sense in which it is also God's will seems to me twofold (a) The one you mention: that God willed the free will of men and angels in spite of His knowledge that it cd. lead in some cases to sin and thence to suffering: i.e. He thought Freedom worth creating even at that price. It is like when a mother allows a small child to walk on its own instead of holding it by her hand. She knows it may fall, but learning to walk on one's own is worth a few falls. When it does fall this is in one sense contrary to the mother's will: but the general situation in wh. falls are possible *is* the mother's will. (In fact, as you and I have so often said before 'in one way it is, in another way it

---

[3] Matthew xxvii.42; Mark xv.31.
[1] See the chapters on 'Human Pain' in Lewis's *Problem of Pain*.

isn't!) (b) The world is so made that the sins of one inflict suffering on another. Now I don't think God allows this to happen at random. I think that if He knew that the suffering entailed on innocent A by the sins of B wd. be (in the deep sense & the long run) *bad* for A, He wd. shield A from it. And in that sense I think it is sometimes God's will that A should go through this suffering. The supreme case is the suffering that *our* sins entailed on Christ. When Christ saw that suffering drawing near He prayed (Luke xxii.42) 'If thou be willing, remove this cup from me: nevertheless not my will but thine.' This seems to me to make it quite clear that the crucifixion was (in the very qualified sense wh. I've tried to define) God's will. I do not regard myself as disagreeing with you, but as holding the same view with a few necessary complications which you have omitted.

Warnie is now definitely better as far as this bout is concerned: but we dare not assume that it is the last. As long as there was no one but him to leave in charge at the Kilns and as long as he is a dipso-maniac it *seems* impossible for me to get away for more than a v. few days: but I don't doubt at all that if it is good for us both (I mean, you & me) to meet and have some happiness together it will all be arranged in ways we can't now foresee.

I've just finished re-reading *War & Peace*. The great beauty of *long* books is that however often you read them there are still large tracts you have forgotten.

Yours
Jack

224

[The Kilns]
27/ 7/ 49

My dear Arthur

My telephone number in College (i.e. from 9 a.m. to 1 o'clock) is 3151: at home (i.e. from 1.45 to night, *except* on Thursdays when I'm usually out) is 6963. I will take the train to Helen's Bay.

A horrid cloud has appeared on the horizon. Warnie shows some signs of getting ill with a nervous complaint he has had before. If he *does*, of course the whole scheme will fall through. I am in an agony of hopes & fears as you may imagine: meanwhile proceed on the assumption that all will be well.

It wd. be better if the door of my prison had never been opened than if it now bangs in my face! How hard to submit to God's will.

Don't tell Jane you haven't got me a room for the whole time. Of course I want to see her but not to stay with her.

Hope for the best.

Yours
Jack

225

Magdalen College
Oxford
27^1/ 7/ 49

My dear Arthur,

Good, I'm glad we are really agreed. The one thing I forgot to say in my other letter (and I think you will agree with it too) is that we make a great mistake by quoting 'thy will be done' without the rest of the sentence 'on earth *as it is in Heaven*'. That is the real point, isn't it? Not merely submission but a prayer that we may be enabled to do God's will *as* (in the same way as) angels and blessed human spirits do it, with alacrity & delight like players in an orchestra responding spontaneously to the conductor.

I don't think I can make a second attempt to get to Co. Down. W. himself is going away (without me) soon and of course I must be on duty then. I'm taking a few short trips (long week ends) instead: there's a difference between that & any Irish holiday long enough to be worth taking. But I have (faint) hopes of another year. He has been completely tee-total now since he came out of hospital. If only he cd. keep it up! Perhaps he will. I had thought, like you, that 'others depending on us' might be an incentive, but you see this broke down as soon as it was tried. I think it wd. work with an ordinary temptation, but not with what is really a recurrent obsession – i.e. almost as much a medical as a moral problem. If we cd. get a 12 months' clean bill of health from him I shd. feel much freer.

The whole affair has done at least this good that it has made us write to one another again! If you call this scrawl writing – my hand has gone all to pot. God bless you.

Jack

---

[1] Possibly a mistake for '29'.

226

[The Kilns]
12. 10. 49

My dear Arthur

I couldn't agree with you more. One of the worst bye-products of a bad habit is the nervous expectations and infuriating vigilance it creates in the sufferer's family, and also in him, if he's trying to fight it. Your recipe is the right one: but, of course, much easier to understand than to carry out. (Wh. reminds me of a book I read wh. recommended as a cure for Forgetfulness – can you believe it – *Memory!*)

I thoroughly enjoyed Jane's visit and wished you had been with us. If there were any changes in her I thought they were all for the better.

Autumn weather here is beautiful enough to break your heart. I've just re-read *The Woman in White*.[1]

Yours
Jack

227

Magdalen College
Oxford
2/ 5/ 50

My dear Arthur

Once again the axe has fallen. Minto was removed to a Nursing Home[1] last Saturday and her Doctor thinks this arrangement will probably have to be permanent. In one way it will be an enormous liberation for me. The other side of the picture is the crushing expense – ten guineas a week wh. is well over £500 a year. (What on earth I shall do if poor Minto is still alive nine years hence when I have to retire, I can't imagine.) The order of the day thus becomes for me stringent economy and such things as a holiday in Ireland are fantastically out of the question. So cancel all. I hardly know how I *feel* – relief, pity, hope, terror, & bewilderment have me in a whirl. I have the jitters! God bless you. Pray for me.

Yours
Jack

[1] By Wilkie Collins (1860).
[1] 'Restholme' in 230 Woodstock Road, where she was to remain for the rest of her life.

228

My dear Arthur

Thanks for your wise and kind letter. Of course your're perfectly right and I *do* try to 'consider the lilies of the field'.[1] Nor do I doubt (with my *reason*: my *nerves* do not always obey it!) that all is sent in love and will be for all our goods if we have grace to use it aright. And thanks too for your immensely generous offer. I can't accept it. She is miserable enough without being deprived of my daily visits. When you and I are meant to meet we shall.

God bless you.

Yours
Jack

229

My dear Arthur

Warnie is now quite restored again. My daily visits to Minto are v. grievous to me, but I don't think things are too bad for her. On her (medically) 'best' days she grouches a good deal and talks about going home, but more often she is childish and incoherent. I don't think she is any *more* discontented than she was at home. Remember that if you can get over to England the Kilns is *now* a house less horrible to stay in than I know it was before and except for an hour in the afternoon when I go to the Nursing Home we wd. have all our time to ourselves. I'd love to have you of course.

I'm fine, as I now get much more exercise. I have spent a good deal of this last fortnight *in* the river.[1] I'm glad you still see dear old Lee. Remember me to him. Did I tell you that a children's story by me is coming out this year?[2]

We have (thank goodness) no dog now, so there'd be no objection to your bringing Peter[3] if you come. Do consider it. God bless you.

Yours
Jack

[1] Matthew vi.28; Luke xii.27.
[1] The River Cherwell which flows past Magdalen College.
[2] *The Lion, the Witch and the Wardrobe* published in September 1950.
[3] Arthur's cocker spaniel.

230

Magdalen etc

31/ 1/ 51

My dear Arthur

Minto died a fortnight ago.[1] Please pray for her soul.

Wd. it suit you if I arrived at your local inn on Sat. March 31st and left on Mon. April 16? Can you let me know by return? And also if the inn cd. have me? If they're fed up with my choppings & changings you can truly tell them that my circumstances are wholly changed.

God bless you.

Yours

Jack

231

[The Kilns]

23/ 3/ 51

My dear Arthur

Naturally, without a Co. Down Ry. time-table I can't tell you what time I'd be at Helen's Bay! But we shall find better uses for your petrol, and I'll come by bus from Oxford St. I'm glad to know there's a 'regular' service and am wondering whether it runs regularly every 5 minutes, every hour, once a week, once a month, or once a century. No doubt I shall find out. Looking forward! – yes, I can't keep the feeling within bounds. I know now how a bottle of champagne feels while the wire is being taken off the cork.

Yours

Jack

Pop!!

---

[1] Mrs Janie King Moore died at 'Restholme' on 12 January 1951, aged 78. Her body was buried in the churchyard of Holy Trinity Church, Headington Quarry, in the same grave as that of Mrs A. H. Moore.

232

My dear Arthur

You were quite right to leave me when you did. A farewell meal is a doleful business: it was much better for me to get my luggage dumped and my berth found & for you to be back at home as soon as possible.

Thank Elizabeth[1] for her letter. She will understand, I am sure, why I don't want to continue the discussion by post: my correspondence involves a great number of theological letters already which *can't* be neglected because they are answers to people in great need of help & often in great misery.

I have hardly ever had so much happiness as during our late holiday. God bless you – and the Unbelievable.[2] *Pas de jambon encore.*

Yours
Jack

233

[The Kilns]
23/ 4/ 51

My dear Arthur

(1.) A Ham had been posted to you to-day.

(2.) My plans, if they fit with yours, for the summer are as follows.

(a.) Short visit to C'fordsburn *with* W. Aug. 10 (arrive 11th) – Aug. 14

(b.) Stay with W. in S'thern Ireland Aug. 14–28.

(c.) Longer visit to C'fordsburn *alone* Aug. 28–Sept. 11th.

Can you be in residence at Silver Hill Aug. 28th – Sept. 11th?

Blessings,
Jack

---

[1] Arthur's cousin-by-marriage, Lisbeth Greeves.
[2] One of Arthur's dogs.

234

> [The Kilns]
> 16/ 6/ 51

My dear Arthur

You're right. Not that I shall be tired of hotels, still less of you, by then, but that I shall be feeling like getting down to a little work. Also, I think you wd. find it a waste both of Lily and of me to have us together.

Love to the Unbelievable and to yourself.

> Yours
> Jack

235

> Magdalen College,
> Oxford.
> 8/ 3/ 52

My dear Arthur

I hope to arrive at Crawfordsburn with W. on Aug. Wed. 20th. He will leave on Aug. Sat. 23d. If agreeable I wd. like to stay on at the Hotel for a fortnight of your society, i.e. sail again on Mon. Sept 8th. Will that suit you? I can't manage the Easter as well.

In the *Last Chronicle*[1] I think all the London parts (the 'Bayswater Romance') a bore and now always skip them. But I think the Crawley parts splendid.

I am wondering how your date with Tchainie went? Give her my love. Blessings.

> Yours
> Jack

236

> Magdalen College,
> Oxford
> June 22d 1952

My dear Arthur

I shall be free to be with you from Sat. Aug. 23d till Mon. Sept. 8th when I sail for L'[iver]pool. These dates cannot be changed but if you like to spend all or any of this time motoring me about Ireland, I

---

[1] Anthony Trollope, *The Last Chronicle of Barset* (1867).

shd. like it v. much and will fall in with any dates (between those two) or any itinerary you choose. Just us two, of course: I wouldn't face any third.* You and I know the worst about each other by now! I look forward to it immensely.

Yours
Jack

* Except the Unbelievable, of course: he has *more* sense than we have!

P.S. But I'd forgotten. My room at the C'burn Inn is already booked for that period. I'm afraid I couldn't manage to pay it *and* other ones as well. Can you decide on your dates at once & then see if the Inn will cancel my room for the period of our tour without charging? If *not*, then I'd better stick to my original plan & you take your motor trip after I've gone. But I hope not. I shall be a little anxious till I hear from you again.
P.P.S. No sharing a room: but you'd hate it as much as I, so I'm safe!

237

Magdalen College.
28th June 52

My dear Arthur
   Splendid. The manageress is right: Aug 21st is my first night at Crawfordsburn. Setting off with you on Mon. 25th will do fine. And *of course* I don't want all day & every day in the car: we think just the same on that subject. I look forward to the trip immensely: the first time you and I have been away together since Portsalon in about 1916![1] This time we shall at least not quarrel about Hair-Oil!

Yours
Jack

[1] See letter of 18/9/16.

238

Magdalen
20/ 9/ 52

My dear Arthur,

No, please don't send H.J.'s *Letters*.[1] The idea of your returning a present was applicable only on the assumption that it was useless to you. And anyway, if they're not much about the books, they wd. be useless to me.

A retired naval captain whom you may have sometimes heard of in the papers (Bernard Acworth)[2] tells me he was at Derryherk shortly before us and says the fishing was just as bad as the food. I wonder what the Magic Major is *really* up to.

I've got a 100 Horsepower cold but feel mentally & spiritually much the better from our holiday. It – and you – have done me lots of good. All blessings.

Yours
Jack

239

Magdalen
11/ 10/ 52

My dear Arthur

James's *Letters* vol. I arrived yesterday. I don't know if I really ought to accept it, James being so much more your kind of author than mine. On the other hand it is too big for an envelope and putting up parcels is one of the many things I can't do. And there seems to be a good deal about books in it after all. Well, thanks very much indeed. Yes, I love my Father's underlinings: the pencil (can't you see him, with his spectacles far down on his nose, getting out the little stump?) so heavily used that, as W. said, he didn't so much

---

[1] *The Letters of Henry James*, ed. Percy Lubbock, 2 vols. (1920). The copy spoken of here, once belonging to Albert Lewis, had been given to Arthur.

[2] Capt. Bernard Acworth (1885–1963) who was the Founder and President Emeritus of the Evolution Protest Movement, served for eighteen years in submarines and commanded the Anti-Submarine Flotilla. He was the author of many books, and shared with Lewis a distrust of Teilhard de Chardin's views on evolution as they are recounted in the latter's *Phenomenon of Man*.

draw a line as *dig* a line.

Term began yesterday, so I have now returned to harness after what has been perhaps the happiest year of my life. I began, appropriately, by cutting myself when I shaved, breaking my lace when I put on my shoes, and coming into College without my keys.

There have been some most perfect autumn days here lately and this is a well timbered country which they suit.

Love to *l'Incroyable* and your good self and all blessings.

Yours
Jack

240

Magdalen College
Oxford
17/ 10/ 52

My dear Arthur,

I've finished vol. I of the Letters of H.J. I announce this not to hurry you but to show that I have enjoyed yr. gift. I'm afraid he was a dreadful Prig, but he is by no means a bore and has lots of interesting things to say about books. Was it you sent me the Northern 'Whig'? If so thanks.

Yours
Jack

241

Magdalen College,
Oxford.
Nov 18/ 52

My dear Arthur

Thanks v. much for the 2d vol. of H.J. which arrived in good order a few days ago. It is really most generous of you. The Letters, even if they had no other interest, wd. be useful as an anthology of all the possible ways of apologising for not having written before – it sometimes goes on for 2 whole pages!

I really feel much as you do about big formal functions, and though I attend many more of them than you, I skip all I can. As I get older I become more impatient of being kept sitting on or hanging about after the meal is over.

I shan't begin the Letters for a few days for I am at present re-

reading Montaigne. Sharp frost here this morning: I wish we could have a walk to enjoy it together.

Love to both of you.

Yours
Jack

242

Magdalen College
Oxford, England
Feb 27. 53

My dear Arthur

I wd. love to come away with you this year again but it couldn't be earlier than last year. I have been put on to examine this year which will keep me busy at Oxford into the first week of August. My jaunt with W. could be made to come *after* my jaunt with you instead of *before* it if you wish, I expect. I hope this doesn't spoil things for you?

Someone has given me *Armadale*. It is clearly not so good as the famous two but well worth reading.[1]

I'm in such pain with *sinusitis* to-day I can't think straight: so if any of this letter doesn't make sense you'll understand! I'm not lecturing at Queen's.

Yours
Jack

Magdalen College,
Oxford.
16th. March 1953.

My dear Arthur,

What between sinus and examinations, poor Jack is sunk fathoms deep this morning. However, we talked over your letter of the 11th. last night, and he asked me to ask you whether Saturday 29th. August to Saturday 12th. September would suit you for the jaunt: to which he is very eagerly looking forward. These dates are tentative, so if you don't like them, please say so. But let us know as soon as possible, as it is part of a 'master plan' and we have all kinds of other things to make fit in with it.

Incidentally, if the dates suit, I hope to be with J. at Crawfordsburn for a few days before you and he set out, and am looking forward

[1] Wilkie Collins's *Armadale* was published in 1866. His 'famous two' are *The Woman in White* (1860) and *The Moonstone* (1868).

to more than one meeting with you. I daresay amongst other things, we may be having a supper with our Jane, and a drive home across the Holywood hills.

Love to Lily, Janie, and any others of my old friends you meet; and kindest regards to those good Samaritans, your neighbours and relations, who gave us drinks that Sunday morning.

Can you forsee any end to this winter?

Yours ever,
Warren

243

Magdalen College
Oxford, England
21/ 3/ 53

My dear Arthur

I hope you weren't shocked at getting an answer from W. instead of me the other day. On Monday I was both rather ill and also engaged in viva-voce examinations from 9.15 a.m. to 5.30 p.m., so I couldn't well write, and I thought you wd. like to have all those dates at the earliest moment.

Yours
Jack

244

Magdalen College,
Oxford.
25th. March 1953.

My dear Arthur,

On looking into the matter further, it would suit me better to prolong our jaunt for another 48 hours, i.e. for me to cross on Monday 14th. September instead of Saturday 12th. The Sunday train service on the English side is practically useless – one train, and *no* restaurant car. Will 14th. suit you?

Yours,
Jack

245

Magdalen College,
Oxford.
July 13/ 53

My dear Arthur

We have both of us been a little flustered, it seems. *First* you wrote a letter of wh. you sent me only part: at least, so I conclude from the fact that it had no signature and broke off in the middle of a sentence. *Then* I got it on a day when I was just going for a journey and lost it. So sorry. The facts are these.

Aug. 20th   W. and I arrive Crawfordsburn.

Aug. 28th   W. departs by L'pool boat.

Sept. 14th   I depart ————

I hope this fits in with you?

R. L. Green has written a v. good Arthurian book for children in the Puffin series[1] – not merely a re-telling of Malory, something much better than that, wh. he explains in the preface. I am sending you a copy when it comes out: if you want to refresh your memory of that cycle, you can get it all here with the 'brasting' left out.

Yours
Jack

246

Magdalen College
Oxford
Oct 6/ 53

My dear Arthur

I have ordered Blackwells to send you a copy of Barfield's ('G. A. L. Burgeon's') book.[1]

I enclose one wh. I found worth reading but don't want to keep. If you don't like it, pass it on to someone else. You'll agree with the author about Noise! I think you'll also find in him an approach to Christianity wh. you haven't v. much met yet & wh. is worth knowing about: it is fairly widely spread here. Of course parts of it are too explicitly R.C. for us but a lot of common ground remains.

Here are some C. M. Yonge titles, all good books: *The Daisy Chain*

[1] Roger Lancelyn Green, *King Arthur and His Knights of the Round Table* (1953).

[1] 'G. A. L. Burgeon' (=Owen Barfield), *This Ever Diverse Pair* (1950).

and its sequel *The Trial; The Pillars of the House; The Three Brides; The Two Sides of the Shield; Dynevor Terrace.* Not so good (but W. differs from me) is *Nutty's Father.*

I wish you had enjoyed our holiday as much as I did! But I expect you're enjoying yourself all the more now. All blessings.

Yours
Jack

I'm still waiting to know what I owe you for petrol.

247

Magdalen College
Oxford
Oct 17/ 53

My dear Arthur

I wonder are you allowing for the fact that in the *Heir*[1] one of the main characters is, and is meant to be, a horrible prig, and the other a man who believes himself to be under (almost) a hereditary curse? This justifies dramatically in both a degree of introspection which may not at all be C. M. Yonge's idea of normal Christian life. Mrs Edmonstone (clearly a good woman) does not show the same trait, nor does Amy.

I shall of course be perfectly happy to spend our joint holiday in the Inn at C'burn this year, if it so falls out. If you are in England I think you might find a few nights in the College guest room not unendurable and I'd try to give you breakfast as late as the servants cd. be expected to bear. (There are, however, clocks that chime the quarters all over Oxford; perhaps that wd. be fatal.)

I'll send you W's book as soon as it is out. I think you'll like it.[2] V. difficult to write to Gundred about J.F.'s death, wasn't it?[3]

This has been the most exquisitely beautiful autumn I can remember.

Yours
Jack

[1] C. M. Yonge, *The Heir of Redclyffe* (1853).

[2] Warren's book, *The Splendid Century: Some Aspects of French Life in the Reign of Louis XIV* (1953) was the first of six works which were to establish him as one of the leading scholars of seventeenth- and eighteenth-century France.

[3] Colonel John Forrest, who had just died, was the husband of Lewis's cousin Gundreda (Ewart) Forrest.

248

Magdalen College,
Oxford.
March 25/ 54

My dear Arthur

W. will be crossing back to England on Aug 30th and I shall then be at your disposal. I couldn't come earlier in the year as I shall be examining till the v. end of July. As for *place* I shall be perfectly content either to repeat last year's excellent menu of Inver and Rathmullan or to try any new experiment if one occurs to you. To me the pleasures of returning to the same place (wh. begins to acquire homeliness) and those of adventuring to a new, tho' different in kind, are about equal in degree. If wd. be wise if you pointed out to both managers that I am an unseasonably early riser and you a light sleeper so that you wd. be greatly obliged if we could be put in rooms *not* adjacent. (This is not meant as a joke!).

If it is convenient for you not to start till Wed. Sept. 1st I have no objection to sleeping at the Crawfordsburn inn on the 30th & 31st.

I happen to have 2 copies of this ugly book in wh. you may find some of the articles worth reading. Joy Davidman's is the best, I think.[1]

I am suffering from a number of small diseases one of which entails daily visits to hospital for 'dressings', but none of them are dangerous.

No author minds having to answer letters in praise of his own book: not even Warnie.

Blessings.

Yours
Jack

[1] He means Joy Davidman's essay 'The Longest Way Round' in *These Found the Way: Thirteen Converts to Protestant Christianity*, ed. David Wesley Soper (1951).

Magdalen College,
Oxford.
2nd. April 1954.

My dear Arthur,

Hurray, I'm so glad that you enjoyed the book, and it was good of you to write. I must re-read that chapter on the army, for you are by no means the first person who has spoken of it as you do. Whether there is to be any more book-making depends on how this book goes; the latest London report is that 'sales are steady, not sensational', which is as good as a beginner can hope for I think. The New York edition came out on the 17th., and of it I have as yet no news – beyond a positively rapturous review in the N.Y. Times, which is all to the good, so far as it goes.

Yes, I too look forward to another meeting. Jack and I plan to come to the north first this year, and then go on to the south – arriving at Crawfordsburn about the 7th August. I've given Jack your message.

Yours ever,
Warren

249

Magdalen College
Oxford
April 13/ 54

Dear Arthur

No, I have no suggestions; I lack knowledge. For one's own peace of mind I think it is best to set a time limit for one's decisions (I mean, decisions of mere pleasure where duty & necessity don't come in) – e.g., that if you haven't thought of a new plan instead of Rathmullan by noon on a certain day, about a week hence, you will at once write to Rathmullan. Also, we might find rooms all booked if we delayed too long. I suppose Sept. 15 is the night for which I shd. book my berth to L'pool? Of course I quite understand that it wd. be hard on Esther[1] if you put me up – and perhaps on you!

Yours
Jack

[1] Arthur's housekeeper, Esther Smith, of Newry, Co. Down.

250

Magdalen College
Oxford
4/ 5/ 54

Splendid. Do I sleep the night of the 15th at Rathmullan & cross to L'pool on the 16th, or leave R. on morning of 15th & cross that night? All the best.

J.

I have more copies of a huge 2 vol. American collection of Eng. poets (preface to Spenser by me) than I know what to do with.[1] Wd. you care for one?

251

Magdalen College
Oxford
August 6, 1954

My dear Arthur,

We ought to have been crossing tonight, but Warnie is in a nursing home (the usual thing). I will get across by hook or crook for my jaunt with you, arriving Crawfordsburn Monday, August 30th. I am writing to the Inn to cancel the original bookings and confirm a room for myself on the night of the 31st. But so many letters to that blasted Inn have gone astray that I'd be very glad if you would walk round and see for yourself that they've got these instructions all right.

Blessings.

Yours,
Jack

---

[1] *Major British Writers*, ed. G. B. Harrison (New York: Harcourt, Brace and Co., 1954).

252

Magdalen College
Oxford
Aug 15/ 54

My dear Arthur

W. and I sail to-morrow & go straight to the South. I hope to be at C'burn on the 30th and have now booked a room there for 30th and 31st. I am sorry you come in for a share of the bother. If I had had my wits more about me perhaps I cd. have spared you: but I am a muddler at the best of times and was then in a good deal of distress. I embark on the 'holiday' with W. full of the gloomiest forebodings. Let me have your prayers: I am tired, scared, & bewildered.

Yours

Jack

[This was to be Lewis's last letter from Magdalen College. He had been persuaded to accept the post of Professor of Medieval and Renaissance English Literature in Cambridge University, which Chair had been specially created for him, and to which he had been elected by a complete unanimity of votes. With the Professorship went a Fellowship to Magdalene College, Cambridge. Though plagued by ill health, and in two minds about leaving Oxford (except that he would be able to come home for the week-ends), he was to be extremely happy at Cambridge, and particularly with his new colleagues at Magdalene. On 29 November 1954 he delivered his Inaugural address, *De Descriptione Temporum*, which was an outstanding success. He was in the process of packing for the final 'move' when the following letter was written.]

253

Magdalen College,
Oxford.
Dec. 4th 54

My dear Arthur,

No: both were 'for keeps'. The J.A. article is from a periodical: the other article wh. you get a bit of is by someone else. What you have got is what they call an 'Off-print'.[1]

[1] The two items were Lewis's 'A Note on Jane Austen', *Essays in Criticism*, IV (Oct. 1954), pp. 359–71 and an off-print from *Res Judicatae*, VI (June 1953), pp. 224–37 of Lewis's 'The Humanitarian Theory of Punishment' and 'A Reply to C. S. Lewis' by Norval Morris and Donald Buckle.

It's all rot to say that a man of your intelligence can't *understand* Barfield's book [*This Ever Diverse Pair*]. Read it again.

Yes: the move looms large and black – all the things to 'see to' and all the decisions to make.

Blessings.

Yours
Jack

254

Magdalene College,
Cambridge.
2/ 6/ 55

My dear Arthur

Thanks for your letter of the 27th May. The arrangements are fine, except that my berth from Belfast to L'pool is booked not for Sept 19 but for Sept 20th. Shall we stay a night longer at Rathmullan or will you book me a room at the C'Burn Inn for the night of the 19th? Which you please. I don't know why you shd. feel such a heavy sense of responsibility; everyone knows that a crust, a cup of cold water and a bed of straw, or even a rug shared with you on a summer seat is enough for me!

Yours
Jack

255

The Kilns,
Headington Quarry,
Oxford
18/ 8/ 55

My dear Arthur

I arrive at Larne on the morning of Friday Sept 2nd and proceed at once to Crawfordsburn. My berth is booked for sailing from Belfast to Liverpool on the night of Tuesday Sept. 20th. Apparently I must have told you wrong, or made such a muddle that no one cd. understand me. I'm really very sorry. If the extra night's booking at Rathmullan can't be cancelled without expense, I will of course, in common fairness pay your share as well as my own. I am looking forward to our meeting v. much.

A nice, dull man from Eire (more W's friend than mine) is to spend the night of Tue. [Friday] Sept. 2nd at the Inn C'burn; so we can't do anything that evening. W. is not coming at all this year.

Sometime after Sept 15 a copy of my autobiography[1] will arrive for you. (You can always sell it or give it as a Christmas present, you know!)

> Yours
> Jack

256

> The Kilns,
> Headington Quarry,
> Oxford.
> 25/ 9/ 55

Dear Arthur

I enclose cheque and hope you are now recovered from the fatigues of our journey. I arrived home with a 100 horse-power cold to find an empty house, W. having been drunk for a fortnight and now in his old nursing home. But it's a lovely autumn morning to day. Blessings.

> Yours
> Jack

257

> As from Magdalene College,
> Cambridge.
> 30/ 10/ 55

My dear Arthur,

How nice to have a letter about a book from you again, even if it's only *my* book.[1] (I mean, it wd. be even more like old times if it weren't mine. But of course it gives me a special, and different, pleasure that you shd. like *this* one.)

W. has now resolved to live as a tee-totaller and is doing splendidly at present. I know you will not cease your prayers.

The other affair remains where it did. I don't feel the point about a 'false position'. Everyone whom it concerned wd. be told. The 'reality' wd. be, from my point of view, adultery and therefore mustn't happen. (An easy resolution when one doesn't in the least want it!)[2]

[1] *Surprised by Joy: The Shape of My Early Life*, published on 19 September 1955.
[1] *Surprised by Joy.*
[2] See note following.

God bless you. That was a famous holiday we had this year. We never exasperated each other less!

Yours
Jack

[The 'other affair' referred to in this last letter involves the highly complex and bitter-sweet relationship Lewis was to have with Joy Davidman who eventually became his wife. Arthur, as we learn from Lewis's letter to him of 25 March 1954, had been sent a copy of *These Found the Way* which contains a short autobiographical account of Joy Davidman's conversion to Christianity, partly through the reading of Lewis's religious books. It would be ideal (and certainly more to my liking) if Lewis could be left to tell what happened between Joy Davidman and himself. Most of it, however, came out in the course of conversations with Arthur, and it must be substantiated from other sources.

Joy Davidman, who came of a secularized Jewish background, was born in New York City in 1915. She received a B.A. degree from Hunter's College in 1934 and a M.A. from Columbia University in 1935. She won considerable acclaim for her book of verse *Letter to a Comrade* (1938) and she published two novels, *Anya* (1940), and *Weeping Bay* (1950). She looked for intellectual satisfaction in Communism, but after several years' flirtation she ended up with a total disillusionment and hatred for it. It was, however, at one of the Party meetings that she became attracted to a fellow Communist, William Lindsay Gresham (1909–63), who also told his story in *These Found the Way*. Gresham, an extremely insecure but gifted novelist, whose *Nightmare Alley* (1946) was made into a film, had already been married and divorced before he and Joy Davidman met and were wed in 1942. The Greshams had two sons, David, born in 1944, and Douglas, born in 1945; and almost coincidental with the Greshams' abandonment of Communism came their conversion to Christianity in 1948.

Partly because of her lifelong ambition to be a writer, and because of her deep appreciation for the great help Lewis's books had given both her and her husband, Joy Davidman began a correspondence with Lewis. This ripened into such affectionate regard for the man himself that she left her children in the custody of her husband and a female friend and turned up at the Kilns in September 1952. After being in England for six months, much of it spent in London, word reached her that Gresham was in love with the other woman. Joy Davidman returned to the United States, and after allowing her husband to divorce her on the grounds of desertion, she returned to England in the summer of 1953 with her two sons. She settled into 14 Belsize Park, London, and sent the boys to Dane Court, a preparatory school at Pyrford in Surrey. After a number of week-end visits to Oxford to see Lewis, and because of her undisguised desire to be close to him, she moved to Oxford and set up house in 10 Old High Street, Headington.

For reasons which remain unexplained, the Home Office refused to renew her permit to remain in Great Britain. (Though it is only a guess, the most reasonable supposition seems to be that her former connections with the Communist Party made her unacceptable.) Lewis had no romantic feelings for her at this time, but he was moved with pity at her plight and the 'other affair' he talked about with Arthur in the summer of 1955 was the question in his mind as to whether or not he should 'marry' Joy Davidman in order to secure her and the children a legal right to remain in this country. When he said that 'the "reality" wd. be, from my point of view, adultery and therefore mustn't happen' he meant that an actual, consummated Christian marriage was out of the question; but he knew that he could, without bending canon law forbidding marriage to a divorced person, go through a legal ceremony which could make it possible for Joy Davidman and the children to remain in England.

It can be argued – indeed it is so argued in the most orthodox circles when attempting to explain and defend Lewis's 'marriage' to Joy Davidman – that because Gresham had entered into a secular marriage before he met Joy, and because her own marriage to Gresham occurred before either of them were Christians, that Joy Davidman was not married (Christian sense) when she met Lewis. That is, if marriage (even a secular one) is *indissoluble* then Gresham was still married to his first wife: if only Christian marriage is indissoluble, William Gresham and Joy Davidman were never married.

Lewis himself was wary of such casuistry and the only thing we can say with certainty is that he took literally – see the chapter on 'Christian Marriage' in his *Mere Christianity* – Christ's own words in Matthew xix.5 that 'For this cause shall a man cleave to his wife: and they twain shall be one flesh', which Dominical utterance is further underpinned by St Paul's insistence in I Corinthians vi.16 that the very act of sexual intercourse between any man and any woman makes the participants 'one flesh'. All of this Lewis believed and urged others to believe, and his words regarding the ' "reality" ' being 'from [his] point of view adultery' would seem to substantiate it. It is also clear that Lewis did not regard a mere civil ceremony a Christian marriage, or, if the couple weren't living together, a union of any particular significance.

While he was considering whether or not he should enter into a civil contract in order to give Joy Davidman and her children English status, the lady was given notice to quit her house in 10 Old High Street, Headington. Acting with the benevolence characteristic of him, Lewis 'married' Joy Davidman in the Oxford Registry Office in St Giles Street on 23 April 1956, thus giving her and the two children British nationality. This was handled as secretly as possible so as to avoid conjecture, Joy Davidman still living in her own house.

Suddenly they had other things to worry about. Though only 41 at this time, Joy Davidman had been suffering so terribly from pains in her right leg, diagnosed as rheumatism, that she was forced to walk with a stick. There followed from this the most extraordinary coincidence I have yet come across. Talking with me about it a few years later, Mrs Austin Farrer, the wife of Dr Austin Farrer who was the Chaplain of Trinity College (and one of the witnesses to the 'secret' civil ceremony) told me that very late on the night of 18 October 1956 she suddenly *knew* something was wrong with her friend Joy. 'I *must* ring her!' she exclaimed to her husband as she dialled Joy Davidman's telephone number. Before the bell could ring, Lewis's legal wife, at home in Headington, tripped over the wire bringing the telephone down on to the floor, at the same time feeling the bone in her leg snap like a twig. With the pain came Katherine Farrer's voice begging to know if anything was wrong. Help was soon at hand, and Joy Davidman was officially admitted to the Wingfield-Morris Orthopaedic Hospital on 19 October, her femur bone having been eaten through by cancer. After some weeks of treatment there, she was transferred to the Churchill Hospital which is just across the road from the Wingfield-Morris.

It was shortly after this that Lewis was writing to Greeves (25 November 1956) – and other friends as well – disclosing the sad fact that Joy Davidman was indeed dying from cancer and that there was 'a real danger that she may die in a few months'. As he further pointed out to Greeves, 'if she gets over this bout and emerges from hospital she will no longer be fit to live alone so she must come and live here. That means (in order to avoid scandal) that our marriage must shortly be published.'

It is perhaps inevitable that those who rejoice in 'daring' to shock the public with intimate details of their private lives are likely to believe that there is a touch of hypocrisy in Lewis's wish to 'avoid scandal'. The thing is too complex for such infirm conjectures. Lewis could not, without embarrassment to both the lady and himself, reveal the precise nature of their 'marriage'. He felt a responsibility for those who had been nourished and often converted by his defence of orthodox Christianity, and because rumours were flying thick and fast, he had the following announcement put in *The Times* (24 December 1956) p. 8: 'A marriage has taken place between Professor C. S. Lewis, of Magdalene College Cambridge, and Mrs Joy Gresham, now a patient in the Churchill, Hospital, Oxford. It is requested that no letters be sent.'

Even then there remained the question of *how* Lewis could avoid the 'scandal' of taking into his house a woman to whom he had not been united by the Christian sacrament of marriage, albeit one who was sadly dying of cancer. Lewis talked the matter over with the Bishop of Oxford, but that very compassionate man, despite the peculiar nature of the marriage in question, was bound by the responsibilities of his high office. He forbade any of the priests in his diocese performing such a ceremony. In the end Lewis turned to his old friend, the Reverend Peter Bide of the Diocese of London, who had, through God's grace, healed others by the laying on of hands.

Joy Davidman had some time earlier been returned to the Wingfield-Morris (now called the Nuffield Orthopaedic Centre) in Old Road, Headington. It was there, on 21 March 1957, that Father Bide laid his hands on Joy Davidman praying for her recovery, and afterwards – because it seemed a good thing to all concerned – he married them. It is in fact this incident that Lewis was recalling in his essay 'The Efficacy of Prayer' (1959). He wrote 'I have stood by the bedside of a woman whose thigh-bone was eaten through with cancer and who had thriving colonies of the disease in many other bones as well . . . The doctors predicted a few months of life: the nurses (who often know better), a few weeks. A good man laid his hands on her and prayed. A year later the patient was walking . . . and the man who took the last X-ray photos was saying, "The bones are as solid as rock. It's miraculous." '

In her surviving years Joy Davidman was to bring Lewis much happiness, for their love was one that grew out of adversity. As Lewis was to say to Nevill Coghill, 'I never expected to have, in my sixties, the happiness that passed me by in my twenties' (*Light on C. S. Lewis*, 1965, p. 63).]

258

The Kilns,
Headington Quarry,
Oxford
5/ 12/ 55

My dear Arthur,

Home for the Vacation to-day and all *very* well here. Thanks for the review, which I hadn't seen. The phrase 'eulogy of pederasty' is a trifle misleading I shd. say![1]

Sorry my handwriting is so awful. I do try! Of course I don't know anything about foreign schools: one gets the impression they are full of spies and informers (which is worse than pederasty) but I dare say one gets it wrongly.

---

[1] The reviewer was writing about *Surprised by Joy* and in particular the chapter (VI) describing Lewis's unhappy years at Malvern College ('Wyvern'). It is not known where it was reviewed, nor by whom, but the reviewer upon sniffing the *word* 'Pederasty' took what was in fact a condemnation of it for a 'eulogy' – a not uncommon 'mistake' for those who will have pornography on any terms.

I admired *The Mill on the F.* last time I read it. The one I can't go back to is *Adam B..*[2]

Happy Christmas.

Yours
Jack

259

Magdalene,
Cambridge.
19/ 2/ 56

My dear Arthur,

'Revelations' about you in *S. by J.*! What if I'd made a few more?

I didn't know Ramsay. I think the evidence for suicide pretty weak. King's Chapel is under repairs. He might easily have gone up to look at the work – squeezed half his body out thro' that hole to see one particular place – lost his head – and slipped through. If one can get one's shoulders thro' an opening, the rest of one will follow easily.[1]

W. was pleased with yr. remarks about his book.[2]

Where you will, next summer. All love.

Yours
Jack

[2] George Eliot, *The Mill on the Floss* (1860); *Adam Bede* (1859).

[1] The obituary of Fr Ivor Erskine St Clair Ramsay (1902–56), Dean of King's College, Cambridge, since 1949, is found in *The Times* (23 January 1956) p. 6. His body was discovered near the walls of the college chapel on 22 January, and while the Coroner recorded a verdict (*The Times*, 26 January, p. 5) of suicide 'while the balance of his mind was disturbed and that he died from injuries compatible with a fall from a height', Lewis, as can be seen, was not convinced.

[2] Warren's second book (dedicated to Jane McNeill), *The Sunset of the Splendid Century: The Life and Times of Louis Auguste de Bourbon Duc du Maine, 1670–1736* (1955).

260

As from Magdalene College,
Cambridge.
13/ 5/ 56

My dear Arthur,

After 9 months of perfect tee-totalism (we flattered ourselves it was a real cure) W. has started drinking again and the elaborate joint holidays he had planned for us in the summer will probably have to be cancelled.

But I want to make *your* and my jaunt sure. May we leave C'burn on Monday Sept 3d and return to B'fast (I to the boat) on Mon. Sept 17th? If all goes *wrong* with W., I shall be arriving at the Inn on Fri. Aug 31: if by any chance he should be well enough to carry out the original plan (or, more probably, *think* himself well enough to drag me thro' that hell) then it will be different, to the extent that I shan't reach C'burn till Aug 1st. But this won't affect *our* (your and my) dates.

You always say (truly enough) that I'm a bad proof-reader. I may be getting proofs of my new Cupid & Psyche story[1] in June. If there's time to send you one copy wd. you care to do me a kindness by going through it? Don't, if it is in the least a bother. You'd have about 10 days probably to do it in, and the book is a little longer than *S. by J.*.

My Doctor friend[1] says that the latter leaves out too much and he is going to supplement it by a book called *Suppressed by Jack*! God bless you. A chat with you wd. cheer me up no end this minute

Yours
Jack

[1] *Till We Have Faces: A Myth Retold*, published on 10 September 1956.
[2] Robert Emlyn Havard (1901–   ) was not only Lewis's doctor but a much-valued friend and a dedicated member of the 'Inklings'. He was educated at Wolverly School, Kidderminster, and Keble College, Oxford. He received his B.A. in 1921, his B.M. and B.Ch. in 1927, and his M.A. and Doctor of Medicine in 1934. He was a Research Student at Guy's Hospital in London, and Asst House Surgeon and later Physician in the Radcliffe Infirmary, Oxford. After serving as a Lt in the Royal Naval Volunteer Reserve between 1943–5, he returned to his practice in Oxford.

261

Magdalene College,
Cambridge.
17/ 5/ 56

My dear Arthur,
The crucial date, from your point of view, is Sept. 3d (third, III^d). My arrival at the Inn will, as you say, depend on circumstances. Our letters crossed. Thanks for yours of the 15th. Yes, Bro. Lawrence[1] is of course right.

Yours
Jack

262

Magdalene College,
Cambridge.
18/ 5/ 56

My dear A.,
I was so busy with a big mail yesterday that I forgot to thank you for saying you'd vet. my proofs. Scrawl your notes (in pencil if you like) on their margins.

Yours
Jack

263

The Kilns,
Headington Quarry,
Oxford
19/ 6/ 56

My dear Arthur,
Here's the proof. I'd like it back in 10 days, but don't on any account let it be a nuisance to you. If you can't finish it without pressing yourself, just send it back unfinished, but put a X at the bottom of the last page you *have* done

Yours
Jack

[1] Brother Lawrence's (c.1605–81) *Practice of the Presence of God.*

264

The Kilns,
Headington Quarry,
Oxford
19/ 7/ 56

My dear A,

I have a letter from Kelsie saying she has heard from Janie that I am going to Donegal in Sept and that she (K.) is also going there in Sept. with her helper Adrian *and* (heaven help us) my cousin John Hamilton[1] and heaven knows who else and hopes we shall meet.

I have replied that I go with you and that we shall not be in one place all the time and that you know all the dates and addresses and that she'd better find them out from you. Don't swear at me too much! I can't remember the addresses & if I'd settled anything with K. on my own I might have gone against your wishes. Her destination seems to be Port Noo. I think we shall have to sacrifice one day to going to see her (by the way, Cherrie Robins is in the party too but hope there will be no trouble beyond that. Incidentally I shd. *like* to see Cherrie. John is, I think, a bore). It will be v. like old times: most of our holidays will be spent in dodging! I can already hear our conversations!

Some day, when you're not rushed, you might write me the Inver and Rathmullan addresses and dates on a P.C.

W. still well, thank God.

Yours
J.

265

The Kilns,
Headington Quarry,
Oxford
Nov. 25th 1956

My dear Arthur,

Joy is in hospital, suffering from cancer. The prospects are *1.* A tiny 100th chance of ultimate cure. *2.* A reasonable probability of

---

[1] Lewis's first cousin, John Borlase Hamilton (1905–   ) was the son of Augustus Warren Hamilton and he was employed in his father's business, 'Hamilton & McMaster – Marine Boilermakers and Engineers'.

some years more of (tolerable) life. *3*. A real danger that she may die in a few months.

It will be a great tragedy for me to lose her. In the meantime, if she gets over this bout and emerges from hospital she will no longer be fit to live alone so she must come and live here. That means (in order to avoid scandal) that our marriage must shortly be published. W. has written to Janie and the Ewarts to tell them I am getting married, and I didn't want the news to take you by surprise. I know you will pray for her and for me: and for W., to whom also, the loss if we lose her, will be great.

Yours ever
Jack

266

The Kilns
Headington Quarry
Oxford, England
5/ 4/ 57

My dear Arthur,

I was meaning to write to you anyway when I got your letter of the 2d – if only to tell you that there will be no likelihood of an Irish holiday for me this year. Next year, almost certainly, I shall be (in the sense I least desire it) 'free'. Joy has now been sent home from hospital, not because she is better but because they can do nothing for her. She is completely bed-ridden – has to be lifted even onto the bed pan – and we have a resident nurse. I know you continue to pray for us. W. is being wonderful. God bless you.

Jack

267

[The Kilns]
Aug. 21. [1957]

My dear Arthur,

They did give me Deep Heat alright as long as the trouble was supposed to be a slipped disc or anything rheumatic. But as soon as the x-rays showed osteoporosis they dropped Deep Heat at once. And I do sleep with [a] board under my mattress. *This* disease is, I fancy, quite different from what you had: the cure, if there is one, depends on getting the system to turn into bone more of the calcium one's ordinary food contains – a question of blood & metabolism.

But enough of this.

Telephone call from Eire to say that W. was dead drunk and they were trying to get him into the Lourdes Hospital. Then, a day or two later, letter from W., now in Lourdes Hospital, to say he has been diagnosed as having a heart complaint wh. will kill him in a year. It *may* not be true – he says anything in his alcoholic spasms – and I've written to the Rev. Mother asking for the facts. It's weary waiting for an answer.[1] It always *might* be true this time.

But perhaps it is a good thing that troubles never come singly. Any *one* of my present woes (Joy, W., myself) wd. possibly affect me more if it was the only one. At any rate, when life gets *very* bad (do you find?) a sort of anaesthesia sets in. There is at least a mercy in being always tired: it takes the edge off things.

Sun this morning for the first time after many days. I hope the view from your house is bathed in it too – I'd love to see it this moment. You must have had a tough time when you and Esther were both laid up. Did Peter make a good nurse?

Yours
Jack

268

[The Kilns]
Sept. 5/ 57

My dear Arthur,

I've now got the *real* news about W., wh. is much less alarming. The heart trouble is slight & curable: it was a bye-product of acute alcoholism and pneumonia.

Sorry about Peter's operation and your wrist. Yes, yes, I've been examined for a whole morning by the biggest pathologist here, had

[1] This is the first time this hospital has been mentioned but it had already played a significant part in Warren's life. As has been seen, Lewis had found it progressively difficult to find his brother a bed in one of the Oxford nursing homes. While Warren preferred Oxford and his brother's company when he was sober, he felt an irresistible attraction to Eire when he was not, and some time in the 1940s when he collapsed from drink in Drogheda, Co. Louth, he found medical and spiritual succour in Our Lady of Lourdes Hospital at Drogheda. The hospital, run by the Medical Missionaries of Mary, was founded in 1937 by Mother Mary Martin which dear and gracious lady – whom I have had the good fortune to know – was to look after Major Lewis whenever he was ill from then on. For more about Mother Mary Martin and her work see *The First Decade: Ten Years' Work of the Medical Missionaries of Mary, 1937–1947* [1948] to which Lewis contributed an essay, 'Some Thoughts'.

instruments shoved up my bottom and specimens sucked out of my marrow, & x-ray photos and all.

God bless.

Yours
Jack

269

Magdalene College,
Cambridge.
Nov. 27th 57

My dear Arthur,

Our news is all very good. Joy's improvement has gone beyond anything we dared to hope and she can now (limping, of course, and with a stick) get about the house and into the garden. My osteoporosis is also very much better. I have no pain worth talking about now: wake up a bit sore in the mornings but that wears off by the time I'm shaved and bath'd. I don't think I'll ever be able to take a real walk again nor to leave off my surgical belt; but I cd. hardly have believed, if it had been foretold me, how little either of these prospects bothers me. I began to get better about 4 weeks before term began. I have to hire a car at the beginning and end of term for the journey because I can't handle the luggage, but I go to & fro by train on week ends quite comfortably. Indeed a corner-seat in a railway carriage is one of my best positions.

I've been writing nothing but academic work except for a very unambitious little work on the Psalms, wh. is now finished and ought to come out next spring.[1]

I like Cambridge better all the time: also my new job – or rather my new leisure for I've never been so under-worked since I first went to school.

Please congratulate Peter on his successful operation. You say nothing about yourself: I hope this means there is nothing but good to say? Give my love to Janie and the Glenmachonians: and give God thanks on my behalf for all His mercies. Bless you.

Yours
Jack

W. is well and busily writing.

[1] *Reflections on the Psalms*, published 8 September 1958.

T.S.T.–S

270

The Kilns,
Headington Quarry,
Oxford
26/ 3/ 58

My dear Arthur,

Nice to hear from you. I don't think I can make any plans for the summer. Joy (how unlike poor Minto) wd. not breathe a word against my going. But, though all goes splendidly, the sword of Damocles hangs over us. How shd. I feel if it descended quite soon and I then felt 'I did not even stay with her while I had her.' If, by God's mercy, all continued to go well for a couple of years it wd. be a different matter.

I suppose it is idle to speak of *your* coming to England? There's a proper spare room here now, and central heating – – and Magdalen*e* is much nicer to stay at than Magdalen. You cd. have breakfast when you pleased in your own sitting room.

Things are wonderful at present. Joy is up all day, can get in and out of cars and go up and down stairs, keeps all the staff in good form, and is (of course) re-decorating the house. You have no idea how lovely it is to have no *nurses* about.

But I've been meaning to write to you about the last of all the nurses, because her conversation was so exactly like that of Miss F's Aunt. Here is a specimen: 'I once nursed a lady on Boar's Hill. When I was taking my patient out in her bath chair we used to meet dear Mr Pilkington. He was looking for bees in the woods. With his binoculars. He always stopped his car to tell my patient. The reason he told her about the bees was that she was a Scotchwoman. You see, she was a whiskey lady.'

I'm correcting the proofs of that book on the Psalms at present.

God bless you, and thank you for your prayers, which I know you will continue.

Yours
Jack

271

The Kilns,
Headington Quarry,
Oxford
2/ 4/ 58

My dear A.,

Yes, yes, of course. If we ever dare to make any plans more than a month or so ahead. I certainly want to bring Joy to Co. Down, and the occasional hospitality of your car wd. be most welcome. As for who is going to do the talking – Joy has the extraordinary delusion that I do most of it anyway. Actually, against you *and* her I shd. have no chance.

I agree. One has long since come to regard Mr Woodhouse[1] as the most sensible character in the book.

God bless you

Yours
Jack

272

Magdalene College,
Cambridge.
May 30th 1958

My dear Arthur,

Here's a copy of W's last book,[1] with my compliments. It has elicited a furious letter from the present representative of the family, The Duc de Guiche; so furious I was releived to find it did not end in a challenge!

And now – wd. you believe it? – Joy is so well that she and I are proposing to visit Ireland and shd. be in Crawfordsburn for 10 days in the first half of July. I need not say how I hope you'll be in residence. Will you?

Yours
Jack

[On 28 August 1958 Lewis wrote to a friend, Mrs Watt, describing the holiday he and Joy had with Arthur: '. . . We had a holiday – you might

---

[1] In Jane Austen's *Emma*.
[1] W. H. Lewis, *Assault on Olympus: The Rise of the House of Gramont between 1604 and 1678* (1958).

call it a belated honeymoon – in Ireland and were lucky enough to get that perfect fortnight at the beginning of July. We visited Louth, Down, and Donegal, and returned drunk with blue mountains, yellow beaches, dark fuchsia, breaking waves, braying donkeys, peat-smell, and the heather just beginning to bloom. We flew to Ireland, for, tho' both of [us] wd. prefer ship to plane, her bones, and even mine, could not risk a sudden lurch. It was the first flight either of us had ever experienced and we found it, after one initial moment of terror, enchanting. The cloud-scape seen from above is a new world of beauty – and then the rifts in the clouds through which one sees (like Tennyson's Tithonus) "a glimpse of that dark world where I was born". We had clear weather over the Irish Sea and the first Irish headland, brightly sunlit, stood out from the dark sea (it's very dark when you're looking directly *down* on it) like a bit of enamel . . .']

273

The Kilns
Sept 15th 1958

My dear Arthur,

(1) The picture gets better every week. You have embodied in it the whole feel of the North of Ireland. I can almost feel the damp (not that I need a picture for that to-day, for it's pouring!) and hear the shushing of that wind. I don't in general like titles (fancy ones) for pictures, but this does again and again remind me of the line from Wordsworth 'The Winds come to me from the fields of sleep'.[1]

(2) After carefully keeping a petrol account with you, did I ever actually remember to *pay*? Let me know. (3) Book enclosed.[2] (4) W's in Ireland. Joy is grand. Both our loves.

Yours
Jack

274

Magdalene College,
Cambridge.
Nov. 3ᵈ 1958

My dear Arthur,

They gave me calcium tablets and little tablets which (for some reason) contain female hormones. I think there was Vitamin-

[1] *Intimations of Immortality*, III, 28.
[2] *Reflections on the Psalms.*

something mixed with the calcium. Also a surgical belt. The pains gradually became less frequent and less severe. I say *pains* not *pain* because so far as I can make out the bone-condition is not itself painful. What hurts is the spasms the muscles go into in order to protect the bones, when you make any unusual movement. I am now almost entirely well again and walked about 2 to 3 miles last week. I still wear the belt till about 3 p.m. But I had a whole week without it lately when it was being mended and this produced a little aching. Whether the belt or the calcium or the hormones or nature is responsible for my improvement, of course I don't know. It *feels* as if it were the belt. No one suggested injections.

We are all well and v. happy. W. as sober as a judge.

Yours
Jack

In haste – just off the train from my week end at home. Blessings.

275

The Kilns
Headington Quarry,
Oxford
25/ 3/ 59

My dear Arthur,

When you wrote you had not heard the news about Janie.[1] Actually, at the moment, I am *feeling* very little (this is often the way) but I know that you and I have had a huge bit of our past hacked away. And even while I write this comic ideas come into my head. She seems to have had the nicest possible death.

Now. We have just been financially knocked flat by a huge surtax on royalties earned 2 years ago, which was a bumper year, long since forgotten and of course spent. I think we shall weather it alright, but we shall have to go very carefully – not perhaps for always but certainly for 18 months or so. Joy and I were talking it over only yesterday and agreed that the Irish holiday will almost certainly have to be given up this year. A great loss! This 'Janie business' makes me feel it worse, as it will you too. Now don't *you* go dying or anything silly!

Has the old lady met her? – the slow head-shake and 'Oh Tchanie, Tchanie'

[1] Janie McNeill died peacefully in her sleep on 23 March.

All well. We ramble about the woods like anything.
I'd give anything for a few hours with you just now.

Yours
Jack

276

The Kilns,
Headington Quarry,
Oxford
1/ 4/ 59

My dear Arthur,

I'm already doing something about J. for Campbell, impelled by a man called Armour who makes the shattering statement 'I always felt that J.M. was a mystic and more deeply soaked in the mystic point of view than anyone I have known' (!!?$\sqrt{-1} \div$?δ!).[1] Well! If so, we missed a good deal. I am shaking with laughter while I write, and I hope you are while you read. Having heard Armour on J. how I wish I could hear J. on Armour.

Are you and I a pair of humbugs? We now miss her dreadfully; while she was alive what a lot of time we spent evading her!

W. says 'I must be like a cat which loves places more than people. What really hurts is the idea of never being in that house again.'

God bless you.

J.

[The 'something' Lewis did 'about Janie' was to write an obituary for the Campbell College magazine *The Campbellian*, Vol. 14, No. 9 (July 1959), pp. 692–3, which, because of its general inaccessibility, is given below in full.]

Molliter Ossa Cubent.

Of Miss McNeill the charitable lady, the teacher, the member of committees, I saw nothing. My knowledge is of Janie McNeill: even of Chanie, as we sometimes called her, for she had the habit, common in some Scotch dialects, of 'unvoicing' the consonant 'J'. Obviously there is a great deal I never knew. Someone writes to me describing her as a mystic. I would never have guessed it. What I remember is

[1] Lewis may have temporarily forgotten him, but John Kenneth Cameron Armour (1895–1975) became a pupil at Campbell College in 1905 and remembered Lewis arriving there in September 1910. Mr Armour had been a Master at Campbell College since 1927.

something as boisterous, often as discomposing but always as fresh
and tonic, as a high wind. Janie was the delight and terror of a little
Strandtown and Belmont circle, now almost extinct. I remember
wild walks on the (still unspoiled) Holywood hills, preposterous jokes
shouted through the gale across half a field, extravagantly merry
(yet also Lucullan) lunches and suppers at Lisnadene, devastating
raillery, the salty tang of an immensely vivid personality. She was a
religious woman, a true, sometimes a grim, daughter of the Kirk; no
less certainly, the broadest-spoken maiden lady in the Six Counties.
She was a born satirist. Every kind of sham and self-righteousness
was her butt. She deflated the unco-gude with a single ironic phrase,
then a moment's silence, then the great gust of her laughter. She
laughed with her whole body. When I consider how all this was
maintained through years of increasing loneliness, pain, disability,
and inevitable frustration I am inclined to say she had a soul as brave
and uncomplaining as any I ever knew. Few have come nearer to
obeying Dunbar's magnificent recipe (she knew her Dunbar):

> 'Man, please thy Maker and be merry
> And give not for this world a cherry.'

277

The Kilns
April 3/ 59

My dear Arthur

Our prospects have suddenly cleared up. We are going to get a fair
amount of refund for erroneously paid tax and also have found
means of keeping more of my own royalties.

This is probably unintelligible, but the upshot is that we CAN
come to Ireland this summer after all. Are you still available? We cd.
take our fortnight any time between June 20 and July 15. Rathmullan, I suppose? Or have you any other idea? I can't tell you how
pleased I am. Joy sends love

Yours
Jack

The Kilns, Kiln Lane
Headington Quarry
Oxford
May 12, 1959

Dear Arthur,

Yes, make it a week at Rathmullan if they can take us. I think we tried later last year and they managed it, so I'm hopeful. On checking our dates I see we can manage any time between June 20th & July 19th – we'll pick a fortnight, more or less to suit you. I suppose we'd better have several days at Crawfordsburn *before* Rathmullan, as before.

September wouldn't do, I'm afraid, because the boys are home from school then. We daren't leave the helpless housekeeper at their mercy, and we're planning to take them to Wales.

I'll be a surprise to you this year – I can walk a mile without tiring, now! I hope you feel as well as I do.

Yours,
Joy[1]

278

The Kilns,
Headington Quarry,
Oxford
12 March 1960

My dear Arthur

I am afraid it is rather an understatement to say that Joy is 'not so well'. The last x-ray test revealed that cancer is returning in almost every part of her skeleton. They do something with radio-therapy, but as soon as they have silenced an ache in one place one breaks out in another. The doctors hold out no hope of a cure; it is only a question of how soon the end comes and how painful it will be. She is still, however, mostly free from pain and able to get about and unbelievably cheerful. We hope to do a lightning trip to Greece by air this vacation.[1] We hardly dare to look as far ahead as next summer.

[1] As hoped, Lewis and his wife were able to spend a fortnight with Arthur, stopping part of the time at The Old Inn, Crawfordsburn and part of the time at the Royal Fort Hotel, Rathmullan, Co. Donegal, returning to Oxford on 10 July.

[1] As problematical as Lewis knew it would almost certainly be, Joy had all her life longed for a sight of the golden isles of Greece, and they did in fact go. The trip, which lasted from 3 to 14 April 1960, was taken with their

I am sorry for your sake that my old friend Peter is going but glad for his. Life is not much use to an animal when it can not longer enjoy its body. They can't, like us, make up for it by reading and talking.

W. is v. well. I have had flu' and am discovered to be suffering from high blood pressure. I have in consequence been put on a very rigid diet!

I think a dentist who, having pulled *your* tooth out, complains about how it affects *his* lumbago, has either no sense of humour or a v. mischievous one!

God bless you. I hope you and I at least will be spared to one another.

Yours
Jack

P.S. Get a cat. They're more suitable for us old people than dogs, and a cat makes a house into a home.

279

The Kilns,
Headington Quarry
Oxford
30 Aug 1960

My dear Arthur

It is nice to hear from you. It might have been worse. Joy got away easier than many who die of cancer. There were a couple of hours of atrocious pain on her last morning, but the rest of the day mostly asleep, tho' rational whenever she was conscious. Two of her last remarks were 'You have made me happy' and 'I am at peace with God.' She died at 10 that evening. I'd seen violent death but never seen natural death before. There's really nothing to it, is there? One thing I'm very glad about is that in the Easter Vac she realised her life long dream of seeing Greece. We had a wonderful time there. And many happy moments even after that. The night before she

friends Roger and June Lancelyn Green, and the day-to-day diary which Roger Lancelyn Green kept of their travels from Athens to Mycenae, Aegosthena, the Island of Rhodes, Crete and other islands of the Peloponnese is printed in full in the *Biography* (ch. XI). What is probably also worth a mention is that, in talking with me about the trip shortly before his death, Lewis said 'Joy knew she was dying, I knew she was dying, and *she* knew *I* knew she was dying – but when we heard the shepherds playing their flutes in the hills it seemed to make no difference!'

died we had a long, quiet, nourishing, and tranquil talk.

W. is away on his Irish holiday and has, as usual, drunk himself into hospital. Douglas – the younger boy – is, as always, an absolute brick, and a very bright spot in my life. I'm quite well myself. In fact, by judicious diet and exercise, I've brought myself down from 13 stone to just under 11.

Yours
Jack

[Joy was taken to the Radcliffe Infirmary early on the morning of 13 July 1960 and she died there that evening. Their friend, The Rev. Dr Austin Farrer (1904–68), who was the Warden of Keble College, conducted her funeral service on 18 July at the Oxford Crematorium where her ashes were scattered.

Lewis considered long what epitaph he should write for Joy and it was during his long illness in July 1963 – mentioned in his last letter to Arthur – that he dictated to me this epitaph which, published here for the first time, is inscribed on a stone plaque at the Crematorium:]

Remember
HELEN JOY
DAVIDMAN
D. July 1960
Loved wife of
C. S. LEWIS

Here the whole world (stars, water, air
And field, and forest, as they were
Reflected in a single mind)
Like cast off clothes was left behind
In ashes, yet with hope that she,
Re-born from holy poverty,
In lenten lands, hereafter may
Resume them on her Easter Day.

280

> Magdalene College,
> Cambridge.
> 25/ 1/ 61

My dear Arthur

Thanks for noting misprint[1] – I'm v. bad at spotting them.

I do hope you'll risk a few days with us when you are in England. We do now have a decent spare room with a double bed nearly as broad as it's long. Or, if it is in term time, this college has a good guest suite, sitting room as well as bedroom (with TV) and you can have breakfast in it by yourself unshaved at any hour you like. Do.

> Yours
> Jack

> Silver Hill,
> 21 Ballymullan Rd
> Crawfordsburn,
> Co. Down.
> 6.5.61

My dear Jack,

I am hoping to fly to London on the 21st June (Wednesday); staying with my friend Will McClurg[1] at 109 Park St. W.1 till Monday 26th; then on to Rege at Plymouth for a week or two.

I thought I might, if suitable, get down to see you for a day or a night at Oxford between 21st & 26th before I go on to Plymouth. If I remember right, Paddington is the station for Oxford. This would be much simpler than Cambridge: besides, I'll only have a dark grey suit (no dinner jacket) &, as you know, am rather shy of all the people one meets in college.

I presume this would have to be the Friday or Saturday? as you will be at Cambridge earlier. This is only tentative. Especially as I've had a little heart grogginess – not serious, the doctor says, but please God I'll be free of it when I leave.

Don't hesitate to say at once if any of those dates don't suit.

Everything is changing. Lismachan (where we saw 'the hedge pig' – do you remember?) is being sold.[2] The four aunts nearly all over 90,

[1] Almost certainly in a proof-copy of Lewis's *An Experiment in Criticism* which was published in October 1961.

[1] Dr William Moncrief McClurg, the osteopathic physician.

[2] 'Lismachan', in Strandtown, was built by Joseph Greeves's brother

have gone elsewhere. I've been re-reading 'Lilith'. This man has a fascination.

Let me know what you think. I suppose there are good trains about 11 AM. or earlier. I suppose you wouldn't be up in London?

Hope you are all keeping well.

Love
Arthur

281

The Kilns,
Headington Quarry,
Oxford
8 May 1961

My dear Arthur

Your letter has brightened my whole sky. I shall, by June 21, be here, not at Cambridge. Can you come on Thurs 22, and stay at least till the morning of Sat 24? – longer if possible. But if you can manage only two nights, make them the Thurs. and Fri., for our 'daily' doesn't come on week-ends and it will not be so comfortable. Also, roads are more crowded. This matters because (D.V.) I'll run up to London in a hired car and we'll drive* back here together – the run down thro' the Chilterns and Thames valley is a pleasant one. By the way, this time you shall have a double-bed nearly as broad as it's long.

I am concerned to hear your medical news. Unfortunately it is just at that point that your letter turns illegible. It looks as if you had HUNT POGGINES. I suppose the first word is HEART, but I can't make out the second.

Yes, all changes. The party gets thinner and I suppose you and I shall be leaving it soon.

A-propos of Geo. MacDonald, some American has written a ghastly psychological study of him, trying to prove that he had an incestuous love for his mother, couldn't bear his father, hated the human race, and delighted in cruelty. I only hope I shall be asked to review it![1]

Yours
Jack

(* Don't worry. I mean we shall be driven! Not me at the wheel)

John Greeves (1831–1917) and it had been the home of that branch of the family till it was sold.

[1] In the end, Lewis didn't review Robert Lee Wolff's *The Golden Key: A Study of the Major Fiction of George MacDonald* (1961).

Silver Hill,
21 Ballymullan Rd
Crawfordsburn
Co. Down
12/ 5/ 61

My dear Jack,

How wonderful of you to make it so easy for me by taking me by car! I've just written to Will to tell him of the arrangement. Thank you so much – D.V. I'll hope to stay with you from the Thursday June 22nd till Saturday June 24th as you suggest. I'm delighted so much [it] has been settled. I can hardly believe it.

In case I forget when writing again, Will's address is: William McClurg, Flat 1. 109 Park Street London W.1 (Phone Mayfair 3889.) I'll go there in taxi. If it would be easier for you if I met you elsewhere, let me know.

The correct translation is: HEART GROGGINESS! In other words, Palpitations – breathlessness etc. But I am much better & had a longer walk this morning. Yes, I wonder how much longer? Aren't I four years older?

The American must be 'knuts' himself. But it might have the effect of drawing attention to G.M. A good thing.

As ever,
Arthur.

282

The Kilns,
Headington Quarry,
Oxford
14 May 1961

My dear Arthur

About our journey from London to Oxford on Thurs. June 22. My Jehu and I might waste a good deal of time finding 109 Park St. W.1, so I suggest, if convenient, you shd. meet us at some station nearer the outskirts. Ealing Broadway at about 12 noon wd. do well. Let me know (at Magdalene, Cambridge) as soon as possible. I am excited at the prospect of meeting again. Heaven send that nothing goes wrong!

Yours
Jack

Silver Hill,
21 Ballymullan Rd.
Crawfordsburn,
Co. Down.
17.5.61

My dear Jack,

Yes certainly – D.V. I'll meet you at Ealing Broadway Tube Station – or wherever the bus from Marble Arch lets me down at that terminal on 22nd June at noon – (not midnight – or AM or PM – or any other M).

I *shall* just bring a handbag, two steamer trunks & a portmanteau (a little shabby) The latter can go in the boot so we'll have plenty of room to stretch our legs!! Without joking – just the handbag (& what I stand up in of course) And please God all will be well.

I'm looking forward to it all tremendously & I'll try & not be a damned nuisance.

Arthur

P.S. Do you think Warren can bear it!!

283

The Kilns,
Headington Quarry,
Oxford
21 May 1961

My dear Arthur

Good. 12 Noon Thurs. June 22d, Ealing Broadway Station. This is not, by the way, exactly a Tube station. It is on the Metropolitan which has become a surface railway by the time it reaches there, so that the E. Broadway Metropolitan station and the ordinary G.W.R. station are one and the same station. Whichever of us gets there first must await the other on the 'down' platform. (There is probably a refreshment room.) I shall bring sandwiches for lunch on the drive.

This is not because I have lost my old preference for hotels, but my usual driver, who is almost a family friend, is unable to come[1] and

[1] Lewis's 'Jehu' and good friend who usually motored him to and from Cambridge and wherever else he wished to go was Alfred Clifford Morris (1914–) who mentions Lewis and other of his distinguished clients in his *Miles and Miles: Some Reminiscences of an Oxford Taxi Driver and Private Car Hire Service Chauffeur* (Abingdon: The Abbey Press, 1964).

his substitute is not a man we could very comfortably take into a dining room. (He is also, by the way, one of the most vociferous bores in England.)

Warnie will be away while you are here. He's not (honest!) running away on your account – it had all been fixed before we knew you were coming.

Yours
Jack

Silver Hill,
21 Ballymullan Rd
Crawfordsburn,
Co. Down.
31st May '61

My dear Jack,

Yes, I understand about the metropolitan station. I'll hope to be there E. Broadway G.W.R. on the down platform on Thursday June 22nd 12 noon. I haven't been away since last May when I saw you, so am looking forward to everything.

Esther[1] is leaving definitely for good when I go. There are snags of course – but it is all for the best.

I'm sorry I won't see Warren & I do hope I'm not being a nuisance. It will be interesting to see all the old haunts again. I can hardly believe that I will.

In case you've lost my London address: – c/o W. M. McClurg – Flat 1. 109 Park St (Quite close to Marble Arch) W.1 Phone 3889 Mayfair. I'll be there on the night of 21st.[2]

As ever
Arthur

---

[1] Esther Smith, his housekeeper, had decided to retire.

[2] The two days together at the Kilns were to be poignantly satisfying, though Arthur was to scribble in the margin of the next letter he received from Lewis 'He was looking very ill'.

This was the last time they were to meet.

284

The Kilns,
Headington Quarry,
Oxford
27 June 1961

My dear Arthur

My trouble has been diagnosed as one v. common at our time of life, namely an enlarged prostate gland. I shall soon be in a nursing home for the necessary operation.

How I did enjoy our two days together!

Yours
Jack

285

The Kilns
30 June '61

My dear Arthur

The trouble turns out to be (what's v. common to our age and sex) a distended prostate gland. I go into the Acland Nursing Home on Sunday for the operation.

Our little re-union was one of the happiest times I've had for many a long day. I hope the cool of the moor-lands will soon set *you* up.

Yours
Jack

286

[The Kilns]
12 Nov. 61

My dear Arthur,

Yes. The *Imitation* is very severe; useful at times when one is tempted to be too easily satisfied with one's progress, but certainly not at times of discouragement. And of course it is written for monks, not for people living in the world like us.

A good book to balance it is Traherne's *Centuries of Meditations*, wh. I expect you know (*Not* to be confused with his poems, which I don't recommend.) There is all the gold & fragrance!

Midway between the two I'd put the anonymous *Theologia*

Germanica[1] (Macmillan's in the little blue Golden Treasury series). This is curiously like the sort of letters we used to write 45 years ago!

Yours
Jack

P.S. I never read St John of the Cross

287

[The Kilns]
24 Nov [1961]

Thanks for review. I always thought Herbert R. an ass, so I don't know whether to conclude that my book is bilge or to revise my opinion of H.R.[1]

I don't think the author of the *Imitation* was ever aware of the beauty of nature as we understand it.

Hope you'll soon be better

J.

288

The Kilns,
Headington Quarry,
Oxford
18 June 62

My dear Arthur,

Some months ago they had decided that I should never be ripe for that operation but must just carry on, always wearing a catheter, on a low-protein diet, and being v. careful about stairs. They let me go up to Cambridge at the beginning of last term, reluctantly, and 'as an experiment'. The experiment has however been a far greater success than was hoped and I am now definitely better than I have been since the trouble began. There begins to be a faint chance that I may be able to have the operation after all and, if so, some day to resume a more or less normal life. But there can be no question of journeys, hotels etc at present. I need to be near a life-line (the plumbing often goes wrong.)

[1] A late fourteenth-century anonymous mystical treatise.
[1] Sir Herbert Read's generous review of Lewis's *An Experiment in Criticism* (1961) is found in *The Listener*, LXVI (16 November 1961), pp. 828, 831.

T.S.T.—T

I had v. much hoped there wd. be a chance of seeing you *here* this summer, but I gather you are an invalid too – you don't make your condition v. clear. This is sad news. If you can get away I shall be here all summer, and W. away for a good deal of it.

Blessings.

Yours
Jack

289

The Kilns,
Headington Quarry,
Oxford
19 Nov 62

My dear Arthur

I am v. sorry to hear you are ill. Especially the heart trouble. I know now what it's like – gasping like a new-caught fish which no one has the kindness to knock on the head.

I wonder does this put the boots on a scheme which was just beginning to form in my mind – that of coming over next summer, if I'm spared, bringing Douglas[1] with me (I can't carry my own bag & there are almost no porters now) and you and I and he spending 10 days or so in a hotel somewhere? You wouldn't find him a nuisance; he'd be out all day once we'd settled in. Any chance? Of course you and I wd. take it v. slow. At need, we cd. even hire someone to drive us to the place.

The talk on Bunyan was a tape-recording – I was actually booming away in my arm chair here![2]

I'm back at Cambridge now but home every week end, and very much better. But still catheterised and still on a low protein diet. There is no question of being really cured without the operation; about which they are persistently vague.

Blessings.

Yours
Jack

[1] Douglas Gresham (1945–   ), his step-son.

[2] The talk Arthur heard over the air on 16 October 1962 on *The Pilgrim's Progress* was afterwards published, with some alterations, as 'The Vision of John Bunyan' in *The Listener*, LXVIII (13 December 1962), pp. 1006–8, and is now reprinted in Lewis's *Selected Literary Essays*, ed. Walter Hooper (1969).

290

The Kilns,
Headington Quarry,
Oxford
18 Dec. 62

My dear Arthur

I am *very* glad to hear you have a housekeeper again; may she be a success!

I shouldn't like the Ship Inn at all, and except for one night (if that happened to be necessary) it wd. be a bad place for Douglas. If we can get no further I'd like one of the little places up the Antrim coast.

All blessings.

Yours
Jack

291

The Kilns,
Kiln Lane,
Headington Quarry,
Oxford
3 March 63

My dear Arthur

On July 28 W, Douglas, and I will be at the Glenmachan Towers Hotel [Belfast], and on the 29th W. will go to Eire. Can Doug and you and I go off somewhere for a week or two beginning on that date? If you don't feel up to driving us to wherever we go, I'll hire a car & driver for the journey. Wd. Castlerock or Glens of Antrim be any good? Portrush only as a last resource. But we want to be pretty quick about booking 3 rooms (it *must* be 3) and about berths for Doug & me on our return journey to England.

I saw snowdrops for the first time last week.

Yours
Jack

292

The Kilns,
Kiln Lane,
Headington Quarry,
Oxford
10 March '63

My dear Arthur,

Good man! There are 3 hotels at Port B[allintrae] – the other two being Ballintrae House and Beach Hotel. If you can't get 3 rooms in Bayview you must locate 2 of us in one hotel and 1 in another or even (as a last resource) one in each of the three. Doug & I will aim at sailing on Mon Aug 12. The *times*, as you point out, are by no means ideal, but we can't manage Sept.

Keep our fingers crossed & keep on saying D.V.

Yours
Jack

293

Magdalene College,
Cambridge.
15 March 63

My dear Arthur

I don't see how to change, for berths, which now a days need fixing as far ahead as hotels, are all fixed, and also all the hotels in the Eire part of our holiday. I can manage stairs now, provided I take them in bottom gear. So do try again. Your letter, forwarded by W., has only just reached me. How difficult it is to *do* anything.

Yours
Jack

294

> The Kilns,
> Headington Quarry,
> Oxford
> 22 March 63

My dear Arthur,
Bravo! As you say, not ideal, but the main object is to have some days together. We're both too old to let our remaining chances slip!
> Yours
> Jack

295

> The Kilns.
> 11 July 63

Alas! I have had a collapse as regards the heart trouble and the holiday has to be cancelled. Let me know how much you are out of pocket for our cancelled bookings at Port Stewart and, as is only fair, I will send you a cheque for that amount.
I don't mind – or not much – missing the jaunt, but it is a blow missing *you*. Bless you.
> Jack

296

> The Kilns,
> Kiln Lane,
> Headington Quarry.
> Oxford.
> 11 Sept 63

My dear Arthur
Last July I had a 'coma' of about 24 hours and was believed to be dying. When I recovered consciousness my mind was disordered for many days and I had all sorts of delusions. Very quaint ones some of them, but none painful or terrifying. I have had to resign my Chair and Fellowship at Cambridge and now live here as an invalid; not allowed upstairs. But quite comfortable and cheerful.
The only real snag is that it looks as if you and I shall never meet again in this life. This often saddens me v. much.

W., meanwhile, has completely deserted me. He has been in Ireland since June and doesn't even write, and is, I suppose, drinking himself to death. He has of course been fully informed of my condition and more than one friend or more has written him strong appeals but without the slightest result. But Paxford and Mrs Miller look after me v. well and if it weren't for that horrid amount of letter writing I now have to do, we could really get on v. well without him.

Tho' I am by no means unhappy I can't help feeling it was rather a pity I did revive in July. I mean, having been glided so painlessly up to the Gate it seems hard to have it shut in one's face and know that the whole process must some day be gone thro' again, and perhaps far less pleasantly! Poor Lazarus! But God knows best.

I am glad you are fairly well and have a housekeeper. But oh Arthur, never to see you again! . . .

Yours
Jack

INDEX

Lewis, Clive Staples 'Jack' [*contd.*]
Irish jaunt with Greeves, 562–5;
collapse and a final farewell,
565–6

BOOKS: *The Allegory of Love*,
19, 324, 409, 467, 474, 477, 479n;
Beyond Personality, 502n, 503;
Broadcast Talks, 493n; *Christian
Behaviour*, 502n; *Chronicles of
Narnia*, 28; *Dymer*, 159, 167,
170, 173, 175, 178, 239, 287n,
296–7, 298, 302, 303, 363, 378,
381–4, 385, 388, 427, 454; ed.
*Essays Presented to Charles
Williams*, 428n, 479n, 501n; *An
Experiment in Criticism*, 555n,
561n; ed. *George MacDonald:
An Anthology*, 507; *Letters*, 32,
224n, 269n, 286n, 289n; *The
Lion, the Witch and the Wardrobe*,
518n; *Mere Christianity*, 502n,
536; *Miracles*, 428n, 504, 510n;
Narrative Poems, 159n, 262n;
Out of the Silent Planet, 486,
492; *Perelandra*, 27n, 492n; *The
Pilgrim's Regress*, 19, 21, 26, 354,
385, 428n, 444–7, 449, 452, 453,
454, 467, 468, 474–5; *Poems*, 510n;
A Preface to 'Paradise Lost',
493n; *The Problem of Pain*, 27,
487, 514n; *The Queen of Drum*,
262n; *Reflections on the Psalms*,
545n, 546, 548; *The Screwtape
Letters*, 492; *Selected Literary
Essays*, 562n; *Spirits in Bondage*,
129n, 216, 250n, 252, 253;
*Studies in Medieval and
Renaissance Literature*, 347n;
Surprised by Joy, 9, 11–12, 13,
26, 38, 157n, 202n, 212, 255,
259, 270, 293n, 308–9, 311n, 314n,
317n, 372n, 534, 538n, 539, 540;
That Hideous Strength, 69n,
494n, 499–500, 504n, 505; *Till
We Have Faces*, 540, 541;
Undeceptions, 323n

POEMS: 'Death in Battle',
237n; 'Irish Nocturne', 270;
'Lilith', 353–4; 'Lullaby', 220;
'Song', 215–16; 'Victory', 255

ESSAYS: *De Descriptione
Temporum*, 532; 'The Efficacy of
Prayer', 538; 'The Humanitarian
Theory of Punishment', 532;
Molliter Ossa Cubent, 550–1;
'Myth Became Fact', 428n; 'A
Note on *Comus*', 347n; 'A Note
on Jane Austen', 532n; 'Notes
on the Way', 507n; 'Some
Thoughts', 544n; 'The Vision of
John Bunyan', 562n

Lewis, Florence Augusta Hamilton
'Flora' (Lewis's mother: 1862–
1908): 13–14, 357, 361, 398

Lewis, Joseph (1856–1908): 13, 43

Lewis, Dr Joseph 'Joey' (1898–
1969): 304, 376

Lewis, Martha (1884–?): 13

Lewis, Percy Wyndham (1884–
1957): 25

Lewis, Richard (1832–1908): 13

Lewis, Richard (1861–?): 13, 324,
453, 456

Lewis, Sarah Jane (?–1901): 13

Lewis, Warren Hamilton 'Warnie'
(1895–1973): INTRODUCTION:
educated at Sandhurst, 11; his
ancestry, 14; compiles the *Lewis
Papers*, 16; dislike of Mrs
Moore, 20–1; attitude towards
Lewis-Moore *ménage*, 22–3; his
alcoholism and last years, 28–37.
EDITOR'S NOTE: disposal of
brother's letters to Greeves,
39–40; the 25 letters reproduced
in *Lewis Papers*, 42. LETTERS: on
leave from France, 66; spends
day in London with brother,
104n; with father and brother at
home for Christmas 1918 and
now Captain in ASC, 240;
learns of brother's infatuation for
Mrs Moore, 257–8; holiday with
brother, 259; transferred to
Aldershot, 278n; admiration of
brother's academic success, 295;
to China in 1927 for 3-year tour
of the Far East, 301n; learns of
father's illness and death, 305–6;
invited to make his home with
Lewis and Moores, 346; last
visits to Little Lea before it is